David Fellman
Vilas Professor of Political Science
University of Wisconsin
ADVISORY EDITOR TO DODD, MEAD & COMPANY

THE URBAN POLITY

THE URBAN POLITY

William O. Winter
University of Colorado

DODD, MEAD & COMPANY
New York · Toronto · 1970

To Alice

PREFACE

Deeply involved today in the urban crisis, we tend to be more than occasionally overwhelmed by the complexity of it. If there are not riots in the streets, at least dirt clogs the gutters and burdens the air and dulls the vision. Or traffic clogs the streets, and a multitude of governments chokes up those avenues of communication so necessary in forming coherent public policy. The city furnishes a seedbed for crimes and other forms of antisocial behavior. It harbors great wealth and extreme poverty. The urban citizen is inordinately wealthy, simply comfortable, or incredibly poor: within arm's reach are the mansion, the townhouse, and the hovel. Judges regard cities as subordinate creatures of legally superior governments; politicians think of cities as places to mass voters for achieving state and national victory; the citizen himself shrugs off political forces that rattle his very door. And so some describe the city as ungovernable; others insist that urban living is unlivable.

The city produces most of the wealth of this and all other nations of the western world, yet city treasuries are typically bare. Here most of the work is done, yet here also are most of the unemployed. The city is hog butcher to the world; it is also a patron of the arts. The city is in perpetual change and perpetual crisis, and only the complexity and the change remain constant.

Since the city, indeed, is itself complexity and constant change, it is a difficult subject to write about. One finds that books about the city are usually partial views of the city. And that is true of this book. Here I have sought to explain the nature of the political environment. Seeking not to lose sight of the socioeconomic, and even the physical aspects of urban life, I have focused upon urban politics, law, and public administration; upon the endless chain that is policy formation and execution; upon power, the uses of power and the access to power; upon systems, mostly value-ladened, sometimes almost valueless; upon programs in realization and in frustration; upon urban theories, both normatively and empirically based. And since the city is an historical organism, I have used history and prehistory to throw perspective on contemporary urban phenomena. And though the urban polity that I write about is essentially American, I have sought data from European and Canadian cities in an effort to avoid provincialism.

While ever seeking the objective statement and stoutly rejecting the hortatory, and while using empirically based judgments to the fullest extent possible, I must readily admit to value biases. For one thing, if I did not impute certain primary values to the urban political system, I would not write about it. For another thing, if I did not think the city and its political environment important, I would write a book about urban sociology or international politics. But since I believe, with Lewis Mumford, that the city is the master institution of civilization, I must write about it, and all the while admit the biases that attend that writing.

Although I wrote this book, I cannot claim it entirely as my own. My wife lent it her great good sense and her constant good nature. My editors —William Oman, David Fellman, and Genia Graves—gave it their critical judgment. My colleagues, both within and outside the academic world, brought to it that measurement of the *Realpolitik* of the city's public life that I, a lone campaigner, could never have given it: Professors James E. Larson, Frank Smallwood, Daniel Grant; Municipal League directors Jay T. Bell and J. Kinney O'Rourke; City Manager Wayne Anderson. Many of my students, often unknowingly, gave it sharpened analysis of both major and minor points. And those who surround me administratively most generously gave it time and effort that had been earmarked for other tasks: Grace Martini, Marilla Senterfit, Betsy Stanek, Joanne Higley, and Nancy Harvey Miller. These people contributed many of the virtues; all of the faults I must claim as my own.

WILLIAM O. WINTER

CONTENTS

PART I

Urban Evolution

CHAPTER 1

The Urban Revolution

Weltstadt: The City Is the World

It was William Wordsworth who voiced the romantic protest against the city when he wrote:

> The world is too much with us; late and soon,
> Getting and spending, we lay waste our powers:
> Little we see in Nature that is ours;
> We have given our hearts away . . .

This is as much an expostulation against the city as that voiced by Thoreau from Walden Pond. It is a protest against materialism, against people crowded in upon one another, against machines and a machine-dominated civilization, and against a retreat of the landscape.

This is a protest. But is it also an indictment? We can be assured that it is only partially so. Is the city materialistic? We know that it is also nonmaterialistic. The city is dominant in scholarship: it peoples and houses the great universities, laboratories, and libraries. It is dominant in the arts: in New York City alone there are over three hundred art galleries and many thousands of artists. Men of letters, musicians, and poets are legion in the city. If the city really stifles the Muse, why do not the galleries, the museums, the libraries, and the laboratories move to the villages, and the artists each move to his own Walden Pond?

There is almost an infinite variety to the city. If the Viennese call their city a *Weltstadt,* it is not only because of a pride of citizenship but also because of a desire to apply a colorful, descriptive noun to this urban variety. Though every major city has a character of its own, and in that sense is local and distinct, it also has a character which transcends the local—and certainly the regional and the national—to encompass the world. One may find virtually all human skills in the city's shops and factories. In the libraries one may find a record of the world's knowledge; in the universities and research laboratories, the learned professionals, who themselves encompass the world's knowledge and seek to enlarge it. Peoples of many tongues gather in the cities—peoples of many races, and peoples from all points of the compass.

Each of the hundred-odd major cities of the world is itself a *Weltstadt,* a microcosm of the world, a small but accurate reflection of what the Greeks called the *kosmos*. And the citizen is—or can become—a cosmopolite (note the root): the urban man who is also a world man. Since the lesser cities are usually tributary to the greater ones, they cannot be disassociated from their fellows. Yet just as Charleston, Philadelphia, Boston, and New York were tributaries of London during the Colonial period, and still assumed a pronounced character of their own, so can today's tributary city assert its own individuality. When it fails to do so, the failure cannot be laid to circumstance, but rather to the poverty of its own spirit.

Emerging Social Patterns of the Western City

The Ecology of the City. All of life is governed by a deeply pervasive interrelatedness, by what Charles Darwin called "the web of life." From this basic truth, which Darwin documented so well in his research, has stemmed a mass of ecological studies, both in biology and in the social sciences. Hawley comments that "in his works Darwin formulated the basic ideas which were later brought together to constitute the theoretical understructure, the frame of reference, of modern ecology. All life was Darwin's province, and he perceived it as a moving system of vital relationships in which were implicated every organism and species of life." [1]

But what is ecology? And why should we discuss it in a book on the politics and government of the city? Ecology is made up of three branches: plant, animal, and human. All three branches are engrossed with the study of how living things are distributed upon the face of the earth and how those living things relate to their environment. Man, like plants and other animals, is profoundly influenced by his environment. Therefore every student of society must be concerned with human ecology.

A brief, accurate, and intelligible description or definition of human ecology is very hard to come by. McKenzie defines it in these terms: "Human ecology deals with the spatial aspects of the symbiotic relations of human beings and human institutions." [2] But this definition is inadequate. As Hawley observes, McKenzie overemphasizes the spatial relationships in the human community to the detriment of the functional relationships, which are equally important. Gist and Halbert agree that the study of the spatial distribution of peoples is an element of human ecology, but they insist that it is only "a starting point in ecological analysis." [3] Hawley attempts to emphasize both space and function in this definition:

[1] Amos H. Hawley, *Human Ecology* (New York: The Ronald Press Co., 1950), p. 5.
[2] R. D. McKenzie, "Human Ecology," in *Encyclopedia of the Social Sciences* (1951 reprint), Vol. V, p. 314.
[3] Noel P. Gist and L. A. Halbert, *Urban Society* (New York: Thomas Y. Crowell Co., 1956), p. 75.

"Human ecology may be defined . . . as the study of the form and the development of the community in human population." [4]

If these definitions do not sufficiently clarify the nature of human ecology, perhaps a history of human ecology as a separate sociological discipline and a description of the principal aims of ecology will do so. Although Charles Darwin was vitally interested in all of human life, especially in its functions and in its adjustments to environmental conditions —as we may see in his *Origin of the Species*—the birth of human ecology is usually associated with the publication of *An Introduction to the Science of Sociology* by R. E. Park and E. W. Burgess in 1921.[5] In less than half a century of existence the discipline has developed a quite extensive literature on the city. Although his concern is by no means exclusively with the city, the human ecologist finds himself turning constantly to the urban community for research purposes. Indeed, if human ecology itself has a branch, it is urban ecology, which may eventually take over the entire discipline.

The urban ecologist has certain concepts which are useful to the student of urban politics. The first of these is the concept of centralization. This is no more than a description of the tendency of people to gather at a central point to satisfy their needs or to carry out their functions. This tendency can be seen in the theatrical districts of cities. Lincoln Center for the Performing Arts in New York City is an example of a publicly decreed kind of centralization. So are the civic centers seen in so many other cities. The central business district, with its grouping of similar retail and financial establishments, is another example of centralization.

The second concept, nucleation, is an extension of the idea and an observable fact of centralization. Most towns and small cities are mononucleated; but polynucleation, long a feature of the large city, is spreading to the smaller ones. Nucleation is essentially a static concept; it is descriptive of what exists at a particular place at a particular time.

The third main concept of urban ecology—decentralization—is highly dynamic. Decentralization, the spreading out of peoples and institutions, can rapidly change the character of the city, cause severe fluctuations in land values, and profoundly change the political configuration of the community.[6] On these problems both urban ecologists and political scientists share the same concerns; both, for example, are vitally interested in annexation of territory by the central city and the incorporation of satellite municipalities in the urban fringe. In short, both are interested in the effect that deconcentration has upon urban man.

[4] Hawley, *op. cit.*, pp. 68–69.
[5] *Ibid.*, p. 8.
[6] See, for example, Amos H. Hawley, *The Changing Shape of Metropolitan America: Deconcentration Since 1920* (Glencoe, Ill.: The Free Press, 1956).

A fourth basic concept of urban ecology is <u>segregation.</u> The ecologist is interested in the tendency of peoples to group themselves according to similar interests, economic standing, race, nationality, and religion. As a scientist, the ecologist wants to know why these things happen, what the results are, and what the social reactions are. He is not interested as a scientist in the impact of such segregation upon the individual personality; this must be left to the psychologist or the poet, or to the novelist, moralist, and clergyman. Here again the interests of the ecologist and the political scientist coincide. The latter is interested, for example, in the politics of segregation illustrated by the rich suburban community which has separately incorporated itself in order to fence out the rest of the urban community.

The fifth and final basic concept is <u>invasion and succession.</u> Robert Frost once wrote, "Something there is that doesn't love a wall, That wants it down." Though the poet's observation was about stone walls in New England, it can equally be applied to society. One group will insist upon setting itself off from society; another group will find that society has built a wall around it. But humanity does not like a wall any more than nature does; and wherever walls are found, there you will also find individuals trying to breach them. This, in somewhat literary guise, is a description of invasion and succession. We are most familiar with this phenomenon when minority groups penetrate residential neighborhoods housing a dominant majority. And we see the culmination of invasion-succession when the dominant majority, fearful of being overwhelmed by the minority group, leaves the neighborhood. But there are other types of invasion and succession. We see it in institutional invasions, and we see it when land use changes through the erosion of zoning codes.

The coincidence of interest of the ecologist and political scientist is very great. Is the ecologist concerned with the spatial distribution of institutions and peoples in the urban community? So is the political scientist. Does he study changing residential patterns? So does the political scientist. Is the ecologist's research concerned with the urban fringe? The political scientist constantly investigates the political life and the political configurations of peripheral urban communities. Does the ecologist view the metropolitan community and seek to explain its mysteries? Many political scientists today are virtually obsessed with metropolitan problems. Thus, our study of the political aspects of the city will be enriched if we remember the intellectual tools of the urban ecologist.

The Influence of the City upon Manners and Mores

Jeremiads against the city are as old as the city itself. Cities are attacked as life-destructive, materialistic, and fleshpots of sin. To many people throughout history, whether peasants or intellectuals, cities were to be repressed or even destroyed, as Sodom and Gomorrah were destroyed in the Bible.

The ideas of Thomas Jefferson, perhaps more than those of any other American thinker, have influenced American ideas about the city. Jefferson's suspicions of the city and of urban life in general are well known. In his ideal commonwealth, which would be almost exclusively rural, governmental powers would be distributed among the rural community, the county, the state, and the nation. But to him the rural homogeneous community best represented the ideal of a republican-democratic society, and he would have preferred that the major portion of governmental powers and functions remain in the rural communities and close to the people. It should be remembered, however, that Jefferson's belief in the desirability of local control of governmental institutions was as strong as his prejudice in favor of the rural community. This should be enough to discount some of his anticity bias.

In a book of not-too-recent vintage, entitled *Cities Are Abnormal,* many of the standard arguments against the city are conveniently assembled. The enforced collectivization or interdependence of the city, runs the argument, is a perplexity to the individual, who really wishes a greater individualism. Because the city has destroyed the neighborhood and the community, the city is prey to crime and corruption. The very congestion of the city, which comes from a primordial urge to huddle into some protective enclosure, invalidates that urge. Because of the devastating nature of modern ordnance, the city is highly vulnerable to attack; and the larger the city the greater its vulnerability. Finally, rural life is the norm of human existence, and urban life represents a substantial departure from that norm.[7]

Yet even the editor of *Cities Are Abnormal* does not, in the final analysis, wish to eliminate the city as such. Rather, he wishes to attack the congested, denatured urban life that has developed in so many of our cities. With this kind of attack even the foremost student of the contemporary city, Lewis Mumford, would agree. Writes Mumford, "We must restore to the city the maternal, life-nurturing functions, the autonomous activities, the symbiotic associations that have long been neglected or suppressed. For the city should be an organ of love; and the best economy of cities is the care and culture of men."[8]

There is little doubt that cities profoundly affect man's habits and other behavior patterns. All of the evidence points in that direction. So let us

[7] Elmer T. Peterson (ed.), *Cities Are Abnormal* (Norman, Okla.: University of Oklahoma Press, 1946), pp. 10–20.

[8] Lewis Mumford, *The City in History* (New York: Harcourt, Brace & World, 1961), p. 575.

look at some of the effects. The city may be a lonely place; and the individual inhabitants, anonymous beings. For some this means tragedy; for others, freedom. For many people the city is a place to hide, a place to escape the pressures of neighborhood, community, and family. If it is a lonely place, it is also a challenging one. And the challenge comes, in good measure, from the anonymity of urban living.

The passion for anonymity may actually lead one beyond loneliness; it will often permit the individual to establish contacts with people of his own peculiar persuasion, unfettered by community pressures. The person who has lived on Skid Row knows how, on the one hand, fifty strangers may live month after month in the same vermin-infested hotel, and how, on the other hand, there is scarcely a bum without a buddy. Here the buddy system is pervasive; here in crude outline is a sample of how anonymity works: an individual surrounded by strangers, but protected from loneliness by a friend or a group of friends.

Of course, one must not overemphasize the anonymity of the urban place. There is probably not a single Western city today which does not contain many closely knit neighborhood units in which the people are accustomed to frequent daily intercourse.[9] In the metropolitan suburb as well as in the smaller cities, one may find tightly grouped neighborhoods. Though these neighborhoods may not have the demographic stability or the personal, gossipy nature of the rural community, neither do they possess the pervasive anonymity of the great apartment-house districts of large cities.

The city has long been the scene of various types of aberrant social behavior. It is the city which houses and nurtures the rebel. If there is a religious, social, or economic cult, it will probably originate within the city and flourish there. Some types of rebellion may be considered wholly destructive; some may represent net social gains. Such types of abnormal behavior as alcoholism, certain sexual aberrations, and crime—all damaging to the city and to society—seem to be stimulated to a degree by urban living. In the crowded quarters of the city, for example, the growing child may very soon lose his illusions about sex—illusions which may be both dynamic and socially constructive—and come to view sexual relationships solely in terms of physical gratification. The city generally, moreover, seems to hold most of the prostitution and the various forms of sexual perversion known to American society.

Crime and various types of nervous and mental disease seem to thrive in the urban environment. We can observe fewer crimes per given unit of population in the rural areas than in the urban, and there seems to be a correlation between the extent of criminal activity and the size of the city.

[9] In Jane Jacobs, *The Death and Life of Great American Cities* (New York: Random House, 1961), one can find some excellent descriptions of such neighborhoods.

There is also some reason to believe that mental disorders are more prevalent in urban than in rural areas.[10]

The Influence of the City upon Family Life

The urban family is not yet a dead institution, nor even a moribund one. Yet various data would seem to indicate that the pressures upon the urban family are sufficient to alter it considerably from the rural or small-town pattern. Let us look at some of these data.

Is the city biologically bad? Some people, when comparing rural and urban birthrates, would insist that it is. A European sociologist has called Vienna a city without a rising generation, a city without progeny, largely because of the low birthrate there. Indeed, from 1951 to 1961, the city's population increased a mere 11,000 (from 1,616,000 to 1,627,000).

It has long been insisted by demographers that the city cannot reproduce itself. If this is an iron law of population which cannot change, then we can assume that any society which becomes predominately or overwhelmingly urban must gradually die. But is this an iron law? Data on American population growth indicate that it may not be so. In 1940 the birthrate per 1,000 population in New York State was 14.7; in Illinois, 16.2; and in California, 16.6. In 1965 the birthrates for these three states were, respectively, 21.4, 23.3, and 22.8. It should be noted that all of these states are highly urban and that in the period from 1940 to 1965 all three states experienced noticeable increases in birthrates at the same time that they were becoming increasingly urbanized. It would seem from these data that even the city is making its contribution to the world's population explosion!

The size of the family unit tends to be somewhat smaller in the city than in the country. In 1965, 15 percent of all American farm families had four or more children under eighteen years of age living at home. Only about ten percent of the nonfarm families fell in that category. Urbanization also seems to have been a factor in the increase in the divorce rate. In 1910 there was roughly one divorce per 1,000 population; in 1965 the rate was 2.5 divorces.[11] On the other hand, it would be well at this point to observe that many of the highly urbanized countries of Europe—England, Belgium, Sweden, and the Netherlands, for example—have far lower divorce rates than the United States.

Collective Services and Controls. Bringing land, labor, and capital together in limited compass, developing an elaborate transportation network, utilizing a complicated banking system, originating and expanding

[10] James S. Plant, "The Personality and an Urban Area," in Paul K. Hatt and Albert J. Reiss, Jr. (eds.), *Cities and Society* (Glencoe, Ill.: The Free Press, 1957), pp. 647–665.

[11] U.S. Bureau of the Census, *Statistical Abstract of the United States: 1966*, pp. 4, 46, and 47.

a vast system of public services and controls, the city becomes a remarkably effective instrument for doing work. Simply by bringing people close together, the city raises immeasurably the economic productiveness of mankind. In the words of one economist, "The principal means through which the city contributes to the economic tasks of mankind is proximity—a physical arrangement whereby people are placed close to other people, workers to employers, producers to consumers, establishments to establishments." [12]

But that proximity alone is sufficient to require vast collective controls. For the city to exist it must have an array of public and quasipublic institutions designed both to serve and to protect. Traditionally, the city's political institutions have been essentially of a protective or regulatory nature. Such protective and regulatory institutions are costly; indeed, as the city grows, the costs of public controls are apt to increase geometrically rather than arithmetically. As an indication of this phenomenon, we can observe the relation of size to police expenditures. For American cities over 500,000 population, per capita costs were $22.04 for police protection in 1966. For cities in the 10,000–25,000 population group, per capita costs were $10.69.[13] Cities, in other words, are much like modern nation-states; they must spend an inordinate amount of money merely for protection.

Increasingly, however, the modern city supplements regulation with service. A truly vast investment of public capital is necessary for urban effectiveness. In an isolated rural county little or no public property is needed; in a city as much as 25 percent of the land area may be in streets and other public ways alone. Vast sums of money must be invested in storm and sanitary drains, water mains, street lighting, transit systems, schoolhouses, and other public buildings.

In order to exist, the city must rely upon a considerable network of laws —statutes, ordinances, administrative regulations—and a very considerable bureaucracy. These laws and the bureaucracy are by no means entirely the city's own. In the average American city there are many other local governments, each with its own bureaucracy and its own set of legal rules. There are also state laws and state agencies and federal laws and federal agencies which are of vital importance to the city. The city, for example, could not possibly exist without a communications system. Of all the important elements involved in such a system, the city probably relies most heavily upon the post office, an instrumentality of the federal government.

Supplementing the manifold governmental institutions are the privately owned, quasi-public companies. In communications and in transportation,

[12] Louis Winnick, "The Economic Functions of the City Yesterday and Tomorrow," in *The Urban Problem, Proceedings of the American Academy of Political Science,* May, 1960, p. 13.
[13] *The Municipal Year Book 1967* (Chicago: International City Managers' Association, 1967), Table 16, p. 450.

particularly, the city must depend upon the telephone and the carriers of goods and people. Although, as we have already seen, a basic reason for the city's existence is proximity—an effort to lessen the disutility of distance —distance still can be a formidable barrier to the city's functioning. Imagine trying to maintain communications between central and outlying fire stations by semaphore or flashing lights! Imagine a company's central office downtown trying to communicate with its outlying retail outlets and warehouses by messenger! So also with transportation and power supply. Without that common carrier, the mass transit system—in some cities privately owned—urban life would be virtually impossible. And power supply, especially electrical power supply, which is of such crucial importance to the city, is normally furnished the urban community by utilities which have a decidedly public character, even when privately owned.

As the social services of the state increase, as public authority intrudes into economic areas once securely held by the entrepreneur, as the city government itself becomes as much a service institution as a regulatory one, politics has tended to increase in importance and economics has tended to retreat. The workweek shortens and family income rises, to use one case in point; and taxes multiply to take care of the automobile traffic, the recreational needs, and the educational and assorted other demands of the released individual. In Brooklyn in 1860, the adult male may well have spent twelve hours a day in the factory, shop, or office. And he had no long weekends. In Kansas City today, the forty-hour week and the long weekend give the urban dweller so much freedom that he finds the greatest portion of his time absorbed with nonwork activities. A striking result of modern urbanism indeed has been to give Everyman the leisure once possible only for the wealthy and highborn.

There is nothing new about the city's being an organism of collective services and controls. That most of the people of the Western world have now become subject to this form of interdependent life, however, is a strikingly new development. And since the city is not only depopulating the countryside, but has already substantially implanted its mores and way of life in the habits of rural folk, an urban culture spreads over entire continents and tends to obliterate the rural-urban dichotomy, sociologically and perhaps even politically. Now most of mankind in the Western world is in close symbiotic relation with his fellows and is highly dependent upon the rest of the community for his daily requirements.

The Phenomenon of Worldwide Urbanism

Cities have their roots in prehistory, in the urban- and food-producing revolutions. The first cities originated in the valleys of the Indus, Tigris, Euphrates, and Nile rivers. Almost simultaneously cities appeared in

China. For five millennia, therefore, man has been acquainted with, if not used to, cities.

The prehistoric urban revolution may have been not a complete one, but rather only the first stage of a development which is now reaching its climax. Although cities have dominated civilization in the past, most of the people never actually lived in them. Now, however, most of the world's population will be gathered into cities. What effect will this remarkable transformation have on the politics, habits, mores, yes, even the arts of humanity? It is useless to conjecture about this transformation. It may be unwise even to suggest that this is the culmination of a revolution which started in prehistoric times. This much we can count on, however: a major change has come over mankind, and this is undoubtedly a change which will pose major problems, some of which simply cannot be lived with but must be solved.

The impact of urbanization has been profound not only in the West, but also throughout the world. In the United States, as we can see in Figure 1-1, there was virtually no urbanization in 1790. By 1960, not only had major urban centers developed, but the rate of urban growth was also accelerating sharply, while the growth rate of rural population was in decline. The number of farm-operator families declined sharply in the decade and a half after World War II, from 5.9 million in 1947 to 2.9 million in 1966. The

Figure 1-1. Rural and Urban Population Growth in the United States 1790–1960

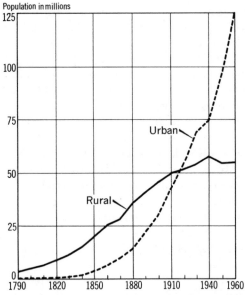

Source: U.S. Bureau of the Census, *1960 Census of Population* (1961), Vol. I, Part A, p. 29.

number of nonfarm families, on the other hand, increased sharply from 31.1 million in 1947 to 45.3 million in 1966.[14]

Urban development in the United States has been characterized not only by the growth of great urban centers and by the rapid urbanization of the population, but also by the development of urban regions. According to a definition of the Urban Land Institute, an urban region is a series of urban counties, including both those clearly metropolitan and those in transition. The region must have a population of at least 1,000,000 people and a population density of at least 180 per square mile.

By this definition the United States "contains 21 urban regions with a 1960 population of 97.7 million—55 per cent of the total. These regions occupy 179,268 square miles of land, or 6 per cent of the surface of the coterminous United States. Thus, in 1960, 55 per cent of the nation's population was located within 6 per cent of its land area included in the urban regions; the remaining 45 per cent of the population was spread unevenly over 94 per cent of the national territory." Of course, urban regions as such are not new to the American scene. Every major city has long had its satellites. But the regions analyzed here are notable (1) for size and (2) for the massing of urban centers. These are the new and novel elements of urban regions which have appeared within the past quarter of a century.[15]

The pattern of urbanization in most Western nations has been similar to that in the United States. In the Orient and Africa urbanization has gone on apace. The underdeveloped countries in both regions strive for urbanization, and there is wide variance among the various nations in the degree of urban development. Although in Japan and Burma roughly one-half of the population lives in the cities, Pakistan is little more than 10 percent urban.

The major African cities—such as Johannesburg, Cairo, Alexandria, Casablanca, and Algiers—tend to lie on the periphery of the continent. Black Africa has few major urban centers, and indeed some of the newer African states have almost no urban population. But though cities are few, towns are numerous. The Niger Republic, until 1960 a part of French West Africa, is a desert country inhabited largely by nomadic tribesmen. Its capital city, Niamey, is about the size of Philadelphia in 1770. Without cities it will be difficult for Niger to maintain an independent existence in the modern world.[16]

---

[14] U.S. Bureau of the Census, *Statistical Abstract of the United States: 1962*, p. 318; and *Statistical Abstract of the United States: 1967*, p. 38.

[15] Jerome P. Pickard, "Urban Regions of the United States," in *Urban Land*, xxv (April, 1962), 3. See also Jean Gottmann, *Megalopolis* (New York: The Twentieth Century Fund, 1961).

[16] Rose Hum Lee, *The City—Urbanism and Urbanization in Major World Regions* (Philadelphia: J. B. Lippincott Co., 1955), Chs. 4, 5; and United Nations, *Demographic Yearbook 1962*, pp. 310–311.

Russia, struggling for an industrialized society, is being forced to urbanize. Though still slightly more than one-half rural, the Russian people are crowding into cities in a fashion not too dissimilar from that which is commonplace in the Western world. The available data seem to indicate that Russia is following the Western pattern of urbanization. From 1939 to 1965, the population of Chelyabinsk increased from 273,000 to 805,000; and that of Moscow (the city proper) from 4,137,000 to 6,366,000. Leningrad increased in population from 3,015,000 to 3,329,000.[17]

Since the city has become so much a part of mankind, what are some of the basic characteristics of the urban phenomenon? In the first place, urbanization is worldwide; it is not limited to the West, as we too often assume; nor is it limited to those places around the world which have felt the influences of Western practices and culture. In the second place, urbanism is as widely extended in time as it is in space. Mankind has known great cities for five millennia, lesser ones for much longer. Thus urbanism is not dependent upon industrialization, mass transportation, or other "modern" innovations. The third characteristic of urbanization is that it gives rise to a social complexity that is not necessarily a function of size. As we shall see by examining American colonial cities, such urban places as New York and Philadelphia, though small in population, were both complex and sophisticated social entities. Even tiny Charleston had an art life superior to that in many a contemporary city of a quarter-million population.

The city is characterized, further, by density and diversity of population. A great many different types of people are grouped together into a relatively small space. Pressed in upon each other, and forced to specialize, the urban group becomes a highly interdependent organism.

Finally, urbanism stimulates a certain degree of personal anonymity, on the one hand, and social fluidity or mobility, on the other. Because of this, as the romantics have pointed out, many men have lost their roots in the urban group, and many urban societies have been hard pressed to develop and maintain adequate standards of social conduct. Because of this the city is the focus for many types of aberrant behavior. Also because of this the city is the hammer which the individual may use to break himself loose from the anachronistic chains of custom and prejudice.

Toward a Metropolitan World. Seeking to identify metropolitan centers around the world, Kingsley Davis used the following criteria: the metropolis is "an area with 100,000 or more inhabitants, containing at least one city (or continuous urban area) with 50,000 or more inhabitants and those administrative divisions contiguous to the city (or to the continuous

---

[17] Kingsley Davis *et al., The World's Metropolitan Areas* (Berkeley, Calif.: University of California Press, 1959), pp. 61–62; and *Demographic Yearbook 1965* (New York: United Nations, 1966), pp. 159–160.

urban area) which meet certain requirements as to metropolitan character." [18]

By using these criteria, Davis and his associates identified 1,064 metropolitan areas in the world. Out of 202 countries and territories examined, 105 were found to contain at least one metropolitan center. Perhaps more significantly, the group found (1) that the highest *rates* of metropolitan growth occur in the world's underdeveloped areas, and (2) that much of the population increase in industrialized societies goes into the metropolitan centers.[19] In a very real sense, therefore, the metropolis seems to represent the culmination of the worldwide urban revolution.

Annotated Bibliography

The textbooks on urban sociology summarize the major features of the city as a social organism: origins and growth, ecology, population, family life, organizational structure, behavior patterns, housing, and planning. Their treatment of urban government is cursory, but no more so than the treatment, in this textbook, of urban society. Rose Hum Lee, in departing somewhat from the usual textbook approach, has three especially valuable chapters on the growth of Asian and African cities. See Rose Hum Lee, *The City—Urbanism and Urbanization in Major World Regions* (Philadelphia: J. B. Lippincott Co., 1955).

There are a number of good treatments of urban ecology, all of value to the student of the city. Noel P. Gist and L. A. Halbert, *Urban Society* (New York: Thomas Y. Crowell Co., 4th ed., 1956), has been widely read, and deservedly so, for over a quarter of a century. It is particularly valuable for its section on urban ecology. A fifth edition of this standard work was brought out in 1964 by Noel P. Gist and Sylvia Fava.

But the definitive work on human ecology is probably that done by Hawley. See Amos H. Hawley, *Human Ecology* (New York: The Ronald Press Co., 1950). Also see J. A. Quinn, *Human Ecology* (Englewood Cliffs, N. J.: Prentice-Hall, 1950). A student of Professor R. D. McKenzie's, who was a pioneer in the development of human ecology, Professor Hawley has attempted, to use his own words, "to develop a full and coherent theory of human ecology." Other useful studies in ecology include James M. Bechers, *Urban Social Structure* (New York: Free Press of Glencoe, 1962); George A. Theodorson (ed.), *Studies in Human Ecology* (Evanston, Ill.: Row, Peterson & Co., 1961); and Roger G. Barker and Herbert F. Wright, *Midwest and Its Children: The Psychological Ecology of an American Town* (Evanston, Ill.: Row, Peterson & Co., 1956).

The geographer, too, has something to say on the points we have reviewed in this chapter. Working on problems connected with the physical growth of cities, urban geographers are concerned with the influence of site upon urban development, the effects of climate and latitude, the impact of regional trends, and the instrumentalities and effects of planning. Although books on limited aspects of urban geography are legion, works that cover the entire field are relatively few. See, however, Thomas Griffith Taylor, *Urban Geography* (New York: E. P. Dut-

[18] *Ibid.*, p. 25.
[19] Jack P. Gibbs and Leo F. Schnore, "Metropolitan Growth: An International Study," *American Journal of Sociology*, LXVI (September, 1960), 160–170.

ton & Co., 1949); Robert E. Dickinson, *City, Region, and Regionalism* (New York: Oxford University Press, 1947); Arthur E. Smailes, *The Geography of Towns* (London: Hutchinson's University Library, 2nd rev. ed., 1957); and Harold M. Mayer and Clyde F. Kohn (eds.), *Readings in Urban Geography* (Chicago: University of Chicago Press, 1959). For a somewhat popular view of the American city from the standpoint of a scholar trained in agricultural geography, see Edward C. Higbee, *The Squeeze: Cities Without Space* (New York: William S. Morrow & Co., 1960). A comprehensive treatment of the American city, written from the standpoint of the geographer, is Raymond E. Murphy, *The American City* (New York: McGraw-Hill Book Co., 1966).

That the city has received cavalier treatment from the intellectuals may be easily seen from the books by Peterson and the Whites. See Elmer T. Peterson (ed.), *Cities Are Abnormal* (Norman, Okla.: University of Oklahoma Press, 1946); and Morton White and Lucia White, *The Intellectual Versus the City: From Thomas Jefferson to Frank Lloyd Wright* (Cambridge, Mass.: Harvard University Press, 1962). Although both books are overstatements, each documents the intellectual's suspicion of the urban place. (And if there is no suspicion, there is invariably disinterest—which makes an effort such as the Whites' doubly trying.) On the other hand, one must be careful to distinguish between criticism of the city's malfunctions and of the city per se. Can the Whites call both Wright and Mumford anticity? Perhaps they can so label the former, but certainly not the latter.

CHAPTER 2

*O*rigins and Development of the City

Take yourself to the heart of a great city; within sight, within sound, within walking distance, you will find visual, tactile evidence of man's greatest triumphs—and his most abysmal failures. There, in asphalt, stone, glass, aluminum, and steel you will see evidence of man's hope and, perhaps, an indication of his ultimate fate. Give me any dream of man, or any activity, and I can give you a city for it, and a street leading up to it, and a building that houses it. For even when the prophet dreams in the wilderness, he must return to the city to implement his dreams.

The city has long been one of two principal tools—the other is language—available for man's use as he adventures into the wilderness. This "wilderness" may be a geographic area which man wishes to conquer, or it may be some part of the natural or intellectual world about which he is curious; in either case, urbanism is at once an adventure and a tool for exploration. Look at the American West—it was a geographic wilderness and adventure came in subduing it. The trappers probed it, but had no power to dominate it. The first settlers, in their sod huts, were overwhelmed by it. Not until he built a city, or an urban settlement of some kind, to stand guard over the countryside was the American able to establish a foothold. Then the advance of civilization was assured, the wilderness conquered and subdued.

All of the unknown is in truth a wilderness, and in attempting to conquer it man has always worked from an urban base. Music, painting, sculpture, literature—all of the arts are, in conception, adventures into the unknown, and one does not generally find centers of art in the country. Nor does one find centers of scholarship or scientific investigation. If you should happen across a laboratory lost somewhere in the cornfields of Illinois—I am thinking of the great Argonne National Laboratory—you are certain to find it near a city, staffed and administered by a university in that city. Trace the slow progress into the unknown region of radioactivity. Its beginning was in a desk drawer in Paris, when a Frenchman inadvertently put a piece of ore near an unexposed photographic plate. The high point of its history was reached in an abandoned football stadium in Chicago, when an Italian successfully induced a "chain reaction" and ushered in the atomic age. The point should not be labored. Without the city we would be impoverished, even as we would be without language.

Origins of the City

The city is the measure of man, and of whatever progress he has made. Without the city, the civilization that we have laboriously built over the past three thousand years could not survive. Indeed, the start of city building marks the beginning of civilized man, as we know him, and the destruction of cities would certainly mark his end. When the Dark Ages descended upon Western Europe, cities ceased to be an important factor in man's existence. Then, when the renaissance of the twelfth century showed conclusively that the long ages of darkness and uncertainty had passed, cities began spreading like the green grass of spring over the face of Europe. It was in this century that old cities began filling up and new cities were established. Nor were these cities mud-and-wattle encampments; they were, on the contrary, strongly made of stone and masonry and heavy timbers. Western man was regaining the confidence in himself that he had lost with the fall of Rome so many generations before; and neither empire nor princedom, but the city itself, showed his new vigor.

The scholar has laboriously described the origin of cities; the poet, too, has concerned himself with the city's birth. Indeed, it is well—even necessary—that we rely upon *both* the poet and the scholar for insight into municipal origins. For the city, being a work of art—"with language itself, it remains man's greatest work of art," Lewis Mumford has observed —often defies rational analysis; and where the scholar's reason fails, the poet or the prophet should be allowed to speak.

The very earliest cities which we know of historically served various purposes: they were centers of religion, of defense, of government, of trade and commerce. These were the earliest functions of the city. Can we not assume that these historic functions provide some explanations for its origins?

Economic Origins. The prevailing explanation for the origin of the city is an economic one: man discovered that he could raise crops and domesticate certain animals. Having thus made his food supply secure, he was then able to progress from a nomadic to a sedentary life—and thence to the urban revolution. This theory has a hard, pragmatic ring to it. To our practical and unpoetic minds today, it must seem obvious that man would need to set up some system of supply before he could erect and maintain the city. Viewed carefully, however, this hypothesis has certain dangers. We can, of course, be reasonably sure that the discovery of cities came close upon the first cultivation of crops and the domestication of animals. The question arises as to whether the economic always preceded the urban revolution.

The anthropologist tends to emphasize the economic origins of the city over all others; yet even he, at times, is willing to minimize the role of economics. Redfield has observed that the urban and food-producing revolutions were simply two parts of one great transformation, but that the urban revolution was the part which changed the minds and habits of mankind. It was the city which produced "novel and transforming attitudes" toward life.[1]

All of this is not to discount the economic origins of the city. Some cities, unquestionably, originated for purely economic reasons, but others doubtless began and flourished from different causes. Just as man himself has motivations other than economic, so his development of the city probably had noneconomic sources as well as economic ones.

Religious Origins. Because man's search for the godhead has always been of central importance to him, one should not be surprised to find in the religious quest a reason for the city's birth. Religion requires an altar; the altar, a temple and sacred ground; and such elements of the religious life cannot always be transported back and forth across the face of the earth by a migratory people. Ancient religion wanted permanence, was nonmigratory, had a strong sense of place.

A sense of place, indeed, has been strong throughout the development of the human race; and religion was, to a considerable degree, responsible for this local loyalty. The Aryan peoples of Asia, ancestors of most of the inhabitants of the Western world, developed a religion which strongly attached them to the soil. Originating long before recorded history, this religion was basically a form of ancestor worship, and it centered around the hearth, where the patriarchs of the family presided, and around the tombs, where they were buried.

Long before history we find that ancient man has transformed his ancestors into gods. The hearth has become the altar of those gods; and the fire on the hearth, a sacred fire, which must not be moved except when the family is in extremity. Look closely, for a moment, at these ancient peoples: "When they establish the hearth, it is with the thought and hope that it will always remain at the same spot. . . . The god of the family wishes to have a fixed abode. . . ." Caught up in his veneration of the dead, the ancient finds himself compelled to settle upon a fixed spot. He has made the hearth into an altar, before which he worships his ancestors, and upon the altar burns the sacred fire, which has instructed him in a new way of life: ". . . the sacred fire taught men to build houses: and indeed, men who were fixed by their religion to one spot, which they believed it their duty not to quit, would soon begin to think of raising in that place some solid structure. The tent covers the Arab, the wagon the Tartar; but a family that has a domestic hearth has need of a permanent dwelling. The stone

[1] Robert Redfield, *The Primitive World and Its Transformations* (Ithaca, N.Y.: Cornell University Press, 1953), p. 5.

house soon succeeds the mud cabin or the wagon hut. The family did not build for the life of a single man, but for generations that were to succeed each other in the same dwelling." [2]

In this chronology, first comes a religion that tells wandering man to stand still. Next come permanent buildings: homes, storehouses, perhaps a palisade for rudimentary defense. Then man has a village, and with a village the beginnings of an urban life.

But we do not need to rely exclusively upon such authorities as Fustel de Coulanges (quoted above) to deduce that religion helped primitive man to develop an identity of place. The paleolithic art in the caves of Altamira and Lascaux, discovered after Fustel's death, shows that more than 20,000 years ago man was habitually returning to one spot and that he prized it perhaps above all others. Having once found this attachment to place—a place for his gods and his art—he had broken through the cultural barrier of his *Wanderleben* and was ready to stand still.

Defensive and Governmental Origins. After five centuries of darkness the people of Western Europe, as we have already seen, rediscovered the art of city building and of urban living. What was the reason for this? "The revival of trade," says Mumford, "is often taken, even by eminent scholars like [Henri] Pirenne, as the direct cause of the civilizing activities that took place in the eleventh century." This is not so, Mumford believes: only when the collection of farmers' huts was walled and made secure against outside depredation did the urban community come into existence. "Note the sequence," advises Mumford. "First the cowering countryside, with its local production and mainly local barter: social life gathered in little villages or in 'suburbs,' as the agricultural settlements that nestled under the castle's walls were called. Then a deliberate physical reconstruction of the environment: the wall: protection made permanent and regular." [3] In the security behind the walls the market place could develop and trade could flourish, but these things came after the building of the city, not before it.

Vergil, in the *Aeneid,* describes the founding of Rome for reasons mystical and heroic, most certainly not economic. The facts here bear out the poet; Rome's site was good for defense, for government, even for worship of the pagan gods. It was not ideal for trade. And again, in the Book of Genesis, Adam is shown disconsolate and inconsolable after having been driven from the Garden of Eden. His wife bears him two sons: Abel, the shepherd, and Cain, the farmer. When Cain slew Abel, he was forgiven by Jehovah, but in punishment God drove him from his own country. This might have been his undoing, except that, in the words of the chronicler, "Cain went

[2] Numa Denis Fustel de Coulanges, *The Ancient City* (Boston: Lee and Shepard, 1873; Garden City, N.Y.: Doubleday Co., Anchor Books, 1956), pp. 61, 62.

[3] Lewis Mumford, *The Culture of Cities* (New York: Harcourt, Brace & Co., 1938), pp. 17, 16.

out from the presence of Jehovah, and dwelt in the land of Nod, on the east of Eden . . . and he builded a city, and called the name of the city, after the name of his son, Enoch." Thereafter the sons of Adam prospered: they had made peace with their God, and they had built a city. The city served as their primary tool to conquer the wilderness, as their primary defense against their enemies, and as the seat of their government.

Man's imagination has often outrun his needs and his capacities. To the nomadic chieftain, proud and egocentric, a rocky hilltop, which was his refuge and the refuge of his people when hard-pressed by tribal enemies, might have seemed the logical place to stay, not merely for the moment, but through the long years. So he put his people to work on crude fortifications, on storehouses and dwelling places. He put aside his tent for a permanent building, to give himself prestige and to give himself comfort. He was the prototype of Kubla Khan, whom Coleridge dreamed of in an opium-induced sleep:

> In Xanadu did Kubla Khan
> A stately pleasure-dome decree:
> Where Alph, the sacred river, ran
> Through caverns measureless to man
> Down to a sunless sea.

Fixed in one spot, members of the tribe were forced to invent ways of supplying themselves with food and clothing. They trapped wild animals and brought them to their fortified village to slaughter as the need arose. They harvested wild rice in the valley. Some of the animals grew tame; the rice sprouted in the rich earth of the cattle pens; the tribe was on the verge of the urban and food-producing revolutions.

Both Mumford and Fustel de Coulanges think of the central walled fortress, where the chieftain lives surrounded by the shanties and ephemeral dwellings of the people, as the primordial form of the city. The archaeologist has unearthed evidence in Palestine that the hunter's camp became transformed into a permanent stronghold. Can we not expect that the village which grew up around the stronghold did so for reasons of defense, and that this village, as Mumford has remarked, represented the "unfertilized ovum" of the city?

Thus, we can say conclusively only that the origins of the city are indeed obscure. But we can also say tentatively that the causal forces that started the urban revolution were probably economic, political, and religious, acting either independently or in concert. Most certainly can we make this modest, though negative, assessment of the evidence: the origins of the city were more than economic in nature. More than simply a place of economic benefit, designed to help man fill his belly and his pockets, the city seemed to arise out of man's mind bursting upward to his gods, out of his need to defend himself, to erect a splendid building, stage a play, maintain a stable government. If man does not live by bread alone, neither does he build his cities merely to feed, clothe, and shelter himself.

From the Tigris to the Tiber

In the valleys of two great rivers of the Middle East, the Tigris and Euphrates, began the cities, and thus the civilization, of what today we describe as the West. Ancient Babylon was great by 2000 B.C. and so was her sister city, Nineveh. Memphis, capital of Egypt on the Nile, had flourished and waned before 2500 B.C. We cannot be sure of the government of these cities, except to know that they had a government. We can say little about their politics, their art, their commerce, their agriculture, or their religion, except that they had these, too.

Emerging out of millennia that seem empty to us, though they surely were not, these great cities suddenly appeared and flourished; then waned and disappeared. Yet even when they disappeared as Memphis disappeared, they did not wholly die; they had started a revolution in man's affairs, a new way of life: urbanism. This new phenomenon was to spread slowly to the entire Mediterranean world and to become the index of man's achievement.

When we think of the ancient world, two cities invariably come to mind: Athens and Rome. Athens we remember for her great art, her ideas and philosophies, her way of life; Rome we remember for her laws and engineering and public administration. Five hundred years before Christ, Athens was entering upon her Golden Age. Considerably smaller in area than the largest American county today, and far smaller in population than our largest city, Athens created a civilization unexcelled, either before that time or since. The men she produced—whether Socrates, Sophocles, or dozens of others—were the artistic and intellectual peers of any men who have lived in the more than 2,000 years since the Athenian Golden Age. No man can consider himself an educated person today unless he has read Aristotle's *Politics* or Sophocles' *Oedipus Rex,* or unless he can distinguish between the Corinthian and Ionic columns of Greek architecture. By the same token, every Western man must consider himself the intellectual heir of the Athenians.

In Athens indeed—this small city-state upon a barren coast—a few men reached the very summit in art and science and a way of life. And in government, too, for government *was* their way of life. Once you have taken the measure of Athens, and all that it represented, you can never again be sure that there is such a thing as progress in human affairs. If the heights were reached between 500 and 400 B.C., what profit is there to dream of progress? That is, unless you dream, with Augustine, of a *City of God.*

The Athenians thought of and explored almost every facet of human life. But thought and intellectual discussion never took them so far away from the everyday world that they could not construct an ideal city. They were practical enough to develop a great fleet and to become a major naval power. In education they insisted upon more than a thorough reading of the philosophers. Realizing that a man is only as good as his body, they insisted also that their youths practice gymnastics with their schooling. It was in this happy combination of thought and action that the Athenians were so extraordinary. Probably no other society has so excellently combined dreams and action. In Athens there was, in a very real sense, no withdrawal from life. Even their art—which modern man so often regards as withdrawal—Athenians considered as the essence of life itself.

The real genius of the Greeks was their ability to integrate—to live life completely. This had an important effect upon their views of politics. Politics was life and life politics. In Jowett's translation of Aristotle's *Politics,* so often quoted, man is spoken of as a political animal. Actually, one could translate Aristotle's meaning by saying, as well, that man is a social, or gregarious, creature. To Aristotle, either version would have seemed valid, for in Athens in its heyday there was no distinction between society and politics, a distinction so often made in the twentieth century. To the Greeks "all men . . . [had to] exercise political authority in order to realize their best life." [4] The Athenian could no more disengage himself from his city than he could turn his back on living itself.

From Greece, the center of the Western world shifted to Rome. For sheer size, for military prowess, for a fine legal sense, Rome was unequaled in the ancient world. Her army and navy made the Mediterranean a Roman sea, and for centuries Rome was to maintain hegemony—though sometimes tenuously— over that sea and all the lands washed by it.

The Romans had a genius for city building. In 1954, as workmen tore down a bomb-gutted building in Vienna's inner city, they found, deep under the foundations, some tile floors and masonry walls. Cautiously excavating further, under direction of the city archaeologist, the workers uncovered the remains of a stone house built by the Romans on the shores of the Danube 2,000 years before. This house, with its ingenious central heating system (the winters on the Danube were, and are, cold and dreary), was a part of the fortified city of Vindobona, situated at one of the northernmost extremities of the Roman Empire. This was one of the deepest of Ro-

---

[4] Lawrence L. Wanlass, *Gettel's History of Political Thought* (New York: Appleton-Century-Crofts, 2nd ed., 1953), p. 41.

man penetrations inland, because Rome, even as Athens before her, was a great naval power, and relied heavily upon the seas for her lines of communication. Vienna, therefore, was never more than an army encampment. The great cities of the Roman world were never far from the sea.

But great cities there were—almost a multitude of them. If the rural peoples resisted the Romans and Roman ways and the strange Roman tongue, the urban dweller rejoiced in them and eagerly sought after Roman commerce and Roman citizenship. Upon the cities Rome relied, not only for commerce and defense, but also for the loyalty that was so necessary to the maintenance of the Empire. After Christianity was adopted by the Emperor Constantine, it spread throughout the Empire; that is, through the cities of the Empire. The rural peoples were not so easily persuaded, and the Roman word for countryman—*paganus*—has been stamped upon our language with the similar word "pagan"—referring to the unchurched, the unbeliever, the heathen.

As the West sank into that great hiatus between the ancient and medieval worlds, the Dark Ages, happily there was kept for us the record of the Greek and the Roman antique civilizations. Although man has doubtless chosen to emulate the Romans more than the Greeks, he should nevertheless be grateful for the example the Athenians held up to him. For the Greeks possessed the scientific and poetic mind; the Romans, only the legal and engineering. As a result the Greeks built great cities while the Romans merely created a splendid municipal administration. It is not hyperbolic to say, therefore, that it is the real task of Western man to go beyond the Romans and seek to capture in his cities the genius of Greek civilization.

Light and Darkness

With the fall of the Roman Empire (476 A.D.) the great urban civilization that Rome had built rapidly crumbled. The barbarians from the north did not really wish to destroy the cities—indeed, they were in awe of them—but, untutored in urban ways, they could manage neither an urban government nor an urban society. The cities slowly emptied; the great part of the people of Europe slid into darkness. Rome in 700 A.D. was a mere shell—a few people rattling around in gigantic ruins.

But while the West languished, the exotic civilization of the Arabs stepped up in tempo. Although Islam destroyed much of the urban life in the Mediterranean world, it soon built quite remarkable cities of its own: Córdova, Cairo, Baghdad. By the eighth and ninth centuries a rich urban life had developed throughout the Arab world.

With Charlemagne, the chaos of Western existence diminished, and the hopefulness of a new age showed itself in the hesitant revival of a few cities. But the Carolingian period was not to mark the beginning of medieval fruitfulness. Before the Middle Ages, in all their greatness, could properly begin, Carolingian centralization had to die, and a new, vigorous localism take its place. When historians have bewailed the particularism of either the Greek world or the Middle Ages, they have simply decried the genius of each age.

With particularism, with the federalizing of the West in the eleventh century, began the medieval period, surely one of the most remarkable ages of man. After its long sleep, the West suddenly sprang to life. By the twelfth century a genuine renaissance was under way; it was a renaissance of city building, and of all of those remarkable human activities associated with the revival of cities: art and learning, curiosity and commerce, religion and citizenship.

Just as the decline of cities was one of the factors that doomed Roman civilization, so their revival signaled a new Europe. The twelfth century itself was a time for the extension of old cities and the founding of new ones. Mumford comments that the building of towns was one of the major activities of the early medieval period. During the Middle Ages in Europe over 2,500 new towns were established.

The urban culture of the medieval period was vital and productive, even measured in purely quantitative terms. During these centuries one of the greatest of all architectural forms—the Gothic—was developed and widely used. A vernacular Latin evolved, and in it appeared a literature of considerable bulk, if not importance. At the same time poets were writing in the idiom of the various regions and peoples: thus Chaucer wrote in Middle English and became one of the literary immortals. The theater had a new beginning in the religious morality plays. Modern universities have their roots in the medieval era. In Paris, Prague, various Italian cities, and elsewhere, communities of scholars (students and teachers) pursued learning with a zest that since then may have been rivaled but has never been excelled.

In politics, too, and in government and commerce the cities dominated the era. Upon the countryside lay the darkness of serfdom. In the cities men fought for freedom and more often than not attained it. Urban life, indeed, demanded freedom from the feudal customs enforced by prince, baron, or bishop—freedom of a new legal system, power to tax, right to transfer and mortgage property; in sum, the power of people (although an elite) to govern themselves.

It was the self-governing city (often described now as the city-state) that dominated most of the medieval world. Sometimes these cities stood almost alone in their respective sovereignties; sometimes they sought strength and protection in federations, such as the renowned Hanseatic League.

Venice was a city that stood alone and still rose to greatness. Founded in the fifth century by people fleeing from the rampages of the barbarians coming down from the north, it was not ideally situated for urban growth. Here was little more than a salt marsh, out of which rose a few dozen islands. The nearest fresh water was miles away on the mainland. At the new city's doorstep was the sea, and in between was the sandbar, which gave protection from the storm-driven tides: a protection but also a barrier, for in order to survive Venice had to get her ships across the bar and out to sea. Since this site was so full of hazards, how could men build a city? How could these many fragments, separated by such a multitude of saltwater channels and canals, come together in an organic, working unit?

Somehow the hazards were surmounted, and by the dawn of the medieval period, Venice was already an important urban center; the Dark Ages had never quite enveloped her. By the thirteenth century she had a great merchant marine and a formidable fleet. Because of her maritime greatness, she was able to reap great commercial rewards from the Crusades. In the latter part of the fourteenth century Venice defeated her great rival, Genoa; by the fifteenth century, she had a merchant fleet of 300 vessels and a navy of 45 galleys manned by 11,000 men.

At the other end of Europe, Lübeck achieved greatness by becoming the center of the Hanseatic League, the largest of all leagues of independent cities. Founded in that remarkable century of city building, the twelfth, Lübeck was fortunately situated on the estuary of the Trave River, a location that gave it a good harbor and an opportunity to engage in the Baltic Sea trade. Its fortunes were linked closely to that trade and to the power and influence of the Hanseatic League.

In government the medieval city was invariably aristocratic. The town councils, however selected, represented the well-to-do commercial class. Yet it is just as well not to emphasize too greatly this aspect of the city, because, aristocratic or not, the urban center represented freedom to the ordinary man; and it was to the city that he looked for a loosening of feudal restrictions. Thus if we do not today regard the government of the medieval town as free, it is only because we have learned to identify freedom with such modern democratic devices as universal manhood suffrage and bills of rights.

But freedom is a relative term; and in the eleventh to fifteenth centuries the urban citizen had only to look through the gates of his city to the countryside, where the serf labored on the land which owned him, to realize just how free the city was and how free he was in the city. Observe this bit of evidence: the great revolts of the medieval period were peasant revolts, not urban ones. It was, indeed, this freedom which gave urban man such pride in his own city. It was perhaps as much in joyful appreciation of his city as it was in strength of faith that he spent generations in building a Gothic cathedral. It was pride in his city that made him build the Rathaus or Hotel de Ville. It was local pride that made him lay out his city and cultivate its growth like a garden. The remarkable, ordered irregularity of the medieval city is still a tribute to the citizen's pride in his city and, as well, to his common sense and keen perception of form.

Modern man builds his industrial city, typically, by first laying out rigid squares, then making the site conform to the engineer's drawing. But the medievalist had respect for the natural contours of the land (fortunately perhaps for him, the bulldozer had yet to be invented), for light and air, for green, open spaces. He meant to live in his city, not flee from it to the suburbs at the earliest opportunity, and he built with care and great skill.

Gradually the medieval period fused into the Renaissance. Contrary to common belief, the Renaissance did not represent a sudden flowering upon a landscape that had previously been desert. Man's horizons widened, undoubtedly; yet the Renaissance did not grow out of dead soil; rather, it came directly from the immense fertility of the medieval period.

The city, its art, and its government were of the greatest importance to the Renaissance man, even as they had been to his earlier counterpart in the Middle Ages. So important were the cities that even some of the Popes were deeply interested in them. G. E. Kidder Smith speaks of "Sixtus V, the great town-planning Pope." [5] City planning as we conceive of it, however, was virtually unknown, either in the medieval or Renaissance period. Planning, in either period, was organic: a slow growth or evolution, by means of which the form of the city was delicately fused with the life of its people. It is no wonder that one hears of no great city planners in the long centuries between the Carolingian and Elizabethan epochs. If a Sixtus V was interested in town planning, it was much as a botanist is interested in an antique oak, itself a classic production of nature in league with time. Perhaps, like the botanist, he would cut off a dead limb here or graft on a branch there, but this was only to cooperate with the generations that had gone before.

Although democracy, as we understand it, was unknown in the Renaissance city, considerable freedom nevertheless existed. Even the despot of the Italian city-state of the late medieval period looked with misgivings on hereditary privileges. Writing of the despot, Jacob Burckhardt observed that "with his thirst for fame and his passion for monumental works, it was talent, not birth, which he needed. In the company of the poet and the scholar he felt himself in a new position, almost, indeed, in possession of a new legitimacy." [6] If this need of the despot for men of achievement did not democratize society, it did help to create a freedom and upward mobility unknown outside the great cities. Thus if one could paint, if he could write,

---

[5] G. E. Kidder Smith, *Italy Builds* (New York: Reinhold Publishing Corp., 1955), p. 90.

[6] Jacob Burckhardt, *The Civilization of the Renaissance in Italy* (New York: Random House, Modern Library, 1954), pp. 8–29.

if he had the urgings of a capitalist or a politician, he could rise to the heights of achievement in the Renaissance cities.

The politics of the Italian city-states is best remembered through the writings of a Florentine politician. A republican in principle, a longtime servant of the Republic of Florence, the leader responsible for introducing a reform that has become a feature of modern democratic states (the citizen army), he is nevertheless remembered largely for his book in praise of the despot. This politician was, of course, Niccolò Machiavelli, and the book was *The Prince*. Machiavelli embodies, in his career and his writings, much of the essentials of Renaissance politics. He might, indeed, be described as one of the first of modern politicians. Showing his devotion to republican principles in the *Discourses* and in his history of his city, he was led (or misled) to praise of the tyrant, possibly by personal ambition for a return to power, possibly by a misplaced devotion to his own city that could insist on any means, however immoral or amoral, if the ends were a stronger state. If his career is, then, not a complete summary of Florentine or Renaissance politics, it is at least an indication at once of the devotion of Renaissance man to his city and of his political parochialism when his thoughts wandered outside the city gates.

From the Baroque to the Modern

By the seventeenth century the city was beginning to feel profound changes. A new agitation of mind and heart—nationalism—was creeping over the face of Europe. A split in Christendom caused men's passions to flame and moved Christians to visit unspeakable enormities upon other Christians. Cities cowered behind their thickening walls, dreading the new ordnance that resulted from the spreading use of gunpowder. The city continued to grow, but for the most part its citizenry had lost its heart to quarrelsome kings and contending bishops. True, in Italy, there was enough vitality left to produce the baroque and enough interest in the Germanies effectively to utilize it. True, also, again in the Italian peninsula and in the Germanies, many cities were able to keep their political identity; but in every case these were delaying actions. Localism was rapidly dying.

German and Italian particularism, extending into the nineteenth century, has often been decried. Undoubtedly, this particularism represented a great falling off from that vital identity so many cities were able to establish and maintain during the medieval and Renaissance periods. Furthermore, the continued political fragmentation of Italy, and much of the Germanies, was sometimes destructive of basic local and personal freedoms. To one interested, however, in the cultural and social vitality of the city, the small city-states and principalities that made up what is now modern Italy and Germany can only be regarded as great good fortune. While London and Paris were sapping the lifeblood of English and French cities in the early modern period, Frankfort and Munich did not have to contend with centripetal forces centered in Berlin; nor did Venice and Genoa need to fear the cultural and social imperialism of Rome.

Politically, too, particularism had its advantages. Petty despotisms could and did flourish in Germany and Italy, but even the machinations of Prussia were held in check by the local patriotism of the citizens in city-state and principality. The fatuous nonsense of Mussolini and the grotesque enormities of Hitler could never appear until nationalism had leveled local loyalties and created the Leviathan.

The Crowded City. One of the evils of the present—misuse of urban land—had its beginnings in the early modern period. Crowding was known in ancient Rome and perhaps, in rare instances, in the medieval city. The countryside was only a few minutes away from the small medieval city, and thus, if the land was crowded with buildings and a street happened to be teeming with people, a citizen did not need to travel miles through slums to get relief from the press of humanity. The medieval city, moreover, could be easily extended. Suburbs were built under the old walls, and these mere settlements were gradually enclosed, so that the city showed a kind of cellular growth, ever enlarging as the need for enlargement arose.

By the sixteenth century the outer walls of the city were rapidly thickening. The new ordnance, especially cannon, required a new kind of protection: no longer could the city be safeguarded by a mere shell of stone or wood. The early medieval city had often used a log palisade for its wall— much like what the frontier forts used for over two centuries in America. The word "burg," not uncommonly a suffix in a modern city's name, originally was Anglo-Saxon for the protecting enclosure or palisade about a settlement. Now the thin medieval wall was no longer sufficient. A great embankment of masonry and earth had to be constructed, and this required substantial capital outlays. As a consequence, the city could not expand without the enormous expense of extending the wall. Since capital for this extension was not easily forthcoming, within the great walls land values rose rapidly, and open spaces disappeared. Splendid buildings, so lovingly put up by the medieval citizenry, were cut off from view by shops and tenements. Buildings crowded upon the land and people crowded into the buildings.

The Soulless City. But if the baroque city was to destroy its heritage— the legacy of the Middle Ages and the Renaissance—the industrial town was to lose its soul entirely. The rapid increase in Europe's population that came with the Industrial Revolution, the enclosures in England that forced the people from the land into the cities, the burdens of tax systems, the ineptitude of municipal and national governments, these and other factors converted the cities of Europe, and later of America, into something little better than pigsties. If a worker, crowded into a hovel in London or Manchester, ever heard the comment of the English jurist, spoken in the best liberal tradition, that a man's house is his castle, he must surely have been moved to sardonic laughter. It is certainly to the discredit of the great liberal era that it concerned itself so much with nation-states and individual rights that it forgot about its cities. Little wonder that the urban proletariat of Europe crawled out of its sewers, at last, to stone not only the despots, but the middle-class liberals as well. Marxism, syndicalism, anarchism, and fascism may have been invented by members of the middle class, but it was the urban proletariat that took these antiliberal doctrines to its bosom.

For the city, the nineteenth century was a terrible century, sowing the winds that are now being harvested by twentieth-century cities as whirlwinds. Lewis Mumford sums it up: "Though the nineteenth century was certainly, in a quantitative way, the greatest era of city building the world had ever known, it created its new urban environment without benefit of art or science. Neither the methods nor the goals of urban planning were understood: for the city itself, as an artifact of culture, had hardly been described; and without knowledge the last century lacked the power to create." [7]

Because city life in this terrible century was destructive instead of humane, much of the constructive work done by the city worker became, for him, fruitless endeavor. For now that the urban was no longer urbane, even work had lost that ennobling quality celebrated by poet and prophet and was transmuted into drudgery. It seemed, indeed, as if the new form of work, industrial toil, would wholly change the character of the city. Probably it is hyperbolic to say that the nineteenth century exactly reversed the nature of urban life as it had previously been, that the serf now belonged to the city, the free man to the countryside. That that reversal did not quite come off is indicative of the good sense of Western man. Yet, in the United States, the trauma of nineteenth-century city life has left its mark in a continuing distrust of the city. The trauma, in Europe, still appears in the ideology of Marx and Lenin (itself a reaction to the heartless urbanism of the last century). The city will not soon cast off the effects of this last dark age.

Summary

For upwards of five millennia Western man has experimented with the city, and for a much longer period he has been involved with the urban

---

[7] Lewis Mumford, *The Human Prospect* (Boston: Beacon Press, 1955), p. 105.

revolution. Arising out of complex forces, the city has shown complex tendencies. Although it may not be the carrier of warfare, the city has often been, as Mumford suggests, a container for violence and an agent of war. If the great city federations of the Middle Ages contradict this judgment, the Greek city-states and those of the Renaissance illustrate it. To the Athenian, as well as to the Florentine, the politics of the world beyond the city wall was essentially the politics of violence.

It was the Athenians who first began developing systematic ideas about the city. In a very real sense their philosophy of the state, or of politics, was a philosophy of the city and its polity. These people who could not think beyond the local citizenry were essentially theorizers about the city.

Oddly enough, modern man has rarely addressed himself directly to the idea of the city. Yet such ideas exist; or they can be derived from the political folk wisdom, from the empirical evidence, and from the systematic philosophy of the modern world. Before we can intelligently review the political phenomenon of the American city, we must see what those ideas are.

Annotated Bibliography

One of the most perceptive books on the ancient city was written a hundred years ago by the French scholar Fustel de Coulanges (Numa Denis Fustel de Coulanges, *The Ancient City* [Boston: Lee and Shepard, 1873]). It may be easily found and purchased in a recent paperback edition (Garden City, N. Y.: Doubleday & Co., Anchor Books, 1956). Among other things, the evidence that Fustel gives of the religious origins of the city is impressive and should weaken—for all time or until better evidence is in—the economic-determinist argument about urban origins. If Fustel is not an empiricist, in modern terms, his scholarship is impressive; and his evidence is more acceptable than much of the faulty generalizations that are made from the findings of archaeological digs.

For the ancient's idea of the city, one can best go to Plato's *Republic*. Far from being an examination of the characteristics of the nation-state, as many scholars have assumed, the work is a Platonic view of the ideal city. And it is probably as good an example of the ancient view of the city as we can come by, though one can never forget the works of Edith Hamilton. See especially Edith Hamilton, *The Greek Way* (New York: W. W. Norton & Co., 1930).

Something of the urbane temper of medieval man may be gotten from Charles Haskins, for his study of the Renaissance of the twelfth century is, in fact, a study of the city during that remarkable period. Published some years ago, it is now available in an inexpensive edition. See Charles H. Haskins, *The Renaissance of the Twelfth Century* (New York: Meridian Books, 1957). Burckhardt's history is essentially a dissertation upon life in the Italian city-states of the fourteenth and fifteenth centuries. See Jacob Burckhardt, *The Civilization of the Renaissance in Italy* (New York: Random House, Modern Library, 1954). One may find in Mundy and Riesenberg a brief but adequate treatment of the medieval city. See John H. Mundy and Peter Riesenberg, *The Medieval Town* (Princeton, N. J.: D. Van Nostrand Co., Anchor Original, 1958). And the eminent Belgian scholar Henri Pirenne has a short, excellent treatise on the same theme, which has had as much effect upon present-day medieval scholarship as the growth of cities had on the medieval period. See Henri Pirenne, *Medieval Cities: Their Origins and the Revival of Trade* (Princeton, N. J.: Princeton University Press, 1925). Pirenne's economic interpretation of history has, of course, been seriously challenged, but the value of his small book remains essentially unimpaired.

The Viennese medievalist Friedrich Heer has produced a one-volume history of the Middle Ages which should be on the shelves of anyone interested in the city between 1100 and 1350 A.D. See Friedrich Heer, *The Medieval World* (New York: The New American Library, Mentor Books, 1963).

No student of the city can safely do without Lewis Mumford. Virtually everything he has written is pertinent, in one way or another, to urban life, but two works especially are essential. See Lewis Mumford, *The City in History—Its Origins, Its Transformations, and Its Prospects* (New York: Harcourt, Brace & World, 1961), and *The Culture of Cities* (New York: Harcourt, Brace & Co., 1938).

CHAPTER 3

The Idea of the City

Because the city is the oldest of all sophisticated human political institutions, a concept of the city does in fact exist in the Western world. In this chapter we shall subject this concept to historical, logical, and empirical analysis by breaking it down into five parts: the self-evident idea, the idea of local equality, the objective idea, the kinship idea, and the ethical idea. With all of these ideas brought together, we can—hopefully—create a theory of the city.

The Self-evident Idea

The View from Athens. The Greeks were deeply concerned with the city and with its polity. Their state was truly Lilliputian, whether viewed demographically or geographically. Athens was as small in population as it was in area; and when Plato conceived of his utopian republic, he was thinking of it as a prototype of his home city. (A population of 5,040 households was ideal, he said in the *Laws.*) Athenian political philosophy was, then, a philosophy of the free city-state, essentially unitary in structure— far more unitary in fact than any geographically extensive nation-state, such as France, could ever be.

If the Greeks did not think of federalism, if they did not write about local self-determination in the modern fashion, the reason was that they conceived of "state" and "city" as essentially interchangeable terms. And since the state was the city, it was above all else local; and there was no need to investigate further into political organization. Forgetting this all-too-obvious truth, forgetting also that the Greek philosophers and statesmen were particularistic almost to the point of self-destruction, we have often misinterpreted Greek ideas. If the great Athenians were political centralists, they still placed their political unity in a local setting. More to our point, these Athenians sought to arrive at an idea of the city. The question now is, What was that idea?

The principal elements of the idea were that an urban place with a surrounding hinterland was ethically self-sufficient; that a reasonably homogeneous elite group within the city, tied together by ancient tribal and religious attachments, should govern; and that whatever were the political relations that might exist between one city-state and another, they must not be of a character to diminish the sovereignty of the home city.[1] Though an Alexander might create an empire, such a political occurrence could only be viewed by the Greeks as accidental, or as not worthy of systematic examination.

Localists and Universalists of the Middle Ages. During the medieval period, the idea of a universal Christian commonwealth, coupled with a rapidly growing urban population in the free cities, reinforced the particularism of the era. In order for the middle and artisan classes in the new cities to flourish, two essential elements were necessary: freedom for the city from irksome exactions, whether of prince, monarch, or bishop; and a trading community that was extended as widely as possible geographically. To a surprising degree the social, political, economic, and religious values of both the people and the leadership in medieval cities corresponded, even in spite of the class conflict that developed.

The artisan viewed the city as an island of freedom, in which he needed to spend but a year and a day to throw off the feudal yoke. The city wall was a psychological symbol of an enriched life as much as it was a physical symbol of protection. The merchant, too, equated the city with freedom, though not in such personal terms, perhaps, as did the artisan. To him the city represented economic and political power as well as physical protection for his family, himself, and his goods.

Moving beyond the city, both merchant and artisan recognized that it was to their own benefit that no barriers to movement of people or goods be raised by robber baron or robber monarch. And thus did a local orientation extend naturally into a universal one. Far from being nationalistic, as their successors were to become centuries later, the medieval merchant and artisan were at once localists and universalists. These were indeed complementary viewpoints, which helped to develop logic and coherence to the system of values of the urban dweller.

The Utopians. If the Greeks and the medieval urban dweller were particularistic, many utopians of the modern period were hardly less so. Sir Thomas More's Utopia of 1516, like Plato's republic, was conceived as essentially a city-state, small in population and geographically circumscribed. More's Utopia was an island containing fifty-four small cities, each of which had a population of about 6,000 families. Thus, by these criteria, Boston, Philadelphia, and Charleston, during the colonial period, were virtually de facto city-states.

Robert Owen's experiments at New Lanark, his abortive adventure at New Harmony, and his later advocacy of "villages of cooperation," were all based on a view of society that was as particularistic as it was socialistic. So

---

[1] See Norton Long's essay, "Aristotle and the Study of Local Government." This is a perceptive examination of Athenian ideas and their application to modern political life. In Norton E. Long, *The Polity* (Chicago: Rand McNally & Co., 1962), Ch. 17.

also with the multitude of utopian communities which spread across the American continent during the nineteenth century: Brook Farm, Oneida, Amana, and countless others. Though economic and social theory—and sometimes religious values—tended to shunt politics to the side in these utopian communities, their particularistic bias is self-evident. The utopians sought to create a sociopolitical community which was small, autonomous, and self-governing. They reached, in short, for the Athenian ideal. They could live in peace with the nation-state if the nation-state did not interfere in their internal affairs, or did not force upon them external relations not of their liking. Here was a striking resemblance, one must admit, to Plato's republic, even though the utopian settlements might differ from the social pattern envisaged by Plato.[2]

Except for the utopians and a handful of commentators upon federalism, few theorists of the modern period have felt it necessary to give more than passing attention to local government. Their assumption has been that any local political grouping, urban or otherwise, is a mere adjunct of the state. Where the Greeks could literally not think beyond the city to a larger political grouping, the moderns have difficulty bringing themselves inward from the national to the local. If the Greeks are responsible for political theory's concentration on the unitary state, as Georg Jellinek has suggested, they can hardly be blamed for it. Their concern was with the city, by nature local and unitary.[3]

The Self-evident Idea as Folk Wisdom. Throughout the English-speaking world, local government is accepted almost without question. It is a fact of nature, one might say rather loosely, which surrounds us and which has always been with us. It is a part of our political folk culture. If we raise any fundamental questions about local government—Is it democratic or elitist? Is it efficient or is it inept?—even these questions are based upon the folk knowledge that local government is always with us and always will be. In the United States, the existence of local government is explicitly recognized in the federal system and implicitly recognized constitutionally, if we consider the fundamental laws of our states as a part of the American constitutional system.

In England, it is probably similarly based. As Professor W. J. M. Mackenzie has remarked, "My . . . conclusion is that in some sense or other local government is now a part of the English constitution, the English notion of what proper government ought to be." [4] Elsewhere in the English-

[2] Even the twentieth-century utopian is often particularistic. Note Broadacre City, in Frank Lloyd Wright, *The Living City* (New York: Horizon Press, 1958).

[3] See Stanley Hoffman, "Areal Division of Powers in the Writings of French Political Thinkers," in Arthur Maass (ed.), *Area and Power—A Theory of Local Government* (Glencoe, Ill.: The Free Press, 1959), p. 114.

[4] W. J. M. Mackenzie, "Theories of Local Government," *Greater London Papers No. 2* (London: The London School of Economics and Political Science, 1961), pp. 5, 7.

speaking world, where the legal systems and even the political attitudes have been influenced by British political institutions, one may find the notion of local government accepted as one of the eternal verities. One might suppose that Americans, Canadians, and Australians, as much as the British, come fitted out with a political Gestalt, into which primordial pattern they fit their governmental structure and powers. Let us remember that wherever Englishmen have gone, whether to Jamestown in 1607, to Bombay shortly thereafter, or to Lagos in 1861, they have taken with them, as a matter of course, their local-government institutions. Mackenzie puts it this way: "The policy of local government in the colonies . . . went through with as little opposition as a proposal for a royal tour."

For the French the situation was both similar and different. The French took overseas their concepts of local government—thus the similarity—but the French concept of local government, largely as an instrument of the central power, was completely different from the English. In Quebec the French did not erect a local-government structure, save in an administrative sense, and when the Constitutional Act of 1791 introduced a limited form of representative government, "The *Canadiens* were neither psychologically nor politically prepared for it." The French Canadians had not been permitted to develop democratically in at least one kind of training ground, local government.[5] And the pattern was repeated in French West Africa, where the French departed from their usual practice to permit some self-government in the Senegalese communes, only to find that they were sorely tried by the independent spirit of the Senegalese.[6] This adventure with a British type of local autonomy greatly troubled metropolitan France and led the government to revert back to the old pattern of rigid centralization. Metropolitan France has itself failed to construct a viable government. Professor Long sums up this failure in one devastating sentence: "One may see in France's apathetic masses a result that Burke foresaw in a metaphysical constitution that denies the necessity of mediating institutions between individual and nation." [7]

It seems, then, that to the English-speaking world the idea of local government is as self-evident as it was to the Greeks or to the medieval urban dweller. But where the Greeks went on to examine the axiomatic idea theoretically, the English-speaking peoples have, by and large, considered a theoretical examination unnecessary. Any attempt to build a theoretical philosophy about local government would simply be superfluous, they have assumed, because folk wisdom itself gives sufficient justification for it.

[5] Pierre Elliott Trudeau, "Some Obstacles to Democracy in Quebec," *The Canadian Journal of Economics and Political Science*, xxiv (August, 1959), p. 298.

[6] Virginia Thompson and Richard Adloff, *French West Africa* (Stanford, Calif.: Stanford University Press, 1957), p. 180.

[7] Long, *op. cit.*, p. 231.

The Idea of Local Equality

Federalism and Pluralism. In the modern era, marked by progressive attachment to nationalism—first by peoples in the West, and then by peoples the world around—the vigor of the local bias seemingly remains unimpaired. Not only does decentralization appear, in arguments based upon formal logic, as the inverse of centralism—thus you cannot pose the idea of political unity without at once entangling yourself with its *bête noire*, political diversity—but it also appears as a kind of recurring political reaction to centralized control in the everyday world. Nationalist sentiment has hardly stilled the states' rights argument in this republic; nor has insistence by the state governments upon complete sovereignty vis-à-vis the city stilled the demands of urban politicians for greater freedom of action. And one cannot shrug off the provincial loyalty of the citizen of Quebec, who seems to think more of his province than of the Canadian nation; nor of the citizen of tiny Gibraltar, who thinks of himself as a discrete political being, distinct and apart from either the British or the Spanish. In the real world of politics Lilliput does indeed thrive alongside the Leviathan.

The Federal Argument. Having stood the Greeks on their heads—those people who "never transcended the limits of the *polis*"—the modern thinker has permitted himself virtually a total engrossment in the nation-state and the idea of sovereignty. The only notable exception to this concentration upon political unity is to be found in the theories of federalism and pluralism. Although both of these theories can have some real use in furnishing a theoretical rationale for the city, their potential for furnishing such a rationale has never been realized.

Though the struggle between the centralist and the decentralist point of view in politics seems, to twentieth-century students, to be one of the eternal facts of statecraft, the Greeks, as we have seen, did not even consider the problem. Nor did the medieval European consider it to any considerable degree. It is a modern struggle, and a modern problem, therefore, that might be dated from the era of Jean Bodin, Cardinal Richelieu, and the long-drawn-out battle of the Huguenots to maintain their autonomous existence in an increasingly nationalistic, absolutist France.

Many observers seem to accept implicitly that a state with a decentralized structure or a community of peoples gathered into small, autonomous political groupings was at long last dispatched by German and Italian unification in the nineteenth century. This assumption ignores, of course, the rise of the federal states, and particularly the United States. In the latter republic, federalism has had untold detractors, even though it has shown surprising strength. Scholars by the score, politicians by platoons and divisions, pundits, right-wingers, left-wingers, and laymen have met countless times to bury the federal system only to find that they did not have a corpse to lay away.

No one would dare say that American federalism has lacked attention. For all that, one can with good reason argue that there is only one document in American political and legal literature that systematically and theoretically examines federalism as a principle of government. That document is John C. Calhoun's *A Disquisition on Government.* In the *Disquisition,* and the *Discourse* which followed, Calhoun's objective was, first, to explain why a decentralized governmental structure was essential to achieve a democratic state and, second, how that decentralized government could best be achieved. Finally, Calhoun's *Theory of the Concurrent Majority* was one of the most ingenious of American theories for supporting a decentralized, particularistic state, and for assuring the protection of geographic minorities from the overweening ambitions of majorities.

Aside from Calhoun's systematic appraisal of federalism, the literature abounds in either matter-of-fact or legalistic inspection of the relation of the states to the federal government, and little else. In other words, American arguments over federalism have tended to pose the question of *centralism* versus *decentralization* legalistically and practically, rather than ethically. Further still, the volumes written on our federal structure, far from giving a basis for urban autonomy, have treated solely of the states vis-à-vis the federal government. By overemphasizing the power struggle between these two levels of government, the federal argument has ignored the cities and has probably even helped to reinforce the arbitrary "sovereign" control of the cities by the states. With Calhoun's ideas, on the other hand, one could proceed to support the ethical autonomy of any kind of political division, let us say, for example, that of a city of 1,000,000 with a home-rule charter.

If one of the basic political values of Americans is that much of the governmental process should be locally controlled, federalism has meant that legally and constitutionally such local control is centered in the states and their instrumentalities. Because of the emphasis upon state sovereignty, the local governments become mere creatures of a higher authority, simply an adjunct of the sovereign will.

Neither Thomas Jefferson nor James Madison—nor Calhoun—systematically considered any other possibility than this; any kind of tripartite federalism was totally foreign to their ideas. On the other hand, if one accepts the original thesis of these men—that pluralism is a major political good—one need not restrict oneself to the specific structure into which any one of the three fitted his ideas.

The Pluralism of Jefferson and Madison. Because Thomas Jefferson's thought had a strong agrarian cast and because a widely diffused free-farmer class could control the state legislature, there was no compulsion within Jefferson's logic to decentralize any further than the state. Since government has an inevitable tendency to tyrannize the people, that much, but only that much, decentralization is essential. Just as centralization is the road to tyranny, so decentralization is the way to a healthy, democratic state. A divided sovereignty, in short, was not only possible; it was absolutely necessary.

But if the states were to have sovereignty over domestic matters, there remained not even a small measure of autonomy for the cities, and this is as Jefferson would doubtless have wished it. It is not that he ignored local government. Quite the contrary, he thought of states divided into counties, the counties into townships, wards, or hundreds, as he variously described them. And the constituency of each was to manage the affairs which accrued naturally to it.[8] Particularly was he impressed with the vigor of the New England township, a startling contrast, he thought, to the oligarchic lethargy of the counties he knew so well in Virginia. In this small, primary, rural unit, Jefferson would place his faith.

Unlike Jefferson, who began with a monistic hope for society—a homogeneous people united in their objectives—and ended up with a pluralistic, decentralized government, James Madison started out with pluralism. The faction, though by his own definition bad, was recognized by Madison in *The Federalist,* No. 10, as inevitable: primarily from differences in wealth "ensues a division of the society into different interests and parties." Since factions are thus inevitable, the task of a people is not to eliminate them—this would be impossible—but to channel their energies toward desirable ends. A significant way to make factions serve socially desirable purposes is by means of social complexity. The smaller the society, the less complex it will likely be; the less complex, the more likelihood of oppression. On the other hand, expand the society, increase its complexity, and "you make it less probable that a majority of the whole will have a common motive to invade the rights of other citizens," as Madison observed.

Does this mean that Madison, recognizing that society was necessarily pluralistic because of economic differences and man's own nature, was nevertheless forced into political monism? In *The Federalist,* No. 10, he saw an advantage in the Union over the states, since a political virus, he thought, would be less likely to sweep the nation than it would a smaller governing unit. But when the nation was swept by anti-Jacobin hysteria in the late 1790's, he was perfectly willing to pen the Virginia Resolution, which would interpose the states between an oppressive national government and the people. It is not surprising, then, that Madison regarded the republican principle as fundamental to any just government, and distribu-

[8] Samuel P. Huntington, "The Founding Fathers and the Division of Powers," in Maass, *op. cit.,* pp. 150–200.

tion of powers geographically as scarcely less important than republican-ism itself.[9]

Although putting the greatest emphasis upon the necessity of a federal, republican government, although insisting upon the reality of a divided sovereignty resulting from the constitution of 1787, Madison still deplored local democracy.[10] Again, this conclusion resulted from his own pluralist theory of society, with its corollary idea of complexity as the safeguard against the excesses of factionalism.

If we were to extend Madison's theory into the twentieth century, we might find that his strictures about local democracy would no longer hold true. Is a complex society more apt to be free than a simple one? Then the great city will be free and the rural village or the rural county in chains. Where can one find greater complexity than in the modern city? Where a greater variety of intellectual, commercial, racial, religious, and social in-terests? One might argue that the intensity of factional contest is greater in the city than in nation or hemisphere. In the city one recognizes not only a vast number of factions, but also a crowded juxtaposition: physical near-ness. Madison's agrarian prejudices and the lack of complexity in commu-nity political life led him to excoriate local government. But being of scien-tific temper, he would doubtless not be led to such conclusions today, even though he might have an atavistic wish for the agrarian republic of his fruit-ful years.

Calhoun's Pluralism. Like Madison, John C. Calhoun was a pluralist, and, like Madison, he has been attacked as antidemocratic (though not be-cause of his political theory, but because of his defense of the southern slaveholding oligarchy.[11] It is true that both of these American polit-ical philosophers denied Jefferson, and in particular denied the Jeffer-sonian concept of an indivisible sovereignty resting ultimately in the peo-ple. But simply to insist that the ideas of these men were undemocratic be-cause of their pluralism and because of their insistence upon a divided sovereignty is untenable. Indeed, this assumption is based, first, on the prop-osition that the larger the group the greater its moral status, and that the national group is thus ethically superior to any smaller group. We shall examine this proposition shortly. Note, however, that when Madison spoke of the superiority of the national group over the local he was basing his judgment on the former's superior complexity, not its superior moral vir-

[9] Madison was a vigorous advocate of the idea that sovereignty could be divided. See Charles E. Merriam, *A History of American Political Theories* (New York: The Macmil-lan Co., 1926), p. 259.

[10] Huntington, *op. cit.*, p. 189.

[11] Clinton Rossiter notes that though Calhoun's "own interest was especially repug-nant to the democratic tradition [this] should not blind us to the broader significance of his intellectual achievement." In *Conservatism in America* (New York: Alfred A. Knopf, 1955), pp. 125–126.

tue. This trap that Madison avoided, however, has snared some contemporary thinkers.[12] Second, this same proposition ignores the criticism of respected modern philosophers that the idea of an indivisible sovereignty, even when resting in the people, can easily lead to totalitarianism. Calhoun's ideas were undemocratic only if his severe limits upon a unitary national will can be described as undemocratic. In an age of hypernationalism, this conclusion could—and has been—easily reached. In a less emotional environment such a conclusion must be suspect.

Calhoun reasoned that all legitimate governments must be based upon rule by the majority: "the responsibility of the rulers to the ruled, through the right of suffrage, is the indispensable and primary principle in the *foundation* of a constitutional government"—the indispensable and primary principle, but not the sole one, because control of the rulers by the ruled still leaves intact an undivided sovereignty in the people, an authority that might become as oppressive eventually as any princely despotism. If society were completely homogeneous, if all people had the same values and the same goals, there would be no reason to worry about such unrestrained majority rule. That such a society does not exist, that every society is made up of "various and diversified interests" (here he is being Madisonian) which are always in conflict is self-evident. In order that one faction might not despoil others, restraints must be imposed upon majority rule. These restraints would come by introducing the concurrent majority into government, in order "to give to each interest or portion of the community a negative on the others." [13]

By the concurrent majority, the consensus of all major groups in the community is obtained before the community may act. If there is no consensus, if one group exercises a veto over the proposed acts of the others, this group today, and all others tomorrow, will be protected against the overwhelming ambitions of the majority. But might this not so impede the governmental process as to bring it to a stalemate? Calhoun thought not. On the contrary, it would bring to society a greater cohesiveness and an enlargement of cooperative interplay among groups. To the degree that the local or partial groups would be secure in their defensive vetoes, to that degree would they become reasonable—willing to participate in the give-and-take of public life. Trying valiantly to show that his essentially negative theory of the concurrent majority must have positive results, Calhoun may have failed to achieve his goal. Yet his is as good a rationale for a pluralistic, federal state as might be found anywhere. His concurrent majority might be described, indeed, as one of the most complete ideological foun-

[12] See William H. Riker, *Federalism* (Boston: Little, Brown & Co., 1964). Riker was evidently trapped by this logical fallacy.

[13] Richard K. Crallé (ed.), *The Works of John C. Calhoun*, Vol. I, *A Disquisition on Government* (New York: D. Appleton & Co., 1854), pp. 12, 35.

dations ever to be constructed by an American for a theory of local government.

The Objective Idea

In spite of the ideas developed by Jefferson, Madison, and Calhoun, most American political theorists have tended to ignore the local constituency.[14] The same is not true, however, of the sociologist and the geographer. In particular, it has been the human ecologist who has been most adventurous, and who has attempted valiantly to construct a theory of the city.

Tracing the City's Movements. To the ecologist the city is a network of sustenance relationships, an idea of commonality. The urban group is interdependent in its daily requirements: local contacts are daily contacts. These conclusions can be deduced; more importantly, they can also be documented by scientific investigation.

Here is an example of such documentation. The automobile that Detroit typically produces, and that the American typically drives, is a high-speed, long-distance vehicle. But by origin-and-destination studies we have determined that it is mostly used for short-distance, low-speed travel. In a large city, most automobile trips will be under thirty miles; in small cities the average trip may be less than five miles. There will be a definite correlation, in other words, between the size of an urban grouping and the average distance of a journey by auto. One does not need to know from the "O-and-D" study what the purposes of the trips are—though the study could be designed to tell us. We merely need to know the average length of all automobile trips, and with that datum we have empirical evidence of the city's existence. The very fact, moreover, that this long-distance machine is held in check by its users emphasizes the local, daily nature of the city.[15]

Delineating the City Physically and Economically. The Built-up Area. Both the sociologist and the urban geographer have sought to define the city in other terms. First, the city is a physically built-up area which may be mapped and even photographed. It is the only political grouping with any commonality at all which will show up, by way of example, on an aerial photograph. If one were to take a high-altitude picture of the New York urban area, he would have on his print a view of a political, as well as a physical, fact. This phenomenon spills over both local and state boundaries to show that those boundaries do not correspond to reality. A similar photograph of Detroit would show the city spanning a great river, which

---

[14] One notable exception to this generalization is the theorist Robert A. Dahl, who has produced an able study of community power structure: *Who Governs?—Democracy and Power in an American City* (New Haven, Conn.: Yale University Press, 1961).

[15] Amos H. Hawley, *Human Ecology* (New York: The Ronald Press Co., 1950), pp. 257–258, 408.

any native Detroiter knows is a national boundary. Clearly delineated on the photograph is a city, a very human development, which has ignored the artificial boundary between two nation-states, and which has taken unto itself segments of the United States and Canada. (Demographic movement also shows Detroit-Windsor to be one city in an ecological sense.)

Area of Intensive Land Use. Similarly, the area of intensive land use can be delineated empirically. This area includes the built-up portion of the city, but extends beyond it to encompass truck farms, nurseries, cemeteries, parks, golf courses—all the multitude of land uses which are such a necessary adjunct of the city, but which do not result in the structural crowding of the land. This use can be mapped. It is another method for objectively defining the city.

Land Values. The third kind of empirical evidence which may be used to define the city is to found in land values. We know that there is a striking difference between urban land value (site value) and rural land value. By

Figure 3-1. *Land Value as a Definition of the City*

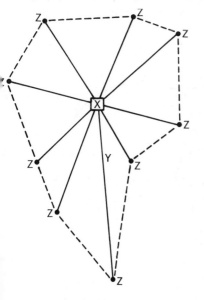
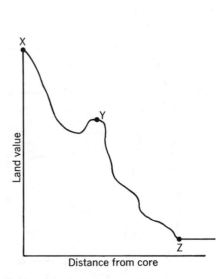

X is the city's core; Y is an outlying business district; Z is the point at which urban or site value no longer affects the price of raw land.

The dotted line connecting the Z points on the various sectors is the boundary between the city and the country. In terms of empirical research these points are, admittedly, difficult to arrive at. Yet even though the Z points may be somewhat arbitrarily placed, we do know that site value extends out into the "country." Indeed, the courts have accepted site value as a rationale for municipal annexation. See *Kansas City* v. *North Kansas City*, 360 Mo. 374, 228 S.W. 2nd 762 (1950).

starting at the city's core and plotting land values as one progresses outward from the core, one should be able to determine roughly where the land is no longer affected by site value, and thus where the city ends and country begins. See Figure 3-1.

Area of Dominance. The final method for objectively identifying the city is the determination of the city's area of primary economic and sociological dominance. This might be called the "trade area" technique. By studying such factors as newspaper circulation, department store and milk company deliveries, church membership in the core city and suburban neighborhoods, the shopping and recreational habits of people in the city's hinterland, one may determine the city's economic and sociological "watershed." If we arrive at a boundary which encloses all of the people who rely on the city for work, play, foodstuffs, and supplies, we have discovered where one city (or one urban region) ends and another begins. See Figure 3-2.

Are these criteria for measuring the extent of the city as valid in the highly urban Western society of today as they were a generation or a half-century ago? An eminent French geographer, Professor Jean Gottmann, describes the urbanized northeastern seaboard of the United States as a megalopolis which stretches from Maine to Virginia.[16] But in this great

Figure 3-2. Delineating the City

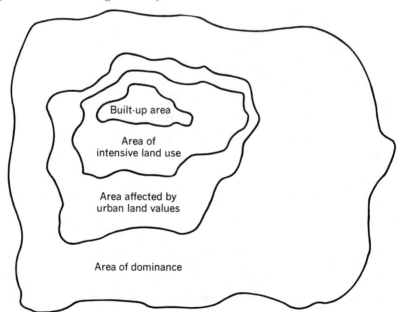

[16] Jean Gottmann, *Megalopolis* (New York: The Twentieth Century Fund, 1961).

urbanized region individual cities are still sharply delineated, or can be delineated by the techniques described above. Even if the region were, someday, to become continuously built-up (a highly unlikely prospect), by one technique or another, discrete urban communities could be distinguished.[17]

A final word needs to be said about the city as an objectively identifiable phenomenon. Politically, the city is usually the built-up area and no more. Similarly, when we use "the city" in our everyday speech, we usually refer to the built-up area. If we were to define the city according to its functions, however, we would reach outward to include a great deal of the country, because this countryside belongs to the city. Wherever it has primary social and economic dominance, there is the city. In the words of an eminent American geographer, "the countryside is set up by the cities to do the tasks which cannot be performed in urban areas." [18] The phenomenon which we finally discover, then, is the urban region—the city (as it is described in commonplace terms) plus the hinterland which the city dominates.

The City Is Politically Distinct. One of the identifiable phenomena of American politics is that local political issues are, to a certain degree, distinct from state and national issues. Tax policy is an issue everywhere in our political system, but in its local guise it is sharply different from fiscal issues posed in Washington or the state capitols. Land use is also of recurring concern to the Congress and to the city councils, but the difference in the issues is a major one. The Congress is concerned with agricultural land use predominantly, while city councils are engrossed with the problems of planning and zoning urban land use.

Do the Congress and the city councils debate urban renewal? Yes, truly, but the arguments are so different that urban renewal nationally and urban renewal locally seem quite different phenomena. Moreover, to continue to use this issue as example, party lines are drawn differently on the local and national levels of government. It makes no difference to a solidly Democratic ward in New Orleans or Philadelphia if a Democratic president and the Democratic leadership in Congress favor urban renewal. Both Democratic ward leaders and neighborhood power blocs are very apt to support

[17] In identifying the "standard metropolitan statistical area" (SMSA), as defined by the U.S. Bureau of the Budget, the U.S. Bureau of the Census normally uses commuting patterns, but if this measurement fails, other criteria are used. These criteria include "such items as newspaper circulation reports . . . , analysis of charge accounts in retail stores of central cities to determine the extent of their use by residents of the contiguous county, delivery service practices of retail stores in central cities, official traffic counts, the extent of public transportation facilities in operation between central cities and communities in the contiguous county, and the extent to which local planning groups and other civic organizations operate jointly." U.S. Bureau of the Budget, *Standard Metropolitan Statistical Areas* (1964), pp. 2–3.

[18] Edward A. Ackerman, *Problems for Resource Development Planning in Southern Illinois* (Carbondale, Ill.: Southern Illinois University Press, 1960), p. 10.

or oppose an urban renewal project on grounds entirely disassociated from party policy in Washington.

Because such local and national groups in the same party are often so distinct, it is not surprising that we find that local political parties rise up in the city and take away control of city hall from one or the other old-line parties. By way of example, during the last quarter of a century, local political-action groups in Kansas City and Cincinnati either have dominated their respective city halls or have constituted formidable minority blocs there.

In summary, we can say that by using a number of criteria we can objectively identify the city. By tracing the movements of the urban population, particularly by means of origin and destination studies, we can determine that the city is a system of sustenance relationships and is interdependent in its daily requirements. By using such objective phenomena as built-up area, intensive use of the land, the extent to which urban land value extends into the countryside, and the city's area of social and economic dominance, we can delineate the city. Finally, by analyzing political issues, we can show that those which are posed locally are often distinct and peculiar to the local political scene. There is, in short, an objective, empirically identifiable idea of the city.

The Kinship Idea

The Inertia of Population. Much has been said over the past decades—perhaps too much—about the mobile nature of the population. That man is constantly in movement can be documented, but much of that movement is purely local in nature. Migration of individuals and groups has been known since time immemorial; neither political boundaries nor great physical barriers have been able to confine people who want to move. On the other hand, people have sedentary tendencies which are perhaps stronger than migratory ones; they will remain in one place in spite of the most powerful forces which would seem likely to drive them from their native heath.

It has been observed that coal miners in West Virginia, Kentucky, and Illinois show the greatest reluctance to move, even though the mines have become mechanized and the workers' source of livelihood has been taken away. This results in pockets of severe unemployment. It results, also, in the willingness of some ex-miners to drive long distances to and from work. In fact, this long-distance commuting documents Hawley's observation that "motor vehicle transportation seems to have introduced a new resistance to migration." [19] In order to keep his roots in his native commu-

[19] Hawley, *op. cit.,* p. 337.

nity, the individual will use every means at hand to keep from migrating. His inertia shows his kinship to locality.

The Ties of the Social Plant and Social Groups. Once settled in a community the family rapidly develops ties which tend to bind it to that place. One invests time, energy, and capital in the social plant: in the home, the church, the lodge, the community theater, the schools—all the public and quasi-public facilities of the community. Entirely aside from the attachment to groups, there is identification with the familiar building, the familiar urban landscape. Things can very easily attach themselves to human affections. One's memories, one's own personal history can so often be found in the physical manifestations of community life that to migrate seems an act of disloyalty, a rejection of one's past.

Stronger yet are the ties to the social groups, both primary and secondary. Since migration means removing oneself from one's family, from a church congregation, from a garden club, from a political association, some individuals will regard such a move with much ambivalence, others with such distaste that movement becomes impossible for them. Fustel de Coulanges has shown us the religio-social attachment even of prehistoric man to his native soil. In spite of the great migrations of history and prehistory, the fact remains that for millennia mankind has not been nomadic. Once settled, man loves to stay settled. The trauma of migration is very real and often very much more than the individual can tolerate.

The Desire to Return. But there are compelling reasons for migration —usually economic—which are sufficient to overcome the individual's attachment to his own, his native land. He pulls up his roots. He migrates. And then the trauma is accentuated. Popular songs and folklore are sentimental indications of the traumatic effects of migration. So, to a degree, is family history: two families in Oregon proudly fix their origins, one of them in Virginia, one in Vermont.

The desire to return is so great that the adult migrant can only with difficulty find himself a new home. Having cut his roots in the "olde sod" he finds it hard to grow them again in the new. Thomas Wolfe, with the artist's insight into human desires, has said that the migrant can never go home again; but whether the migration has been across the sea, or from farm to city, many will still try to return. Observe the nineteenth-century European migration overseas. Involving an estimated 60 million persons, it was one of the great demographic movements of history. Yet of that 60 million, about 20 million returned home.[20] One can only speculate about the number, in addition, that would have liked to return, had economic and other factors not intervened.

Regional Loyalty. Sometimes the local loyalty that we have been review-

[20] Hawley, *op. cit.*, p. 331.

ing has a larger compass than the urban neighborhood, the town, the village, or the farm. It will reach outward to include a region of more or less extensive territory, which is still small enough for the individual to know intimately. Nathaniel Hawthorne is supposed to have said that New England was as large a place as could ever claim his loyalty, and Henry David Thoreau had the selfsame type of regional feeling.[21] Nor has the passage of a century dimmed that passionate devotion to place which the New Englander today still so deeply feels. Similar examples abound in the United States alone; we need not look further for them though they are worldwide. The Texan is very much like the Vermonter in his attachment to his state. Although William Faulkner created a world all his own in Yoknapatawpha County, he rarely left his home in Oxford, and indeed once said that if he were ever compelled to choose between Mississippi and the United States, he would choose Mississippi.

It would seem, then, that local loyalty in various guises strongly grips the individual. Because of the inertia of the population, the ties of the social plant and the primary and secondary groups, the attachment to place which shows up so poignantly in the migrant's desire to return home, and the extended local loyalty to a region—so often and so variously expressed —we can only conclude that the individual's identification with a highly localized place is very real and altogether common.

The Ethical Idea

The last hypothesis which we must examine is whether there is a moral quality to the local group that can help establish an idea of the city. All free societies struggle to accommodate both unity and diversity, and to maximize them; yet these two sociopolitical values, though of highest worth, can be reconciled only with greatest difficulty. As Reinhold Niebuhr has remarked, the good society constantly steers between the Scylla and Charybdis of anarchy and tyranny.[22] This is not to say that unity invariably leads to tyranny (though the despotic states, whatever their political facades, are always in fact unitary). Nor does it mean that diversity must lead to anarchy (though the extreme diversity of our political system in 1787 caused many politically sensitive men to call for a unifying constitution). The meaning is that somewhere between the shoals of unity and diversity lie the deep, safe waters of democratic sociopolitical organization.

For a free society to maximize political unity, it would need to create a world-state. To maximize diversity it would need the small Greek city-state.

---

[21] Lewis Mumford, *The Golden Day* (New York: Boni & Liveright, 1926), p. 112.

[22] Harry R. Davis and Robert C. Good, *Reinhold Niebuhr on Politics* (New York: Charles Scribner's Sons, 1960), p. 182.

Although these ideal models seem further away from twentieth-century man than at any time in history, we can nevertheless use them for the moment to speculate upon the basic problem of reconciling unity and diversity. Let us begin by stating two hypotheses:

1. If man were governed by the city-state, he would be compelled to seek unity through confederation or conquest, even as did the ancient and medieval city-states.

2. On the other hand, if he could create the world-state, he would immediately need to decentralize power, so that all power would not rest at the center. As Kelsen, a centralist, has observed, "democracy . . . may be centralized as well as decentralized . . . but decentralization allows a closer approach to the idea of democracy than centralization." [23]

If 3,000 years of recorded political experience has taught man anything, it is this: that concentrated power usually calls for division, and divided power for concentration. The problem of reconciling unity and diversity seems an inevitable consequence of political life. During the past several centuries of vigorous—and sometimes virulent—nationalism, the local group has been on the defensive. Indoctrinated with national values, obsessed with national goals, Western man retains his local loyalties, but does so almost surreptitiously. He is shamefaced about local attachments. Such emotions are for provincials, not for the educated or the worldly!

By becoming nationalistic, the modern world has become centralistic. By emphasizing centralization, modern man has assumed that unity is an absolute good which must take precedence over lesser goods, simply because they are, by his definition, lesser. The objectives of a local group are less important, the reasoning continues, than the objectives of the national group, because, ultimately, the larger the group the greater its moral force. Our purpose, here, is not to attack this hypothesis, at least not frontally. Rather, it is to ask whether the local group does not have at least as secure an ethical base as the larger national group.

Political organization will probably follow the loyalties of the people, and as we have seen, there is a striking loyalty to place observable in the local group. Political organization also will follow certain economic and sociopolitical phenomena which, by objective criteria, can be shown to exist. That the city is objectively identifiable is an indication of its reality. Because it is real, economically and socially, it will be given reality politically. If the law, or formal political organization, denies this reality, ethical tensions will inevitably result: there will grow up an informal organization which will deny the law and insist upon an ethical validity of its own.

But for our purposes of the moment, it does not matter whether the law is

---

[23] Hans Kelsen, *General Theory of Law and State* (Cambridge, Mass.: Harvard University Press, 1945), p. 311.

based upon myth rather than fact. That problem we shall consider in succeeding chapters. We are concerned here with the idea of the city, and the
moral basis for that idea. In our value system, that which is artificial has
less validity than that which is real. Since all modern governments,
whether democratic or despotic, regard the city as an artificial being, it is
little wonder that the city (or local group) has little moral force.

Yet the city has far greater objective reality than any other political entity. In our own constitutional system, the states and the nation are considered real, in defiance of objective criteria which indicate their artificiality.
The city, on the other hand, has greater objective reality than either state
or nation. If such reality gives moral force to a group, we must assume the
superiority of the city to constitutionally higher government.

The argument can be extended. Within the small group, face-to-face
contacts are frequent. The person is a person, not a number on a punch
card, to be fed into a sorting machine. As a group grows, face-to-face contacts diminish proportionately; personal relationships are reduced in importance. The larger the group, the greater the necessity of its acting im-
personally. With the reduction of personal relationships, as Aldous Huxley
has observed, "imagination has to take the place of direct acquaintance,
behavior motivated by a reasoned and impersonal benevolence, the place
of behavior motivated by personal affection and a spontaneous and unre-
flecting compassion." Since most people are incapable of "reasoned and
impersonal benevolence," it necessarily follows that the morality of the
larger group is inferior to that of the smaller. Huxley, again, insists that
"individuals and small groups do not always and automatically behave
well. But at least they can be moral and rational to a degree unattainable
by large groups." [24]

If we assume that the individual, easily, quickly, and without highly organized indoctrination, identifies himself both with the small local group
and with the entire human community, we can see immediately that such
identification is a threat to any larger group which lies between the city
and the world. Thus it is to the advantage of the large group to seek to
suppress both local and universal sentiments. To the large group, as Niebuhr has observed, "every immediate loyalty is a potential danger to higher
and more inclusive loyalties." (Jean Jacques Rousseau saw this, too, when
he argued against partial associations in the state.) Moreover, as the group
grows larger, its selfishness will increase vis-à-vis the total human community. "It will be more powerful and therefore more able to defy any social
restraints which might be devised. It will be less subject to internal moral
restraints." The larger the group, the more difficult it will be for it to retain
cohesiveness and maintain a common purpose. Conflict with other groups,

[24] Aldous Huxley, *Grey Eminence* (New York: Harper & Bros., 1941), pp. 311–312.

indeed, becomes the one factor that can hold the large group together; it is the "seemingly unavoidable prerequisite of group solidarity." [25]

We can argue, then, that the moral basis of the local group is at least as great as that of larger groups, that, indeed, it may well be superior to that of all larger groups, save only the total human community itself. Political diversity, represented by the autonomy of the local group, becomes superior to any kind of unity except that represented by the world-state. In terms of contemporary politics, the local becomes superior to the national, and at least equal to the international.

And yet we still have not said enough. We do not need, in practical politics, to assume the absolute superiority of the local group to the larger group; we need only to assume its equality. We need only to follow that lesson of political experience which we have already reviewed: divided power calls for concentration; undivided power, for decentralization. Huxley sums it up very well: "The art of what may be called 'goodness politics,' as opposed to power politics, is the art of organizing on a large scale without sacrificing the ethical values which emerge only among individuals and small groups. More specifically, it is the art of combining decentralization of government and industry, local and functional autonomy and smallness of administrative units with enough over-all efficiency to guarantee the smooth running of the federated whole." [26]

Summary

Because it is so much with us, local government can easily be thought of as an integral part of our constitutional system. In England, according to W. J. M. Mackenzie, the same reasoning is valid. Local government seems to be a kind of "natural" outgrowth of the political experience of the English-speaking peoples. To this degree they are particularistic, regardless of whether their governments are organized on federal or unitary bases.

Historically, other peoples have also been particularistic. The Greeks thought in terms of a city-state, a small localized political group, and they did not think beyond this local, intimate form. In the medieval period, artisan and merchant, though highly prizing the city as a haven of freedom, showed themselves capable of going beyond the Greeks by developing such federations as the Hanseatic and Rhine leagues. Beginning with Sir Thomas More's *Utopia,* the modern period has seen a wealth of utopian literature built around the small, autonomous group. The utopian communities of the nineteenth century made concrete the utopias envisaged in literature.

[25] Davis and Good, *op. cit.,* p. 85; see also Reinhold Niebuhr, *Moral Man and Immoral Society* (New York: Charles Scribner's Sons, Scribner Library, 1960).
[26] Huxley, *op. cit.,* p. 312.

Although local government today is largely taken for granted, it features prominently in what might be called the democratic catechism. Major exceptions to modern concentration on political centralization, moreover, may be found in the theories of federalism and pluralism.

Of all the American political theorists who have influenced the development of this republic, Jefferson, Madison, and Calhoun are probably the most important to the city. Madison's theory of complexity can be used to give an ideological base for the local autonomy of a highly complex urban community today. Calhoun's *Theory of the Concurrent Majority* is a prime weapon of defense for the geographic minority, whether local or regional.

Although the local group has an uncertain base in modern political theory, there is no uncertainty as to its existence in fact. Of all political groups, the local urban group is the only one which is objectively identifiable by a whole series of criteria. Empirically, we can establish the city's being a gathering together of individuals interdependent in their daily requirements. The city is local, distinct, discrete. It has a built-up area and an area of intensive land use; it includes territory in which urban land values dominate and an even greater region, the economic and social needs of which it supplies. It also has a political distinctiveness, inasmuch as local political issues are so often dissimilar to state and national ones.

We can establish the very strong attachment that the individual develops for the local community. The ties of the social plant and social groups, the resistance to migration, the desire to return, the recurrence of regional loyalties, all are factors that can be established to show the reality of the city.

This reality, empirically established, confounds the insistence of the law and current philosophy that the city is artificial. It is not the city which is based upon myth, but modern man's regard for the city. It is the city's reality which must give it moral force, since in our value system the real is more worthy than the artificial.

Reinhold Niebuhr has observed that all good societies steer constantly between the Scylla and Charybdis of anarchy and tyranny. Although every free society must resolve the problem of unity opposed to diversity, this problem can never even be approached politically unless the ethical position of the local political group is recognized. If that position is ignored as it is in nationalistic, totalitarian states, then diversity is sacrificed to an all-encompassing unity. Without a value justification, in other words, it is questionable whether the city can exist as a truly viable political entity.

Annotated Bibliography

Very little has been done in this century to try to develop a political theory of the city, and thus the few works that have appeared stand out, if for no other reason than the scarcity of the literature in the field. A comprehensive series of essays that could be used as a starting point in developing such a theory may be found in Arthur Maass (ed.), *Area and Power: A Theory of Local Government* (Glencoe, Ill.: The Free Press, 1959). In seeking to find a theoretical base for the explanation of political integration and fragmentation at the international and metropolitan levels of political interaction, Karl W. Deutsch and others have produced some intriguing insights into the nature of both urban and international life in Philip E. Jacob and James V. Toscano (eds.), *The Integration of Political Communities* (Philadelphia: J. B. Lippincott Co., 1964).

The most eclectic student of the city in this century has been Lewis Mumford, and one can hardly think of urban man in any category without using ideas that Mumford has already considered. Only at great risk, therefore, can one ignore Mumford's two principal books on the city, *The Culture of Cities* (New York: Harcourt, Brace & Co., 1938), and *The City in History* (New York: Harcourt, Brace & World, 1961).

Amos H. Hawley arrives at an ecological theory of the city in his *Human Ecology—A Theory of Community Structure* (New York: The Ronald Press Co., 1950). Nisbet sees in nationalism and other forms of political centralization causes for an increasing sense of alienation in modern man and argues that the loss of community and a vital pluralism can have serious consequences for a free society. See Robert A. Nisbet, *The Quest for Community* (New York: Oxford University Press, 1953); this was also published by Oxford as a Galaxy Book in 1962, under the title *Community and Power*. In two other works one can find a good deal of empirically based theory. George K. Zipf develops gravity models of attraction between and among urban centers in his *Human Behavior and the Principle of Least Effort* (Cambridge, Mass.: Addison-Wesley Publishing Co., 1949). And Ralph Pfouts gives us some cogent examples of measuring regional urban influence by means of such empirical data as retail trade patterns and telephone calls in F. Stuart Chapin, Jr., and Shirley F. Weiss (eds.), *Urban Growth Dynamics* (New York: John Wiley & Sons, 1962).

Anwar Syed summarizes American theories on local government in his *The Political Theory of American Local Government* (New York: Random House, 1966). Three valuable works on pluralism are Harold Laski, *A Grammar of Politics* (New Haven, Conn.: Yale University Press, 2nd ed., 1930); Kung Chuan Hsiao, *Political Pluralism* (New York: Harcourt, Brace & Co., 1927); and Mary P. Follett, *The New State* (New York: Longmans, Green & Co., 1918). The fifth impression of the Follett volume, 1926, is to be preferred, because of the introduction by Lord Haldane. Max Weber's sociohistorical analysis of the city, a widely respected essay, can be found in Max Weber, *The City*, trans. and ed. by Don Martindale and Gertrud Neuwirth (Glencoe, Ill.: The Free Press, 1958).

PART II

The Urban Setting in America

CHAPTER 4

Village into Metropolis:
A Sketch of Urban Life in America, 1607–1914

Early American Cities

On a spring day in May, 1607, the first permanent settlement of English-speaking peoples in America was founded, and the settlers proudly named it Jamestown, after their king. Swampy and pest-ridden, the site did not lend itself to city building, and Jamestown was never to become a great city. Probably the settlers never meant it to be great: Jamestown was to be a beachhead in the war against the wilderness, nothing more. If it served this purpose well—and it did—then it fulfilled its function in history.

But if the swamps and the sand on which Jamestown was situated did not encourage urban life, there were other sites along the coast which made great cities almost inevitable. The splendid heights above the St. Lawrence River, where the French established Quebec in 1608, practically assured the growth of a large urban center. Fine natural harbors from Boston southward determined that five cities were to be the principal centers of urban life during the American colonial period: Boston (1630), Newport (1639), New York (1609), Philadelphia (1682), and Charleston (1670). The only city away from the sea that could rival these five was Williamsburg, seat of the College of William and Mary, where so many of the architects of the American republic received their training.

From the founding of Jamestown to the start of the Revolutionary War, cities had a century and a half to get a foothold in the New World. However, it was not until the middle of the eighteenth century that any kind of lively urbanism showed itself in the English colonies. At first the settlements along the coast were like Jamestown: nothing more than beachheads in the war against the wilderness. To the people living in their crude log shelters, the ships riding at anchor in the harbor were safety and good sense, law and order. We commonly make the mistake of assuming that the new settlers severed their ties with Europe when they set sail for America. Actually, the nearest Indian village, perhaps an hour's journey inland, was farther away in spirit and in culture than England, a grueling six-weeks' voyage to the east. The white settlements were always mere physical extensions of Europe; and regardless of the violence of the personal revolt that had led them to leave their homes, the settlers remained thoroughly European.

If for no other reason than the urban background of many of the settlers, cities in the New World were inevitable. It is surprising that they did not develop sooner. Wealth was lacking, true enough, and so were people; but no considerable amount of wealth and no great mass of people are needed to build a genuine city with a genuine urban life. The colonists themselves were to prove this in the two decades immediately preceding the American war for independence.

Appearance of a Genuine Urbanism

Although many indices of urbanism are used to define the city, one that is usually overlooked is the existence and flourishing of various art forms. As soon as the public building is erected, not merely with the purpose of meeting administrative needs, but also with an eye to art, just then begins a real urban sense. The same is true with other art forms. Although we tend to date the city from the year in which its charter was first conferred, the real city may antedate that year of "origin." Boston, without a charter during the colonial period, was still very much a city. Its art life gives empirical evidence of its being truly urban. Perhaps that evening in 1757 when a Handel oratorio was performed in Boston (probably its first colonial hearing) is the day that we should speak of as the birth of the *city* of Boston.

The sudden flourishing of the arts is, indeed, one of the surest indications we have that by 1770, after almost a century and a half of European settlement, a real urban life had come into being in America. Charleston was hardly more than a village—4,000 people were counted there in 1770—and Philadelphia and New York, measured by population, were little more than large towns. Yet the theater in these three towns reached into every corner of the dramatic arts: from frivolous farces to Shakespearean tragedies. "During the three seasons of 1772–4, regular playgoers in each city could have seen more than seventy plays, farces, and ballad operas, including many of Shakespeare's dramas in the eighteenth-century versions. In fact, even in the present century New York has not offered a better repertoire." [1]

As early as 1736 Charleston had a theater on Dock Street, and there "such plays as Farquhar's 'The Recruiting Officer,' Addison's 'Cato,' and 'The Orphan, or the Unhappy Marriage' were performed. No subterfuge, such as was later used in New England to accomplish the presentation of plays in the guise of moral improvers, was ever necessary in the fun-loving little city of balls and horse-racing." [2]

[1] Carl Bridenbaugh, *Cities in Revolt* (New York: Alfred A. Knopf, 1955), p. 370.

[2] Robert Molloy, *Charleston, A Gracious Heritage* (New York: D. Appleton-Century Co., 1947), p. 54.

By the middle of the eighteenth century, New York, too, was exhibiting an urge to greatness. The predecessor of Columbia University, King's College, was chartered in 1754; and in the same year the New York Society Library was founded. "Lectures on scientific topics, and others illustrated with stereopticon views entertained the public. . . . The theatre was also a popular form of amusement, and though the plays were usually of a lighter vein, serious dramatic performances, such as 'Cato,' 'Richard III,' and 'Romeo and Juliet,' were presented." [3]

Thus did an urban consciousness spread through the colonies. Even though the wilderness was but the journey of a day or two to the west, the colonists were fully aware of the central importance of their small cities.

In form, too, cities were developing a consciousness of symmetry and even of beauty. In some of the towns of colonial America, especially in New England, there was a genuine attempt to construct an urban environment which combined functionalism and esthetics. Beginning with the town common, of no standard shape or size, the New England town builders placed their churches, town halls, stores, and houses in a kind of random order around the green open space of the common. Streets ran to the common and away from it in a way that suited the people rather than the slide rule of an engineer, or the finances of a real estate developer. A sense of form alone, it is true, was not sufficient to make the New England village into a city. Yet here was a striking example for the city to follow. Even today, occasionally, there survives a town square—such as the one in Norfolk, Connecticut—which for simplicity and functional beauty cannot be excelled, in the New World or the Old.

In the South the cities may have looked more as if they came from the drawing board than from the habits of the people, but they, too, had a more "natural" design than most present-day cities. This was especially true of Charleston. Whereas the New England town grew outward from the town common, Charleston seemed to develop from the periphery inward. Centuries before, many a medieval town really began in its villages several miles away and came to its climax in the complex street pattern of the inner city. So it was with Charleston. In the fifty-odd major plantations surrounding it the city really began. Each plantation was a village. Centered around "the Hall," or plantation house, the cabins and workshops of field hands, bricklayers, and blacksmiths gave the appearance of a small urban grouping. From these plantations, the roads and waterways gradually drew the countryside into Charleston itself. Though the gridiron street pattern might have conveyed a sense of rigidity, life itself denied the pattern.

---

[3] Arthur Everett Peterson and George William Edwards, *New York as an Eighteenth-century Municipality* (New York: Longmans, Green & Co., 1917), pp. 215–216.

Governing the Colonial City

The corporate, or governmental, existence of the colonial city was based upon a charter granted by the royal governor, or the proprietor, of the colony in which the town was situated. Upon its corporate birth the city assumed the rights and obligations of its English counterpart overseas.

Like most other public authorities, colonial cities had relatively few governmental functions. They could own and manage property, sue and be sued, own and manage various municipal enterprises, maintain the peace, and adjudicate disputes. The form of government would not be totally unfamiliar to us today. At the center of municipal authority was the council, made up of the mayor, councilmen, and aldermen. Concentrated in the council were all powers of the city—legislative, executive, and judicial.

This local government, like the society in which it functioned, was aristocratic rather than democratic. Sex, property, racial, even religious qualifications reduced the electorate to a relatively small percentage of the inhabitants. A city father may have loved his wife, been fond of his servants, and kind to the blacksmith who shod his horses, but he would have been incredulous if you had suggested that these important members of his household should participate in affairs of state.

In Philadelphia the city was a "close" corporation, which removed the government even further from the people than in many sister towns. The government there was made up of a self-perpetuating governing body. Whenever a vacancy occurred on the council, either by death or resignation, the remaining members elected a man of substance to fill the empty chair. If this practice offends our democratic and equalitarian sensibilities today, we should remember that such forms of government fitted the traditions and values of the colonists. Except for a few Tom Paines, Jacksonian democracy would have been regarded by the colonists, of whatever class, as the rankest heresy.

Because the city had not too much to do, the revenue problem was not particularly acute. The property tax furnished some income; fees and charges drawn from municipal docks, ferries, and other enterprises added other funds to the city coffers. Late in the seventeenth century, New York used the special assessment for the first time in the New World. In lieu of taxes the citizen often had to contribute labor or other services to the city. Thus, the householder might be required to maintain the street in front of his property. Just as social affairs are often used today to raise money for worthy causes, so in the colonies balls and other forms of entertainment drew money out of the pockets of the burghers to finance a street or fill in a swamp.

The evidence seems to indicate, in summary, that from the founding of Jamestown in 1607, to the first shot of the Revolutionary War fired on Lexington Common one spring day in 1775, stretched a period which saw the development of a genuine urban culture in the New World. At least a half-dozen urban places, though small in population, could be called real cities. In politics and art, in commerce and industry, in education and philosophy, these cities could rival or excel cities of today with many times their number of inhabitants. These small cities, crowded between the wilderness and the sea, could not rival Vienna or Rome, Paris or London, "but they did more than match the provincial cities of Europe, especially those in the British Isles." [4] In a few short years the English colonists had created a genuine urban life.

The Revolutionary City

Without the city the American revolt against the British crown could never have happened. Above all else, the city furnished the communications network for revolt. Few, if any, leaders of the Revolutionary movement were outside the influence of urban life. Embattled farmers may have stood their ground in Massachusetts, and fired the shot heard 'round the world, but if the feverish councils of merchants and artisans and lawyers had not been in session in the cities, the shot would have been fired in vain. Even though the working people were, for the most part, not enfranchised, they fell to the task of making a revolution with much enthusiasm. These "valuable, but sometimes troublesome, allies," as Beard calls them, "furnished the sinews for stoning English stamp agents, demolishing statutes, sacking official residences, and heaving cargoes into harbors. While merchants resolved solemnly and petitioned gravely, artisans shouted hoarsely and rioted vigorously, shocking the timid gentry of store and warehouse who hoped that the business of resisting British measures might be conducted with the decorum of the counting room." [5]

One of the remarkable facts of the American revolt against Great Britain was that although over 95 percent of the people were engaged in agriculture, this was not an agrarian revolt. Perhaps it could not be called an urban revolt, either, but note how often commercial considerations entered into the rising anger of the colonies against the mother country. The "great" cities along the coast, from Boston to Charleston, seethed with protest against the British restrictions on their trade and on their local political autonomy. And so the cities led the way.

[4] Bridenbaugh, *op. cit.*, p. vii.
[5] Charles A. Beard and Mary R. Beard, *The Rise of American Civilization* (New York: The Macmillan Co., 1934), p. 100.

As soon as the ties with the mother country had been broken, in fact if not in law, the cities lost their legal reason for being. Obviously, a charter granted in the name of the crown now had no standing. This gap was soon filled by the legislatures of the various states, which proceeded to grant, or extend, charters to their cities. This action introduced two novel elements into American city government. Where the city had formerly been the creature of the executive will centered in the central government, it now became a creature of the legislative will centered in the state, or regional, government. When the British forces of occupation moved out of New York on November 25, 1783, for example, the city was momentarily without a government. The Council for the Southern District of New York, however, had already been set up by the state legislature, and this council quickly took over the affairs of the city.[6]

In truth, New York still had its basic law, the Montgomerie charter of 1731: it had been ratified and continued in effect by the New York Constitution of 1777. Although this new state constitution had entirely changed the legal basis for the city charter, the charter itself remained basically the same. As so often happens, war and revolution had little effect upon the structure of the city's government.

In December, 1783, the qualified electors of New York chose their new aldermen and assistant aldermen. Upon their election, the Common Council of the City of New York was again in existence. But the council was not complete. Under the charter, the mayor and recorder were also members of the council, and they had to be appointed by a state body headed by the governor. Other officers of the city were also still missing. The clerk, sheriff, and coroner had to be appointed by the same state body which appointed the mayor and recorder. The people, under the charter, were to elect the assessors, collectors, and constables. But since these offices could be filled later—it was a mayor that the city needed most of all—in January, 1784, the Common Council recommended to Governor DeWitt Clinton that he and his state board appoint the celebrated lawyer and patriot James Duane as first postwar mayor. Clinton and his advisers complied, and on February 7, 1784, Duane was inducted into office.

Throughout the colonial period the mayor had been a most important officer in the city, although this importance stemmed more from the nature of the man than from strength built into the office by the charter. Because leading citizens always filled the office, they lent it their prestige. Moreover, although the term of office was only one year, it was the custom for mayors to be reappointed again and again. These customary practices were revived

[6] The source for the following material on the New York City government is Sidney I. Pomerantz, *New York: An American City, 1783–1803* (New York: Columbia University Press, 1938).

in post-Revolutionary New York. Duane served for six years; Richard Varick, his successor, for twelve. But after Varick's long tenure, the mayor's time in office tended to shorten. In 1834, undoubtedly because of the stimulus of the Jacksonian revolution, the office was made elective.

The New York mayor's presidency of the Common Council gave him considerable legislative power, even though he could vote only in case of a tie. As presiding officer, or member of several courts, moreover, the mayor had considerable judicial powers. Administratively, he had not too much to do, because the city's administration was rudimentary, but he "made numerous appointments and had extensive licensing powers. He named the high constable, the chief marshall and his deputy marshalls, the deputy clerks of the market, markers and sealers of weights and measures, a deputy water bailiff, scavengers, cartmen, inspectors of hay, public porters, packers, cullers, and common criers."

Here, then, was an official to be reckoned with. Adding the powers and privileges of the ofice to the personal prestige of the men who occupied it, one cannot wonder that the people of the city looked upon their mayor with more than a little awe. Considering the status of the office, it is not at all strange that DeWitt Clinton resigned from the U.S. Senate in 1803 to become mayor of New York.

The pattern of city government found in New York was repeated, without too much variation, in other cities of the Revolutionary and early republican period. The Baltimore Charter of 1796 set up a bicameral council —an innovation—and a mayor with veto power. The mayor was not responsible directly to the people; he was chosen by an electoral college.[7] In spite of such structural deviations, however, it is probable that the Baltimore city government functioned much like that of New York and other cities. In the mayor and council were concentrated all the powers of the city: legislative, executive, and judicial. Furthermore, because of general property restrictions upon office-holding and the exercise of the franchise, the city hall was dominated by a rather select circle of merchants and professional people. Jeffersonian mistrust of cities and Jacksonian insistence upon the right of every man to an elective office—whether that of mayor or garbage man—had neither of them yet been felt by the sedate and orderly men in city hall. There was quick energy in the municipal chambers, and great local patriotism, but little soul-searching. As the years moved toward 1828, the city fathers were unaware that the election of a frontier general to the Presidency of the United States in that year would signal the end of the great golden age of American cities. It is just as well that they did not know.

[7] Arthur W. Bromage, *Introduction to Municipal Government and Administration* (New York: Appleton-Century-Crofts, 2nd ed., 1957), pp. 12–13.

The Antebellum City

"In the year 1825," wrote Vernon Parrington, "the little city of Charleston, with its fourteen thousand whites and more than fourteen thousand blacks, was perhaps the most delightful spot in America. The mecca of plantation fashion and the capital of plantation politics, it prided itself on its genial and distinguished society. It was the last stronghold in America of the older pride of aristocracy. . . . Despite the large admixture of French Huguenot blood the manners and prejudices of the aristocracy retained the pronounced British cast that came down from pre-Revolutionary times, and if Dr. Johnson could have stepped from Fleet Street of 1780 to the Charleston of 1825 he would have felt almost at home." [8]

But if all was well-ordered and conservative in Charleston, conditions were quite otherwise in northern cities. Washington, only recently laid out on the swampy banks of the Potomac by the Frenchman L'Enfant, was unprepossessing. And still farther north, in the cities of New England, a new and ugly force had shown itself. Crude and unfettered capitalism was turning urban life into a maelstrom. A real urban proletariat, as real as anything in England or on the continent, was taking shape. The new capitalism very quickly disposed of the idea of the city which had, seemingly, taken such good root in New England in the eighteenth century. The examples of Newport, of Boston, and of many a New England village were forgotten. The city lost form, shape, the sense of esthetic completeness; it became a workshop, grimy, disordered, and lacking pride. It became now, not a place to live in, but a place to exist in, not a corporate being, but an instrument of exploitation.

One need only look at the condition of the working class to measure the corruption of civil conscience. An organization of laborers to provide minimum protection against the whims of their employers was regarded as a criminal conspiracy. In 1836, when the state of Massachusetts moved to legislate protection of child workers in factories, it could go no further than to prohibit employment of children under fifteen years of age that had not had three months of schooling the previous year.

In the new industrial city of America a greater part of the population lived with little hope. Not uncommonly, men, women, and children worked twelve hours a day, seven days a week, in mines and factories that seemed to be designed by some malevolent god to ruin the bodies and crush the spirit of humankind. The worker's only escape from this industrial slavery was injury, as a result of which, because there was no chance of com-

[8] Vernon L. Parrington, *Main Currents in American Thought* (New York: Harcourt, Brace & Co., 1927), Vol. II, p. 109.

pensation, he quickly starved. Or an economic depression could throw him out of work, in which case he also starved. Neither the moral code of the capitalist, who controlled the industrial wastelands, nor the rudimentary eleemosynary laws of the city and state gave the worker any protection. Contracting debts that he could not pay was a crime, and pauperism was virtually so. The paltry sums raised by the city's poor tax were totally inadequate: a ration of fat pork here, a scuttle of coal and some mittens there; this was all the city attempted to do, or even thought it should do, for its unfortunates. And private charity, too, was just as negligible.

If the Industrial Revolution was tearing apart urban life, still another force was adding to the disorder. War, revolution, and famine were driving the Irish, Germans, and other Europeans to the promised land beyond the seas. Unhappily, the promise did not materialize for most of them. Out of the frying pan into the fire is a succinct description of many an immigrant's change of homeland. Of course, the new American at least had hope, if not for his own future, then for the future of his children and grandchildren. With the future always nebulous, however, was this hope much reward to the exploited immigrant? The brutal fact is that the Irish and the Germans had bought a pig in a poke, and all they could do was make the best of it. Given the politics of the nineteenth century, the immigrant had none of the power—even if he had had the imagination—to change the urban environment. The 1844 religious riots in Philadelphia, which killed at least 30 and wounded 150, indicated the bankrupt nature of the urban spirit in the industrial city.

Just as the rush of Puerto Ricans and southern Negroes to the northern cities during the past decades has overtaxed the city, so the rush of immigrants in the nineteenth century completely overwhelmed the city's capacity to meet the needs of its inhabitants. Housing and the public services were inundated by the flood of people. Fires could not be fought, nor an adequate supply of water furnished the people; streets were more often than not a mess of mud and garbage. Human, animal, and inorganic wastes piled up within the city, so that at times it seemed to function primarily as a diseased organism infecting impartially the great, the not-so-great, and the insignificant.

Faltering attempts were made by the city to raise the level of the public services. In this period came the first organized fire companies, and some rather ingenious machines for firefighting were produced in the North. After a disastrous fire in Fayetteville, North Carolina, in 1831, the Boston fire department sent, as a gift to the people of Fayetteville, a Boston-built fire engine.[9] A central water supply, too, was being thought of and built in many a city, to aid firefighting and also to fight disease. But how could the

[9] Guion Griffis Johnson, *Ante-Bellum North Carolina* (Chapel Hill, N.C.: University of North Carolina Press, 1937), p. 135.

city supply pure water in the days before Pasteur? Or how could it fight a fire in a tinderbox?

Not every city of the antebellum period, it is true, can be described as a wasteland. In the new West there were urban places that had not yet felt the stranglehold of rapid industrialization. For every Lowell there was a Cincinnati, the Heidelberg of the Ohio; or a St. Louis, where Charles Dickens found houses he liked, houses with a French shrug about them; or a New Orleans, where age already sat gracefully upon streets and buildings of a French or Spanish character. And there were the towns which existed chiefly to service the frontier: Chicago, Milwaukee, San Francisco.

Concerning a Few Utopias

It was the enormity of misery in the industrial city that contributed to Karl Marx's drive to produce his blueprint of a perfect society. This same stimulus moved Robert Owen, François Fourier, and Ralph Waldo Emerson to think in utopian terms, of utopian towns. Where Marx began at the top of the political and economic pyramid, these other utopians started at the base.

The nineteenth was a gigantic century in America. Civil war, industrialization, the winning of the West, and the building of cities all assumed epic proportions. Smaller in scope, but greater in dreams, were the dozens of attempts to build the perfect city, and thus the perfect life. At Brook Farm, in New England, many a Transcendentalist came down off his craggy eminence to strive for a microcosmic social perfection. Robert Owen, having tested his visions of the ideal commune in Scotland, displaced those strange celibates, the Rappites, from the shores of the Wabash and at New Harmony started upon the construction of his version of utopia. In Iowa, the Amana colonists, and on the distant shores of Great Salt Lake, the Mormons, were attempting to construct the City of God.

Whether these communities represented the burgeoning of a religious spirit or a reaction against the inhumanities of the industrial city, they assumed similar patterns. In an economic sense they were communistic: individual ownership of goods (except for personal belongings) was not tolerated; the community owned the land, the factories, all the productive and distributive machinery. In addition, the communities were socially and politically regimented. Since the ideal way of life had already been created by the dreamer, the role of the individual was to fit himself to that ideal. In this perfect city, where equality was absolute, the individual, paradoxically, was lost. Indeed, this had to be: those societies which were most democratic—note Brook Farm and New Harmony—soon disappeared. But those ruled by the iron hand of a religious oligarchy—the Amana colony is an example—survived for generations.

While the utopians were attempting to build the city upon the basis of absolute equality of man—before God or before the Machine—the southerners thought of their commonwealth in terms of absolute inequality. Every society, they insisted, was based upon the exploitation of labor. "The only difference between your system of factory slavery and ours of chattel slavery," they told the North, "is that we are honest about ours, and you are not."

The South, indeed, was caught up in what Parrington so eloquently describes as "the dream of a Greek democracy." This is not surprising. Perhaps the greatest of ancient civilizations had been built in Athens, and Athens, to use the words of a famous nineteenth-century American, was half slave and half free. The southern intellectuals were not slow to see the parallel. Refusing to recognize the moribund nature of the slave system, they looked to the plantation and its peculiar system of labor, and there put their hopes for the future. That this was a kind of utopianism cannot be denied. The plantation society which southern intellectuals dreamed of existed only here and there even in the South—in the tidewater section of Virginia, around Charleston, in the lower Mississippi Valley. The average slaveholder owned only a few hands and often worked side by side with them in the field. The master was often as crude as the servant.

Around Charleston the plantation was a factory in the field; it was also a village that was a satellite to the central city. This was the prototype of southern dreams: a social, political, economic aristocracy, in which the workers labored productively in the fields and the intellectuals studied law and philosophy by day, and went to a ball or to a play by William Shakespeare at night. If Charleston—brilliant city surrounded by industrious plantation villages—had been representative of the South, the romantic dream of a Greek democracy might have been realized. But it was not. And the utopia which the southerners thought of as so very complete ended like all utopias—in incompleteness. Instead of a Greek democracy the southerners soon found themselves despoiled of their property, their cities ruined, their young men dead or lame, their hopes blasted.

And so the utopianism of the nineteenth century failed. Although the utopians had dreamed of the ideal society and sought to create the ideal city, their dreams had to give way to capitalistic individualism. This burgeoning force, at least partially created by the city, was to have a profound effect on urban development.

Mr. Jackson's Egalitarianism

The equality of man had been talked and written about a great deal since that day in 1776 when Thomas Jefferson published his thoughts on the subject for the world to read. Until 1830 few people, except radicals like

Tom Paine, had thought of equality as being much more than equality before the law—in itself a splendid concept, but quite different from the point of view of the levelers.

In class-conscious England, the Chartist movement, during the 1830's, was demanding what its proponents called "real" equality. In class-conscious America, the frontiersman, whether in Illinois or Tennessee, held himself up as good as any rich capitalist, plantation owner, or intellectual. And so egalitarianism swept the land, and for convenience we link it with the name of President Andrew Jackson, who was himself not the cause, but the result of the popular revolt.

The new equality of man had a profound effect upon the structure of government in America and upon the access to political power. Property qualifications for voting or office-holding, which had been used almost everywhere until 1830, now were drastically lowered, or eliminated altogether. During colonial times, and for fifty years of republican history, the city and nation had been governed by an aristocracy. For all its faults, this group of merchants, planters, and professional people had approached government seriously and respectfully. Here was an institution of man, they thought, to be treated as an art, not as a plaything.

Nor did they think government was to be used exclusively as a tool to advance the economic self-interest of a particular class. The economic determinists deny this: many a sneer has been directed at the men who wrote the Constitution of 1787 on the grounds that they were acting, not for the good of society, but for the good of their pocketbooks.[10] Unquestionably, the men who labored in Philadelphia through the summer of 1787 had economic motivations. Perhaps they wished to protect their own economic interests. But to deny them other motivations, just as stong, just as influential, is to adopt the bankrupt philosophy, so prevalent during the past century, that man *does* live by bread alone.

To the people enfranchised by the Jacksonian movement toward absolute equality, the government became a tool, pure and simple, of their economic self-interest and of their own emotional self-justification. Nowhere can you find a better example of this than in state and local government. Take the constitution of Illinois. In the summer of 1818 a group of highly capable men gathered in a little village on the banks of the Mississippi River and wrote a short, simple document that the people ratified a few months later. This document provided for an elective governor and legislature; all other state officials, administrative and judicial, were to be appointed. Thirty years later, this state charter was set aside, and the constitution of 1848 provided that a long list of administrative and judicial officials should be elected. This same sort of change was taking place in most of the

---

[10] See, for example, Charles A. Beard, *An Economic Interpretation of the Constitution of the United States* (New York: The Macmillan Co., 1913).

other states, and by this means the "long ballot" was introduced into American government.

In local government the change was equally drastic. Both urban and rural government shuddered violently from the Jacksonian earthquake; and many a city hall, or county courthouse, found its foundations cracked as a result, and its roof sagging. "Elect them all," was the cry across the land. "Every man a politician" seemed to be the watchword of every party and every faction.

In the cities the change introduced a new structure and a new kind of politician. City governments had been far removed from the people. The city council had been an exclusive club; the franchise had been severely restricted. Jacksonian political surgery swept away this aristocratic past in a few short years. Not only did the new laws and charters call for election of mayors and councils, but they also provided for the election of clerks, auditors, attorneys, magistrates, health commissioners, tree inspectors, police chiefs, and snowshovelers. The new structure of urban government, in short, if not a travesty of democratic responsibility, was at least an affront to common sense. The Jacksonians had created a hydra-headed monster that could not function, that could not even breathe fire from its countless nostrils. There is, indeed, some reason to believe that the ineffective government resulting from the Jacksonian revolt helped to produce the rise of a new elite—the boss and his political machine.

These were some of the results of a philosophy of government that held firmly to the idea that anyone was capable of filling a public office or job. If a carpenter who could never saw a straight line had a glib enough tongue to talk his way into the job of health officer, then he deserved the job. If a cripple could do no other useful work, then a public office was a means of furnishing him a pension. And even if a capable person were elected and developed a professional attitude toward his job, he should be replaced before he could stake out a permanent claim to the office.

In sum, the Jacksonian ideology had both negative and positive effects upon urban government. It helped democratize an institution that had been far removed from the people. But in doing this it so atomized both the city's political and administrative structure that it contributed to its own decay into a crude form of elitism. The legacy to cities of the Jacksonian ideology was hardly a productive one.

Bosses and Boodle

On April 9, 1865, when Lee surrendered to Grant, the cities of the South were either ruined or prostrate. But the cities of the North and West and in the border country were humming with activity. Vastly stimulated by the war, industrial capitalism needed only peace to realize the fruits of political and economic dominance.

The cities were not prepared, however, for the people and machines that settled upon them like locusts. Brooklyn had a population of 202,000 in 1854; in 1865 it had acquired almost 100,000 more people; and by 1900 the population exceeded 1,000,000, five times the number of people a half-century before. And the machine came just as rapidly: "At the conclusion of the Civil War, there were fewer than five hundred factories in Brooklyn. Five years later the number had doubled. By 1880, Brooklyn had 45,587 men working in 5,201 factories turning out products valued at $177,-223,142." [11] Late and soon, getting and spending, Brooklyn laid waste its powers. And in this it was not alone.

Now, truly, the great cities of America, and most of the lesser ones, became mere adjuncts of the factory, the counting house, and the tenement. Nor had the urban population, seemingly, any will to be otherwise. Inundated by people from the farms and by immigrants from overseas, the cities were simply not equipped to offer even the minimum of necessities to most of their people. Even if there had been a will to do so, no legal or administrative machinery existed to enable them to meet the situation. Held in thrall to the states, with weak councils and weaker executives, the cities were truly giants in bondage.

Into this limitless confusion, this power vacuum, stepped a new figure, the political boss. Here was the answer to some of the most pressing dilemmas facing the city. What to do with the atomization of power in city hall? Concentrate the power, extralegally, in the hands of the boss. How to wring concessions from the state house? Let the boss, with his thousands of controlled votes, issue the commands. What to do with the nameless multitude, enfranchised but ignorant? Let the boss herd them into one political party or the other. The Jacksonian insistence that all should rule had, for the cities, ended in the rule of a new and crude elite.

This was a gaudy period, this urban period between the Civil War and World War I, and we will probably never see the likes of it again. "Honorable" Tweed in New York, "King" James McManes in Philadelphia, Colonel Ed Butler in St. Louis: these typical bosses filled their own pocketbooks with gold and in doing so robbed the city at every turn. So adept were they that, even as they stole, they often stole legally. George Washington Plunkitt, one of the lesser buccaneers in Tammany Hall, spoke virtuously of honest graft: any reasonable person, he thought, should concede him the right to steal within the law.

In Brooklyn there held sway for some thirty years a mighty man who was perhaps the first political leader to carry the name of "boss." Hugh Mc-

[11] Harold Coffin Syrett, *The City of Brooklyn, 1865–1898* (New York: Columbia University Press, 1944), pp. 12–13. 140, 235.

Laughlin ruled the Democratic machine in Brooklyn from shortly after the Civil War until the turn of the century, when Brooklyn lost its political identity to the greatly enlarged city of New York. Across the East River in Manhattan, Richard Croker, William Tweed, John Kelly, and other Tammany bosses came and went, but Hugh McLaughlin still issued his orders from Kerrigan's auction rooms on Willoughby Street and had the satisfaction of seeing them obeyed.

However corrupt McLaughlin and his counterparts were, we cannot take this corruption as a complete and unqualified condemnation of the boss. Lustful of power though he was, the boss nevertheless made gains for the city which the reformer often failed to achieve. For one thing, he tied up the loose ends of the governing structure; with all of the waste attending his rule, he paradoxically achieved a certain amount of efficiency which the Jacksonians had cavalierly ignored. For another thing, he gave a sense of fulfillment to the oppressed minorities which he appeared to represent. What Anton Cermak did for the Czechs in Chicago, Ed Crump later did, though to a lesser extent, for the Negroes in Memphis. A mess of pottage for each minority group? Truly. Yet the pottage was far, far more than either had ever had before.

The sway of the boss over the party, however, did not always mean that he controlled city hall. In the swashbuckling decade following the Civil War, when graft and thievery reached even into the office of the President, there were outraged reformers crying for the blood of the pirates. On more than one occasion the reformers ousted the machine from city hall, and the city, for a while at least, had honest government. Usually, the surest route to reform lay through the mayor's office, and thus the struggle between the grafters and the reformers centered there.

In Buffalo the reform element placed in the mayor's chair a man who, if not overly burdened with imagination, was still the soul of probity itself. Grover Cleveland, soon to be President of the United States, came to be known as the "Veto Mayor" because he overruled so many bills ground out by the machine-dominated city council. Because of his record in Buffalo, Cleveland went to Albany; and Albany, as we should all know by now, is only an arm's length from Washington.

A similar man rose to head the city of Brooklyn. As a result of the efforts of State Senator Frederick Schroder, former mayor of the city, the legislature in Albany passed, in 1880, a special law applying only to Brooklyn. Called the "single-head bill," it was a revolutionary departure from the usual type of city government in postwar America. Departing completely from the Jacksonian tradition, the authors of the bill provided for a strong mayor and a short ballot. Only the mayor and aldermen, comptroller, and auditor were popularly elected. "For the first time, the council was reduced in power and restricted in its opportunity to interfere directly with administration, and this led to a new synthesis of mayor-council relations in which the mayor was given undivided authority over administration." [12]

With the office of mayor powerfully strengthened, the only remaining need was to find a man who could fill it. Brooklyn had such a man in Seth Low, a young, wealthy entrepreneur. When he assumed office in 1882, Low had more power than any other mayor in the United States. Showing his resolution to direct his administration forcefully, he announced that "the acceptance of any appointment at my hands will be evidence to the community that the gentleman accepting it has personally given me his assurance that he will without delay give me his resignation whenever I ask for it." [13] Thus the department head in Brooklyn was, at long last, put in the same relation to his chief as the department head in the federal government was to the President.

The success of the new charter was assured by Mayor Low. So well known did Low become, in fact, that he was to author a chapter in the famous commentary of Lord Bryce upon the American commonwealth. This was in spite of the fact that Bryce thought American city government the one conspicuous failure of American democracy.

The rise to power of Seth Low in Brooklyn was one of the first indications that a new class was to assert itself in urban politics. The men and women of this group were middle class (though newly risen—Dahl calls them the "ex-plebes"), with the self-confidence that seemed to come from money, status, and achievement. This new class possessed a new ideology. Although the strong executive in Brooklyn, and the spread of the system to other cities, might be regarded as a return to the prestigious mayor of the colonial and early republican city, it is unlikely that the reformers of the turn of the century had that aristocratic example in mind. Rather, they seemed to be operating from a set of values which they had already proved (at least to their own satisfaction) in their business and professional lives. For the new class, including such eminent political leaders as Woodrow Wilson, the proper view of city government was essentially an apolitical one: strong executive leadership, efficiency, merit appointment of administrative personnel, "businesslike" management, and rejection of politics.

Not all reformers, however, operated in the spirit of the Lows and the Wilsons. Three quite remarkable mayors who appeared around the turn of the century illustrate how reform leaders could at one and the same time strike massive blows at corruption and still build stable political organizations. Identifying themselves with the needs of the urban poor, mayors Hazen Pingree of Detroit (1889–1896), Samuel M. ("Golden Rule") Jones of Toledo (1897–1904), and Thomas L. Johnson of Cleveland (1901–1909) fought for municipal ownership of utilities, free public services such as

---

[12] Arthur W. Bromage, *op. cit.*, p. 265.
[13] Syrett, *op. cit.*, p. 109.

kindergartens, playgrounds, and concerts, and various other programs of social welfare. Reform in their hands extended beyond the middle class and developed such mass support that they deserved the title of reform bosses.[14]

Environmental Changes

As American cities sought to strengthen their political systems they faced other problems. Because of rapid growth, in both territory and population, the city had to find some way to transport its masses. Horsecars were too slow, and so the overhead railway came into use. Although a blight upon the urban landscape, the "El" did serve the people's needs for fast transport. The cable car made its appearance in San Francisco and spread widely throughout America. Soon after Lieutenant Frank J. Sprague installed the first electric trolley in an American city in Richmond, Virginia (1887–1888), the "streetcar" revolutionized urban transport. Boston built the first American subway (1895–1897), and New York soon followed suit.

For years the gaslight had, romantically but ineffectively, lighted the streets of the city. The invention of the arc lamp in the 1870's added countless lumens to every square foot of street surface in America. As the illumination of streets spread, it was resisted in some places. A St. Louis mayor, arguing against street lights at the turn of the century, ungrammatically cried, "You have the moon yet—ain't it?" [15] But such outcries did not stop the lighting of the city streets.

To make the city habitable, the wastes of urban living had to have proper disposal. In some cities, sewage was still running away to the nearest river in open trenches, and the outdoor privy was common; but cities began making significant efforts to carry the wastes at least outside their boundaries. For the most part, raw sewage was dumped into watercourses, although some cities began using the filter bed or farm irrigation system to give partial treatment to the raw wastes.

Garbage disposal was taken care of in a variety of ways. Even in great cities, the chickens or pigs in the backyard ate the remains of the family meals. Farmers collected garbage to feed to swine, and some cities ran—and for a profit—their own pig farms. Chicagoans, a wit of the period commented, simply kicked around their garbage until it dried up and was carried away by the wind. By 1900, some cities were burning garbage and other wastes. New York and other cities on the sea loaded their garbage on scows. These "honey barges" were then towed out to sea where their cargoes

[14] Charles N. Glaab and A. Theodore Brown, *A History of Urban America* (New York: The Macmillan Co., 1967), pp. 213–215.
[15] Joseph Lincoln Steffens, *The Shame of the Cities* (New York: McClure, Phillips & Co., 1905), p. 38.

were dumped in the water, with the hope that not too much of the litter would get back to shore.

Water was a problem for every city. Those urban centers fortunate enough to be on rivers or freshwater lakes—St. Louis and Chicago, for example—had all the water they needed at their doorsteps. As industrialization progressed, however, these sources became increasingly subject to pollution. New York, like other cities along the coasts, found its only source of fresh water was in the hinterland, and to the hinterland it went. In 1892 New York completed the New Croton aqueduct to supply nearly 300 million gallons of fresh water to the city daily, and with this pure supply assured, the city had only one-half as many deaths from typhoid fever as Chicago and Philadelphia, cities with contaminated water supplies.

Impure water did not hamper one important function of the city, however. Though citizens might complain that their drinking water was not hygienic, still the impure water would put out fires. Since fire had always been a nemesis of cities, this was no small advantage. The distribution of water under pressure to all parts of the city was advanced both as an aid to healthful living and as a safeguard against fire. Thus, as water distribution systems spread, as more and more cities employed professionally trained firefighters, and as firefighting equipment improved, one of the great natural enemies of cities was fought with increasing effectiveness.

Progress in the arts was also being made by some cities during this period. In 1881 the Boston Symphony was organized; two years later, in New York, opera lovers opened the Metropolitan Opera House, though few other cities, except New Orleans, found the money for this expensive art. Some cities, such as St. Louis and Cincinnati, where the German population was large, developed an active musical life. But most urban Americans could not go beyond Gilbert and Sullivan.

Painting, sculpture, and architecture were vigorous arts, but not distinguished. Architecture had for itself a kind of glad madness at the "fin de siècle," and the "gingerbread" house, or the city hall built to resemble a castle on the Rhine, was not an uncommon sight. The virtue of the style was that it did not have the bloodless severity of some of the functional architecture of the mid-twentieth century.

Although American painting and sculpture were not generally outstanding, distinguished Americans grew interested in these arts. After spending many fortunes on European paintings and other art objects, sons and daughters of the robber barons passed them on to their cities. In some cases the institutions which received the gifts were organized and run as nonprofit corporate enterprises—for example, the excellent museum at Worcester, Massachusetts. In other instances, private philanthropy was quickened by the investment of municipal funds, both in the acquisition of art treasures and in buildings to house them. In 1904, after the St. Louis

World's Fair, the city government adapted a great hall for use as an art museum and levied a tax for its support. And Chicagoans built their Art Institute on city park land near the lake front.

The theater was as popular as the other arts. Thought of largely as an entertainment rather than an art medium, the stage occasionally gave the city a view of things above the ordinary. But the greater part of the time the stage was occupied by such worn vehicles as the famous abolitionist drama by Harriet Beecher Stowe, which not even the most doctrinaire abolitionist had ever regarded as good theater. A Minnesota editor commented wearily one day in the 1890's that *"Uncle Tom's Cabin* . . . appeared at the opera house last night. The dogs were poorly supported." [16]

Tax support of the theater was not great; yet there were evidences of it. Although no major city operated theaters as a municipal function, as cities were doing in Europe, the municipality often provided a place where players could perform. The opera houses and the civic auditoriums were as necessary to the traveling company as an audience. Thus with the theater, as with other art forms, the city showed some dim awareness of the vital importance of the arts to civic life.

The city gave increasing attention to library and lecture hall, and a great deal of public money went into both facilities. Parks, too, got a share of the city's budget, because perceptive city leaders were beginning to realize that open spaces were essential to urban life. Central Park was begun in the 1850's. Its 840 acres, previously littered with shacks and ranged by pigs and goats, became, after the Civil War, one of the great parks of the world. Across the river, Brooklyn laid out its fine Prospect Park. Although unduly expensive—Boss Hugh McLaughlin made a pretty penny out of it by buying up land and selling it to the park commission—the work was finally completed, and the results justified the expense. Cities to the west—Chicago, St. Louis, Cincinnati, San Francisco—were also purchasing land to keep it in the public domain. No such imaginative plan as that of a green belt to surround the city ever appeared, however, and open spaces appeared only occasionally, almost as a civic afterthought.

The High Tide of Reform

By the late nineteenth century, reform was at white heat. The appearance of the strong-mayor form of municipal government gave hope to the reformers; the decline of the special legislative act freed cities, somewhat, from the whims of the state legislature. With the introduction of constitutional home rule in Missouri in 1875, partisans of local self-determination for cities took heart and proclaimed a new day for local government.

[16] Arthur M. Schlesinger, *The Rise of the City, 1878–1898* (New York: The Macmillan Co., 1933), p. 291.

But the political effectiveness of the reformers varied. Here and there the boss was routed and city hall cleaned up, but never for long. Invariably, the machine counterattacked. Lincoln Steffens, Ida Tarbell, and other muckrakers found cities in chains at the turn of the century, partially because the boodlers were never long absent from council chamber or mayor's office. Thinking that they could gain strength by union, the reformers banded together in the National Municipal League in 1894, and with this there began a consistent reform movement.

After the turn of the century two additional forms of municipal government appeared in America. The Galveston flood resulted in the development of commission government, which was to flourish briefly and then fade. In Staunton, Virginia, and Sumter, South Carolina, began, almost simultaneously, a plan of government which was to revolutionize many a city. Soon labeled the council-manager form of city government, this plan centralized administration under a city manager, who in turn appointed his department heads. The city manager, like the strong mayor, represented a striking break with the Jacksonian concept of government by elective amateurs and gave hope for a new day in municipal affairs.

If the strong mayor and city manager sought to arrest the chaos in the city's administrative structure, so also did the city planner attack the physical disorder in the urban community. The planner arrived on the municipal scene about the same time as the city manager. If the manager has had a more immediate effect upon the city, perhaps it is because the planner has had the more difficult job.

What were the results of the almost frantic activity of the urban reformer during the late nineteenth and early twentieth centuries? Professor Schlesinger insists that "the record as a whole was distinctly creditable to a generation which found itself confronted with the phenomenon of a great population everywhere clotting into towns. No other people had ever met such an emergency so promptly or, on the whole, so successfully." And yet Schlesinger himself is forced to add, "What most impresses the historical student is the lack of unity, balance, planfulness, in the advances that were made. Urban progress was experimental, uneven, often accidental: the people were, as yet, groping in the dark." [17]

If we cannot identify precisely the results of the reform movement, we can at least say with some accuracy that the list of ideas which came out of the reform period was impressive:

1. Strong executive leadership (strong mayor and city manager).

2. Professionalization of the public service, and development of a career service.

3. City planning.

4. The short ballot.

[17] *Ibid.*, p. 120.

5. Nonpartisanship and at-large election of councilmen.
6. Popular democracy (the initiative, referendum, and recall).
7. Municipal home rule.
8. Efficiency, economy, and responsibility in government.

These ideas represented a kind of middle-class commitment to structural reform and ideological values that often had little or no appeal to the broad range of urban citizens. That few reform leaders had the mass appeal of "Golden Rule" Jones of Toledo, for example, undoubtedly accounted for the political failure of the reform movement in so many instances. That a majority of reformers failed to follow the example of Mayor Thomas L. Johnson of Cleveland undoubtedly separated them from the urban poor and disinherited and thereby both eroded their political base and kept them from achieving social goals of importance to the whole city.

Reform ideas, nevertheless, coalesced into a political ideology of urban reform that was to influence the American city for generations to come, and that was to have an almost equal impact on the twentieth-century Canadian city. And though this ideology is under attack in the 1960's, its strength is still formidable, as we shall see in the following pages.

Annotated Bibliography

By all odds the best two histories of Colonial America are Carl Bridenbaugh's *Cities in the Wilderness* (New York: Alfred A. Knopf, 1955), and *Cities in Revolt* (New York: Alfred A. Knopf, 1955). Tunnard and Reed have written an engrossing history of American architecture, which also has a great deal to say about American life in general. See Christopher Tunnard and Henry Hope Reed, *American Skyline* (Boston: Houghton Mifflin Co., 1955). Although overdone in spots, the Whites have written well about the attitude of American intellectuals toward the idea of the city in Morton White and Lucia White, *The Intellectual Versus the City: From Thomas Jefferson to Frank Lloyd Wright* (Cambridge, Mass.: Harvard University Press, 1962).

Schlesinger could qualify for the title of urban historian because of the excellence of one book alone—Arthur M. Schlesinger, *The Rise of the City, 1878–1898* (New York: The Macmillan Co., 1933). Richard C. Wade, *The Urban Frontier* (Cambridge, Mass.: Harvard University Press, 1959), traced the rise of cities from 1790 to 1830, and the beginnings of an urban civilization in the western United States. A useful and instructive book of readings which reviews urban development from the Colonial city to the present-day metropolis is Charles N. Glaab's *The American City—A Documentary History* (Homewood, Ill.: The Dorsey Press, 1963). Also see Charles N. Glaab and A. Theodore Brown, *A History of Urban America* (New York: The Macmillan Co., 1967).

To have a look at utopias is to have a look at man himself, and thus every student of the city of man should know Lewis Mumford's *The Story of Utopias* (New York: Boni & Liveright, 1922; The Viking Press, Compass Books, 1962); and Charles Nordhoff's *The Communistic Societies in the United States* (New York: Harper & Bros., 1875; Schocken Books, 1965). See also "Communistic Settlements," in *Encyclopedia of the Social Sciences*, Vol. IV, pp. 95–102.

CHAPTER 5

The City and Its Superiors

By 1914 the urban reform movement had spent its initial force and had propounded its major ideas. It was then that the reformer set about to consolidate his gains. His expectations were that home rule was to strike blow upon blow at city subserviency to the state; that the initiative, referendum, and recall were to bring democracy into city hall; that the short ballot and strong executive leadership would drive the Jacksonians out of the city; that nonpartisanship was to cut the tie with the major political parties, if not to exclude politics from municipal affairs altogether; and that civil service reform was to create a popularly responsive bureaucracy staffed with professionals and technicians. His philosophy was expressed in the words of a 1917 amendment to the Denver city charter: "the administration of the city . . . shall be nonpolitical, with economy and good service as its aim and purpose"!

But urbanization confounded both reform and reformer. That the city was too dynamic to be held within the bounds of any rigid system of ideas can be seen both in the ideological and practical developments that have swept over it in the past half-century.

That urban government has become one of the most dynamic aspects of American political life can be seen from the vast growth of urban budgets, from the increase in the number of urban governing units, from state and federal case law bearing directly upon city life and politics, and, no mean criterion, from the mass of literature that comes from academic observers of and active participants in the urban political struggle. This outpouring of literature indicates a special change in what we might call the ideological view of the city. Urban ecology, small-group theories, role-perception studies, quantification of data, sociopolitical investigations into the behavior of voters, administrators, and political leaders—all have produced an empirical frame of mind which is, to say the least, strikingly different from the old reformer's intellectual stance. Even political theory has not gone untouched. Observe the struggle between elitist and democratic theory, joined in the community-power-structure studies of political scientists and sociologists.[1] This battle has seen such pluralists as Robert Dahl throw down the gauntlet to monist Floyd Hunter. But perhaps the most important result, to the city, has been not in the diverse and contradictory find-

[1] See Lyman Kellstedt, "Atlanta to 'Oretown'—Identifying Community Elites," *Public Administration Review*, XXV (June, 1965), 161–168.

ings, but in the introduction of strong new empirical elements in the methodology of urban study and in the realization among scholars that the city contains a gold mine of data on political behavior and that these data can lead to explanations, not only of local, but also of national and even international political behavior.[2]

In addition to the academic reassessment of urban life and politics, there have been at least two other major developments which the reformer did not contemplate: (1) the profound urbanization of the continent, with a consequent rise of the metropolis, and (2) the radical increase of intergovernmental interdependence. This change in the relations among city, state, and federal governments, as striking as urbanization itself, we could without hyperbole describe as the intergovernmental revolution. It is the purpose of this chapter to describe some parts of that revolution.

The City and the State: A Symbiotic Relationship

The multitude of political relationships between city and state are of massive importance to the quality of urban life and government. Some of these relationships are contained in the law: the state constitution, the statutes, and the case law; others may be found in the struggle between parties or party factions, in the maneuverings of political leaders, and in the day-to-day contact of chief executives, department heads, and other high administrative figures.

The intergovernmental revolution has struck both the state and the local bureaucracy. In 1914 the administrative contacts of the local health officer with comparable state officials were few and far between; one can indeed find virtually no contacts except those of a purely legal nature. But today state and local health officers are constantly and closely in touch with each other. The same is true with police officers, engineers, educators, librarians, planners, finance officers, and all other officials. And in this contact, what is more, policy is not only executed; it is made. In their multitude of interactions, the state and local bureaucracies have entered the policy arena and have significantly changed state and local relations.

State Administrative Aids and Controls. Technical Aids. To catalog all of the types of technical aids given to the city by the state is one way to describe the change in state-local relations. There is hardly a department or agency of any state which does not, from time to time, extend a helping hand to the city or its sister governments. There is hardly a department that does not seek, at times, to control city administration. Indeed, the very doctrine of absolute legal dependence of the city upon the state, though an

[2] An attempt to relate certain aspects of political behavior at the metropolitan and international levels may be seen in Philip E. Jacob and James V. Toscano (eds.), *The Integration of Political Communities* (Philadelphia: J. B. Lippincott Co., 1964).

anachronism, may stimulate a certain noblesse oblige on the part of governors, legislators, and administrators. If the city is the creature of the state, the logic of that relationship is that the parent assumes responsibility for the child.

In public safety, health, finance, education, many kinds of public works, planning, personnel, and administrative management, the city benefits from state technical aids. It is pertinent to note here that in economic terms alone the man-hours spent by state personnel on local government problems represent a large indirect investment by the state in local affairs. It is also pertinent to note that state technicians influence local policy and are in turn influenced by local policy.

State aids to the city's public safety functions are numerous and varied. Not only do the state police and the state fire marshal stand behind the local police and fire departments to offer reinforcement in extremity, but they also offer help ranging from training of public safety personnel to identification of criminals.

A good case in point is the Oklahoma State Bureau of Investigation, which offers nine major services to city and other local law enforcement departments. Data on all missing and wanted persons reported by local police are kept on file in the bureau. Each month a state bulletin lists wanted persons and articles stolen but not yet recovered in each jurisdiction. The bureau's photographic and criminal identification sections are involved constantly in helping the local departments identify the criminal and his modus operandi. By means of the bureau's telephoto service, photographs and documents of interest to police departments may be sent or received nationwide. The polygraph (lie detector) requires both equipment and skilled personnel: these are available at the bureau's central office. Not infrequently the handwriting in a document, or even the typewriter used, is central to "breaking" a case. Experts at the bureau can tell whether a signature is genuine, whether there have been erasures on the document, and even whether a check was torn from a particular stub. The firearms and chemical laboratories are equipped to make ballistics tests on weapons as well as to identify blood and other types of stains, dust particles, hair and fibers, paint, glass, and poisons.[3]

In health, as in public safety, the state stands ready to serve the local governments. State health laboratories test municipal water supplies, and sanitarians advise city officers on technical problems of water supply and purification. If health hazards lie outside the city limits, the state officers will help the city to abate them. Sewage disposal and the setting up and operation of sanitary landfills for rubbish and garbage disposal are matters upon which the state offers advice and assistance.

[3] Oklahoma State Bureau of Investigation, *Services of State Bureau of Investigation* (Oklahoma City, Okla.: the Bureau, undated).

Because so many officials of smaller cities are elected or appointed to fill jobs for which they have had no previous training, the state offers a wide variety of in-service training facilities to local personnel. In this regard, the state university has, in recent years, assumed major importance. Operating health seminars, management institutes, fire and police schools, specially designed short courses for assessors, finance officers, civil defense personnel, stenographers, police and court officers concerned with juvenile delinquency, and recreation directors, the state university eventually penetrates into nearly every aspect of city government. Nor does the university neglect those people concerned with the arts: little-theater managers, band and orchestra directors, architects and influential laymen concerned with civic art (plazas, fountains, preservation of buildings of historical interest and artistic integrity), and library administrators come to the campus for training and advice. It is to the university, also, to which the city must look for a constant supply of skilled urban administrators. Most state-supported universities have recognized the need for educating city managers, city planners, police officers, civil engineers, and other urban administrators. But because of the great demand for trained personnel by other governments and by private business as well, the supply of such personnel has not kept up with the demand, and many observers feel that there is a manpower crisis facing the city.[4]

When a state highway department makes soil tests on the site of a new street, when state auditors help a city with a new accounting system, when the state civil service commission aids the city's personnel testing program, the city is getting service of considerable value, at little or no cost. Where the city runs the public schools, the state office of education will offer a wide variety of technical aids to the school department.

Although a considerable part of the mass of technical aids offered the city by the state are on a take-it-or-leave-it basis, many of them are compulsory. In matters of finance, especially, the compulsory features of state aid are very evident. The same compulsory language is often found in the statutes governing city health activities.

Reports and Inspections. Requiring reports from cities serves two valuable purposes: (1) it assures the state of information necessary to evaluate performance standards; and (2) it results in a body of data essential to state, local, federal, and even private agencies. Financial data furnish a good example of both purposes. The various levies against property, income from those levies, types and yield of nonproperty taxes, purchasing methods, budgeting and accounting techniques, per capita costs of various services —all of these data are useful to governors and state legislators, mayors and councilmen, citizen groups, scholars, and administrators. Many efforts

[4] See Municipal Manpower Commission, *Governmental Manpower for Tomorrow's Cities* (New York: McGraw-Hill Book Co., 1962).

have been made in the past to evaluate the efficiency of one city government as compared to another, all without notable success. If such a thing were possible, city officials, and the citizenry at large, would have a valuable tool to measure their community against others of comparable size and wealth. One of the reasons that this comparison has been virtually impossible is that no body of data exists which furnishes the raw material for evaluation. But as standardized reporting increases in scope (especially when reinforced with computerized data banks), the possibility of valid comparisons between and among cities becomes more easily realizable.

With reports, as with technical aids, the response of the cities may be either obligatory under the statutes or purely voluntary. That voluntary performance can yield most satisfactory results is shown by the success of the U.S. Bureau of the Census. The encyclopedic *1967 Census of Governments,* for example, is made up of material gathered without compulsion. Indeed, the federal government has no power to require reports of the cities and other local governments, save by means of a contingency clause attached to a grant-in-aid. An example of successful voluntary compliance at the state level is found in the Illinois statute which gives the state auditor authority to collect certain basic data from cities, villages, and incorporated towns. After more than a decade of vigorous administration and polite persuasion the auditor has obtained almost 100 percent compliance.

Although the legal requirement that cities furnish reports to the state is perfectly within the state's rights, local officials tend to look askance at such compulsion. For one thing, they point out, the compiling, checking, and mailing of data take time and money. It ill behooves the very state government which puts so many onerous restrictions on the city's taxing power to demand that the city spend money for state benefit, where those funds are so badly needed for local purposes. It would ease the burden upon the cities if the state would offer local governments grants-in-aid to help finance the reports. Thus would the state influence local action without demanding it, and thus would it also take on a share of the cost of compiling the data.

If state funds are being spent on city streets, the state highway department will want to know whether the street is being built to proper standards (or at least to the standards that the department considers proper). A report, however, is by its very nature historical; it details action which has already taken place. Although past errors discovered in the report may be corrected in the future, the state may not be willing to wait for reports but may prefer to send out inspectors to check while work is going on. Inspections by the state fire marshal may duplicate fire inspections by the city, particularly of public institutions such as schools, but may at the same time reveal fire dangers overlooked by the city. State health inspectors may find laxness at the city's filtration plant and advise the operators to eliminate potential dangers to the city's health.

Inspectors who operate in such fields as health and safety and finance and education will sometimes issue orders; but more often they will advise city officials and offer assistance to accomplish the desired ends. If a city keeps its accounts on a cash basis, for example, it is unlikely that inspectors from the state auditor's office will order the books put on an accrual basis. Rather they will advise it, and then offer the city assistance to do the job. A comment made in the 1930's is still valid today: "Most local officials are entirely willing to accept state advice and assistance when it is clearly designed to further the interests of their municipalities." [5]

If the inspector offers advice or assistance and sometimes gives an order, he is also in a strategic position to check on the compilation of reports, to see whether the data are valid and are presented in intelligible form. In other words, the inspectors can greatly enhance the value of the reports by being at the elbow of the individual who compiles them.

State Administrative Intervention. Because the state is responsible, in legal theory, for every action of the city, it may feel compelled to intrude into the most intimate details of local political life. This is substitute administration: the state takes over local administrative functions and policy formation, either on a temporary or permanent basis.

When law and order completely break down in the city, the governor sends in the state police or the National Guard. By a declaration of martial law, the state can virtually set aside all local government and, on a temporary basis, rely on military officers under command of the governor to direct the city, and on military forces to administer it. Similarly, the state is apt to step in when there is a complete breakdown of administration in the two vital public services of health and finance. The Local Government Board in New Jersey, for example, may send into a city in distress a local administrator of finance to act as a kind of receiver for the city.[6]

Although substitute administration is usually rationalized on the grounds that it is but temporary, sometimes it turns into a long-lasting fixture of local government. The people of St. Louis have learned this fact well over many decades. When St. Louis was plagued by internecine struggles between Confederate and Union sympathizers during the Civil War, the state of Missouri set up its own agency to administer local police affairs. One hundred years later the state still controls the police through a board of commissioners, all of whom, except for the mayor, are appointed by the governor. Though nominally a department of the city government, the police agency functions directly under state law. The city must support the department, but it has no budgetary control over it. When the board sub-

[5] Robert K. Carr, *State Control of Local Finance in Oklahoma* (Norman, Okla.: University of Oklahoma Press, 1937), p. 219.
[6] Bennett M. Rich, *The Government and Administration of New Jersey* (New York: Thomas Y. Crowell Co., 1957), p. 356.

mits a budget to the mayor and council, they have little alternative but to approve it. Thus in 1960 the board announced that in the 1961 session of the state legislature it would ask not only for higher wages for the St. Louis police but also for more policemen for the force. The increased expense would, of course, be borne by the city government. Because of state control of the police, over 20 percent of the city's budget is completely outside the purview of the people, the mayor, and the city council.

If temporary, substitute administration can be of great value to the city in distress. But if permanent, it can become a major impediment to the city's control of its own affairs. It might even be described as a form of political dishonesty if it is camouflaged by a spurious local complexion.

Financial Aids of an Administrative Nature. According to the popular mind, local governments—and particularly the city and the county—are ridden with graft. The local official has his hand in the till, extracting as much wealth from it as he can before being discovered by a righteous citizenry or the agents of the law. Popular myth on this score, as on so many others, is hardly an accurate description of the situation. The city's road to financial perdition is far more apt to be paved with good intentions than with vicious ones. In short, the city official needs help more than chastisement.

The real trouble with the local government's conduct of its own affairs is that so often it does not have in its administrative staff that expert knowledge which is required to carry out effective financial policy. Nor does it have the financial resources to acquire the expert administrators who are necessary. Only the larger cities, or the richer smaller ones, can afford finance officers and accountants as regular administrative personnel.

So much for the most important reason for state financial aids of an administrative nature. But there are other reasons, with less substantial logic underlying them, for state administrative aids for local finance. And this goes as well for administrative controls. The states have used faulty administration in some local jurisdictions to rationalize intervention in all jurisdictions. For example, as a result of pressure-group activity, the states have required or sought to cajole cities into unnecessarily expensive types of financial reporting. This is particularly true of reports submitted directly to the people. Publication of the annual budget (in minute detail), tax levies, assessment rolls, and other technical data may be good sources of income to local newspapers, but is rarely enlightening to the citizenry at large. Such reports, when printed *in extenso,* are rarely read, and even more rarely understood. Yet the newspaper lobby at the state legislature insists on the state's requiring or encouraging them. Though considered a form of aid, at least by the state, to the local citizenry, the device fails in its purpose and causes the diversion of badly needed funds into subsidies for the local press.

In tax administration, the states aid the cities in a variety of ways, and this kind of aid, according to the Advisory Commission on Intergovernmental Relations, might well be extended: "States should provide their local units with technical assistance by serving as a clearinghouse of information on tax experience in other parts of the State and country, by providing training facilities for local tax personnel, by giving them access to State tax records, and where appropriate, by employing sanctions against State taxpayers who fail to comply with local tax requirements." [7] One of the time-honored aids of this character is that given to the local administrators of the general property tax. Except for Hawaii, where the state administers the tax, most states rely heavily upon local administration, with the state offering technical advice and training facilities to local administrators. [8]

One of the constant perplexities of finance administration in cities is the preparation and marketing of bond issues. In this matter the states can be of very considerable help to their cities. North Carolina, by means of the Local Government Commission, approves and then markets all local bonds. Because of centralized marketing and because the stamp of approval of the commission is highly respected by bond buyers, North Carolina "municipals" are readily sold, and at advantageous rates. [9] Similar to the North Carolina plan, except that it is optional, is the Virginia system. The state agency markets bonds if requested to do so by the local body.

In Michigan, as in North Carolina, a state commission supervises local indebtedness. The Municipal Finance Commission must approve all bond issues (including special assessment bonds), but does not market them. Similarly, the Louisiana Bond and Tax Board exercises almost complete control over local borrowing, but small appropriations and staff have hampered its operations. Like its counterparts in Michigan and North Carolina, the board must rely more on persuasion than coercion. [10]

Connected with the New Jersey Department of the Treasury, a local government division has truly extensive control over municipal finance. The division may prescribe procedures for receipt, custody, and disbursement of city funds; stipulate forms to be used in various finance operations; require that the city designate a finance officer as comptroller; and issue rules and regulations governing municipal finance administration. [11]

Although financial aids and controls are most often institutionalized in

[7] Advisory Commission on Intergovernmental Relations, *Local Nonproperty Taxes and the Coordinating Role of the State* (Washington, D.C., September, 1961), p. 7.

[8] For a comprehensive review of the states' role, see Advisory Commission on Intergovernmental Relations, *The Role of the States in Strengthening the Property Tax*, 2 vols. (Washington, D.C., June, 1963).

[9] Robert S. Rankin, *The Government and Administration of North Carolina* (New York: Thomas Y. Crowell Co., 1955), pp. 385–387.

[10] Advisory Commission on Intergovernmental Relations, *State Technical Assistance to Local Debt Management* (Washington, D.C., January, 1965).

[11] Rich, *op. cit.*, p. 355.

tax commissions, departments of finance, or offices of the state auditor, they will also be found in various line departments responsible for the administration of grants-in-aid. State grants for roads, streets, and bridges, when channeled through the highway departments, are subject to control by those departments. Not only does the department control the physical design of the improvements; it will specify how state funds are to be received by the city and how the city will disburse them. And then it will send its own auditors to check on its procedures. Indeed, the city may well be supervised by several groups of state auditors, each group representing a different state agency. And only one group will probably be interested in an overall investigation of the city's finances. A duplication of function? Indeed it is. But the state is jealous of its prerogative to specify precisely about the expenditure of its grants.

How can we evaluate state administrative aids to the cities, whether in budgeting, assessment and collection of taxes, debt administration, or accounting methods? Although much of this supervision—whether obligatory or otherwise—is productive, one authoritative source describes it as "unsatisfactory as now administered in most states." [12] Another way to view the matter is in terms of the size of the individual city, and the professional quality of its administrative staff. Because professionalization of the municipal service usually increases with size, the larger cities probably have less need for the various state administrative aids than the smaller ones. Detroit, in other words, could get along without the Michigan Municipal Finance Commission much easier than could Escanaba.

In closing this section on administrative aids of a financial nature, we need to note that the cities receive substantial money grants from the states. In the fiscal year 1966, intergovernmental revenues received by the cities amounted to approximately $4.1 billion. The great bulk of this money— about $3.3 billion—came from the states, mostly in the form of grants-inaid or shared taxes.[13]

Joint State-Local Action. Because of the legal relationship of city and state, many state functions are carried out by the local governments. Joint administration of a project or the joint carrying out of a function, however, is comparatively rare. But it does exist, and can fruitfully be expanded. When a state patrolman directs a glut of traffic at one city intersection and a city traffic officer performs the same function at another, the two public safety officers are engaged in a concrete display of cooperative administration. This kind of thing, though, is sporadic. Cooperative action at the administrative level can be, and sometimes is, continuous.

By providing the site for a park, the state of California has joined with

[12] International City Managers' Association, *Municipal Finance Administration* (Chicago: ICMA, 1962), p. 34.
[13] U.S. Bureau of the Census, *Statistical Abstract of the United States: 1967*, p. 435.

Santa Monica in a recreational enterprise that benefits both state and city. Operating expenses of the park are met by parking fees. If California had waited until budgetary allotments had permitted it to build the park, years might have elapsed. If, on the other hand, Santa Monica had not had the land available, it might have had difficulty financing the beach park. But the city and the state, by joining forces, got immediate results.

Possibly the greatest helping hand that the state can offer the city is in assignment of equipment and personnel to aid the city, either in setting up new programs or in expanding old ones. Just as the federal government has assigned health personnel to aid the states, so a number of states frequently send engineers, sanitarians, health education officers, and even doctors to aid local health departments. Though on loan, these administrative officials function as local officers and may actually work locally for months, or perhaps several years, at a time. An example of this kind of cooperation was found in Wisconsin's 1960 transfer of William D. Rossiter, chief of the Wisconsin fire-marshal division, from the state capital to Milwaukee, where he took up offices in the headquarters of the city fire department. Such aid to local governments can have as much value as substitute administration, without the disadvantages of that extreme solution to a community's problems.

When discussing the subject of state-local cooperation in personnel matters, one cannot ignore the part played by the state university. For years, schools of education have furnished school systems with both teaching and administrative staff made up of students working for the baccalaureate or an advanced degree. Although this procedure is rationalized on the ground of apprenticeship training for fledgling teachers and administrators, there can still be no doubt that the inexperienced personnel is of some help to the school system. So, also, in recent years universities have sought to place young men in training positions in the offices of mayors and city managers, in public works departments, and in fire and police departments. This is almost always a mutually beneficial arrangement: young men get training, and the city gets additional manpower at very low cost. In equipment, as in personnel, the state can be of aid. State highway departments can make available to cities a goodly amount of expensive equipment which the city, even if it could afford to pay for it, could not use frequently enough to make the use economical.

Like cooperation between and among the units of local government, state help to the city on a cooperative basis has great promise. If the current trend continues, we shall see in the latter part of the twentieth century an expansion of cooperative endeavors between and among all levels of government, and between and among all types of governmental authorities.

Effectuation of Aids and Controls. A variety of administrative techniques are used to implement state aid to the cities and state control of municipal functions. One of the decisions a state must make is whether to concentrate aids and controls in one agency or department, or permit them to be dispersed throughout the state administrative structure. In short, the problem is dispersed versus centralized administration.

New Jersey and North Carolina, as we have already seen, have gone a considerable distance along the road to centralized financial aid and control. New Jersey set up a department of local government in the 1930's, which, from the title, would seem to indicate that it was designed to concentrate all state-local relations at one spot in the administrative organization. But subsequent developments have shown this not to be the case. When the department was given divisional status in the Treasury Department, the true nature of the activity was evident: its purpose was financial oversight of local government.

Pennsylvania probably comes as close as any state to the centralization of administrative aids and controls in one department. From the Department of Internal Affairs the state advises local government officials in legal, financial, and managerial affairs; and the publications issued by the department are authoritative guides for local action. The department's Bureau of Municipal Affairs is especially busy with the review of assorted general-obligation bond issues and numerous other matters.

Though aids and controls may rest on an informal base, more often than not they derive from the constitution; statutes; and administrative orders, regulations, and ordinances. The growth of administrative rule-making and adjudication during the twentieth century has been phenomenal throughout the Western world. Although municipal law has not escaped this trend, a nineteenth-century rigidity still pervades it. Constitutions strictly bind the cities, and statutes specify in minute detail the most intimate conduct of municipal life. To make matters worse, the courts, staffed by judges who know little about the governance of the city, hear arguments by counsel who have little general or special knowledge of the complexities and necessities of urban government.

Yet in spite of the archaic nature of municipal law, some progress has been made in administrative rule-making and adjudication. As we have seen above, the New Jersey local government division may issue a variety of regulations bearing upon municipal finance. In health matters, a state agency may issue a cease-and-desist order directing a city to stop dumping raw sewage into a watercourse. A state housing department may approve or disapprove the mayor's appointments to the local housing board, an action that may not be rule-making per se, but one that has rule-making effect.

But the surface has been no more than scratched. State rule-making and adjudicatory commissions could be set up to approve incorporation of cities and villages, to settle disputes between and among cities and other local units over annexations, to determine fiscal capacity of cities. As we shall later see, constitutional and statutory limits on the taxing and borrowing powers of municipalities are often unrealistic because they give no attention to the fiscal capacity of the community. Rule-making power fixed in a state commission, however, could give a flexibility to financial and other controls that could never be achieved by statute or constitution.

At the policy level, state legislatures have long had standing committees on municipal affairs. As the legislative power of the governor has grown over the past decades, moreover, some of the states have seemed interested in establishing in that high office an adviser for urban affairs. At the request of Governor Nelson Rockefeller, the New York legislature in 1959 created in the executive office a new agency called "Office for Local Government"; and less than a year later the governor of New Hampshire established, in his office, a division of municipal affairs.[14] In 1961, Missouri established a permanent local government commission; and in 1963, Governor John Love of Colorado appointed a 100-man commission to look into all aspects of local government.

The work of the Colorado 100-man commission culminated in the passage of legislation in 1966 which created a Division of Local Government. Major responsibilities assigned to the division were (1) to advise the governor and the General Assembly on local government problems, (2) to integrate state efforts in aid of local governments, (3) to act as an information and research center, (4) to encourage intergovernmental cooperation, and (5) to publish an annual compendium of local government fiscal data.

Such offices, which numbered 16 in 1967, may well effect a change in state-local relations from both the policy and the administrative standpoint. The local government secretariat may be able to expand state-local cooperation, raise the effectiveness of both state and local services, and—no insignificant point—enhance the stature of the governor himself. It might also serve to educate some governors in the significance of urban government.

The City and the Federal Government

When Chicago Police Commissioner Timothy O'Connor, in 1959, called in the police courtesy cards of accredited representatives of sixty different foreign countries, Swedish Consul Gösta Oldenburg protested that his immunity to arrest was assured by treaty between his country and the United States government. Somewhat taken aback by the prospect of the city's creating an international incident if the Swedish consul or any other foreign representative were arrested, the commissioner hastily restored the courtesy cards.

[14] *Public Management*, LXII (April, 1960), 90.

This experience of the Chicago police commissioner dramatizes the position of the great city vis-à-vis the world at large. It also illustrates some of the traditional contacts that the city has with the federal government. Whenever a city has lain on an international boundary, whenever it has received foreign ships or planes in its ports, whenever it has had foreign consuls or a great number of foreign visitors, it has been projected into the world at large.

Just as the city's relations with people and things that cross national boundaries involve it with the federal government, so other constitutional matters involve the city. In civil rights the city is, under the Fourteenth Amendment, deeply involved with the federal government. And the Civil Rights Act of 1964 may be expected substantially to affect city-federal relations.

Nor does the city-federal relationship remain strictly unilateral: there is a strongly reciprocal element to the relationship. In the financing and administration of elections, the city, together with the county and the state, aids and even subsidizes the federal government. Remember that there is no such thing as federally financed and administered elections in the United States. Furthermore, in carrying out their law enforcement functions, cities lend invaluable service to the nation in combating narcotics traffic, protecting the currency, and suppressing genuinely subversive activity—three objectives of primary concern to the federal government.

But in the last analysis, the federal contacts that have had massive impact upon the cities derive from the national government's spending power. It is, in short, the grant-in-aid which has been the vehicle that has revolutionized federal-city relations over the past few decades.

City-Federal Relations to World War II. Although one study has indicated that in 1930 there were as many as 77 federal services to municipalities, these contacts had relatively little impact on municipal government's overall operations.[15] City officials knew full well that their governments operated within a constitutional federal system. They knew that the national government's financial policy, its control of interstate and foreign commerce, its operation of the postal system, its policy toward internal improvements, its sovereign immunity to taxation, and its power to make war might singly or together affect the city. If national action helped the city, political leaders would shout hurrah; if federal policy hurt the city, the leaders would denounce it, though few would take the picturesque tack of Mayor Wood of New York, who, in 1861, called for secession of his city from the state and the Union.

Mayors and councilmen, often professional politicians, might be in a po-

[15] J. C. Phillips, *Municipal Government and Administration in America* (New York: The Macmillan Co., 1960), p. 124.

sition to make or break governors and senators, and a big-city mayor might cause the President to tremble for his political life. The men of city hall, as political power centers, might loom large on the Washington scene or in the state capitols. Often they might use their cities for the benefit of their parties in state and nation, and often this might be a disadvantage to their cities. The city's treasury and the efficiency of its government might, time and again, be sacrificed by these men for the sake of state and national party victory.

And yet, for all that, the city and nation were never close. The controlling, overwhelming legal fact was that the cities were creatures of the state, to be touched only now and then by the nation. This was the way it was in 1924 when Professor William Anderson wrote a revealing essay on federal-city relations for the *National Municipal Review*. Noting the constant— and irrevocable—drift of population to the cities. Professor Anderson prophetically called for closer ties between the central government and the cities, in order that they might, in union, approach the complex riddles posed by the urban areas: "the national government must be called upon to cooperate and to assist in the solution of municipal problems." [16] Though not anticipating in this essay the massive use of grant-in-aid that was soon to come, Anderson did specifically recommend that a bureau of local government be established in the federal bureaucracy, to act as an information agency and to help establish liaison between the city and the central government. Thus, he anticipated the establishment of a cabinet department devoted to urban affairs in 1965.

In 1924 the cities were riding the crest of business prosperity. Though rumblings of agrarian unrest were coming from the hinterlands, city fathers were perfectly confident of themselves and, if anything, more confident of the remarkable business techniques, the industrial apparatus, the cultural achievements, the architectural triumphs, and the scientific and technical skills that had been built up so rapidly in American cities over the previous few decades. Surely these vast facilities were enough to discount the future. Surely this mass of brain and muscle could not be overwhelmed by any force, however large. You could as easily reverse the flow of all the rivers on the continent as quiet the peripatetic, charging, clanging, stentorian urban giant that sprawled over the landscape.

The notable decade of the 1920's, which Frederick Lewis Allen remembers so well in *Only Yesterday*, gripped entire cities and, of course, the city halls as well. Only occasionally did some Jeremiah—an H. L. Mencken, a Sinclair Lewis—give warning. And so, when the urban defenses were broken through by the disastrous financial crisis of the early 1930's, when the city, for all its triumphs, turned beggar, city hall was as unprepared as

[16] William Anderson, "The Federal Government and the Cities," *National Municipal Review*, XIII (May, 1924), 293.

state capitol or the White House for the emergency. Occasionally, a city under an intrepid mayor, such as Dan Hoan of Milwaukee, could at least make the best of things. Hoan, for example, never defaulted on a bond issue and never failed to meet a payroll. But Hoan was a rare mayor and Milwaukee an even rarer city.

If the cities could not save themselves, where were they to turn? The states were as hard-pressed as they; even when state officials wished to act, they often butted into rigid state constitutions that immobilized them or into a prostrate economy which could not support them. The triumph of the moderately left-wing New Deal, in 1932, and the inauguration of President Roosevelt, in March of 1933, changed the situation visibly. The cities found themselves with a godfather—and a rich one. Roosevelt's concern for the "Forgotten Man," who usually lived in the city, was sufficient in itself to motivate him to go to the city's aid. But there were other stimuli: though called a country squire, Roosevelt was no more a typical American farmer than was Thomas Jefferson. Indeed, much of his family's wealth had been accumulated by means of urban, capitalistic enterprise. And since much of his life had been urban, the President was emotionally attached to the urban scene, and he was, therefore, sensitive to the city's plight.

After March 4, 1933, the new administration in Washington moved swiftly to relieve the plight of the cities. Soon, by means of the Works Progress Administration and the Public Works Administration, the city's unemployed were building streets, repairing sidewalks, enlarging the reptile house at the zoo, building a school auditorium, laying out parks. In terms of physical plant, the city's gain could only be called a bonanza. Though much waste undoubtedly resulted from the lack of planning for the various projects, the city, as a corporate body, received physical properties of great value, virtually without cost to the local budget.

At the same time municipal finance suffered a sea change. The special assessment went into eclipse, not to reappear as an important element of public finance for two decades.[17] Some municipalities, having a heavy debt structure, almost turned turtle in the heavy financial seas; federal municipal bankruptcy legislation helped save some of them. The federal grant-in-aid became, for the first time in American history, of crucial importance to the city.

During the 1930's, Washington was peopled with the impatient. Theoreticians, utopians, young men in a hurry hit upon an idea at a coffeehouse in the morning, carried it to Congress in the afternoon, and celebrated their victory at cocktails in the evening. And just as the utopians of

---

[17] See William O. Winter, *The Special Assessment Today* (Ann Arbor, Mich.: University of Michigan Press, 1952).

the nineteenth century had sought to create the ideal city, so these utopians of the 1930's began to build their "perfect" urban communities. The result was the creation of nearly a hundred communities, each entirely new, each built from the ground up, many constructed after the ideal precepts of Ebenezer Howard and Patrick Geddes.[18] The towns themselves are still in existence—note Greenbelt, Maryland—but the excitement of their builders is gone.

New federal projects of a less utopian cast were set up and have endured. Using the grant-in-aid as the carrying agent for most substantive programs, the federal government sought to advance public housing, public health and sanitation, slum clearance, public transportation, education, welfare, and vocational rehabilitation. Most of these programs necessitated some kind of direct federal-city contact.

City-Federal Relations Since World War II. Today there is hardly a federal department or agency that does not, at one time or another, have some contact with the city government. The U.S. Bureau of the Census relies upon cities to report a great mass of data to the bureau or to its agents, and the city in turn relies upon the census reports to help form municipal policy. Municipal police departments rely upon the crime reporting and training facilities of the U.S. Department of Justice, and city police cooperate with federal police on many fronts. Fire departments receive grants-in-aid and information from the U.S. Office of Civil Defense and may be aided in emergencies with loans of equipment from that agency. The U.S. Bureau of Mines will advise sewer departments on dangerous sewer gases, and the U.S. Public Health Service will aid the same department in solving some perplexing problems of sewage treatment. The city which dumps raw sewage into an interstate river system may find itself in trouble with federal authorities, but may obtain federal funds to aid in the building of sewerage facilities.

Even the U.S. Department of Agriculture in its operations will affect the city. Agricultural food surpluses will be handled by city welfare departments. The county agent, a quasi-federal official, will advise the city on a tree program. By payments on land in the urban fringe, the department enables owners to hold transitional land off the market. And the department has been known to sponsor urban research.

Of recent years the city's involvement in the military policy of the central government, always considerable, has increased a hundredfold. Once places of refuge militarily, cities are now prime targets for supersonic aircraft and missiles bearing atomic bombs and warheads. Another major war would surely be a struggle of the great powers to eliminate enemy cities: the

[18] Paul K. Conkin, *Tomorrow a New World: The New Deal Community Program* (Ithaca, N.Y.: Cornell University Press, 1959).

nation which first lost its cities would first be prostrate. Little wonder, then, that the city is anxious for the nation to look to its defenses—and just as anxious for the great nations to keep the peace.

Less dramatically, but no less importantly, the central government's military procurement policy deeply and vitally affects the city's economic life. In St. Louis, for example, the largest employer is McDonnell Aircraft Company, which subsists almost exclusively on military contracts from the central government. Because of a diversified industrial base, St. Louis might not suffer too greatly if peace were effected in the Cold War, but the shock would nevertheless be great. Heavy defense spending, in short, may be vital to a city's economic health (and thus to its political stability).

In the postwar years, a truly remarkable amount of attention has been given to the relations between and among units and levels of government in this republic. The two Hoover commissions, authorized in 1947 and 1953, though primarily devoted to questions of federal administrative efficiency, nevertheless could not avoid attention to some of the problems involved in state and local government. At the same time that the second Hoover Commission was carrying on its work, the Commission on Intergovernmental Relations, popularly known as the Kestnbaum commission, was delving into the innermost recesses of federal, state, and local relations and activities. As the Hoover and Kestnbaum commissions were at work, their activities were watched with the greatest interest by the governors and mayors of the states and cities of the United States.

As a result of the governors' interest, a new commission, the Joint Federal-State Action Committee, was established in July of 1957, and its members were appointed by the President and the chairman of the National Governors' Conference. Although primarily concerned with federal-state relations, the committee made recommendations of great significance to American cities. Indeed, its second report (December, 1958) included four recommendations which, if carried out, would have eliminated or altered federal aid to cities for vocational education, sewage treatment, natural disasters, and to a certain extent urban development, housing, and planning. At the same time, the United States Congress, which has always been a veritable hotbed of particularistic sentiment, was interesting itself, formally, in the problem of federal-state-local relations. A subcommittee of the House Committee on Government Operations held extensive hearings throughout the United States in 1956, 1957, and 1958, largely to get the opinions of mayors and governors on matters bearing upon intergovernmental relations.

During the second session of the 86th Congress, a new body called the Advisory Commission on Intergovernmental Relations was established. It began operations early in 1960. This twenty-six-member, bipartisan commission was to provide advice and assistance to the President and the Congress on all phases of intergovernmental relations, especially those that directly pertained to the federal grant-in-aid program. The commission's studies were to range from research into the problems involved in intergovernmental cooperation to the allocation of revenue sources among the various governmental levels. The membership of the commission has included governors, senators, and representatives in Congress; federal administrators; state legislators; private citizens; mayors; and county officials. One of the most impressive facts about the establishment of this commission was that for the first time in the history of the republic a permanent commission was instituted with the authority to concern itself not only with the classic problems of federalism—that is, relations between the states and the federal government—but also with the problem of local relationships with the states and the central government.[19]

For the two major American political parties, the local party organization is of crucial importance to victory at the polls, whether at the local, state, or national level. Because of this power of the local political group and because the mayors of the larger cities are more often than not in control of their local political organizations, the mayors speak with stentorian voices in the state and national councils of the parties.

Adding to the influence of both mayors and other city officials in national affairs are the National League of Cities (NLC) and the U.S. Conference of Mayors (USCOM). Both organizations have offices in Washington, D. C., and here both, either singly or together, constitute an effective lobby for American cities. In the spring of 1960 the two organizations joined together to present an identical fourteen-point urban affairs plank to the two major party platform committees. Democratic mayors of New York City, Philadelphia, Chicago, Madison, St. Louis, and Nashville presented the plank to the Democratic Platform Committee; and the Republican mayors of Los Angeles, Syracuse, Norfolk, Fort Worth, Seattle, and Knoxville presented the same plank to the Republican Platform Committee.

Although the platforms finally hammered out by each of the major parties did not follow all the recommendations, a substantial portion of the fourteen-point urban affairs plank did get favorable attention from both parties. In the words of an official of the National League of Cities, "what the 1960 platforms seem to disclose after comparison with their predecessors is [that] the cities' critical importance to the Nation's future has been finally recognized by both parties and that municipal governments will not have to fight the battle of growth and decay almost completely alone for much longer."

[19] For an exhaustive report on the origins and goals of the Advisory Commission on Intergovernmental Relations, see Deil S. Wright, "The Advisory Commission on Intergovernmental Relations: Unique Features and Policy Orientation," *Public Administration Review*, XXV (September, 1965), 193–202.

The NLC-USCOM urban affairs plank recommended the creation of a federal department of housing and urban affairs with cabinet status. The Democratic platform of 1960 pledged that a national Democratic administration would "give the city dweller a voice at the Cabinet table by bringing together within a single department programs concerned with urban and metropolitan problems." [20] Although the Republican platform did not so specifically follow the NLC-USCOM recommendation, it did call for improved liaison between the federal, state, and local governments.

Each year during the early 1960's, the pressures upon the Congress and the President for a cabinet-rank department of urban affairs mounted. Supported strongly by the urban delegations in Congress and by a number of pressure groups, including the National League of Cities, President Kennedy sought the creation of such a department in 1962, but was frustrated by the House of Representatives. Finally in 1965, a bill to establish the U.S. Department of Housing and Urban Development (HUD) passed both houses of Congress, and the President signed it into law in September of that year.

The original agencies of the new department were the Federal Housing Administration, Urban Renewal Administration, Public Housing Administration, Community Facilities Administration, and the Federal National Mortgage Association. Of basic importance to the city, but left out of HUD's program, was mass transit. This element of the city's life, however, was recognized in the Department of Transportation, which came into being in 1967.

The secretary of HUD was charged by the enabling act to advise the President on policies which would aid urban areas, to coordinate federal programs in housing and urban development, to provide technical assistance to state and local governments, and to consult with governors and state administrative heads on various aid programs.

Urban political leaders publicly hailed the new department, but privately often expressed somewhat more limited approval. And there were major newspapers that reviewed the new act in less than glowing terms. The *Atlanta Journal,* which had opposed the bill, called it a "sad, lamentable truth" that the measure would not have been necessary "had the states and their rurally dominated legislatures (Georgia is a prime example) been decent, fair and honest in their relationships with their own cities." A little sardonically, the *San Francisco Chronicle* observed that the man in the new cabinet post would have the greatest chance to come to the aid of his country since Jefferson made the Louisiana Purchase. His task would include the education of the President of the United States, "the total re-education of some Governors (if that is achievable), and a [sup-

[20] Democratic National Committee, "The Rights of Man," platform adopted by the Democratic National Convention, July 12, 1960, p. 40.

pression of] the bulldozers and wrecking balls that knock down the old and beautiful just for the hell of it"! [21]

One further item needs to be added to the rapidly lengthening list of federal attempts to build up rapport with the states and the cities. In 1965 President Johnson designated the office of the Vice President as the principal federal liaison agency with the local governments, and the Office of Emergency Planning, headed by former Governor Farris Bryant, to accomplish the same purpose with the states.

This sketch of intergovernmental studies and activities over the past two decades does not do full justice to the interest exhibited by politicians, administrators, and laymen in intergovernmental processes and relationships of this republic; but it does indicate the depth of the interest and the amount of effort that is being made to explore intergovernmental relations —federal, state, and local. One could certainly expect mayors and other city officials, and perhaps certain state officials, to be concerned with the relation of the city to the central government, as well as to the state government. One should not be surprised, moreover, to find interest in the Congress, particularly because of the local bias so often exhibited by members of Congress. But when all of these officials combine with the President, the governors, and nationally influential laymen in examining the problem, one can be sure that these matters are of basic concern to the very future and continued well-being of the republic. Still further, the virtual explosion of federal urban legislation during the middle 1960's gives compelling empirical evidence that the city is of prime concern to national politics. Let us turn, therefore, to specific federal-city relationships.

Financial Relations. Acquisition of federal property in cities over the past quarter of a century has seriously eroded the tax base in some localities. As early as the middle 1930's there was general recognition that federal ownership of property was having an impact upon state and local financial systems. In 1955 the Kestnbaum commission recommended that substantial payments in lieu of taxes be made by the federal government to local governments, and gradually various specific programs have evolved, such as aid to "federally impacted" school districts, which show federal recognition of a financial obligation to the urban community. Still, in the opinion of most local officials and many detached observers, this recognition is partial and insufficient. As long as the federal government continues to ignore its obligation to the city for municipal services to federal property and indeed to federal employees, just so long will the local governments continue to subsidize the federal government by supporting, from local revenue sources, services and activities that are essential to the effective administration of federal responsibilities throughout the country.

---

[21] Quoted in *Nation's Cities*, III (October, 1965), 15.

Possibly the most important aspect of federal-city financial relations, and indeed perhaps the most important aspect of all federal-city relations, is centered in the grant-in-aid. Income from federal grants has become so important a part of municipal revenue that cities would be hampered in their operations if the federal government were to discontinue these grants. Without going into the substantive aspects of the programs which the grants support, we should nevertheless examine some of the advantages and disadvantages which the grants embody.

Based upon the spending power of the federal government, a grant of authority contained in Article I, Section 8, of the U.S. Constitution, the grant-in-aid is a federal appropriation given to the city for certain specific objects. Almost invariably these grants from the central to the local governments are restricted; that is, the monies must be spent for certain specific programs and may not be diverted into the general fund of the city to be spent wherever need arises. Although, theoretically, the city is free to reject the controls from the central government imposed by the grants-in-aid, it may do so only by refusing the money, and this, considering the dire financial straits of most cities, is of course very difficult to do. After the acceptance of the grant, the city is compelled to follow the strictures laid down by the federal government in the enabling or the granting legislation. These strictures apply even though only a small percentage of the total program may be financed by the federal government. The city's acceptance of a small federal grant, therefore, may mean that it must spend not only the federal money but a sizable amount of its own money according to federal requirements.

So much has already been said about grants-in-aid to the city, from both state and federal governments, that we need here only to glance briefly at some of the advantages and disadvantages of federal grants-in-aid to the cities. First, we can safely say that the grants-in-aid have helped the cities to expand their service functions. In housing, planning, education, urban renewal, and public works, the cities have benefited significantly from federal money. Because the service level of the city's administration has been raised by this money, we can probably safely assume that the federal programs have enabled the cities to become more effective governing units than they were in the past. On the other hand, it is probably safe to assume that some local power and discretion have been taken away from the citizens of the city itself and deposited in the central government. The federal grants also seem to have caused some shift of power from the local governments to the state governments. Just how important these shifts of power have been and whether they have been counterbalanced by the prestige which the city gains from an increase in the service level caused by the grants-in-aid is impossible to say.

Still another characteristic of federal aid is to be found in what might be called the visibility of the aid program. This visibility stems from a peculiar characteristic of our news media. When a federal grant is received by a city, it is the federal action that more often than not gets the headline, while the action of the local governing body and the money to be spent upon the same program by the local government are given only passing attention. A case in point is the building and maintenance of streets and highways in this country. Although the amount of state and local money expended for this purpose exceeds federal outlays by about two times, there is, nevertheless, a tendency by the news media to treat federal expenditures as the most important item in this particular field of public works. A citizen is apt to conclude, therefore, that the federal government is primarily responsible, financially, for the construction and maintenance of highways and streets. For example, in 1965–1966, state and local governments spent $8.8 billion on streets and highways; the federal government, $4.1 billion.[22] Just how much effect this has on the prestige of the cities is impossible to detect, but that there is some damage to that prestige is unquestionable.

As we shall see later on in our discussion of urban renewal, administrative jargon has labeled some federal grants as "seed money." This phrase refers to the mobilization of local capital, both public and private, which has been stimulated by federal money. A federal expenditure of $10 million, for example, may stimulate a further expenditure of local capital by the city and private investors of as much as $100 million. Thus, the federal money sows the seed and a major plant grows from it. While recognizing the great value of this "seed money" in the mobilization of local capital, we should not forget a signal disadvantage to such aid: its contribution to the disintegration of local government, particularly metropolitan government. Because of the multitude of uncoordinated aid programs, federal aid has probably increased rather than lessened the enormous problem of governing the urban community.

In addition to stimulating local action, the grants also act as an equalizing device. Some urban renewal, for example, can be carried on alone by the richer cities; the poorer ones can do nothing at all without federal aid. One of the frequent criticisms of federal grant-in-aid programs, however, is that they are not really a very good equalizing device. A grant-in-aid program which is ideally constructed, say the critics, would give only moderate grants to the richest city, and massive grants to the poorest.

Varying the Impact of Federal Funds on Local Decision-Making. Of all the questions that arise over federal aid to state and local governments, none has more emotional content, none gives rise to more debate, and certainly none calls forth more clichés than the degree to which such aid is used to influence or coerce local policy-making. Few informed observers of

---

[22] U.S. Bureau of the Census, *Governmental Finances in 1965–66*, GF, No. 13 (August, 1967), 22.

American federalism would doubt that the central government does indeed exercise some control by means of the purse strings, but most of them would probably disagree over the extent and importance of such control. Even where control admittedly exists, it will simultaneously offend the values of those who hold that the essence of democracy is decentralization and diversity and upset those who support increasing centralization and unity more or less in conformance with the French model. Thus, for some groups the control is bad because they want little or none; for others it is bad because it is too weak.

We shall attempt to take the measure of this problem, first by use of a case study to illustrate how in a power struggle between city and central government, the city is not necessarily helpless. Secondly, we shall look at the Heller and other plans for decentralizing power in federal grant programs.

Mayor Daley Versus U.S. Commissioner of Education Keppel. Sometimes federal direction of the local effort is implied in a statute; sometimes it is openly stated, though rarely so openly as in the Civil Rights Act of 1964. In Title VI of that act, Congress boldly pronounced the policy of withholding federal money from public schools that were still racially segregated. This section of the act was designed to speed compliance by public school systems in the Deep South with the 1954 decision of the Supreme Court in *Brown* v. *Board of Education of Topeka*. It soon became obvious, however, that the act would affect not only southern schools but northern ones also.

Since there had been months-long demonstrations against the Chicago public schools by civil rights groups during the spring and summer of 1965, the U.S. Commissioner of Education, Francis Keppel, decided to hold up $32 million in federal funds promised the Chicago schools until the complaints about segregation had been investigated. He decided, in other words, to invoke the Civil Rights Act. Mayor Richard Daley was disturbed. Although the Chicago school system has never been formally under the control of the mayor, he does appoint the school board, and there is little doubt ever expressed by Chicagoans that he cannot control it in fact, whenever he so desires. In this case, Mayor Daley had stoutly defended his school board against the protests of the civil rights groups, and he quickly made it plain that he would not permit the U.S. Commissioner of Education to humiliate him and his city. The rectitude of the commissioner's decision, then, was not the question at issue. Nor was it whether the commissioner had the legal right to act. The question was: Who had the political power?

If anyone had any doubts about Mayor Daley's power, the mayor soon put those doubts at rest. If he did not actually talk with the President, all the evidence indicates that the President heard the arguments of the Chicago political leader and sympathized with them. At the same time, rumors started around Washington that the House Government Operations Committee, headed by one of Daley's political subordinates, Representative William L. Dawson, was readying itself to investigate Commissioner Keppel. It is not surprising, therefore, that the commissioner quickly capitulated, conceding all points to the mayor.

Although the city had won the fight in the first round, some face-saving negotiations remained to be carried on between Mayor Daley's representative, the president of the Chicago school board, and an undersecretary of the U.S. Department of Health, Education, and Welfare. The agreement between the city and the federal authorities resulted in the city's getting the federal money and its continuing the programs it already had in existence.

There is no telling, from this case, on which side virtue lay. One can only tell where political power rested. With the law on his side and with a sizable amount of federal money to be used to influence local action, Commissioner Keppel found himself completely frustrated by power politics. That he had support in Congress for his policy was indicated by the distress of Representative Adam Clayton Powell, the Harlem Democrat who was chairman of the House Education and Labor Committee, over his capitulation. He also had the support of civil rights groups which could muster votes in both the Senate and the House. He probably was not, therefore, wholly naïve politically in thinking that he could crack the whip over the Chicago school system.

The commissioner's basic mistake, in all probability, was the same one so often made by scholars, laymen, and bureaucrats in assessing the nature of the federal grant-in-aid programs. If the law specifies that certain conditions be met by the city before federal money will be forthcoming, the conclusion is too easily reached that the matter is simply one of compliance with the exact terms of the law. This is, however, usually not the case. The real decisions as to who will control whom may be made by informal negotiation or by such political power plays as this one pulled off by Mayor Daley. The federal grant-in-aid programs must always be evaluated in terms of these informal aspects.

The Heller and Other Plans. Impressed by the apparent need for federal aid to state and local governments, and convinced that signal disadvantages lay within the standard conditional grant system, various individuals and organizations during the 1960's offered plans for a more rational ordering of the grants than the traditional system affords.

Of all of these models, the Heller plan became the best known, perhaps because its author, Walter W. Heller, was chairman of the Council of Economic Advisers under both Presidents John F. Kennedy and Lyndon B. Johnson. This plan proposed, in essence, a means of using federal fiscal power in aid of the hard-pressed cities and states but of simultaneously withdrawing federal fiscal control over those polities. To paraphrase Heller, the plan was offered as a means of using federal affluence to help meet the problems of local effluents.

Central to the plan was what Heller called per capita revenue sharing. Its essential elements were, first, that a federal rebate to the states would be fixed in terms of a certain percentage of the federal income tax base. Thus if taxable income under federal income tax laws amounted to $300 billion for a particular year and the percentage of rebate were set at 2 percent, the total grant to the states would be $6 billion. Second, the funds would be distributed to the states on a per capita basis. Third, the states would receive this money annually as a matter of right, and as a result of simple accounting procedures. Fourth, there would be routine restrictions, largely of an accounting and reporting nature, attached to the monies. If substantive restrictions were added, such as a requirement that the states conform to Title VI of the Civil Rights Act, they would be kept to a minimum also.

The Heller plan would affect the federal relation in several ways. It would have a very definite equalizing effect among the states in that the poorer states would be getting back more money than their citizens paid the federal government under the 2 percent formula, and the richer states would get back less. The states would also be relatively free to spend the money without restrictions, and this freedom would have a decentralizing effect on policy-making in the American federal system. There would be, still further, a progressive impact upon the state revenue systems, since the federal income tax base is less regressively oriented than the tax bases of most states.

But, one might ask, how would the Heller plan help the cities? Without aid to local governments in general—the cities as well as the other local governments—the plan would surely not serve its purpose. But local aid would inevitably flow from the plan, according to its author, even if indirectly. Reapportionment of the state legislatures will make them more sensitive to local needs. States, moreover, have a good record in coming to the aid of their local governments, although the urban areas are often slighted. One must rely upon the states to be fair to their local governments, even though one may wonder whether the metropolitan areas especially would be fairly treated were the Heller plan to become national policy.[23]

The other notable plan for federal aid to the local and state governments is the one which would permit the citizen to credit against his federal income tax liability at least a portion of the income tax which he has paid to

---

[23] Walter W. Heller, *New Dimensions of Political Economy* (New York: W. W. Norton & Co., 1967), Ch. 3.

his own state.[24] This tax-credit plan, in its various guises, would probably stimulate both states and cities to enact their own income taxes (some of the plan's critics have said that it would coerce states and cities to enact income taxes) and would eliminate the federal government as broker or intermediary in the federal fiscal relationship. One of the significant disadvantages to the tax-offset plan would be the lack of a built-in equalization element among the various states.

Major Federal Programs in Urban Areas. Transportation. During the past quarter of a century, federal aviation activities have been of substantial importance to urban areas. Before 1933, airports developed largely with municipal and private capital. After 1933, major federal contributions to airport development began via the various work relief programs. The Kestnbaum commission estimated that $400 million in federal funds were spent on airports in the 1930's.

The Federal Airport Act of 1946 provided that $500 million a year should be expended on airports over a seven-year period. In 1950, this period was extended for five years. Under this program the federal government assumed 50 percent of the cost of the given project. The rest of the money came from the city governments, although in a few instances the state governments also contributed a share to the program. In 1966 Congress extended the Federal Airport Act, and thus federal aid to airports, through fiscal year 1970.

The civil aeronautics administrator is responsible for developing and keeping up-to-date a national airport plan, though there is no way in which he can make or compel the cities to conform to it. Major airports in the nation—for example, Kennedy International in New York and O'Hare International in Chicago—have been built largely on a self-liquidating basis with local funds, and thus their development has been mainly beyond federal control, except for technical aspects of design.

The city's role in civil aviation has been largely overlooked. With airports just as we have already observed with other governmental functions, a federal grant tends to push into the background the substantial contributions of the grantee; the popular imagination tends to be excited by federal activity and at the same time to forget the activity of the local government. Still another factor to consider is that the larger cities of the nation maintain those air facilities which are crucial to the operation and development of air transportation. In 1959, for example, the 41 largest cities spent approximately $72 million on airport development and operation, or about

[24] See, for example, Advisory Commission on Intergovernmental Relations, *Federal-State Coordination of Personal Income Taxes* (Washington, D. C.: The Commission, October, 1965), pp. 15–19; and Committee for Economic Development, *A Fiscal Program For a Balanced Federalism* (New York: The Committee, June, 1967).

60 percent of the total amount spent by all cities in the United States during the same year. In 1965–1966, capital outlay on construction of air transportation facilities amounted to $226 million (local governments), $84 million (federal government), and $31 million (state governments).[25] While the large cities get federal aid for their airports, they are much more apt to rely upon their own resources, including levies upon the air transportation industry itself, to maintain and develop their air terminals. A good deal of the federal effort, on the other hand, is expended upon hundreds of smaller airports around the country which are not now economically viable and possibly never will be. Without question, therefore, it is upon the larger cities that the aviation industry must heavily rely for development and expansion.

The federal government contributes materially to the support of water transportation routes by dredging rivers and harbors, by maintaining navigational aids, and by regulating rates charged by interstate carriers. This activity can and does contribute materially to the economic development of the city. The federal regulation of types of interstate carriers such as railroads, pipelines, and bus and trucking firms is also of direct importance to the city. And federal aid to the states and the cities for the construction of highways and urban streets aids that circulation of personnel and matériel which is so necessary to the life of the city.

Except for air transportation subsidies, federal aid in the general field of transportation has been a disappointment to many urban leaders, perhaps to most of them. With the cities strangling in a glut of traffic, the federal interstate highway program has served to increase the importance of the automobile to the city's movement pattern. Because of this emphasis on the automobile, mass transit has gotten short shrift from the federal government, even though it has not gone entirely unnoticed.

Although every city with a master city plan has, in effect, a coherent policy statement on the local transportation complex (whether this overall plan is actually carried out, of course, is another matter), the federal government has never had a central plan nor a central planning agency for transportation. Federal policy has been found in any number of unrelated statutes and in the rules of various unrelated agencies, boards, and commissions.

When the new cabinet-level Department of Transportation was established in 1967, however, federal policy took a new tack by recognizing both local transportation needs and the necessity for some kind of unity in federal transportation planning and programming. Among other things, the basic statute directed the secretaries of the Departments of Transportation, and Housing and Urban Development to cooperate on a study of urban

[25] U.S. Bureau of the Census, *Governmental Finances in 1965–66*, GF, No. 13 (August, 1967), p. 25.

transit problems. Since high-speed transit between and among cities, moreover, is of major importance to urban life, the Office of High Speed Ground Transportation was switched from the Department of Commerce to the new transportation department. In addition, a most important obligation imposed on the new department was that it should, again in cooperation with Housing and Urban Development, plan for urban transportation systems that will fit into national and local needs. Finally, showing its strong integrative bias, the legislation provided for some departmental control over air, highway, and rail transportation.[26]

Education. Although the typical administrative pattern in the United States is for education to be conducted by local school districts which are independent of the city, the number of cities containing the schools as departments of the city government is sufficient for some comment on federal aid to education to be pertinent at this time. Current federal programs for schools can be broken down into several categories: (1) substantial aid, both in funds and in foodstuffs, for school lunch programs; (2) aid to schools in the so-called "federally impacted" areas; (3) aid in the teaching of such vocational subjects as home economics, agriculture, and the mechanical arts, and such academic subjects as science and foreign languages; and (4) general grants which first came into use with the passage of the innovative school aid bill of 1965.

Although federal aid to state and local school systems is not large when compared with the total expenditure for education, it is nevertheless an item to be reckoned with. Out of a total expenditure on schools of about $18 billion in 1959, the federal government contributed $826 million to aid the state and local governments in fulfilling their educational responsibilities. In 1965–1966, state and local expenditures had increased to $30.2 billion, and federal to $4.6 billion.[27]

The startling rise in federal expenditures on public education from 1959 to 1966 indicates that the great debate of the past decades over federal aid to education has largely been won by its proponents. But far from being an index of federal domination of the educational system, the data rather show a growing political consensus that education, like most other domestic programs, should become a cooperative responsibility of all three levels of government.

Recreation. To the frenetically active American in his 300-horsepower automobile, a visit to a national park, such as Yosemite or Yellowstone, has long been the symbol of a truly satisfying summer vacation. But therein lies

---

[26] *U.S. Government Organization Manual 1967–68* (Washington, D. C., 1967), pp. 396–413.

[27] U.S. Bureau of the Census, *Governmental Finances in 1959*, G-GF59, No. 2 (September 30, 1960), p. 18; and *Governmental Finances in 1965–1966*, GF, No. 13 (August, 1967), p. 22.

a difficulty: national parks, as well as other federal facilities, are often so far removed from major population centers that only by considerable effort can the urban citizen reach them. Although it is probably true that most of the visitors to Yosemite National Park live in the San Francisco and Los Angeles metropolitan areas, it remains that most federal facilities are not conveniently accessible to the urban citizen. Very few cities, for example, are as fortunate as Nashville, Tennessee, where a large federal lake was built on the Cumberland River for navigational, power, and flood-control purposes, and where the lake, being at the city's front door, can be developed as an important recreational center for the entire Nashville metropolitan area.

There has traditionally been little recognition by the National Park Service of the importance of developing recreational areas in or adjacent to urban centers of population. In 1958 Congress gave weak support to federal participation in recreation by establishing an Outdoor Recreation Resources Review Commission which was to attempt to evaluate and recommend general recreational goals for all levels of government in the United States. The final report of the commission was submitted to the President in January, 1962.

Although parks and recreational facilities will continue to be largely the responsibility of the state, the cities, and the counties, the political pressures will mount for the federal government, in making its vast expenditures for the development of natural resources and in opening up new parks and forests, to consider the recreational needs of the urban citizen. The great expanse of federal lands in the West can be regarded as a prime resource for recreation.

In recreation, intergovernmental cooperation shows promise. On a federally built reservoir, the state installs and operates a state park, and the city constructs and maintains a swimming beach. Or the city builds a great lake high in the Rocky Mountains, as Denver built Dillon Reservoir, and assigns its recreational development to the U.S. Department of the Interior. In this way not only can the particular facility in question be utilized to its full capability, but also the financial burden of development can be spread among two or three levels of government.

Water Policy. For many of the desert cities of the Southwest and the Pacific Coast, federal water policy is of life-and-death concern. The dramatic struggle of Los Angeles for water over the past half-century is excellent documentation of the necessity for the federal government's including the needs of great urban centers in its water policy. Situated between a dry desert on one side and a watery, salty desert on the other, Los Angeles has had to reach far beyond its boundaries for fresh potable water.

At the turn of the century the city and the surrounding urban community were supplied from the Los Angeles River and various dug wells. Realizing that these sources were totally inadequate to the growing city's needs, the city fathers determined upon an aggressive policy to expand the city's water supply sources. The result was the Los Angeles aqueduct, 233 miles long, which stretched across the desert to the eastern slopes of the Sierra Nevada Mountains. The city began getting mountain water in 1913. This new supply gave Los Angeles such an abundance of water that communities were eager to join themselves to the city. Spectacular annexations resulted. When the city outgrew this source of supply, it extended its aqueduct 100 miles to the north, so that the total length of the city's aqueduct is now approximately 350 miles.

In the meantime, pressure from those elements of the Los Angeles metropolitan area which were still outside the city, and from other metropolitan areas in southern California and Arizona, was to a considerable degree responsible for the construction of the Hoover and Parker dams on the Colorado River. These dams were, of course, financed by the federal government. Simultaneous with this federal action, a local governmental authority, the Metropolitan Water District, was authorized by popular vote to spend the formidable sum of $220 million for an aqueduct from the river to the Pacific Coast. With this new supply, the thirst of one great urban complex was at least temporarily sated.[28] To climax this remarkable history of intergovernmental cooperation, in 1960 the people of California approved a bond issue of $1.75 billion to build an aqueduct some 500 miles long—in effect, a man-made river—from the Feather River in the north to the metropolitan areas of Los Angeles and San Diego in the south.[29]

Federal recognition of the city's needs for water was a long time coming. Although flood control and navigation programs were of considerable economic importance to the city, these aids faded into insignificance compared with water supply. Finally, in 1958 the federal water supply act authorized the U.S. Corps of Engineers and the Bureau of Reclamation to include urban water supply in their planning and construction of dams and reservoirs. As we shall see, however, in Chapter 17, the politics of water is played in deadly earnest, and the partisans of navigation, flood control, and irrigation—particularly the last—will fight the city's use of a federal supply of water that is by no means limitless and can never be.

Housing, Urban Redevelopment, and Planning. Since we shall devote separate chapters to the housing of the urban population and to the planning and renewal of cities, no more need be given here about these pro-

---

[28] Nelson M. Blake, *Water for the Cities* (Syracuse, N. Y.: Syracuse University Press, 1956), pp. 286–287.

[29] Reginald C. Price, "Some Decisions in the State's Development of California's Waters During the 1960's," *Public Administration Review*, XXV (December, 1965), 290–296.

grams than a general summary statement. For housing and community re-development, the federal government spent $1.6 billion in 1965–1966, and the state and local governments together, $800 million.[30] That the federal government is assuming approximately 70 percent of the burden of this activity fully indicates the importance of the federal program to the city.

Very little public housing was known in the United States before the advent of the New Deal in the 1930's. In Austria, by contrast, the city of Vienna was investing a sizable proportion of its annual budget during the 1920's in housing for lower-income groups. In the middle 1930's, when public housing became a reality in American cities, this housing was either built by the federal government or substantially supported by it. During World War II, public housing activities largely lapsed, except for those directly connected with the defense effort. Federal housing policy finally came to maturity in the housing acts of 1949 and 1954.

The recognition that public housing could not be considered by itself but must be integrated with the development of the city in many other respects was first introduced into federal law by the Housing Act of 1949. This act provided federal assistance for various types of programs directed toward the elimination of blight in urban areas. Both loans and grants-in-aid could be made by the federal government to the cities for such redevelopment.

The concepts of urban development and urban renewal have been evolving for several decades. After the recognition of urban redevelopment in the Housing Act of 1949, the federal government moved on to a larger concept of the program in the Housing Act of 1954, under which the federal government made available both grants-in-aid and loans to local governments for urban renewal purposes. And under the same act the federal government offered grants of up to 50 percent of the cost to aid urban communities with populations of under 25,000 to develop city plans.

For more than a decade the Congress made, in virtually every session, substantial additions to the federal housing and urban renewal legislations. Thus the Housing and Urban Renewal Act of 1965 provided for:

1. Rent supplements for lower-income families.

2. Grants of 50 percent for basic water and sewer facilities.

3. Grants of 66⅔ percent for neighborhood health and recreation centers serving low- or moderate-income families.

4. Grants to cover the interest for debt incurred in acquiring land for future public use.

5. Open space assistance: grants increased from 20 percent to 50 percent for acquisition of open space; for development of the open space; and for

[30] U.S. Bureau of the Census, *Governmental Finances in 1965–1966*, GF, No. 13 (1967), p. 22.

acquiring, clearing, and developing open spaces in the built-up parts of the city.

    6. Grants of 50 percent for urban beautification.

    7. Grants of 66⅔ percent for demolition of unsafe structures.

    8. Grants of 66⅔ percent to 75 percent for concentrated code enforcement in deteriorating areas.

    9. Urban renewal grants.

    10. Urban planning grants.

In 1966 Congress made an important addition to housing, planning, and urban renewal legislation in passing the Demonstration Cities and Metropolitan Development Act (popularly known as the "model cities law"). Designed to encourage unity of programs and administrative agencies at both the local and national levels, the new policy emphasized the use of a wide variety of existing attacks upon urban blight and the concentration of these attacks upon specific cities, and neighborhoods within specific cities, in order to effect a change in the total urban environment.

Health and Welfare. For general health, hospitals, and public welfare, all governments in the United States in 1965–1966 spent approximately $15.4 billion. Of this amount, the federal government spent about $6.6 billion; a greater amount ($8.8 billion) was expended by the state and local governments from their own resources.[31] These figures indicate the importance attached to health and welfare by all levels of government in the United States.

The federal government contributes to the health of cities in a variety of ways, not only by means of its own health program, but also through grants-in-aid and other aids to local health administration. Under the so-called Hill-Burton Act, passed in 1946, the federal government has contributed substantially to the construction of new city hospitals by grants-in-aid of up to one-third of the cost of such hospitals.

Since 1948, when the Federal Water Pollution Control Act was passed, the central government has taken increasing interest in the health problem posed by the pollution of watercourses, rivers, and lakes in the nation at large. Until the early 1960's most of the federal grants to reduce water pollution were used by the municipalities for the construction of sewage treatment plants; paradoxically, no federal money was available for building sewerage distribution systems. Thus, if a community was faced with the financial impossibility of building such a distribution system, even though it was able to build a sewage treatment plant by obtaining federal aid, it had no way of getting the sewage to the plant. Such are the problems of intergovernmental relations!

Because public action in meeting the problem of water pollution finds

[31] *Ibid.,* p. 22.

general acceptance by the community, the success of local, state, and federal governments in arresting extreme pollution can be anticipated. With air pollution, however, it is quite a different matter. When the city attempts to specify the type of furnace that will be put in a private dwelling, when the city intimates that it might insist upon the motorist's installing a device to absorb some of the noxious elements from his car's exhaust fumes, when city health officials protest that airborne wastes from atomic explosions set off by the federal government might be eliminated, the sensitive political nature of the air pollution control problem is evident. Although the federal government has timorously moved against air pollution, as in the Clean Air Act of 1963, it had not by 1969 taken really major steps toward helping the states and local governments with the problem.

The growth of the political-administrative relations of the city to state and federal governments over the past two or three decades amply documents the intergovernmental revolution in the United States. Not only does this growth illustrate the concern for urban government—even urban culture—that has penetrated into state and federal policy; it just as well illustrates how the city has become a de facto partner in the federal arrangement.

But the association of the city with the state has an aspect other than the one pictured in the preceding pages. This is the legal relation. Though formed in the nineteenth century, this relation has tended to be static rather than dynamic. We need now to examine that static relationship and to inquire into its effect upon the city.

Annotated Bibliography

In the 1950's a United States government commission did valuable work in clarifying intergovernmental relations: local, state, and national. The Kestnbaum commission (Commission on Intergovernmental Relations) submitted its report to the President in 1955, *A Report to the President for Transmittal to the Congress* (Washington, D.C.: U.S. Government Printing Office, June, 1955). In addition to this final report, in itself a valuable summary of the commission's findings, there are a number of supplemental reports of merit.

Another commission, the Advisory Commission on Intergovernmental Relations, was established by act of Congress in 1959 "to give continuing attention to intergovernmental problems." Made up of governors, mayors, members of Congress, and other public figures, the commission assembled a professional staff, and taken together, the staff reports constitute possibly the best extended comment on intergovernmental relations in existence. For a list of commission publications, see Advisory Commission on Intergovernmental Relations, *Ninth Annual Report* (Washington, D.C.: The Commission, January 31, 1968).

W. Brooke Graves has made the most exhaustive recent commentary on the American federal system and has very logically extended it to include federal-local, state-local, and interlocal relations. See W. Brooke Graves, *American Intergovernmental Relations* (New York: Charles Scribner's Sons, 1964). And somewhat in the same vein is the examination of one of the most striking developments in intergovernmental relations in Roscoe C. Martin, *The Cities and the Federal System* (New York: Atherton Press, 1965).

In 1946, upon receiving a grant from the Rockefeller Foundation, Professor William Anderson and his associates embarked upon the ambitious project of examining critically and minutely the major areas of federal-state-local relations in the state of Minnesota. Although not always directly pertinent to municipal government, the study reveals the complex, delicate balance of public powers and functions between and among the three great levels of government in Minnesota. Professor Anderson's summary (see No. 10 below) is particularly valuable to the student of cities. See William Anderson and Edward W. Weidner (eds.), *Intergovernmental Relations in the United States as Observed in the State of Minnesota* (Minneapolis, Minn.: University of Minnesota Press). The following series of ten monographs compose the study: (1) Forest Talbott, *Intergovernmental Relations and the Courts* (1950); (2) R. A. Gomez, *Intergovernmental Relations in Highways* (1950); (3) Robert L. Morlan, *Intergovernmental Relations in Education* (1950); (4) Laurence Wyatt, *Intergovernmental Relations in Public Health* (1951); (5) Ruth Raup, *Intergovernmental Relations in Social Welfare* (1952); (6) Francis E. Rourke, *Intergovernmental Relations in Employment Security* (1952); (7) Paul N. Ylvisaker, *Intergovernmental Relations at the Grass Roots* (1956); (8) William Anderson, *Intergovernmental Fiscal Relations* (1956); (9) Edward W. Weidner, *Intergovernmental Relations as Seen by Public Officials* (1960); and (10) William Anderson, *Intergovernmental Relations in Review* (1960).

With its increasing importance as a local governmental unit, the special district needed a definitive study to define its place in the web of governing authorities in the United States. Very adequately meeting this need is John C. Bollens, *Special District Governments in the United States* (Berkeley, Calif.: University of California Press, 1957). Connery and Leach describe the belated interest of the federal government in the cities. More than a catalog of the urban functions of the central government—in itself an important contribution to the literature —the study is a critique of the President, the Congress, and the bureaucracy vis-à-vis the American city. See Robert H. Connery and Richard H. Leach, *The Federal Government and Metropolitan Areas* (Cambridge, Mass.: Harvard University Press, 1960).

CHAPTER 6

Creature of the State—A Profile of Municipal Law

Judge Dillon's Rule

Surely one of the paradoxes of history is that the city, the master institution of civilization, has rarely been its own master. Except for the Greek city-states, the free cities of medieval and Renaissance Europe, and perhaps the autonomous cities of feudal Egypt, the city has most of the time been subject to the legal and political dominance of a higher power.

The birth, life, and death of the American city are today as subject to the state's overlordship—one is tempted to say arbitrary authority—as was the city of Rome under the emperor-philosopher Marcus Aurelius or Paris under Louis XIV. We need only to look at the rule pronounced by the nineteenth-century American jurist Judge John F. Dillon to begin to be aware of the extent of this sovereign power over the city's destiny. The municipality may exercise only those powers expressly granted to it by the state, or powers necessarily and clearly implied from those expressly granted, or those which are essential to the municipality's performance as a corporation. Any fair and reasonable doubt must be resolved against the city! To quote Judge Dillon, "it would never do to allow corporate powers to be assumed and exercised except for purposes and on terms previously defined by the legislature." [1] In sum, the city is a creature of the state, completely subservient to the constitution and laws of the state.

From these facts we can deduce certain legal characteristics of the city. It is, first, a segment or part of a larger political group empowered to act as a political unit. As a municipal corporation it possesses the delegated authority to exercise (1) corporate powers (perpetual succession, acquiring and holding property, suing and being sued, making contracts); (2) governmental powers (police, taxing, regulation of commerce, and others); and (3) proprietary powers (engaging in a wide range of money-making enterprises). These powers are all strictly construed.

The city, village, or incorporated town (to use the more general titles) is also a fully developed municipal corporation; that is, it is a general-purpose authority which performs a wide variety of governmental func-

---

[1] John F. Dillon, *Municipal Corporations* (Boston: Little, Brown & Co., 5th ed., 1911), Vol. I, p. 88.

tions. As such, it is distinguished from the quasi-municipal corporation —the county, township, school, and other limited-purpose districts— which have not attained full corporate status. Finally, the city is primarily a local-service institution, designated to function locally in order to meet local needs. These generalizations lead us to a consideration of how the municipal corporation comes into existence, how it lives, and how it can be abolished.

Birth, Life, and Death of the Corporation

Because the city is a creature of the state, it must be created by means provided in state law. Originally, at least in Anglo-American experience, the city attained corporate status as a result of an executive act. Thus during the colonial period the prevailing custom was for the municipal charter to be conferred upon the city by the king or by the governor or proprietor. After the Revolution this authority passed to the newly created state legislatures. More specifically, what had once been an executive act now became a legislative one.

There are today three ways to incorporate and control the municipal corporation: (1) by special act of the legislature, (2) by general act, and (3) by certain miscellaneous means. We shall consider each in turn.

Incorporation and Control by Special Act. For a century after the states assumed authority over the cities, the special act was almost universal. By means of a special law the legislature brought the municipal corporation into existence and provided for its structure of government and its powers by a charter applying only to the city designated in it. Subsequent special acts would expand upon the original act of incorporation, and occasionally general acts would also apply to the city. In the 1870's, goaded into action by their scandalously opprobrious treatment by the state legislatures, as H. L. McBain once described it, cities moved to obtain constitutional amendments to the state constitutions which would ban such local acts. In this effort they were largely successful, and only a handful of states today still retain the special-act system.

The special-act system had some very important characteristics. It not only put the city at the mercy of the state legislature; it also burdened the legislative body with much local legislation. But the system was by no means wholly destructive of the city's interests. Since the local act of incorporation was often written at the urging of the local citizenry and with their political wants in mind, it had a flexibility and local orientation that no general act could ever attain.

A case in point is North Carolina, where the cities have long had general acts available to them, but where the special act is still extensively relied upon. Far from indicating a tendency by the legislature to interfere in municipal affairs, the special acts usually originate at the specific request of the local officials. "For over 40 years," comments John L. Sanders on North Carolina, "the statute books of this state have offered four optional plans of municipal government, plans which appear to offer a city substantial freedom to run its own affairs without legislative intermeddling. Yet scarcely a dozen cities have adopted any of these plans. The reason, paradoxically, is that these stock plans, by forcing the city adopting them into a legislative-fixed standard pattern of organization and powers, deprive the city government of . . . flexibility and freedom. . . ." [2] By means of the special-act system, on the other hand, the city is able to attain that flexibility and freedom. In short, the experience of North Carolina alone has been sufficient, in this century, to show the special-act system in a constructive guise.

Incorporation and Control by General Act. Incorporation by general act, the system now generally used in the United States, presupposes that a community, having gained a certain size—and a degree of political self-consciousness—will utilize the provisions of general laws already on the statute books. The standard form of action is for the citizens of the community to initiate incorporation proceedings by petition. But, as they do so, certain statutory requirements must be met.

The community itself must meet certain standards. It must usually con-

Figure 6-1. The Contorted City

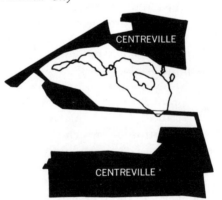

This striking figure shows the outlines of a midwestern city incorporated in the late 1950's. An administrative and political anomaly, this city is doomed by shape alone to an uncertain existence. Such miscarriages could be avoided if adequate standards for incorporation were established by statute, particularly if a state agency were given the power to administer the law. They could also be inhibited by the central city's having a veto over suburban incorporations.

[2] John L. Sanders, "The Proposed Constitution of North Carolina: An Analysis," *Popular Government,* February, 1959, p. 9.

tain a minimum number of people, or have a minimum population density per square mile. It must have some area but usually not too much; that is, the proposed municipality must not be too large geographically. It may need to be compact in form, with all of its area contiguous. (See Figure 6-1.) Taken altogether, the standards for incorporation are quite easily met, and corporate status is normally very simple to come by regardless of whether it makes sense or nonsense. How many communities have incorporated without a sufficient tax base to support themselves? Or with boundaries that could be emulated only by a contortionist? Or because of the purely negative reason that if the area remained unincorporated it would be annexed by an adjoining city? One of the reasons for the political fragmentation of the local community, which we shall examine presently, has been the relatively easy incorporations permitted under the general statutes.

The petition itself must meet certain stipulations. Its very form may be outlined in the statute. But the most important requirement of all is the one governing who may sign and how many must sign. The Ohio statutes provide two methods of petitioning. According to one method, the petition must be signed by not less than 10 percent of the freeholders residing in the area, and in no case may there be fewer than thirty signers. By the second method, no fewer than thirty qualified persons may sign the petition.[3]

When the petition bears a sufficient number of signatures to meet the statutory requirement, it must go to a court or board of proper jurisdiction for review. The county court has jurisdiction in Texas, the county board in Missouri, and the county board or the board of township trustees in Ohio. Since the function of this reviewing agency is purely ministerial, it has the sole duty of examining the petitions for conformance to the law. Beyond that it has no competence. In other words, it must answer the question: Are the requirements of the law met? It usually has no competence to ask: Is this incorporation desirable or necessary?

Finding that the petitions are in order, the reviewing jurisdiction usually must call an election, which a majority vote will win. (Sometimes a court or other body of proper jurisdiction may order incorporation without an election.) The election results are then certified, often to a state officer such as the secretary of state, and the newly incorporated city or village proceeds to elect its officers.

Having incorporated under the general act, the municipality must live under it and other acts. But the states and cities learned very early that the general-act system had such an inherent inflexibility that substantial innovations needed to be made to mitigate that rigidity. These changes might

[3] Francis R. Aumann and Harvey Walker, *The Government and Administration of Ohio* (New York: Thomas Y. Crowell Co., 1956), p. 420. Also see *Page's Ohio Revised Code Annotated* (Cincinnati: W. H. Anderson Co., 1954), Title 7, Sec. 707.03, 1966 Supplement.

be classified as follows: (1) permissive legislation, (2) legislation (permissive or obligatory) addressed to one class of cities, (3) optional charters, and (4) home rule.

A permissive act is one which permits, but does not compel, a city to act. Such an act is, to a degree, a contradiction. Because law is a means of controlling society and the relations of individuals and groups within society, we think of it as compulsory. Because law is an attempt to bring regularity into man's affairs, to give him certainty for today, tomorrow, and the day after, we think of it in the Biblical terms of "Thou shalt," rather than "You may." The same does not hold true, however, with municipal law. The general acts of the states abound with legislation which may be used by the city, but which is in no way forced upon it. An example of such a permissive act is one which gives the city power to adopt the council-manager form of government, and which specifies the procedure for the adoption of the new government. Rather than requiring by compulsory general law—by legislative fiat—that all cities adopt this form of government, the state simply makes it available to those communities in which political forces are strong enough to bring it to popular vote.

Legislation by class of city is an attempt to recognize that cities vary greatly one from the other. Usually based upon population (directly or indirectly), an act directed toward one class of city will contain powers not available to cities of another class, or restrictions not bearing upon municipalities of another class. It may be compulsory: for example, all cities with populations of 100,000 to 200,000 may be required to pay their firemen and policemen a minimum of $400 per month. Or it may be permissive: all cities with populations of over 200,000 may be permitted to establish museums of art.

Such a classification of cities has been extensively used, particularly as a device for increasing the flexibility of the otherwise rigid general-law system. The system often fails in application, however, because it establishes purely arbitrary standards of classification, because it may encourage discriminatory legislation, and because it still retains a considerable element of rigidity. If a city of 190,000 population wishes to establish an art museum, why should it be prevented from doing so by a statute that arbitrarily stipulates that only cities over 200,000 may establish such municipal institutions? In short, the classification system must inevitably be arbitrary.

It may also be discriminatory. Much legislation which clears the Illinois General Assembly applies only to cities of over 500,000 population. Now it so happens that the only city of this size in the state is Chicago. Therefore, all legislation of this class, though couched in general terms, is really special and local in application.

Still, discrimination may be favorable or unfavorable to the city. One city or a small group of cities may be singled out for legislative displeasure.

On the other hand, the political forces in the legislature may be such that a few cities could gain an objective that all cities together could never achieve. Chicago has, in effect, a charter all its own because of the section in the Illinois statutes applying only to cities over 500,000 population. Though the city is still legally dependent upon the state, "as a matter of practice . . . the state legislature is usually responsive, almost without question, to proposals for change initiated by the city except when they involve questions of taxation or licensing." [4] Although the courts have long held that classification may not be so used as to become a mask for special legislation, many of our greatest cities—notably New York and Chicago—are beneficiaries (and sometimes victims) of special legislation in the guise of general acts.

The optional-charter arrangement is a variation upon the two methods discussed immediately above. The legislature enacts several laws which, in form and effect, are true city charters. The charters are available to cities, but not forced upon any city. They are, in a word, permissive. In Massachusetts, New Jersey, and more than a dozen other states, optional charters give the cities a considerable variety of choice in their selection of forms of government—strong-mayor, council-manager, and others. In some instances the city may even select from among variations upon the same form of government. Thus in Massachusetts, Plan D and Plan E are available, the former a council-manager form with a standard ballot, the latter a council-manager government with proportional representation. In New Jersey, where the best example of the optional-charter system exists, at least fifteen different plans of government are available to cities, including several variations upon the mayor-council and council-manager forms of government.[5]

Does the optional-charter plan provide the necessary flexibility, under the general law, to enable cities to meet their individual needs? From an ideal standpoint, it probably does not. Practically, however, especially as the system is used in New Jersey, it achieves its purposes of heightened flexibility and widened local discretion.

The fourth method for introducing flexibility into city-state legal relations is municipal home rule. But home rule is so important that it must be discussed at some length in a subsequent chapter. Here we need only observe that the home-rule method is the most ambitious one available for permitting the city to operate within the general laws of the state, on the one hand, and to make allowance for local custom, needs, and political de-

[4] Gilbert Y. Steiner, "Administrative Reorganization in Chicago," *Illinois Government*, No. 11 (September, 1961). It should be added, however, that this optimistic view of legislative response is not shared by Chicago officials.
[5] Bennett M. Rich, *The Government and Administration of New Jersey* (New York: Thomas Y. Crowell Co., 1957), p. 353.

sires, on the other. Classic home-rule doctrine may be stated thus: onl
when a city is permitted to draft and amend its own charter can it truly b
said to have reached that level of political individuality which will enabl
it to utilize its full potentialities.

Incorporation and Control by Miscellaneous Means. If a city attempts t
incorporate under a general statute but for some reason a flaw in the pr
ceedings develops during the attempt, it may still be recognized by th
courts as a de facto municipal corporation. In other words, it is recognize
as a corporation in fact, though not in law. To a layman this may seem
distinction without a difference, since the municipal corporation exis
and its past acts and obligations are regarded as legally binding.

At least two points of very considerable interest should be raised abo
the de facto corporation. In the first place, the courts have long recognize
that a de facto officer may exist, but not a de facto office. Yet all offices a
de facto in this kind of municipal corporation, a clear contradiction of th
general rule. In the second place, as we have seen, the city is utterly depe
dent upon the state for its creation. The general rule of municipal law
that the local political group has no capacity for the creative act. Indee
such a creative act implies a measure of sovereignty, which, again, exis
solely in the state.

Yet where the local political group, in seeking corporate status and
corporate personality, departs from the general act, however minutely an
whether consciously or otherwise, is this not a creative act of its own, whic
the courts later recognize as legally and constitutionally possible? Has n
the law been forced to admit that a shade, a shred at least, of local discr
tion does in fact exist? And if this admission is made, what happens to th
theorem that the state's authority over the local political group is comple
and undiluted?

There are two other miscellaneous ways in which an urban place m
attain corporate status. One is by implication and the other by prescri
tion. Even when the municipality has not complied with significant prov
sions of the general act of incorporation, the courts may recognize that
exists by implication. The necessary element in the court's decision here
whether the state legislature has conferred upon the city powers which on
a municipal corporation could exercise, such as the power to annex ter
tory.

When corporate existence has been established by proof that the mun
ipal corporation has functioned as such over a long period of time, ev
though there is no record of its having been formally incorporated, th
courts will recognize its incorporation by prescription. This is roughly an
ogous to the ancient rule in the law of domestic relations that a common-la
marriage may establish certain rights—in property, for example—which a
as valid as if a formal marriage contract had been effected and consu
mated.

Whether a municipal corporation is de facto or whether it is recognized by implication or prescription, it still exists under the general or special acts of the state to which it is subject, and it is, of course, controlled by those acts.

Death of the Municipal Corporation. One of the basic attributes of a municipal corporation is that it has the right of perpetual succession. It may extinguish itself or it may be abolished by the state, but otherwise it continues indefinitely and in perpetuity. If it is depopulated, if all evidences of its physical existence disappear, if it is gone as truly as ancient Ur of Sumer, this is of no matter to the law. Only the state or the local political group acting under state law may abolish the city.

If the state constitution is silent on disincorporation, the legislature has the sole power to provide for it. The only notable exception to this rule is that a disincorporation must not so violate personal or property rights that it will be repugnant to the Fourteenth Amendment to the U.S. Constitution or perhaps the bill of rights of the state constitution. In states where special acts are still permitted, the legislature may disincorporate a municipality by such an act. In most cases, however, disincorporation is effected in much the same way as incorporation, that is, by local initiative and utilization of the state law.

As a practical matter, why should a city eliminate itself? Corporate status is, after all, highly prized. One reason is that municipal functions may be adequately performed by another level of government. Thus in Montgomery County, Maryland, where county government has reached high standards of performance, certain groups have advocated the disincorporation of various municipalities in the county. The county government would then assume all municipal functions. But the ordinary reason for the death of the corporation—and this is not too frequent—stems from the consolidation of two or more cities. Consolidation may take the form of one city's absorbing another or of two or more cities' joining together in an entirely new municipal corporation. In either case one or several corporations are eliminated.

Disincorporation of the quasi-municipal corporations is far more frequent than the abolition of the municipal corporation itself. Such disincorporation will usually occur by special act or by local initiative under general acts. It may also occur through simple annexation by a neighboring municipality. The law varies greatly on this point.

Liability of the Municipal Corporation

One attribute of the municipality, as we have seen, is its capacity to sue and to be sued. Although the state and federal governments may not, with certain exceptions, be brought into court without their consent, the city shares this immunity only if it is carrying on a state (or governmental) function; and even then its position is uncertain. Since the liability of the municipality is a crucial element in its existence and may even sometimes explain its success or failure as a government, we need to examine the factor at some length.

Contractual Liability. When the municipality enters into a legal contract, the general rule is that it is bound by the terms of that contract until the instrument expires or its stipulations are met. Contractual obligation may be involved, not only in relationships based upon an instrument formally labeled a contract, but also in situations where a contract may be inferred from municipal action.[6] Although the city has no obligation to enter into a contract or to grant a franchise, once it has done so, it is bound to meet its solemn obligations.

But, one might exclaim, may not an emergency or a radically altered situation make it imperative that a city break a contract? The law admits of this possibility and provides that the bonds of a contractual obligation may be altered or broken under the police power or by use of eminent domain. But justice demands—and the courts are always there to enforce the demands—that the individual be safeguarded even here in the enjoyment of his property rights. The extent of the police power is by no means limitless, and eminent domain is limited also to being exercised for a public purpose and only upon the payment of just compensation.

Civil Liability of Officers. Legal action may be taken against the municipal officer himself, either by action at law or in equity, by use of the so-called extraordinary writs. Any party thinking himself aggrieved may appeal to court for a writ of injunction. This writ, often called the strong arm of equity, may be issued against an officer of the city to compel him to act or cease to act. Although sometimes used by the perpetually quarrelsome citizen (and what city does not have one or two of them!) or by political dissidents who resort to the courts because they cannot achieve their aims at the ballot box, the injunction is an effective tool for permitting judicial examination of real or fancied grievances against an official.

The quo warranto is a form of action designed to test the right of a city official to hold office. Since it is essential to orderly government that each public servant have a clear title to his office, the desirability of this remedy speaks for itself. The same is true with mandamus. A municipal official may not be willing to perform a ministerial duty; to compel him to do so a citizen appeals to court for a writ of mandamus to compel him to act. At times the official himself may be unsure whether the act in question is discretionary or ministerial and will welcome a court hearing to clarify his position.

[6] Charles S. Rhyne, *Municipal Law* (Washington, D.C.: National Institute of Municipal Law Officers, 1957), Sec. 10-3, p. 259.

Another of the extraordinary writs is the writ of habeas corpus. Most frequently the writ is used to require police officials to bring into court someone they are detaining. The purpose of the writ is not necessarily to free the individual, but to permit the court to examine the official reasons for his detention. Finally, it may on occasion be necessary to use the writs of prohibition and certiorari, particularly when quasi-judicial tribunals of the city threaten to overstep their authority.

City officials—and on occasion city employees—may be sued in contract or tort. It seems that, simply as a matter of course, a municipal official would never incur personal liability when executing a public contract, yet occasionally the courts are called upon to examine precisely this point: Did the official in fact obligate himself as well as the city? Similarly, the question arises as to whether, by action or inaction, the officer or employee was guilty of a tort. Personal liability here often hinges upon whether the officer was acting without or within the law. Thus, in an illegal arrest the officer is normally held to have committed a tort against the person illegally detained. But further consideration will be given this subject presently.

Criminal Liability of Officers. An officer may act in such a way as to make him criminally liable for his acts. Such is the case where an official absconds with the municipal treasury, when a police officer is criminally negligent in handling firearms so that someone is hurt, or when a water department employee drives a departmental vehicle at breakneck speed through the city and maims or kills a citizen. Since no man is above the law, the official or employee cannot claim immunity for his wantonness simply because he is a public servant.

Tort Liability. The traditional rule in municipal law is that municipalities may be sued on legal contracts and that city employees may be held liable on civil or criminal grounds. But—again traditionally—neither city nor official may be sued for tort unless (1) there has been statutory authorization for such action, or (2) the function is (a) proprietary rather than governmental and (b) ministerial rather than discretionary. In some respects the tradition still holds; in others, as we shall see, it has been seriously eroded.

Immunity to suit lies in the antique concept that the sovereign cannot err. This patent absurdity has been explained away by such practical arguments as the one that liability could make administration of public affairs so difficult that it might stop the wheels of government. Yet both the state government and the federal government have permitted themselves to be sued for tort, and the cataclysm has not occurred. And city officials, sorely tried by suits for alleged torts, can point out that cities still function in spite of the judgments against them. Since immunity has never extended to contracts or to the civil and criminal liability of officers, we are interested solely, at this point, in the allegedly tortious action of the city or its agents which might lay it open to suit.

A tort is any wrongful act, not involving a breach of contract, for which a civil action will be sustainable. It might be gross negligence: the city fails to repair a broken sidewalk, and someone falls and is injured. It might result from an illegal act: a police officer illegally arrests and detains an innocent citizen. It might be carelessness or a shocking lack of judgment: a school bus driver fails to stop his vehicle at a railroad crossing, and several children are killed. A tort, in other words, causes personal injury or property damage. It may result in death, injury, or financial loss. The city, in acting (or in failing to act, for that matter), has caused an injury. Is there any reason for the city's not paying damages? [7]

The courts and the state legislatures tend, more and more, to answer this question in the negative. As we move toward an expanded social-service state, the tendency in all matters is to try to shift individual burdens to society. Expanding the tort liability of the city is but one indication of this trend. With such major states as Illinois, New York, California, Wisconsin, and Michigan in the lead, we seem to be moving rapidly toward the point where municipal tort liability will be so enlarged that the immunity of the corporation will be largely a matter of history. What will be the result of this deterioration, or elimination, of the city's immunity?

In the first place, it will raise the costs of government. No longer immune from suits for alleged torts, the city can expect to have to defend itself in court more frequently than before, and this will raise administrative costs. The city must also insure itself with a private company or self-insure (that is, carry its own risks), either of which is costly. To the city official, worried by the city's perpetual budget difficulties, this added cost may be reason enough to wish for the halcyon days of governmental immunity. To the individual who likes to set the city apart from the rest of society, it is not the cost but the very fact of extensive liability which is distressing. Does this not, he will ask, lower the status of the city? To the person, however, who is ready, even anxious, to shift some of the burdens of life from the individual to the city, the deterioration of the immunity doctrine is merely a change in the law which is to be heartily welcomed.[8]

Secondly, the court will no longer have to face the perplexing—one is tempted to say foolish—problem of determining which functions of the city are governmental and which are proprietary. In the past, when the immunity doctrine was at the height of its vigor, the prevailing concept was that a city performed certain functions—police and fire protection, for ex-

---

[7] See, for example, "Municipal Liability for Failure to Provide Police Protection," *Fordham Law Review*, XXVIII (Summer, 1959), 316–322.

[8] For a lawyer's concurrence in this point of view, see George G. Coughlin, "The Shame of Immunity," *National Civic Review*, LIV (September, 1965), 409–412.

ample—as an agent of the state. Because these functions were governmental by definition, the city acquired the state's immunity in their performance. On the other hand, other functions, particularly those of a business-like or utility nature, were proprietary (sometimes also described as private or corporate). The city was immune from tortious action when the alleged injury involved a governmental function. It could be sued when the function was proprietary.

To the layman, any action of the city must logically be considered governmental, since the city is a governmental body. In a few instances the state courts adopted this commonsense point of view. But it was standard practice for the courts to attempt the impossible—to seek a distinction between governmental and proprietary functions. One positive result of the deterioration of the immunity doctrine is that this most confused region of the law can finally be charted. With little or no immunity to be had, the law need no longer worry itself over a purely arbitrary distinction between two sets of municipal functions.

One final question needs to be asked. Will lack of immunity, except insofar as it raises governmental costs, seriously damage the city's operations? Some uneasiness is felt by local officials on this point. The city has always been very suable; in other words, it has long been considered fair game for those who have suffered real or fancied injuries. Will a decrease in immunity increase the city's suability? The evidence, so far, is uncertain. But state legislatures have been moved by the pleas of local officials to attempt to establish limits to the city's liability.[9] In fact, many municipal league officials feel that the state legislature, not the courts, should work toward the solution of the problem of sovereign immunity. These officials hold that if the city's immunity is to go by the board, the orderly way to do it is by statute, with some built-in protection for the city, rather than by judicial fiat.

Municipal Imperialism: Annexation and Extraterritoriality

The city must have its allotted share of the earth's surface in order to exist. A city without area would be as much an anomaly as a sea without water. Laid out in the first place by a special act of incorporation, or by procedures specified by constitution or general act, the boundaries of the city must retain a certain flexibility. It is to this flexibility, whether it concerns the expansion or contraction of the corporate limits, that we must now address ourselves.

---

[9] See "Governmental Immunity in Illinois: The Molitor Decision and the Legislative Reaction," *Northwestern University Law Review*, LIV (November–December, 1959), 588–605.

But, first, a word of caution. Annexation is a method of absorbing unincorporated territory, that is, territory not within the limits of a municipal corporation such as a village, incorporated town, city, or similar type of government. Territory within the jurisdiction of a quasi-municipal corporation (county, township, school, and other special districts) is also usually regarded in the law as unincorporated. Rarely does the law permit annexation of incorporated territory.

Annexation by Special Legislative Act. During the era of the special act, roughly 1776 to 1870, the original boundaries of the city were determined by the state legislature, and any alteration in them was similarly set forth by special statute. In a few states this method is still followed. Thus, when the corporate limits of Atlanta were extended by a major annexation in the early 1950's, it was accomplished by special act of the Georgia legislature.

This method of annexation illustrates the general rule that annexation is solely within the jurisdiction of the state legislature unless the constitution provides otherwise. As we shall see, however, the state legislature may delegate this authority to the municipality by general act; or it may allow for an element of local discretion in a special act. Thus, while providing for a specified extension of the boundaries, a special act may require that local approval of the annexation be given by popular vote.

As we have already seen in our discussion of incorporation by special act, the method has the great advantage of flexibility, and this advantage is readily apparent in annexation proceedings. At its best a simple and straightforward system for enlarging the city, the method is not widely applied simply because the special act itself is so frequently forbidden.

Multilateral Determination. The annexation method most widely used by American cities requires that both the city and the suburban area consent to the annexation. Although the responsibility for the decision falls upon the local community, the community speaks with various voices rather than with one: consent must come from two, or perhaps even three sources (on occasion, for example, the city must consent, and also the property owners as well as the general population of the area annexed).

Widely used, this method of annexation has undoubtedly contributed greatly to the Balkanization of the urban community by permitting fringe neighborhoods immediately outside the corporate limits to inhibit the geographic expansion of the central city. It permits a tiny minority to obstruct the will of the great majority. It seriously impedes the planning and administration of the natural urban community. And by often forcing the decision to popular vote, it assures the injection of highly emotional irrelevancies into the determination of corporate boundaries.

The difficulties of multilateral determination do not mean, of course, that the cities which must use the system are ipso facto denied the possibility of expansion. Various forces, both political and administrative, may act to overcome the obstacles. There are cities that sedulously woo the suburbs in order to bring them into the corporate limits. Milwaukee has had for years a department of annexation designed precisely for this purpose. Other cities withhold water and sewer service to force the suburbs to come in. Subdividers and other real estate men, conscious of the importance of city services to property values, often constitute a pressure group, both influential in the fringe and friendly to annexation. Neighborhood improvement groups, wishing police and fire protection, zoning, and other services offered by the central city have shown considerable political effectiveness when the annexation issue comes to a vote. That a city can annex even under the system of multilateral determination was shown in 1959–1960 when Oklahoma City expanded from 80.5 square miles to 433 square miles in one mightly leap outward. But Oklahoma City either is made of sterner stuff than most cities or is more fortunate politically than the great majority.

Judicial Determination. Sometimes labeled the Virginia plan of annexation, after the state in which it is most effectively used, judicial determination is a method by which the question of whether the city may annex territory is presented to a court for a decision on the legality and desirability of the expansion. Since annexation has traditionally been considered a political matter, the submission of the matter to a court of law represents a rather considerable departure from customary procedures in most states.

In Virginia annexations a special court of three judges is convened. After hearing arguments by counsel, both favorable and unfavorable, the court then renders its decision. Because these decisions have been overwhelmingly favorable to the annexations desired by the cities, the system has been described as a "not-so-judicial" method of expanding the corporate limits. To many county and other local officials in Virginia, who think their units are harmed by the annexations, the system seems prejudiced in favor of the city. On the other hand, the system is apparently well established in Virginia precisely because annexation decisions are not made by city, county, or suburban area, but by a disinterested outside party.[10]

Although judicial determination of annexation is not entirely unknown in other states, it is rare enough to be described as a significant departure from customary practice. But because it effects the separation of the annexation question from the hurdy-gurdy of politics, city officials in many of the states following the course of multilateral determination have eyed the Virginia plan with considerable longing. In Illinois the state municipal league, representing approximately 1,000 cities and villages, has strongly supported legislation roughly modeled on the Virginia plan. So far, how-

---

[10] Chester W. Bain, "Annexation: Virginia's Not-so-judicial System," *Public Administration Review*, XV (Autumn, 1955), 251–262. Also see Bain, *Annexation in Virginia* (Charlottesville: The University Press of Virginia, 1966).

ever, because of the weakness of the cities' influence in the legislatures, the plan has made little headway.

Unilateral Determination. A few days before the Kansas City annexation of 1949 went into effect, the police and fire departments sent officers and official vehicles into the new area to map out administrative districts for the protective services. The officers were greeted like the advance units of an invading army. Latent hostility was everywhere, and active hostility was not unknown. A Kansas City officer in his squad car was arrested by a local constable! In the entire 20 square miles there were few people, apparently, who welcomed the prospect of becoming citizens of the central city.[11] But there was no way of knowing whether the people favored or opposed the annexation: Kansas City had absorbed the area by amending its charter and there was no way for the suburban population to express its will on the matter.

This episode illustrates the primary feature of unilateral annexation the central city initiates the proceedings and effects annexation without consulting the fringe taxpayers and citizens. Sometimes called the Missouri Texas plan of annexation, after the two states which have pioneered in its use, unilateral determination has enabled the larger cities of those states to effect some startling changes in their boundaries. Dallas increased in area from 50 square miles in 1945 to 280 square miles in 1960. After annexing 187 square miles in 1960, Kansas City had an area of 316 square miles; in 1943 it had contained only 58 square miles. Other cities—Houston, San Antonio, Fort Worth, Austin, and many more—have also engaged in truly sensational geographic expansion.

What are the procedures used in unilateral annexation? In brief, the annexation is usually effected either by charter amendment or by ordinance the exact method is determined by the home-rule charter. The charter of Austin provides that the city limits may be expanded simply by an ordinance passed in the usual fashion. No referendum is necessary. The Kansas City charter stipulates that the corporate boundaries may be altered by charter amendment, and the amending process requires proposal of the amendment by council resolution and its approval by popular referendum

Whatever the details of the procedure, the controlling factor is that the central city decides whether to annex, and there is little that the fringe-area inhabitants can do except gnash their teeth in frustration. They can, it is true, attack the reasonableness of the annexation in the courts, and thus they have that much protection.[12] And once having gotten voting rights within the city, they might attempt to get themselves deannexed. This may

---

[11] See William O. Winter, "Kansas City Leaps a River," *National Municipal Review* XXXIX (October, 1950), 445–449.

[12] See *State ex rel. Kansas City* v. *North Kansas City*, 360 Mo. 374, 228 S.W. 2nd 76 (1950).

neuver, indeed, was attempted in Kansas City after an annexation in 1950, but it failed.

As a result of a variety of pressures upon the Texas state legislature, a new municipal annexation law became effective in 1963. Under this law the unilateral annexation powers of Texas cities have been restricted. For cities of over 100,000 population, for example, the power to annex unilaterally is limited to a five-mile zone surrounding the existing city limits. For all cities the annual rate of annexation must not be in excess of one-tenth of the corporate area. Thus a city of 100 square miles may unilaterally annex 10 square miles in one year; in the next it could absorb an additional 11 square miles of area.[13]

In recent years Tennessee has joined the ranks of Missouri and Texas by providing a system of statewide unilateral annexation. Initiated by the Tennessee Municipal League, subsequent to the constitutional convention of 1953, the statute provides for annexation by ordinance, with attacks on its reasonableness possible in the courts. Under the statute Nashville was able to complete a notable annexation of 43 square miles in 1961.[14]

What are the disadvantages of unilateral determination? It does not permit the people in the area to be annexed to have a voice in the decision, even though it may raise their taxes and burden them with expensive municipal services they do not want or need. It may encourage the city to annex rashly and to bring in largely agricultural lands. (In the 1949 Kansas City annexation about 85 percent of the land was still being farmed.) It may be a device to aid the land speculator and may stimulate untimely land subdivision. And it may cause competitive land-grabbing among cities.

What are the merits of unilateral annexation? It helps reduce the fractionalization of the urban community by checking the growth of satellite cities and villages. It enables the city to annex an area on the verge of urban development with less difficulty than by other methods.

But is it proper in a democratic society to force a group of people into a city? Proponents of unilateral annexation in Missouri and Texas stoutly maintain that it is. They will ask, "When the law permits a tiny minority in the fringe to thwart the will of the great majority in the central city, is that democratic?" And they will ask the question particularly if the fringe is an integral part of the city and separated from it only by an artificial political boundary. If the city acts unreasonably and a group thinks itself hurt, it can still have its day in court.

Deannexation. For a city to seek to draw inward is unusual; nevertheless, the law provides for deannexation of territory. For the most part, deannex-

[13] Stuart A. MacCorkle, *Municipal Annexation in Texas* (Austin, Tex.: Institute of Public Affairs, University of Texas, 1965), pp. 28–30.

[14] Daniel R. Grant and Lee S. Greene, "Surveys, Dust, Action," *National Civic Review*, L (October, 1961), 466–471.

ation procedures follow those set out for expansion of the corporate limits, except that rarely does a section outside the city have a voice in the matter as it does in the general multilateral plan of annexation.

Deannexation is normally a political question which will be handled by legislative or popular action. The courts will intervene only if statutory procedures are not followed, or if certain property and civil rights are violated. When San Antonio found in the early 1950's that it had overextended itself in annexing 80 square miles of incorporated territory, it sought to deannex a portion of the newly acquired land area. Thereupon a taxpayer and citizen of the area challenged the action on the grounds that the value of his property would be adversely affected if it were deprived of city protection and services. The court upheld his position and overruled the deannexation.[15]

Although the change of city boundaries almost never involves federal constitutional guarantees, precisely just such a point did arise in Alabama in 1960. The city of Tuskegee prevailed upon the state legislature to deannex by special act sections of the city where Negro residents predominated. Deprived of their municipal citizenship, a group of Negroes appealed to the courts, and the U.S. Supreme Court, in *Gomillion* v. *Lightfoot,* held that the deannexation was a patent attempt to deny political rights to a certain group and thus was repugnant to the Fifteenth Amendment.[16]

Extraterritoriality. The corporate limits of the city are of basic importance because the exercise of municipal powers usually ends at those limits— usually, but not always. In certain situations the city may extend its powers beyond its limits into unincorporated territory. This extension is extraterritoriality.

The extraterritorial rights of the city might be classified as both legal and extralegal. In the former class are those many instances in which the city is given the right to abate nuisances both within the corporate boundaries and without. That this kind of authority is very old is indicated by statutory permission given the city of Monroe, Michigan, in 1837, to abate and remove all nuisances within the city and beyond, to a distance of one-quarter mile in any direction. Such authority has long been granted to cities across the land. Another long-standing legal right of extraterritorial effect is in the ownership and control of property. Most cities of any consequence have airports, waterworks, parks, and other properties of great value beyond their corporate limits, and they may exploit these properties largely according to their own ordinances.

[15] *City of San Antonio* v. *State ex rel. Criner,* 270 S.W. 2nd 460 (1954).

[16] 364 U.S. 339 (1960). Mr. Justice Whittaker, in a concurring opinion, argued that the local act was a violation of the equal protection clause of the Fourteenth Amendment. See also Bernard Taper, *Gomillion* v. *Lightfoot—The Tuskegee Gerrymander Case* (New York: McGraw-Hill Book Co., 1962).

The extension of the city's police power beyond its limits, anticipated by abatement-of-nuisances legislation, has greatly expanded during the twentieth century. Chicago, at one time, sent inspectors to the East Coast to check upon a harvest of oysters which was to be sold within the city. In the inspection of milk, city officers may regularly visit dairies not only beyond the corporate limits, but even beyond state boundaries. And they may specify production safeguards as to the purity of milk which the dairyman will violate only at the risk of losing his market.

Perhaps the most important use of extraterritorial police powers is the control of land use beyond the city limits. This control may extend to one, two, three miles or more in any direction from the boundaries, and may include such matters as approval of street plans, requirement of open spaces, subdivision control, and general zoning of land use. Under state enabling legislation, Raleigh, North Carolina, zoned all the area lying within one mile of the city limits. When a resident of this region started building a trailer court, the city sought to enjoin the project and the state supreme court held that the zoning ordinance was a proper use of the police power and could be enforced by injunctive relief.[17] In a number of other states the courts have upheld extraterritorial zoning.

In describing other forms of extraterritoriality as extralegal, one needs to make clear that the law countenances this authority but does not contemplate it. The city, under the law, may set up binding rules which govern the extension of sewer and water services to newly developed neighborhoods beyond the corporate limits. If the city refuses to extend these services, it is very effectively imposing its will upon a group of people outside its borders. In Cincinnati, for example, the city has followed the practice of turning down petitions for water main extensions if they are planned for an area not suitable for urbanization. Although a public health officer might question this practice, the city could explain that chaotic urban sprawl on its outskirts is ultimately disadvantageous not only to the community's health but also to its economic, political, and esthetic development.

Another form of extraterritoriality covers the use of the taxing power. Income and sales taxes, in particular, tend to have extraterritorial effect. When the city of St. Louis enacted an income tax shortly after World War II, it had a profound effect on the entire metropolitan region. Because the tax was levied both upon residents of the city and upon those who worked there but lived elsewhere, it touched people who resided outside the city, even those from another state. A similar Detroit levy reaches even beyond national boundaries, since it taxes the incomes of Canadians who work in Detroit but live in Windsor, Ontario.

Similarly, the sales tax reaches the pocketbook of the person who lives

[17] *Raleigh v. Morand*, 247 N.C. 363, 100 S.E. 2nd 870 (1957).

outside the corporate limits but shops in the city. In one midwestern town of 20,000 a large new shopping center was annexed to the city, largely at the initiative of the firm which was promoting the development. Much of the population served by the new stores lived outside the city limits, but with the levy of a sales tax these people began helping to pay for city services.

Extraterritoriality, like annexation, is an important method for extending the city's influence into suburban areas. But extraterritoriality may go much further afield than annexation and may even have the effect of extending the city's influence into another state or to the international level. It is, in short, a municipal tool of a dual nature (both legal and administrative) which the city would sorely miss if ever deprived of it.

Annotated Bibliography

The most complete as well as convenient source on municipal law is Eugene McQuillin's *The Law of Municipal Corporations* (Chicago: Callaghan & Co., 3rd ed., 1949). A handy one-volume reference is Charles S. Rhyne's *Municipal Law* (Washington, D.C.: National Institute of Municipal Law Officers, 1957). For British local-government law see Sir Ivor Jennings, *Principles of Local Government Law* (London: University of London Press, 4th ed., 1960); and W. O. Hart, *Hart's Introduction to the Law of Local Government and Administration* (London: Butterworth & Co., 1957). A minor classic in the running comment on the law of city government is Barnet Hodes, *Law and the Modern City* (Chicago: The Reilly & Lee Co., 1937).

For a legalistic view of annexation, see Frank S. Sengstock, *Annexation: A Solution to the Metropolitan Area Problem* (Ann Arbor, Mich.: Legislative Research Center, University of Michigan Law School, 1960). More administratively and politically oriented is Stuart A. MacCorkle's *Municipal Annexation in Texas* (Austin, Tex.: Institute of Public Affairs, University of Texas, 1965). For a full appraisal of judicially determined annexation, see Chester W. Bain, *Annexation in Virginia—The Use of the Judicial Process for Readjusting City-County Boundaries* (Charlottesville, Va.: The University Press of Virginia, 1966). One may get a quick review of the law of extraterritoriality in Frank S. Sengstock, *Extraterritorial Powers in the Metropolitan Area* (Ann Arbor, Mich.: Legislative Research Center, University of Michigan Law School, 1962).

CHAPTER 7

The Search for Local Autonomy

The Anachronism of the City's Legal Position

The city is a creature of the state; its every move, indeed its very mood, is dictated by the constitution, the statutes, and the case law of the state which has given it life, which controls it, and which may alter or abolish its corporate existence. Respect for the law is not enough for the city official; he must live in dread of it. What may seem to him reasonable and eminently in the public interest will often turn out to be, according to Mr. Justice Dillon's grim reasoning, either against the law or outside its bounds. Picture the city official who supports a policy which he thinks is in the public interest only to find it branded illegal. To the official's constituents an illegal act is an illegal act. They do not understand the fine points of *ultra vires* (outside the law; utterly void) and strict construction, and the official who acts in the public interest (but technically outside the law) is equated with the embezzler who walks off with the municipal treasury. After all, an illegal act is an illegal act!

It is precisely this situation which so bedevils local officials. Product of those hoary twins *ultra vires* and strict construction, the environment in which the city exists is generally restrictive and often stultifying. Product also of the discredited philosophical idea that sovereignty is indivisible, the city's legal situation stifles initiative and inventiveness and puts a premium on inactivity. There is little doubt but that the concept of indivisible sovereignty is as harmful to the development of municipal law as it is to the development of international law.

The anachronism of the city's legal position stems from at least three major sources: (1) the inadequacy of the legal talent available to the city, (2) the general stance of the law vis-à-vis the city, and (3) the idea of an indivisible sovereignty which rests in the state. Let us consider each one in turn.

The Inadequacy of Legal Talent. *Lack of Training in Municipal Law.* Very few lawyers have had anything but the most rudimentary training in municipal law. Many law schools do not offer even a basic course in it, and when they do it is by nonspecialists. Yet a large number of lawyers, whether of the bench or the bar, must make far-reaching decisions about the legal posture of the city or some other local government. If, too often, the decision is made without that sophisticated grasp of municipal law which the city can legitimately expect of its legal counsel or of the judge who hears the case, surely one reason is the lack of specialized training.

To one who has observed the operation of the city or any other local government over a period of years, the role of the legal counsel will seem inordinately large. The tendency of the city attorney to speak ex cathedra is so prevalent that it is accepted as part of the local council's legislative life. The dread of the law, the knowledge that the city is in an exposed position legally, and the positive stance which attorneys so often assume (or are forced to assume)—all of these factors add to the legal counsel's power in policy determination. It is no wonder that the attorney for a state league of cities in the Midwest once exclaimed in exasperation that the most important single legal problem of his member cities was not so much municipal law itself as the city attorney's lack of expert knowledge of it.

Only if expert opinion other than that of the legal counsel can be readily available to the city council can that body arrive at an independent legislative judgment. Such expertise may come from the attorney for the state municipal league, from the few law firms who have on their staffs men who specialize in municipal law, from university scholars, from the legal staffs of large cities, or from professional administrators, such as city managers or school administrators. An example might be used to illustrate the point.

A Michigan city was about to embark upon an ambitious street improvement program to be financed largely by special assessments. The city attorney protested that the program was beyond the scope of the city's home-rule powers and that if tested in court as a result of a taxpayer's suit, it would be declared *ultra vires*. The city manager argued, just as strongly, that the program would be popular and would probably not be challenged, and that even if it were the city should not be turned away from attempting to put into effect good public policy simply because of the possibility of suit. The council followed the advice of the city manager and passed the necessary ordinances to get the program in operation. It was never challenged in court.

Lack of Specialization. Although there are upwards of 90,000 local units of government in the United States and all of them hire legal counsel, there is a surprising dearth of lawyers who specialize in municipal law. We might stop to examine, for a moment, why this is so. One reason, as noted above, is that the law schools have virtually ignored municipal law, and lawyers thus have little or no opportunity for formal training in this special field. There is, moreover, a general attitude among members of the local bar that any lawyer is fitted to be the city's legal counsel, whatever his background. This is somewhat similar to one's taking the position that an obstetrician might just as well be called in on a heart case as a cardiologist.

Another reason is that cities too often do not take advantage of their capacity to hire full-time legal talent. This is particularly true of cities in the middle and lower population ranges. Sometimes a city which could easily support full-time legal counsel divides its resources and hires two part-time professional men—such as a city attorney and a corporation counsel—even though there is rarely a distinction between them save in title alone. The attitude of the local bar, as noted above, may be responsible for this situation. More often, the legal position is a political plum, even under city-manager government, and the attorney who is appointed is identified with the winning party or faction.

Still another reason for lack of specialists in municipal law is the dispersed nature of local government itself. If all the local units in an urban community were to join together, the chances of hiring a full-time legal staff would be greatly enhanced. Instead, with the urban area split up into jealous, competing cells, each government must have its own (part-time) attorney.

Even if all of this is true, one might ask, why do not legal firms specializing in municipal law develop to meet the local governments' need for expertness? Indeed, there are many such firms; most of the great metropolitan areas have them. But there has not developed the widespread practice in law, as there has in engineering, of consulting firms which concentrate upon supplying local government legal needs. And so the practice remains of filling positions with legal generalists instead of specialists.

No Career Service. A further reason for the inadequacy of the city's legal talent is to be found in the absence of a true career service in municipal law. Long after police work and municipal finance—to name only two municipal specialties—became careers, and even as city management developed into a profession, no professional corps of municipal lawyers came about. Where other professional groups developed strong regional and national organizations, municipal attorneys did not join into a nationwide fraternity until the National Institute of Municipal Law Officers (NIMLO) was formed in 1935. This was in spite of the fact that the lawyer had been an important city official since colonial days. And the impact of NIMLO on local government legal counsel, for all its excellent work, has not been great.

No Chain of Command. A final reason for the inadequacy of the city's legal talent may be found in the attorney's position in the administrative hierarchy. Sometimes elected, sometimes appointed by the council, he usually sits in a detached position, outside the administrative chain of command, with no specific responsibility to the chief executive office. Yet he is, above all else, a staff officer, distinguishable from the finance officers or the city planner only by the nature of his training.

In the days of the city boss, the attorney was independent of central authority in a formal sense, but informally he was subservient to the real source of power—the boss. Contemporary city charters seem to indicate that the attorney is to be subject to the will of the executive both formally and informally. The strong-mayor charter of Honolulu provides that the corporation counsel and the prosecuting attorney be appointed and removed by the mayor. The mayor appoints the metropolitan attorney of Nashville, and the council-manager charter of Kansas City, similarly, stipulates that the city attorney shall be appointed by the city manager.

Viewed with detachment, the attorney's functions and prerogatives represent one way in which the city and state have sought to reach a modus vivendi. This modus vivendi, as it so happens, has meant emphasis upon sovereignty of the state and the subservience of the city to the state, and both sovereignty and subservience are anachronisms in terms of modern politics. But if the attorney has contributed to the anachronism of the city's legal position, he is still a relatively minor cause of it. Of far greater importance is the set of ideological assumptions—the norms—which underlie the law. We must now look at these norms, posit other norms in opposition to them, and show that current rules are not necessarily the eternal verities that they are purported to be.

The General Stance of the Law Vis-à-vis the City

Dominance of the Nineteenth Century. The character of the city is summarized in the legal description of a municipal corporation, which we reviewed in Chapter 6. As a body politic and corporate, created under central law, it may sue and be sued, own and transfer property, and possess a common seal. With the right of perpetual succession, it becomes a lasting repository for the right of the urban group to conduct its public affairs. As a creature of the state, however, the municipal corporation acts, at times, as agent of the state; is subject to the constitution and laws of the state; and usually has the power to enact only subordinate forms of legislation, such as ordinances and resolutions.[1] Although the city may be created by the state legislature with or without consent of the local residents, almost without exception the initiative for creation rests with the local electorate, and the state does little more than provide procedures for incorporation and its certification.

Thus the municipal corporation is a creation of state sovereignty; it must act as an agent for that sovereignty, though its primary raison d'être is to supply local needs. It is democratically controlled, either by direct expression of the local majority will or by a republican (indirect) expression of

---

[1] See Charles S. Rhyne, *Municipal Law* (Washington, D. C.: National Institute of Municipal Law Officers, 1957), pp. 1–4; *Black's Law Dictionary* (St. Paul, Minn.: West Publishing Co., 4th ed., 1951), pp. 1168–1169; Charles M. Kneier, *City Government in the United States* (New York: Harper & Bros., 1957), Ch. 3; Charles W. Tooke, "Municipal Corporation," in *Encyclopedia of the Social Sciences* (1951 reprint), XI, 86–94; Eugene McQuillin, *The Law of Municipal Corporations* (Chicago: Callaghan & Co., 3rd ed., 1949), Sec. 15.01.

that will. And it may enact binding rules of conduct and procedure which are not law, but which may often have the effect of law.

The idea of the legal nature of the city can be traced to the Roman Empire, when Roman legalists invented the *municipium* to permit cities of the Empire a limited freedom, always subject to the sovereignty of Rome. This duality is still one of the hallmarks of the city in Anglo-American law and is very evident in Germany today, although it has virtually disappeared in France. The present basic law of West Germany provides that the cities "must be guaranteed the right to regulate under their own responsibility all the affairs of the local community in accordance with the laws." [2] However, efforts by local authorities to obtain for cities (and counties) a kind of equal status with the *Land* (roughly comparable to an American state) and federal governments have failed.[3] In France, the city is, in law at any rate, completely an agent of the central sovereignty. (Communes have locally elected councils, but they are closely supervised by the central government.)

Although the city's duality was established in ancient Rome, it was nineteenth-century jurisprudence that fixed the mold, and it is the nineteenth century which still dominates the city. This romantic, nationalistic century left an indelible mark not only upon the physical city but also upon the very ideology on which the city is based. If we consider 1914 to be the "real" end of the century, we find that a surprising number of great names in letters and politics were concerned, at one time or another, with some form of localism: Thoreau and Emerson with Brook Farm, Calhoun with the concurrent majority, Henry George with the single tax, Lincoln Steffens and his fellow muckrakers with municipal corruption. Wilson's insistence on self-determination for the people of Austria-Hungary was surely in part an extension of the American identification with the idea of local self-government.

Scholars by the score were concerned with aspects of the city and its political existence: in France, Fustel de Coulanges and Henri Pirenne; in England, Sidney and Beatrice Webb; in Germany, Max Weber, Hugo Preuss, and the scholars associated with the *Hansischer Geschictsverein*. In the United States, scholars and men of affairs became deeply involved with the municipal reform movement; such men as W. B. Munro, Grover Cleveland, Charles A. Beard, and Theodore Roosevelt helped to originate the municipal reform movement at the turn of the century and to advance its

[2] Amos J. Peaslee, *Constitutions of the Nations* (The Hague: M. Nijhoff, 2nd ed., 1956), II, 34–35.

[3] Arnold J. Heidenheimer, *The Governments of Germany* (New York: Thomas Y. Crowell Co, 1961), pp. 161–162. We must except, of course, the cities of Hamburg and Bremen, each of which is both a city and a *Land* (state) in the Federal Republic of Germany (West Germany).

interests through the first two decades of the twentieth century.[4] As we have already seen, the municipal reform movement, growing to maturity before 1914, propounded a set of ideas and ideals which, for better or for worse, still dominates our thinking about the city and its politics.

In the law the interest was also extensive. When the great Michigan jurist Judge Thomas M. Cooley argued for the "absolute" right of local self-government, he was saying that state policy was in no way superior to local policy, and that the state could not legitimately interfere with the self-determination, if you please, of peoples in the city and its immediate environs.[5] It was not Cooley, however, but the Iowa jurist John F. Dillon who was to carry the day. As mentioned previously, he spoke of absolutes, too, but of a different kind: the absolute dependence of the city upon the state.[6]

Dillon produced his first dissertation on the American municipal corporation in the early 1870's, and for the next half-century the latest editions of Dillon's *Municipal Corporations* furnished an almost exclusive point of reference for police judge and U.S. Supreme Court justice, for corporation counsel and attorney general, for state legislature, city council, and (in matters pertaining to Washington, D.C., and territorial cities) the U.S. Congress. If nineteenth-century industrialization substantially affected the urban environment, of no less effect were the ideas of Mr. Justice Dillon upon the city's legal position.

That the legal dependence of the city upon the state had been accepted before Dillon is, of course, a matter of record. But it had never become dogma. That the city still benefited from Jefferson's identification with localism and particularism is shown by Cooley's dictum in *LeRoy* v. *Hurlbut*, which came in the same decade of Dillon's first publication of his *Municipal Corporations*. And yet, note that both positions were stated in terms of absolutes, or diametrically opposed norms. Here was none of the flexibility of either Jefferson or Madison; here were dramatically opposed positions based more nearly on Hegelian idealism.

This is not the place to mount an attack upon idealistic, a priori judgments, but it might be proper at least to observe that both Cooley and Dillon rejected empiricism out of hand and that each used the same ideological method, though they arrived at different ends. Dillon swept the field of all Cooleyite opposition, but Dillon's easy victory was over a fellow idealist.

---

[4] Arthur M. Schlesinger, *The Rise of the City* (New York: The Macmillan Co., 1933); and Frank M. Steward, *A Half-century of Municipal Reform* (Berkeley, Calif.: University of California Press, 1950).

[5] *People ex rel. LeRoy* v. *Hurlbut*, 24 Mich. 44 (1871).

[6] One of the most extraordinary opinions written by a jurist of the nineteenth century came from Mr. Dillon's pen, and it illustrates the rigid character of his legal mind. See *McCord* v. *High*, 24 Iowa 336 (1868). In this case Dillon wrote of the "absolute rights" of property, which compelled the court to assess damages against a local official simply because there was no other remedy available.

The issue in municipal law of idealist against empiricist has never been joined.

The Hyperactivity of the Courts. An elementary fact of the city's legal position is the overwhelming influence of the courts. Playing a role in the life of the city far greater than their more celebrated involvement in state and federal affairs, the courts enter into the most intimate details of municipal policy-making. Though the line between the legislative and judicial functions of the federal and state governments is more than occasionally blurred, the boundary can hardly be said to exist at all in municipal affairs. The legal formulas stemming from Dillon's rigid idealism constitute an irresistible temptation for judicial involvement in municipal policy-making.

One of the reasons for the courts' importance in urban affairs is the ease with which the judicial process may be utilized to attack the city. The city is eminently suable. It is not enough that it may be haled into court because of an alleged violation of an individual's constitutional rights; nor is it enough that the citizen, thinking himself injured by ordinance or administrative act, may petition the court for relief. Such safeguards are sufficient controls upon the state and federal governments, but not upon the city. There is a vastly more potent challenge to every conceivable municipal act—the challenge of a taxpayer's suit.

This peculiar creature of municipal law makes possible suit by an individual with no direct personal interest in the matter (save his interest as citizen and taxpayer) and without having sustained direct personal injury. It can be said without exaggeration that about all one needs to bring a taxpayer's suit against the city is a certain amount of determination and some financial resources. True enough, the litigant must show sufficient interest (from a technical legal standpoint) in the matter, but this is a relatively easy task.[7]

When, in the summer of 1961, the Portsmouth, New Hampshire, school committee voted to waive a $405 tuition fee so that an African student could attend the city's high school, a local citizen threatened a taxpayer's suit to nullify the committee's action. Basing this threat upon his belief that tuition could not legally be waived, the citizen lectured the committee on its responsibility to be frugal with public money. His interest, in other words, was to attack public policy. Without having any direct interest in the case, except as resident and taxpayer, without suffering any direct, personal injury, the Portsmouth citizen was able to take his complaint to court. As an example of the use of the taxpayer's suit, these details could be repeated time and time again with only slight variations.

---

[7] Rhyne, *op. cit.*, Sec. 31–3, pp. 792–794. It is especially noteworthy that the taxpayer's suit is a "class bill" filed in defense of the common interest of the city's taxpayers. It must be clearly distinguished from the type of suit in which the taxpayer seeks to redress private injuries. See McQuillin, *op. cit.*, Secs. 52.01 and 52.02.

It is of more than nominal interest that little or no objective analysis of the taxpayer's suit has ever been undertaken.[8] From the evidence available, however, one can fairly safely assume that:

1. The suits are primarily an attack on public policy.

2. The suits are brought, largely, by persons in the upper socioeconomic strata of the community.

3. They quite often represent minority attack upon majority power.

4. Always a threat to public action, they increase the possibility of judicial veto over policy decisions, and possibly influence those decisions in much the same way that threat of gubernatorial veto influences legislative decisions.

5. They stimulate judicial intervention in urban policy-making.

Strict Construction and Ultra Vires. As every student knows, even if he has had no more than high school civics, the federal government possesses delegated powers and the state possesses reserved powers. This same student rarely knows that the city is also a government of delegated powers. But its resemblance to the federal government stops there. Because the delegated powers of the federal government have been interpreted broadly, there are few realms of governmental activity which are closed to the Congress, the President, and the federal courts.

If the activity of the city covers a vast territory—as varied almost as life itself—the reason is that the city has won the right to such variety by constant appeal to the state legislatures for permissive authority to act and by constant struggle with the courts to accede to that action. As Arthur Bromage has pointed out, the broadly interpreted law or constitutional stipulation is standard for the federal government.[9] For the city it is as rare as the melodic line in twentieth-century music.

Whereas the courts usually give the federal government the benefit of any doubt that may be entertained over its taxing, spending, military, postal, foreign, and other substantive powers, the city will normally have all doubts resolved against it. Where the elastic clause in the federal Constitution has been stretched to include a wide variety of implied powers, in municipal law an implied power may be derived from a specific grant only under the most severe conditions. Influenced by nationalism, bemused by the idea of sovereignty, the courts have, in spite of periodic aberrations, had no overwhelming difficulty in arriving at a broadly conceived view of federal power. From Marshall to Holmes, Cardozo, and Black, the reaction of the U.S. Supreme Court to the expansion of federal power has been varied, indeed, but if the trend were plotted it would be seen tending to-

[8] A good summary of its more obvious characteristics may be found in "Taxpayers' Suits: A Survey and Summary," *Yale Law Journal*, LXIX (1960), 895 ff.

[9] Arthur W. Bromage, *Introduction to Municipal Government and Administration* (New York: Appleton-Century-Crofts, 2nd ed., 1957), p. 108.

ward greater freedom and flexibility. With the city the trend has been quite otherwise.

Strict construction, as applied to the city, is hard to define briefly. We have already examined the gist of Dillon's rule. Eugene McQuillin's rule, sometimes held to be a slight relaxation of Dillon, does not give any real guidelines. It holds that the municipal corporation has those powers which (1) are expressly conferred upon it by state law or local charter, (2) may be clearly implied from those powers expressly granted, and (3) are essential to accomplish the purposes and objectives of the municipality.[10]

The greatest misfortune is sometimes found to have a subordinate benefit, and this is true of strict construction. "What is strict or liberal construction is . . . measured by results. The court may insist on a close observance of statutory language and achieve a liberal result, or it may read inferences into the statute and reach a decision denying power to local governments." [11] If the strict constructionist position of the court at a given time, however, results in a decision favorable to the city, this must be taken as a rare accident rather than a significant advantage.

If the city goes legally adventuring, it will of course cast about for some kind of basis for its acts. It will rarely seek to establish a policy which can have no basis in law whatsoever. Thus the city's legal counsel, if challenged, will ask for a liberal interpretation of the law (sometimes the law or constitution will specifically direct the courts to interpret the city's powers liberally).[12] In the minds of the judges, the basis for action may be so tenuous that even liberal interpretation of the law could not permit the action. In such a case the ordinance or administrative action is completely outside the law—void or *ultra vires.*

The monolithic power of the state in its relation to the city is no better illustrated than by the common-law doctrines of *ultra vires* and strict construction. They are, in fact, often very difficult to separate. Not only laymen, but lawyers and judges also, have difficulty in clearly making a distinction between them.[13] An action that appears to the city merely to require a liberal construction of existing statutory authorizations may appear to the court as so totally without basis in law as to have no connection with any legal authorization and thus to be *ultra vires.* A planning case will serve to illustrate the point.

---

[10] McQuillin, *op. cit.,* Sec. 10.09.

[11] John H. Vanderzell, *The Scope of Municipal Power as Interpreted by Pennsylvania Courts* (Harrisburg, Pa.: Department of Internal Affairs, 1961), p. 7.

[12] Art. X, Sec. 1, of the constitution of Alaska stipulates that "liberal construction shall be given to local government powers." Rhyne observes that where the existence and extent of municipal powers has been determined, strict construction no longer applies. But of course this is begging the question; the damage has already been done.

[13] See McQuillin, *op. cit.,* especially Sec. 29.10, for a definition and discussion of *ultra vires* and some of the confusion that attends it.

Downers Grove, a Chicago suburb perplexed by the rapid growth of population affecting the periphery of most of the Western world's metropolitan centers, sought to meet the crisis in part by passage of a subdivision control ordinance. This ordinance provided that no subdivision could be approved until the subdivider had deposited $325 per lot with the municipality for use by the schools to construct new buildings or to purchase land in the newly developed neighborhoods.

When the ordinance was challenged in the courts, the village argued that the practice was legal under the statute which authorized cities and villages to require that subdividers provide for streets, alleys, and public grounds in conformance with the municipality's master plan. But the court would have none of this reasoning. Admitting that the payment of $325 per lot into an educational fund would have advantages over the dedication of land, the court held that "the statute does not authorize this technique." [14] The essence of the court's reasoning was that under state law the municipality had no educational function. Yet any objective analysis of the relation between the city and school governments shows that it is very close indeed. Traffic and crime control, juvenile delinquency, parks and recreation, library services, planning, public health—some of them are directly educational (the library and recreation functions, for example)—and others are of compelling concern to the family, the school child, and the school administrator. The Illinois court, however, reasoned from the ideological base set for it by Justice Dillon and very narrowly defined the educational function.

The Downers Grove decision, with a multitude of others like it, points up the importance of the courts in forming urban public policy. That they do aid in policy formation is taken as axiomatic by most observers. As Judge Dillon himself once observed, "while the function of the judge is pre-eminently declarative, it is also necessarily, though subordinately, legislative: that is, he inevitably makes law in and by the process of administering it." [15]

The inevitable result of strict construction and *ultra vires* in municipal law, however, is not to make the judge's legislative function a subordinate one but, on the contrary, a principal one. So long as these concepts grip the law, the courts will enter constantly into the legislative prerogatives of the local bodies of government. By holding the city strictly accountable to the statute, by insisting that the city may not act in absence of the sovereign nod from the state, and by resolving all doubts against the city, the law not only permits, but requires the courts to legislate. This system is in essence oligarchic: much of public policy is determined for the urban citizen by

[14] *Rosen* v. *Village of Downers Grove,* 19 Ill. 2nd 448, 454; 167 N.E. 2nd 230, 234 (1960).
[15] John F. Dillon, *Municipal Corporations* (Boston: Little, Brown & Co., 5th ed., 1911), p. xxi.

agents beyond his control. To say that this situation puts the cities at the mercy of judicial whim is perhaps to state the case too strongly; yet one needs only to read extensively in the case law on cities to see how very important is judicial whim to the fate of the city. Even a court disposed toward the most rigid kind of strict construction will engage in legal legerdemain to approve of a local ordinance, the objective of which it approves. And then the selfsame court will fall back upon the hoary cliché of *ultra vires* to explain why it overrules a measure which does not fit into its preconceived notions of the proper function of a city.

When the city of Philadelphia sought to support an opera company by providing for a maximum expenditure of $25,000 annually to be used in aid of opera performances, the state supreme court ruled the appropriation illegal.[16] But when the city allocated substantially greater sums for a trade fair, the court was able, though with some difficulty, to permit the action to stand. As later observers have pointed out, the only difference between the two cases was in the court's attitude toward what a city should or should not do. Obviously no music lovers, the judges could not stomach the thought of the city's supporting the arts, but aiding a trade fair was quite a different matter.[17]

Such judicial whim is so commonplace that almost everything we have said about strict construction seems endangered. If the courts are really so arbitrary, is it valid to speak of any principles, whether Dillon's rule, liberal construction, *ultra vires,* or others? Actually, the rules do stand, in spite of the notable exceptions to them. These exceptions, far from vitiating the importance of the rules, simply serve to show the extent to which cities are subject to judicial overlordship. The cities, bound to the rigid letter of the law, have little chance of breaking out of the legal straitjacket.

Municipal Law as Sublaw. Municipal rule-making may not be considered law at all but merely a subordinate category which to the citizen appears to be law, but which is usually not recognized as such by the courts. And its legislative power is not really that, but is rather quasi-legislative power. The classic position of the law is that the state does not delegate to the city any of the sovereign's legislative power, but only an inferior right to make rules which cannot be recognized as legislative. Thus have the courts "solved" the problem posed by the maxim that none of the legislative power may be delegated, and they have solved it by a legal trick.

This legal myth is an affront to the empirical evidence that lies at hand. Why is a zoning ordinance which may control the use of property valued in the hundreds of millions a mere rule, while a statute for the relief of Widow Jones and her mites is a law? In some home-rule states, cities have per-

[16] *Kulp* v. *Philadelphia*, 291 Pa. 413; 140 A. 129 (1928).
[17] *Stegmaier* v. *Geeringer*, 218 Pa. 501 (1907), and *Sambor* v. *Hadley*, 291 Pa. 395 (1938), cited in Vanderzell, *op. cit.*

suaded the courts to accept the position that a municipal ordinance may be equal to or even superior to a state statute. This does not mean that the law has broken through the barrier, however, but only that a little water has lapped over the brim.

There are several paradoxes in this situation, aside from its not representing the real world. The city is democratically controlled and probably as responsible to the will of its citizens as the state or federal government. Some would argue that it is much more responsive. But its ordinances are of the same genus as the rules of an administrative tribunal which is far removed from the people. If the law reflected reality, it would certainly use democratic responsiveness as a normative criterion to measure the status of a governmental body's rules, but such responsiveness to the popular will is given short shrift by municipal law.

There is a revealing contrast to be made between the city and other government corporations created under the state law. The state university is sometimes described as a municipal corporation in the creative statute that serves as its charter, yet the university is an autonomous entity which often enjoys a far greater freedom of decision than the city. Did the city of Philadelphia have difficulty subsidizing the performing arts? The university does not. A city without explicit statutory authority would most certainly run afoul of the law if it attempted to operate a hotel and restaurant. The public university operates both dormitories and restaurants without so much as a by-your-leave from the state legislature.

Many state universities have virtually become little cities, catering to every imaginable undergraduate whim. The student center is a vast amusement palace; "buildings and grounds" has become a great public works department. Within the confines of the campus are medical doctors, lawyers, merchants, and plumbers. There are experts in every known field of human endeavor. There are theaters, radio and television stations, post offices, hospitals. There are ballrooms, stadiums, golf courses, swimming pools. There are orchestras, even dancing girls. And all of this is done by a municipal corporation in the name of education. Education is the magic wand that changes dross into gold; it is the open sesame that permits this modern Ali Baba's entrance into the mountain's treasure trove.

Here we have municipal corporations of two types. One educates—and is given carte blanche. The other watches over civic life—and is beggared. Once again we see the law's imperviousness to reality; once again we see the use of the legal trick to perpetuate and extend the divorce from reality.

The Idea of an Indivisible Sovereignty in the State

Elements of the Modern Idea of Sovereignty. The propositions we have so far examined are significant, but they still do not enable us to probe to

the heart of the matter. To examine the very life source of the law's anachronism, we must examine the idea of sovereignty and its remarkable impact
upon the city's legal existence.

Sovereignty has these main elements, as stated originally by Jean Bodin:
(1) it is centered at one spot and is indivisible; (2) it is an inalienable possession of the king; (3) it cannot err; and (4) it is absolute. All other power
falls before the might of the sovereign; though the sovereign may grant the
right to others to make decisions, he may withdraw that right at will.

Bodin, very much a sixteenth-century man, sought a rationale for the
growing power of the French monarch, a power that even then was close to
absolute. And thus he "invented" sovereignty; centered it in the throne;
and made it absolute, indivisible, and incapable of error.[18] But though he
was a monarchist and favored a strong central government, he was not at
all a totalitarian in the contemporary sense. Although a Catholic, he advocated tolerance for the Huguenots; although an advocate of centralized
power, he wanted local discretion for local communities and a good deal of
freedom for private associations within the state.[19] As a Christian, he firmly
believed that there were bounds beyond which the state could not venture:
even the sovereign state could not transgress the laws of God.[20] Although in
sixteenth-century terms Bodin was a tolerant man, who surely would have
been affronted by the reductio ad absurdum to which others took his ideas,
his introduction of the idea of sovereignty into modern thought had
great dangers. As Lewis Mumford comments upon the baroque period:
"Real men and women, real corporations and cities, were treated in law
and government as if they were imaginary bodies; whilst artful pragmatic
fictions, like Divine Right, Absolute Rule, the State, Sovereignty, were
treated as if they were realities." [21]

Thomas Hobbes was willing to go far beyond Bodin. No power might be
advanced against the king, save for one reason and one reason alone: if he
could no longer protect society from either internal or external enemies.
Then, and only then, did any of the elements of society have the right to
seek to replace the king's sovereignty with another.[22]

Although Hobbes was to base the organization of his state in the people
—the act of creation centered in the social contract—he was not to put
the moral base in the popular will. This was to be left to Jean Jacques

[18] Jean Bodin, *Les Six Livres de la République* (1576).
[19] Stanley Hoffman, "The Areal Division of Powers in the Writings of French Political
Thinkers," in Arthur Maass (ed.), *Area and Power* (Glencoe, Ill.: The Free Press, 1959),
p. 115.
[20] Bodin, *op. cit.*; J. W. Allen, *A History of Political Thought in the Sixteenth Century* (London: Methuen & Co., 1957), Part III, Ch. 8.
[21] Lewis Mumford, *The City in History* (New York: Harcourt, Brace & World, 1961),
p. 366.
[22] Thomas Hobbes, *Leviathan* (1651).

Rousseau. When Rousseau developed the concept of the general will, gave it all the attributes of sovereignty, and centered it in the mass of the citizenry, he clothed sovereignty with an irresistible democratic appeal.[23] By adding to this the ideology of nationalism, history created that incredible edifice, the true Leviathan. In it we see a political power which is not only limitless, indivisible, incapable of error, and centered in one spot, but which is also directed by the national will (that is, the general will combined with the national consensus). Now vox populi has truly become vox dei.

This strange combination of ideology and history did not develop without resistance. In the United States alone the Founding Fathers were devoted to the idea of limited government. In seeking to translate this belief into governmental structure they created a federal state; they fenced government in with personal guarantees in both state and federal constitutions; and they distributed the powers to govern among three great compartments of government. In doing so, they put forth an essentially new idea of sovereignty. It was no longer limitless, because of personal guarantees in the state and federal constitutions. The clear assumption of the Founding Fathers was that the sovereign will could err and must be controlled.

But was sovereignty still centered and indivisible? Harold Laski has commented on the difficulty of finding the locus of sovereignty in the United States.[24] Is there a determinate authority which is the ultimate source of power? If there is, it can only be found in the amending article to the U.S. Constitution. Let us pause for a moment to examine the situation which the amending article has established. Speaking broadly, we may say that the convergence of two forces is contemplated by the amending article —a kind of national consensus must propose the amendment, and massive local agreement (three-fourths of the states) must ratify the proposal. When this convergence occurs, we find the ultimate source of authority. Here, if anywhere, is power: pristine, illimitable, centered, and indivisible. Before such force all obstacles must crumble.

And so we come out by the same door wherein we went with Bodin *et alia*. But do we? From Bodin to John Austin sovereignty was conceived as a power, not only limitless and indivisible, but also constantly applied. Never may the sovereign relax; he has an awful burden which he may never shift to other shoulders. Intermittency is unthinkable; it is a contradiction which cannot be allowed. Sovereignty is a ship's master who may never leave the bridge nor even remove his hands from the helm. Moreover, sov-

---

[23] J. J. Rousseau, *Contrat Social* (1762).
[24] Harold Laski, *A Grammar of Politics* (New Haven, Conn.: Yale University Press, 2nd ed., 1930), Ch. 2.

ereignty is single, a unity. From the viewpoint of the Bodin school, it must ever stem from a single source and can never be subject to a veto. (Notice that one must always think of sovereignty in this context as an expression of national will, whether by the monarch or the general will.) Permit the intrusion of any partial will, as Rousseau might have described it, and you have destroyed sovereignty. If this partial will becomes a geographic or regional minority which can veto a national decision, you have wholly changed sovereignty as conceived by the Bodin school.

Yet this is precisely the change effected by the architects of the American federal system, although they did not explain their own decisions in completely systematic terms. This was done for them later by John C. Calhoun in his theory of the concurrent majority. By Calhoun's reasoning the majority will could easily be equated with sovereignty of the Bodin sort and would inevitably result in tyranny. Although the convergence of the national and regional wills in the federal amending article did not entirely satisfy Calhoun—the theory may have been satisfactory, but not the operating results—his general concurrence with the Founding Fathers is unmistakable. It was only that with Calhoun the kind of convergence found in the amending article must be extended by giving the regional minority an operational veto upon the center. If Calhoun agreed with the Bodin school at all, it was at this point: sovereignty could not be an intermittent factor in the governing process. If it were, as contemplated by the amending article, its prerogatives might well be usurped by the center, the central government. Thus the regional minorities, which have a constituent veto, must also be given an operational veto at the center. This is perhaps the major objective, for example, of his proposal to set up a dual presidency.

That the men who molded American federal institutions were engaged in a full-scale assault upon the Bodin concept of sovereignty should by now be obvious. Their position was to be reinforced from another source—by Anglo-American pluralists, particularly of the early twentieth century. Even Bodin, as we have seen, conceived of a pluralistic society, with vital local institutions, under the tutelage of a monistic state. Although the twentieth-century pluralists arrived at conclusions that sometimes resemble Bodin's, their emphasis was quite different from his. In one of the best statements of contemporary pluralism, Harold Laski assails the whole idea of sovereignty and asks that it be abandoned.[25] The federal state itself divides sovereignty, and it is noteworthy that of all those who developed the modern idea of sovereignty—Bodin, Hobbes, Rousseau, Bentham, Austin —only Austin wrote after the federal state had been fully explored. In fact, argues Laski, Austin's theory of sovereignty—an ultimate, unrestrained authority which habitually gives commands—is filled with error. If there

[25] Laski, *op. cit.* See especially Ch. 2, "Sovereignty."

is an ultimate power, it is often hard to find, as in the United States. If sovereign power is limitless, no modern state possesses sovereignty; indeed, no sovereign anywhere has ever possessed limitless power.

But is there a power which habitually commands? Laski does not think so. Though it is true that command is the essence of law, there is a plethora of statutes which are permissive, which say "You may" rather than "You shall." (Laski might well have looked to American local government for countless examples of this phenomenon.) If permission to act is given, the alternative of not acting also exists. What happens, then, to the habitual power to command?

The emphasis of the pluralist is upon the disparate, complex nature of modern society: the countless groups organized with legal permission (note again the permissive nature of much of the law), the numerous voluntary associations which are extralegal in the fullest sense of the word, even local governments which are as much a part of the sociopolitical landscape as the flora and fauna are of the natural world. The pluralist is bent upon a "scientific" explanation of society. After discovering the nature of society, he then seeks to set up an institutional framework (including the law) which is consistent with that nature.

Laski, G. D. H. Cole, John N. Figgis, and A. D. Lindsay in England and Mary Follett in the United States were concerned with social, economic, and religious as well as political groups. In arguing for the self-governance of such groups, they did not deny that the state must have some kind of ultimate authority, if for no other reason than that society needed a coordinating agent. This ultimate, coordinating power might possibly be described as sovereignty, but in an entirely different guise from the sovereignty conceived of by Bodin and his successors.

Since society must always be thought of as federal in nature and since the countless voluntary associations in society are no less sovereign than the state itself—such was Laski's reasoning [26]—it naturally follows that sovereignty, far from being indivisible and constant, is divided and intermittent. The ultimate source of authority in the state, by the reasoning of the pluralists, takes on a close resemblance to sovereignty in the U.S. Constitution. Though an amendment may level all opposition, it is highly intermittent, and it recognizes the pluralistic nature of society by requiring a concurrence of local wills with the national.

Added to the literature of the early twentieth-century pluralists are the observations of numerous American scholars on the American party system. These studies veer heavily toward matters of national concern, how-

[26] *Ibid.*, pp. 59–60; also note that both Otto von Gierke and F. W. Maitland maintained that many groups develop naturally and have real personalities rather than artificial ones.

ever, and the end result is that such scholars concentrate upon national party organizations and the national pressure groups. In the literature of this nature, the central government is related to the national groups, the state becomes a unity, and the assumption is implicit that sovereignty is centered and indivisible.[27] The pluralists of two generations ago were not so limited in their perspectives.

If the federal theorists among the Founding Fathers and subsequent thinkers, together with the pluralists, did not thoroughly dispose of the idea of sovereignty as conceived of by the Bodin school, the modern French philosopher Jacques Maritain has completed the task in perhaps the best recent statement of the logical inconsistencies in the idea.[28] Sovereignty in its original meaning, according to Maritain, was never sufficiently tested. As a result it has caused no end of confusion, both politically and juridically. Many jurists have challenged the concept on juridical grounds. Robert Lansing, for example, would shift sovereignty from the nation-state to the international community. But Maritain is not content with a limited, juridical examination of the concept. Rather, he wishes to consider it in terms of political philosophy where, he insists, it properly belongs.

In doing so, he relies upon Georg Jellinek (*Recht des modernen Staates*), who held that sovereignty was once a political concept which became transformed into a legalism to support the burgeoning nation-state. And thus, argues Maritain, we must eliminate the concept of sovereignty, "not because it is an antiquated concept, or by virtue of a sociological-juridical theory of 'objective law'; and not because the concept of Sovereignty creates insuperable difficulties and theoretical entanglements in the field of international law; but because, considered in its genuine meaning, and in the perspective of the proper scientific realm to which it belongs (which is political philosophy) this concept is intrinsically wrong, and bound to mislead us if we continue using it."

The task, then, is to examine the meaning of sovereignty and attempt to discover whether it exists. Genuine sovereignty has two aspects: (1) it is a natural and inalienable right to supreme independence and supreme power, and (2) it is a right to an independence and a power which are supreme absolutely and transcendentally (over, above, separate). Is either the body politic or the state sovereign in these terms? The body politic may approach the first criterion, but never reach it. It cannot possibly achieve the second. If there is to be an authority which is supreme, absolutely and transcendentally, it must be alive and apart—separate from the thing

---

[27] For example, see Karl Loewenstein, *Political Power and the Governmental Process* (Chicago: University of Chicago Press, 1957), Ch. 12, "Pluralism."

[28] Jacques Maritain, "The Concept of Sovereignty," *American Political Science Review*, LIV (June, 1950), 343–357.

upon which it exercises its power. Yet how can the body politic be over, apart, and separate from itself? This is the "nonsensical notion which is at the core of Jean-Jacques Rousseau's *Contrat Social.*"

If the body politic cannot be sovereign, of how much less weight is the claim of the state to such authority! The state is simply a part and an instrument of the body politic. The state "has neither supreme independence with regard to the whole or supreme power over the whole, nor a right of its own to such supreme independence and soverign power." In short, it meets neither of Maritain's criteria: "The State is not and has never been genuinely sovereign."

Maritain's a priori analysis of the logical inconsistencies in the idea of sovereignty is amply reinforced by empirical evidence. If a state in the American union—or a province in Canada—is not sovereign, no more so is the modern nation-state, in spite of the posturings and more-than-occasional inanities of national leaders. Yet the full force of the idea of a pure and undiluted, limitless and constant power resting in the state is still felt by the city. In such a way has unreality been translated into a very real fact of the city's existence. But, then, such political existentialism is hardly out of the ordinary in the apparently real world of politics.

Impact of the Idea of Sovereignty upon the City. During the medieval period, the prevailing concept of a universal Christian community, both temporal and spiritual, permitted a remarkable freedom of cities and of the urban populace. During the Italian Renaissance, Florence, Venice, and other city-states developed an art, a scholarship, and a way of life that rivaled fifth-century Athens two millennia previously. But beginning with Bodin the kind of particularism so familiar in ancient Greece, in medieval Europe, and in Renaissance Italy rapidly declined, until it was eliminated altogether in the nationalistic fervor of the nineteenth century. The only countermovement to this concentration of power at the political center is to be found in the development of the federal states. Yet even federalism, at least in the United States, was not to have the effect of heightening municipal autonomy.

Sovereignty has a great deal to do with the modern city even though the city, paradoxically, represents the inverse of sovereignty. The position of the city vis-à-vis the state cannot be adequately examined without a constant recurrence to sovereignty in its modern guise. There is involved in the concept of sovereignty a strong absolutist element. To quote Maritain, "The two concepts of *Sovereignty* and *Absolutism* have been forged together on the same anvil." And this absolutism shows itself in municipal law. As creature of the state, the city is absolutely and completely under control of the state government or of the state's body politic. If the destruction or emasculation of the city cannot be accomplished by statute, it can surely be done by constitutional amendment.

That such destruction by legalistic cataclysm will not occur and that, indeed, the city exists by a custom which is so strong that the state could not possibly (perhaps even "constitutionally") destroy it out of hand are political facts of life. Although these facts lessen the absolutist stance of the law, they do so only to a limited degree. The reason is that beginning with the absolutist position, the state does not intend to destroy the city, but only to control it. Exercising its sovereign prerogative, the state assumes a "donative" role. It gives to the city and it gives again, but always with conditions, and very severe conditions, attached to the gifts.

The Donative Role of the States. Like a doting parent, overly fond of a not-so-bright child, the state visits its largess upon the city. The gifts or grants of power and money are of two kinds: (1) grants to the urban body politic at large, in its corporate capacity, and (2) grants to certain partial groups within the urban body politic. The first type of grant is the one we examined at length in the preceding chapter, the one with which Dillon's rule is concerned. It is a grant which must be strictly construed and which upon repeal would leave the city without power to act.

Restrictive though the first type of grant is, the second type has an even greater impact upon the city's powers. By the exercise of the donative power of the sovereign, the state grants to various special-interest groups within the city a corporate existence which permits certain functions—education, parks and recreation, transportation, water supply, sanitary and storm drainage, library policy and administration, housing and urban renewal—to be removed from the control of the city. So also with the dwellers in the outer reaches of the urban community. Extreme state permissiveness allows such peripheral groups to incorporate into villages, cities, or special districts. Without a really effective capacity to lobby in the state legislature—even when combined in a state league—the cities find the special-interest groups within the urban community often more effective in gaining positive legislative response than they.[29] The final result of the donative role is the atomization of the urban body politic.

The Fault of Federalism. Though Dillon, the rigid idealist, effectively cut the city off from the sources of American particularism, the results were not entirely his: federalism and the federalist theorists were partly to blame. So engrossed have American thinkers been with a defense of the states, on the one hand, or a rationalization of increased federal power, on the other, that there has been no time to consider the city. From Jefferson to the present day the great debate over centralization versus decentralization has been in terms of state and federal power, and the local body has been given short shrift. Here again sovereignty is involved—and the city is left out. The theoretical problems of the one and the many, of unity and diver-

[29] York Willbern, "The States as Components in an Areal Division of Powers," in Maass, *op. cit.*, Ch. 4, p. 79.

sity, are inevitably translated into questions of federal-state relationships.

The contradiction in our long-standing debate over federalism lies here: it admits the existence of a pluralistic society, admits that governmental and political pluralism results from the American social milieu, but refuses to recognize that local governments may reflect the diversity as truly as do the states. Perhaps this is inevitable. The centralist dislikes the federal system, wants greater control at the center, perhaps dreams wistfully of the day of federalism's demise. He attacks the states because they are the foundation stones of federalism. It is their freedom of action which stands in the way of complete sovereignty at the center. The decentralist counterattacks by defending state sovereignty, and he has no time to deploy his forces in defense of the city. And thus one denies a self-evident pluralism, while the other forgets the full extent of it.

Maritain Again: Sovereignty Beclouds the Real Issues. Are the issues beclouded by the concept of sovereignty? Maritain thinks so. The sovereign state erroneously thinks of itself as possessing a power which is absolutely supreme: "As a result, the pluralist idea is not only disregarded but necessarily rejected. Centralism, not pluralism, is required." It is unnecessary to point out that the centralization of power, whether in the state or the central government, makes little difference to the city. In either case it has lost the constitutional resources necessary for an autonomous existence.

If the courts are not fully aware of the impact of the idea of sovereignty upon the city's existence, they have fully felt its effect. Constantly referring to the sovereignty of the state and federal governments, neither state nor federal courts consider the city worthy of a life or character of its own. Remember, however, that in a handful of home-rule states the courts have spoken of "local sovereignty." Enamored of the word "sovereignty," the courts use the phraseology common to Bodin, Hobbes, and Rousseau: "the uncontrolled will of a sovereign power." [30] "Sovereignty" means supremacy in respect to power, domination, or rank.[31] It is supreme domination, supreme jurisdiction, absolute, uncontrollable power. Yet it remained for a nineteenth-century Kentucky court to warn that the words "sovereign state" are "cabalistic words, not understood by the disciple of liberty. . . . It is an appropriate phrase when applied to an absolute despotism, [but] the idea of sovereign power in the government of a republic is incompatible with the existence and foundation of civil liberty, and the rights of property." [32] Thus did at least one court anticipate the criticism of sovereignty by twentieth-century theoreticians.

The judgment of one court, however, was not enough; most of them have remained bemused by the concept of sovereignty. A federal circuit court, in

---

[30] *Aetna Casualty and Surety Co.* v. *Bramwell,* 12 F. 2nd 307, 309 (1926).

[31] *Brandes* v. *Mitterling,* 196 P. 2nd 464, 467, 67 Ariz. 349 (1948).

[32] *Gaines et al.* v. *Buford,* 31 Ky. (1 Dana) 481, 501 (1833).

1838, summarized judicial opinion which has remained essentially un-
changed to this day, at least vis-à-vis the city. Before the U.S. Constitution,
"the states were sovereign in the absolute sense of the term." Although certain limits are imposed in the Constitution, "the states are still sovereign,"
and this sovereignty rests in the people and not the government itself.
Moreover, the sovereignty is inalienable: "A state cannot divest itself of its
essential attributes of sovereignty." [33]

We have seen how the courts have used the classical definition of sovereignty in considering the autonomy of the state in the American federal
system. It is absolute, at least within the state's sphere of operation; it is
indivisible and may not be alienated; it is constant, rather than intermittent; and it is, by implication, over, above, and separate from the local body
politic. It is not enough to argue that the courts have been speaking from
habit, and that they "knew" the state might be autonomous but not sovereign. To the city the state's sovereignty has not only been very real; it has
also been as sweeping as in Jean Bodin's conception of it. Let us see, in
specifics, how this has affected the city.

The Specific Effects. Somewhat loosely, but nevertheless accurately, we
can describe the first effect as a cultural one. The climate in which the
courts view the city is an unfriendly one; it is entirely favorable to the state
and unfavorable to the city. And no wonder: the state is sovereign, the city
merely the creature of the sovereign.

The second specific effect is found in prevalent judicial opinions that the
state's sovereignty is indivisible and inalienable, that although its powers
of sovereignty may be delegated, every presumption must be against the
state's intention to surrender sovereign powers.[34] This interpretation
strongly supports the nondelegability of legislative powers, which leads to
the status of municipal law as sublaw and to the inevitable vagaries of judicial interpretation of the "sovereign" will. Absoluteness, too, makes its contributions. The idea of a sovereignty which is absolute was indispensable to
Dillon in the development of his dogma of total municipal subserviency to
the state. And it has led many a court astray in a fruitless search for legislative intent. This "discovery" of legislative intent is a commonplace legal
fantasy which often results in a substitution of the court's will for the city
council's.

The concept of sovereignty has a third specific connection with municipal law. This is found in the element of separateness. The sovereign state
stands apart from and over the subject city, as surely as Bodin's sovereign
king stood over and apart from his subject Frenchmen. This is little more
than a master-servant relationship. The city must be at all times amenable

[33] *Spooner* v. *McConnell et al.,* 22 Fed. Cas. 939, 943 (1838).
[34] *Corpus Juris Secundum,* "States," paragraph 2 (Brooklyn, N.Y.: The American Law
Book Co., 1953).

to the will of the state.[35] Cooperation—which implies volition as well as joint action—is impossible: all must be according to the master's will.

And finally, there is constancy. State sovereignty never relaxes. Though in fact the state's exercise of its awful authority is intermittent, the courts hold fast to the theory of constant application. There are many interstices in the law which the city will inevitably take advantage of. The city will often operate extralegally and without challenge in the courts, and the state will have no opportunity to exercise its sovereign authority. Yet for all these facts the courts hold to the fiction of constancy.

It is here that we will rest our case against the law's stance vis-à-vis the city. We must now turn to a discussion of a trend in municipal law which is directly counter to Dillon and which has challenged categorically most of the old and classic concepts of sovereignty. This is the idea of municipal home rule.

Municipal Home Rule

The Beginnings of a Movement. Almost at the same moment that Dillon was publishing the first edition of his *Municipal Corporations,* political leadership in Missouri was formulating an idea which was to become the only direct challenge ever made to the Iowa jurist's dogma that the city is utterly subservient to the state. This challenge was placed in the provisions of the Missouri constitution of 1875, which allowed St. Louis and other cities of over 100,000 population to exercise the right of local self-government under charters of their own making. Immediately there arose in Missouri the question of whether the constitution had given with one hand and taken away with the other. It had, on the one hand, conferred rights of local self-government and, on the other, made those rights subject to the constitution and general laws of the state. Note the exact wording of the constitution: "Any city having more than 100,000 inhabitants may frame and adopt a charter for its own government, consistent with and subject to the Constitution and laws of the state. . . ." [36] The ambiguity of this phraseology is immediately apparent; it was to plague the courts for generations—and it still plagues them, as we shall see below.

Four years after Missouri originated constitutional home rule, California adopted it. Two other states, Washington in 1889 and Minnesota in 1896, introduced home rule before the century was out. Today about one-half the states grant home rule to their cities.

Just what had Missouri attempted to do by the invention of home rule? First, it had sought to put the cities to a degree beyond the reach of the

[35] *Ibid.,* "Municipal Corporations," paragraph 3.

[36] *Constitution of Missouri* (1875), Art. IX, Sec. 16. The provision applying to St. Louis was similarly worded.

legislature. Regardless of the ambiguous phraseology, that was indeed the intent, and the courts over the years have recognized it. Second, it had sought to create a form of local particularism by giving the city power to "frame and adopt a charter for its own government." Third, it had put this extended local power in the constitution and had made it self-executing. Since only a constitutional amendment could retract that grant of power, the cities were assured of autonomy, that is, unless the courts ruled otherwise.

The attitude of the courts, in fact, was to be crucial, both in Missouri and in all the other states which were to adopt home rule. That home rule put a considerable strain upon judicial reasoning—and upon judicial scholarship—is evident from the case law. At the same time that Dillon and his successors were creating the dogma that the city was a creature of the state, which meant in reality that it was wholly subject to the policy decisions made by the governor, the legislature, and the courts—at the same time that this was happening, the sovereign people were voting into the state's constitution a series of provisions that looked very much like a substantive grant, not only of power, but also of rights, to the people of the city. Were the courts to believe that what was one day a subservient creature of the state could by approving a home-rule charter become an autonomous unit the next? Could the courts believe that the constitutional intent was to create an *imperium in imperio* for one city—or two, or three, or a hundred —while all others were confined by Dillon's rule?

Judges did not know what to believe, not simply because the strongest current in municipal law was tending in the direction of municipal subserviency, but more importantly because home rule originated as a fact without a theory. It has remained so largely to this day.

Basic Elements of Home Rule. Broadly speaking, home rule is of two types, legislative and constitutional. When using legislative home rule, the state attempts by statute to confer upon the city substantial rights of local self-government, including the right to a locally determined charter. Although some states, notably Wisconsin and Michigan, failed in this endeavor because the statutes were declared unconstitutional, several states broke through the judicial barrier. Of these, Connecticut has probably had the most fruitful experience. From 1957 through 1961, forty new charters were drafted (and thirty-one approved), and twenty-eight old legislative charters were revised by Connecticut municipalities. Fifty-six municipalities appointed one or more charter commissions during that period.[37]

Legislative home rule permits the municipality to possess its own charter

---

[37] Connecticut Public Expenditure Council, *Connecticut's Home-rule Law* (Hartford, Conn.: The Council, 1962). By 1963, seventy-two municipalities had appointed charter commissions. Connecticut Public Expenditure Council, *CPEC News*, XV, May–June, 1963, unpaged.

of government, locally drafted and locally approved (though sometimes state approval is also needed). But since the charter is based upon statute, it is directly subject to legislative will. Because of this chance of legislative interference, most local political leaders have sought constitutional rather than legislative home rule.

Constitutional home rule may come in one of two forms: self-executing or nonself-executing. In the former, the constitution stipulates in detail the procedure for a city's convening a charter commission, drafting the charter, and finally approving or not approving it. In originating constitutional home rule, Missouri provided for the self-executing type, which most students of the problem regard as the desirable one.

Nonself-executing home rule is a constitutional grant of power to the city, but the city may not take advantage of the grant until the legislature passes the necessary implementing laws. Since the legislature might not be willing to act, home rule can be denied cities even though permitted in the state constitution. This was precisely what happened in Pennsylvania. For three decades Article XV of the Pennsylvania constitution gave the legislature authority to grant home-rule powers to cities generally or to cities of a certain class, but the legislature did not act until the late 1940's, and then acted only to permit Philadelphia to draft and adopt a city charter.[38] On the other hand, the Michigan legislature acted immediately to implement the home-rule amendment of 1908.

Procedures for framing and adopting home-rule charters, whether found in constitution or statute, usually fall into a classic sequence. Action leading to home-rule status begins with the election or appointment of a charter commission. When convened, the charter commission proceeds to draft a new charter or to add amendments to the old one. During its deliberations the commission may have the power to employ expert advisers, to hold hearings, or to request information from any office of the city government. Upon completing the draft of the proposed charter, the commission turns it over to the governing body of the city, which then submits the proposed charter to a vote of the people. If approved, the charter's schedule then governs the change from the old form of government to the new. In some cases, state approval is necessary for final ratification of the charter; in other cases, no state action is necessary, although the law may require that the new charter be filed with an officer of the state government.

This is a composite of procedures in the hundreds of home-rule cities in the United States. A composite description, too, may be made of the amending process in home-rule charters. Amendments may be proposed by

[38] J. D. Crumlish, *A City Finds Itself* (Detroit, Mich.: Wayne State University Press, 1959), Ch. 3. The enabling act, passed in 1949, provided that cities of the first class (Philadelphia) could frame, adopt, and amend home-rule charters. Two years later Philadelphia voters ratified the city's first home-rule charter.

a charter commission, by the city council, or by an initiative petition. Ratification may be—and usually is—by vote of the people. Individual charters will, obviously, vary from this pattern.

What does a home-rule charter contain? After a general statement of purpose in the preamble, the charter will usually state the name of the corporation, the boundaries, and the methods of annexing and deannexing territory. Some charters will delineate wards and election precincts. The next article will deal with corporate powers, usually with a general statement that the city may exercise the powers of local self-government which are not forbidden it by constitution or statute. Such a general statement is often followed by an enumeration of specific powers, with an added proviso that the listing of powers is not meant to be restrictive—that, indeed, the city has the right to use powers of local government not to be found in the enumerated powers. Thereupon, the charter will take up the organization and management of the city: the legislative body, the executive, the city courts, and the principal municipal departments and officials. Then, retaining the flavor of early twentieth-century reform, the charter will often provide for the initiative, referendum, and recall. Finally, there come the amending article and perhaps the schedule, which soon becomes a dead letter, because its function is merely to provide for a transition from the precharter government to the changed form.

The Effectiveness of Home Rule. Perhaps the only statement that can be made about home rule, without fear of challenge, is that since practice varies so greatly from state to state and city to city, one can generalize about it only with the greatest difficulty. In spite of this difficulty, however, some generalization is possible, indeed necessary.

That the courts have been severely tried by the mass of home-rule litigation is without question. When faced with a constitutional grant of the power of local self-government to the cities, the courts must find a way to live with such a constitutional provision. This grant of constitutional autonomy, we should remember, must be interpreted by a judicial mind conditioned by Dillon's rule of municipal subserviency and dominated by the classic idea of state sovereignty. The situation of a judge faced with a home-rule problem is similar to that of a man who has two native tongues and who is also, in effect, virtually a native of two differing (and perhaps incompatible) cultures. Just as such a man may find himself sometimes confusing his tongues and using a wrong culture pattern in one society or another, so the courts may be severely tried in trying to switch from one legal milieu to another.

Picture how difficult it must be for a court to consider a case involving a non-home-rule city and then one involving a municipality with a charter adopted under a self-executing provision of the state constitution. The difficulty is so great, in fact, that many, if not most, courts cannot make the transition. There are few guides to give the learned justices a sense of orientation. In 1939, for example, the court of appeals of Ohio decided upon a case involving Youngstown, a home-rule city. In the decision the following statement appears: "Upon adoption . . . [the] charter became the organic law of that city and by reason of the new distribution of governmental power therein *a sovereign power* was created. . . . *The city is supreme* over matters of local self-government . . . and the provisions of its charter will repeal statutes in conflict therewith subject to the limitations of Section 3, Art. XVIII of the constitution, as amended." [39] One can almost hear the judicial sigh of relief in the use of the grand old phrase "a sovereign power" and the familiar concept of supremacy. Oddly, of course, sovereignty and supremacy were used in a topsy-turvy fashion—to the advantage of the city—but think of the comfort the court must have had as it trod new ground in the familiar, treasured footwear!

No doubt there has been a great deal of romanticism surrounding home rule. The enthusiasm of the reformers of the late nineteenth and early twentieth centuries for a heightened civic consciousness, commendable though it was, often gave a touch of unreality to the reforms they proposed. The zeal of those reformers is still of widespread influence today, and it has probably led many advocates to emphasize the "should" of home rule rather than the "how" or the "why." This enthusiasm has had other effects. Held away from their goal of municipal autonomy by judicial unfriendliness, as well as by the grim realities of politics, a portion of the advocates of home rule have become disenchanted and have been willing to give up the battle altogether. It is better, they conclude, that the city throw itself on the tender mercies of the legislature than dwell in the never-never land of home rule.

Another fact about home rule is that one can prove almost any point of view by citing chapter and verse. It has been nearly a century since Missouri discovered this system of state-local relations, and both the literature on the subject and the case law are voluminous. Further, the points of view are highly varied. Not only does the effectiveness of home rule vary from state to state, but also from city to city. This clutter of experience and opinion, joined with the ambiguity of the law and a general lack of judicial understanding, led the Chicago Home Rule Commission to conclude in 1954 that home rule is "a symbol almost wholly void of substantive content and meaning." [40] But is this true? Is such a generalization itself meaningless when measured against the experiences of specific home-rule cities? Is it

---

[39] *City of Youngstown et al. v. Park and Recreation Commission,* 22 Ohio Opinions 186, 187–188; 39 N.E. 2nd 214, 216 (1939). Italics mine.

[40] Chicago Home Rule Commission, *Modernizing a City Government* (Chicago: University of Chicago Press, 1954), p. 309. But see "Report of the Mayor's Temporary Committee for Home Rule and Charter Recommendations," Chicago, May 7, 1953 (mimeo.),

not as unreasonable to condemn home rule out of hand as it is to support it without qualification?

In politics one must nearly always seek to achieve limited gains. A qualitative leap forward is hard to achieve and even harder to make secure, as the history of political revolutions shows us. The apologists and enthusiasts for home rule have sought to achieve this great leap forward, but they have been restrained, partially because of environmental circumstances, partially because the strong spring tides in the law have been running the other way. Home rule was born in a nationalistic century, with an emphasis upon concentration of power at the political center. It grew up during a period when the absolute dependence of the city upon the state was being elevated to a position of dogma. It matured in a rural environment, in which the seemingly natural distrust of the city was heightened by the corruption of city politics. Only the reformers supported it; and though they must be given credit for its continued existence, they too eventually weakened it by their hortatory arguments and by their emphasis upon the "should" rather than the "how" or "why." Relatively few sought after a detached appraisal. Even fewer attempted to construct ideational underpinnings for home rule.

Assaulted by natural enemies, ineffectively defended by its friends, home rule nevertheless appears to have achieved some limited gains. In order to evaluate these gains, we should first recall that the city in America was largely governed by special acts until the late nineteenth century. Although this arrangement gave flexibility to state-local relations, it also made the city greatly subject to legislative whim. The widespread change to control by general law lessened somewhat the interference of the legislature, but at the same time introduced a certain rigidity into the city's relationship with the state. Home rule, if nothing else, was an attempt to achieve a status for the city which neither the special-act nor the general-law system could create: freedom from legislative intervention *and* a considerable amount of flexibility. Have these goals been achieved?

Control over Form of Government. The consensus of most students of the problem is that the home-rule city has greater control over its form of government than the city not having a locally drafted charter. In Ohio, "the home rule amendment has provided . . . [cities] with control over the *form* of their governments. The strait jacket of uniformity that bound Ohio's cities before 1912 has been discarded." [41] For perhaps a majority of all home-rule cities elsewhere the same generalization will apply. Form of

for a statement supporting home rule. It is interesting to observe that the revisionists who reject home rule fall into the same trap as the reformers: their reactions are a priori, almost wholly without an empirical base.

[41] Francis R. Aumann and Harvey Walker, *The Government and Administration of Ohio* (New York: Thomas Y. Crowell Co., 1956), p. 417.

government is so obviously a matter for local choice that the courts have no difficulty in deciding that that is a question for the city's electorate and representative officials to decide.

It is true, of course, that the phrase "form of government" usually has a limited connotation. Whether to change from a weak-mayor to a council-manager system is clearly within its meaning, as are other considerations like whether to combine the offices of comptroller and treasurer into a new department of finances, whether to put urban renewal into the plan department or give it separate departmental status, or whether to combine the police and fire departments into a combined department of public safety.

On the other hand, since form and structure are very much a part of the political environment, autonomous control over these elements may be very important to a particular urban community. The home-rule charter, for example, has been the vehicle used by many cities to drive toward political change. Though more often than not the proposed changes have been rejected at the polls, such major innovations as those achieved by means of home-rule charters in Nashville and Miami–Dade County show that autonomy in organizational matters is of no little significance.

Opportunity for Local Decision-Making. Setting organizational matters aside, we can find another result of home-rule authority: it permits an enlarged opportunity for local decision-making. For one thing, it has stimulated a great deal of variety. Among the 237 Michigan cities and villages that by 1960 had adopted home-rule charters, widely varying governmental powers and structures were present. Arthur Bromage has observed that "Michigan municipal home rule has been conducive to flexibility in organization and most functions. But fiscal home rule, in the sense of power to levy diversified taxes, is not yet indubitably established." [42]

In Arizona the experience of cities with home rule has been as varied as in most other states. By 1960, ten of the twenty-five Arizona cities eligible for home rule had adopted charters and about 80 percent of the state's urban population lived in home-rule cities. Six of the ten cities adopted charters between 1957 and 1960. Although general state law applies to all cities, "where a charter provides the power, a home-rule city may act in conformity with such power not only in matters of local concern, but also in matters of state-wide concern . . . when the state legislature has not appropriated the field. . . . A home rule city is not required to look to the legislature for authority before exercising a power, but to its own 'organic law,' and its charter may provide for the exercise of powers even though they have not been delegated to cities by the state legislature." [43]

[42] Arthur W. Bromage, *Municipal and County Home Rule for Michigan* (Detroit, Mich.: Citizens Research Council of Michigan, October, 1961), p. 11.

[43] David A. Bingham, *Constitutional Municipal Home Rule in Arizona* (Tucson, Ariz.: Bureau of Business and Public Research, University of Arizona, November, 1960), p. 35.

When St. Louis was confronted by a financial crisis in the late 1940's, it turned to its home-rule charter for relief. This basic document gave the city the general power to tax, and both the city's political leaders and legal counsel felt that an earnings tax would be a permissible home-rule act. Following up this decision, the city council passed a one-fourth of one percent levy upon the gross earnings of individuals and the net earnings of corporations. The levy applied to residents and nonresidents alike.

Challenged before the state supreme court, the earnings tax was held invalid.[44] Surely one of the worst-written decisions ever to come from a court of last resort, the reasoning in the decision was the despair of city legal counsel all over the state. After the first wave of consternation, city hall looked over the destruction and found that all was not lost after all. At least there was hope of relief from the state legislature. The city's reasoning went something like this: The ice has been broken, we have levied and collected an earnings tax, and we have spent some of the money. Although the legislature is unfriendly and would never have given us the earnings tax of its own volition, we can now show that the city will face disaster unless a statute legalizes the earnings tax. The legislature cannot say "no" to us.

And they were right. With much grumbling the legislature did legalize the tax and permitted the city to extend it at 0.5 percent until July, 1950. Once more the city entreated and once more grudgingly got an extension to April, 1954. By 1953, however, it seemed that the city's luck had run out. The governor seemed to be sympathetic, but he would not act. Because the tax could be saved only by a special session of the legislature, the governor informed the city that he must be given assurance of legislative interest in the city's plight before he would issue a call.

Fortunately for St. Louis a determined mayor sat in city hall. A former professor of engineering at Washington University and a maverick Democrat, Raymond Tucker embarked upon a tour of the state to convince even the legislators deep in the Ozark Mountains of the justice of the city's case. So well did he impress the legislators that the governor consented to call a special session, and the legislature approved, once more, an extension of the earnings tax. After a Gargantuan effort St. Louis had won its argument. The *St. Louis Post-Dispatch* made the very apt comment, however, that "through no fault of his own, the mayor had to spend more of his first year in office as a legislative lobbyist than as a man in the mayor's chair."

Did home rule enlarge St. Louis's capacity to make local decisions? Some observers think so. In the first place, under its charter St. Louis passed the earnings tax. Without home rule, nothing of the sort could have been done. Once it had the tax, it was able to persuade the legislature to validate it and several times to extend it. Without the initial home-rule action, runs

[44] *Carter Carburetor Corporation* v. *City of St. Louis*, 356 Mo. 646; 203 S.W. 2nd 438 (1947).

the argument, no amount of persuasion could have gotten the legislature to act.

In the second place, the final authorization in 1954 specifically gave the city authority to amend its charter to permit a permanent earnings tax. In September, 1954, such an amendment, offered at a special election, passed by a vote of six to one.

Finally, the St. Louis earnings tax case shows what might be done if an unfriendly court does not stand in the way and if the constitutional home-rule provision is made clear-cut rather than ambiguous. Ohio cities, for example, never had the trouble visited by an unfriendly judiciary upon St. Louis. When Toledo passed an earnings tax under authorization of its home-rule charter, the Ohio supreme court approved it. Similarly, a number of home-rule cities in Colorado have levied sales taxes without the need of asking the state legislature for permission to do so.

The enlargement of opportunity for local decision-making comes in unusual ways. Under the general statutes, Texas and Missouri cities are limited to awkward annexation procedures. But home-rule cities in both states have largely freed themselves from the statutes by entering annexation provisions in their own charters. The result has been that such major cities as Kansas City, Dallas, Houston, and San Antonio have been able to anticipate municipal growth by annexing land on the verge of urban development.

The comment is often made that home rule is the darling of theorists, of a hard core of political scientists and lawyers who are not willing to look at the record and report the failure of home rule. Far from being the sole supporters of home rule, such theorists are actually in a tiny minority. The greatest support for home rule comes from that most practical and hard-headed of men, the municipal official. Not only do these practical men support constitutional home rule; they also, in states with legislative home rule, seek to have it entered in the constitution. The same is true of municipal leagues. If an isolated state league has rejected constitutional home rule and local charter-drafting out of hand, it is a random action that stands out because of its uniqueness. All the municipal leagues in states with home rule, as well as the national body, the American Municipal League, argue strongly for an extension of home rule, rather than its abandonment.

Lessening the Burdens upon Legislature and City. Another gain that seems to result from home rule is the decrease in the number of local bills both the city and the legislature have to act upon. The trials and tribulations of St. Louis in its long-drawn-out earnings tax struggle is illustrative of the burdens placed upon the city by home rule interpreted à la Mr. Justice Dillon. In Connecticut, with legislative home rule, the decreased burden on the legislature is clearly indicated by Figure 7-1. In 1957, when the home-rule act was passed, 234 local bills were passed by the general assembly; in the 1961 session only 76 local bills were passed. In 1957, 17.3 percent of all bills passed by the general assembly were local bills; in 1960 only 7.4 percent of the bills passed were local ones. Such are the possibilities inherent in home rule for decreasing the burden upon the legislature and, by the same token, the burden upon the city in its dealings with the legislature.

Of course, if power and prestige are involved, the legislature—or its members—may not regard the decrease in local bills as an unmixed blessing. If the mayor, for example, is a political rival of the legislative members from his district, those legislators may well seek to enhance their own power and undermine the mayor's by sponsoring bills to satisfy local power blocs. This is, in fact, a summary of the history of wage-and-hour legislation for policemen and firemen throughout the United States. Legislators are often only too happy to grant benefits to these municipal employees, particularly since such favors will endear them to public safety personnel and to the trade union bloc as well. And since such legislation costs the state nothing, the legislator is in the happy political position of being able to confer costly benefits which do not require additional state taxation: it is the city that must scramble for the funds.

Inhibiting Ripper Legislation. Wage-and-hour legislation for public safety personnel of cities is but one example of twentieth-century type of ripper legislation by which legislators, without having to spend a cent of the state's money, can often sponsor legislation which appeals to special-interest groups and power blocs in the urban community. Politically, these legislators are the benefactors of enforced municipal spending. A wide variety of special and general laws, in addition to public employees' wage-and-

Figure 7-1. Percentage of Local Bills to All Bills Passed by Connecticut General Assembly since Passage of the Home Rule Act

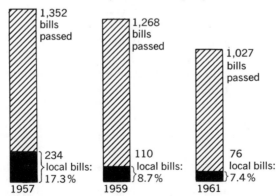

Source: Connecticut Public Expenditure Council, *Connecticut's Home Rule Law* (Hartford, January, 1962), p. 5.

hour legislation, fall into this category: pension and retirement laws; health and education measures; acts bearing upon utility rate-making, especially in sales outside the municipal boundaries; legislation giving counties the prerogative of taxing the city to offer urban services to the unincorporated fringe; arbitrary tax and debt limits. The list is virtually endless. Whether these statutes are permissive or compulsory, they usually represent a reduction, if not in municipal autonomy, at least in control over its finances.

Home rule has not greatly reduced the amount of such ripper legislation, nor have pious calls upon the legislature to exercise self-restraint. Neither the pure politician, nor even the statesman, will be able to resist the temptation of gaining political advantage without political cost.

Local officials and leagues of officials offer various solutions to this problem. The Illinois constitution provides that certain general, special, and local laws applying to the city of Chicago must be ratified by a majority vote of the Chicago citizenry. The Japanese constitution of 1947 has a similar provision applying to all special laws affecting a single local public entity. Rodney Mott and Jefferson B. Fordham have both proposed a more inclusive and more practical method for placing responsibility upon the state. Each wants state legislation which would impose financial burdens upon the city to be restricted in some fashion, normally by requiring that the state assume responsibility for the extra expense.[45] Such an addition to the home-rule section of the state constitution might effectively restrict irresponsible legislative action.

A New Tack—The Concurrent-Powers Approach. One of the most challenging plans for heightening the effectiveness of home rule is the one advanced by the National League of Cities. In brief, the plan provides that a city or county may exercise any legislative power which (1) is not denied to it by its own charter, (2) is not denied by general state law to all cities and counties, (3) is not denied to cities and counties of the class within which the particular local government falls, and (4) is "within such limitations as the legislature may establish by general law." [46]

The home-rule amendment to the Kansas constitution passed in 1961 comes close to satisfying these criteria. Although under the amendment Kansas cities may not draft their own local charters, they may enact two types of ordinances which substantially decrease their dependence on the state legislation. The first type is the regular ordinance, by means of which "a city can legislate on any matter of local affairs or government as long as the Leg-

[45] J. B. Fordham and the Committee on Home Rule, American Municipal Association, *Model Constitutional Provisions for Municipal Home Rule* (1953); and Rodney L. Mott, *Home Rule for America's Cities* (Chicago: American Municipal Association, 1949).

[46] *Model State Constitution* (New York: National Municipal League, 6th ed., 1963), Sec. 8.02, p. 16. For commentary on this provision, see pp. 96–98 of the same edition.

islature has remained silent on the subject." The second type is the charter ordinance. A statute which is not applicable to all cities of the state may be changed by charter ordinance. Thus any statute which applies to a particular class of cities or which in any other way has limited rather than general application may be set aside in a given city by a charter ordinance. In effect, this substitutes "the wisdom of local officials for that of the state legislature." [47]

Summary

That home rule has not lived up to the hopes of its sponsors cannot be questioned, yet a careful analysis of the data indicates that cities have developed some degree of additional autonomy under home rule. As Sayre and Kaufman have commented on the experience of New York City, home rule has not resulted in "unfettered local self-government," but it *has* meant greater local autonomy than the city would have had without it.[48] So long as the urban polity will not accept complete political domination by the state, just so long will urban leadership seek after home rule.

Annotated Bibliography

An interesting study of the effects of newly granted home-rule authority on Philadelphia politics is J. D. Crumlish, *A City Finds Itself* (Detroit, Mich.: Wayne State University Press, 1959). Flawed in many spots, this case history nevertheless gives some valuable insights into what happens in a city when the dead hand of state sovereignty is lifted somewhat from local policy-making. A very old work on home rule that can still be read profitably for its legal insights is Frank J. Goodnow, *Municipal Home Rule* (New York: The Macmillan Co., 1895).

First, H. L. McBain and then, later, J. D. McGoldrick summarized the history of home rule and the development of the law around it, from the beginnings of the movement to 1930. See H. L. McBain, *The Law and Practice of Municipal Home Rule* (New York: Columbia University Press, 1916); and J. D. McGoldrick, *The Law and Practice of Municipal Home Rule, 1916–1930* (New York: Columbia University Press, 1933). A monographic study that states succinctly many of the basic legal and administrative problems of home rule is Rodney L. Mott, *Home Rule for America's Cities* (Chicago: American Municipal Association, 1949). An historical examination of the roots of the home-rule movement, written by a political scientist, is Thomas S. Barclay, *The St. Louis Home Rule Charter of 1876: Its Framing and Adoption* (Columbia, Mo.: University of Missouri Press, 1962). For a discussion of much of the current thinking on home rule, see the

---

[47] James W. Drury, *Home Rule in Kansas* (Lawrence, Kans.: Governmental Research Center, University of Kansas, 1965), especially pp. 64–65.

[48] Wallace S. Sayre and Herbert Kaufman, *Governing New York City* (New York: W. W. Norton & Co., 1965), p. 586.

Model City Charter (New York: National Municipal League, 6th ed., 1963). James W. Drury explains the Kansas experience in his monograph *Home Rule in Kansas* (Lawrence, Kans.: Governmental Research Center, University of Kansas, 1965). There is yet to be written, however, an extended empirical study of the effects of local autonomy on the life of the city polity.

CHAPTER 8

The City and Its Peers

Geographic and Vertical Disintegration

Coming into Honolulu, either by sea or by air, the traveler sees a magnificent island of 600 square miles, and a great city with military bases, villages, and pineapple plantations in its hinterland. From the heart of the city the traveler can progress easily into the countryside—up over the Pali, to the windward side of Oahu, or out by Waikiki toward Diamond Head. Physically, as one goes outward, the city diminishes to a few scattered houses, farms, or estates; the country takes its place.

Were Honolulu a typical American city, the traveler would already have crossed several political boundaries before reaching the country. But Honolulu is anything but typical. Over the entire area of the island of Oahu lies but one local governing authority, the city and county of Honolulu. And not only is this unity decades old; it is also politically acceptable. When, for example, the Honolulu charter commission of the late 1950's was petitioned to make separate political units of the city's suburbs, it easily resisted this pressure.[1] Since the Honolulu charter makes no attempt to distinguish between city and county, politically and legally they are the same. Combined, the city and county perform every major local governmental function, except education, and the only reason that Honolulu does not administer the schools is that in Hawaii education is primarily a state responsibility.

Select at random any American urban area the size of Honolulu in population and geographic extent, and then compare the two. You will find a startling difference in the local government structure. Whereas the one is simplicity and unity, in effective combination, the other is complexity and diversity. Dozens, sometimes hundreds, of local governments are crowded together, stacked one upon the other, and stretched outward from the center, over an area no larger than the island of Oahu.

The typical urban area in the United States is fragmented both horizontally and vertically. The man who works at the center of the area and lives at the periphery is apt to cross a dozen political boundaries going to work. The owners of the building which houses his office, moreover, are apt to be subject to the tax levies of several overlapping governments, and to

[1] Norman Meller, "Centralization in Hawaii: Retrospect and Prospect," *American Political Science Review*, LII (March, 1958), 106.

control by others, which may have no taxing power but which may nevertheless have some legal hold upon property and persons. And this is true
for practically all urban areas of over 10,000 population.

Both the general-purpose governments (cities, townships, counties) and
the special districts contribute to the urban community's governmental
fragmentation. Because state law is of crucial importance, the number of
local governments varies greatly from state to state. If the legal environment is conducive to local government fragmentation, population, as such,
seems to have a secondary effect upon it. Note, from Figure 8-1, that Illinois
has more governmental units than any other state in the union, whereas
New York, with twice the population, has less than two-thirds the number
in Illinois.

The reasons for urban fractionalization are numerous. Some of these are
of strictly local character: some of them are general. Of the latter, the more
important ones should be listed. First is the failure of cities to annex the
urban fringe. Second is the egocentrism of special-interest groups: the insistence upon political independence and corporate status for their own

*Figure 8-1. Number of Local Governments
in Ten Most Populous States: 1962*

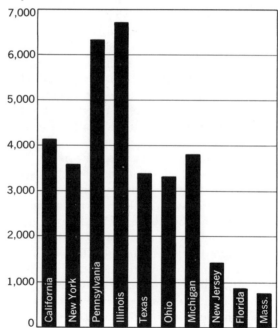

Source: U.S. Bureau of the Census, *1962 Census of Governments*, "Graphic Summary"
(1964), Vol. VI, No. 5, p. 2. The states are ranked according to 1965 data. See U.S. Bureau
of the Census, *Statistical Abstract of the United States: 1966*, p. 11.

group projects. Third is the number of unrealistic limitations put upon local taxing and borrowing power: in order to evade those limits, new taxing and borrowing jurisdictions must of necessity be organized. Fourth is the perplexing matter of boundaries and service areas: sometimes it is difficult, if not impossible, to make service, or functional, areas coincide on a rational basis; and because of this difficulty, special governments are set up to manage a special functional area. Fifth, the attempt to fit essentially rural-type governments—the township in the northeastern states, and the county elsewhere—to the urban scene has added rigidity to local government and has contributed to its disintegration. A sixth reason, which cannot be regarded as unimportant, is the mistrust of local government exhibited so often by state and federal officials, a mistrust that may be at least an incidental cause of fragmentation.[2]

Geographic Fractionalization. City, village, township, county, and special district revolve around the hub of the urban community like the earth and its sister planets revolve around the sun. (See Figure 8-2.) Since these governments have a large degree of political independence—and complete legal independence—one from the other, the urban community is governed from a variety of centers and with varying degrees of political vitality. To map the urban community, whether large or small, is to draw a spider's web of jurisdictional boundaries.

Figure 8-2. Geographic Disintegration of the Urban Community

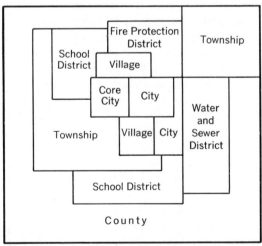

[2] For a study that finds little or no federal influence on fragmentation in local airport development, public housing, and urban renewal, see Daniel J. Elazar, "Fragmentation and Local Organizational Response to Federal-City Programs," *Urban Affairs Quarterly*, II (June, 1967), 30–46.

Geographic fractionalization stems principally from satellite communities which have incorporated in the urban fringe. In order to understand this phenomenon we must return to the nineteenth century when, under the stimulus of industrialization, the American city began to feel the stir of might and to push outward from its point of origin.

The original corporate limits of the city, whether laid out in the Colonial or early republican period, usually enclosed a built-up area plus some considerable amount of raw land around the business and residential sections to allow for the city's expansion. Gradually, this expansion belt filled up, and population spilled over the corporate limits into unincorporated territory. When this fringe became of sufficient importance to merit inclusion within the city, the city annexed it, and with that annexation the city once again achieved a unity.

But then the annexation process became fouled with legalistic and political particularism, and the central city was soon powerless to absorb the population that continued to spill over its limits. As a result, the city was rapidly surrounded with newly incorporated cities and villages which were, in fact, satellites to the main urban body, but which, under the strictures of municipal law, were of equal status to the central city. With the appearance of the electric streetcar in Richmond and the steam and electric interurban transit systems, the spread of population away from the central city was accelerated. The urban fringe grew apace and so did the Balkanization of the urban community.

In all of this the central city was caught between Scylla and Charybdis. Not only was it powerless to annex the urban fringe—because of awkward state law, because the natural community was divided by state or national boundaries, or because of political antipathy that built up in the suburbs. It was also incapable of preventing the random incorporation of every little population center that appeared within its orbit. Here again, state law was lax. Following the spurious doctrine that self-determination of peoples should be applied, even to the smallest of population groupings, the law permitted citizens to incorporate themselves with remarkable ease, either into municipal corporations or special districts. If the law of domestic relations had permitted children of eight or ten to embark upon the seas of matrimony without the by-your-leave of their parents, a no stranger situation would have developed than that of the incorporation movement in the urban fringe.

We need only to check at random among the nation's cities to observe the effect of this phenomenon upon the urban community. In Los Angeles County there are the central city of Los Angeles and forty-nine satellite cities; in Marion County, Oregon, there are Salem and sixteen satellites. Sangamon County, Illinois, includes the core city, Springfield, and twenty-three satellite municipalities. Southern and border cities are not so perplexed, it is true, by this Balkanization, though it still exists. Galveston has only two cities surrounding it; and in Jackson County, Missouri, there are eight satellites around the core city of Kansas City.[3]

In some instances the municipality which now appears as a satellite was not one originally. Former President Truman's home town, Independence, was incorporated at approximately the same time as Kansas City and did not become a satellite until comparatively recently. Some proud citizens of Independence would even yet protest—and vehemently—that their city is not a tributary to Kansas City, yet the growth of the latter in area and influence has served to overwhelm the smaller city.

The same is true of the enclave, surely one of the strangest growths in the American urban jungle. The enclave is an incorporated and independent community existing within the parent city and entirely surrounded by it. Hamtramck, although surrounded by the city of Detroit, nevertheless maintains its corporate independence, and within Kansas City there is an enclave which in turn contains another enclave. Like Independence and tributary cities of its type, the enclave is sometimes as old as its parent city and has been reduced to subordinate status in the urban complex only by the mysterious interaction of history, politics, geography, and economics.

Although the city, village, and other incorporated urban places are principally responsible for the Balkanization of the urban complex, other types of local governmental units contribute to it. In those states where the township still exists, the urban fringe is often governed, in part, by that political anachronism. The township, though of a basically rural character, sometimes administers such urban activities as poor relief, assessment of property, and water supply. A quarter of a century ago, Arthur Bromage saw the township dying on the vine. But academic and political logic are not the same, and under the impact of urban conditions, the township has raised its sleepy agrarian head and sought to meet the needs of the vital urban community. That it has not done so is largely the fault of design: the machine built for the country lane cannot accommodate itself to the city street. Only by radical alteration of the township can it be made to fit the urban scene with any degree of satisfaction. And then it is far closer to the true city than to the traditional township.

Where the county is combined with the city—as in St. Louis, San Francisco, Baltimore, Denver, Honolulu, and the major cities of Virginia—the county is ipso facto a city. Indeed, in combination with the city it almost completely loses its identity as a county. These situations are exceptional, however, and when the county overlays an urban complex, it tends to concentrate its urban services in the unincorporated sections. Police and fire protection, planning and zoning, public works, and other urban type ser-

[3] U.S. Bureau of the Budget, *Standard Metropolitan Statistical Areas* (1964), pp. 16, 21, 27.

vices of the county, often supported in large part by property in the cities and villages, redound largely to the benefit of the inhabitants of the unincorporated urban fringe. Although regarded as an injustice by the people of both core and satellite cities, the supply of urban services by the county goes on and contributes to the community's Balkanization.

Largely a product of America's urbanization, the special district has assumed ever greater importance in the urban community over the past half-century. In the twenty years from 1942 to 1962, the number of special districts (excluding schools) increased from 8,299 to 18,323. If we add school districts to the list—and schools are special-district governments par excellence—we find that in 1962 there were 55,342 of these units in the United States. Most special districts furnish only a single public service. Thus school districts furnish educational service; fire districts, fire protection; water districts, "city" water. As one may observe from Figure 8-3, except for the school districts, a majority of the districts supply a strictly urban type governmental service.

Special districts have been growing for various reasons, including many of those previously listed as contributing to Balkanization: to evade debt and taxing limits, to satisfy the political egocentrism of special interests, to take advantage of state and federal aid, and to bypass the perplexing problem of boundaries and service areas. In the last regard, it is often far easier

Figure 8-3. Number of Special Districts,
by Function: 1962

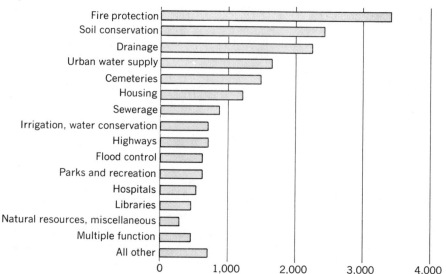

Source: U.S. Bureau of the Census, *1962 Census of Governments,* "Graphic Summary" (1964), Vol. VI, No. 5, p. 3. Schools are excluded.

to set up a special district than it is, for example, to expand the city's boundaries. Since the people of the fringe areas want, and often need, only partial municipal service, such as water supply or fire and police protection, they will strongly resist annexation to the city. And even when they feel in need of all the major city services, they often prefer incorporation as a separate municipality rather than annexation to the central city.

Thus the Balkanization of the urban community in the United States goes on apace. Nowhere else in the Western world has such a situation developed. Although the European urban area often has a certain diversity to its government, rarely has this diversity deteriorated into chaos. Vienna has grown outward to absorb such ancient villages as Grinzing, but Grinzing is an integral part of the city, rather than an enclave like Hamtramck. On the other side of Vienna is Klosterneuburg, a city of medieval origin that has become a satellite to the central city in the metropolitan complex, and population has spilled slightly over the southern and eastern boundaries of the city—but only slightly. There is, in short, virtually no such thing as an urban fringe around Vienna.

Hamburg has no major fringe problem yet, though it is uneasily eyeing population movement into Schleswig-Holstein and Lower Saxony. Since Hamburg is a city and state combined, the inflexible boundaries will create a fringe problem and resulting Balkanization as they have in American urban areas. On the other hand, probably one of the important reasons for setting up the new Paris and London metropolitan governments in the early 1960's was that the two regions had grown outward to such an extent that they were afflicted with profound Balkanization.

A Modern Babel. If geographic disintegration were the only organizational problem of the urban area, the situation would be difficult enough. But when functional disintegration is added to the urban scene, the disorganization is almost beyond the scope of rational analysis.

Much has been said, and more has been written, of the city as a natural growth which seems to be beyond human agency and human control. To a certain extent, this could be said of all urban governments. Looking at the cluttered maze of public authorities in the urban area, one is tempted to conclude that the whole process comes from the machinations of a group of malevolent gods. Yet, upon close examination, we can see that the clutter stems, point by point, just as surely from the law, politics, and emotions of the urban community, as the litter on a downtown street results from the sloppy habits of the passersby. Only if one maintains that law, politics, and urban emotions stem from nature—admittedly not a wholly untenable argument—can he insist that the present urban chaos derives from natural forces.

Functional, or vertical, disintegration is the piling up of governments, layer upon layer, over the central city and its satellites. Both general-purpose and special-purpose governments overlay the city and offer a variety of urban services. Although in certain instances the superimposed governments may have boundaries which are coterminous with the city's (see Figure 8-4), more often than not the boundaries do not coincide. If the core city occupies only one section of a natural drainage area, it cannot easily set up an integrated system of levees and storm drains. A special district results. The same thing can occur with transportation. In metropolitan areas, particularly, there needs to be an integrated transportation system which covers the entire metropolitan region. Again, a special district is set up to supply one service—transportation—to the "natural" service area.[4]

Traditionally, the county has overlaid the city and extended far beyond it. Because of the large area of its jurisdiction, the county's boundaries are much more apt to include the bulk of the urban area than are the core city's. This condition has led some enthusiasts to propose the county as the logical, and indeed inevitable, government for the urban area. In fact, however, the county does not appear to hold much promise for the government of the urban area in the decades immediately ahead. If the county moves as slowly in the future as it has in the past, the late 1960's and the 1970's will see no substantial change in either its powers or its governmen-

Figure 8-4. The Modern Babel—Vertical Disintegration of the Urban Community

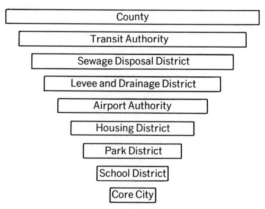

The resident of the core city in the American urban community is apt to be governed, not only by the city, but also by several other public authorities. Residents of suburban satellite cities may find themselves in a similar situation, with the municipality and many other governments involved in making and implementing public decisions. Since these governments speak with many political tongues, one may truly use the medieval language of the Wyclif Bible to describe the situation: "Therefore was callid the name of it Babel, for there was confoundid the lippe of all the erthe." Gen. xi.

[4] Viewed from a perspective other than the one presented here, the areawide, special-purpose district also represents a form of functional integration. See Ch. 9 of this volume, "Governing the Metropolis."

tal structure. A chaotic administration, a limited set of governmental powers, and rigid boundaries do not offer much hope to the urban community. An extended geographic area is about the only advantage the county has over the city. While this is an asset not to be depreciated, it is still vastly inadequate as a rationale for the urban government of the future.

If the attempt to make governmental boundaries correspond with service areas is one of the basic reasons for functional disintegration, it is not the only one. Statutory and constitutional limits upon the taxing and bonding powers of local governments often require that special districts be set up to avoid those limits. Thus if a city has bonded itself up to the limit imposed upon it by state law, and if it is levying both general property and non-property taxes to the full extent of its legal capacity, any expansion of function or service level will be seriously inhibited.

Community sentiment, let us say, is strongly in favor of an ambitious park and recreation program which will require a great deal of money, both for capital outlay and for operating expenses. Without the legal capacity to raise taxes or to issue further general obligation bonds, the city is powerless to meet community demands. But there is a way around the arbitrary fiscal restrictions imposed by the state law. By setting up an independent governmental unit—a park district—the community is able both to tax itself and to issue bonds for park and recreational purposes. The upshot of the matter is that the "protection" to the community of the state fiscal limits has been useless, the community has gotten its park and recreation program, and the community's governing structure has been further complicated by a new political unit.

As we have already seen, both the state and federal governments have contributed to functional disintegration. The Port of New York Authority, set up by New York and New Jersey and consented to by Congress, overlays New York City. Perhaps made necessary because of the artificial division of a single urban complex by state boundaries, this authority nevertheless adds to the fractionalization of the New York urban area. For less substantial reasons, the various federal housing acts stimulate the conformance of local housing authorities to an organizational arrangement prescribed in Washington. In the words of Professor William Anderson, "Congress and the national administration have encouraged the creation of new special districts or public authorities in the fields of public power development, public housing, soil conservation, rural electrification, watershed control, and hospital construction . . . new types of public entities . . . that might have been assigned, in large part at least, directly to existing counties or cities." [5] Once again, the functional disintegration of the local com-

---

[5] William Anderson, *Intergovernmental Relations in Review,* Vol. X of *Intergovernmental Relations in the United States* (Minneapolis; Minn.: University of Minnesota Press, 1960), p. 116.

munity is advanced, and by an authority far, far removed from the local area.

Another reason often advanced for the creation of governmental authorities independent of the city is that the function involved must be kept "free of politics." This is the old and hackneyed rationale, given throughout the country west of the Allegheny Mountains, for separate school districts. Since it is obviously impossible to keep politics out of any governmental process, and since schools are governmental bodies subject to political decisions, the argument has little validity.[6]

Still another reason for functional disintegration of the urban area lies strictly within the area itself. Local forces, local power centers, vying with each other for status, influence—and public money!—create a political situation which can result in either pleasing diversity or functional chaos. But this competition of interest groups and the results of this competition are so important that they can be noted adequately only in a separate division of this discussion.

The Political Egocentrism of Local-interest Groups

One of the phenomena, surely, of the group within the local American society is its urge to achieve political distinctiveness, or separateness, from other groups. This psychological necessity for "apartness" explains, for example, the feverish anxiety to incorporate settlements in the urban fringe before they are absorbed by the parent city. Of even greater importance in the growth of the special district, this egocentrism has materially complicated the local governmental scene in America.

Let us turn to public recreation again, as an example of group egocentrism. Dissatisfied with the attention given to recreation by municipal officials, a certain interest group decides to work for the creation of a separate government with recreation as its sole function. Following procedures established by state law, the interest group circulates a petition which calls for an election to approve setting up a special district and which, usually, specifies the proposed district's boundaries. If the group is able to get a sufficient number of signatures to the petition—and this is normally not difficult—the petition is presented to an official designated by statute, and he, finding the petition in order, issues the call for an election.

In presenting its case for the incorporation of a special-purpose recreation district, the sponsoring group will use a variety of arguments and will employ both fact and fiction to advance its cause. Because the city has insufficient funds for recreation, and insufficient interest in it, the program

---

[6] For an extended discussion of this subject, see Thomas H. Eliot, "Toward an Understanding of Public School Politics," *American Political Science Review,* LIII (December, 1959), 1032–1051.

suffers, argue the members of the group, and our children wander in the streets with nothing to do. The city, furthermore, has an inadequate reserve of bonding power to permit the issuance of general obligation bonds for capital investment in recreation land and improvements. Nor are city boundaries reasonable: within the proposed recreation district is a rich industrial area which the city has been unable to annex.

These arguments are persuasive; the voters approve the creation of the recreation district, and the recreation aficionados have achieved their real objective: "apartness," governmental independence. At the same time, the interest group has ignored the inherently superior capacity of the city to carry forth a fully developed recreation program. And thus the recreation enthusiasts have achieved group ego-satisfaction, but whether they have advanced long-range recreational goals is at least questionable.

As if the internal pressures on a community were not enough, external stimuli are applied to push the urban area toward functional disintegration. Although the federal government's role in supplying these external stimuli may be at times important, it is the state which furnishes the major ones. A state department of health encourages a fringe community to set up an independent water district—an example of Balkanization; then the city annexes the area, and the special water district may still exist within the city proper. Or annexation is stopped altogether by the very existence of the district.

The state legislature may itself take a hand in the matter. Rhode Island fire districts are created by the legislature; the Chicago Transit Authority was set up by the Illinois general assembly; the Bay Area Air Pollution Control District was established by special act of the California legislature. In the last two instances, however, the legislatures of Illinois and California had no other practical alternatives than to create special districts. Given the fractionalized nature of the Chicago and San Francisco metropolitan areas, it is no wonder that the legislatures sought a solution to a regional problem by setting up special districts.

The nadir is reached in the creation of special districts when private business, purely for reasons of private gain, propagandizes for an independent governmental authority. John C. Bollens cites an instance of business concerns promoting the creation of a sanitary district solely for the purpose of selling supplies and equipment to the district. One of the results of this selfish venture was the laying of sewer lines far in excess of present or anticipated needs.[7]

Going through the catalog of special districts, one finds a vast number which are directly representative of discrete groups within the urban community. The school districts reflect the orientation of education devotees

[7] John C. Bollens, *Special District Governments in the United States* (Berkeley, Calif.: University of California Press, 1957), p. 15.

and of the professional educators; the park districts reflect the interest of recreation enthusiasts; library districts, of library enthusiasts; airport authorities, of the tiny group of flying enthusiasts who are willing to spend $5,000 an hour of the public's money to keep themselves airborne on weekends; and so on through the long list of special governmental districts and authorities. While many reasons may move these special-interest groups to promote and maintain "independent" local governments, their egocentrism is so important that it becomes at times the overwhelming compulsion in their political actions. To be subject to the overriding authority—budgetary or otherwise—of the city council is offensive to them, and they will struggle mightily to free themselves from the city. In doing so, they stimulate and advance the functional disintegration of the urban community.

The Use and Abuse of Authorities

The temptation of the zealot, upon viewing the diversity of local government, is to follow the advice of the poet and "destroy this sorry scheme of things entire, and mold it nearer to the heart's desire." This sort of utopianism, however, while appealing in its simplicity, does not take into account the realities of local political behavior. As with any governmental system, as soon as the idealist has destroyed the time-sanctioned political structure, with all of its faults, he must hasten to construct his ideal system. Untried and a priori, this system is apt to reproduce the faults of the *ancien régime* and add some new ones of its own. Since we have explored the disintegration of the local community, and, at least by implication, condemned many of the elements contributing to that disintegration, we must examine the situation from a different point of view. Otherwise we may fall into the error of the zealot and be led into the rigid, idealistic trap of destruction and attempted reconstruction.

The facts are that even the lowliest of governmental units often contribute something of value to the amenity of the local community. And since all of us, willy-nilly, spend all of our working and leisure hours within the limits of a locality, we must respect the local unit for what it is. One should move to alter or destroy it only when he has overwhelming evidence of its failure politically. With the empirically reinforced judgment that it is only the rare local government which does not contribute necessary elements to the governance of the community, we can approach the problem of the fractionalized local scene with logic, tempered by common sense and sound data.

First, we must recognize that the urban community, while a unity, is also a combination of disparate elements. Strong, high walls split the urban area, both vertically and horizontally. To change the metaphor, for all the centrifugal forces that create and mold the entire community, there are equally numerous centripetal forces that have creative influence.

Although this pragmatic point of view may be abused, it is nevertheless representative of a middle position taken by those who cannot agree with the advocate of the status quo ante, or with the idealist who wants the urban community reconstructed in the image he himself has of it. The community can be very much alone in its efforts to improve its own governing institutions. Because political, economic, and social forces may bear upon it from afar, its only course of action—either of offense or defense—may be to use whatever instruments are at hand to achieve its objectives. The phenomenal growth of the special district is caused in some part by this down-to-earth pragmatism.

The element of group defense is another motivation for the creation of a multitude of governmental units in the urban community. Here special districts share the honors with townships, counties, and satellite cities. The attempt in 1958 to force unity upon the Nashville metropolitan area was voted down, in part because the people of small, unincorporated communities in the county were content with the services rendered by the county. In addition, these people, who were a geographic minority in the outer reaches of the urban area, voted against "metro" in order, so they thought, to safeguard their historic, small-town way of life.[8]

Condemning "authoritycin"—the word itself his most felicitous invention—Professor Joseph McLean has admitted that some utilization of special districts is necessary, and indeed inevitable. Rather than insisting upon their total elimination, he calls for restraint in their use. He warns of an "overdose of authoritycin" which "may produce not only confusion but may serve as an embalming fluid in the body politic. General government is in danger of being superseded by a set of authority-type ganglia directed by a small, weak brain."[9]

No better example exists of the necessity of the special district and, at the same time, of its limitations than that of the Port of New York Authority. Created by interstate compact between New York and New Jersey, it overlays the great New York metropolitan area—an area which includes part of Connecticut as well. Hardly a single-purpose district, the authority operates airports, tunnels and bridges, a grain elevator, port and dock facilities, bus and truck terminals, a rapid-transit system, and warehouses. The governing board is appointed by the governors of New York and New Jersey, and the policies of the board are subject to veto by the governors. Even though the authority has no taxing power, it is no beggar crouching at the

---

[8] Daniel Elazar, "Metro and the Voters," *Planning, 1959* (Chicago: American Society of Planning Officials, 1959), pp. 69–76.

[9] Joseph E. McLean, "The Use and Abuse of Authorities," *National Municipal Review*, XLII (October, 1953), 444.

back doorsteps of the state governments in wait for handouts. Quite the contrary, the authority lives well—some would say lavishly—on fees and service charges, sale of revenue bonds, and subventions from the state and federal governments. The authority began the 1960's with a staff of 4,000 (and a director paid $60,000 a year); from 1956 through 1965 the gross operating revenues of the authority increased from $76 million to $179 million, and its funded debt from $325 to $856 million.

The first of the great public authorities in the United States, antedating the Tennessee Valley Authority by over a decade, the Port Authority was patterned after the Port of London Authority. Negotiations between the states of New York and New Jersey over the interstate problems of the New York port area resulted in the interstate compact of 1921 which set up the authority.

It was not waterborne traffic, however, but another form of transportation—the automobile—which gave the Port Authority a fertile field of operations. The authority built the George Washington Bridge over the Hudson River in the 1920's and then constructed three other bridges. It acquired the Holland Tunnel in 1931 and later built the Lincoln Tunnel. During the 1940's, the authority extended itself into another major field of transportation by acquiring La Guardia and New York International airports from the city of New York, Newark Airport from the city of Newark, and Teterboro Airport from private owners. The only major transportation facilities in the New York metropolitan area not under Port Authority administration are rail and subway commuting systems (except for the relatively minor Port Authority Trans-Hudson System and the important highway transit systems). Even though the authority has power to plan for and even operate a transportation complex for the entire New York metropolitan area, it has never tried to attack the perplexing problem of the rail, bus, and subway mass-transit systems. One commentator observes that the authority has failed "to fill the need for a transportation agency capable of handling the total problem of the area." [10]

It is this failure, according to its critics, which constitutes a major fault of the Port Authority. Anxious to venture into no activity which is not a sure revenue-producer and which cannot, therefore, be self-amortizing, the authority has assiduously avoided the mass-transit problem in the New York metropolitan area. One of its primary objectives seems to have been not to jeopardize its fine standing in the bond market. To those people who think of the transportation problem as a unity, the authority's piecemeal approach, which skims the cream from the bottle and leaves the rest of the milk to sour, is the key to both the authority's financial success and its limited role as a public transportation agency.

[10] Wilfred Owen, *The Metropolitan Transportation Problem* (Washington, D.C.: The Brookings Institution, rev. ed., 1966), p. 177.

Another important fault of the Port Authority, as seen by its critics, is lack of political responsibility. That the design of the authority's structure was precisely to remove it from the hurdy-gurdy of precinct politics is no answer. Even the veto that the governors of New York and New Jersey have over the operation of the authority, the one real political control written into the authority's compact, has apparently been ineffective. "Theoretically," pronounced the New York legislature's Temporary State Commission on Coordination of State Activities, "the Governor can himself study, or assign staff to study, in detail the Authority's activities. Actually no such detailed supervision is or has been carried on, and the veto power has rarely been exercised." The Temporary State Commission concluded that there is need "for a device which would encourage an overall evaluation of Authority problems, programs, and accomplishments." [11]

Thus the Port Authority, like its sister agencies all over the country, has come around a full cycle, back to its point of departure. Set up with the object of solving a public problem in a "nonpolitical" fashion, it is being roundly criticized for perching so far above and beyond politically responsible sources of authority that its power has become autocratic. The vox populi, which is accustomed to sound with Jovian accent, has been reduced, in the case of the Port Authority, to an ineffectual murmur. Having been insulated from the people, say the critics, the authority has moved outside the people's ken.

One method for increasing the political responsiveness of the authority has been used in Pittsburgh. The Pittsburgh Urban Redevelopment Authority, created in 1946, had by January, 1960, seven redevelopment projects completed or under way, six of which had received no federal assistance, and seven more in the planning stage. Perhaps the most successful —certainly the best known—of Pittsburgh's redevelopment projects is the one involving the blighted fifty-nine acres at the "Golden Triangle." In 1945, the tax income from this area was approximately $293,000. By 1959, even with a sizable amount of the area incorporated into nontaxable Point State Park, the tax yield was approximately $548,000. Not so well known, but equally successful, was the South Side redevelopment project, which resulted, among other things, in the construction of eleven new open-hearth furnaces by Jones and Laughlin Steel Corporation at a cost of $70 million.

In its own way, then, the Pittsburgh Urban Redevelopment Authority has been no less successful than the Port of New York Authority. But there

[11] Temporary State Commission on Coordination of State Activities, "Staff Report on Public Authorities under New York State," Legislative Document No. 46, 1956, pp. 559, 560. For a popular critique of the Port Authority, see also Edward T. Chase, "How to Rescue New York from Its Port Authority," *Harper's Magazine,* CXX (June, 1960), 67–74.

is a substantial difference between these agencies: the Port of New York Authority is a special district, which enjoys a substantial amount of freedom from political responsibility to the state governments which created it; the Pittsburgh authority is subordinate to the city government and, indeed, is an arm of that government. In Pennsylvania, a city's redevelopment authority may be set up by ordinance or resolution, with the five-member board appointed by the mayor. Thus the Pittsburgh authority has been as much an instrumentality of the city government as a regular line department, except that it has been able to act with somewhat more freedom than a department. Since Mayor David Lawrence of Pittsburgh was both a strong mayor and an effective political leader, the redevelopment authority was more thoroughly integrated into the city's administration than it would have been if a less effective political and administrative leader had been in city hall.

In sum, we can see that the special governments have performed significant governmental services, that they have filled a gap that general governments, such as the city, sometimes could not fill. It is not, therefore, the use of "authoritycin," but its abuse, that has contributed so greatly to the fractionalization of the local community's government. If the special government is used judiciously in local government—used, indeed, with maximum restraint—it can perform necessary service without at the same time contributing to the community's political disintegration. Indeed, in the large metropolitan community it may represent the only reasonably available form of political integration.

A Sword for the Gordian Knot?

At times there is objective need of governmental unity within the urban area, regardless of the population of the "real" city. If there is a storm drainage or flood problem, if air pollution has become a major worry to health officials, if the service area of the library or the art museum extends to the farthest definable limits of urban occupation, then there may be pressing practical reasons for breaking through the barriers of territorial fractionalization. For equally substantial reasons, it may be necessary to lessen or eliminate the vertical or functional fragmentation of the community. What methods are available for achieving the political integration of the urban community?

Annexation by the Central City. Few indeed of the roughly 5,400 cities and villages of over 2,500 population in the United States have no urban fringe. This urban area, which lies outside the corporate boundaries of the city, has some pronounced characteristics. It is peopled by men and women who are urban in occupation, in habits, and in desire for urban service. Land *use* is varied (it is both urban and rural in nature), but land *value* is usually so far above the value of surrounding rural lands that it can only be designated as urban. Because of "inflated" value, much of the land is in a transitional state, and even where the use might be considered agricultural, it is a far more intensive kind of use than is typical. And so in the environs of the city one sees truck farms, greenhouses and nurseries, riding stables, and other "agricultural" uses that are essentially urban.

This urban fringe is a part of the city in reality, though it is separated from the legal city by the corporate limits. As we have seen earlier, the cities are not wholly at fault for permitting this separation of the urban fringe from the city proper. Whatever the cause of it, annexation can be an effective means of eliminating it. Although many of our largest cities are effectively checked in their territorial growth by the surrounding wall of satellite municipalities, there still remains in this republic a great block of cities, large and small, which can stem the tide of Balkanization by aggressive annexation policy.

It is not the ring of satellite cities and quasi-urban governments in the fringe which acts as the greatest deterrent to territorial expansion of the city. It is the doctrine of self-determination of the urban fringe, written into the law of most states and into the political folklore of suburban America, which has been the real obstacle to annexation. Just as Kansas City, Dallas, Houston, and San Antonio have greatly arrested horizontal disintegration by annexing hundreds of square miles of the urban fringe, so other major cities, and most minor ones, can follow the same course of action. (See Table 8-1.) They are capable of jumping the hurdles of folklore and the law.

Some Questions about Annexation. What are the proper criteria for determining whether an unincorporated area is suitable for annexation to a city? By traditional standards the area should be (1) compact—it should as nearly as possible approach the square or the circle in form; (2) contiguous—the area should be physically connected with the city; and (3) urban in character. It is this last criterion which presents such great difficulty. In common practice, land use determines whether the area is urban or nonurban. But though use may be an indicator, land value is perhaps more pertinent from an empirical standpoint: agricultural use of the land persists long after the land has acquired urban value. Moreover, if a city wishes to maintain a greenbelt around its periphery, it might annex some territory with the purpose of keeping it open. For example, as a result of Oklahoma City's bold annexations of 1959–1960, "farm areas have been brought in under agricultural zoning, and these could guarantee the city its own food-producing 'greenbelts' unless or until rezoned. The city's planning commission can now insist on new subdivisions with adequate streets, sewers, schools, and parks." [12]

[12] "Oklahoma's Second Land Rush," *Architectural Forum*, CXVIII (June, 1961), 115.

Table 8-1. Notable Annexations by American Cities, 1952–1965

City	Year	No. Sq. Mi. Annexed	Est. Pop. Area Annexed	Annexation Initiated by
Charlotte, N. C.	1959	33.10	44,000	SC
Dallas, Tex.	1956	38.06	ND	ND
	1958	35.09	7,000	C
Dothan, Ala.	1956	36.10	2,000	ND
El Paso, Tex.	1955	34.50	40,000	C
	1956	33.00	50,000	ND
Flagstaff, Ariz.	1958	49.24	1,500	F
Houston, Tex.	1956	187.63	140,000	ND
	1965	86.99	6,769	C
Kansas City, Mo.	1954	48.11	18,000	ND
	1960	187.00	30,300	C
Lubbock, Tex.	1958	45.20	6,500	SC
Mobile, Ala.	1956	76.80	30,000	ND
	1960	68.55	28,430	C
Oklahoma City, Okla.	1959–60	352.30	ND	C
	1960	137.60	ND	ND
Phoenix, Ariz.	1959	57.40	118,681	ND
	1960	78.40	62,775	C
	1965	23.04	8,000	F
San Antonio, Tex.	1952	79.88	42,000	C
San Diego, Calif.	1958	41.90	1,000	FC
	1960	43.50	25	FSCO
	1963	50.00	129	F
Tampa, Fla.	1953	46.00	95,000	FC

Code: C=city; S=real estate subdividers; F=fringe-area residents; O=others; ND=no data.
   Source: *The Municipal Year Book* (Chicago: ICMA, 1953 through 1966); *Architectural Forum*, CXVIII (June, 1961), 114.

Another question of importance is: Should cost be a determining factor in annexation? The charge is often made, sometimes legitimately, that the city is all too willing to annex territory which has a lucrative tax base—industries, shopping centers, high-income neighborhoods—but shies away from low-valuation sections—working-class neighborhoods, badly developed subdivisions, and neighborhoods with bad servicing or social problems. This tendency results in crazy-quilt municipal boundaries which are an affront to reasonableness.

   The rule of thumb in municipal finance is that residential districts usually cost more to administer than they return to the municipal till in tax money. Industrial and commercial districts, on the other hand, yield more in tax returns than they take out of the budget in service expenditures. The trouble is that this generalization is based on the old-fashioned dependence of the city upon the general property tax. With sales taxes, income taxes, and service charges coming to the fore in city finance, the validity of the generalization is in peril. Since industrial, commercial, and residential areas of the city, moreover, are obviously interdependent, it would follow that an annexation program might logically aim to absorb all such areas.

Community growth is almost certain to have an impact upon the city's financial position.[13] Whether the city will benefit from growth or will be adversely affected by it, however, may depend considerably upon its annexation policy. When Kalamazoo, Michigan, by vigorous annexation, doubled its size in four years, the city was taking a calculated risk that revenues would not lag drastically behind expenditures. Happily for its budget, the end of the four-year period showed the city with lower per capita operating costs and fewer city personnel per capita than before annexation.[14] For all the fiscal burdens imposed by annexation, in other words, the city was able to lower unit costs, an objective determinant of long-term fiscal success.

Should annexation be forced upon either the suburbs or the city? To the municipal official, enforced annexation is not only a necessary element of good law but a desirable one. "We reject the untenable idea," reads a statement of the influential National League of Cities, "that dwellers within . . . 'fringe areas' . . . should be given a veto power over the . . . destiny of the city." [15] It is probably accurate to say that a majority of state legislators do not agree with this point of view.

Without a doubt, one of the factors contributing most to local government Balkanization has been the ease with which groups can incorporate themselves, whether as full municipal corporations or as quasi-corporations. Enforced annexation is a way to meet this problem by absorbing fringe areas before they incorporate separately. Directed to this same end is a device introduced in Arizona, which provides that a city or village may forbid incorporations within an urban area adjacent to its corporate limits. (The urban area is defined by statute.) If the city refuses to annex the area, then and only then may the county board act upon a petition to incorporate.[16]

Does annexation solve any basic community problems? As we have already suggested, it probably does militate against that Balkanization of the urban fringe which results from the growth of satellite communities. It can also aid in planning community growth. If the community is truly a "natural" area, a seamless web, then political unity may be a corollary of the

[13] See Walter Isard and Robert E. Coughlin, *Municipal Costs and Revenues Resulting from Community Growth* (West Trenton, N.J.: Chandler-David Publishing Co., 1960).

[14] Charles H. Elliott, "A City Compares Costs after Annexation," *Michigan Municipal Review*, May, 1959, pp. 113–115.

[15] American Municipal Association (now National League of Cities), *Basic Principles for a Good Annexation Law* (Chicago: The Association, May, 1960), unpaged.

[16] *Public Management*, XLIII (August, 1961), 186.

larger unity, and annexation a means of achieving it. Moreover, as one commentator has suggested, annexation may result in the reurbanization of the fringe territory, by heightening the service level and controlling land use.[17] Politically, it means that the fringe inhabitants have an immediate and lasting voice in the public councils of the city. The city is no longer deprived of the suburbanite's influence, and the suburbanite is no longer helpless to shape the political destinies of the city of which he is an integral part.

On the other hand, annexation may become little more than an instrument of the land speculator. This happened in Santa Clara County, California, and the result was a degree of urban sprawl so alarming to the farmers that they began to regard the city as their natural enemy (not a very difficult attitude for farmers to develop, after all!). As a result, an agricultural pressure group pushed a law through the California legislature establishing an agricultural zone in the county into which subdividers could not intrude.

Such measures of desperation, however, are only a stopgap. As land values are forced up by urban growth, the farmers, too, will be enticed by the high prices. Ultimately, they will be forced to join with the city to preserve both productive land and open space. Annexation, in and of itself, may be an aid or an obstacle to achievement of this objective. There is no reason that all the territory within the city should be heavily built up. Only from a narrow, traditionalist point of view can the city be regarded as a user of land solely in the highly intensive sense. By purchase of land for parks and forest-preserve areas, by condemnation or negotiated purchase of the developmental value of land, by an imaginative use of the taxing power, and by vigorous zoning policies, the city can, if it has the will, control the development of its fringe areas. Annexation may be useful here, as useful as extraterritoriality and cooperative zoning with the county.

Another question of importance is: Should the state intrude, administratively, in annexation matters? That the state customarily intervenes in an other-than-administrative fashion is obvious from the foregoing discussion: the statutes control annexation procedures, by and large, and the courts often play a crucial role even outside Virginia. But administrative intervention is a comparatively new phenomenon. Minnesota set up a municipal commission in 1959 with the power to review and to deny both annexation and incorporation proposals. And in California, the Governor's Commission on Metropolitan Area Problems has recommended that essentially the same method be used.[18]

[17] Jerome G. Manis, "Annexation: The Process of Reurbanization," *American Journal of Economics and Sociology*, XVIII (July, 1959), 353–360.

[18] Stanley Scott *et al.*, *Local Governmental Boundaries and Areas: New Policies for California* (Berkeley, Calif.: Bureau of Public Administration, University of California, February, 1961), p. 1.

The question of political accommodation is implicit in every discussion of annexation. Viewing the American, Canadian, and European city empirically, one finds a strong tendency toward unity in the smaller cities. But when the city grows to middle size, the strain toward diversity becomes strongly pronounced. And increasing size seems to emphasize the diversity. Since annexation is a unifying force, at least geographically, we might expect to find relatively slight resistance to it in the smaller cities, but a stiffening resistance as we move our observation to larger and larger cities. Whether this hypothesis is valid has never been rigorously tested, and therefore we can only say that there are some indications of its validity, but that they are by no means conclusive. The larger the metropolis, the greater its governmental diversity. Every metropolis of middle size and above, as we shall see presently, is marked by pronounced geographic fractionalization. There seems to be, moreover, massive resistance among both American and Canadian suburbanites to a loss of political identity to the great central city, and this resistance shows up in state and provincial councils. If these observable phenomena do not establish the validity of the hypothesis, they at least indicate it is worthy of further investigation.

Consolidation of Governments. Consolidation is a means of bringing together into some kind of unity both general-purpose governments and special districts. That it can be spectacularly successful is shown by the consolidation of school districts over the past two decades.

Perhaps the oldest type of consolidation is between and among general governments. Cities consolidate with cities, and counties combine with cities. City-county consolidation has been eminently successful in some urban areas in unifying power and services. The city of New York overlays five counties and has largely absorbed their activities. In Philadelphia, Baltimore, Denver, St. Louis, San Francisco, and Honolulu, one government handles all the elements of city and county government. In 1949, Baton Rouge, Louisiana, effected a partial consolidation with East Baton Rouge Parish, which resulted in what was basically a single legislative body for the city and parish, and a single executive, a mayor-president, elected from both city and parish at large. In spite of these successes, however, consolidation of the city with other general governments has made no major impact upon American local government. To combine city and county, or city and city, seems to be almost as difficult as combining nation-states in the international community. Consolidating the city with special governments has not been practiced widely; still, it can be an effective means of reducing vertical disintegration, whether achieved by formal or informal means.

One type of consolidation which shows promise theoretically but which has little political force behind it is the unification of the school and city governments. Partly because of the egocentrism of interest groups and partly because of the myth that schools, by being independent, can be kept free of political pressures, most public schools over the country have been set up as autonomous governmental authorities. This independence has resulted in the duplication of functions, sometimes of equipment and even personnel, has caused the school district often to work at cross-purposes with the general government, and has usually created excessive competition and rivalry between the two principal public spending agencies of the community.

One way to insure against working at cross-purposes is to combine the schools with a new metropolitan government (as in Nashville, Tennessee), or if that is impractical, to combine the schools with the other major general government, the county (as in Arlington County, Virginia). We have had enough experience with the schools operating as a part of the city government to know that the system will probably not seriously harm the educational program and may substantially benefit it. Both large cities and small ones now operate the schools as integral parts of the city administration or, at the very least, exercise control over school personnel and school budgets.[19]

In New York City the school system is a part of the city government; in Lake Forest, Illinois, the mayor appoints the school board for the grade-school system, and the council must approve the school budget. Chattanooga and St. Paul have long since made their schools a part of the city government. When the charter commission in Nashville was drafting the charter for the metropolitan government that was eventually approved by the voters in 1962, certain interest groups sought freedom for the schools from the city. This pressure was effectively resisted by the commission, and public education remained a department within the city government.

Interlocal Cooperation. If annexation is unlikely and consolidation legally or politically impossible, another possibility for integrating the community is to set up cooperative arrangements between and among the various local governments. City-county cooperation has long been utilized by alert local officials both to increase the effectiveness of local government and to reduce its costs.

The county may also perform services for the city on a contract basis. Possibly the best example of this type of interlocal cooperation is the California "Lakewood Plan." In the Los Angeles metropolitan area, where the county furnishes, on a contract basis, police, fire, public works, and other services, there has resulted a kind of functional consolidation. A California legislative committee reported that in Los Angeles county, "county operation of municipal type services is something that has developed through the years, originally as an answer to the needs of the rapidly urbanizing

[19] See, for example, N. B. Henry and J. G. Kerwin, *Schools and City Government* (Chicago: University of Chicago Press, 1938).

unincorporated areas in the county and lately as an answer to metropolitan government. It should be noted that through the functional consolidation device, Los Angeles county has been able to achieve as much or more metropolitan government than several areas which have undertaken extensive metropolitan governmental reorganization." [20]

Although only a handful of counties in the United States are in a position to supply the kind of service of which Los Angeles county is capable, three county services widely offered to cities and villages (as well as to other local governments) are election administration, public health controls, and assessment and collection of the general property tax. The city-county health department, or the department which is wholly the county's, is a practical device for eliminating much conflict and duplication in local health administration. Often, too, property-tax administration can be more economically carried on at the county level than by the city. The city manager of Berkeley, Missouri, found in the early 1960's, for example, that the city could turn over tax collection to St. Louis county and save money even after paying the county's service charge.

To illustrate all that can be done in both the traditional and the newer city-county relations, the city of Wichita and Sedgwick county, Kansas, within a relatively short period:

1. Created a metropolitan area planning commission and department.
2. Created a city-county health department.
3. Created a city-county civil defense department.
4. Jointly completed a $20 million floodwater diversion works.
5. Maintained a city-operated, jointly financed sanitary landfill.
6. Conducted elections under supervision of a single county election commissioner.[21]

In some jurisdictions, fruitful cooperative arrangements have developed between cities and schools. One or the other of the governments will handle purchasing, some personnel and fiscal matters, recreation, and legal affairs; or the functions will be handled jointly. Thus the city and schools of St. Joseph, Michigan, have organized a joint recreation program to bring the resources of the school system and the municipality under central management. A gymnasium, city and school playgrounds and athletic fields, and city beaches and parks are all brought together without costly duplication of expenditures, facilities, and personnel. Milwaukee makes available to the Milwaukee school district the facilities of its legal and finance depart-

[20] California Assembly Interim Committee on Municipal and County Government, *Final Report, Assembly Interim Committee Reports, 1957–1959* (Sacramento, Calif.: General Assembly, 1959), Vol. 6, No. 10, p. 7.

[21] Frank H. Backstrom, "Advantages and Disadvantages of Municipal Consolidation," *Mayor and Manager,* III (March, 1960), 5, 18. For recommendations concerning city-county cooperation generally in Kansas, see *National Civic Review,* LIV (January, 1965), 42.

ments to service and sell school bonds. According to the findings of the Greater Toledo Municipal League, a privately supported research organization with no public connections, the city of Toledo aided the public schools and the university with assistance in excess of $16 million in the period 1946–1958.

One sure way to develop interlocal cooperation is to bring the local bureaucracies into a working harmony. With this end in view, the International City Managers' Association and the American Association of School Administrators sponsored three meetings in 1963–1964—East Coast, Midcontinental, and West Coast—between city managers and school superintendents, with political scientists and professors of education as added participants. These meetings gave the chief administrative officers of the two main spending units of local government a chance to exchange views and perhaps to reach toward a modus vivendi.[22]

Many possibilities exist for interlocal cooperation in the conduct and finance of city, school, county, and other local elections, which are numerous and expensive to administer. On April 2, 1957, three local jurisdictions in Springfield, Missouri—city, school district, and county—held a joint election. By combining the use of judges, clerks, and polling places, the cooperating governments not only saved the voters time and trouble, they also saved the taxpayers approximately $5,000.[23]

When they are well organized, the larger units of local government— whether city, county, school, or park district—are in a position to lend a helping hand to many other local governments which are geographically close. Training is a good case in point. In the city's academies, the St. Louis police and fire departments train policemen and firemen from cities and villages of the metropolitan area without charge. Similarly, in financial administration, public works, and even legal affairs, the large city can give assistance to the small ones.

That a sewerage system can be operated over a large region by intermunicipal cooperation is remarkably evident from the Detroit experience. The central city's sewage treatment plant, interceptors, and laterals are being planned and built to serve a population of 4,000,000 by 1980. In 1960 the system served an area outside the city of over 200 square miles, and cities and villages numbering over 50.[24] And it has been extended since that date.

The extent of interlocal cooperation varies from state to state. After a

---

[22] See Archibald B. Shaw (ed.), *Realities of Intergovernmental Relations* (Washington, D.C., and Chicago: American Association of School Administrators and International City Managers' Association, July, 1964). This is a report on the Midcontinental conference.

[23] Missouri Public Expenditure Survey, *Possible Areas of Cooperation Between City of St. Joseph, Buchanan County, St. Joseph School District* (Jefferson City, Mo.: The Survey, January, 1959), pp. 5, 7.

[24] Clyde L. Palmer, *Detroit's Role in Providing Sewage Treatment Service to the Metropolitan Area* (Detroit: Detroit Department of Public Works, undated mimeo.).

survey in 1958 the Pennsylvania Department of Internal Affairs discovered 617 agreements linking 1,794 cities, boroughs, townships, counties, and school districts throughout the state. A New York study, which excluded schools and other special districts and New York City itself, found 345 contracts for fire protection and numerous other contracts for water supply, sewage disposal, lighting, and snow removal. From 18 to 32 fields of cooperation are open, by law, to cities, counties, villages, and towns. [25] A 1965 survey in New Jersey discovered 757 interlocal contracts and agreements in existence.[26]

Cooperation between and among the multitude of local governments cannot only reduce both vertical and horizontal disintegration; it can also materially increase the effectiveness of local government. Although each local government, down to the tiniest hamlet, has a tendency to guard its autonomy as jealously as any Balkan kingdom, one way for any local government to preserve autonomy, paradoxically, is by functional cooperation. As of 1967 some 32 states permitted it by statute (Connecticut, Indiana, Virginia, New York, and Ohio are some of the states that have authorized intergovernmental cooperation and contractual agreements in the past decade).[27] Even where no statutory authority exists, municipalities and other local governments have found ways of coming together in mutually satisfactory cooperative arrangements.

One of the failures of intergovernmental cooperation has undoubtedly stemmed from a failure of communications. The legal and jurisdictional walls dividing the urban community have probably served to foul the channels of communication between and among peoples, political leaders, and administrators involved in public policy. But if this has been a problem, it has not gone unnoticed; indeed, urban communities have made valiant efforts to increase the level of communications between and among peoples and governments. The Association of Bay Area Governments in San Francisco and the Greater Hartford town meeting are but two examples of a multitude of approaches to the search for greater communication among local governments.

Summary

Annexation, consolidation, and intergovernmental cooperation, used singly or in concert, cannot cure the American urban community of either its Balkanization or its vertical disintegration. They are only partial reme-

[25] New York State Department of Audit and Control, *Interlocal Cooperation in New York State* (Albany, N.Y.: The Department, 1958), p. 29.

[26] Advisory Commission on Intergovernmental Relations, *A Handbook on Inter-Local Agreements* (Washington, D.C.: The Commission, March, 1967), p. 11.

[27] *Ibid.*, p. 23.

dies; they give only partial answers to the riddle. But they can increase the effectiveness of the city and her sister governments. If they do not cut through the Gordian knot, the reason is perhaps that the sword does not exist. Unity in local government, such as in Honolulu and Nashville, can be achieved only rarely. That cities will continue to strive for it, however, goes without question; that it will escape the grasp of most urban communities seems to be inevitable. Instead of seeking an absolute, perfect unity, therefore, the urban community will seek increased coherence in policy and administration. If it cannot eliminate competing governments, it will reduce tensions. If it cannot eliminate duplication, it will strive to minimize duplication. Ultimately, it may substitute pluralism for chaos by building effective communications systems among peoples and governments.

Annotated Bibliography

A political scientist and a professor of education some years ago examined the relationship between the schools and the city governments in cities of over 50,000 population. Showing the value of city-school coordination, this work is as fresh and pertinent today as it was in 1938. See N. B. Henry and J. G. Kerwin, *Schools and City Government* (Chicago: University of Chicago Press, 1938). For an extended discussion of the Lakewood Plan, see Samuel K. Gove, *The Lakewood Plan* (Urbana, Ill.: Institute of Government and Public Affairs, University of Illinois, May, 1961). A great deal of factual data on interlocal cooperation may be found in the *1962 Census of Governments,* especially from the first volume in the series. See U.S. Bureau of the Census, *Governmental Organization,* Vol. I (1963). Bollens' work on special districts has a good deal of intergovernmental comment. See John C. Bollens, *Special District Governments in the United States* (Berkeley and Los Angeles: University of California Press, 1957). A concise summary of the role of special districts in the United States may be found in the Advisory Commission on Intergovernmental Relations, *The Problem of Special Districts in American Government* (Washington, D.C.: U.S. Government Printing Office, May, 1964). An indispensable source book on intergovernmental relations is W. Br ooke Graves, *American Intergovernmental Relations* (New York: Charles Scribner's Sons, 1964). Since formal and informal communication systems are vital for productive intergovernmental relations, the metropolitan council is potentially valuable for achieving such systems. See Royce Hanson, *Metropolitan Councils of Government* (Washington, D.C.: Advisory Commission on Intergovernmental Relations, August, 1966). Interesting examples of intergovernmental cooperation may be found in U.S. Department of Housing and Urban Development, *Cooperative Ventures in Urban America* (Washington, D.C.: U.S. Government Printing Office, May, 1967). Considerable data on the extent of interlocal cooperation, as well as numerous examples of model statutes, constitutional provisions, and contracts and agreements are included in Advisory Commission on Intergovernmental Relations, *A Handbook for Interlocal Agreements and Contracts* (Washington, D.C.: The Commission, March, 1967).

CHAPTER 9

Governing the Metropolis

The Metropolis, Great and Small

According to the commonplace definition, the metropolis is a large city with a wide range of stores, shops, skills, and peoples. It is an entertainment center where one may go to a nightclub, a professional football game, or a fine restaurant. It is a cultural center with a university or college, fine libraries, a symphony orchestra, and an art museum. It is a place where one may see a professional troupe perform legitimate theater.

What would be the population of such a place? Few people would concern themselves about this question, or if they did, they would not worry about any precise figure. So long as the urban center would not deny them the services and amenities they expect, a city could contain 3,000,000 or 300,000 and still be thought of as a metropolis.

The Census Definition. Obviously such an imprecise definition of a metropolis is not suitable for either scholarly or statistical use. Seeking to establish a precise definition, therefore, the U.S. Bureau of the Budget, acting with the advice of a federal committee, has developed the concept of the "standard metropolitan statistical area" (SMSA), which is used by the U.S. Bureau of the Census, by other public bodies at all levels of government, and by research agencies. The principal criteria of the SMSA are:

1. Each SMSA must include a city of 50,000 population or more, or two contiguous cities having a combined population of 50,000 or more (the smaller city must have at least 15,000 population).

2. At least 75 percent of the labor force in each county in the SMSA must be engaged in nonagricultural pursuits.

3. In New England the city and town, rather than the city and county, are used in defining the SMSA. Population density for each of these units must be at least 100 persons per square mile if the unit is to be included within the metropolitan area.

4. Further criteria for determining whether the county may properly be included within the SMSA are commuting patterns, newspaper circulation, and other factors.[1]

Defining the Supermetropolis. The difficulties in defining a metropolis are only too clearly evident from the criteria used by the Bureau of the Cen-

[1] U.S. Bureau of the Budget, *Standard Metropolitan Statistical Areas* (1964), pp. 1–2.

sus. At one end of the spectrum is the city which is possibly too small to be a metropolis; on this point, many scholars and laymen would agree. But can it also be that there are now in existence urban communities which are too large to be included within the term metropolis? Some scholars are beginning to think so. The French geographer Jean Gottmann uses the term "megalopolis" to describe major cities lying close together. The megalopolis is a type of urban region characterized by "manifold concentration" and by "polynuclear structure." It is to be found at three points in the United States: the northeast Atlantic seaboard; the industrialized Midwest, between the Great Lakes and the Ohio River; and the California seaboard.[2] British geographers and planners have also recognized the great urban region which is more than a metropolis, but they seem to favor the word "conurbation" to describe the phenomenon.

Not to be outdone, the U.S. Bureau of the Budget has designated "standard consolidated areas" in New York–Northwestern New Jersey and Chicago–Northwestern Indiana. Each standard consolidated area includes two or more SMSA's "in recognition of the special importance of even more inclusive metropolitan statistics." There will doubtlessly be more of such areas designated by the bureau in the future.[3]

The Metropolis Defined Politically. A metropolis thus may be defined differently by statistician, sociologist, geographer, or philosopher. To the political scientist the metropolis is a phenomenon which must be governed, and the political definition must reflect the exigencies of the governing process.

What is this metropolis that the political scientist views? It is, first of all, a continuously built-up area in and around a major city: the central city, suburbs, and immediately surrounding hinterland. It is, secondly, an urban community tied together by diurnal interchanges and daily needs. For example, the point at which the metropolis ends might be placed somewhere in the vicinity of the last stop of the commuter train. A third characteristic of the metropolis as viewed by the political scientist is the large number of local governments and governmental agencies which service and control the urban community. Although the community is in a very real sense self-governing, the public policies are formed by numerous constituencies, not one of which ever includes the entire community. As a result, the policies which are formed in the metropolis are often in conflict or contradiction. This is the Balkanization and the results of such Balkanization which we discussed in the preceding chapter.

Finally, the political scientist accepts the standard metropolitan statistical area as a definition of a metropolis, but with substantial exceptions.

[2] Jean Gottmann, *Megalopolis* (New York: The Twentieth Century Fund, 1961), pp. 23–25.
[3] U.S. Bureau of the Budget, *Standard Metropolitan Statistical Areas* (1964), p. 43.

The definition of the SMSA is at best arbitrary—at worst, misleading—from a governmental standpoint. Its great virtue is that it gives us a bench mark, a standardized point of reference, from which to begin a discussion of the metropolis.

These criteria are set up in reference to the American metropolis. But most of them—especially the first three—are useful in examining the Canadian and the European metropolis.

Metropolitan Growth in the United States

According to the U.S. Bureau of the Census, there were 96 United States metropolitan areas in 1930, 140 in 1940, and 168 in 1950. Using a slightly different definition, the bureau identified 212 metropolitan areas in the United States in 1960 and 231 in 1967 (including the three Puerto Rican SMSA's of San Juan, Ponce, and Mayagüez).

In analyzing the growth of major metropolitan regions of the United States, Jerome P. Pickard has found that the number of such areas with a total population of 250,000 or more increased from 23 in 1910 to 77 in 1960. During the decade 1950–1960, all metropolitan areas gained in population except for Wilkes-Barre, Pennsylvania, which declined by 14 percent. Overall population in these major metropolitan areas increased by 19 million, or 22 percent. For the United States at large, 68 percent of the national growth went into the major metropolitan areas.[4]

The growth of the metropolitan area, as Amos Hawley observes, has been one of the most significant types of population movement during the twentieth century in the United States. This population movement has caused the metropolis to change not only in number of units and number of people but also in shape. The nineteenth-century city was fairly compact; the twentieth-century city, or metropolitan urban aggregate, extends widely over the landscape. This latter phenomenon has given rise to the geographic disintegration we have already examined. It has also caused the central city in the metropolitan area to contain less and less, proportionately, of the population in the metropolitan area. (See Table 9-1.) In 1910 the central cities of the metropolitan area contained approximately 77 percent of the population of those areas.[5] But in 1960 the central city population was only slightly more than half the population of all metropolitan areas. In the 212 standard metropolitan statistical areas in 1960, 58,000,000 people lived in the central cities and 55,000,000 lived outside.[6]

[4] Jerome P. Pickard, *Metropolitanization of the United States, Research Monograph No. 2* (Washington, D.C.: Urban Land Institute, 1959), p. 16; and Pickard, "Metropolitan Area Growth in the United States, 1950–1960," *Urban Land*, February, 1960, pp. 3–6.

[5] Amos H. Hawley, *The Changing Shape of Metropolitan America* (Glencoe, Ill.: The Free Press, 1956), pp. 1, 2.

[6] U.S. Bureau of the Census, *1960 Census of Population* (1961), Vol. I, Part A, p. 25.

Table 9-1. 1960 Population of Selected Urban Areas and Their Central Cities

Core City	Population of Core City	Population of Urbanized Area	Percentage in Core City
New York	7,781,984	14,114,927	55.1
Chicago	3,550,404	5,959,213	59.6
Los Angeles	2,479,015	6,488,791	38.2
Philadelphia	2,002,512	3,635,228	55.1
Detroit	1,670,144	3,537,709	47.2
Baltimore	939,024	1,418,948	66.2
Houston	938,219	1,139,678	82.3
Cleveland	876,050	1,784,991	49.1
Washington	763,956	1,808,423	42.2
St. Louis	750,026	1,667,693	45.0
Milwaukee	741,324	1,149,997	64.5
San Francisco	740,316	2,430,663	30.5
Boston	697,197	2,413,236	28.9
Dallas	679,684	932,349	72.9
New Orleans	627,525	845,237	74.2

Source: U.S. Bureau of the Census, *1960 Census of Population* (1961), Vol. I, Part A, Table 22, pp. 40–49.

The Role of the States and the Federal Government

Since the states furnish the legal basis for local government, the metropolis is today a reflection of the constitutional and statutory framework which the states have built. This legal framework has enabled the metropolis to govern itself, by and large, but it has also very often had the effect of hamstringing experiment with differing governmental devices in the metropolitan community. But the law is not the only point at which the metropolitan area makes contact with the states. As we have already seen in a preceding chapter, the states offer to all cities and other local governments numerous administrative services and grants-in-aid, particularly for highways, roads, streets, and schools.

The federal government also offers to the metropolis various grants-in-aid and administrative services, the most important of which are to aid urban renewal and public housing. In addition, much federal money for arterial streets and highways comes to the metropolis via the states. Finally, joint federal and state action by means of the interstate compact is often important for metropolitan regions lying in two or more states. Note the Port of New York Authority, for example.

That the states and the federal government must come to the aid of the metropolis seems to be an inevitable result of the rapid urbanization of the United States. For the most part it is the states which must act, though often with the aid of the federal government. Luther Gulick has summarized what the states can do and how the federal government might complement their efforts.

In the first place, according to Gulick, the state must review its constitution and laws and alter them to fit the new facts of metropolitan life. There must be a new definition of "home rule," one appropriate to the "new age of metropolitan regionalism." Moreover, since the metropolis is apt to spill over state lines, the state must work with the federal government to develop interstate compacts and agreements, both to serve the metropolis and to enable the metropolis to serve itself. As Gulick further observes, many local service problems are apt to extend far into the hinterland, far beyond the recognizable limits of the metropolis. If the metropolis is to have clean water and clean air, for example, both state and federal action are often necessary.

The states are the funnels through which much of the federal aid destined for urban areas is channeled. Since this aid is highly fragmented and disjointed, the states should do everything in their power, according to Gulick, to bring some order out of the chaos. Furthermore, "the governors can pressure the federal government into doing a better job in rationalizing its several programs." The states must plan for and with the metropolitan areas; they must gather many facts needed in governing the metropolis. They must aid in the control of land use, in order to control extensive as well as intensive uses and to preserve open spaces.

Finally, the states must reexamine entirely the financial underpinnings of the metropolitan governments. The states' control of tax and other revenues, the rigid and unscientific control of local debt, the sometimes unrealistic and sometimes nonexistent regard for fiscal and revenue administration—all these things require serious reexamination.[7]

It may thus be seen that without the aid of the states and the federal government, the metropolis will continue to drift. The finest local leadership, the most active and imaginative local body politic, singly or in concert, cannot meet the problems of the metropolis without the aid of the larger and legally superior governments.

The Vital Center

Every metropolis has a center which dominates the entire community. Usually it is a single city, as with Chicago, Denver, New York, or Los An-

[7] Luther Gulick, "The Role of the State in the Solution of Metropolitan Area Problems," in Stephen B. Sweeney and George S. Blair (eds.), *Metropolitan Analysis* (Philadelphia: University of Pennsylvania Press, 1958), pp. 165–179. Also see Robert H. Connery and Richard H. Leach, *The Federal Government and Metropolitan Areas* (Cambridge, Mass.: Harvard University Press, 1960). There were 31 SMSA's which crossed state lines and at least 28 others which extended to state lines in 1964. See U. S. Bureau of the Budget, *Standard Metropolitan Statistical Areas* (1964), pp. 4–42.

geles. Sometimes it is split up into two, three, or even more centers, no one
of which dominates, as in Minneapolis–St. Paul or Albany–Schenectady–
Troy. That the core or heart of the metropolis is vital to its existence is
obvious even to the most casual observer. Here is the center for recreation
and entertainment, for business and industry, and for public administration. Since the vital center is often also the political center, here one may
find the principal political leaders of the entire urban community, and
here one may also see the headquarters of the governmental bureaucracy,
whether represented by police headquarters or a civil courts building.

The vital center is the central city or cities which form the hub of the
metropolis. We might best think of this center as a business, industrial, and
residential community which originally encompassed the entire urban
community but which now makes up only a part of it. In a very real sense
the center must fulfill two functions: (1) to meet the needs of its own citizenry, and (2) to service the entire metropolitan area and even beyond.
Since many central cities have failed in the first function, they have imper-
iled the entire metropolis.

If there is rot at the core, eventually the whole organism will be affected
—not only the metropolis itself, but the entire region and perhaps the entire nation. If the central city should decay and die, and if the metropolis
should then spread over the landscape in a kind of amorphous glob, there
would first of all be an immediate and substantial increase in transportation costs. And not only the costs but also the problems of moving people
and goods would mount drastically. Second, the elimination of the center
would result in the spreading of slums and further profound economic dislocation. In the words of Jean Gottmann, "urban real estate would lose
much in value; the whole capital invested in buildings, services, and the
highway system itself would be devalued. The share of all the national
wealth now vested in the central cities is so great, though difficult to estimate precisely in dollars and cents, or even in percentages, that one can
hardly visualize how the nonurban parts of the national economy could
shoulder a serious depression of urban values." [8]

Very often the plight of the central city has appeared in the deterioration
of even its immediate downtown area. In 1948, writes one observer, "the
landmarks of Philadelphia's days of glory were lost in an ever-widening
jungle of slums." [9] The "Golden Triangle" in Pittsburgh was well tar-
nished. And within walking distance of the Capitol building in Washington, D.C., one could find some of the world's worst slums. The waterfronts
in Boston, Detroit, and St. Louis—all of them near the downtown area—
were suffering progressive decay.

[8] Gottmann, *op. cit.*, p. 689.
[9] Ernest Havemann, "Rebirth of Philadelphia," *National Civic Review*, LI (November, 1962), 538.

But it was not the downtown areas alone that felt this spread of blight. By traveling in almost any direction from Chicago's Loop—except into the lake itself, of course—one could find seriously decayed areas. So much decay had invaded Chicago's South Side that many despaired of its ever becoming rehabilitated. The Mill Creek section in St. Louis was simply one great slum. Just the evidence of physical deterioration alone would have led one to the conclusion that the central city was moribund and could never be brought back to life.

During the 1950's a dramatic reversal took place, however. Revitalization of the city, increased federal aid, and economic prosperity combined to reverse the strong tidal sweep toward decay. In Philadelphia, a home-rule charter, strong mayors, and a vigorous citizens' movement "lit the fuse and set off a tremendous explosion of civic pride, resolution, and active participation in local government." [10] In Chicago, Mayor Richard Daley, firmly in control of his own party, not only reformed city hall but also combined with important community leaders and various interest groups to effect a virtual rebuilding of vast areas of Chicago's South Side. Pittsburgh business leaders united with city hall to make the "Golden Triangle" once again golden. Fort Worth showed imagination in commissioning Victor Gruen to produce the now world-renowned Gruen plan for redevelopment of the urban core.[11] So far, however, the citizens and leaders of Fort Worth have not been able to muster a sufficient consensus to put the plan into operation.

This rebuilding of the central city has not been accomplished without certain failures. Jane Jacobs likens some of the new projects to well-groomed cemeteries. According to some critics, Boston has cut the heart out of her downtown by artless use of expressways, as has Nashville. But in spite of all the mistakes that have been made, various central cities over the past decade have shown remarkable vitality, at least in the central business district. There is indication that the central city may be able to pull itself out of its slough of despond and once again become the vital center.

Metropolis and Suburbia

Although some metropolitan communities may be virtually without suburbs, usually the suburb is as common to the metropolis as traffic jams. What accounts for the outward population movement and consequent growth of the suburbs? According to Gist and Fava, at least two major forces are responsible for this phenomenon.[12] The first of these is transpor-

[10] *Ibid.*, p. 541.

[11] Victor Gruen, *The Heart of Our Cities* (New York: Simon & Schuster, 1964), pp. 214–220.

[12] Noel P. Gist and Sylvia F. Fava, *Urban Society* (New York: Thomas Y. Crowell Co., 1964), pp. 184–186.

tation. Although the railroad and the electric streetcar had caused some linear movement away from the city by the end of the nineteenth century, it has been the automobile and its companion the expressway which have given the urban population sufficient mobility to spread over the countryside.

But high-speed, relatively inexpensive transportation is not the only cause. The twentieth-century cultural pattern is equally responsible. People value getting away from the dense city into the "garden city." They value the homogeneity of the suburb, which can literally put a wall around itself in order to stave off the threat of invasion by people who have different incomes, different values, different religion, and perhaps a different color of skin. The single-family dwelling, moreover, has become a symbol of the good family life.

The suburban movement has been most pronounced in Canadian and American cities, but European and Japanese cities are experiencing an outward movement of population that may eventually become as strong as it is on the North American continent. Still, only a relatively few cities throughout the world as yet know the suburb in the Canadian-American sense.

When thinking of the growth of the suburb, one is apt, too often, to think of it as a flight from the central city. It is that, of course, but other elements are involved. There is movement from the older suburbs to the newer ones. There is movement from the rural areas and the small towns directly into the suburbs, a movement which departs from the classic pattern in which the family moves first into the central city and then later into the suburbs.

What are the characteristics of the suburbs which surround a metropolis? In the first place, they are highly diverse. They are governmentally diverse: note the 1,060 local governments (mostly suburban) which existed in the six-county Chicago metropolitan area in 1962. They are also highly diverse when measured by socioeconomic standards. Even as the central city developed its own specialized areas with varying racial, national, and socioeconomic groupings, the suburbs tended to do the same. Scarsdale, New York, has the highest average family income in the United States; Kinlock, Missouri, is one of the poorest communities in North America—yet both are suburbs. Some suburbs resemble a well-kept garden; others, a garbage dump. And contrary to popular superstition, some cities, particularly the smaller and newer ones, are populated by higher socioeconomic groups than their suburbs.[13] Finally, there are some smaller cities of defined metropolitan character with virtually no suburbs at all. (See Table 9-1.)

With all this diversity, there is inevitably a great deal of pluralism. A

[13] Leo Schnore, "The Socio-economic Status of Cities and Suburbs," *American Sociological Review*, XXVIII (February, 1963), 76–85.

vigorous community spirit exists in some suburban areas; a myopic parochialism exists in others. A metropolitan planning commission in the Chicago area had this to say about the political pluralism of the area:

> There is operative at the metropolitan level a kind of local urbanism that takes on many of the characteristics of the nationalism found on a higher governmental level. At the metropolitan level, as at the national level, there is a devotion to the history, traditions, folkways, politics, housing arrangements, zoning laws, and a hundred other things individually associated with each of the communities in the area. Few such communities will cheerfully abandon this spirit of localism and acquiesce in the adoption of a new governmental system.[14]

On the other hand, Charles E. Gilbert has found in the Philadelphia suburbs that local identification is conditioned by the socioeconomic character and place of employment of the population. People of higher education and social rank tend to identify strongly either with their own municipality or the Philadelphia region in the large, but people of lower social rank and education seem much less inclined to identify with the whole metropolis: they are far more apt to be locals than cosmopolitans.[15]

For all of this particularism, there is a second characteristic of suburbia: identity with the central city. This may seem paradoxical, yet it certainly exists. When A. J. Liebling wrote a series of articles for the *New Yorker* magazine which were anything but complimentary to Chicago, he received a great many letters of protest from the city and its environs. "The most catamountainous of all came from the suburbs; the people who wouldn't live in the city if you gave them the place rose to its defense like fighters off peripheral airfields in the Ruhr in 1944." [16]

No discussion of the large metropolis should be made without mentioning the general excellence of city government in many of the fringe satellites. The government of Glencoe, Oak Park, or Evanston is superior, by certain standards, to the government of the city of Chicago. The same is true of Cambridge compared with Boston, of Shaker Heights compared with Cleveland, of University City compared with St. Louis, or of Berkeley compared with San Francisco. If a metropolitan government were to absorb any of these communities, the very probable result would be deterioration in their governments.

Still another characteristic of the suburbs, which has important economic and social as well as political consequences, is the extensive rather

[14] Northeastern Illinois Metropolitan Area Local Governmental Services Commission, *Metropolitan Area Services, Second Report of the Commission* (Urbana, Ill.: Institute of Government and Public Affairs, University of Illinois, March, 1959), p. 6.

[15] Charles E. Gilbert, *Governing the Suburbs* (Bloomington, Ind.: Indiana University Press, 1967), pp. 29–30.

[16] A. J. Liebling, *The Second City* (New York: Alfred A. Knopf, 1952), p. vii.

than intensive use of land. Although the older suburbs are becoming more and more densely occupied, the number of families per acre or per square mile is usually far lower than in the central city. The American city has a voracious appetite for land. Not only does the single-family dwelling require, normally, a minimum of 5,000 square feet, one-eighth of an acre; the modern industrial plant also tends to occupy space horizontally rather than vertically.

Although it is the fashion nowadays to debunk both the suburb and suburban living, these phenomena are very much with us and must be lived with. If suburbia represents a problem, it also represents an opportunity. Indeed, the relation of suburbia to the central city probably represents the central problem of the metropolis. We should keep this in mind as we examine the governmental devices used in metropolitan areas.

Metropolitan Reform

That the metropolis suffers from a superfluity of governmental units must be evident to the most casual observer of metropolitan affairs. Although not every metropolis in the United States suffers from the progressive geographic and functional disintegration which we described in the preceding chapter, most of them do. The result is a frustration of the governmental process which not only inhibits the implementation of public policy but which also causes popular disenchantment with local government.

In his analysis of 112 metropolitan surveys, Daniel R. Grant identified at least four sources of this frustration and disenchantment. First, the metropolis often has no governmental instrumentality which can adequately furnish areawide governmental services, nor has there been, in the second place, any way to eliminate the many inequities which have arisen in the financing of governmental services. Third, the unevenness of service levels has been a source of great dissatisfaction. When one community in the metropolitan area is relatively stable and is enjoying a multitude of high-quality governmental services, there is frustration in another community which is hard put to furnish even the most basic ones. Finally, the democratic responsiveness of the multitude of governmental units varies. The surveys seem to make the point that the very complexity of the governmental process, in and of itself, is apt to militate against democratic responsiveness.

Because these conditions and these sources of frustration exist in almost every metropolis in the United States, one can find this theme consistently recurring throughout the metropolitan surveys: some kind of uniformity must be established if the metropolis is to govern itself properly. The unity may be of a very limited type, such as that represented by a metropolitan public-transit authority or a metropolitan water and sewerage authority, or the unity may be of a very broad and inclusive type: one government, and one government alone, to control the metropolis and see to its public needs.[17]

Western man has had a considerable experience with the metropolis. Out of this experience, out of the multitude of investigations, surveys, and studies, have come various fruitful approaches and systems for governing the metropolis. We should now look at some of those systems.

The Urban County. As pointed out in previous chapters, the county in the past has not made a particularly effective contribution to the urban governing process. But history, contrary to the popular adage, does not necessarily repeat itself. Is it possible that the county in the future will be able to convert itself into an effective governing instrument in the urban community?

There are a few counties in the United States today which indicate that the answer to this question might be yes. Arlington County, Virginia, and Montgomery County, Maryland, both lying on the fringes of the Washington, D.C., metropolitan area, are two such counties. But if there is to be a bellwether to lead the flock out of the rural wilderness, it will probably be Dade County, Florida.

The Experience in Dade County. Nothing short of a revolution has been achieved in Dade County within the past few years. Even if the revolution should come to naught, it is still impressive. Including all of the Miami standard metropolitan statistical area, the county government has been rejuvenated and reorganized to the point that it has become the metropolitan government for Miami. How did such a development come about? And what has been its success?

City-county consolidation proposals were presented to the voters of metropolitan Miami in 1947, and both proposals failed. Voting again in 1953 on a proposal to abolish the city of Miami and transfer all its functions to the county of Dade, the voters rejected the idea by a margin of only 980 votes out of 54,292. Immediately after this election the city of Miami created a board, named the Metropolitan Miami Board, to study the governmental problems of the city and its urban environment. The board requested the services of the University of Miami, and the university in turn engaged the Public Administration Service to do the actual survey of the metropolitan area.

In a subsequent report the members of the survey staff recommended that a metropolitan government for Miami, surrounding municipalities, and Dade County be established. In order to accomplish this objective, advised the report, a state constitutional amendment should be adopted, per-

[17] Government Affairs Foundation, *Metropolitan Surveys: A Digest* (Chicago: Public Administration Service, 1958), pp. 5–6.

mitting Dade County to frame a home-rule charter which would convert the county government into a genuine metropolitan government. But the report recommended that "the creation of the metropolitan government need not and should not carry with it the extinction of separate municipal governments in Dade County." [18] Unlike so many other metropolitan communities, Miami acted immediately upon the recommendations of the organizational study. After the adoption of a home-rule amendment to the state constitution, the county convened a charter commission to draft a home-rule charter, and it was approved by a narrow margin in May, 1957.

The charter provided for a board of county commissioners made up of five commissioners elected from as many single-member districts, five other commissioners nominated from the districts but elected at large, and one commissioner from each city of 60,000 population or over. By setting up the office of county manager and by other administrative stipulations, the charter effected a complete administrative reorganization of the county.

Among the powers which the charter conferred upon the county were most of those necessary to give the new metropolitan government control over areawide problems. In this respect, as in most others, the charter reflected the recommendations of the Public Administration Service study. The county was given areawide control over traffic and transportation, public safety, planning, health, welfare, and recreation; over libraries, museums, and other cultural facilities; over zoning, housing, and urban renewal; and over the levy and collection of taxes and special assessments. Although Article 5 assured the continuance of existing municipalities, the charter gave the county commissioners control over the authorization and creation of new municipalities.

Immediately after the new government had established itself in the county building, formidable opposition to it arose. The city of Miami, which had been principally responsible for the study by the Public Administration Service out of which the home-rule charter grew, led the other municipalities of the county in a concerted attack upon the new charter. Scarcely more than a year after the adoption of the charter, an amendment giving the municipalities wide-range autonomy came to a vote. It was rather decisively defeated.[19]

The infighting continued. In 1963 no fewer than ten amendments to the charter were proposed, and, of these, four received approval of the voters. These four provided for a council of nine members, all of whom were to be elected at large. One of these candidates, the amendment also provided,

---

[18] Public Administration Service, *The Government of Metropolitan Miami* (Chicago: The Service, 1954), p. 88.

[19] Reinhold P. Wolff, *Miami Metro: The Road to Urban Unity* (Coral Gables, Fla.: Bureau of Business and Economics Research, University of Miami, 1960), p. 129.

was to run as mayor and serve as permanent chairman of the council. Other changes were to make the sheriff elective instead of appointive, to increase the difficulty of charter amendment by the initiative, and to set up a modified Missouri plan for the selection of judges serving on the metropolitan court.[20]

What is the future of metropolitan government in the Miami region? After almost a decade under the new charter the metropolitan community is seeing comparatively few changes. Sniping at Metro will probably continue to be politically *de rigueur* for suburban councilmen, residents in the unincorporated areas of the county, chambers of commerce, and an assortment of other interest groups. Observers have seen two warring camps in Miami–Dade County, one represented by the "consolidationists" and the other by the "localists," and it has been the conflict between these two groups that has kept metropolitan politics in turmoil.[21]

The 1963 amendments may result in substantial change in the strength of metropolitan government or little change at all. Thomas J. Wood believes that the elective sheriff and the separately designated mayor may weaken the manager's position. On the other hand, he also suggests that the members of the new council, elected at large, could develop a more cosmopolitan point of view than former members, and that possibly "under a commission composed of men with this outlook, Metro will move ahead more rapidly in some fields." [22] All of this is conjecture. We can safely say only that the revolution in local affairs which has hovered on the Miami horizon like a Caribbean hurricane has not swept the country. Possibly the only important result of the establishment of Miami Metro, indeed, has been the complete reorganization of the county government. Relatively few of the long list of substantive powers which the county is authorized to exercise under the home-rule charter have as yet been utilized.[23] In the first few years of its existence, the politics of Miami Metro has been the politics of frustration.[24]

The Lakewood Plan. Beginning in 1954, Los Angeles County offered services on a large scale to cities on a contract basis. Because Lakewood, California, was the first of these contract cities, the label "Lakewood Plan" has become the usual designation of the system. As previously mentioned, for a local, indigenous approach to meeting some of the problems of the

[20] Thomas J. Wood, "Basic Revisions in Dade Charter," *National Civic Review*, LIII (January, 1964), pp. 39–41.

[21] John C. Bollens and Henry J. Schmandt, *The Metropolis: Its People, Politics, and Economic Life* (New York: Harper & Row, 1965), p. 507.

[22] Wood, *op. cit.*, p. 41.

[23] Wolff, *op. cit.*, pp. 129–131.

[24] For a somewhat more optimistic view of the success of the metropolitan government, see Edward Sofen, *The Miami Metropolitan Experiment* (Bloomington, Ind.: Indiana University Press, 1963), pp. 211–219.

metropolis, the Lakewood Plan seems to fit well into the southern California environment. Its being politically acceptable outside California is, at the moment, questionable.

Domination by the Central City. There are various methods by which the metropolis may be organized to permit domination of it by the central city. Such dominance may be achieved by the Honolulu system, by the energetic annexation of the surrounding territory, by city-county consolidation, and finally—though an unlikely possibility—by giving the city statehood within the federal system.

The Honolulu System. As described in the previous chapter, the Honolulu metropolitan area is the only one in the United States in which there is now no geographic disintegration and in which it cannot easily take place in the future. One government, the city and county of Honolulu, covers the entire island of Oahu.

Honolulu has also been saved, up to the moment at least, from vertical or functional disintegration. When Honolulu's home-rule charter was approved by the electorate in 1958 and then ratified in 1959 by the territorial legislature, the laws of the Territory of Hawaii recognized only one local government for the entire island of Oahu. Since statehood, the constitution and laws of the state of Hawaii have not changed the situation. Thus the Honolulu metropolis is governed by one local government and one state government.

With 75 percent of the population of Hawaii living on the island of Oahu, with the governor of the state living in Honolulu itself, with the city hall across the street from the statehouse, it would not be surprising if the state should take an active hand in the government of the metropolis. In fact, it already does. Though the police department is financed by the city, it is administered by a board appointed by the governor.[25] Tax assessment is a state function, as is operation of the schools. Care and maintenance of the school buildings is a local function.

Because of its unusual situation, and because Hawaii has a tradition which supports concentration of governmental authority, the Honolulu metropolis has achieved both a geographic and functional unity which probably can never be duplicated anywhere else in the United States. But if Honolulu cannot stand as a model for other American communities, it can, as Charlton Chute has observed, serve as a challenge to traditional thinking about the metropolis.[26]

Annexation. As we have already seen in an earlier chapter, annexation is a means of sometimes arresting and sometimes defeating geographic disin-

[25] *Charter of the City and County of Honolulu, Hawaii,* Art. VII., Sec. 7–101; *Revised Laws of Hawaii* (1955), Secs. 150–152.
[26] Charlton F. Chute, "The Honolulu Metropolitan Area: A Challenge to Traditional Thinking," *Public Administration Review,* XVIII (Winter, 1958), 7–13.

tegration in communities, both large and small. During the decade of the 1950's the central cities of all standard metropolitan statistical areas in the United States increased in population by 4,581,000. If they had not annexed territory, they would have gained in population by only 767,000.

Annexation is effective only if the central city has relative freedom to absorb outlying territory, only if its expansion has not already been choked off by the incorporation of satellite communities, and only if strong separatist tendencies have not developed in the area. As one may see in Table 9-2, only Texas' cities, by and large, seem to meet these criteria.

Table 9-2. Core-City Dominance Achieved by Means of Annexation

Core City	Population of Central City—1960	Population of Urban Fringe—1960
Amarillo, Tex.	137,969	none
Austin, Tex.	186,545	612
Beaumont, Tex.	119,175	3
El Paso, Tex.	276,687	441
Lubbock, Tex.	128,691	598
Midland, Tex.	62,625	649
Raleigh, N.C.	93,931	none
Topeka, Kan.	119,484	16
Tyler, Tex.	51,230	509
Wichita Falls, Tex.	101,724	380

Largely by means of annexation the small metropolis has sometimes achieved a remarkable governmental unity. Because of the freedom with which the Texas home-rule city may annex territory, it is not surprising that Texas cities dominate this table.

Source: U.S. Bureau of the Census, *1960 Census of Population* (1961), Vol. I, Part A, Table 22, pp. 40–49.

Although annexation may show real usefulness in establishing the dominance of the central city, even where it may be freely used it has a major weakness. A city, by means of annexation, may achieve geographic unity, but it still may be visited with progressive vertical or functional disintegration. It is this problem that annexation is not designed to meet.

City-County Consolidation. The combining of the city and county seems almost as difficult in American local government as the joining of nation-states in the international community, yet efforts to consolidate still continue. In 1961–1962 two major consolidations were achieved—Virginia Beach and Princess Anne County, Virginia, and Nashville and Davidson County, Tennessee—and one lesser one—South Norfolk and Norfolk County, Virginia. On the other hand, the consolidations of Memphis and Shelby County, Tennessee and of St. Louis and St. Louis County, Missouri, were firmly rejected by the voters in November, 1962.

The Nashville Metro. By all odds the most important city-county consolidation effected in recent years was that approved in June, 1962, for Nashville and Davidson County, Tennessee. Voting on a proposed home-rule charter, the electorate of metropolitan Nashville approved decisively the organization of a new government with jurisdiction over approximately one-half million people and 533 square miles of territory. The favorable vote, a surprising one considering the difficulties, came after more than a decade of effort on the part of Nashville citizens to correct some major deficiences in the government of the metropolitan area. The first major step in the effort was probably represented by a study published in 1952 which recommended, among other things, extensive annexations by the city of Nashville and the assumption by Davidson County of responsibility for county-wide functions.[27] In 1957 state legislation was passed which permitted the establishment of metropolitan charter commissions, and shortly thereafter a Nashville commission went to work drafting a charter. Providing for a consolidation of the city and the county, the charter was rejected by popular vote in 1958.[28]

But sentiment for a new metropolitan government would not die. In 1961 the question of whether to call together a new charter commission was approved by a favorable vote in both city and county. This commission proceeded to draft a charter similar to the one in 1958; and, as we have already seen, it was approved.

The charter achieves some important objectives for one of the larger metropolitan areas of the South. It creates a new metropolitan government, known as "The Metropolitan Government of Nashville and Davidson County."[29] It provides further for a metropolitan mayor—a strong mayor—and a metropolitan council of forty-one members including the vice-mayor, who is the presiding officer of the council and who is elected at large, five members elected at large, and thirty-five members elected from single-member districts. The metropolitan council possesses all the legislative powers of the old city council and the county court.

One of the most unusual features of the charter is its provision for two services areas, a general services district and an urban services district. The former includes all of the area subject to the jurisdiction of the metropolitan government; the latter all the area included within the former limits of the old city of Nashville. The urban services district is designated a separate municipal corporation, with a three-member urban council having the sole function of levying property taxes within the district. But the urban

[27] Community Services Commission, *A Future for Nashville* (Nashville, Tenn.: The Commission, June, 1952), p. 3.

[28] Daniel R. Grant and Lee S. Greene, "Survey, Dust, Action," *National Civic Review*, L (October, 1961), 466–471.

[29] *Charter for the Metropolitan Government of Nashville and Davidson County, Tennessee* (April, 1962), Art. 1, Sec. 1.01 (as approved June 28, 1962). See also Daniel R. Grant, "Consolidations Compared," *National Civic Review*, LII (January, 1963), 10–13, 29.

council is wholly subject to the authority of the metropolitan council and exists solely for the purpose of levying taxes for urban services not needed in the outlying sections of the metropolitan area.

Because of the historically close relationship between the city and the schools in the Nashville area, the metropolitan home-rule charter of 1962 provided for consolidation of the school function with other local functions. Members of the metropolitan school board are appointed by the mayor and confirmed by a two-thirds majority of the whole council. Although the school board is given a measure of autonomy under the charter, the school function is still clearly an integral part of the metropolitan government. The operational school budget, for example, is prepared by the school board for presentation to the metropolitan council. If the budget, as approved by the council, is in the opinion of the board insufficient to meet operational school needs, the board may, by a two-thirds majority of all its members, adopt a resolution which not only proposes an additional general property tax levy for the schools, but which also "calls for and initiates a referendum election to determine whether such additional tax should be levied." [30] By means of this unusual feature, the metropolitan council retains effective control over the school budget, and at the same time the school board is given the opportunity of initiating a tax referendum in case it feels that the council's levy is inadequate.

But what will happen, one might ask, to the satellite municipalities under the new charter? This problem is one which charter drafters met with considerable effectiveness. Although each suburban city continues in existence until it voluntarily gives up its charter, it may not annex territory. It may contract with the metropolitan government for the administration of any of its governmental functions. And no new city may be incorporated within the area of the metropolitan government.

We can see, in summary, that Nashville has taken a major step in the direction of unified metropolitan government. By eliminating much horizontal and functional disintegration, by establishing a strong executive authority and comprehensive powers in the metropolitan government, and by providing for differential service areas, the metropolitan home-rule charter is a strikingly novel attempt to change the character of metropolitan government of a major urban complex.

There are inadequacies in the Nashville charter, at least from the reformer's standpoint. The metropolitan tax assessor, for example, is elected; and because certain constitutional officers could not be eliminated by the charter, the register of deeds, sheriff, court clerk, public defender, and other officials must still be elected on a not-so-short ballot. Whether this affront to classic reform ideology will have political significance is a factor difficult to measure.

[30] *Ibid.*, Art. IX., Sec. 9.04.

Nashville has not achieved the unity of Honolulu, but it shows remarkable similarity to the Pacific metropolis. The difference between the two is that the unity in Honolulu is well established. In Nashville, it is relatively new; and whether it will survive, only time and local politics will tell.

Consolidation in Baton Rouge. In 1949, the people of the city of Baton Rouge and the parish of East Baton Rouge voted to bring the two governments together into a partial merger. The accentuation of metropolitan problems by population growth, governmental fragmentation of the community, and the relatively static character of public service capacities had convinced local political leaders, or a sizable proportion of them, that the governmental powers and resources available to them were inadequate to the task of meeting the public needs of 150,000 people.

Obviously a compromise, the new metropolitan government was, like Gaul, divided into three parts: the city (six times larger in area than formerly), the rural area, and the industrial districts. The legislative power of the government was placed in two councils—a city council of seven members and a parish council of nine members. But council membership overlapped: all seven city councilmen also served on the parish council. A single executive, a mayor-president, was to direct the administrative effort.

How has the Baton Rouge experiment fared in the two decades of its existence? Observers have called it successful, first, because it has survived and, second, because it has shown itself capable of adaptation to a changing environment. These two criteria of success are, to say the least, impressive.[31]

Separate Statehood. In their interminable fights with the state legislatures, the major cities of the metropolitan regions have sometimes longed for the independence of the state in the American federal system. Why should we, metropolitan leaders have asked themselves, continue beholden to state legislatures dominated by farmers and small-town lawyers and merchants, and to governors who often turn their backs on the cities? These metropolitan leaders know that some cities in Western federal systems—notably Hamburg, Bremen, and Vienna—have achieved the status of city-states. Although the advantages of this status to Vienna have been minimal, since Austria is a federal state in name only, Hamburg and Bremen have gained considerable autonomy from being city-states within the German federal system.

Metropolitan leaders know, too, that statehood would effect a monumental change in metropolitan government in the United States. Instead of being dominated by an archaic legal system, as they are now, the great cities of America would achieve substantial autonomy in finance and all

---

[31] William C. Havard, Jr., and Floyd L. Corty, *Rural-Urban Consolidation: The Merger of Governments in the Baton Rouge Area* (Baton Rouge, La.: Louisiana State University Press, 1964).

other functional areas; and—no insignificant change—each would have two senators in the United States Congress. A still further possible result of statehood might be that state boundaries would no longer arbitrarily divide a metropolitan region.

But, of course, separate statehood for the metropolis must be counted as little more than an idle dream. This is at least true for North American cities. Although Canada, the United States, and Mexico have governments that are federal in character, it seems unlikely that any North American city will be able to achieve the autonomy or the political separateness of Vienna, Hamburg, or Bremen. Under the U.S. Constitution, for example, no territory can be taken from a state without its consent, and it is unthinkable that any state would give up the rich tax base to be found in any metropolitan region. If the idea of the city-state will not die, that is only an indication of its logical validity. But an idea which has logical validity will often not have an iota of political strength.

The Federated Metropolis. To a great city beyond the Canadian border Americans may look for a working model of the federated metropolis. On January 1, 1954, the Toronto federation came into being. Because Toronto has had a number of years' experience with federation and because it has been studied and examined exhaustively, we need to take the measure of it. On January 20, 1953, the Ontario Municipal Board issued a series of recommendations pertaining to the Toronto metropolitan area which immediately gained the sympathetic attention of Premier L. M. Frost of the Province of Ontario. At the premier's instigation, legislation to carry out the main recommendations of the municipal board was introduced into the Ontario Parliament and the legislation was passed.[32]

In making its recommendations, the Ontario Municipal Board was concerned with the strategy of the possible. The board was concerned with meeting metropolitan-wide problems and, at the same time, with avoiding not only the objections to the continued independence of local governing units but also the objections to their consolidation. The goals which the board had in mind can be seen from the following significant quotation from its recommendation:

> The Board has also quite frankly attempted to prepare a plan which may be considered acceptable and practical and not too far in advance of the existing general level of public opinion and information in the whole metropolitan area. No form of government, national, provincial, or local, can be expected to survive for any length of time unless it satisfies the great majority of the people it is intended to serve. The Board is convinced that there is a growing sense of metropolitan unity

[32] Winston W. Crouch, "Metropolitan Government in Toronto," *Public Administration Review,* XIV (Spring, 1954), 85–95.

in the Toronto area and a widespread recognition of the need for a better form of local government. It is also convinced that at the present time and perhaps for a long time to come there will be an equally strong demand for the preservation of truly local units of government and a general recognition of their value.[33].

The municipal board wished to achieve a system, in short, which would at once be administratively effective and politically acceptable. A decade of experience has indicated that the board was remarkably astute in its evaluation of the Toronto situation. Unlike Miami Metro, the Toronto plan has seemingly enjoyed a wide degree of public acceptance: it has resulted in a metropolitan government which has proved to be effective enough to survive without the kind of continuous assault to which Dade County has been subjected.

At the outset, the government of the Toronto metropolis, formally known as the Municipality of Metropolitan Toronto, was made up of a federation of thirteen municipalities—the city of Toronto, three villages, four towns, and five townships. The metropolitan council, with twenty-four members plus a chairman, was composed of members who had their seats ex officio—by virtue of their being officers of the constituent municipalities. Only the chairman of the council, elected by the council itself, was not an ex officio member. The city of Toronto had twelve members on the council, and the twelve suburban municipalities had one each.[34]

Following the federal idea, the Toronto plan has sought to establish essentially three jurisdictional areas: (1) over those functions which are exclusively metropolitan, (2) over those functions which may be exercised concurrently, and (3) over those functions which are exclusively local. Metro was given exclusive authority over assessments, capital borrowing, and public transportation, police, and licensing. It shared jurisdiction with its constituent municipalities over water supply, sewerage, education, health, and a number of other functions. Only fire protection and the collection of local property taxes were functions which still rested exclusively with the city, the villages, the town, and the townships.

Has the Toronto federation been a success? John G. Grumm, in 1959, gave a qualified "Yes": "The federation plan has the great, overwhelming advantage that generally it will be more feasible politically than consolidation." [35] Frederick G. Gardiner, the intrepid chairman of Toronto Metro for almost a decade, would answer "Yes" with even fewer qualifications. The metropolitan government has shown itself to be a master of public-

---

[33] The Ontario Municipal Board, *Decisions and Recommendations of the Board* (Toronto, Canada: The Board, January 20, 1953), p. 89.

[34] John G. Grumm, *Metropolitan Area Government: The Toronto Experience* (Lawrence, Kans.: Governmental Research Center, University of Kansas, 1959), pp. 9, 19.

[35] *Ibid.*, pp. 19, 44.

works programming. The water capacity of the metropolis has been doubled; some $60 million has been invested in sewage disposal facilities; 150 new schools and 259 additions to old schools have been added to the educational plant. Above all, federation has reduced the tensions between and among the various governing units of the metropolis. As Frederick Gardiner put it, there is a "built-in liaison between the local councils and the metropolitan council which results from having the metropolitan council composed of persons elected to the local councils." [36]

Frank Smallwood, viewing the difficulties from a somewhat different perspective in 1963, identified the three major problems of the Toronto metropolitan government as (1) a growing imbalance in financial resources among the constituent units; (2) "the failure to achieve a cohesive spirit of metropolitan unity among these members; and (3) the reluctance on the part of Metro and its members to deal decisively with a number of important commitments and responsibilities." [37]

The growing consensus that some revision was necessary in the metropolitan government of Toronto resulted in the appointment of a Royal Commission in 1963 to look into Metro problems. After working for two years, the commission reported that the metropolitan organization should be retained, but that the thirteen municipalities should be consolidated into four cities, and that these cities should make up the constituent units of the metropolitan government.[38]

Following the temper if not the detail of the Royal Commission's recommendations, the Ontario Parliament, in 1966, passed legislation which altered the formal structure of Toronto Metro in several ways. In place of the thirteen municipalities, the new law provided for six cities varying from a population of 91,000 to 682,000. The membership of the new Metro council was increased to thirty-two, with the council to elect as its chairman either one of its own members or an outside person. In order to make representation on the council proportionate to the population of the constituent units, each city was given one representative for approximately 50,000 people. Thus the smallest unit, East York (population, 91,000), was given two representatives, and the largest, Toronto (population, 682,000), received 12 members.[39] The membership on the council retained its ex officio character.

Since the new government came into being as of the first of the year 1967,

[36] Frederick G. Gardiner, "Getting Things Started," *National Civic Review*, LI (January, 1962), 11.

[37] Frank Smallwood, *Metro Toronto: A Decade Later* (Toronto: Bureau of Municipal Research, 1963), p. 17.

[38] *Report of the Royal Commission on Metropolitan Toronto* (Toronto: The Province of Ontario, June, 1965), p. 200.

[39] Frank Smallwood, "Toronto's Metro Is Reconstructed," *National Civic Review*, LV (November, 1966), 590–591.

the experience with it has been insufficient to enable one to evaluate the merits of the change. Since the constituent units are all of rather considerable size, however, and since representation on the Metro council is roughly proportionate to population, one might expect a priori that fewer tensions would develop in the new government than in the old.

Other Aids to Metropolitan Unity. Metropolitan councils of government have been taking a role of increasing importance in the larger metropolitan areas, both in the United States and abroad. Much more than regional plan commissions, the councils aim at the establishment of rapport among metropolitan leadership and at a semblance of coherence in policy-making; and they have been set up from London to San Francisco.[40] Perhaps the most ambitious council organization of the 1960's was that proposed in 1966 for the Detroit region. Calling for representation from the city of Detroit, 6 surrounding counties, 106 other municipalities, 109 townships, and 165 school districts, the plan envisaged a general assembly, in which each government would have a voice, and a 35-member executive committee. Each type of government (cities, counties, townships, and school districts) would constitute a voting bloc, and three out of the four blocs would commit the council to a particular policy. The existing regional plan commission would be placed under the authority of the council, and the member governments would foot the bill for its operations.[41]

What of the future of such councils? Victor Jones views "voluntary metropolitan associations of local governments as the most promising development in our federal system." And Royce Hanson insists that the "councils of governments offer one of the most productive means of translating plans into action for many of America's metropolitan areas." [42] Whether such promise can be translated into reality presents a major challenge to urban leadership.

Linked with metropolitan councils will be the use of the special district, whether single or multifunctional. For those who like to think of limited goals—the people who think of politics as the art of the possible—special districts seem to be the only method, very often, by which a single function or series of functions can be administered on a metropolitan-wide basis. Politically, it seems to be much easier to set up a sewerage district or a transit authority than it is to achieve an areawide, general-purpose government.

---

[40] See Royce Hanson, *Metropolitan Councils of Governments,* Report M-32 (Washington, D.C.: Advisory Commission on Intergovernmental Relations, August, 1966); and Norman Prichard, "Reorganization of Local Government in Greater London," *Metropolitan Viewpoints,* I (November, 1966).

[41] See "Council for Detroit Region Proposed," *National Civic Review,* LV (October, 1966), 524–526.

[42] Victor Jones, "Associations of Local Governments: Patterns for Metropolitan Cooperation," *Public Affairs Report,* April, 1962, p. 4; and Royce Hanson, *op. cit.,* p. 35.

In St. Louis during the 1950's, where only sewage disposal was administered on a metropolitan-wide basis, dissatisfaction with the lack of metropolitan government led to an ambitious study of the problem by John Bollens and his associates. The Bollens study recommended a multifunctional metropolitan district government which, among other things, would assume responsibility for general property tax assessments, would control the areawide road and mass-transit systems, would partially control land use, and would absorb the functions of the metropolitan sewerage district.

As soon as a board of freeholders was convened to write a new home-rule charter for the proposed metropolitan government, it was immediately apparent that the limited-objectives point of view had its political deficiencies. The board very quickly polarized, with one group supporting the special district recommended by the survey and another strong group fighting for consolidation of city and county into a metropolitan county. The special-district idea won by a narrow margin, and when the board presented its charter to the people, it was soundly defeated. Three years later, in 1962, the municipal-county idea, which called for a total reorganization of the governments of St. Louis and St. Louis County, was taken to the polls. In a statewide vote involving a constitutional amendment, this idea too was soundly defeated.

A few months later, however, in early 1963, the Bi-State Development Agency, organized some years earlier under an interstate compact between Missouri and Illinois, absorbed all mass-transit lines operating in the St. Louis metropolitan region. For the first time in the history of the urban area a metropolitan function was taken over by a truly metropolitan agency, that is, by a public authority empowered to operate in both the Illinois and Missouri sections of the metropolis. (The metropolitan sewerage district has jurisdiction over the Missouri section only.)

From the limited evidence at hand, we can probably assume that most metropolitan areas will be forced to rely on the single-function or multifunctional district to meet areawide problems. Although, when viewed from an abstract, theoretical point of view, most special districts in the United States may well be either unnecessary or undesirable, it must be admitted that, particularly in the larger metropolitan areas, the special district does have a certain utility and would be difficult to dispense with. If the special district absorbs only genuinely metropolitan functions, it will not materially disturb existing local governments in the metropolitan area. This is an advantage politically, and it is also an advantage if one regards the large metropolis as essentially a pluralistic community in which the existing communities and villages will do battle to maintain a degree of local autonomy. Another point in favor of the special district is that it may more easily cross state lines than any other form of local government. The

Port of New York Authority is a classic example of this situation, as is the previously mentioned Bi-State Development Agency in the St. Louis metropolitan region.

But a basic problem with the special district—that of democratic control—remains unresolved. This problem can be ameliorated, on the other hand, if a number of single-purpose special districts can be merged into a single multipurpose district. John Bollens suggests one, or at most two, multifunctional districts for a single metropolitan area.[43] And he follows up this suggestion in the study of the St. Louis metropolitan area by recommending a single multifunctional district to take over all areawide functions in the Missouri portion of the St. Louis metropolitan area.

Few of the problems of metropolitan government can be solved without state assistance. That the states are not unaware of this fact is evidenced by a resolution passed by the Governors' Conference in July, 1962, which called for the states to move "promptly to assert vigorous leadership and to provide effective assistance with respect to problems of governmental structure, finance, and planning in metropolitan areas. . . ."[44] Some states have already set up planning commissions, such as the Northeastern Illinois Metropolitan Area Planning Commission for the Chicago area, in order to facilitate metropolitan-wide planning. Minnesota has a state commission with the power to forbid wildcat incorporations in metropolitan fringe areas. American states might take a leaf from the book of various Canadian provinces, where, either by special legislation or by order of an administrative board, local government boundaries may be adjusted to fit new situations.[45] Furthermore, as an aid to greater state awareness of urban problems in general, some states, as we have already seen, have set up offices fixed with the responsibility of a continuing study of local governmental problems.

Finally, the state itself might assume the active administration of one or more metropolitan functions. Thus a state department of public works, for example, could undertake control over transportation and sewage disposal and could administer those functions from a state rather than a local level. As we shall see presently, this idea essentially has been advanced for the Tokyo metropolitan area.

---

[43] John C. Bollens, *Special-district Governments in the United States* (Berkeley, Calif.: University of California Press, 1957), pp. 260–261.

[44] "Resolutions Adopted by the Governors' Conference," *State Government,* XXV (Autumn, 1962), 256. The Council of State Governments has recommended a single multipurpose authority for the metropolitan area, with representation on the governing body from the councils of existing units. *The Book of the States, 1964–1965* (Chicago: The Council of State Governments, 1964), p. 112.

[45] K. Grant Crawford, *Canadian Municipal Government* (Toronto: University of Toronto Press, 1954), pp. 68–71.

The Foreign Metropolis

That American cities are not alone as they wrestle with metropolitan problems has already been evident from our review of the situation in Toronto and other Canadian metropolitan centers. Looking farther afield, we can see that in Europe and Asia also cities face the metropolitan dilemma.

The Reorganization of the London Government. Perhaps the most ambitious plan for the governing of a large metropolis anywhere in the world was the one offered for London by the Royal Commission on Local Government in Greater London. Set up in December, 1957, by the British government, this commission, which soon became known after the name of its chairman as the Herbert Commission, reported unanimously on a plan for the Greater London area in October, 1960. Most of the commission's recommendations were supported in a government white paper submitted to Parliament in November, 1961. And in February, 1962, the House of Commons supported the proposals set up in the white paper by 302 votes to 198.

During its three years of work, the commission rejected some major ideas: (1) that metropolitan power should be transferred to the central government, (2) that metropolitan government should be carried on by additional ad hoc authorities, and (3) that interlocal cooperation between and among existing local units of governments in Greater London could solve the metropolitan problem.[46] The commission recommended, rather, that a two-tier system of government for Greater London be set up, with a single government encompassing the entire area and with 52 boroughs of 100,000 to 250,000 population making up the lower tier. These 52 local governments, reported the commission, should replace a hodgepodge of 112 governments which had had a hand in governing Greater London. Since the government favored boroughs with a minimum population of 200,000, however, the Greater London Act, which cleared Parliament in 1963, provided for 32 boroughs in the lower tier.[47]

The Herbert Commission report, as one might expect, had both its supporters and its critics. Professor William Robson, insisting that the government of Greater London was in a crisis, argued that some kind of reformed local government for Greater London must be set up or centralized control from Whitehall would result. Observing that the Herbert Commission was not in the least doctrinaire about its approach to local government, except perhaps for "a conviction that local self-government is good in itself," Rob-

[46] L. J. Sharpe, "The Report of the Royal Commission on Local Government in Greater London," *Public Administration Review*, XXXIX (Spring, 1961), 73–92.
[47] Frank Smallwood, *Greater London: The Politics of Metropolitan Reform* (Indianapolis, Ind.: The Bobbs-Merrill Co., 1965), pp. 280–282.

son strongly supported the major part of the commission's recommendation. In a summary of his views, Robson wrote that "it will be a calamity if
the Report of the Herbert Commission is rejected or put into cold storage." [48]

Lining up almost solidly against the Herbert Commission's recommendations, as well as those of the white paper, were the representatives of the
Labour party, both in the local councils and in the Parliament. Because the
London Labour party was solidly in control of the London County Council, according to Robson, and because the London County Council would
be abolished if the recommendations of the Herbert Commission were carried out, the Labour party opposed the commission's recommendations on
the grounds of political self-preservation. Peter Robshaw, writing in 1961,
refused to admit the validity of Professor Robson's thesis that there was
a crisis in the government of Greater London. Making a frontal assault
upon the recommendations of the Herbert Commission, Robshaw proclaimed that "the humanity of local government is in danger of being lost
if we try to force community needs and services to fit a tidy administrative
scheme or an academic theory." [49]

If Labour was quite solidly opposed to and the Conservatives were generally in support of the commission's position, these were by no means the
only elements involved in the vigorous political battle which began after
the commission submitted its report. Joining with the London County
Council and the London Labour party in denouncing the plan were the
county councils of nearby Surrey and Kent and the London Teachers' Association. Other groups expressed opposition; but, except for the teachers,
their opposition was muted during most of 1961—until, that is, the government issued its white paper in December, 1961. Thereupon, mounting
attacks forced the government to retreat and then, in March, 1962, to coun-
terattack by forcing favorable votes in both the House of Commons and the
House of Lords on the general principle of metropolitan reform.[50]

This tactic was not to still the critics of the plan, however, and during the
summer of 1962 the opponents joined forces in the Committee for London
Government, which began circulating a protest petition against the government bill with the aim of getting 500,000 signatures on it. But the
government was not to be deflected from its purposes, and with a secure
majority in Parliament it pressed forward with its reform plans during the
remainder of 1962.

Throughout 1963, there was bitter infighting in both houses of Parlia-

[48] William A. Robson, "The Reform of London Government," *Public Administration*, XXXIX (Spring, 1961), 59–71.

[49] Peter Robshaw, "Another View on the London Government Royal Commission,"
Public Administration, XXXIX (Autumn, 1961), 247.

[50] The author is indebted to Smallwood, *Greater London*, for the remainder of this
discussion.

ment over the government bill. After the bill finally cleared Commons (where more than 1,000 amendments were offered), it ran into equally heavy Labour opposition in the House of Lords. The longest session of Lords on record came during debate on the bill. But the Conservatives were able to force the bill through, and it received Royal Assent in July, 1963.

"Why," Frank Smallwood asks, "should the supposedly innocuous issue of local governmental reorganization possess such a pervasive political wallop?" For one thing, the Labour party was as securely entrenched in the London County Council as the Socialist party in the city of Vienna. Just as the Socialists in Austria could be assured of power as long as they controlled Vienna, so Labour could use its power over the British capital to advance its goals, both locally and nationally. Viewing the reorganization as a sly Conservative plot to gain political advantage at its expense, the Labour party fought it tooth and nail. That Conservative hopes and Labour fears were premature is indicated by the sweeping Labour victory (sixty-four Labour seats to thirty-six Conservative) in the first election of the new Greater London Council membership in 1964. But the Conservative victory in the council elections of 1967 may show that those hopes and fears were not entirely groundless.

Another reason for the vigor of the contest over reorganization lay in the high hopes of Labour for the comprehensive school and the equally high order of disenchantment Conservatives had with the idea. Beginning in 1947, the London County Council had experimented widely with the comprehensive school and had sixty of them in operation when the reorganization plan was proposed by the Herbert Commission.

The comprehensive school represented to Labour a blow at what it regarded as an otherwise tradition-bound school system which served to reinforce the strength of a class society. The Conservatives, on the other hand, regarded the comprehensive school program as an attempt to destroy quality education, or at least to dilute that quality. And so the clash over reorganization represented a clash of educational philosophies. More than just a structural reorganization, in other words, the governmental changes recommended for London by the Herbert Commission and later approved in modified form by Parliament gave many participants in the battle very high stakes to fight for. In this regard, the London struggle is representative of metropolitan political activity throughout the Western world.

Metropolitan Government in Tokyo. On the other side of the world from London, and in a land and culture far different from that of England, metropolitan Tokyo faces the problems of planning, traffic control, water supply, urban sprawl, and many others that are not too unlike those faced by Western cities. The government of the metropolis is divided into two levels: the Tokyo Metropolitan Government at the top and a host of smaller units at the bottom (23 partially self-governing wards, eleven cities, and three counties). Although the system seems reasonably stable, the metropolitan government has been attacked both by the national government and by the constituent units, especially the wards. In 1962, national agencies offered two reorganization plans, under both of which the Tokyo metropolitan government would lose many of its powers to the central government and to the wards. It is not surprising that the Tokyo metropolitan assembly in June, 1962, strongly attacked both ideas, with the argument that if Tokyo metropolitan government is not by any means perfect, "the cause may be attributed to a lack of a centrally-and-locally coordinated plan and to the Central Government's various financial restrictions upon metropolitan administration." [51] The central government's plans were not implemented.

Summary

In spite of the welter of evidence concerning the metropolis, whether it be in the United States or abroad, it is difficult to arrive at many conclusions which will be equally valid for all metropolitan centers and for any length of time. This is in spite of the easily documented fact that the problems which face metropolises around the world are very similar except perhaps in those which are largely nonindustrial.

In this chapter we have been talking about two quite different phenomena, each of which is called a "metropolis." The metropolis of Chicago, New York, London, or Tokyo is quite different from the metropolis with a core city of 100,000 population and a limited urbanized fringe area. Although we have sought to encompass both phenomena in our discussions in this chapter, the wide differences between them should always be kept in mind.

The small metropolises, which make up the great bulk of the American metropolitan centers identified by the U.S. Bureau of the Census, are basically units which can be governed in a unitary fashion. There is very little logic in having a Grand Rapids, a Lubbock, or a Sacramento governed by a large number of jealous and competing local authorities. The ideological monism with which most scholars approach the urban community in the twentieth century has the strength, when applied to such communities, which only logic reinforced by an abundance of evidence can give to any idea. It is the annexation policy of Amarillo, or the consolidation of Nashville and Davidson County, which seems to point the way to governmental unity in an urban community which is in itself a unit. Unity, moreover, seems to have a considerable measure of political acceptance in the smaller metropolis.

[51] "New Metropolitan System Contemplated in Government Circles," *Tokyo Municipal News*, XII (August, 1962), 1.

For the large metropolis—let us say arbitrarily for the one which exceeds 500,000 population—the unity approach loses much of its force and unquestionably a good deal of its logic. Large metropolises, after all, are usually a central city plus a conglomeration of smaller cities and other governments, closely joined together. If the great metropolis is something more than a bunch of suburbs in search of a city, as a wag once characterized Los Angeles, it nevertheless does not usually achieve the unity of one with a population of 100,000, either demographically or politically. It is not surprising, therefore, that most of the studies of the large metropolis have recognized the presence of both a unity and a diversity in the great urban center. Using the term somewhat loosely, we can conclude that the large metropolis is a "natural" federation. This was one conclusion of the Herbert Commission in London. This was the conclusion of Arthur Bromage when he wrote that "development of a full-fledged federation appears to be the only course of action if the theory of self-government is to be carried to the metropolitan level." [52]

Change, of whatever kind, comes hard in the metropolis, because people view the metropolis differently; and with the difference in viewpoint will come political conflict. In addition to these differences in values are differences in personal advantage. There seems to be an inevitable growth around every formal structure of an informal organization that has both meaning and utility to a variety of people and groups. And although destruction of the formal structure may not mean the elimination of the informal one, it will generate sufficient fear, as Scott Greer has said, to mobilize the status quo. Any change, once again, comes hard.

It is altogether possible, nevertheless, for the metropolis to be governed in a reasonably efficient and democratic manner. It is also quite possible, as we have seen, for major reforms to be achieved in metropolitan government. Whether the metropolis is to be governed as a unit or whether it is to be governed by a two-tiered structure depends largely upon the politics of the given situation. We can be sure, therefore, that governing the metropolis will remain one of the great political problems of this age, and perhaps of the ages that lie ahead.

Annotated Bibliography

Because the social studies are closely interrelated, no examination of the political metropolis can be truly fruitful without extensive reading in sociology, economics, and geography. Some of the recent works of this nature which should be read by every political scientist interested in the metropolis are books by the French geographer Gottmann and the sociologist-political scientist Greer. See Jean Gottmann, *Megalopolis* (New York: The Twentieth Century Fund, 1961);

[52] Arthur W. Bromage, *Political Representation in Metropolitan Agencies* (Ann Arbor, Mich.: Institute of Public Administration, University of Michigan, 1962), p. 94.

and Scott Greer, *Governing the Metropolis* (New York: John Wiley & Sons, 1962). The economist Raymond Vernon has sought to summarize and interpret the findings of the ambitious New York Metropolitan Region Study and to formulate projections of the region's development to 1985. See Raymond Vernon, *Metropolis, 1985* (Cambridge, Mass.: Harvard University Press, 1960).

Rarely have the scholars and staff members of a metropolitan survey finished their tasks and then, after a passage of time to give them perspective and after a reexamination of their data to give them further insight, written and published an analysis of their own research findings. Yet this is precisely the course taken by John C. Bollens and his associates. After concluding a survey of the St. Louis metropolitan area in the late 1950's, they published an extensive reexamination of their study in 1961. See John C. Bollens (ed.), *Exploring the Metropolitan Community* (Berkeley, Calif.: University of California Press, 1961).

Case studies of metropolitan government abound, most of them the result of scholarly group effort. A historical review of these efforts may be found in a fairly recent publication. See Government Affairs Foundation, *Metropolitan Surveys: A Digest* (Chicago: Public Administration Service, 1958). The fate of most of these surveys has been to gather dust on library shelves, but at least two have led to striking changes: Community Services Commission, *A Future for Nashville* (Nashville, Tenn.: the Commission, June, 1952); and Public Administration Service, *The Government of Metropolitan Miami* (Chicago: the Service, 1954). Two intensive studies of the political changes in Nashville are contained in books by Booth and Hawkins. See David A. Booth, *Metropolitics: The Nashville Consolidation* (East Lansing, Mich.: Institute for Community Development and Services, Michigan State University, 1963); and B. W. Hawkins, *Nashville Metro: The Politics of City-County Consolidation* (Nashville: Vanderbilt University Press, 1966). And the Miami–Dade County experiment has been more than adequately treated by Wolff and Sofen. See Reinhold P. Wolff, *Miami Metro: The Road to Urban Unity* (Coral Gables, Fla.: Bureau of Business and Economics Research, University of Miami, 1960); and Edward Sofen, *The Miami Metropolitan Experiment* (Bloomington, Ind.: Indiana University Press, 1963). One of the latest case studies to appear is a book of readings on the Detroit metropolitan area. See Robert J. Mowitz and Deil S. Wright, *Profile of a Metropolis* (Detroit, Mich.: Wayne State University Press, 1962). For Toronto, see *Report of the Royal Commission on Metropolitan Toronto* (Toronto: Province of Ontario, June, 1965).

But the case study of the metropolis, for all of its merit, has the serious deficiency of being an isolated study in space and time. Not only may the metropolis change from decade to decade, but the truths found in one metropolis may also be irrelevant in another. That a scientific view of the metropolis, if one is to be had, must involve perspectives and generalizations of wide application is a proposition that now has wide acceptance. Scott Greer attempted to reach this level of valid generalization in *Governing the Metropolis,* mentioned above. So did Janowitz, Wright, and Delany, even though their data were drawn from the Detroit metropolis. See Morris Janowitz, Deil Wright, and William Delany, *Public Administration and the Public—Perspectives Toward Government in a Metropolitan Community* (Ann Arbor, Mich.: Institute of Public Administration, University of Michigan, 1958). By extensive use of the literature on metropolitan government and by recourse to his own practical experience in the city government of Syracuse, New York, Webb S. Fiser has written a study of the metropolis which successfully reaches the level of valid generalization without, however, having the catholicity of Scott Greer's treatment. See Webb S. Fiser, *Mastery of the Metropolis* (Englewood Cliffs, N.J.: Prentice-Hall, 1962).

Other books of value in metropolitan area study are by Stephen B. Sweeney and George S. Blair (eds.), *Metropolitan Analysis* (Philadelphia: University of Pennsylvania Press, 1958); the editors of *Fortune, The Exploding Metropolis* (Garden City, N.Y.: Doubleday & Co., 1958); Amos H. Hawley, *The Changing Shape of Metropolitan America* (Glencoe, Ill.: The Free Press, 1956); Tax Institute, *Financing Metropolitan Government* (Princeton, N.J.: The Institute, 1955); and W. A. Robson, *Great Cities of the World* (London: George Allen & Unwin, 1954).

A sample of excellent monographic studies should include "Metropolis in Ferment," *The Annals*, CCCXIV ((November, 1957); "A Symposium on Metropolitan Regionalism," *University of Pennsylvania Law Review*, CV (February, 1957); Advisory Commission on Intergovernmental Relations, *Factors Affecting Voter Reactions to Governmental Reorganization in Metropolitan Areas* (Washington, D.C.: The Commission, May, 1962); Arthur W. Bromage, *Political Representation in Metropolitan Agencies* (Ann Arbor, Mich.: Institute of Public Administration, University of Michigan, 1962); and the study of the Baton Rouge consolidation, William C. Havard, Jr., and Floyd L. Corty, *Rural-Urban Consolidation: The Merger of Governments in the Baton Rouge Area* (Baton Rouge, La.: Louisiana State University Press, 1964). An extended administrative study of the New Orleans metropolis may be found in L. Vaughan Howard and Robert S. Friedman, *Government in Metropolitan New Orleans*, Tulane Studies in Political Science, Vol. VI (New Orleans: Tulane University, 1959).

Undoubtedly the most complete summary of the findings and of the literature on the American metropolis is John C. Bollens and Henry J. Schmandt, *The Metropolis: Its People, Politics, and Economic Life* (New York: Harper & Row, 1965); and the best book by an American scholar on a foreign metropolis is Frank Smallwood, *Greater London: The Politics of Metropolitan Reform* (Indianapolis, Ind.: The Bobbs-Merrill Co., 1965).

Valuable background material for the study of both the Western and non-Western metropolis may be found in Kurt Steiner, *Local Government in Japan* (Stanford, Calif.: Stanford University Press, 1965); and R. P. Dore, *City Life in Japan* (Berkeley, Calif.: University of California Press, 1958). A paperback edition of the latter was published in 1965. See also Brian Chapman, *Introduction to French Local Government* (London: George Allen & Unwin, 1953); Samuel Humes and Eileen Martin, *The Structure of Local Governments Throughout the World* (The Hague: Martinus Nijhoff, 1961); and Mark Kesselman, *The Ambiguous Consensus—A Study of Local Government in France* (New York: Alfred A. Knopf, 1967). For a selected bibliography on the governmental problems of metropolitan areas throughout the world except for the United States and Canada, see D. Halász, *Metropolis* (The Hague: Martinus Nijhoff, for the International Union of Local Authorities, 1st ed., 1961; 2nd ed., 1967). And, finally, the charters or basic statutes for Baton Rouge, Nashville, Dade County, Toronto, London, and Seattle may be found in Joseph F. Zimmerman (ed.), *Metropolitan Charters* (Albany, N.Y.: Graduate School of Public Affairs, State University of New York, 1967).

PART III

Governing the City

CHAPTER 10

*F*orms of City Government

Importance of Structure

Shortly after the end of World War II an aircraft made the first controlled flight through the sound barrier. Although man had long since built tools which could send projectiles aloft at tremendous speeds (from rockets fired by the Chinese to cannonballs aimed against the walls of a late medieval city), never before had man himself exceeded the speed of sound. The universal excitement over breaking the sound barrier thus was amply justified.

Now the event is commonplace: whoever has been within 30,000 feet of a jet aircraft—and who has not, in these days?—knows the explosion-like turbulence of the air called the "sonic boom." Yet no person who lived through the excitement created by the first sonic boom will forget the lengthy discussions over aircraft form and structure that it engendered. Not only engineers and mathematicians but laymen in general discussed air foils, power plants, instrumentation—esoteric problems of how to construct a machine that could safely conduct man into the serene regions beyond the speed of sound.

All of this is but a dramatic example of how the machine has affected our everyday thinking. Being machine-minded, we tend to become wholly mechanistic in our values and our philosophy. If a new machine can produce 10,000 clothespins per hour whereas an old one could produce only 1,000, we replace the old with the new. When motorcars, or even books, can be produced on an assembly line, we substitute efficiency for craftsmanship; and only occasionally does someone protest the inhumanity of the new mechanics. More production means more and cheaper goods, and more goods mean a better life. This is our answer to the artist or philosopher who would challenge progress; this is the measure of our faith in the machine.

Our interest in form and structure extends not only to machinery, but also to many of our institutions. One of the basic divisions in American Christian churches centers about the mechanics of religious organization. Whether the local church should be controlled by the congregation or the bishop—whether, in short, the best form of church organization is congregational or episcopal—has called forth reams of clerical and lay debate.

In state and national politics, too, the discussion of governmental structure goes on apace. We hear, constantly, praise of our form of government. We talk a great deal about the proper role of the courts or the legislative bodies. We debate the proper functions of the governor or the President. Never do we really, however, question the *basic* structure of either the state or the federal government.

The situation is different, however, in local government. We may accept the basic structure of state and nation, but we are far from agreeing on any one pattern of local government. One of the great debates that has stirred urban Americans over the last half-century has been the argument over the proper form of municipal government. During that period some 2,000 cities and villages have adopted the council-manager form. In hundreds more the question has been put to the voters, and council-manager government has been rejected. In some of these cities the vigor and intensity of the campaigns has been exceeded by the debate on no other issue—state, national, or international.

These political battles, these arguments over forms of city government have broken friendships, impaired business relationships, and even divided church congregations. Council-manager government is, to some people, as American as Tom Sawyer; to others, as subversive as the Kremlin. In one city during the campaign to adopt council-manager government, a college professor, speaking in favor of the change, was accused by a local patriotic group of advocating overthrow of the government. In another city, the manager was pictured, in cartoons and in verbal propaganda, as a carpetbagger who would move into the city, dominate it for awhile, and then move on to other fields of exploitation. These debates over structure, even though they sometimes engender more heat than light, nevertheless strengthen the citizen's awareness of his importance to the city. On such issues he can participate directly in the decision. On other matters, he can do little but fume or write his congressman.

Yet both the reformers and the standpatters put far too much emphasis on the mere mechanics of government. Government might bear some resemblance to the machine or to the factory, but the too-mechanistic approach to the city or any other government is sadly amiss. So often with council-manager government, the reformer believes that he has the means, at last, to cure at a blow the main ills of his city government. The standpatter uses the other side of the same coin: he fears that change to city-manager government will put a strong man in city hall and reduce his influence, increase his taxes, and subject his city to control by an outsider.

Both of these positions are mechanistic; both attribute too much importance to the structure of government. There has been a prolonged tendency in the literature on American local government to ignore the informal organizations that seem to exist within every administrative structure and that seem to influence every part of the daily life of the institution.

On the other hand some academicians, and even an occasional administrator, have been led to the other extreme of emphasizing the informal systems in administration almost to the exclusion of the formal structure. That this primary emphasis on the informal, however, is as hazardous as the older involvement almost exclusively with the formal is indicated by the following comment: "to say that . . . informal structures are not completely determined by the formal institution is not to say that they are entirely independent of it. For informal organizations develop in response to the opportunities created and the problems posed by their environment, and the formal organization constitutes the immediate environment of the groups within it." [1] Structure, in other words, is always important, and because it is, let us look now at the formal governmental organizations which exist in American cities.

Forms of Government Characterized by the Weak Executive

The Commission Plan. On a stormy Friday evening, September 7, 1900, the people of Galveston, Texas, sat down to dinner. Few of them gave any thought to the weather. If any citizen of this city built on sand listened to the sound of the Gulf of Mexico pounding on the beaches, he did so with a sense of pleasure rather than alarm. To every Galvestonian—and there were 37,000 of them—the sea was a source of good, not evil. The sea brought commerce from around the world, piled up money in the local banks, put delicacies on the citizen's table, cooled his house, gave him constant pleasure. On this September evening in 1900 it would have been hard to convince anyone of the sea's malevolence.

After dinner a few people went out to look at the storm. Already breakers were pushing into the front yards of the houses nearest the sea. It was obvious that the Gulf would soon be in the town. But no real Galvestonian would be alarmed by a foot of saltwater in his backyard. Since the highest point of the city was a mere 8.7 feet above sea level, seawater had at one time or another washed through virtually every street in town. Houses were built on platforms, high and sturdy, to defeat the rising waters. The city was confident of itself; it felt no alarm; it went to bed for a good night's sleep.[2]

At four o'clock the next morning, Joseph Cline, chief clerk of the

[1] Peter M. Blau and W. Richard Scott, *Formal Organizations—A Comparative Approach* (San Francisco: Chandler Publishing Co., 1962), p. 6.

[2] Much of the following description of the Galveston disaster is taken from John Edwards Weems, *A Weekend in September* (New York: Henry Holt & Co., 1957).

weather bureau station in Galveston, got out of bed and with a sense of uneasiness looked out into his backyard. Although the Cline residence was over five blocks from the Gulf, the sea was already there. With great perturbation, Cline realized that the storm was worse than he had predicted.

Throughout Saturday morning the waters rose steadily. About eleven o'clock a group of people, some of them strangers, gathered at the railroad station wanting to flee the city. They were too late; the last train out of Galveston had left the city shortly after nine o'clock. Late in the morning, Henry Ketchum, son of Galveston's chief of police, tried to get to the beach on horseback. Two blocks from where the beach had once been, surf forced him back.

When it was that the first house broke up, no one knows; but it was probably in the early afternoon. As soon as that structure collapsed, the sea took up the debris and threw it against the next houses. The weakest of them fell, and the sea gathered more debris. This process continued until each wave was a huge battering ram—part water, part debris—hurled against the city. By nightfall, death and total destruction ringed the city. Four hundred people huddled into the city hall. When the tower and third floor collapsed under the pressure of 120 mile-per-hour winds, the police chief had to keep order by gunpoint.

By Saturday night, half of Galveston was destroyed; the rest was severely damaged. One-sixth of the population was dead or injured. Public sanitation was reduced to the level of the jungle; food supplies were short; the city had no fresh water. Hungry, thirsty, injured, often without adequate clothing and shelter, the Galvestonian wondered how much longer he could stay alive.

The looting began on Sunday morning, and the mayor put all able-bodied policemen on the streets. The soldiers stationed at Fort Crockett —those who had not drowned—supplemented the police. But seventy policemen and thirty soldiers were not enough. The mayor began swearing in citizens as temporary policemen.

As soon as the storm abated on Sunday morning, the city moved quickly to rescue the victims trapped under the debris. Some of them were never reached; many who had survived the storm died in the wreckage simply because the rescue team could not reach them. An emergency almost equal to that of rescue was the identification and burial of the dead. To this task the city—both its official personnel and its citizenry—moved with grim urgency. Many of the dead were taken by barge out into the Gulf and buried in the sea that had destroyed them. Other bodies were buried in the sand where they were found.

Clearly, the city was not paralyzed. Both the city's people and its emergency government moved decisively to meet the overwhelming emergency. Help eventually came from the outside, true enough; but for the most part the city doctored its own wounds, and it did so with a rather novel governing apparatus.

When disaster struck Galveston on that September weekend in 1900, the city had a weak-mayor form of government. The council was elected, twelve aldermen from as many wards. This was a government which had sometimes been inadequate to the city's needs in normal times; it was wholly inept in disaster. Moreover, the legal concept of the city as a creature of the state of Texas was ludicrous under the present circumstances. And since no city has any considerable amount of emergency powers, it was inevitable that Galveston should be forced to act extralegally.

At two o'clock Sunday afternoon a group of leading citizens met at the call of the mayor to organize a relief committee. This group, called the Central Relief Committee, immediately became the de facto government of Galveston.[3] Several basic characteristics of the committee helped explain its success in bringing an ordered existence back into the city. First, there was the quality of leadership found on the committee. As with the medieval city, the colonial town, and the city in the early days of the republic, the "real" leaders of Galveston became, at one and the same time, its political leaders. The committee, moreover, was not only a deliberative body but an action group; to each of its members it assigned a responsibility which belonged to that person and to him alone. Thus was the monumental task of reconstruction parceled out: distribution of food, water, and other supplies; maintenance of order; handling of city funds and city correspondence; burial of the dead; care of the injured.

Still a further factor in the committee's success was the virtually total support of the community: an overwhelming public consensus. Some might protest the lack of drinkable water for both people and animals and others might cry out at the primitive conditions of the hospitals; but no one would say that water supply and care of the injured were not tasks that should be done, and done regardless of cost. Such consensus and social cohesiveness are as inevitable corollaries of disaster as they are of war. They simplified greatly the task of governing the wrecked city.

A final advantage resting with the committee was that it was a de facto government, not one in law. Released from the dead hand of Dillon's rule, the city did not need to wait for the consent of the state to accomplish its task. The great seas took away many things from Galveston, but at the same time they gave the city something it had never had before, and has not had since: a vast amount of governmental power which no one would question. For a fortnight Galveston was a free city.

Believing that they had discovered a new form of government with revolutionary possibilities, the citizens of Galveston went to the Texas legisla-

[3] Central Relief Committee, *Report* (Galveston, Tex.: The Committee, May 2, 1902).

ture some weeks after the flood and requested a new city charter, which incorporated the basic elements of the de facto government set up as the Central Relief Committee on September 9, 1900. Under the second postdisaster
charter (the courts had ruled the first one unconstitutional), the city council was made up of a mayor and four commissioners elected from the city at
large for two-year terms. Each of the five elected officials was given a city
department to administer; the members of the council, collectively, became
the legislative authority of the city; individually, they made up the executive branch.

Commission government, as it developed, had some elements that en-
deared it to the municipal reformer. The most clear-cut of these elements
were (1) the short ballot and (2) the concentration of all municipal power
in the council.

The first of these characteristics—the short ballot—struck down the
practice, inherited from the Jacksonian era, of electing a vast array of local
officials—administrative, legislative, and judicial. Under the commission
plan, in its pure form, the only city officials elected were the commissioners
themselves. (Sometimes one may find an elective traffic judge, or other official, but these are only incidental variations from the norm.)

The reformer also cheered the concentration of power in the council as a
truly significant development in American city government. Too long had
American cities, he argued, unimaginatively copied the theory and practice of separation of powers and checks and balances as they were used in
the state and national governments. The reformer did not see, however,
that far from being new, Galveston's concentration of power in the council
was a return to early American experience: in colonial cities the bulk of
municipal power—executive, legislative, and judicial—had been centered in legislative bodies.

Some elements of the commission plan were soon to disenchant the reformer and lead him to seek other governmental devices. Since the council
retained all of the power of the city, at least in theory, there was no room for
a strong executive: the mayor was but another member of the council, a
kind of superior among equals, if indeed he was that. By ordinance or resolution the council set both legislative and administrative policy, and the
mayor was in no position to assume a role of policy leadership.

Nor was he in a position of administrative leadership. After members of
the council set policy collectively, they carried it out individually. Each
member of the council was administrative head of a department: he was, in
short, both administrator and legislator. If the commission was made up of
five members, the city automatically had five departments. Thus, in Illinois, the statutes provided for departments of public affairs, accounts and
finances, public health and safety, streets and public improvements, and
public property. The mayor headed public affairs; each of the four com-

missioners headed one of the four other departments. The structure of government was simple; the responsibility for governing was firmly fixed in the members of the council. (See Figure 10-1.)

Other features of commission government were more representative of reform ideology than of the plan itself. The commissioners were usually elected at large, rather than from wards, in order to give the council (it was argued) a broad, instead of a parochial, point of view. More often than not the commissioners were elected on a nonpartisan ballot. Party government, so the reformers thought, was good for the state and nation, but not for the city. Often, too, the initiative, referendum, and recall were tacked on to commission government, and in some states—Illinois is again an example —these triplets of reform became a distinct feature of commission government.

Hardly more than a decade after the destruction of Galveston, the critics

Figure 10-1 Formal Organization of a Commission Government

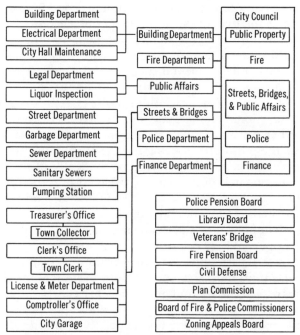

The government of East St. Louis, Illinois, gives a good deal of insight into how formal administrative arrangements are made in commission government. More important, in the case of this city, is the invisible government behind the organization chart: the mayor, as political leader, is in firm control of both policy and administration.

Source: William O. Winter *et al., Organization and Management of the Government of East St. Louis* (Carbondale, Ill.: Southern Illinois University, 1961), p. 1.

of the commission plan were as numerous as its friends. Probably the two most glaring defects identified by the foes of the system were (1) the absence of clear-cut executive authority and (2) amateur administration.

Since all authority was concentrated in the council, it would seem, at first glance, that the maximum of concentrated authority was achieved by commission government. This was not, however, the case. Although the council as a body could, and did, act in a legislative and executive capacity, it could not by itself administer policy. Policy administration became divided and isolated into many islands of responsibility. If the commission was made up of seven members, seven men were responsible for administration of civic policy. Each commissioner felt that the department he headed was his own, to do with as he pleased. Jealous of his prerogatives, he expected the other commissioners, when they sat as a council, to keep their hands off the internal affairs of his department.

What if a majority of the commissioners, using their prerogatives as councilmen, decided to "interfere" in the affairs of a particular department? Although this could, and did, happen, it was apt to be sporadic: some unusual circumstance, such as a public scandal, for example, might force the commission to flout the norms and intervene.

It has been the history of the commission plan, in other words, for the majority to exhibit the utmost reluctance to gang up on a man and dictate to him on matters of departmental concern. If the majority interferes, will not every commissioner thenceforth live in dread that he will someday be singled out for councilmanic dictation? To be safe in one's own department, the commissioner reasons, one must be strictly neutral toward problems of the other departments. In such a system every commissioner fears, above all else, the possibility of being forced into a minority position. Not only will his department suffer; if he is permanently in the minority, his prerogatives as monarch of his particular island of responsibility will be destroyed. Thus, "I'll scratch your back, if you'll scratch mine" is his motto.

If internal dissension does develop, the results are just as striking. A permanent majority opposed to a permanent minority splits the city's administration wide open. Where departments were once uncoordinated, but at least neutral toward each other, now they are active enemies. Here is separation of powers in its most virulent form. But instead of the classic separation—legislative, executive, and judicial—this is separation in the administration itself. Here is a perfect situation for buck-passing. The majority will insist that malfunctioning of the minority department is causing the failure of the city's administration; the minority will insist, with equal justification, that the majority has hamstrung the minority departments.

The reformer discovered—or thought he had discovered—a second major weakness of commission government: amateur administration. The little centralized executive authority that existed under the plan was held by amateurs—the council. Moreover, the heads of the departments were commissioners, who were themselves unschooled in the intricacies of departmental management. How many commissioners of public safety knew anything about the use of fog or foam in fighting fires? How many commissioners of finance understood the intricacies of accrual accounting systems or special-assessment financing of local improvements? In justice to a great many intelligent and industrious commissioners it could be said that after years in office some commissioners developed a remarkable knowledge of affairs in their own departments. But until a commissioner did develop such an expertise, he was either (1) superfluous (he let his subordinates run the department) or (2) dangerous (he insisted upon interfering in departmental matters about which he knew nothing).

Whether these arguments of the reformers were at all times legitimate is at least questionable. Certainly British local government seemed to get along reasonably well with a kind of segmented administration run by councilmanic committees—by amateurs, in other words. But legitimate or not, from an objective point of view, reform disenchantment with the commission plan had devastating effects politically. By 1920 the commission plan had become a weed in the garden of reform, thereafter to be fought rather than nurtured.

Weak-mayor Government. Almost every schoolboy is aware that the republic has had both weak and strong Presidents. The Constitution of 1789 was so written, and it has so developed in the intervening years, that the office of President expands or contracts, according to the wishes and political philosophy of its occupant.

Not so with the office of the mayor. Most cities with the mayor-and-council form of government have weak mayors. This is not because the person who occupies the office is himself a mere cipher; it is rather because the weakness has been built into the office itself.

Although the strong executive in American government—whether strong mayor, governor, or President—has very considerable power, both executive and legislative, the power of the weak mayor is inconsequential. Ostensibly the head of the executive branch of the city government, he is head in name only. A multitude of boards, commissions, and independently elected officials operate departments and activities free of his direction. No actual direction of the administrative effort of the city is possible. The long ballot which results from this system, moreover, presents the voter with a multitude of decisions he probably is not capable of making and assures the existence of a whole platoon of amateurs operating the city's administration.

In the appointment of department heads the mayor must act with the advice and consent of the council; and the council, being jealous of the mayor's few prerogatives, insists strongly on being directly involved in the appointing process. If the mayor wishes to remove the officials appointed by him, the council usually may, under the law, checkmate him and refuse to permit the removal. Authority is further divided, moreover, and the mayor's command over administration greatly weakened by the constant interference of council committees in the administrative affairs of the city.

Perhaps the greatest weakness of the mayor is found in the budget-making process. In the evolution of democratic government throughout the Western world, the responsibility for compilation of the budget has been fixed, to an ever greater extent, in the hands of the executive. Thus the executive budget has become a fixture of democratic governments, a kind of sine qua non of effectiveness. In the weak-mayor organization, by contrast, everyone is a budget-maker—the independently elected administrative officials, the mayor, the department heads, the council itself. A process which by its very nature needs central direction is scattered throughout the organizational structure of the city. Comprehensive financial planning, whether for the year ahead or the decade, becomes a virtual impossibility.

In other legislative matters the executive authority is equally weak. The weak mayor in Illinois cities is typical. Under the Illinois statute the mayor has three distinctly legislative powers: (1) he is presiding officer of the council; (2) he may deliver messages to the council, stating his legislative program; and (3) he may veto entire ordinances or strike out sections of ordinances by use of the item veto.[4] These may seem to be important powers. If fully exercised, they would be, but custom and usage have dictated that the veto be rarely used and that the mayor never come up with a legislative program which he states in a message to the council. As presiding officer of the council, moreover, he is expected to function as a member of the team rather than leader of it. The statutes may even forbid his voting except in case of a tie.

If the mayor is put in a nebulous situation, how much more so is the council. Because of its plethora of administrative duties the council finds it impossible to stick to its own last. To a certain extent the council's situation here resembles that of its counterpart under commission-type government. Not only does the council have administrative burdens of a major sort—partial direction of the administrative effort through council committees, approval of appointments and removals of the mayor, budget-making (shared with the mayor, independent administrative officers, department heads, and sometimes various boards and commissions)—but it also has to tussle with the minutiae of administration—approval of incidental purchases, negotiation of contracts and bond sales, selection of the

---

[4] *Illinois Revised Statutes* (1957), Ch. 24. Art. 9, Secs. 27, 44, 48.

type of street sweepers to be purchased, purchase of soap for the city hall lavatories.

It may well be that the council enjoys such things. Councilmen, like water, seek their own level; and many councilmen are happiest when "debating" the merits of various brands of traffic-marking paint. In such things they feel at home; in the discussion of great issues facing the city they are lost. Soon the classic circle evolves: the capable, well-educated citizen, impatient with the mass of administrative detail, turns his back on a councilmanic seat; the citizen of narrow perspective yearns for council duty precisely because he can busy himself with the minutiae of the position.

We can see, then, that weak-mayor government is faced with as many perplexities as the commission type. The mayor's position is weak and futile, though some have risen above it; the council is so burdened with administrative detail that it tends to neglect the larger problems of the city until they are forced upon its attention; the election of a number of administrative offices makes a muddle of administration; and the resulting long ballot presents the voters with decisions that they are usually disinterested in making. If, in other words, leadership (political, legislative, or executive) is a necessity for effective government, the weak-mayor system is hardly the way to obtain it.

Forms of Government Characterized by the Strong Executive

Strong-mayor Form. A strong mayor heads each of the ten largest cities in the United States. Because of his central position, his role in the city government resembles that of the President or the governor in nation and state.[5] In New York or Philadelphia, St. Louis or New Orleans, San Francisco or Chicago, you will find the mayor fixed with very considerable executive and administrative authority. He is, moreover, important in the formation of legislative policy. Much like the governor or the President, the strong mayor, if he chooses, can be the chief legislative officer of the city. Like our state and national executives, too, he is an influential party leader, whose voice will be listened to with respect. Because of the city's abject legal subserviency to the state, the mayor must be heard, especially in the state capitol, if he wishes to make an effective record for himself in office. Success or failure for the strong mayor may hinge not so much on

[5] "The expectations of the electorate," observe Sayre and Kaufman of the mayor of New York, "of the organized groups of all types, and especially of the communications media, center sharply upon the Mayor. His office is the most perceptible, the most impressive; it is taken for granted that he has the most power and thus the capacity to act vigorously in the solution of the city's problems great and small. Failure to meet these high expectations is taken to mean not lack of vigor in the office but in the man." In Wallace S. Sayre and Herbert S. Kaufman, *Governing New York City* (New York: W. W. Norton & Co., 1965), p. 657.

how he administers city affairs as upon his effectiveness in dealing with the governor and the state legislature.[6]

In the strong-mayor form of government, we find the familiar system of separation of powers and of checks and balances. The city council is fixed with legislative authority. Meeting frequently, the council originates legislation, deliberates upon it by means of standing committees or committees of the whole, and then passes it. The legislation then goes to the mayor for his approval or veto. If the mayor vetoes the measure, it will return to the council where it may be passed over his veto. If he signs the measure, it becomes law. In either case, after an ordinance is formally approved, it becomes the responsibility of the mayor to see that it is properly administered.

Thus the powers of policy formation and policy execution are sternly separated—at least in theory. In fact, this stern separation is greatly modified by the operation of checks and balances. The mayor usually has a legislative program he publicly announces and vigorously supports in the council. In its policy deliberations the council can no more ignore the mayor than the Congress can ignore the President. The mayor, moreover, is a newsworthy figure. His public statements are announced through the press and over the air. He is able to present his views on legislation far more adequately than councilmen can normally present theirs. He is sometimes, moreover, president of the council.

But the council may intrude itself into the mayor's administrative domain. With a standing or special committee the council may carry out investigations of the mayor's conduct of his administration, investigations which often are influential and sometimes embarrassing. The council may impeach the mayor. Its ultimate control of the budget—a control, it is true, which it must share with the mayor—can have far-reaching consequences upon the city's administration. The council may also, at times, confirm certain mayoral appointments; by passage of a civil service ordinance it can revolutionize municipal personnel practices.

In this give-and-take between mayor and council the electorate itself may have an important function. In fact, it is no exaggeration to say that the people are included in the municipal checks-and-balances system much more directly than in the state and national governments. The mayor and councilmen may be recalled from office by an aroused citizenry. A powerful pressure group in the city may initiate legislation by petition and get it approved by the electorate, thus bypassing the mayor and council altogether. In various referenda, too, the voice of the people must be heard. If the mayor and council agree upon an ambitious capital improvements

---

[6] For a case study of the strong mayor vis-à-vis the state government, see William O. Winter, "Mayor Stumps the State," *National Municipal Review*, XLIV (June, 1955), 302–306.

program, they must first get the voters' approval to a bond issue before the program can be effectuated.

The separation of powers and checks-and-balances system is not the only distinctive characteristic of the strong-mayor plan of city government. The council is usually unicameral, though occasionally remnants of the old bicameral system are still to be seen. In Detroit and Denver the mayor and council are elected on nonpartisan ballots, but this is an exception to the rule; in most instances the mayor and council are elected as Republicans or Democrats.

The council is usually small; the mayor is the real and effective head of the administrative departments of the city. (See Figure 10-2.) Only the mayor, the councilmen, an auditor, and perhaps the municipal judges are elective; thus the short ballot prevails. Financially, the mayor prepares the budget; the council passes upon it. In budget administration the mayor may have the power to make allotments to the various departments, and by this means he may control the departmental rate of spending throughout the fiscal year.

As in state and national governments, the relationship of the legislative and executive branches is of crucial importance. Because the mayor and council are so often elected on a partisan ballot, control of both by the same party is essential to a smoothly working, indeed, a responsible, government. If the Democrats control the mayor's office and the Republicans the council, endless bickering, purely on partisan grounds, is apt to result. Just as crucial is the attitude of the mayor toward his role in the government. The strong mayor must make up his mind whether he wants to be a leader or an administrative cipher. By midcentury the norm had been pretty well established that he should be a leader. Indeed, the very word "mayor" so connotes leadership that the people are mystified by the mayor under the weak-mayor and commission systems; they are surprised that the mayor under those systems is not the strong executive they automatically assume him to be, and they seem equally surprised when a "strong" mayor is sometimes rendered ineffective by politics, law, or informal power groups within his own government.

If the mayor chooses to be an administrative cipher rather than a strong executive, that decision is usually his own. Sometimes, it is true, outside circumstances, or unusually capable and aggressive councilmanic leadership, will force him to take a limited role in such important matters as policy leadership. But usually the decision rests with him. Thus Martin Kennelly, mayor of Chicago from 1947 until 1955, was so convinced of the separateness of the mayor and the council that he was deeply reluctant to make even casual suggestions to the council. This attitude, of course, greatly reduced his effectiveness as mayor. It also unquestionably disappointed his constituents in their expectations of him. Not that Mayor Kennelly's posi-

Figure 10-2. Organization of Strong-Mayor Government

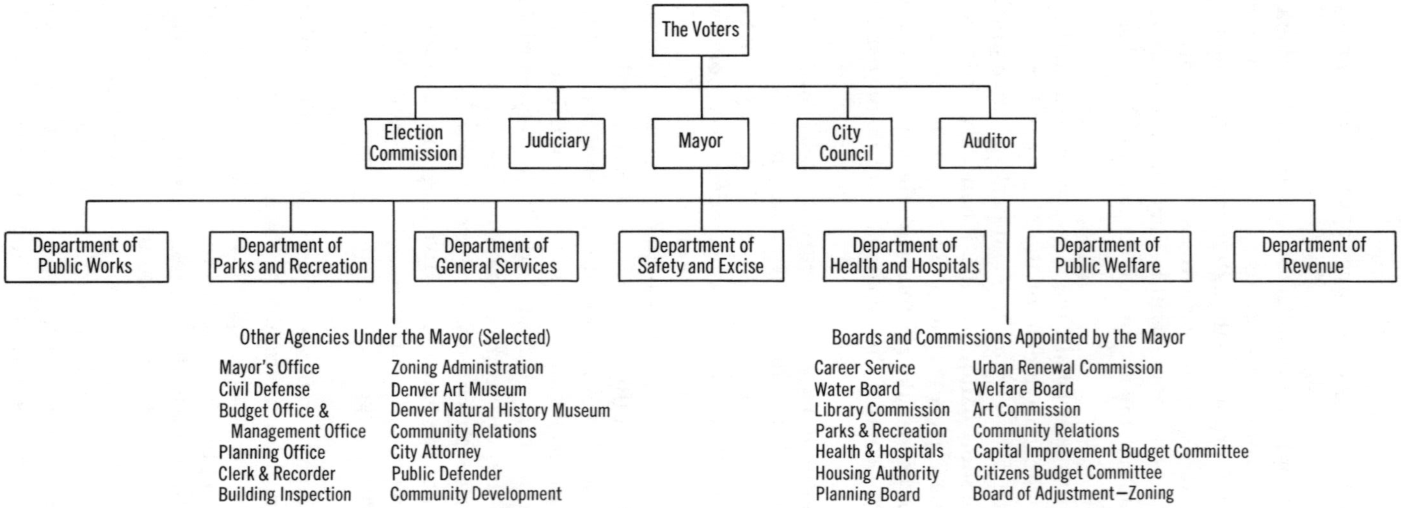

The Voters

Election Commission | Judiciary | Mayor | City Council | Auditor

Department of Public Works
Department of Parks and Recreation
Department of General Services
Department of Safety and Excise
Department of Health and Hospitals
Department of Public Welfare
Department of Revenue

Other Agencies Under the Mayor (Selected)

Mayor's Office
Civil Defense
Budget Office & Management Office
Planning Office
Clerk & Recorder
Building Inspection
Zoning Administration
Denver Art Museum
Denver Natural History Museum
Community Relations
City Attorney
Public Defender
Community Development

Boards and Commissions Appointed by the Mayor

Career Service
Water Board
Library Commission
Parks & Recreation
Health & Hospitals
Housing Authority
Planning Board
Urban Renewal Commission
Welfare Board
Art Commission
Community Relations
Capital Improvement Budget Committee
Citizens Budget Committee
Board of Adjustment—Zoning

Source: City and County of Denver, Colorado, Auditor's Annual Report, 1966, p. 14.

tion was not perfectly rational; it was just that it did not conform to the political expectations of the citizenry of mid-twentieth-century Chicago.

The structural evolution of the strong-mayor form of government, we can say in summary, has followed a general tendency in American government to strengthen the role of the executive. In the mayor himself is concentrated a very considerable amount of power—administrative, legislative, and political. If he chooses to exercise this power fully, the strong mayor is apt to be not only a power within the city but a person of consequence in the state or nation. The mayor, then, is the central figure in strong-mayor and council government, and this unquestionably accounts for much of its effectiveness.

Council-Manager Government. No waves battered upon a helpless town, nor did fire, plague, or famine—the other three horsemen of the Apocalypse—invade the city. The whole thing started quietly, unobtrusively. In the small Virginia city of Staunton began, in 1908, a new technique in governing the American city which was to have startling consequences and which was to stir up as much controversy as almost any other issue in American politics. This was the birth of council-manager government.

In Staunton the members of the council were weary of the mass of administrative detail that constantly accumulated. Thus assailed by the minutiae of civic life, they took an apparently reasonable and logical step: they hired a general manager as full-time administrator of the city government. The administration, wrote John Crosby, president of the Staunton Common Council, in 1911, "is under the control of the general manager who takes the place of council committees, and has full charge and control of all the business of the city, gives bond for the faithful performance of his duty and is responsible to the council." [7]

Although the Staunton plan was a leap into the future, it was, like all things developed ex tempore, a rather crude device. A refinement of Staunton's innovation came in the form of the Lockport proposal. Lockport, New York, had been boss-ridden for years, yet there seemed to be no way to break the grip of the machine on city hall or to pull the boodlers' fists out of the city treasury. The Lockport Board of Trade brought in a proposal, authored by Richard S. Childs, to change the city council to a small body with five members, who would then appoint a city manager. To this manager would be delegated the administrative authority of the council. Embodied in a bill introduced into the 1911 session of the New York legislature, the proposal died in committee; but the Lockport plan itself was heralded all over the United States. [8]

Civic leaders of Sumter, South Carolina, read of the proposal, liked it,

[7] John Crosby, "The Staunton Plan," *The Annals*, XXXVIII (November, 1911), 878.
[8] F. D. Silvernail, "The Lockport Proposal," *The Annals*, XXXVIII (November, 1911), 884–887.

and began council-manager government in that city in 1912. A year later, the National Municipal League introduced the plan in its model city charter, and this most influential of all national civic groups has supported council-manager government ever since.

Commission government, having entered upon the national scene in September, 1900, was now in competition with a new order of civic government. At first, it looked as though the hurricane at Galveston had produced a more popular article than had the Staunton Common Council, Mr. Childs and the Lockport business leaders, and civic officials in Sumter. While a mere handful of cities accepted council-manager government, cities by the dozen adopted the commission plan. But the race was like the proverbial one between the tortoise and the hare. Off to a slow start, the council-manager plan was rapidly outdistanced by its rival. Something was needed to dramatize the city-manager idea. This dramatization, in some degree, came with the adoption by Dayton, Ohio, of council-manager government in 1914. Paradoxically, Dayton had just had a great flood which had visited upon the city considerable damage. Civic leaders thought that the experience with the disaster called not for a commission but for a city manager, and one was appointed shortly after the flood.

Yet the real dramatization of the new form of government in Dayton's city hall came rather from its remarkable achievements during a period of normality than from its success during disaster. The city manager in Dayton achieved an administrative revolution. "By centralizing purchasing and revamping budget procedures, he cut unit costs. A garbage-reduction plant and a sewage-treatment plant were built; the waterworks were enlarged; miles of streets and sidewalks were paved; a comprehensive city plan was adopted; and a thousand acres of parks and playgrounds were added." [9] The drama of great public works in one city increased the popularity of council-manager government far and wide.

The success of the city manager in a large city was really all that urban leaders needed to convince them of the value of centralized administrative power and the necessity of a professionally trained manager. With the Dayton success to point to, civic leaders moved energetically, in their cities and in their state legislatures, to introduce council-manager government into American city halls. By home-rule charter, or under permissive legislation of the respective states, an ever greater number of cities turned to the manager plan.

In the meantime, commission government had reached the high point of its success. By 1920 the race was not to the swift, but to the slow. Discredited in the minds of the reformers, commission government, after a spectacular sweep over the country in the first decade and a half of the century, lost its

[9] Arthur W. Bromage, *Introduction to Municipal Government and Administration* (New York: Appleton-Century-Crofts, 2nd ed., 1957), p. 293.

motive force. Like a great army without unity of command, it had sudden, temporary success. But after the first victories it was forced into fighting rearguard actions for the remainder of the campaign. Its rival, by contrast, has seen little but success in a half-century of urban campaigning, and now is stronger than it ever was in the past.

Not every city with council-manager government, of course, made good on the promises of reform. Kansas City, which adopted the plan by home-rule charter amendment in 1926, was firmly ruled by Boss Tom Pendergast until 1939. Concentration of administrative command in the office of the city manager did nothing to inhibit the rule of the boss; indeed, it was an aid to Pendergast's corruption of city hall, because the city manager was as completely controlled by the boss as the lowliest day laborer on a street gang. When the machine was finally driven out, it was not because of any efforts made by the manager or anyone in his office. It was because a reform civic group, the governor of Missouri, and the federal district attorney all combined forces and attacked the machine from different quarters.

There is a sequel to the Kansas City story. For twenty years the reform group controlled city hall. From his office atop the splendid thirty-story municipal building which Tom Pendergast had built, City Manager L. P. Cookingham, one of the outstanding men in the profession, operated a city administration that, from the standpoint of administrative efficiency, was unimpeachable. In the spring of 1959, however, the reform group lost control of the city council; Cookingham was forced to resign; and ominous predictions were voiced about the city that the machine had returned. After several years of maneuvering, the reform party came back to power, elected the mayor and a majority of the city council, and brought in a widely known city manager with a long professional career behind him.

The Kansas City experience with the city-manager plan is instructive. It shows that the plan, like any other form of government, can be corrupted. Just as a bad driver can wreck a fine automobile, so bad politics can wreck council-manager government. Indeed, the political environment, as Kansas City so well illustrates, continuously influences all elements of the governing structure of the city: the council, the manager himself, and the office of the manager. Neither in Kansas City, nor in any city, can politics be kept out of city hall, in spite of the hopes of some reformers that it can be.

Whereas the manager plan was twisted beyond recognition during its first years in Kansas City, it functioned true to form in Cincinnati. Boss-ridden and corrupt, the city was taken over in 1926 by a charter committee, itself a coalition, which, like the Kansas City reform group, was made up of Democrats, Republicans, and independents. Having thrown the rascals out, the charter committee built itself into an effective political party, which has ever since spoken with a loud voice in municipal councils.

The Great Depression of the 1930's was a testing of all governments at whatever level of operation. During this period of testing the council-manager idea stood up exceedingly well. Throughout the decade the movement continued to grow. And though the evidence is certainly inconclusive, it is probable that those cities with strong-executive systems (whether council-manager or strong-mayor) rode out the economic storm better than those with weak executives.

World War II forced municipal leadership to put its problems on the shelf. After the war the problems were dusted off, and new ones were brought in from every quarter of the city. Faced with an overwhelming number of jobs to do, many cities turned to the trained administrator for aid. In 1945, there were 613 cities with council-manager government in the United States and Canada, and by the end of 1966 the number had increased to 2,113. (See Figure 10-3.)

Events in Illinois give a microcosmic view of council-manager developments in the postwar era. In 1951, only 13 cities and villages in the state used the council-manager form of government, and in some of those the plan lived rather tenuously by ordinance. In 1951 the Illinois General Assembly passed an enabling act which permitted all cities except Chicago the option of adopting council-manager government. This broke the dam, and the flood of reform rolled over the Illinois prairies. In most of the major cities of the state, pitched battles were soon raging over the question

Figure 10-3. Growth Rate of Council-Manager Governments, 1920–1966 United States and Canada

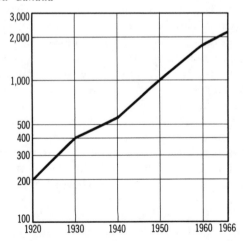

Except for a falling-off in the 1930's (notice the flattening tendency on the curve), the growth rate of the council-manager system has been remarkably constant over the past fifty years (semilog. scale).

Source: *The Municipal Year Book 1967*, p. 536; *1960*, p. 500; *1950*, p. 528; *1941*, p. 575. (Chicago: ICMA.)

of whether the city-manager plan should be adopted. By 1959, there had been over 60 elections in which the plan was an issue. In most of them the plan won voter approval, so that only eight years after the passage of the enabling act there were 53 cities and villages with city managers.

In summary, though the council-manager plan has not been without its problems, a half-century of experience with it has convinced civic leaders in American cities of its potentialities. Its sustained growth alone is evidence, if not of its worth, at least of its political appeal. Just as telling is the popular satisfaction it has created in the cities in which it has been tried. By 1966, only 90 cities and counties had permanently abandoned the plan by vote of the people.[10] If the proof of the pudding is in the eating, it appears that this particular one appeals to the tastes of the civic electorate.

Essence of Council-Manager Government. To the superficial observer the manager plan returns to a classic feature of American government, separation of powers. So prevalent is this belief that proponents of council-manager government often advertise it in their own communities as a "return to traditional principles of American government." This view of the manager plan is largely fallacious: powers are fused, rather than separated. It is not unusual for a statute or charter to say specifically that all municipal powers are concentrated in the city council. And in operation the system illustrates the principle of fusion of powers rather than separation.

The really distinctive feature of city-manager government is separation of function, or, rather, it is the unification of powers, joined with the separation of function. The plan is neither one nor the other: it is both. And the plan cannot be properly understood unless these elements are thought of not as two concepts but as a single, indivisible whole.

All power is concentrated in the council; this is done by statute or charter. Thereupon, the function of administration is delegated to the office of city manager, and there those functions must rest. (See Figure 10-4.) Thus the Springfield, Missouri, charter provides that "all powers of the city shall be vested in an elective council," and Article III of the Greeley, Colorado, charter reads: "the corporate authority . . . shall be vested in . . . the city council."

Although the administrative function must remain in the manager's office, the council retains overall policy control by controlling the city manager himself. Since the manager is hired by the council, has no contract, and may be fired by the council at any time, the council should be in the driver's seat. That it always is not, that the manager may at times come to dominate the council, is surely an excellent indication of how formal systems may be affected by politics and personality.

---

[10] See Arthur W. Bromage, *Manager Plan Abandonments* (New York: National Municipal League, 1954); *The Municipal Year Book 1967* (Chicago: ICMA), pp. 88–89. Twenty-five other places abandoned the plan but later readopted it.

Figure 10-4. The Organization of Council-Manager Government Kansas City, Missouri

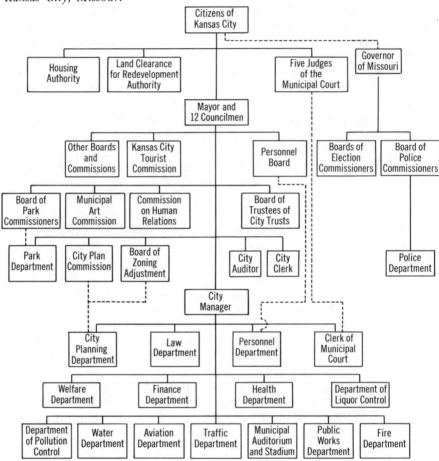

Source: City of Kansas City, Missouri, *Annual Financial Report, 1965.*

In hiring the manager, the council has complete discretion to pick and choose among candidates for the position. Just so that the council shall feel itself in full command of the situation, the statutes and the charters make it perfectly clear that the discretion of the governing body of the city is complete. Because some councils have hired local party hacks as managers, some few voices have been raised to insist that state law or local charter should specify minimum qualifications for the office, or that such a provision should be embodied in the state constitution. The Austrian constitution, for example, provides that the "director of the administrative offices of the municipality must be a legally trained administrative official." [11] The trouble with specifying such minimum qualifications is that there is no general agreement that the best training for a city manager is a legal one or one of another character. If for no other reason, therefore, than a lack of agreement on what a manager's training should be, city councils will probably retain full power to hire the city manager, unrestricted by constitutional, statutory, or charter provisions.[12]

When the council hires the manager, it fulfills one of its most important administrative duties, but it does not end them there. Setting overall administrative policy, surveillance of administrative action, and, in case of necessity, discipline, or discharge of the city manager—the citizen can expect the council to perform all of these general administrative duties and at the same time leave specific administrative tasks to the manager.

The city manager, in turn, must perform his duties with some considerable administrative skill and at the same time keep the people and the council informed of his decisions and activities. Although an administrator of the policy set by the council, he must necessarily participate at times in the formulation of policy. Because of his training in municipal affairs, as well as because of his intimate knowledge of the city's administration, the manager will find the council relying on him as an essential adjunct to the decision-making process. The manager compiles the budget, for example, and presents it to the council; this in itself is a major step in the formulation of policy. In the debate on the budget document, he may be asked by council members to explain various items and even argue for them. His comments will inevitably be influential on the final decisions of the council.

Aside from its basic characteristic of unification of powers and delegation of administrative function, the council-manager plan has other important features. One is that it invariably results in the professionalization of the public service. The manager himself is usually a professional, and he insists upon trained personnel as department heads. As a result of a personnel code, hiring and advances in rank and salary are based upon merit and performance. With his salary fixed at a professional level, with tenure no longer tied to the success of his friends at the polls and with advancement upward through the ranks always open to him, the city employee develops the morale and the expertise of a professional public employee. Still another feature of council-manager government is the wide utilization of staff aids. Budgeting, purchasing, personnel, public relations, planning—

[11] Art. 119, Sec. 5; taken from *Die Oesterreichischen Bundes-Verfassungsgesetze* (Wien: Manz Verlag, 1948). The translation is my own.

[12] Out of 991 managers surveyed by the ICMA in 1964, 392 had received their bachelor's degrees in political science and public administration; 146 in other social sciences; and 208 in engineering. *The Municipal Year Book 1965* (Chicago: ICMA), p. 515.

these staff functions, professionally administered, often appear for the first time in a city with the introduction of council-manager government.

Invariably, the council-manager plan points toward the short ballot. The general principle is that no officer with administrative duties shall be elected by the people. The corollary of this principle is that the manager's office stands at the head of an administrative hierarchy which includes the entire administrative organization of the city. Although remnants of the long ballot remain in a few council-manager cities, they are gradually being eliminated.

Though not necessarily characteristic of the council-manager plan itself, the techniques of direct democracy are so often to be found in council-manager charters or statutes that many assume them to be essential elements of the plan. The initiative, referendum, and recall, however, are just as often connected with other forms of municipal government and thus cannot be considered peculiar to council-manager government.

Council-Manager Campaigns. During the past half-century, several thousand communities over the nation have been divided by the question of whether to adopt council-manager government. Often waged with great bitterness, the campaigns can tell us a great deal, if not about the plan, then surely about public attitudes toward the plan.

In these campaigns the manager plan has, on the one hand, been pictured as a sudden jump upward to nirvana, or, by its opponents, as an equally sharp descent into the seventh depth of purgatory. The city manager himself has been pictured as a saint or a devil; he is thought of, in short, as an abstraction that does not exist, in the spirit or in the flesh, in heaven or on this earth.

During a campaign for adoption of the plan in one city, a veterans' organization called upon a college professor to discuss the plan with the membership. In general, the audience was evenly divided between opponents and proponents of the plan. But the opponents were the most vociferous in support of their opinions, the principal one being that the proposed change was tantamount to revolution. The following edifying colloquy developed between the speaker and a member of the group.

OBJECTOR: This looks to me like overthrow of the government.

PROFESSOR: Well, I think that's a bit too strong; this is a change, yes, but hardly an overthrow of the government.

OBJECTOR: You're throwing out the mayor and the aldermen; if that isn't overthrow, I don't know what is.

PROFESSOR: May I remind you, sir, that the state statutes provide that the people . . .

OBJECTOR: Sure, the people. But what people? A minority brought this whole thing up, and if a minority overthrows the government, that's overthrow in anybody's book.

PROFESSOR: As I was saying, the statutes provide for an orderly transition from one form of government to another. I would like to refer you to Chapter 24, Article 20 of the *Revised Statutes,* which read . . .

OBJECTOR: Looks like overthrow of the government to me.

If not a revolution, the plan can be objected to on many other grounds by those who fear it. It is a device invented by businessmen on Main Street to protect their interests at the expense of the interests of the workingman. The plan is spendthrift—"Look at the salary we would have to pay the manager, and the salaries of all his expensive aides." It is a violation of home rule, the right of a city to determine its own destiny. It may fit 10,000 other cities and work well in all of them—"But our city is distinct; we are getting along fine as we are." Furthermore, it is something new—"We don't take easily to new things around here." Finally, it is supported by the internationalists—"Look at the city managers themselves, organized into the International City Managers' Association!" Such irrational positions reveal some of the prevailing popular attitudes toward council-manager government, which, even if never in the majority, can profoundly influence the government of a city.

Summary

The forms of municipal government fall easily into two main types—those with the strong executive and those with the weak. Within the latter type are the weak-mayor and commission forms, neither of which gains much contemporary critical acclaim and both of which are being reduced in importance, at least in cities over 10,000 population.

The city seems to have thrown in its lot with the strong-executive type of government. The apparent necessity of central administrative direction and the strong compulsion to professionalize the urban services—these and many other factors have led to the spread of strong-executive types of city government. In the past, and especially the recent past, the proponents of the council-manager form of government have had remarkable success in winning cities over to the plan. Even if this growth does not continue, some form of centralized administrative power, handled by professionals, seems to have general acceptance by civic leadership. The trend toward the strong executive has been one of the really striking developments in American state and local governments over the past half-century. There is every reason to believe that this trend will continue, and even accelerate.

Annotated Bibliography

Although Blau and Scott give some excellent discussion of the interrelationship between formal and informal organization in a bureaucracy, very little of that important phase of the governing apparatus is to be found in the literature on local government. See Peter M. Blau and W. Richard Scott, *Formal Organizations—A Comparative Approach* (San Francisco: Chandler Publishing Co., 1962). Formal structure and legal niceties have been the traditional, ongoing concern of commentators on council-manager government, almost wholly to the exclusion of a consideration of politics within and without city hall. See Leonard D. White, *The City Manager* (Chicago: University of Chicago Press, 1927); Harold A. Stone, Don K. Price, and Kathryn H. Stone, *City Manager Government in the United States* (Chicago: Public Administration Service, 1940); and Richard S. Childs, *Civic Victories* (New York: Harper & Bros., 1952).

Except for occasional journal articles, both the weak-mayor and commission forms of government have been ignored for almost a half-century. On the other hand, much has been written on strong-mayor–council systems, though it tends to be limited to individual cities. See, for example, Wallace S. Sayre and Herbert S. Kaufman, *Governing New York City* (New York: W. W. Norton & Co., 1965); and Robert A. Dahl, *Who Governs? Democracy and Power in an American City* (New Haven, Conn.: Yale University Press, 1961). There is, of course, extensive literature on the resourceful, colorful mayor.

CHAPTER 11

The Rules of the Game

Because the city is a political organism, politics in all of its various forms envelops it. Along Main Street; here and there in the clubs, the taverns, the residential neighborhoods, the churches, the pool halls, the union meetings, the chamber of commerce; at the service club luncheon, during the annual meeting of the civic betterment league, at the height of play during the Friday evening session of the Verduredale chowder and marching society—everywhere, in every city activity, politics will inevitably, at some time or other, intrude.

Strangely, however, the intruder may not be called "politics." Indeed, a discussion of who might be the next Republican nominee for President may be cut off by such a statement as, "Let's quit talking politics, for heaven's sake, and decide how we can help pass the school bond issue."

Truly, one of the most remarkable characteristics of urban politics is the custom of describing this phenomenon as nonpolitical. Because reformers over the last half-century have tried to divorce local from state and national political activity; because local officials by the tens of thousands are elected to office without party backing and without formal party designations on the ballot; and because, somehow, civic issues—so people feel—are not the same as political issues, the myth has grown up that much of urban politics is not politics at all. The myth is so strong that the community leader is commonplace who prides himself upon being above politics, and who will at the same time engage energetically in supporting candidates for school board, in bringing pressure upon the city council for a new library, in fighting a bond issue, or in supporting a charter amendment. And the myth is so strong that if you were to point out to such a leader that he is as actively engaged in politics as the Democratic county chairman he would regard your remarks as an incredible joke.

The basic aim of this analysis is to challenge that myth. Whatever the activity of the city, it almost inevitably involves conflict. Before the city can decide to act—or decide not to act—conflict must somehow be resolved. And it is precisely this resolution of conflict that is the essence of politics. Politics, therefore, is ever-present in all urban communities (even in those that try most valiantly to suppress it), first, because conflict is ever-present and, second, because somehow the city always develops ways to manage that conflict.

Conflict, even when it is largely irrational, needs some kind of rational structure to make it productive; and local politics has developed that kind of rationality. Rationality, in other words, has been introduced into an irrational scheme of things by means of formal organizational arrangements, such as determination of voter eligibility, specification of methods for nominating and electing city officials, and the structuring of issue elections. It is to these formal electoral systems that we must now turn.

The Mechanics of Elections

The state is no less the master of the electoral process in the urban community than of any other aspect of urban political life. On the one hand, in a city without either a home-rule or special-legislative charter, one will find virtually all of the electoral mechanics set out in statute and case law. On the other hand, because of constitutional provision or statutory grant of authority to the city, one may need to look to the charter or code of ordinances for the specific mechanics of the electoral process. For a home-rule city all four sources may need to be used, and indeed, probably a fifth source, the case law.

Electoral mechanics, of course, include the dates that regular elections may be held and the exact procedure by which the city may set the dates for special elections. Mechanics include, also, the hours that the polls must stay open, how the election officials shall be chosen, the form of the ballot, the finance of the elections, and a host of varying details, all designed to maintain the integrity of elections.

Who May Vote? Most of us are aware of the gradual expansion of the franchise over the past one hundred years. Whereas once the electorate was severely restricted by property and religious qualifications and whereas women were disenfranchised—along with aliens, criminals, and imbeciles —now the ballot is freely given to nearly all those adults in American cities that take the trouble to fulfill certain procedural requirements. Even in the southern states the battle for the franchise has largely been won by the urban Negro. If the Negro is still disenfranchised in the South—a century after the Fifteenth Amendment!—this irrational aspect of American politics will be found usually in the rural counties, rarely in the cities.

The urban voter must, of course, meet the usual qualifications set out in constitution, statute, or local charter and ordinance. Age is an invariable qualification, and usually one must have reached his twenty-first birthday. In Georgia and Kentucky, however, the minimum age for voting is eighteen; in Alaska, nineteen; and in Hawaii, twenty. At least one Canadian province too, departs from the norm: in Saskatchewan the minimum voting age is eighteen.[1]

[1] Kenneth G. Crawford, *Canadian Municipal Government* (Toronto: University of Toronto Press, 1954), p. 141.

The second major prerequisite for voting is citizenship. Although there were state laws, at one time, which permitted aliens to vote, particularly if they had applied for citizenship, now all states require citizenship status; and four (California, Minnesota, New York, and Utah) require that the former alien must have been a U.S. citizen for at least ninety days before he becomes a qualified voter.[2]

Perhaps the most difficult of all the standard voting qualifications to explain briefly is that of residence. All the states have some kind of residence qualification for voting, and these qualifications are sometimes supplemented by local requirements. The majority of state laws stipulate that a qualified voter must have resided at least a year in the state, three months in the county, and thirty days in the voting district or precinct. When there is a great deal of population movement, both within the city and between and among cities—certainly a characteristic of our urban society—many people will invariably be disenfranchised for that reason alone. Moreover, the legal residence of an adult may be in doubt, as in the case of a college student or a businessman temporarily transferred from one city to another. And what of new residents just brought into the city by annexation?

In South Dakota these problems are partially met, at least for state residents, since no elector "who has changed his residence from one county or precinct to another loses his right to vote in his former county of precinct until he acquires voting residence in the new one."[3] It is pertinent to note that some Canadian cities meet the problem in another way by permitting nonresidents to vote on occasion.[4]

A fourth major requirement for voting is registration. The individual who believes that he meets the age, citizenship, and residence requirements of the law must present himself to the proper official, identify himself, and perhaps offer proof of his eligibility. If the official finds that his credentials meet the legal requirements, his name is then entered upon the registration books; he is often given an identification card, and then he is entitled to vote in subsequent elections. In some places, registration for city elections is separate from that for other elections (in Mississippi and the Territory of Guam, for example). In other places, the individual's registration card may entitle him to vote in county, state, and national elections, but not necessarily in city and school elections. It is not unknown for no registration at all to be required in school elections; and in at least two states, Illinois and Texas, lack of municipal registration seems relatively commonplace.[5]

[2] *The Book of the States, 1960–1961* (Chicago: The Council of State Governments, 1960), p. 20.
[3] *Ibid.*, p. 21, footnote "ac."
[4] Crawford, *op. cit.*, p. 141. (In 1959 the Winnipeg City Council voted to continue permitting owners of property in the city to vote in city elections even though they reside elsewhere.)
[5] *The Municipal Year Book 1963* (Chicago: ICMA), p. 75.

A number of state constitutions contain specific requirements for registration previous to voting in city elections. Usually in such cases, the constitutions either require city registration as a constitutional mandate or stipulate that the legislature shall set up such requirements by general law. States with such specific constitutional requirements include Alabama, Kentucky (cities and towns of 5,000 population and over), Louisiana, Maryland (for Baltimore), Mississippi, North Carolina, Oregon, Rhode Island, Virginia, Washington (cities and towns of over 500 population), and West Virginia.[6]

Registration of voters may be either permanent or temporary. Although the former is to be preferred for several reasons, there is little question but that it raises the costs of election administration. Because the city or the county must meet these costs, and because both units are always hard-pressed for funds, this is no small argument in favor of temporary registration. Nevertheless, a 1963 comprehensive survey of 574 cities of over 25,000 population found that 509 of the cities required registration and that the form of registration in 438 of them was permanent.[7]

Various incidental qualifications for voting appear in American cities. A few states impose general literacy qualifications, and these strictures may be either obligatory or permissive for the urban voter. Taxpaying and property-owning qualifications will usually not be imposed for general city elections, but will sometimes be required for tax-rate and bond-issue elections. In such cases, the municipal electorate falls into two classes: those who may vote in all elections and those who may vote, in addition, on fiscal referenda.

Nominating Candidates for Office. Aside from remembering that nominations and elections in the city are controlled by state constitutions and statutes—as with the remainder of the electoral process—we should recognize a singular fact of municipal elections: they are as separate from state and national elections as municipal politics itself. Even those elections in which Democrats and Republicans contest for public positions in the traditional partisan manner are very apt to be separate. Did you vote for mayor in 1968? The odds are that if you did, you did not do so at the same time you voted for President, governor, and senator, or even county sheriff. The reasons for this practice are several. Partly, it is the result of the clear, admitted intent of those who have drafted the constitutions and statutes—and the charters—over the past half-century. The local consensus has been that the municipal election, like that of the schools, should be something distinct and apart. This is quite unlike the thinking on county elections, by contrast, and it is thus not surprising that county officials are elected on the same ballot with state and national officials.[8]

---

[6] Legislative Research Drafting Fund, *Index Digest of State Constitutions* (New York: Columbia University Law School, 2nd ed., 1959), pp. 454–455.

[7] *The Municipal Year Book 1963* (Chicago: ICMA), pp. 74–75.

[8] Clyde F. Snider, *Local Government in Rural America* (New York: Appleton-Century-Crofts, 1957), pp. 271–273.

Another reason for the separate character of the city election is the wide variety of issues which must legally be presented to the voters. Particularly because of the general use of popular democracy, which we shall look at presently, the city electorate is called upon to decide a wide variety of issues which may be proposed at any time. This condition has a profound impact upon urban elections. Nonpartisanship is still another reason for the separateness. But since we shall consider that phenomenon in the following chapter, it is sufficient now simply to mention it.

In filling a public office by popular election, the first problem is to select the proper candidates to stand for that office. There must be a winnowing process—some way, in other words, to nominate *candidates* for office.

The colonial city usually found it unnecessary to use a selective device to winnow from the running either the politically weak or the downright incompetent. If the caucus appeared, as it did in the late colonial city, it was still a rarity, because there were few cities of any size, and because the franchise was severely restricted or simply unused. How could one talk of a nominating process in the case of a close corporation such as Philadelphia or Norfolk? Nor was there any need for a nominating procedure in colonial New England, where the town meeting was used to govern even the largest city, Boston. That there were informal agreements on whom to present at the town meeting is an assumption we can make even if it is difficult to verify. Such agreements could probably be described as forerunners of the formal nominating process—but only forerunners.

As cities grew and the franchise was extended, the realization spread among thoughtful community leaders that some device must be developed to cut down the number of candidates for office in the final election. During the nineteenth and early twentieth centuries four main devices appeared: the caucus, the convention, the direct primary, and—the dominant one today—declaration of candidacy.[9]

The Direct Primary. For the contemporary city the first question to be raised about the direct primary is whether it is partisan or nonpartisan. (Whether it is open or closed is of comparatively little moment to city politics.) The partisan primary is one in which the political party participates as an integral and necessary element in the proceedings. Though we usually think of the partisan primary as one in which the two major American parties are involved, in city politics the parties may be local ones, with no formal ties at all to the two major state and national organizations.

In the partisan primary each individual actively seeking office identifies himself as a party adherent, and he seeks the party's nomination for the office he desires to fill. On the ballot he is labeled as a Democrat, a Republican, or a member of a local political group. His efforts are directed to getting the support both of party leadership and of the rank and file of

[9] *The Municipal Year Book 1963* (Chicago: ICMA), p. 8.

party members. As a contestant in a *party* election (which is simply another name for the party primary) he competes against other members of his own group for the party's favor.

Though no absolutely unimpeachable data exist on the matter, we can nevertheless say with a good deal of certainty that the great majority of city officials are elected on a nonpartisan ballot and as the result of a nonpartisan nominating device. Without stopping to argue the point that a formally nonpartisan nominating process—as well as the subsequent general election—may in fact be intensely partisan, let us see how the nonpartisan primary differs from its partisan brother.

The ballot is, of course, without party designations. If a stranger were to view it, he could not tell whether the individuals whose names appeared there were party members or wholly without party ties. The voter, then, is without party aid or other guidelines of a partisan nature in casting his ballot. He is, that is, if he is politically inactive; and since much of the city's electorate *is* politically inactive, the generalization must hold. Since party membership, moreover, has no relevancy in the voting, the citizen does not have to establish party affiliation to obtain a ballot. In this sense, all nonpartisan primaries are "open."

Up to this point we have viewed the primary from the voter's perspective. Now, what of the candidate himself? To get his name on the primary ballot, the candidate, as a general practice, must obtain a minimum number of signatures of qualified voters on a petition and submit the petition to the designated election official of the city. This procedure governs both the partisan and nonpartisan primary; in fact, it is equally uncomplicated for the candidate in the primary of either type. Although it may seem a paradox that one might run in a party primary without adequate proof of party membership, loyalty, and regularity, the fact is that tests of such identification are so lax, or so nonexistent, that almost anyone who *calls* himself a partisan may run in the party primary.

Upon filing the nominating petition, a small fee may be required of the candidate. This fee is usually so nominal that it will not deter the filing of frivolous or hopeless candidacies.

The Convention. This is a formal party conclave to which delegates are elected by the party membership for purposes of nominating candidates and setting party policy. Most American citizens are familiar with the convention process only through the national nominating convention. The reason is not hard to find. Only a handful of states still use the convention method, and only 3 percent of the 571 major cities (25,000 and over) surveyed by *The Municipal Year Book* in 1962. (See Table 11-1.)

The Party Caucus. The partisan caucus, in which designated party officials nominate candidates, is a kind of vestigial tail of politics, left over from the nineteenth century. Perhaps not so much so is the nonpartisan

Table 11-1. *Methods of Nominating Candidates*
in Cities of over 25,000 Population—1962

	Number of Cities Reporting *	Percent Filing *				
		By Individual Candidate	By Voter Petition	By Direct Primary	By Party Convention	By Other Method
Form of Election						
Partisan	157	31	13	41	6	5
Nonpartisan	414	64	26	8	†	8
Form of Government						
Mayor-council	186	46	15	33	5	8
Commission	58	52	21	21	0	9
Council-manager	322	61	28	13	2	4
Population Group						
Over 500,000	19	53	37	26	0	16
250,000 to 500,000	26	42	27	35	0	8
100,000 to 250,000	72	53	22	21	6	6
50,000 to 100,000	150	53	23	21	3	5
25,000 to 50,000	307	57	21	18	3	5
All cities over 25,000	574	55	23	20	3	6

* When figures are totaled horizontally, sum may be larger or smaller than 100 percent, resulting from the failure of some cities to report data in this field, while others reported more than one method for nominating candidates.

† Less than 0.5 percent.

Source: *The Municipal Year Book 1963* (Chicago: ICMA), p. 80.

caucus. Fourth-class cities in Washington may provide by ordinance for such caucuses,[10] and a dozen or more suburban municipalities in the Chicago metropolitan area nominate candidates for both city and school positions by this method. But, for the most part, the caucus is used in the American city even less than the convention.

Declaration of Candidacy. This nominating device is of two types: the declaration without the petition and the declaration with an accompanying voter petition. Although sometimes considered two separate devices— and for not insubstantial reasons—we shall here consider the two parts as essentially divisions of a single method.

As one may observe from Table 11-1, 55 percent of American cities of over 25,000 population use the simple declaration of candidacy as their

[10] Bureau of Governmental Research and Services, *Municipal Government in the State of Washington* (Seattle: The Bureau, University of Washington, 1962), p. 59.

nominating method. Another 23 percent require an accompanying petition. Since we have already placed the two types under one category, we can easily verify from the figures in Table 11-1 the overwhelming importance of declaration of candidacy as a nominating method.

The charter of Boulder, Colorado, gives us an excellent example of this method. Under Article III, the nominating petition must begin with an affidavit, by means of which the candidate swears to his qualifications (qualified elector, twenty-five years of age, and a five-year resident of the city) and to his intent to stand as candidate for election. After the affidavit comes the "Electors' Petition," on which the signatures of no fewer than twenty-five and no more than thirty-five qualified and registered electors must appear. After the petition is filed with the city clerk and the clerk finds it in order, the candidate is nominated; and his name shall appear on the election ballot.[11]

The Write-in. Not, strictly speaking, a nominating method, the write-in is nevertheless a means by which an individual may place his name, or have it placed, on the ballot for the final election. Some ballots may actually invite the write-in by providing lined spaces for the voter to indicate his preference. The write-in candidate, too, may willingly aid the voter by distributing stickers with his name printed on them, so that all the citizen must do is to affix the object to the proper place on the ballot.

Qualifications of Nominees. An integral part of all nominating methods is checking upon the qualifications of the candidates as required by statute or charter. Normally, a candidate must meet all of the standard qualifications for voting which we reviewed earlier. In addition to being a qualified elector, he must usually have been a resident (that is, a citizen) of the city for some years longer than that required for a voting residence; and he must be a mature adult (where maturity is measured in years rather than emotional stability!). The Honolulu charter provides that: "Any citizen of the United States not less than thirty years of age who has been a duly qualified elector of the city for at least three years prior to his election shall be eligible to fill the office of mayor." [12] To be eligible for election to the Honolulu city council, one must be a citizen of the United States, a qualified elector of the city for two years, and a resident of his councilmanic district for at least one year. These provisions are typical for American cities.

Critique of Nominating Methods. What is the best method of nominating candidates for municipal office? The answer would be a simple one if we could say that declaration of candidacy, in its two forms, being so widely used, has met the test of time and thus is obviously the best. But such an answer is not sufficient, and so let us look further into the question.

[11] *Charter of Boulder, Colorado,* Art. III, Secs. 22–27.
[12] *Charter of the City and County of Honolulu, Hawaii,* Art. V, Sec. 5–102; Art. III, Sec. 3–104.

First, the nominating method must be fitted to the type of election being used. Is it party-controlled, or is it nonpartisan? The question is a very pertinent one. As Table 11-1 shows, almost half the cities with partisan elections use party-oriented devices for nominating candidates (either the direct primary or the party convention). If municipal leadership wishes to stimulate party competition—even between strictly local parties—the direct primary or the party convention will be used. Of these two, the convention possibly has the advantage of increasing party control over candidates, is relatively inexpensive (both to the city and to the candidate), and does not open the public wounds in the party that characteristically result from the direct primary.

Second, what type and size of community are we talking about? There is serious doubt that declaration of candidacy is a suitable method for making nominations in the larger cities. In small cities, those where the politics of acquaintance is an evident phenomenon, it seems to work without major difficulty, especially if the elections are nonpartisan. Inherent drawbacks to this nominating method, however, are that it stimulates the filing of frivolous candidacies, or at least presents no obstacles to them, and that plurality election often results. (Perhaps we should remember here that the frivolous candidate is one who stands for election even though he is without organized support and thus has virtually no chance of being elected. The wealthy Chicagoan Lar ["America First"] Daly is a good example of a frivolous candidate, though such candidacies are by no means restricted to the wealthy.) If the plurality difficulty is met by a runoff election, that stratagem simply makes the first election, in effect, a direct primary.

We can draw the conclusion that declaration of candidacy, with or without the accompanying petition, does not furnish an adequate filtering process for larger cities. The citizen finds it too easy to place his name on the general-election ballot. On the other hand, in smaller cities the filtering process seems to be taken care of by informal types of selection. The experience of Colorado cities is to the point. Whereas declaration of candidacy has worked adequately for most of the home-rule cities in the state—which means most of the major ones—in Denver rarely is there a municipal election that does not require a runoff. Thus, though nominally Denver nominates by declaration of candidacy, because of the frequency of the runoff, the system has become in fact a blood brother to the direct primary. The criterion of inadequacy, here, is the use of the runoff primary. When the data reveal absence of the runoff, we can assume the adequacy of declaration of candidacy as a nominating device. When the runoff keeps occurring, we can assume its inadequacy.

In the final analysis the two central criteria for gauging the worth of various nominating methods are size of city and existence or nonexistence of formal partisanship. If the city is small and nonpartisan, in the formal sense, declaration of candidacy has such significant advantages that few would question its use. If the city is large and partisan (again, in the formal sense) the method that will fit best is the party convention or the direct primary. For the city in between, the wise decision must be made according to the degree to which the city resembles one of the two extreme types.

Electing Candidates

The methods of nominating and electing candidates obviously complement each other. Once the nominating process has been carried through, the names of those nominated are printed on the general-election ballot or placed in the voting machines. After the votes are cast, the winning candidate for a given office is selected on the basis of a majority vote, a plurality, or a system of counting used in one or the other of the proportional-representation (PR) systems. Since majority election is commonplace and its definition so evident, we need to look at it no further.

Plurality election is one in which the winning candidate receives more votes than anyone running against him, but still not a majority of the votes cast for that particular office. Eugene C. Lee observes that "a feature of municipal elections that is quite dissimilar from state and national balloting is the relative frequency of elections won by less than a majority vote." [13] Of the 499 cities surveyed by Lee, 61 percent reported that no runoff was necessary in case of the lack of a majority vote. This means, by logical extension, that in some 300-odd cities of over 25,000 population, plurality election is often to be expected.

If plurality election offends the democratic instincts of the city body politic, the runoff becomes the means of making the final selection. In Denver, where declaration of candidacy (with supporting petitions) is the nominating device used, the charter provides that if no candidate for mayor receives a majority vote in the general election, then the two persons with the highest number of votes must run against each other in a runoff election.[14] The same rule applies to candidates for auditor and city council.

This system, used in Denver and in at least 100 other cities of over 25,000, not only prevents plurality election. It, in effect, sets up a direct-primary system without designating it as such. As we have already seen above, the general election becomes the primary and the runoff the final election.

Various schemes of proportional representation (PR) have been used in various cities, and are still used or are still available. Probably the most important of these schemes is the Hare system, though others include

[13] *The Municipal Year Book 1963* (Chicago: ICMA), p. 79.
[14] *Charter of Denver, Colorado*, Secs. C1.1–4, C1.1–4(2).

cumulative voting, limited voting, and various other types of preferential systems, such as the Grand Junction (or Bucklin), the Nanson, and the Ware.[15]

The most important reason for using any kind of PR is to assure minority voice in the councils of city government. Both the Hare system (for legislative bodies) and the Ware system (modeled after the Hare, but used to fill single offices) assure minority representation without fail. Yet the latter has been rarely used in the United States, and the use of the former has rapidly declined over the past two decades. Why this is so stems from certain characteristics of the systems which are endemic to them. One might even go so far as to say that these systems are "un-American," not in the sense that they are undemocratic, but rather in the sense that they seemingly do not fit well into American political life or into American political thinking. This is *not* to say that they are not rational systems, but rather that they do not live well in certain political environments. Observe, for example, that while no system of proportional representation has had more than passing acceptance in American cities, the Hare system—or variations upon it—has been rather widely used in some nations of the British Commonwealth.

Under the Hare system, city councilmen are elected from the city at large or from plural-member districts. Because of the nature of the voting process, there is no necessity for making nominations: this knotty problem is simply eliminated because the need no longer exists. The names of all candidates are listed on the ballot, usually, in American practice, without party identification. The voter then marks his ballot by numbering his choices according to his preferences: his first choice is rated one, his fifth choice five, until he has run through all the candidates. After the polls close, the counting begins. Although not particularly complicated, this process is lengthy, and the results of the election may not be known for a day or so. Both candidates and citizens stew in the juices of their own frustrations as they await the results.[16]

Because proportional representation *seems* complicated to the voter, because it may break down party control over elections, and because of certain other factors, the system has never had great popularity in American cities. New York City used it for a decade before discarding it to the cheers of those who had claimed that the election of a handful of Communists and other leftwingers to the city council rendered the scheme suspect! Cincin-

[15] An excellent description of the last three systems, used mainly to choose among candidates for a single office, may be found in Jewell Cass Phillips, *Municipal Government and Administration in America* (New York: The Macmillan Co., 1960), pp. 189–190.

[16] For a comprehensive explanation of the system, see G. H. Hallett, *Proportional Representation—The Key to Democracy* (New York: National Municipal League, 1940).

nati, in 1957, abandoned the system partially because of the election of a militant Negro councilman.[17]

Limited voting is presently being used in Philadelphia, and here and there among American counties. Because the Philadelphia voter may cast ballots for only five of the seven at-large seats on the city council, two minority councilmen are almost certain to be seated.[18]

Cumulative voting has been used for more than a half-century in selecting members for the lower house of the Illinois general assembly. Three members are selected from each legislative district, and the citizen has three votes which he may distribute among candidates as he sees fit. Although some Illinois cities long had the option of adopting the same method for selecting members of the city council, none ever used the option.

The Hare system of proportional representation and the various systems of preferential voting are, from an ideal standpoint, not only wholly consonant with democracy, they are also much more sophisticated techniques than the single-vote-per-office approach we generally use in American politics. Subject, of course, to operational faults—what electoral system is not? —these systems of voting can be designed to measure public sentiment with considerable accuracy and to give the greatest possible minority representation.

But we must remember, on the other hand, that PR is not the only method for assuring minority representation on legislative councils. One of the oldest methods for electing city councilmen—election by wards—can assure minority representatives on the council. The city, as we know from casual observation, is divided into sections, the residents of which differ widely in race, economic worth, national origins, and even party affiliation. If ward boundaries are honestly drawn—not gerrymandered— people of like background in any one section will be able to secure representation on the council.

Ballots: Long and Short. As the Jacksonian revolt swept the country in the 1830's and 1840's the cities and the states felt the impact to a greater extent than did the federal government, at least in a structural sense. That the Jacksonian movement had salutary effects upon the city—extension of the franchise, for example—no one could deny. Nor could anyone deny that the results of the movement, the sweep of a spurious egalitarianism, the introduction of the plural (or fragmented) executive, the shortening of terms of office, and the curbs put upon the right of an officeholder to succeed himself—both increased the electorate's capacity for irrational politi-

---

[17] Edward C. Banfield and James Q. Wilson, *City Politics* (Cambridge, Mass.: Harvard University Press, 1963), p. 307. For an extended examination of the Cincinnati situation, see Ralph A. Straetz, *PR Politics in Cincinnati* (New York: New York University Press, 1958).

[18] Phillips, *op. cit.*, pp. 188, 280.

cal behavior and reduced the possibility of the development of coherent leadership patterns.

But experience teaches, even in politics. After a few generations of experimentation with Jacksonian methods, thoughtful people began considering a return to other forms of government. These second thoughts about Jacksonian methods led to a challenge of the long ballot; more specifically, they led to the short-ballot movement and to the National Short Ballot Organization, established in 1909. The aim of the movement—to shorten the ballot—was simplicity itself. It was, that is, on the surface. The colonial and early republican city often had the short ballot, and there was probably less need for it in 1780 than in 1900. Why, then, did the movement need a war chest, an organization and a membership, publicists, and a program?

The reason was that in order to shorten the ballot one needed completely to reorganize city hall. Most of the long list of elective offices had to be eliminated so that only the mayor and councilmen would be elected. It is no wonder that the short-ballot enthusiasts soon became closely identified with those forms of municipal government which made the short ballot almost inevitable: the strong-mayor, the council-manager, and (momentarily, before it fell from favor) the commission.

The reformers had remarkable success with the city, made modest gains with the state, and came a cropper with the county. Yet even in the cities, remnants of the Jacksonian reliance on the long ballot still remain. It may very well be that elective clerks and treasurers, auditors, attorneys, fire marshals, and assorted other urban officials are anachronisms; but elective they still remain in many urban jurisdictions. V. O. Key's comment on the long ballot in state governments applies equally well to city governments: the "multiple executive remains and becomes at times a block to effective administration; at others a haven for incompetence; and on occasion, a means for obstructing the evident majority will." [19]

Aside from the administrative problems the long ballot presents, confusion of the voter is an inevitable result. V. O. Key again sums up this confusion with a felicitous phrase, "the lottery of the long ballot." And indeed the long ballot is a lottery. In making his selections from among a list of candidates for administrative office the voter has few criteria, either objective or subjective, to guide him. He votes blindly. Blind voting is, in fact, one effective means by which the voter can reduce the burdens which the long ballot would impose upon him. It is also a means by which a political organization keeps control of city hall.

Even though the long ballot no longer presents a major problem to

[19] V. O. Key, Jr., *American State Politics: An Introduction* (New York: Alfred A. Knopf, 1956), p. 198.

American cities, "enlightened" charter drafters will still retain elective administrative officers, because of community custom and traditions, and try to reconcile such officers with strong-mayor or council-manager forms. Oddly enough, sometimes they can successfully make the reconciliation. An elective clerk may, by charter or statutory mandate, be subject to the city manager or the strong mayor in the performance of his office; even his office hours may be under control of the chief executive or chief administrative officer. If the possibility remains that he will, because of his political power in the community, seek independence, this is still but the faintest penumbra compared to the long dark shadow once cast over the city by the long ballot.

The ghost of the long ballot, in other words, has not been laid. But the reformers have won a victory, a notable one, and most observers nowadays would insist that at least this reform victory must be celebrated.

Vox Populi—Vox Dei

The voice of the people, in a democracy, is virtually the voice of God. Here lies the ultimate capacity to make public decisions. Here, too, lies that mysterious element, sovereignty. In the people rests the creative power to give birth to the state, to control it, to change it or upset it. The people speak with an awful voice.

But *how* do they speak? We think of the United States as a republic, where, according to republican principles, public decisions are made by elective representatives of the people—the executives and the legislatures —or by agencies staffed and controlled by the popularly designated officials—the courts and the bureaucracy.

We are governed, in short, by republican principles. But is this generalization completely true? Or even partially so? The answers to these questions depend upon what level of decision-making one is studying. Republican principles? Yes, surely, at the national level. Republican principles? To a large extent in forming state policy. Republican principles? An argument could be made that a major part of the controlling decisions in local government are made according to the principles of direct democracy. The city, in other words, *may* be more a democracy than a republic.

The means by which the city was transformed into a partial democracy were those three forms of direct popular participation in decision-making —the initiative, the referendum, and (to a degree) the recall. Thought by many scholars to have been borrowed from Switzerland at the turn of the century, direct democracy also derived in part from the American past.[20] As observed some years ago, "popular decision upon issues of public policy

---

[20] F. L. Bird and F. M. Ryan, *The Recall of Public Officers* (New York: The Macmillan Co., 1930), p. 2.

had become firmly ingrained in the political mores of the American people long before the Swiss form of the referendum was suggested for adoption." [21]

Partly borrowed, partly indigenous, popular democracy became the darling of reformers and subsequently took firm hold on city government. It has been particularly evident in the charters of commission-type and council-manager cities and is often thought of as an essential characteristic of those forms of government.

The recall permits the citizen to challenge the right of an elected official to continue in office, the initiative gives the voter a chance to propose legislation himself; the referendum enables the voter to say "Yea" or "Nay" to proposed ordinances or charter amendments. Let us look at each procedure in turn.

The Recall of Public Officials. In a Midwestern city some years ago, the city manager decided that the fire chief, being physically incapable any longer of directing his department, should be forced into retirement. Thinking it would be both politic and wise to test opinions other than his own, he first polled the city council and found that four members favored the proposed action and only one member opposed it. Given a feeling of security with such an overwhelming majority behind him, the manager removed the chief from active duty.

The opposition member—a woman—immediately brought out recall petitions against the other four councilmen. In a recall election they lost, and new members were elected. The first business taken up by the council was to fire the manager by a 5 to 0 vote!

If this is a sensational example of how the recall may be used, it also is an instructive one. Note the elements: (1) a single issue, unrelated, as far as the public was concerned, to the broad field of municipal policy information; (2) a dissident faction, with a determined leader (a woman whose advice was scorned!); and (3) direct public intervention in a matter on which it simply was not competent to judge—the capacity of an administrative official to do his job.

Most dispassionate observers would probably decide, from this example, that (1) the city manager had acted reasonably and with good sense in forcing the fire chief's retirement, and (2) his good work had been undone by the sentimental reaction of the voters. They might conclude, therefore, that the recall was a poor route to travel if the city wished to reach the goal of sound policy formation. But is this true? Let us take some other examples.

In 1942 F. R. Buechner, newly appointed city manager of Superior, Wisconsin (he had served less than a year), was summarily removed from his position by a majority of the city council. Suspecting that the council majority wished not so much to get rid of the city manager as to wreck council-manager government, a number of community leaders immediately brought out recall petitions against members of the council. In the subsequent election all of the councilmen who had voted to fire the city manager were recalled, and candidates supporting council-manager government were elected. The newly constituted council immediately rehired Mr. Buechner, and he served without serious challenge until his resignation (at his own volition) some five years thereafter.

In the spring of 1959, a recall election in Little Rock, Arkansas, turned upon a highly emotional public issue—racial integration of the public schools. The city had been deeply perplexed for more than two years over a federal court order directing the school board to permit the admission of Negro children to schools previously limited to white students. The segregationist majority of the board, aided and abetted by a segregationist governor, seemed determined to flout the court's will. The moderates on the board were equally determined that the public school system would not be wrecked by segregationist intransigence.

The moderate group in the city, early in May, 1959, began circulating petitions asking for the recall of three segregationist members of the board (the fourth segregationist member had resigned). Immediately thereafter the opposing faction brought out petitions against the three moderate members. When both sets of petitions were filed, they were found legally sufficient, and the county board of election commissioners set the date of the election for May 25. The issue was clearly drawn: Was the segregationist or the moderate position to prevail? Or to put the matter another way: Would the voters support those who were unalterably opposed to social changes, or would they indicate a willingness to accommodate to change? Although the vote on May 25 was close, the moderates on the board were retained, and the segregationists were recalled. And obeying the electoral mandate, the board of election commissioners appointed three moderates to fill the vacancies on the board.[22]

To bring recall action against an official, the individual or group must petition against him. One of the oldest devices used by democracies, the recall petition goes far beyond the kind of petition envisaged, let us say, in the U.S. Constitution. Far more than a petition for redress of grievances, the right guaranteed in the First Amendment, the recall petition is a direct challenge to the official's continuance in office.

In order for the petitioners to force a call for an election, a minimum number of electors must sign the petition. A typical charter or statutory

[22] Henry M. Alexander, "The Little Rock Recall Election," *Eagleton Institute Cases in Practical Politics* (New York: McGraw-Hill Book Co., 1960), Case No. 17.

provision is that 20 percent of the number of those voting for mayor in the last election constitutes the minimum of signatures necessary. Another typical provision is that the official petitioned against must have served in the office for a minimum period, this in order that a loser in an election may not immediately seek the recall of his successful opponent. The proper city official then reviews the petition. If it meets the statutory or charter mandate, he certifies this fact to the city council, which must call an election.

What happens if the council refuses to carry out its legal obligations? The usual remedy is appeal to the courts for a writ of mandamus. If the city is determined to fight the dissidents, legal action may be long-drawn-out and costly. In the early 1960's recall petitions against certain councilmen in an Illinois city were held up in court, and only after almost two years and several thousand dollars in legal fees were the reformers able to force the issue. Then the recall was held only a few weeks before the incumbents' terms ran out!

In the recall election itself the challenged official may simply be running alone—on his record. If he loses, the city must hold a subsequent election, or the council (or some other authority) may appoint a successor to fill out the unexpired term. On the other hand, the recall election may be a contest between the challenged official and the person wishing to succeed him.

Though having the characteristics, on the surface, of republicanism, the recall often resembles the initiative and referendum in practice. One issue or another is apt to trigger the affair, and the issue overshadows personalities. The mayor or manager fires a popular city employee; the council passes a tax increase; the city refuses to bargain collectively with the garbage collectors—where the issue is of importance there may be very little substantive difference between the recall and the referendum.

One element of the recall which is often overlooked, largely because its effect is so difficult to measure, is the use of it as a threat. Theodore Roosevelt had this element in mind when he described the recall as a club behind the door. An incident from Michigan illustrates the point.

Immediately after World War II a group of newly returned veterans fell into conflict with the school board. More was at issue than conduct of school affairs; this was a battle between generations. On the one hand, there were the board members, all over forty, all securely established in the community, all equally secure in the knowledge that they knew what was best for the local schools. And there, on the other hand, were the veterans: young—not a one had yet reached the age of thirty, confident of their own importance—had they not just won the greatest war in history? Never for a moment doubting the righteousness of their cause, the veterans met with the board in a bitter session and threatened, the very next day, to bring out recall petitions against the board members if the board did not change its policy. Shaken by the prospect, the board gave in to the veterans' demands. Youth had been served!

Just how important the threat of recall is to the formation of municipal policy can only be guessed at. Like any threat, to be effective it must not be empty. The challengers must be willing, if the threat is not heeded, to expend the energy and the funds necessary to carry out the threat. If they do not, their influence will probably be reduced to zero. In some respects the threat of recall doubtless resembles the executive threat of veto. We know both of them are used, and, deductively, we must conclude that they both can influence the actions, if not the opinions, of public officers. The strong mayor may alter the course of particular legislation by his threat to veto it if it is not changed. So also may a dissident faction within the city influence both legislation and administration by means of the threat to recall the election official. We still, however, do not know the real importance of the threat.

Although available to a sizable portion of American urban voters, the recall has not been greatly used outside California. Whether it is of significant value to the democratic government of an American city cannot be determined conclusively. One can only say with certainty that it exists, that it is always a potential threat to the security of those in power, and that it can be used, for good or for ill, by a dissident group which wants to challenge city hall.

The Initiative. More widely used than the recall, the initiative is a means of converting the electorate at large into a legislative body. The central element of the process, again, is the petition, which is circulated among the qualified voters for their signatures. Usually the number of signatures required by charter or statute is not so large as for the recall; 10 percent of those voting in the last general city election is probably close to the average.

Strictly speaking, the initiative has two forms. In using what we shall call Form One, the political-action group must first draft the proposed ordinance, and the draft (or a digest of it) must appear on each sheet of the petition. Below the draft is room for signatures of the electors. Each citizen must sign for himself: a wife, for example, may not sign for her husband who is out of town. When the sheet carries a full page of signatures, the petition bearer signs it himself, and in doing so swears that he has personally witnessed all of the signatures and that, to the best of his knowledge, the signers are all qualified voters of the municipality.

After the petitioners have obtained a sufficient number of signatures, they present the petition sheets in a bundle to the city's election officer. If the document is in order, two types of action may then result, depending upon whether the petitioners are proposing an ordinance or a charter amendment. A proposed ordinance may be presented to the council for action; and if the council approves it, the ordinance becomes part of the city code. If the council turns it down, the proposal must then go to the voters for approval or rejection. If the petitioners are seeking approval of a charter amendment, the city council must normally call upon the electorate for a final decision on the matter.

The most significant fault in this form of the initiative is the responsibility of the petitioners for drafting the proposal. No matter how well conceived, no matter how desirable or statesmanlike, if the proposal is poorly drafted it is apt to cause endless trouble after approval. Since no satisfactory method of correcting this fault has yet been developed—and probably never can be—it will remain a central point of argument for those who view the initiative with disfavor.

There is a first cousin to the initiative—we shall label it Form Two—which calls for the initiation of policy by the people without the attendant drafting of a proposed ordinance or charter amendment. A neighborhood group wishes to set up an improvement district in order to finance a street or sewer by special assessment. A good-government organization wishes to propose a change from the weak-mayor to the strong-mayor form of government. Another group wants a change to home-rule status. In each case group action leads toward institutional change. The people, in other words, *initiate* public policy. This kind of practice needs to be underscored with an example.

The city of Crestfallen finds, after a special census, that it has soared above the 5,000-population mark and now is constitutionally eligible for home-rule status. After a series of study meetings sponsored by the League of Women Voters, some interested citizens form the Crestfallen Home-rule Committee and begin circulating petitions. Upon receiving the petitions, the city clerk finds them legally sufficient and recommends to the city council that an election be called. Subsequently, the council calls the election, the people elect a charter commission, and the commission proceeds to draft a proposed charter. The charter receives majority approval from the electorate, and Crestfallen is a home-rule city.

The important observation to be made here is that the originating cause for home rule was citizen action. As a result of that action, basic changes came about in political structure and, possibly, in political alignment.

This latter form of action avoids a major difficulty of Form One. Indeed, a contrast of the two forms clearly shows up the deficiencies in Form One. Form Two, in the first place, corrects the significant fault in Form One. A home-rule action committee does not draft the proposed charter, nor does a neighborhood group fashion a complex special-assessment program. The people simply take the initiative: they start a movement. Theirs is the creative, democratic act; thereafter, republican institutions—the charter commission, or the council—take over to give the act refinement, even sophistication. Sometimes this ends the matter. At other times there is a third step: the voice of the people speaks through an election to ratify or nullify the proposal.

Second, Form Two circumscribes popular initiative, or at least gives it direction. Action by initiative petition is often simply advisory. It may become compulsory, but the compulsion is so severely channeled, as in the case of the home-rule movement, that republican formality can be used as a balance to democratic enthusiasm. There is, moreover, only a certain sector of public policy available to the people under Form Two. The classic initiative, by contrast, may open up the entirety of public policy formation to initiative action, and thus greatly enlarge the potential for disruptive action.

Another difference between the two forms of the initiative is that Form One is used much less frequently than Form Two. Even in California, where Form One first appeared (in Los Angeles in 1906) and where it is available to the citizens of every city and county, the initiative in classic form has probably had relatively little effect upon local decision-making.[23]

The Referendum. By far the most widely used of all the forms of direct democracy is the referendum. It is to be found in three forms: (1) the compulsory referendum, (2) the advisory referendum, and (3) the referendum by petition (sometimes called the initiative referendum).

The Compulsory Referendum. It would be difficult indeed to overemphasize the importance to local policy formation of the compulsory referendum. Changes in forms of government; financial measures, such as bond issues and tax increases; annexation of territory; the sale or purchase of property; new charters or amendments to old ones—all of these basic policy decisions, as well as a multitude of less basic ones, must be approved by the urban electorate before they become binding.

The compulsory referendum made an early appearance in American politics. Some of the first state constitutions were approved by popular vote; in 1818 Connecticut required that proposed state constitutional amendments be ratified by the people.[24] During the nineteenth century, to quote Key and Crouch, "a wide variety of statutory questions came to be more or less customarily submitted for popular decision . . . . In the local field, bills affecting the scope and form of local government went to a popular vote, as did bond issues, tax rates, liquor laws, city charters, and numerous vexed questions." [25] Urged on by the progressive movement at the turn of the century, both state legislatures and reform groups added the initia-

---

[23] Winston W. Crouch *et al.*, *California Government and Politics* (Englewood Cliffs, N.J.: Prentice-Hall, 2nd ed., 1960), pp. 93–94.

[24] Duane Lockard, *The Politics of State and Local Government* (New York: The Macmillan Co., 1963), p. 263.

[25] Key and Crouch, *op. cit.*, p. 491.

tive referendum to local decision-making. The compulsory referendum thus considerably antedated the referendum by petition in city politics.

Usually required by constitution, statute, or local charter, the compulsory referendum is as familiar to the citizen as the election of city councilmen or school board members. One can say with confidence that most of the really crucial decisions made in American cities today must, because of the compulsory referendum, be concurred in by the people directly. To city politics this circumstance adds dimensions found to a much lesser degree in state politics, and not at all in federal.

The crucial importance of the compulsory referendum can be seen from the experience of a Midwestern city over a period of about three years:

May, 1960	School bond issue	*Failed*
September, 1961	Bond issue to build a fire station and buy ladder truck	*Failed*
January, 1962	School bond issue in altered form	*Failed*
March, 1962	Park and recreation bond issue	*Failed*
July, 1962	Fire protection bond issue (slightly altered)	*Passed*
September, 1962	School bond issue (greatly reduced over former proposals)	*Passed*
March, 1963	Proposal to maintain school tax rate at current levels	*Passed*

Note the major decisions that resulted from these elections. Physical expansion of the schools was held up for two years while the school population was increasing drastically, and community leaders had to decide that half a loaf was better than none for the public educational system in order to pass the second bond issue. Increased fire protection was stymied for over nine months, but eventually was approved substantially according to the original plan. An ambitious parks and recreation program was badly defeated, so badly indeed that it was not immediately brought up again. Reduction in the school tax rate was only narrowly defeated. Success here simply meant maintenance of the status quo.

Can we draw any conclusions from this example? Whether the popular decisions were good or bad depends on one's value judgments, and thus we need not label them here. We can, however, say with confidence that the experience of this Midwestern city was typical, that the decisions were significant, and that the community's civic life was substantially affected by those decisions.

The financial life of the community's public institutions revolves around the compulsory referendum. Both tax rates and new forms of taxation are typically subject to this kind of referendum, as is the raising of the community's debt level. Financial planning, whether of an annual sort as in the operating budget or for the years ahead as in the capital improvements budget, hinges upon ratification or rejection of tax rates and bond issues at the polls. All municipal programs, from promotion of health and safety to support of the arts, are affected by this legislative power resting in the hands of the people.

Often a program must be approved twice by referendum before it becomes established municipal policy. Does the city wish to build a planetarium? First, the charter may have to be amended to give the council substantive authority to act, and then general obligation bonds must be issued to pay for the project. Both of these policy decisions normally must be approved at the polls. And that may not be the end of the matter. Since the city must raise not only the capital to be invested in the planetarium, but also the funds to operate it, there may be need for an increase in the general property tax. Likely as not, this too will need popular approval.

In order to get to the heart of the matter, we need to ask two questions. First, is the compulsory referendum necessary to secure responsible city government? And second, has the referendum had substantially adverse effects upon urban community life?

One answer to the first question may be given by pointing to the national government. If one concedes that the Congress and the President have acted responsibly in their legislative activities over the decades, one must also be ready to admit that the compulsory referendum is not a sine qua non of responsible government. We might similarly comment on the state legislatures and governors, though they are, to an extent, restricted by compulsory referenda.

If this is not a sufficient answer, let us look elsewhere. There is a popular belief that city councils simply cannot be trusted with the determination of tax or indebtedness levels. The councils must be limited in their action on such matters by statute, charter stipulations, or the compulsory referendum —or possibly by all three. Yet in literally hundreds of American cities where the compulsory referendum tends to apply, the property tax rates are less than the statutory or charter maximums. Why are the rates not up to the maximums? It is not because of need, because it is a rare city that has enough money in the general fund. The reason is that the normal political controls exercised through representative channels apply to the council.

In the 1950's the statutory limit on Chicago's general-fund levy expired. Since the compulsory referendum did not apply, the city council was able to increase the levy at will, and there were dire predictions in subsequent years that the council would indeed raise the levy even to confiscatory levels. Although the general-fund levy did go up, the increase was gradual, and there was no evidence of a popular revolt against it. Cook County legislators introduced bills in the Illinois general assembly at intervals to reimpose the ceiling, but Mayor Daley's cohorts were able to beat down each attempt.

Little or no evidence, in other words, exists to support the myth that the compulsory referendum is essential to responsible city government. Indeed, many examples can be garnered, as we have seen, to show that councils are quite responsive to the popular will even when the referendum is not there to prod them into responsibility.

The answer to the second question—Has the compulsory referendum had substantially adverse effects upon urban community life?—is even harder to come by. One may find examples to support both a "Yea" and a "Nay" to the proposition, but examples are by no means conclusive evidence. We know that the compulsory referendum serves, in effect, as a popular veto. From that knowledge we can legitimately assume, deductively, that the referendum serves as a brake upon representative actions, and that it thus forces the electorate into a negative role. We know further, however, that this same popular veto has an affirmative aspect: the people's representatives in city hall must form policy with the veto constantly in mind. These representatives must thus seek good ideas to which the people will react positively at the polls.

Any concluding statement about the compulsory referendum must of necessity contain two types of generalizations: one that is based upon reasonably good evidence and another that seems reasonable deductively. First, we know that the referendum is expensive: making public decisions by means of the ballot is a far more costly process than making them by representative institutions. Second, we know that irrelevancies often crop up in referendum campaigns and serve to divert attention from the real issues.

After surveying the literature, Duane Lockard offers impressive evidence that irrelevancies do indeed become commonplace in referendum campaigns. Although scientific opinion overwhelmingly supports the addition of fluorides to the city's water supply to enhance the dental health of children, probably in more than half the cities in which the question has gone to popular vote in recent years the people have said "No." An example of one argument often used against fluorides is that the chemical is poisonous if swallowed in quantity—an obvious irrelevancy. One may kill oneself from overeating, but that fact does not argue against the intake of food.[26]

One final comment needs to be made about the compulsory referendum. In many urban communities ratification by the electorate of basic policy decisions—new charters, charter amendments, changes in form of government—is perhaps a necessary result of popular sovereignty. The charter of government and radical changes in policy may need the stamp of legitimacy which can be given, at least in the American city, only by popular ratification. Perhaps it is here that we find at last the real functional value of the compulsory referendum: to legitimate the most basic decisions of the local polity.

The Advisory Referendum. The second form of referendum is of an advisory nature. The city council needs—or feels that it needs—advice from the people on a matter of public concern, and the council "polls" the citizenry by means of an election. Would the people approve fluoridation of the water supply? How does a majority of the voters—or a majority of those willing to take the trouble to vote—feel about an increase in the property-tax rate or the imposition of a sales tax? Do the people believe it wise for the council to issue $2 million in revenue bonds to modernize the sewer system? Should the council authorize the mayor to designate one day each year as United Nations Day?

Questions of considerable and lesser moment may be within the competence of the council to decide. But for reasons of politics, because of a desire to find out community thinking, or perhaps simply because of lack of courage, the council may wish to submit a variety of proposals to the people.

Since the advisory referendum is sparingly used, no conclusive judgments can be made about it, but the suspicion lingers in the minds of seasoned observers that when it is used the advisory referendum is a device for passing the buck. The council simply does not have the courage to make the decisions that are essentially its own.

The Referendum by Petition. The referendum by petition—the third form—is a different breed of cat from the two preceding types. As with the classic-type initiative, the petition is used to bring the electorate directly into decision-making. The steps commonly followed are these:

1. The council passes an ordinance which, by law or charter provision, must not go into effect for a certain period of time. On occasion, however, an emergency provision may provide that it may go into effect immediately.

[26] Duane Lockard, *op. cit.*, pp. 267–270.

2. An objecting group circulates a petition against the ordinance and submits it to the city clerk.

3. The clerk checks upon whether the petition is in order. Are there a sufficient number of signatures, and has each citizen signed in his own hand? Has the petition bearer sworn to the sufficiency of the petition? These are some of the substantive questions the clerk must raise.

4. The clerk certifies the petition to the council, which may then repeal the ordinance or order a referendum election. An alternative course of action is for the council to vote that the petition does not meet all the legal standards. It will refuse, then, either to call an election or to repeal the ordinance. In such a case, the petitioners may seek a remedy at law, usually asking the court for a writ of mandamus to compel the council to act. If the petition is in order and the council refuses to repeal the ordinance, it must call an election. A majority vote will then determine whether the ordinance stands or falls.

What have been the results from the use of the referendum by petition? Has it justified the hopes of the progressives at the turn of the century, or has it merely been disruptive of orderly, representative government?

Neither extreme has been realized, except in unusual circumstances. For one thing, the referendum by petition has been only of minor importance compared with the compulsory referendum. No one will ever know precisely how much use its sponsors expected to be made of it, so that one cannot say that they would be disappointed with its limited utilization. Because of its limited use outside California, it has been of little moment to local decision-making, and all arguments concerning it must turn around that central point.

Has the referendum by petition been disruptive of the governing process? In the commission-type cities of Illinois, various fiscal measures have been held up and some have actually been rejected by referendums. For instance, city automobile license fees, sales taxes, parking meters have been turned down. But virtually every one of the seventy-odd cities in this class had, by 1960, installed parking meters and levied automobile and sales taxes. In terms of the overall experience of these cities, in other words, the referendum by petition has made little or no difference.

Has this kind of referendum enabled a dissident group to harass and bedevil the administration in power? Yes, surely, in certain instances. The Touchette faction of the Democratic party (in the Illinois section of the St. Louis metropolitan area) was able to mount two attacks on the majority faction led by Mayor Alvin G. Fields of East St. Louis by petitioning against two crucial city ordinances. In one instance, the Touchette group won its point and seriously embarrassed its opponents. In the other case, the Fields wing challenged the petition and had its challenge upheld in the courts. But this example is unusual. There has been no significant harassment in Illinois, because the referendum by petition has been so little resorted to. Apparently the same generalization applies to California cities.[27]

Has the referendum by petition raised unduly the costs of making local decisions? Even if we discounted the expense of printing and circulating the petition, since these are private costs, we would still have to admit that financing a referendum election, especially if it is a special one, could create a budget deficit—in itself illegal in some states! A good case in point is the celebrated referendum, held in 1958, on the question of whether Los Angeles should build a stadium for the Dodgers' baseball club in Chavez Ravine. Both sides spent considerable sums on publicity before the election, and the election itself was costly.[28] If such elections were often held, the social costs of local decision-making would be raised significantly. But, again, the infrequency of such elections makes it difficult to argue that the referendum by petition is a material financial burden on the community.

Summary

Popular democracy has two major elements: (1) the age-old referendum and initiative that were already in evidence early in the nineteenth century and that are, indeed, almost as old as the republic; and (2) the initiative, referendum, and recall (IRR), developed by the progressives in the first years of the twentieth century and copied, in part, from the Swiss experience.

The IRR, espoused by the progressives, has realized neither the fears of its opponents nor the hopes of its supporters. In all of its three parts, the IRR represents a kind of political escape valve: when the political pot boils, there must be some means to let the pressure escape, and the IRR can do just that.

To underscore this point we might use the reasoning of a U.S. Supreme Court justice, concurring with the majority in *Baker* v. *Carr*, a case that bears directly on the relation of the city with the state.[29] In his concurring opinion, Mr. Justice Clark observed that since the Tennessee legislature had refused to reapportion the state's legislative districts and since the people could not initiate reapportionment legislation, the only remedy lay in the courts. Justice Clark was saying, in effect, that the pressure of the urban population for equal representation in the Tennessee legislature could have been relieved by the initiative, if only it had been available for use.

This kind of reasoning is as applicable to city politics as to state. If the initiative had not been available to the urban electorate—in either one or

---

[27] Crouch *et al.*, *op. cit.*, p. 93.
[28] *Ibid.*
[29] 369 U.S. 186 (1962).

both of its forms—literally hundreds of cities would never have been able to adopt council-manager government.

The other element of popular democracy—one might be tempted to call it the indigenous element—is essentially the compulsory referendum and Form Two of the initiative. This older of the two major elements has significantly influenced the course of the city's political development. Whether the influence has been for good or for ill depends largely upon one's point of view and upon the circumstances of each particular episode, but its significance cannot be doubted.

Neither can these other characteristics: (1) expense—this is a costly way to form public policy; (2) democratic orientation—both elements of popular democracy substantially modify the representative principle; the compulsory referendum, because of its widespread and frequent use, especially so; (3) intrusion of irrelevancies; (4) popular education—electoral campaigns preceding votes on issues undoubtedly serve to inform the voter and may even give him a vital sense of participation in the governing process; (5) the stamp of legitimacy—when limited to ratification of charters or charter amendments, popular approval may give a necessary legitimacy to the basic law of the city.

Annotated Bibliography

Two quite adequate introductions to urban politics are well worth reading. See Duane Lockard, *The Politics of State and Local Government* (New York: The Macmillan Co., 1963); and Edward C. Banfield and James Q. Wilson, *City Politics* (Cambridge, Mass.: Harvard University Press and Massachusetts Institute of Technology Press, 1963). Of the two, the Lockard study is the superior, principally because it gives attention to issue politics, a feature of the local political environment ignored by Banfield and Wilson. Although limited to Florida cities, the study by Gladys Kammerer and associates cannot help but intrigue the student of local politics; and it will give him data and generalizations that could well apply throughout the United States and Canada. See Gladys M. Kammerer *et al.*, *The Urban Political Community* (Boston: Houghton Mifflin Co., 1963).

Sayre and Kaufman give us a conceptual framework for studying the political institutions of great cities. See Wallace S. Sayre and Herbert Kaufman, *Governing New York City* (New York: Russell Sage Foundation, 1960; and W. W. Norton & Co., paperback ed., 1965). And if Robert A. Dahl's examination of more than a century of politics in New Haven is not yet a classic, the reason probably is that it has not been in print long enough. See Robert A. Dahl, *Who Governs?— Democracy and Power in an American City* (New Haven, Conn.: Yale University Press, 1961).

For an old study of the recall which still has more than historical value, see F. L. Bird and F. M. Ryan, *The Recall of Public Officers: A Study of the Operation of the Recall in California* (New York: The Macmillan Co., 1930). The only drawbacks to the Key and Crouch inquiry into the initiative and referendum are its age and its limitation to California. See V. O. Key, Jr., and Winston W. Crouch, *The Initiative and Referendum in California* (Berkeley, Calif.: University of California Press, 1939).

CHAPTER 12

Those Men in City Hall

In the past half-century, city politics has suffered a sea change. In place of the flamboyant boss, in place of the worker and the dispossessed, the new mayor and the city manager have come into city hall; and the middle class has come into the public and private councils that ultimately direct and govern the city. And with this change in class dominance have come a different set of ideas and values and a strange new professional group—could we call it an "elite corps"?—to implement the ideology and values of the middle class.

The old order is gone, or nearly so. And with it have gone the slipshod methods, the saloon politics, the charismatic leader, the unaudited accounts that sum up urban politics at the turn of the century. With it also has gone (some would say) an essential humanity—that individual, non-ideological approach to politics which marked the city machine and made it so remarkable. This was the approach, viewed another way, that not only gave the lowliest citizen access to the leader but also gave him—and this is more important—a certain feeling of equality and rapport with those who sat in the halls of the mighty.

Truly, the city has suffered a sea change into something rich and strange. Has it also suffered—in the modern, non-Shakespearean sense of the word —an alienation from a substantial portion of the citizenry? Has it gained the world only to lose its soul? These are questions that we must keep in mind as we contrast the boss-ridden city of earlier years with the middle-class city of today.

The Twilight of the Boss

Boss rule of the American city arose in the 1840's. Twilight had engulfed the boss and his machine by the 1940's. Although the boss and the machine were still to dominate such big cities as Chicago and Philadelphia and such lesser ones as Gary and East St. Louis, they were anachronisms in a wholly changed political environment.

The century in which the boss grew strong enough to dominate city hall (and many if not all of the satellite governments surrounding city hall), in which he reached into the state house and even into the White House, and in which he finally declined—this was the century of the immigrant. The immigrant created boss and machine and carried them to the heights of power. The passing of the immigrant—more than any other factor—caused the decline of the boss.

This is not, of course, the whole story. It took more than simply the immigrant to establish Boss McLaughlin in Brooklyn by the 1850's and more than the passing of the immigrant to destroy the Pendergasts, Crumps, Hagues, and Curleys, who wielded great power even as late as the 1930's.

The power of the boss and his machine rested on a firm base. There were (1) a poor, generally exploited working class, very large and poorly educated and (2) a violent party spirit which the boss could nurture and utilize. Furthermore (3) a deep sense of identity existed among ethnic, religious, and national groups: the Irish were very Irish, the Jews very Jewish, the Germans, Negroes, Italians, all highly self-conscious; and all were conscious, too, of the latent hostility of the outside world. There was in addition (4) a well-developed spoils system and a kind of social-service system to ease the burdens of the poor: jobs, sinecures, favors, baskets of food, scuttles of coal. And finally (5) there was a dedicated, ruthless, dramatic, committed, charismatic leader. The idea that politics is a game is a recent invention in the city. To the old-time boss, politics was very real and very earnest. He got pleasure from it, yes; but it was still a profession, not a game. The stakes were high and the rewards were most material indeed. One could get rich in politics. How else could one rise out of the dehumanizing factory ghettos of New York or Chicago or San Francisco, or out of the coal pits of Pennsylvania or Illinois? There were other ways, it is true, of gaining success, but for the surefooted and the talented, politics was an open sesame to the treasure house.

A rich literature has grown up around the boss and the machine—and with good reason. The boss not only represented one of the most colorful aspects of American politics (perhaps *the* most colorful aspect); he also made some real contributions.

The most important of these contributions was the unifying effect the boss had upon urban government. Broken into fragments by the Jacksonian insistence upon the long ballot, the city could barely function through its legally recognized officialdom. The mayor was a cipher; a considerable list of elective executive officers competed among themselves for power and prestige; the council was hamstrung by impossible restrictions upon its power. Some kind of extralegal force had to unite the fragments, and that force was supplied by the boss.

When state legislatures were being bought and sold by representatives of the railroads, the streetcar companies, and other robber barons, the boss furnished the city some protection from the depredations of the state politicians. Often, it is true, the quid pro quo was as great as the ravages of the aggressors would have been. This was the case with Boise Penrose in Philadelphia and the state of Pennsylvania. But then look at the Chicago bosses, who always seemed to have a perverse loyalty to the city and who, unsavory as most of them were, were far more sensitive to urban needs than the men who ran the state legislature or, for that matter, the Congress.

Boss rule had other advantages. The good boss—using the adjective without its ethical connotations—was a builder. He paved and guttered the streets; he built sewerage systems and civic plazas; he erected schools. If the city hall in Kansas City is an imposing structure (though hardly an architectural triumph), a skyscraper soaring above all other buildings in the city, a monument to a corrupt political machine, it is as much an indication of Boss Tom Pendergast's perverse pride in his city as it is of his desire to get rich. Some might well condemn the boss for the inordinate cost of such public works, but they would at the same time have to admit that without him much less work in the city would have been done.

The boss, too, humanized an urban society that was as careless of human values as the institution of slavery—perhaps more so. Life in the mill towns of New England or in back of the stockyards in Chicago furnished prime examples of man's inhumanity to man. To the worker caught in this socioeconomic maelstrom the self-seeking politicians in city hall seemed to represent a positive good. What harm could they do him, him who had nothing? On the contrary, they had much to offer him. When no one else had the faintest concern for his plight, they gave him material aid. And, equally important, they gave him psychic aid: friendship, a sense of having an influential person accessible to listen to his complaints and his woes. This access to power, influence, and a sympathetic ear was very real and undoubtedly represented one of the great intangible assets of the machine.

And so the machine and the boss were at times not only politically essential, but also socially useful. Why, then, has the great age of the urban political boss passed away? The principal reason is that the boss, like the dinosaur, could not adapt to a radically changed environment. His personal cupidity, as Banfield and Wilson suggest, was partially responsible for this rigidity.[1] Tom Pendergast of Kansas City had an insatiable appetite for money, and that was one of the things that ruined him. By contrast, Mayor Richard Daley of Chicago has lived a simple, almost spartan life. He has adapted to a changed environment and has survived, and so has the Chicago political organization of which he is head.

But this is not all. As the middle class absorbed the immigrants, or a goodly portion of them; as middle-class values penetrated even into the working-class precincts; and as honesty, efficiency, and professionalization became political ideologies of great potency, the nondoctrinal machine became as out of place in politics as the dinosaur in the natural world. The machine that had once existed for itself alone, without an ideological base

[1] Edward C. Banfield and James Q. Wilson, *City Politics* (Cambridge, Mass.: Harvard University Press and Massachusetts Institute of Technology Press, 1963), p. 124.

of some kind, simply could not survive. These were the changes to which the boss could not adapt. These changes, far more than the introduction of social-welfare services by Washington in the 1930's, were responsible for the decline of the boss.

The Quest for Leadership

One of the prevailing characteristics of democratic government during the twentieth century has been the unceasing quest for leadership. The quest has been reduced, more often than not, to the invention, or development, of formulas that would enhance the power of the executive. In the American states the formula has been to shorten the ballot, hand over increasing fiscal powers to the chief executive, and give the governor added responsibilities of a legislative nature. In parliamentary systems (with the notable exception of the French), the tendency has been to increase the power of the government—the prime minister and his cabinet—at the expense of the legislative body.

A similar trend has been much in evidence in American cities. Beginning with the introduction (or the revival) of the strong-mayor form of government in Brooklyn and accelerating with the invention of council-manager government, the change has at least touched all cities of any size in both the United States and Canada and has radically altered both structure and leadership patterns in most of them. Observe the office of mayor. Before 1930, it was so unimportant that most political bosses disdained to occupy it. In his classic study of twenty bosses, Professor Harold Zink found that eighteen had chosen to control the city from a vantage point other than that of the mayor's office.

The bosses that have survived to the present day, on the other hand, have usually been mayors. Richard Daley of Chicago, David L. Lawrence of Pittsburgh, Orville L. Hubbard of Dearborn, and Alvin Fields of East St. Louis—to use examples from both large cities and small ones—each found being mayor necessary to maintain control over the organization. That one reason for this is the magnified importance of the mayor's office can hardly be doubted.[2]

Mayors: Strong and Stronger

The strong-mayor system of government, examined briefly in Chapter 10, follows the principles of separation of powers and of checks and balances—but only to a degree. The strong mayor is quite often in a much

[2] *Ibid.,* p. 121.

stronger position vis-à-vis the legislative body than the President or the governor. Some of the reasons for this may be found in the powers of the office; some, in the character of the city council; still others, in the local political situation.

A list of the typical powers of the strong mayor shows their formidable nature:

1. He is, in fact, chief executive. The short-ballot movement has swept away, in strong-mayor cities, all but the last vestiges of the separately elected administrative officials who would be a challenge to the mayor.

2. He serves a four-year term, with the right to succeed himself.

3. His is a full-time position, with a respectable salary attached to it. (If he is independently wealthy, he nevertheless finds that the salary adds strength to his political purse.)

4. He has important legislative powers: veto and perhaps the item veto; capacity to recommend legislation to the council, either by formal messages or other devices; and the power to call the council into special session.

5. He has general executive powers: to exercise administrative supervision over all departments and agencies, either personally or through his immediate staff or department heads; to create or abolish administrative positions; to make temporary transfers of positions; and to administer a contingency fund.

6. His power to appoint and remove personnel is quite considerable: his immediate staff aides, without council approval; his department heads, with council approval on appointments but not on removals; the members of city boards and commissions, with council approval on appointments but with removal usually for cause only.

7. His fiscal powers are notable: he compiles and submits the operating budget to the council; he controls the rate of spending of administrative agencies; he negotiates and concludes numerous contracts not requiring council approval; he negotiates gifts of land and money to the city; and through his comptroller he preaudits all agency expenditures to assure that they are consonant with his policy and the council's.

This considerable capacity of the strong mayor to govern is one of the essential stepping-stones to effective political leadership. Too much of late has been said by the student of "politics" in derogation of "structure" and of the contribution of structural reform to the kind of decision-making that eventually occurs in the city. Although it is true that many students of the city, particularly American scholars, have overly concentrated upon the effects of structural reform, the fact remains that structure is as much a part of the warp and woof of city politics as balloting or the activity of pressure groups. With a firm structural base the mayor can move toward real political leadership; without it he is hampered or completely frustrated. Formal structure, in other words, is an integral part of urban politics and affects the political situation profoundly.

The Rise of the New Mayor. Albert Ames of Minneapolis and Henry Ziegenheim of St. Louis, both of whom muckraking Lincoln Steffens damned so eloquently at the turn of the century, were old-fashioned political types who resembled each other closely. And they both controlled their city halls with similar, if corrupt, finesse.

When Arthur Naftalin won the mayoralty of Minneapolis in 1961, once more the Minnesota city and St. Louis were directed by men strikingly similar in background, technique, and accomplishment. In 1948 Arthur Naftalin received his Ph.D. at the University of Minnesota, where he taught for over a decade before being elected mayor of Minneapolis. Raymond Tucker taught civil engineering at Washington University and was active in civic affairs for years before he was elected mayor of St. Louis in the 1950's. Both men were intellectuals; both, middle class; each one came off the university campus to enter politics successfully; each one possessed most of the intangible elements of leadership.

Has the mayor changed so radically elsewhere during the past half-century? Though no unimpeachable empirical data exist on the subject, most observers would agree that he has. College professors do not usually sit as chiefs of the city—and perhaps it is just as well that they do not—but the character and quality of the mayor have changed noticeably, even since the 1930's.

Mayor Daley, a machine politician who has given Chicago its best city government in a century, openly stated at one time that he would follow the professors. And this was no idle boast. He made the late Carl Chatters, an authority on municipal finance and a long-time lecturer at the University of Chicago, his comptroller in 1955. In order to clean up the police department after the scandals of the early 1960's, Daley brought in Professor Orlando Wilson of the University of California at Berkeley to serve as his police commissioner. Nor is Daley exceptional. Both Mayors Robert F. Wagner and John V. Lindsay of New York have relied heavily upon the intelligentsia, both academic and lay.

Far and wide, the strong mayor has sought, usually successfully, to develop his own brain trust of bright young men (and women) who are working energetically to extend the ideals (if not the ideas) of the college classroom into the political market place. If it is incongruous to see a former college professor serving as police commissioner of Chicago, it is hardly less so to see a university-trained, tennis-playing, Unitarian bachelor as the administrative assistant to the Irish-Catholic mayor of East St. Louis.

"From charisma to reason" might be the title of a discourse on this change in the mayor's stance. Although the city manager has been used frequently to illustrate the triumph of middle-class ideals in urban politics, the strong mayor establishes the point equally well. His is the speech laden with facts, ideas, even ideology. He himself is the user of charts rather than the teller of tales.

Does this retreat from humor and theater, this safe, scientific approach to politics, mean that the mayor cannot at the same time be a consummate politician, even a statesman? From those who assume that the politician must have charisma to be an effective leader, the answer is simple: the new mayor has never developed the qualities of leadership.

But this answer misses the point. Just as Thomas Mann could live the life of a prosperous *Bürger* and still produce great literature, so can the new mayor develop his art of politics. Moreover, both the style and ideals of urban politics have changed. There are contemporary Big Bill Thompsons in every city who would like to bring the color, the theater, yes, and the irresponsibility of former years back into city hall, but they are thwarted by the change of political style. The characteristic of urban politics nowadays is understatement rather than flamboyance. And so long as that style governs, the mayor will reflect it.

The Leader: Professional Model

When the small Virginia city of Staunton, in 1908, employed a full-time general manager to serve as the chief administrative officer of the city, the members of the council doubtless assumed that the new manager would exercise leadership of a technical or professional nature. Being a technician he would have nothing to do with decision-making of a political nature. The same assumptions, apparently, were made by the city councils of Lockport, New York, and Sumter, South Carolina.

But the council members of these three cities overlooked a very crucial point: the importance of information to the decision-making process. Not being prescient, they had no means of knowing that the city manager would be forced, willy-nilly, into a policy role. Nor did they know that city councils, like all other legislative bodies throughout the democratic world, would be forced, by the increasing complexity of government, to give up authority to the professionally staffed executive departments.

The retreat of the amateur before the professional has been a prevailing characteristic of democratic political forms during this century. It has affected the nation, and it has profoundly affected the city. Nowhere is this retreat more evident than in council-manager government, which in its various forms has swept over North America (the United States and Canada), Ireland, and northern Europe, for in council-manager government the nonelective professional takes over as chief executive of the political unit. If presidents and strong mayors, backed up by their professional staff men, have assumed powers formerly exercised by legislative bodies, they are still fundamentally amateurs. The national bureaucracies in Washington and London, and the local ones in New York and Chicago, may have acquired inordinate power over governmental decisions, but that power still ebbs and flows, in considerable part, according to the commands of the amateur or the nonbureaucrat, whether mayor, president, or prime minister. Only in the council-manager city does the bureaucrat sit in the office of the chief executive. This is the simple, elemental fact of council-manager government. It is this fact which gives the city manager his special character.

According to the theory and the fact of council-manager government, as we have seen in Chapter 10, all the power that the city possesses is placed in the council. Having had this responsibility placed in its hands, the council then proceeds to delegate its administrative authority to the office of the city manager. By charter or statute the council may be (and usually is) denied the right to abolish the office of the manager or substantially to reduce the authority delegated to that office. The council retains the power to determine who will sit in the office and how long he will remain there.

Subject, therefore, to the confidence of the council, the manager has general oversight over enforcement of the city's codes and ordinances. His administrative responsibility is considerable and, indeed, tends to resemble that of the strong mayor: supervising all departments and agencies, making work assignments, and requiring reports, both formal and informal, in order that he may be kept informed of what is actually going on in the city.

The city manager appoints and removes department heads and staff aids, and he advises the council on numerous personnel matters: salary increases, pay scales, position classification, and personnel codes. He often appoints members of boards and commissions and may be an ex officio member of such agencies.

His fiscal powers include making the annual operating budget and submitting it to the council. In league with his finance officers, he must make crucial decisions in budget compilation which will affect the future of the city and his own future in the city. He must make similar decisions, though of longer range, in making and revising the capital improvements budget and the capital improvements program.

And then there is his role in policy-making. This role is so important that it subsumes all of his powers. In carrying out this role the manager must of necessity become a political force in the community—or, if you please, a politician. We need, therefore, to examine this role at some length.

In terms of formal rights and duties, the manager attends all council meetings (his presence is normally *required*) and engages in discussion that takes place at those meetings. If this is not debate as it is used in other types of legislative deliberations, it is nevertheless a very close approximation of debate. The manager may be asked by a council member to give his professional judgment on the matter at hand, or he may volunteer such a judgment and then be required to defend it. He may be challenged from the floor by a citizen and be forced to defend a policy in being or a policy proposed. In fact, then, if we refuse to be blinded by legal niceties, we must recognize the city manager as a nonvoting member of the city council, who does engage in debate on proposals before the council.

Because of the resources and trained personnel at his disposal, the manager is the principal fact finder. Unlike other legislative bodies, the council typically has no professional staff of its own, and its main reliance, therefore, is upon "the administration" for information.

Having most of the facts, the manager cannot escape making policy decisions. This seems to be the consensus of both managers themselves and academic observers. Arthur Bromage holds that all top management personnel are, at the very least, people whom councils inevitably have recourse to in making decisions. Pfiffner goes even further, insisting that "city managers are unanimous in believing that they have responsibility for initiating policy and that their councils expect them to be 'idea' men. The crucial consideration is not 'whether' they participate in the policy-making process, but 'how' they do it." [3] C. A. Harrell, long one of America's outstanding city managers, argues that "the manager properly participates in the policy-making process." As the knowledge of municipal affairs grows, continues Harrell, "the alternative courses of action to be considered by a city council dwindle." [4]

The City Manager as Politician. Up to this point we have hedged on the question: Is the city manager a political leader? Now we must face the question squarely. But, first, we must ask: What is a politician?

We must categorically deny that to be a politician one must be an elective official. All the evidence supports us in this denial. We do not expect appointive cabinet officers in either the state or national governments to be other than politicians. Nor does one need to wear a party label to be a politician. Thousands of city councilmen, who certainly are politicians, are elected on nonpartisan ballots and often literally do not have party affiliations. Still further, one's being a professional does not necessarily stand in the way of one's being a politician. Any number of medical doctors who head local and state departments of health are immersed in politics.

The best single criterion of a politician is whether the public official formulates public policy and seeks to persuade others to concur in that pol-

[3] John M. Pfiffner, "Policy Leadership—For What?" *Public Administration Review,* XIX (Spring, 1959), 122.

[4] C. A. Harrell and D. G. Weiford, "The City Manager and the Policy Process," *Public Administration Review,* XIX (Spring, 1959), 107, 104.

icy. By this test the city manager is a politician.[5] Even the managers' professional society, the International City Managers' Association, made tacit admission of this fact when, in 1952, the sentence in the managers' code of ethics reading that "The manager is in no sense a political leader" was changed to read that the manager is a community leader.[6]

The manager is also a politician because he must establish a kind of political rapport with the community. In this the mayor and council may help; so also may whatever local political group there is that supports council-manager government. But the manager may abdicate his responsibility to establish rapport only at the risk of destroying himself, the government in power, and even the form of government. If the manager has no political sense and no political information, he is a threat to all those around him. Paradoxically, the manager should be in a position to advise community leaders on community politics. He may well be one of the best sources of political information available to the mayor and council.

The manager is still further a politician because, willy-nilly, he must bear a certain amount of political responsibility. He is responsible to the council, but also, in a larger sense, to the community. Does he owe his official life to the council? Hardly less so is the council indebted to him. Should his actions, his personality, or the policies he espouses upset the community, the council will bear the brunt of community displeasure, perhaps by means of the recall or at the next general election. If he is successful, popular, and respected, community regard cannot but favorably reflect upon the mayor and council.

The manager is a public personality, and whatever he does (or does not do) has public consequences: there will very likely be a public accounting. Is this not the essence of politics?

So far we have relied upon authority and essentially deductive analysis to bring us to the conclusion that the manager is in some part a politician. Can we reinforce this estimate with evidence of an empirical nature? By use of a sociological research tool—"role perception"—we may be able to throw some additional light upon the character of the manager as a politician. If both managers and councilmen perceive the manager as doing the same things, this "role perception" should give us some empirical evidence of reality.

The manager plays many roles, all of them intertwined and inseparable. As an administrator he compiles the budget and sees to its being a technically correct document before he presents it to the council. As a politician

[5] For an able debate on this point, see H. G. Pope, "Is the Manager a Political Leader? No," and Gladys M. Kammerer, "Is the Manager a Political Leader? Yes," *Public Management*, XLIV (February, 1962), 26–33.

[6] See Duane Lockard, "The City Manager, Administrative Theory and Political Power," *Political Science Quarterly*, LXVII (June, 1962), 224–236.

he must make policy decisions on revenue and expenditures which will inevitably excite controversy. Observe that even a reduction in taxes and the cutting of expenditures will disappoint the expectations of groups and individuals, and this disappointment will stimulate them into political activity. It is an eternal verity of politics that any budget which the executive proposes to the legislative body—decreased, stable, or greatly expanded —will be a disappointment to some elements of the population.

How, then, does a manager react to specific situations of a political nature? According to a study by J. J. Carrell, the managers and councilmen of six cities agree overwhelmingly that the manager:

1. Speaks for the council on policy matters, either proposed or already in being.

2. Compromises, on occasion, with pressure groups.

3. Lobbies in the state capital on matters affecting the city.

4. Initiates policy proposals more frequently than any single councilman.

5. Defends the city against local political attacks.

6. Resists the demands of local taxpayers' groups if he feels those demands are unjustified.[7]

On the other hand, Carrell's data show that managers and councilmen differ on some major points. A majority of the managers involved in the study agreed that they were not content to leave policy matters to the council, but a substantial majority of the councilmen thought that the manager stuck pretty largely to his administrative tasks while they determined policy. (If the councilmen seemed to contradict their previous statements on the manager's role, perhaps it was because they saw a distinction between the initiation and final determination of policy matters.)

Most managers, still further, agreed that they did not bring the council into consultation on budget matters during the drafting of the budget. Councilmen thought they did.[8] The managers, in other words, thought of "their" budgets as strictly executive ones. The councilmen tended to think of the budget as a joint executive-legislative effort.

Although these data were drawn from a very small sample of six cities and thus must be regarded as tentative, they do tend to reinforce the judgments of some of the most acute observers of the politics of council-manager government. They seem to indicate that the manager does indeed play a significant political role in his community. But the data also indicate, according to Buechner, that there is a built-in strain in the relations between manager and council. If the Congress, or the state legislature, has always been restive under a strong, policy-oriented executive, no less so is the city

[7] J. J. Carrell, *The Role of the City Manager, Public Affairs Monograph Series,* No. 2 (Kansas City, Mo.: Community Studies, 1962), Tables 2.3, 2.4, 2.5; pp. 10–15.

[8] *Ibid.,* Table 2.6, p. 16.

council. The evident lack of agreement in some of the perceptions of councilmen and managers about their respective roles is at least an indication that councilmen are willing to question the policy role of city managers.[9]

The Mayor and the City Manager. The position of the mayor under council-manager government has always appeared as somewhat of an anomaly to large numbers of people. Because, traditionally, the office of mayor—even that of weak mayor—has had certain dignity and responsibility, some charter drafters have regarded the office as a potential threat to the position of the manager and simply have not provided for it. Thus, the city charter of Berkeley, Missouri, written in the 1950's, omitted the office of mayor altogether. The councilman-at-large who received the largest number of votes was automatically designated president of the council, and the president was strictly a legislative officer, with none of the appointive powers or ceremonial functions which the mayor so often retains. Perhaps just as important, he did not have the title of mayor, with all of its historical meaning and all of its connotations of importance.

It may be that the mayor's position is one of the unresolved problems of council-manager government, particularly as regards political leadership. In the suburban council-manager cities outside New York, Chicago, or San Francisco, this does not seem to be a problem, nor is it usually one in university communities. But in the larger cities and in the smaller ones where middle-class values are not dominant, few categorical statements can be made about the position of the mayor vis-à-vis the manager.

The varied history of council-manager government in Kansas City illustrates this point. When the city was bossed by Tom Pendergast, the city manager was Henry F. McElroy, a complex man who was regarded, even by his enemies, as having some of the characteristics of a sound public servant. Under Pendergast there was no question of the locus of political leadership: McElroy ran the city's business, not its politics.[10] The mayors were mere ciphers.

With the triumph of reform in the late 1930's, L. P. Cookingham became city manager, and for almost twenty years he dominated the city government with the force of his convictions and his personality. When the reformers were forced out of power in the late 1950's there ensued several chaotic years which saw managers come and go, and a mayor struggling with a situation that was beyond him. The return of reform forces in 1963 brought with it the election of Mayor Iluse W. Davis, who immediately showed himself to be intent upon political leadership. Stumping the city

[9] See John C. Buechner, *Differences in Role Perceptions in Colorado Council-Manager Cities* (Boulder, Colo.: Bureau of Governmental Research and Service, University of Colorado, 1965).

[10] A. Theodore Brown, *The Politics of Reform, Publication No. 116* (Kansas City, Mo.: Community Studies, 1958), p. 52.

for a one-half-cent earnings tax in the autumn of 1963, he persuaded the voters to approve the tax by a vote of almost two to one, and many thought it a personal victory for the mayor himself.

From this brief case history one can derive very few generalizations. And yet the disquietude over the role of the mayor under the council-manager plan continues, and a few cities have moved toward the type of mayor who can be a real political leader if he is so disposed. Political leadership was the goal in Toledo and San Diego. It may have been the goal in Dade County, Florida, though the political situation there is so confused that only the intrepid dare make interpretations of it.

By means of a charter amendment Toledo sought to strengthen the policy hand of the mayor by providing for his direct election. Supported by the Toledo Municipal League, a privately directed reform group, and by other reform elements as well, the charter amendment was thought of as a means of strengthening council-manager government.

A political upheaval which eventually resulted in the ouster of city manager George Bean, in 1961, led the citizens of San Diego into a reconsideration of council-manager government in that city. The citizens' charter review committee, reporting in 1962, recommended that the salary of the mayor be increased from $12,000 to $18,000 annually "in order to provide him with additional status and to compensate him for an extremely arduous and time-consuming job." The mayor should also, according to the citizens' committee, make an annual state-of-the-city message to the council, which would, in effect, be a statement of his legislative program and which would strengthen his hand in policy formation and in political matters generally.

The intent of the committee was clearly stated in its report: "It is the thought of the Committee that in a city of the size of San Diego, the position of mayor should be strengthened . . . to permit him to become the chief policy making officer. On the other hand, *the members of the Committee did not feel that the position of mayor should be so altered as to put in jeopardy the council-manager form of government.*" [11]

When the voters of Dade County amended the county charter to provide for both an elective sheriff and an elective county mayor, one observer viewed these developments with misgivings. There could be far more conflict between the sheriff and the manager than there was between the manager and his appointed chief of public safety, thought Thomas J. Wood. Furthermore, "another possible source . . . [of] friction is the relationship between the county manager and the new mayor, the permanent chairman of the [county] commission. In the absence of strong commission leadership, the county manager has from time to time been the Metro

[11] Citizens' Charter Review Committee, *Report* (San Diego, Calif.: The Committee, August, 1962), p. 8. Italics the committee's.

spokesman. . . . A county mayor may become a rival to the manager." [12]

From this evidence we can assume that a good deal of uncertainty exists in the larger council-manager cities over the role of the mayor vis-à-vis the city manager. If the experience of Kansas City, Toledo, San Diego, and Dade County indicates a trend, then certainly the mayor will become increasingly important politically, and the manager's importance in that regard will diminish. Perhaps this is inevitable in the larger cities; we should remember that Mayor Charles R. Taft of Cincinnati, in spite of his city's long and successful experience with the council-manager plan, recommended against its adoption in Philadelphia.

If this development continues, the council-manager and strong-mayor governments of the larger cities may become indistinguishable. In both forms the mayor will clearly be the political leader, and the professional manager or administrative officer will take care of the directorial functions. In all of this discussion so far we have considered only mayors and city managers. But no consideration of leadership in the city is complete without an examination of the council. We must now take up that task.

In Quest of Policy—The City Council

Because there are over 17,000 city councils in the United States, one would expect to find considerable variety among them. Yet generalize we must. Or, to put the matter another way, we must attempt to construct a prototype—a model—of a city council, which will probably never reflect reality for any one of them, but which nevertheless will give us a sense of what each one is really like.

The candidate for city council must usually be a U.S. citizen, a citizen of the state, and a resident of the city and perhaps of the ward for a given period of time. (Usually the requirement is for a period of residence longer than that needed to qualify him for voting.)

Councilmen are elected from wards, at large, or (rarely these days) by a system of proportional representation or weighted voting. Sometimes nomination is from wards, and election is from the city at large. At other times, some councilmen will be nominated and elected from wards, and others nominated and elected at large, so that the city will have, presumably, representatives of both the parochial and general interests on the same council. Election *tends* to be nonpartisan.

Once on the council the member has certain privileges: compensation (usually low or nonexistent), freedom from arrest when going to or from council meetings, and freedom of speech during debate in the council chambers. He is subject to certain types of control by the council itself: the

[12] Thomas J. Wood, "Basic Revisions in Dade Charter," *National Civic Review*, LIII (January, 1964), 39–41.

council seats him—and therefore may refuse to seat him. The council also has the right to discipline or expel him.

The council determines its own rules of procedure and the time and frequency of meetings (subject, usually, to certain charter and statutory restrictions and stipulations). Councils meet frequently throughout the year. Their meetings may be highly structured, with a published agenda and with meticulous observance of parliamentary procedure. Or they may be highly informal, with no set agenda and with hardly a glance at standard procedure of any kind.

The council is organized under a presiding officer: the mayor, a president elected from the city at large, one of the council members (designated by the council itself), or the councilman who received the highest number of votes at the last election. This presiding officer has the power to vote, engage in debate, recognize members, appoint committees of the council, and rule on points of procedure.

The clerk of the council, who keeps the minutes and other records, is usually the city clerk, a full-time public officer. If he doubles in brass as the chief administrative officer of the city, he may be the nearest thing to a city manager that some small cities will ever have. The clerk may also be the only staff which the council possesses. Staffing—research and other legislative aides—is generally inadequate for all councils, even the larger ones. This means that the council, in order to get facts, must rely upon the amateur method of recourse to its own members or upon "the administration." This circumstance tends to lessen the long-range influence of the council upon policy and to increase the influence of the executive.

By building up expertise among its own membership, the council may stand firmly against this trend. Many a councilman of long tenure has become as expert in municipal finance as the finance director himself. But even though he does become knowledgeable, he nevertheless does not have the staff aides available to the full-time administrative experts. (Some councils, like the state legislatures and the Congress, are providing for their own experts. Thus the Denver city council has a legislative analyst who makes studies, conducts research, and prepares recommendations for the council.)

The committee system may aid the council, in this regard, or it may detract from its performance. If the council is large, almost invariably it will divide itself up into standing committees—finance, public works, recreation, and others—which are permanent, subject-matter adjuncts to the council. There are also special ad hoc committees, often including citizen members, to make studies and report to the council. And the citizen members may be professional experts in their own right. Thus a physician, let's say, is made chairman of the councilmanic-citizen committee to study a public health problem.

A similar aid to the council may come from commissions and boards that are advisory to the operating departments. The plan commission, composed of, say, an architect, a lawyer, an engineer, a housewife, and a retired real estate broker, may give the council advice, reinforced not only by the general competence of its members but also by data accumulated by the professional staff of the plan department.

If staffing bears upon the character of the leadership that comes out of the council, size may be no less influential. On the surface, the number of people on the council appears to be an irrelevancy. But whether it is or is not is a question that we must examine.

The Relation of Size to Leadership. For the most part, the more than 17,000 city and village councils in the United States are small bodies, rarely with more than a dozen members. They are, in fact, little more than committees. The reason for this is to a large degree historical: it rests in the zeal of the reformers over the past half-century. The idea of the small council was first popularized by the rapid spread of the commission plan following the 1900 disaster in Galveston. By the time that form of government had spent its force, the council-manager plan was a lusty young giant that could carry and nurture the idea. And by that time, the idea of a small council had become an article of faith to the reformers. It remains an article of faith.

What are the virtues of a small council? No systematic rationale ever developed around it. (One does not need, of course, a systematic rationale for an article of faith.) Aside from the general assumption that small councils are more effective than large ones, some mayors and managers seem to believe that small councils are easier to work with than large ones and that the unanimity which so often results from small-council deliberations is a virtue that must be treasured. This might be described as the "united front" syndrome of local politics.

Whether the large council is actually inferior to the small one is a question that we cannot answer conclusively. There is a mass of opinion on that score, but not much evidence. That the large council is different from the small council, on the other hand, we can decide fairly easily. The differences are observable.

In the first place, the large council can be the more representative simply because the constituency of each councilman varies inversely with the size of the council. We can presume deductively, therefore, that a councilman can be more "representative" of 10,000 people than he can be of 20,000. True enough, if the presumption is challenged, we can only say that this *seems* to be so.

But we can be surer about the second point: that the large council is more apt to split into blocs or factions than the small council. Is it more diverse and thus less easily managed than the small council? We might presume this, but we want more than presumption. We want evidence, empirical evidence, if you please.

We can get much of this evidence from the experimental work of sociologists and social psychologists over the past thirty years with the small group. Before we go into the relevance of small-group theory to the organization of city councils, however, we must first have a quick glance at the meaning of "small group."

Small-group analysis emphasizes face-to-face contact, communication, and constant interaction of the members, one with the other. The group may range in size from two to two dozen, but the ones tested experimentally usually have from five to nine members, the size of the average city council. Although one cannot summarize the vast amount of small-group research in a sentence, one can be sure of this: research has established that the small group (1) exists, (2) permeates all of society, and (3) vitally affects the behavior of group members.

Small-group experimentation has painstakingly and elaborately established the fact that the conformance of individual behavior to that of the small group is very marked indeed. And this conformance seems to vary with the size of the group: the smaller the group, the greater the conformance. Or to put it another way, the smaller the size, the greater the *pressures* are for the individual to conform to the group.[13] He may not conform, it is true, but the pressures for him to do so will increase as the group grows smaller.

The pressures will be felt by the individual member only so long as the group remains a group or, in other words, only so long as the group does not split into subgroups. Whether it does split up depends upon a number of variables, but the variable which seems to control all groups is numbers. The size of the group appears to be crucial. James found, for example, that groups of eight or more tended to split into subgroups.[14] Even though this is by no means conclusive evidence of scientific truth, it does coincide with the experience of observers that large councils, even those which are nominally nonpartisan, are subject to factionalism. In small-group terms this would simply mean that in the large council, small-group pressures upon the individual members are sufficiently dissipated to permit an opposition to develop.

If we could establish that large councils have a tendency toward factionalism not appearing in small councils, would we have found out anything of importance? And, more particularly, would we have found a factor of

[13] Sidney Verba, *Small Groups and Political Behavior—A Study of Leadership* (Princeton, N.J.: Princeton University Press, 1961), pp. 12, 22, 23.

[14] John James, "A Preliminary Study of the Size Determinant in Small-group Interaction," *American Sociological Review*, XVI (1951), 474–477.

importance to leadership in the city? To answer these questions, we must revert from evidence to values.

For a council to exercise leadership, its members should be intelligent, well informed, and representative of the major elements of the community, both functional and geographic. It should also be a medium in which strong conflicts can be resolved to the best advantage of the community. Such conflicts are indeed resolved in councils both large and small. But the methods of resolution are different, and the difference may be significant.

In the small council the conflicts are resolved on a private, personal basis. Not only is public airing of policy difference minimized; it is discouraged. Like any small group the council develops a social structure of its own—it has become a society in microcosm—with its own rules and its own mores. "We must keep our dissension within the family" or "We must present a united front to the community for the sake of the public good" are the felt or expressed reactions of the group. Public dissent by a member of the group, particularly if it occurs again and again, is viewed as nothing less than disloyalty to the group, and the group reacts first by trying to absorb the dissenter and then, if that stratagem fails, by ostracizing him.[15]

In the large council the situation changes radically. In a group numbering fifteen instead of five, the lone dissenter has now become a leader of a minority faction. Reinforced by members who are willing to follow his lead, he can now fight the majority, even if that majority is allied with the administration (the mayor or the manager). And in marshaling his forces he will look for support outside the council. The council majority now finds itself faced with challenge in the council meetings, in the press, and before various community forums. Teamwork and the united front are out the window.

And so we have different ways to resolve conflicts. Which is better? That the small-council type of resolution has worked reasonably well in literally hundreds of communities over decades of experience is probably true. And yet this system is an affront to one of our most dearly held democratic preconceptions: that an opposition party or bloc in the legislative body is essential to the formation of good public policy. What would the British Parliament be without Her Majesty's loyal opposition, or Congress and the state legislatures without minority-party opposition? What happens to council leadership when conflicts are resolved privately? We cannot answer these questions, because each citizen must make his own evaluation of them.

We do not know enough about the behavior of councils, either large or small, to say very much about them categorically, but we can legitimately

---

[15] See Olmsted's instructive summary, in Michael S. Olmsted, *The Small Group* (New York: Random House, 1959), pp. 111–117.

challenge the easy assumption so widely accepted over the past half-century that the small council is ipso facto good and the large one necessarily bad. We can also assume that the organization of the council has an influence upon the leadership it gives to the community. This point can be clarified somewhat in our ensuing discussion of leadership.

What Is Leadership?

The forms of leadership exercised in the city will depend, in some part, upon the city's political system or mode of organization. The type of executive, the organization of the council, partisanship or nonpartisanship, and the uses of direct democracy will all have their effect. The leadership arising from the strong-mayor system with a large, partisan council elected from wards will probably differ substantially from that stemming from the council-manager system with a small, nonpartisan council elected at large. And the extent to which direct democracy is used will add another variable to the leadership pattern. Although structure affects leadership, it does not give us insight into quality, character, and behavior: the real mysteries of leadership.

Insofar as quality and character are concerned, leadership of a political nature revolves around power. But power is of at least two types: that possessed by the government itself and that inhering in the office. If the city is weak as a government, what does it matter that the charter provides for a strong mayor? By the same token, how much meaningful leadership can a weak mayor perform in a city with a vast reservoir of power, in which the long ballot and constant recourse to direct democracy interdict any kind of central control? Power is an inescapable adjunct of leadership. The leader, of course, must have the power to effect a balance of power, both internally and externally. Internally, since blocs develop within all organizations, the leadership role is to see "that a balance of power appropriate to the fulfillment of key commitments will be maintained." [16]

Leadership also presupposes a set of objectives or goals. These may be personal aggrandizement (economic or political), party welfare, or civic achievement. They may even be, to borrow from Freud's typology of human aspiration, money, fame, power, and sex! They may be personal popularity and continued success at the polls—nothing more. Or they may be creative and utopian: nothing less than a complete change in the face of the city will satisfy them.

The goals of the leader have such variety that they need a measure of classification. That they may be positive in nature is so readily evident that we need not document the point. The leader believes in "progress," in

[16] Philip Selznick, *Leadership in Administration* (Evanston, Ill.: Row, Peterson & Co., 1957), p. 64.

change in the direction of better governmental structure, more hardware (streets, bridges, parks, public buildings), and expanded programs. He is a "change agent," to use the cant indulged in by some social scientists. The very word "leader" evokes such a prototype in the minds of people at large. But this concept is too limited. The goals of the leader may be purely negative or a combination of the positive and the negative.[17]

When Mayor Martin H. Kennelly of Chicago, using the separation-of-powers rationale, refused to intervene actively in council affairs in order to get his ideas adopted, he was negating his own hopes that the council would agree with him. His conflicting goals tended to balance out to zero.

When the main passion of the city manager is to be popular and to placate those who are unhappy with him, his main goal is to preserve the status quo. He has assumed, in other words, essentially a negative stance. When a councilman turns maverick and fights his own party, or faction, he is setting his goals (or program) ahead of his party's, and thus his position is a negative one. On the other hand, his real goal may be positive: he is in actuality fighting for a strong bargaining position within his party (or faction), rather than for his openly avowed objectives.

The leader may, in brief, be wholly engrossed in seeing that things *don't* happen. The reason for this very often is that his goals are interior ones; they are psychic or emotional. He is engrossed in power qua power. The city, or his own segment of it, may decay at his feet; he will enjoy the power and ignore the decay. He is sure that action will alienate far more people than inaction. Action might disturb the coalitions, alliances, friendships, and agreements—the delicate threads he has so painstakingly woven into his own political tapestry (that work of art, that lovingly constructed, carefully balanced design!). A move of any fashion might pull or break a thread, and mar his own creation.[18]

After we have considered these characteristics of the leader, have we done enough? Can we neglect his personal traits? Obviously we cannot. The personal traits of the potential leader may help his rise to power, they may hinder it, or they may have marginal effect. We must be cautious about the personal-trait approach, therefore, simply because it may yield significant results or none at all. How typical the remark, "Who would ever have thought that *he* would be a leader?"—a way of saying that the individual concerned had few of the traits popularly associated with leadership. This is not to say that personality has no effect upon leadership, but only that it

[17] Verba, *op. cit.*, p. 119: "It would be unfortunate if the concept of leadership did not let us consider under it those leaders whose specialty is thwarting the group."

[18] That this is a view of the politician held by some minority-group members is indicated by the distrust with which he is regarded by militant Negro leaders. See James Q. Wilson, *Negro Politics, The Search for Leadership* (Glencoe, Ill.: The Free Press, 1960). The more strongly held the ideological position, the greater the tendency to regard *all* politicians as of this type.

is the one factor in many, rather than the dominant or exclusive one. As Verba observes, "the trait theory [of leadership] has gone into disrepute largely on the basis of studies that have shown a lack of agreement on the personality traits of successful leaders." [19]

And so we have structure, power, goals, and personal traits—all descriptive of leadership. At this point the discussion of the political leader usually stops. But we must go on to consider another important element —style.

The Style of Leadership in City Hall. Wilson classifies the styles of Negro leadership as militant and moderate. Although these styles, according to Wilson (in 1960), are of leaders who do not hold public office, a look at them will give us a good introduction to the styles of leadership in city hall.[20]

The Negro militant seeks status for his race, even at the expense of temporary gains in terms of new schools and an expanded welfare program. Although he distrusts politicians, including those of his own community, he seeks objectives that can be embodied in law. He is impatient; he oversimplifies the problem. Like all dedicated reformers, he wants to "remake this sorry scheme of things entire, and mold it nearer to the heart's desire."

The moderate, on the other hand, seeks limited goals—and immediate ones. Perhaps he will settle for the oiling of streets to lay the dust in Negro neighborhoods, or for a "lighted school" program to get the kids off the streets at night. If he does not admire politicians as a group, he at least will work with them. Oddly enough, however, he does not put too much faith in laws as such, because he knows that, even after the very good law is passed, the city will doubtlessly continue to lumber along on its old intolerable course. Time means a great deal to him, but he knows that his group will not achieve the millennium in one generation. He assumes, in other words, a stance very close to that of a politician. And, indeed, most of the politicians will come from his ranks. The officeholder in city hall is almost sure to be a moderate on all public questions.

Style According to Small-group Theory. According to small-group theory, a fragment of which we have already looked at, leadership is a group process. It is not so much the position, the power, or the goal-orientation of the leader—or, for that matter, his personal traits—which produce him as it is group interaction.[21] The style or function of leadership in a small group (and let us think of a particular small group, the city council, during this analysis) is a dual one: it must be both affective and instrumental. Affective leadership directs itself toward maintaining the cohesiveness of the group and satisfying the needs of its members (for praise, companionship,

[19] Verba, *op. cit.*, pp. 129–130.
[20] Wilson, *op. cit.*
[21] The succeeding analysis relies principally upon Verba, *op. cit.*, Chs. 6–8.

defense against outside threats). Instrumental leadership is goal-oriented: the leader wants to get on with the group tasks, he wants production. A particular leadership *act* will be either affective or instrumental; indeed, a single act may very well involve both aspects.

Several studies indicate that the most effective leadership combines both the affective and instrumental elements. If the leader keeps both elements in balance he will have achieved the optimum. But therein lies a real dilemma. The affective and the instrumental are really Scylla and Charybdis, between which it is very hard to steer a true and safe course.

The purely instrumental leader may be so engrossed in achieving group objectives that he completely neglects personal relations. The result is not only that he loses rapport with the group and is cut off from it, but also that the hostility which the group members develop toward him interferes with the instrumental goals. This reaction was shown by the experiments carried out by Ronald Lippitt and Ralph White under the direction of that remarkably inventive scholar Kurt Lewin. The directives of the authoritarian leader of the small, experimental group were grudgingly followed by the members, but only so long as the leader was present. As soon as he left the room and the external pressure was removed, the group no longer complied with his directives.

The difficulties which face the instrumental leader are further documented by the experiments of Robert F. Bales and his associates. Invariably, the member whom the group rated high for ideas and overall guidance was not well liked. In other words, the instrumental stance of the member had interfered with his affective relations.[22]

If the instrumental leader is confronted with a dilemma, no less so is the affective leader. In his efforts to placate group members, to get them to like him, and to maintain warm personal relations with them, the leader may virtually abandon his instrumental goals. Even if external forces do not punish both leader and group for lack of achievement, internal factors having the same effect may crop up. Certain personal satisfactions such as praise, more pay, reelection may be denied the members simply because their tasks are not accomplished. This denial causes resentment, which in turn causes hostility against the leader. And so the affective relation which the leader has so laboriously nurtured can be marred or even destroyed by the lack of instrumental accomplishment.

Small-group research, then, shows that from within the group itself come a number of conflicting expectations: the leader is expected, at one and the same time, to be instrumental (formal, avoidant, task-oriented) and affective (informal, indulgent, companionable). The group member himself is apt to expect the leader to emphasize affective relations over instrumental

[22] A summing-up of Bales's argument and research may be found in Robert F. Bales, *Interaction Process Analysis* (Cambridge, Mass.: Addison-Wesley Publishing Co., 1950).

goals. But the external force or authority has different expectations. Whether this force is represented by the directorate of a company interested in the achievement of production goals or by community power groups wanting effective program performance, the pressure upon the leader is to get the job done—to achieve instrumental goals. The leader is at the point at which a number of opposing forces converge, and he is caught in the middle.

These conflicts will invariably affect the group. First, leader motivation is affected. Leaders in both ongoing and experimental groups must face the dilemma presented by the recurring incompatibility between group acceptance and group direction. Faced with adverse reaction from members of the group ("negative affective reaction"), the leader becomes reluctant to see that the job is done, or he develops a certain immunity to hostility. Bales indeed suggests that the good instrumental leader *must* develop such an immunity.

Second, the conflict of forces affects group accomplishment. Stable leadership, necessary to the accomplishment of instrumental tasks, is difficult to achieve because of conflicting demands for accomplishment, on the one hand, and satisfaction of the personal, emotional needs of the members on the other. If a balance cannot be achieved both between the internal and external demands and between the instrumental and affective goals, the group will either fall apart or continue to operate at high levels of tension. The question, then, is: How do group leaders maintain a satisfactory level of affective relations at the same time that they keep their instrumental activities at a satisfactory level?

Achieving Affective and Instrumental Leadership. The key to the question, according to Bales and others, lies in differentiation—splitting the leadership role into the affective and the instrumental. The investigator has verified this phenomenon experimentally; the small group does in fact show the development of *two* leaders, one affective and one instrumental.

Does this differentiation of roles, by two separate members of the group, tend to accentuate conflict or resolve it? It has the latter result, if we accept the findings of Bales and Slater. The two leaders "interact" one with the other more than with any of the remainder of the group. They exchange ideas with one another more frequently than with the rest of the group, and they agree with each other more frequently. They are, in a word, complementary. They establish a coalition which is highly important, perhaps even absolutely necessary, to the effectiveness of the group. By his capacity to placate and pacify, the affective leader smoothes the way for the instrumental leader, and his position is in turn reinforced by the satisfaction derived from group instrumental attainments. This is the leadership structure that develops in experimental groups. Does the same phenomenon occur in ongoing groups?

At first the difference between the two types seems considerable; then it seems to diminish. The *two* leaders that appear in experimental groups often are absent in the ongoing group. The *single* leader in the latter group assumes his position by virtue of an outside authority (in political systems he may be either appointed or elected), and this fact legitimizes his leadership. He may soften his instrumental role by pointing out to members of the group that certain tasks must be accomplished because of outside demands; he thus shifts the responsibility for action to someone or something other than himself. The group members no longer need feel that they are forced to submit to his arbitrary will; indeed, by the very act of explaining the necessity of performance because of outside pressures, the leader will build up affective satisfactions in the group.

In some ongoing groups dual leaders may develop, similar to those that appear in experimental groups. One investigator found that the best way for immigrant groups in Israel to adapt to their changed circumstances was by means of a dual leadership pattern. The old leadership (religious, personal, traditional) tended to the affective needs of the group; a new leadership directed itself toward the instrumental tasks: accommodation to the political and economic forces of a radically changed environment. It may be that many political societies, large or small, need such a bifurcation of leadership in order that the maximum of instrumental achievement and affective stimulation be achieved.

Still another dilemma faces the leader. Should he be a conformist or an innovator? Since every group develops its own norms of behavior, the leader is expected to conform to those norms. At the same time, however, in order to lead, he has to be imaginative and must produce ideas which vary from the norms. He must thus be a deviant. Once again the leader finds himself in an ambivalent position. Because he must be a conformist par excellence—he must be like the members, or even more so—and because he must be representative of group characteristics to the outside world, he comes to personify group values and group norms. At the same time, outside forces or internal group needs may require him to deviate. This means that he is under pressure to conform to the norms and to violate them. Thus develops the conformist-innovator dilemma.

Just as it is difficult for the leader to balance the instrumental and the affective in order to get performance without destroying group morale, so he finds most elusive the precise way by which he can innovate without losing group acceptance. If change there must be, however, the leader has no alternative but to seek that elusive way, and small-group findings suggest that he may find it.

The leader may achieve nonconsensual change, that is, a kind of change in which acceptance by group members plays little or no part. In a time of great stress or emergency, the leaders may be forced to act not only against the wishes of group members, but also contrary to their values. As long as the group recognizes that the unpopular acts are necessary, however, the change may be effected without an internal upheaval.

The leader may also use his "acceptance capital" to sponsor change without unduly risking his position. If he has acquired high status, if the group has learned to lean heavily on his guidance, if he has earned a considerable amount of respect and admiration, he may be able to use these political assets to sponsor change without undue risk of group rejection. Obviously, since he cannot measure precisely just how much capital he really has, he may use up his reserves before he has his program in being.

Another way that the conformist-innovator dilemma may be overcome is by changing leaders, a harsh method as many a mayor and city manager can testify, but one that is effective. If the old leader has accepted group norms even more strongly than has the group itself, for example, he may be unable to meet the demands for change which even the most conservative member may recognize. By calling in a new leader, one not so committed to the old values, the group may be able to mitigate pressures for change from the outside. Group members may, moreover, find it easier to accept change by an outsider than by someone familiar to them. They may be willing to suspend the rules temporarily for the new leader, and during this period he brings about the needed changes.

A historical parallel might strengthen this small-group finding. Beset by internal strife the Italian city-states of the medieval period found it expedient often to bring in a *podestà,* an uncommitted outsider, to administer the city, perhaps only for a year. Appointing his own subordinates (the *stato,* whence came our word "state"), the *podestà* was sometimes able to reduce disruptive party conflicts and, at the same time, to develop a body of skilled urban administrators.[23] This is a classic example of the new leader who, simply because he is uncommitted, can bring about change. This is also a description of what actually happens, sometimes, in council-manager government.

Finally, the leader may obtain change in other ways. He may do so (1) by projecting the responsibility for it upon another (a scapegoat, perhaps); (2) by attributing it to the demands of the situation; or (3) by obtaining group participation in making the decision to change.

The Pertinence of Small-group Theory to Politics

It must be obvious by now that the evidence gathered from the small group, either experimental or ongoing, corresponds at many points to

[23] Max Weber, *The City,* trans. and ed. by Don Martindale and Gertrude Neuwirth (Glencoe, Ill.: The Free Press, 1958), p. 45. Also see Friedrich Heer, *The Medieval World* (New York: The New American Library, 1964), p. 81.

commonsense observations on politics, particularly at the "intimate" local level. And even where there is no such correspondence, small-group findings can raise some basic questions about the fashion in which local politics is carried on.

Council Organization and Leadership. One such question, as we have seen, has to do with the optimum size of the city council. The great bulk of city councils number fewer than ten members, and they fit ideally, therefore, into the category of the ongoing small group. If we cannot yet say that unanimity is invariably the goal of small-group deliberations—if we cannot say that this is a law of nature!—we at least have enough data to question whether the small council is, indeed, the positive good the reformers proclaim it to be.

The workings of the small city council seem to bear out small-group findings. When there is conflict within the council, the members seek to resolve it privately and behind the scenes. Many times public questions can *best* be resolved privately. But the point of this debate is over the assumption that they should *always* be so resolved. We can legitimately challenge that value judgment, and using small-group findings, ask the question: Should not the council be large enough so that it will "naturally" split and present a *public* minority to the city?

Probably a main reason for the reformers' espousal of the small council is their strong emotional identification with the efficiency concept of government. They are, in other words, highly instrumental in outlook. (The affective leader smacks too much of the old-time boss, whose interests were to cater to the whims of his supporters and to feather his own nest.) And the small council fits well into this ideal model. Its instrumental character is very evident. It is a working committee; it seeks energetically to resolve conflicts within itself as soon as they appear; it is not constantly burdened with a ragtag opposition that bedevils the majority.

Other organizational views of the council further illustrate this point. The council whose members are elected at large is best because it can depreciate the parochial, neighborhood point of view and consider only the good of the city as a whole. This is a highly instrumental outlook! And if the instrumental value is the most important one to be developed, the at-large council may be the type to be used. There are indications that the councilman elected at large wants achievement above all else—and achievement in terms of the needs of the entire community. Admittedly, isolated personal wants and neighborhood objectives get in the way of accomplishing the overall plan. As long as all councilmen are elected at large these localized, individual needs may be subordinated to the generalized needs, or overlooked altogether. But let the councilmen be elected from wards or districts, and you run a great risk that they will give voice to the local interest and perhaps overwhelm the general interest. Even if some members are elected at large and some from districts, the risk still remains that the affective district councilmen will overwhelm the instrumental at-large councilmen.

Whether this risk does, in fact, exist has yet to be established (what a challenging subject for investigation!). But this is the hypothesis upon which most of the reformers seem to act. Observe that the great majority of council-manager charters in American cities provide for councilmen elected at large. And the Model City Charter, which stands as a kind of codification of the value systems of the reformers, also provides for election at large.

And so we see that the reform thinkers act as though they had read small-group literature and sought to put it into practice. Being instrumental in outlook, they want the council organized so that it is instrumental rather than affective: small and elected at large. Because the large council may split into a public majority and a public opposition and because the ward-elected councilman may give voice to local, parochial, and individual wants, it may sacrifice instrumental goals for affective ones.

Although we cannot be sure that this reasoning is correct, small-group data seem to bear it out. These data can be, therefore, a basis for challenging reform ideology in very specific terms. And even if we cannot use empirical evidence to prove or disprove a value judgment, we can set up our own values more easily than if we had no empirical base whatsoever.

Small-group Findings and the Roles of Manager and Mayor. For the most effective leadership, the strong mayor in today's city is forced to perform both affective and instrumental roles in his relation with the city council and with the electorate at large. In the everyday vernacular of politics, if he tries so hard to push his program through that he neglects his political fences, he is not long for public life. On the other hand, if he spends all of his time politicking, he may seriously jeopardize his substantive goals.

How can he solve this dilemma? Since he is a politician (perhaps even a professional one) and an amateur at administration, he will quite naturally assume the affective role and delegate the instrumental role to such a subordinate as a chief administrative officer or managing director. This is precisely the *form* of government found in Honolulu and other strong-mayor cities. Whether the substance is there would be a fruitful subject for investigation. But at least small-group theory suggests a way for the mayor to solve his problems of leadership.

Similarly, city managers must be both administratively competent and politically astute—both instrumental and affective—if they are to achieve success. Many managers seem to have a natural talent for combining these roles. Over a period of years, given some failures, of course, they are able to achieve a viable balance and thus solve their own leadership dilemmas.

But many other managers, perhaps even a majority of them, find the balance always elusive. They simply cannot combine the affective and the instrumental satisfactorily. Having been schooled in the instrumental, they are apt to veer sharply in that direction. If this results in disaster for them, and perhaps even for the manager plan itself, they can insist that they were performing their roles as technical administrators, the way God and the civic reformers expected them to.

The principal difficulty with council-manager government may be precisely this: an insufficient number of city managers who have a talent for properly balancing the instrumental and the affective. And if we assume that this is somehow an inborn talent, the schools cannot fill the gap by turning out more technically trained administrators. Does small-group theory offer a solution to the problem?

We have seen that in experimental groups, and sometimes in ongoing ones, a form of dual leadership occurs. The two leaders, one instrumental and the other affective, interact frequently one with the other; they tend to agree with each other; and their personal relations are warm. This could be taken as a model for council-manager government to conform to. The manager assumes the instrumental role while the mayor takes care of the affective.

Some cities seem to be veering in this direction. Observe Toledo and San Diego. The trouble is that in practical matters it is very difficult to tell where the instrumental ends and the affective begins. The manager himself may never know, except intuitively, where the boundaries are, even when he is performing both roles himself. How much more difficult will it be in the case of dual leadership!

Still another difficulty is that each leader is thought of as confined to one role, clearly demarcated, and one role alone. But must this always be so? Should the mayor always be cast in the affective role and never in the instrumental? Should the inverse be true with the manager? Could not the roles shift according to time, situation, and the exigencies of the moment? These questions, of course, small-group data cannot answer, but they arise logically from analysis stimulated by small-group literature.

If the literature of the small group does not give us answers to the problems of leadership in the city, it at least points us in the direction that further investigation might take. For this direction we are indebted to all those investigators who have painstakingly explored the intricacies of small-group phenomena.

Annotated Bibliography

The bibliography on the boss is so rich that one can never make more than a gesture toward indicating its extent and variety. A classic study of the boss is a book on one of the most powerful of all urban leaders, Frank Hague of Jersey City. See Dayton D. McKean, *The Boss* (Boston: Houghton Mifflin Co., 1940).

Lincoln Steffens identifies some of the remarkable characteristics of the boss and gives us some still-valid generalizations about urban politics in *The Shame of the Cities* (1905) and in his *Autobiography* (1931), both now to be found in various editions. In his novel about a big-city boss (quite obviously James Michael Curley of Boston), Edwin O'Connor was able to show how an urban political leader could survive on his charismatic qualities long after his apparent usefulness to the city was gone. See Edwin O'Connor, *The Last Hurrah* (Boston: Little, Brown & Co., 1956). Still useful is Harold Zink's *City Bosses in the United States* (Durham, N.C.: Duke University Press, 1930).

Although literally reams of material have been written about the city manager, very little of it rises above mere technical considerations of the manager's job. Exceptions to this generalization are the following: John C. Bollens, *Appointed Executive Local Government: The California Experience* (Los Angeles: Haynes Foundation, 1952); and Gladys M. Kammerer, C. D. Farris, J. M. DeGrove, and A. B. Clubok, *City Managers in Politics: An Analysis of Manager Tenure and Termination* (Gainesville, Fla.: University of Florida Press, 1962).

Equally sparse is perceptive material on the mayor. Although mayoral biographies are legion, few if any are sufficiently analytical to furnish valid generalizations about the office. Lockard gives a penetrating analysis of the municipal executive (both the mayor and the city manager) that might well be expanded into a full-scale study of these political leaders. See Duane Lockard, *The Politics of State and Local Government* (New York: The Macmillan Co., 1963), especially Ch. 14. Sayre and Kaufman summarize the dilemmas faced by the mayor of New York, and perhaps most other big-city mayors, throughout their study of the government of New York City. See Wallace S. Sayre and Herbert Kaufman, *Governing New York City* (New York: W. W. Norton & Co., 1965), especially Ch. 18.

Obscured by the strong executive even more than their counterparts at the state and national levels, city councils generally receive consideration only in reference to the strong mayor and the city manager. Sayre and Kaufman represent an exception to this rule, as do the perceptive essays by Arthur W. Bromage: *On the City Council; A Councilman Speaks;* and *Councilman at Work* (Ann Arbor, Mich.: George Wahr Publishing Co., 1950, 1951, and 1954, respectively).

Sidney Verba does a remarkable job of summarizing the literature on the small group which is pertinent to the study of leadership. See Sidney Verba, *Small Groups and Political Behavior—A Study of Leadership* (Princeton, N.J.: Princeton University Press, 1961). Bell, Hill, and Wright digest much of the rest of the literature on public leadership and then add to their review a bibliography of almost 600 items. See Wendell Bell, Richard J. Hill, and Charles R. Wright, *Public Leadership* (San Francisco: Chandler Publishing Co., 1961).

Finally, one can benefit considerably, in the study of the mayor and city manager, by reading Selznick's essay on leadership. See Philip Selznick, *Leadership in Administration* (Evanston, Ill.: Row, Peterson & Co., 1957). And two books on the office of mayor in New York City and Milwaukee contain unusual insights into the methods by which the city's chief executive operates: Theodore J. Lowi, *At the Pleasure of the Mayor—Patronage and Power in New York City, 1898–1958* (New York: The Free Press, 1964); and Henry W. Maier, *Challenge to the Cities—An Approach to a Theory of Urban Leadership* (New York: Random House, 1966).

CHAPTER 13

Who Governs the City?

Robert A. Dahl asks the question "Who governs?" in the title of his study of urban politics in New Haven, Connecticut.[1] It is a disturbing question. Considering the vast differences in wealth, in social position, in education, motivations, and interests, the question seems almost impossible to answer, even for one community. One of Dahl's main points is that in terms of the formalities of the democratic process (the right to vote, the right to free exchange of political ideas, the right to run for office and to organize politically, and the honest conduct of elections), one can give a simple answer: the people govern.

But do they? On the face of it, it is obvious that the mechanics of democracy furnish essential avenues to control by the people. The city, in fact, has almost a superfluity of devices to assure popular control. And yet, going behind the mechanics of democracy, we must face some disquieting questions. Do the people rule all of the time—or only some of the time—or sometimes not at all? And if they cannot rule a city of 150,000, can they possibly ever rule a state or a nation?

A decade before Dahl, Floyd Hunter asked the same questions about the urban community, though in sociological rather than political terms.[2] In his study of Atlanta, Hunter asked people of widely varying backgrounds to identify the leadership of the city. Upon analyzing his data he found that a mere handful of people made all the important decisions and that a somewhat larger, though still very restricted, group implemented those decisions. The decision-makers were almost invariably people of considerable wealth and were rarely responsible to the community in a democratic sense. Indeed, only four governmental officials were among the forty decision-makers whom Hunter identified, and only two of those—the mayor and the city treasurer—were elective officials.

Both Dahl and Hunter raised their questions and gave their answers to the question "Who governs?" by studying, in each case, a single community. Because of their case-study techniques, their findings might have general application to the American city. One generalization on which they concur, which describes both New Haven and Atlanta, is that the sources of power are varied. And yet this is a very limited agreement.

[1] Robert A. Dahl, *Who Governs?—Democracy and Power in an American City* (New Haven, Conn.: Yale University Press, 1961).
[2] Floyd Hunter, *Community Power Structure* (Chapel Hill, N.C.: University of North Carolina Press, 1953).

Dahl uses the term "from oligarchy to pluralism" to describe the political history of New Haven. Here in Dahl's own words is a summation of a hundred years of politics in a single American city: "Within a century a political system dominated by one cohesive set of leaders had given way to a system dominated by many different sets of leaders, each having access to a different combination of political resources. It was, in short, a pluralist system. . . . An elite no longer rules New Haven." [3]

According to Hunter's analysis, the city is governed quite differently. Far from being pluralistic, far from showing a wide variety of power sources, the control of the city is essentially of a monolithic nature. There is a single group or clique which makes the important decisions; and if there is another group involved, it is not competing but subsidiary, a managerial subgroup which has the task of implementing the decisions made by the elite. That there is some variety (of opinion and resources) within the select circle of the powerful is evident from Hunter's work, and it is here that Hunter and Dahl meet in very limited agreement. But for the most part Hunter stands for the monolithic view of community power; Dahl, for the pluralistic.

To begin an examination of these monistic and pluralistic viewpoints, we might glance back to city bossism in its heyday for an example of an apparently monolithic political system at work. One of the reasons, undoubtedly, for the outrage with which most American observers viewed the classic boss was not only his corruption and selfishness but also his violation of the political ideal of pluralism. Bossism was bad, ran the argument, because the system worked to suppress various legitimate sources of power which a democratic society would (and should) permit and even nurture.

Viewed realistically, however, not even the most powerful, most autocratic boss was wholly individualistic and arbitrary. In himself and in his rule a large number of varying groups and individuals found satisfaction: national and religious minorities, racial groups, neighborhood interests. In the boss there converged a large number of power currents, stemming from the many groups or subgroups which he represented and to which he gave a measure of satisfaction. Thus boss rule had a varied base and contained within itself a kind of submerged pluralism.

Most contemporary *political* studies of the urban community agree that control is now essentially pluralistic. And this perspective is perhaps best illustrated in the recent literature by Dahl's study of New Haven. The *sociological* investigations, on the other hand, are apt to find that the city is controlled by an elite. And Hunter gives one of the best examples of this perspective in his *Community Power Structure*. This conflict in evidence, this quarrel over monism against pluralism, is the subject to which we must address ourselves during the greater part of this chapter.

[3] Dahl, *op. cit.*, p. 86.

The Sources of Community Power

In our analysis of community power, we are concerned, first, with the nature of power and, second, with the sources of power. Third, and finally, we will consider the ways in which power is organized in the community and directed toward the achievement of political ends.

The Nature of Power. The nature of power is so elusive that many a competent observer of politics has pursued the appearances of power without understanding its realities. It has been observed that students of the community have had no consistent conception of power.[4] Although they have agreed on the basic approach to the community—empirical analysis—they have defined power in such various ways that the "facts" point to radically different conclusions. How else could empirically based studies describe the community as monistic, on the one hand, and pluralistic, on the other?

We shall conceive of power here as the capacity of a group and its leaders to reach an enduring consensus over objectives, in terms of both ends and means, and to achieve most of those objectives over a period of time. The elements of power, then, include (1) the setting of goals. The group must have the capacity to resolve differences within itself and arrive at a clear-cut, lasting consensus. By means of a happy combination of instrumental and affective leadership, or by strong member identification to a set of values—or by both—the group must arrive at a certain degree of peace and order within itself. If it does not have this capacity, the integrity of the group will be seriously threatened, and the common effort will be seriously weakened.

Power also means (2) that the group must have a capacity to agree on the means to the end as well as the end itself. If there are doctrinaire supporters of differing methods of achieving goals, this division may be even more of a threat to the group's ultimately acquiring power than differences over goals. Within a reform group that is seeking power, to use a practical example, there may be full agreement that a major capital improvement program for the city is absolutely necessary, but some members may be so dedicated to the idea of financing on a pay-as-you-go basis that they reject any suggestion that funds must be borrowed. This lack of agreement over ends could easily split the group and frustrate its efforts to achieve power.

Still another element of group power is (3) achievement. Not that victory is essential all of the time—even the most ruthless of dictatorships, backed by the awful presence of the nation-state, must know defeat some of the

---

[4] Robert Presthus, *Men at the Top* (New York: Oxford University Press, 1964), pp. 3–4. For a succinct analysis of influence and power, see Robert A. Dahl, *Modern Political Analysis* (Englewood Cliffs, N.J.: Prentice-Hall, 1963), Ch. 5.

time—but a certain minimum degree of success is essential to power. Success in politics must be defined as positive achievement and negative achievement. An example of the former would be a group's assuming control of city hall; of the latter, a minority group's frustration of majority objectives. If power cannot rest in a group that meets continuous defeat, neither, perhaps, can it be retained by that group which invariably wins, because success in the latter case may simply mean that the group has abandoned all goals purely for the sake of expediency. It is content to have the shadow of power without the substance.

Power is, therefore, group capacity, first, to reach agreement and then to drive toward the realization of group goals. The group may *have* power without being *in* power. It is apparent that office and legal status have no absolutely necessary connection with this concept of power.

But power has more than this operational meaning. It must have (4) some kind of moral content. The group seeks moral sanction to its power from outside itself. Whether it is "in power" or "out of power," it likes to think of itself as working for the good of the community, which is another way of saying to itself that it is reflective of the *real* will of the community. Since it and it alone reflects this *real* will, it must logically serve as trustee of the power which is not its own but the community's. Thus, in some mystic sense the group feels that it has acquired the moral right to speak and act for the entire community. To say, "We know what's good for them," is merely to claim that the group has knowledge of the community's real will.

Power is really not power until it acquires this moral aura, and the group does not truly have power until it has this moral certainty. This is as true of the group "out of power" as it is of the group "in power," but the latter is probably the better one to illustrate the point. The latter group must convince not only the community but its own members that it is far more than representative of the community; it *is* the community.

In the struggles that often erupt between city hall and the school board, for example, a conflict over objectives may be only one of the sources of difficulty. "Does not the community really want excellent schools above all else, and do we not best represent those real desires?" ask the members of the school board, either implicitly or explicitly. By putting the highest priority on good teachers, a fine school plant, and an expanded curriculum, the board is simply following the real desires of the community. Moreover, if the board wins out over the competing city council, it is apt not only to be reinforced in its moral certainty, but to gather additional adherents at one and the same time. A new school will usually win more friends than enemies for the board. Increased services are apt to stimulate an increase in loyalties.

As Nisbet says of the European nation-state of the nineteenth century, "it was . . . not easy to tell from the appearance of a specific social reform whether it had been motivated by basically humanitarian or military-nationalist motives." [5] Probably the school board, like the nation, wants to achieve its goals and at the same time to stimulate loyalty by meeting popular needs. And this success serves further to convince the group in power that it has correctly interpreted the community will and thus has the moral right to govern.

The Sources of Power. The Political and the Apolitical. By defining power as a process of group interrelationship, we have already made strides toward discovering its sources. That we are still far from those sources, however, must be evident from our incapacity to tell which groups have power and which ones actually wield it. The task of identification is an onerous one.

We shall assume that the inhabitants of any given urban community may be divided into four categories politically: (1) the active, (2) the passive, (3) the alienated, and (4) the apolitical. We shall also assume that in all four categories power exists, at least potentially, and that, since it exists, it should be identifiable.

The first three categories are all of them essentially made up of political types. The actives are those who are involved with public issues, who wish to be a part of the decision-making process, and who have sufficient political resources to enable them to influence others beyond their immediate family or other primary group. The actives in a community are usually not numerous.

The passive types, considerably more numerous than the actives, take a certain interest in public affairs, if for no other reason than out of a sense of public duty. That they can be mobilized on political questions every political activist is aware, and much of the strategy of local political campaigns is built around the attempt to lure the passive group away from its disengagement. The passive type has a deeply felt aversion to political controversy. Although it may be relatively easy to get him to vote and even to contribute money to a cause, he will not publicly commit himself. He may be well informed; he may have a civic conscience. He may work his head off to raise a public subscription for a swimming pool but refuse to take any active role in the passage of a bond issue for the same purpose.

The third category of citizen is the alienated type. Much indeed has been written about alienation in modern society. As Nisbet has observed, "alienation, frustration, the sense of aloneness . . . are major states of mind in Western society. . . ." [6] That they were not unknown in fifteenth-century Florence or nineteenth-century Boston does not soften the harsh

---

[5] Robert A. Nisbet, *Community and Power* (New York: Oxford University Press, Galaxy Books, 1962), p. 165.

[6] *Ibid.*, p. 245.

fact of their existence today. The alienated man makes the alienated citizen (or noncitizen), and he will inevitably affect the city—and indeed the whole of democratic society. What, then, is alienation? Or, in particular, what is political alienation (since alienation is very much a political as well as a social phenomenon)?

The alienated citizen is one who feels a deep sense of frustration vis-à-vis politics. He rejects politics and the political order because he feels that they have cut him off from self-realization. Or he has rejected them because they have rejected him. They have made him feel like a child, unloved and unwanted, who has nothing whatever to offer the community. And they (politics and the political order) have cut him off from power. Just as society has denied him access to those groups which have any capacity to develop power (in the sense defined above), so politics and the political order have similarly closed doors in his face. He becomes suspicious, sullen—perhaps, as Presthus suggests, slightly paranoid. Only in terms of alienation can one understand the rage with which the depressed wards of a city regard the civic reformers' plea for at-large election of the city council. Loss of "his" alderman will only increase the alienated citizen's feeling of powerlessness, frustration, and disenchantment.

And yet he is still political. If the rejected lover has become a foe, he is nevertheless still acting in terms of the same emotion, although considerably transformed. A good deal of empirical research has indicated the propensity of the alienated to vent his wrath upon the community whenever the opportunity presents itself. Full of aggressions against those who, very literally, have hurt him, he eagerly awaits every opportunity to strike at them.[7]

The fourth type of citizen—the apolitical—has no political orientation whatsoever. He neither accepts politics (actively or passively) nor rejects it. He simply does not recognize that politics exists; in no way does it intrude into his consciousness or into his activities. He is the esthete; he is the junior executive who is so frequently transferred by his company that he scarcely has time to glance at the community. He is the professor of astronomy or Renaissance literature; he is a hedonist, wrapped up in pleasure or what he thinks of as pleasure. He is, in short, the apolitical.[8]

If this type of citizen is truly apolitical, why should he even be men-

---

[7] See J. E. Horton and W. E. Thompson, "Powerlessness and Political Negativism: A Study of Defeated Local Referendums," *American Journal of Sociology*, XLVII (March, 1962), 485–494; also Duane Lockard, *The Politics of State and Local Government* (New York: The Macmillan Co., 1963), pp. 268–269, for comment on this phenomenon and further references to it.

[8] Greer uses the term "isolates" to describe a type of apolitical individual in a suburban community. Scott Greer, "The Social Structure and Political Process of Suburbia," *American Sociological Review*, XXV (August, 1960), 514–526.

tioned in any discourse on politics? First, he should be considered because
the apolitical individual (or a group of apolitical individuals) may have
great *potential* influence on the city's political life. Dahl's Rodney Brown,
a man of great wealth who was interested only in gracious living and the
ballet, is an example of such an apolitical individual with great latent
power.[9]

Second, he should be mentioned because we have no assurance that the
apolitical man will remain so all his life. If we could be sure of his remaining so, we could wash our hands of him; and neither our discourse nor the
democratic process would be any worse off. But there we are again; we cannot be sure that some kind of political stimulus will not reach him, or that
some kind of changed condition will not force him into a political act. The
esthete suddenly realizes that there is a local-option election tomorrow and
that by means of the ballot he must strike a blow for the Good Society. And
he may also bring some of his apolitical friends to the polls.

Who can know the consequences of this act? The pebble tossed upon the
smooth, apolitical surface of his mind may cause ripples which, defying the
laws of physical motion, can never quite disappear. This is by no means the
Esthete Transformed, the apolitical become the Good Citizen. In all probability politics will never intrude again into his life. Yet who can be sure?

Least of all can the political activists be sure. Knowing that they cannot
discount the apolitical individual entirely, they must, therefore, take him
into account. He will feature in all of the activists' plans and will influence
them. If the apolitical man has no power as such, therefore, he nevertheless
affects the uses and deployment of power, all quite unknowingly.

We can assume deductively, because there is little empirical evidence on
the matter, that the apolitical and unpredictable man is the great unknow-
able of politics. Those who endeavor to apply standards of measurement to
politics are here faced with the unmeasurable.

Elites and Other Systems. We have already posed the argument over
monism versus pluralism of which Hunter and Dahl are representative.
Now having analyzed the political configuration of the community, we are
in a better position than formerly to expand upon the points of view represented by Dahl and Hunter and to introduce a new concept, elitism.

The monistic state is one in which the ultimate power lies in a sovereign
authority which may be either democratically or autocratically controlled.
In the hands of Jean Jacques Rousseau, monism had all the surface appearances of democracy, but underneath was totalitarian. Since the General Will was the ultimate expression of authority in the state, since it
could never err, and since all "partial" associations (which might claim the

[9] Dahl, *Modern Political Analysis, op. cit.,* pp. 47–48.

people's loyalty and dilute the sovereign authority) must be discouraged, Rousseau's ideas furnish a good base for autocracy.

But the monistic state need not be autocratic. If those partial associations which Rousseau feared flourish within society, there will develop numerous centers of power, no one of which can control the state. Thus the state which is monistic in constitutional and legal structure may be pluralistic in fact—that is, in the way in which political, social, and economic conflict is resolved. One might legitimately claim that without such pluralism within its body politic the monistic state must of necessity be autocratic.

In the pluralistic state the fragmentation of power is institutionalized in the constitution and laws. Pluralism in the United States is institutionalized in the federal system and in such local political experiments as municipal home rule. Popularly it finds expression in American distrust of bigness—big unions, big corporations, big government, and, for that matter, big cities. And yet the institutions of pluralism could so lose their substance that a formally pluralistic state would become monistic. If an all-powerful elite controlled political decisions, then pluralism of structure would be a mere façade.

We have used pluralism in a previous chapter to give a rational justification to the urban community's being and individuality. If the centers of power in the republic are legion, if power seems to arise inevitably out of a diversity of forces, both geographic and functional, why then is not the urban community a reflection of this diversity and entitled to an exercise of power in its own right? Is not the myth of sovereignty in the state belied by the facts? And should not, therefore, legal and constitutional strictures be made to conform to political reality? Such was the gist of the argument for some form of genuine local autonomy. But in that argument we were considering a kind of statewide, or even national, pluralism which is exterior to the urban community. If we move inside the community, our approach to pluralism must change. And so must our approach to monism.

Structurally, the urban community is at least somewhat pluralistic, not only in the United States but also in much of the remainder of the Western world. This community (or "natural" city) usually has at least three or four, and may have hundreds, of separate governments, each of which is independent of the others. Because of this diversity of form one is apt to assume, without further evidence, that there is a diversity of control.

The evidence gathered by the sociological monists, such as Hunter, challenges this assumption. Real control of the community, they say, is not pluralistic but monistic. But they do not call the phenomenon "monism"; they call it, rather, "elitism." And this is not a change from language to jargon. "Monism" smacks too much of the nation-state or of Rousseau's undiluted sovereign authority vested in the General Will. We can hardly use such a word to describe power in a modern city.[10] Regardless of how harsh and unfriendly it sounds to the democratic ear, "elitism" is the word that must be used. The literature of "community-power" research resounds with the word, and we shall therefore bow to current usage.[11]

When Hunter made his study of Atlanta in the early 1950's he found that the city of 500,000 was controlled by a minuscule group numbering but 40 people. Here, truly, was control by an elite, which was made up largely of economic "notables," that is, people who controlled the economic life of the community. This analysis and its results tended to follow the "Middletown" studies of the Lynds some two decades earlier. Hunter's work also let loose a flood of "community-power" research, which, if critical of Hunter at times, did not pretend to disprove his elitist conclusions. Therefore we find a wide variance between the sociologist's view of who governs the community, and how, and the political scientist's view. This is essentially the elitist position opposed by the pluralist.[12]

Elitism versus Pluralism. In order to evaluate the validity of the two positions we must first look at the evidence. Both positions rest upon a somewhat limited empirical base—mostly upon evidence drawn from a relatively few case studies. The one notable exception to this statement is the pluralist's reliance upon structure as well as dynamics to bolster his case.

The diversity of governmental structure in the urban community is so well documented that one never wants for evidence on this point. The 1957 and 1962 censuses of governments, so painstakingly put together by the U.S. Bureau of the Census, give sufficient evidence of this diversity to satisfy even the most meticulous of empiricists. And the pluralist can legitimately insist that this very diversity of structure must mean a diversity of control, without going any further into the matter. Around each of the corporate and separate entities within the urban community there tends to develop at least one power group—at least one, and perhaps several.

This conclusion is reinforced by the "dynamic" studies of community politics. Dahl found that New Haven politics was characterized by a system of "dispersed inequalities" which gives rise to a pluralist democracy. Scoble found that Bennington, Vermont, was pluralist in the sense that no one group had complete power in the community.[13] In his study of Edgewood

[10] See Presthus, *Men at the Top, op. cit.* (above, n. 4), for a very pertinent comment on this point, especially at pp. 10–11, fn. 7.

[11] "Oligarchy" is, of course, the best word of all, because it has such a definitely political meaning. In his study of New Haven, Dahl uses "oligarchy" and never so much as raises "elite" or "elitism" to the dignity of a place in a subtitle.

[12] Presthus, *op. cit.,* p. 38.

[13] Harry Scoble, "Leadership Hierarchies and Political Issues in a New England Town," in Morris Janowitz (ed.), *Community Political Systems* (Glencoe, Ill.: The Free Press, 1959).

and Riverview, New York, Presthus found the latter the "closer approximation to the traditional pluralist model." In Edgewood, however, his evidence supported "earlier research of sociologists who found a tendency toward elitism in community power structures which were usually dominated by economic elites." [14]

Those who see a monolithic power structure in the community rely essentially upon evidence that a few economic "notables" command enduring positions of influence within the community. They read the evidence with a strong bias toward a form of economic determinism. The reasoning goes something like this: if a man has wealth and social status, if these attributes are enduring (which they usually are), and if a goodly number of people identify this person as a man of influence, then we can safely conclude that he is in reality a part of the power elite.

There are several significant flaws to this reasoning. The first is the assumption that wealth and status are the only significant sources of power. This may be true of economic power, but whether it applies to political power is, to say the least, a dubious proposition. There are many sources of political power. As Dahl found in New Haven, wealth and social standing are sources of power, but so also are legality, popularity, and control over jobs and sources of information.[15] And we can assume reasonably that this list does not exhaust the possibilities.

A second flaw is to be found in the techniques used for identifying community leadership. One can seriously question whether the reputational technique, for example, can do more than isolate both those who are actually and potentially leaders.[16] The actual and the potential are intermixed. And, of course, the reservoir of potential leaders can only be touched. Many a potential leader, by definition, will not have established a reputation sufficient to put him on a list of nominees.

Time represents a third flaw. Even if we assume that all of the leaders which we identify are massed together into one coherent, effective elite (a risky assumption, at best), how can we then conclude that tomorrow or next month a rift will not appear in the erstwhile united front? The palace revolution is a familiar enough political phenomenon to make us suspect any theory relying too heavily upon a stable elite. Moreover, opposition may arise not only from within the elite itself; it may also arise from the outside. The latter phenomenon was observed by Booth and Adrian in a case study of a Midwestern city and led them to conclude that the "sudden appearance of a new leader and the rather easy modification of the community leadership structure seem to lend support to those who have suggested

---

[14] Presthus, *op. cit.*, pp. 431, 430.
[15] Dahl, *Who Governs? op.cit.* (above, n. 1), Bk. IV.
[16] Presthus, *op. cit.*, pp. 57–61.

that social scientists tend to over-emphasis [of] the solidity of the community power structure." [17]

Fourth, the elitists, in their economic-determinist position, depreciate
the importance of the electoral process. The ad hoc power groups, taken
together with the popular referenda, are in themselves enough to force us
into use of the hackneyed reminder about the best-laid plans of mice and
men. Even if there is an elite that governs the community, it will be frustrated more than occasionally by defeats at the polls on public issues.

A fifth weakness of the elitist position is to be found in the administrative structure of the urban community. As we have seen previously, the
pluralist assumes that the great diversity of governmental units in most
urban communities will give rise to a diversity of power groupings. The
number of units can be established empirically. Whether this plurality of
units establishes a plurality of control remains a question. But we can be
sure of this: the elitist has never effectively challenged this assumption.

Sixth, and finally, the elitist glosses over the *quality* of both leadership
and political participation. One of the reasons he does so is that quality is
an exceedingly hard factor to measure. Yet dare we neglect it? We have experimental evidence from small-group findings that quality of leadership is
indeed a crucial factor. That the instrumental and the affective are essential qualities of leadership has been reasonably well established by experiments with the small group, but has been ignored as a matter for systematic
investigation by the investigator into community power. If a group of people retains effective control over an urban community for an extended period, is this a kind of hard-core, elitist rule? Or is it effective democracy, in
which the leaders so satisfy the great majority (the actives, passives, alienated, and even apolitical), and in themselves so reflect the community
ethos, that they are representative in the full democratic sense?

The leader, as we have seen from small-group findings, is as much a
prisoner of the group as the group is dependent upon him. In community
politics much the same situation is in evidence. As Dahl so cogently observes, "Viewed from one position, leaders are enormously influential—so
influential that if they are seen only in this perspective they might well be
considered a kind of ruling elite. Viewed from another position, however,
many influential leaders seem to be captive of their constituents." [18]

Participation must be considered too. We all of us assume much too easily that political participation means voting, organizational and committee membership, contributions to political funds, attendance at meetings,
writing letters to the newspapers—in short, all of the devices used by the

[17] David A. Booth and Charles R. Adrian, "Elections and Community Power," *The
Journal of Politics*, XXV (1963), 117.
[18] Dahl, *Who Governs?* op. cit. (above, n. 1), p. 89.

typical activist. But is this all that participation means? What of the great passive group that gives tacit consent to public decisions, this group whose members *feel* that they are participating in the decisions mainly because they agree with them? Is not this a kind of vicarious participation which ebbs and flows according to the political capacities of the leader? If this kind of vicarious participation does not exist, a considerable number of otherwise astute political leaders are operating on false premises.

The probabilities are—or at least this is our hypothesis—that although for the apolitical, participation is a meaningless consideration, for the three political types it may be overt, covert, or vicarious. Thus the relation between and among leader and follower, leader and leader, follower and follower involves a complicated symbiosis which we only barely, as yet, understand.

In summary, there is a substantial difference in the manner with which various scholars regard control in the urban community. And this difference is by no means the result of sociologists' and political scientists' interpreting the same data from differing viewpoints, though such biases can be expected. That elitism exists in some communities cannot be denied. One can expect, deductively, that the greater the homogeneity the greater the possibility of elite control. Observe, for example, the manner in which some well-to-do metropolitan suburbs are governed.

By the same token, one can expect a diversity of control in a diverse community, especially one that is diverse both structurally and demographically. Did Presthus find Edgewood elitist, while Dahl discovered in New Haven strong pluralistic elements? Perhaps a major reason was that New Haven is relatively more diverse than Edgewood. Perhaps these data and conclusions simply bear out Madison's idea of complexity as a safeguard against monolithic control.

If we cannot say conclusively that the American urban community is pluralistic, we can surely say—though all the evidence is not in, by any means—that it *tends* in that direction. But we need to throw further light on this matter by examining the organization of community power.

The Organization of Community Power

The three truly distinctive features of politics in the urban community are (1) nonpartisanship, (2) issue politics, and (3) corporate structure. And from these features the organization of power takes its peculiar cast.

That the great bulk of city, school, and other local officials are elected on nonpartisan ballots is a well-established fact of local government. That most public issues are not identified with either the Republican or Democratic parties is also established. And this condition gives local politics a peculiar cast. Yet the distinction should not be overemphasized. If nonpartisanship dominates the local scene, so also does politics. Nonpartisanship does not eliminate politics, but it does change the nature of political activity.

Another kind of distinctiveness is added by issue politics. Nationally, we may argue over recognition of Red China, federal aid to education, and curbing the power of the Supreme Court, but we never have a chance to vote on such issues directly. On the other hand, taxation, indebtedness, urban renewal, public health measures, education, and other issues of public concern to the city we must quite frequently decide by popular vote.

The corporate structure of the community is no less important in giving local politics its distinctiveness. The use of the appointive professional as chief executive, whether of school or city, is known nowhere else in the American political system. While this is a structural peculiarity of importance to the political situation, it is by no means the exclusive one. The division of the "natural" city into independent and rival jurisdictions— this Balkanization of the community—gives excellent opportunity for a multitude of little sovereignties to develop and to add further differences to the urban political scene.

The Impact of Nonpartisanship. One of the shibboleths of reform politics in the city is nonpartisanship. Together with a small council elected at large, the council-manager plan, the efficiency and economy ideal, and the short ballot, it represents a principal part of the reform ideology. It is one of the accepted myths of the middle-class, good-government fraternity.

State politics, on the other hand, is dominated not only by a vigorous partisanship, but also by the party labels, organization, and traditions of the two major political parties. This presents us with the first anomaly of nonpartisanship: that the parent government of the cities, schools, and special districts which meet the public needs of the urban community should be controlled by the Democratic and Republican parties while the local units are overwhelmingly nonpartisan.

The only local unit, in fact, which has continued to operate in the image of the parent government is the county. County government is undoubtedly the most partisan of all local units, at least in the traditional sense; and the county, wherever you find it, tends to be part of the warp and woof of state politics. Hardly touched by twentieth-century ideas about the governing process, the county courthouse is still the seat of the philosophy that the game of politics must be played daily, incessantly, without remission.

And here is yet another anomaly. Taken together, the counties are the least useful to the urban community of all the other local units. One wonders why they remain upon the urban political landscape at all, except as a vestigial tail to such a municipality as Nashville or Honolulu. That is, one wonders until he becomes acquainted with American political logic, and then he suddenly realizes that the real strength of the county lies not in its capacity to serve and satisfy the body politic, but in its proven worth to the Republican and Democratic parties. Having lost most of its political base in the cities, schools, and special districts, each political party holds on for dear life to the county. And so the county becomes, in substantial part, a servant not to the community but to the party.

What Is Nonpartisanship? The municipal reform movement, getting under way about the turn of the century, put nonpartisanship on its masthead along with home rule and other innovations.[19] As the reform movement gained headway and took within its fold, first, the commission and then the council-manager form of government, the nonpartisan ballot became an integral part of reform in city hall. And it has remained to this day one of the elements of change which reformers most enthusiastically fight for.

The classic definition of nonpartisanship is that no party labels appear on the ballot and that no overt connection is maintained between nonpartisan political activity and the old-line political parties. In practice, however, nonpartisanship has come to mean that the city is controlled by a coalition of dissident Republicans and Democrats, or by other groups and individuals outside the confines of the two major parties. In school elections, nonpartisanship means that a coalition of the school bureaucracy and such satellite groups as the Parent-Teachers' Association opposes an amorphous opposition made up of taxpayers' groups, standpatters, and temporary groups organized around the issues and personalities of a particular election.[20] Such coalitions and such opposing forces tend to be found in all types of nonpartisan elections, whether they involve candidates for office, candidates and issues, or simply issues (such as those posed by referendum or initiative proposals).

Nonpartisanship as Viewed by the Reformer. There are many reasons advanced in support of nonpartisanship. Undisturbed by party labels and alliances with the old-line parties, reform sentiment is able to grow and flourish under one roof, and reformers are able to congregate into a single group. The lack of party labels, moreover, involves people who do not want to "get into politics." Even though the nonpartisan election may embody the essence of politics, popular opinion may have it otherwise.

Another rationale for nonpartisanship is that it enables members of the minority party to participate in public decision-making. If the Democratic or Republican party tends to dominate the local government and this domination continues over the years, the members of the party which is second

[19] See Edward C. Banfield and James Q. Wilson, *City Politics* (Cambridge, Mass.: Harvard University Press and Massachusetts Institute of Technology Press, 1963), pp. 154–155. The authors find that in those states where the progressives were the strongest fifty years ago nonpartisanship is most pronounced.

[20] See Thomas H. Eliot, "Toward an Understanding of Public School Politics," *American Political Science Review*, LIII (December, 1959), 1032–1051.

in strength are in effect denied access to local policy-making. A contrast between the mayoralty of Chicago and that of Detroit might illustrate this point. Both cities tend to be heavily Democratic. In Chicago, the Democrats have held the office of mayor since the departure of Big Bill Thompson from the political scene in the early 1930's. On the other hand, Mayor Albert E. Cobo of Detroit, one of the outstanding mayors of the city of recent years, was a Republican. The evidence would seem to indicate that he never could have been elected mayor had he not run on a nonpartisan ticket.[21]

A final reason for the existence of a nonpartisan election is that it is a means of recognizing and emphasizing the validity of local political issues. That there is no Democratic or Republican way to pave a street, to plan and zone, or to operate an art museum is a commonplace way to state the case for nonpartisanship. The experience with nonpartisan elections over the past half-century gives us ample evidence that nonpartisanship does indeed emphasize local programs over state and national issues.

By contrast, both of the major political party organizations have been all too prone to ignore local problems and local issues and to use city hall as an organizational redoubt to be held at all costs, not in the interest of the city, but for partisan advantage in state and national contests. Has nonpartisanship weakened the political party, as some observers claim? If so, then it is perhaps no more than the parties deserve for their cavalier treatment of the city. The truth is that in a rurally dominated political environment the parties have not done well by the cities.

Nonpartisanship: The Disenchanted View. One of the most telling arguments against the nonpartisan position is that it nurtures the myth that public decisions can be made outside politics. Simply by cutting the ties with the two major parties and by striking party labels off the ballot—or so goes the myth—one can take a large area of public decision-making out of politics. Up to this point the myth is not damaging, although it is admittedly a denial of the facts. But when it is extended further, when one hears otherwise perfectly intelligent people assert that "We must take the city and the schools out of politics," it becomes mischievous, an assault upon the very essence of the democratic process. In school affairs this is particularly evident. Not only must local educational policy be kept pure of public controversy; it must also be separated from the public at large, kept safe in the hands of the professional administrators and a few "tame" laymen. And yet this is perhaps the most important of all public functions (federal, state,

---

[21] Another reason for Cobo's success might have been the low sense of party identification among Detroit voters. See, for example, Samuel J. Eldersveld *et al., Political Affiliation in Metropolitan Detroit, Michigan, Governmental Studies,* No. 34 (Ann Arbor, Mich.: Institute of Public Administration, University of Michigan, 1957), pp. 11–12, 42–43.

or local) and second in costliness only to national defense. Policy on such a matter will be subject to political decisions; indeed, educational policy will inevitably be subject to politics.

The attempt to take politics out of politics is no more futile than it is to expect the voter to mark his ballot more intelligently without the party label than with it. Since the nonpartisan ballot emphasizes the individual candidate over coherent group effort, a measure of chaos is apt to appear in every election. One characteristic of this disorder may be seen in the "name" candidate. Hellmut Weltschmerz has had many years in public office and has served the city honorably and well. But he has a distant cousin, a ne'er-do-well, who also announces for the city council and whose name (the same name) appears with his on the ballot. Not only is the German community confused, but so also is the rest of the city. Detroit has, from time to time, had problems of this nature.

Although the smaller city has not been troubled as much as the large ones with this phenomenon, it is bothered with a roughly similar problem. Where the city council is elected on a nonpartisan, at-large ballot, it is difficult for minority group members to be elected. Persons with non-Anglo-Saxon names find success at the polls far more difficult than the Smiths and the Joneses. And Negroes, even with their normally Anglo-Saxon names, are understandably pessimistic about their chances at the polls.

Does this result stem from the nonpartisan or the at-large character of the election? This is a question that we cannot resolve, given the evidence at hand, though certainly both elements are important. The argument of compelling interest to us, at this point, is that the partisan election could correct this political maladjustment.

Partisan election is easily adaptable to the balanced-ticket approach, which is so familiar to veteran politicians throughout the country. The balanced ticket is one in which all of the major elements of the community —racial, national, and religious—are represented on the party-supported "slate." Such a slate is not only possible in a party election; it is an asset, perhaps even a necessity, in those places where the candidates run at large or from plural-member districts. Only the partisan election, in other words, can achieve the obvious democratic goal of representation of minority interests.

We have already seen the possibly disturbing influence of the small council on open, public debate. That this influence is exaggerated by the nonpartisan election is a logical deduction. If an opposition starts to develop on the council, it can be snuffed out by the pressure of the majority upon the minority members. If these members were supported by a party, on the other hand, their opposition, far from being regarded as a treacherous assault on group solidarity, would simply be an outgrowth of playing the game. In fact, the opposition might be able to develop into a small group itself and evolve a measure of party discipline unheard of in large legislative bodies. But regardless of such small-group "heresy"—as it may be regarded by some students of politics—party election could logically be expected to develop some badly needed public opposition on some city councils.

Does nonpartisanship cut party channels between the city, and state and federal governments? All appearances indicate that it does. Most state governors and legislators, and of course all congressmen and the President are elected on partisan bases. Because of the utter dependence of the city upon the state, this severance of political ties can be serious indeed. As the experience of the county clearly shows—and the township, too, in some states —these units of local governments, which are anachronisms in the urban community, survive mainly because of their strong political ties with the state legislature. Does the state league of cities have difficulty getting its legislative program through the general assembly? One reason may be, though we have little evidence on the point, that the nonpartisan official has less impact on the opinions of the legislators than the partisan one.

A still further objection to nonpartisanship, as it appears in many cities, is that it is a façade without reality. Although the fifty aldermen in Chicago are elected on a technically nonpartisan basis, no one who knows Chicago politics would venture to suggest that they are in fact nonpartisan. Most of the recent mayors and councilmen of Detroit can be identified as Republicans and Democrats. The same is true in Denver. Although San Francisco is nominally nonpartisan in city elections, the city often elects Republican mayors, in spite of the fact that registered Democrats outnumber Republicans almost two to one. Obviously this situation distresses the Democrats, and nonpartisanship seems to be on the wane. During the hotly contested San Francisco mayoral election of 1963, the New York *Times* quoted an unidentified politician as saying that there is a "trend away from nonpartisanship, long one of the distinctive features of California politics." [22]

The Impact of Issue Politics. We have already seen that constitutions, laws, and charters require constant recourse to the people, in order that they may be approved or disapproved as public-policy questions. Our task now is to determine how this habit of urban life affects the organization of political power.

Local government in the United States is, to a considerable extent, government by plebiscite. In the decade 1952–1961, for example, there were 64,110 long-term state and local bond issues.[23] We can safely assume (1)

[22] October 13, 1963, p. 54. Lee, in his study of nonpartisanship in California, found some opinion to the effect that the Republican party was helped by it and the Democratic party harmed. See Eugene C. Lee, *The Politics of Nonpartisanship* (Berkeley, Calif.: University of California Press, 1960), pp. 34–35.

[23] *The Municipal Year Book 1962* (Chicago: ICMA), p. 235.

that the bulk of these were city and school issues, (2) that most of the issues were voted on in compulsory referenda, and (3) that probably 20,000 to 30,000 additional bond issues were proposed and rejected. (We can extrapolate from other evidence sufficiently to enable us to make such a rough estimate.) And these were only bond referenda. Think of all the other types —health and welfare, housing, urban renewal, tax increases, ports and airports, industrial development, recreation, and many others.

There are thousands of instances in which public policy must be made by plebiscite. The stakes are high; they have an immediacy, an abiding personal interest for the citizen; and they are issues on which the citizen can act directly. He has only to pick up his telephone or cross over to his neighbor's door—across the hall or across the street—to enter into the hustings. With the slightest effort, in other words, he can be in politics. It does not take much money (the great bugaboo of so much of contemporary American politics); it only takes time and a certain firmness of conviction.

But such action is no isolated action. That is, it may be, but usually is not. The action takes some form; it becomes a part of the activity of a group more or less in agreement with the individual on the goals to be attained.

What are these groups, and how do they function? With respect to issue politics they may be of three major types: (1) the ad hoc group, (2) the more-or-less-permanent political action group, and (3) the pressure organization, such as the local chamber of commerce, which does not have political action as its primary purpose, but which from time to time will engage in political activity. We should take a look at each of these major types.

The Ad Hoc Group. This group is organized around one issue or a series of related issues. It develops a formal political organization with officers, a secretariat, treasury, committee structure, a platform, and ward, precinct, and block workers. With most of the accoutrements of the political party, and often with much more esprit than that exhibited by the local Democratic and Republican organizations, the group goes forth to battle.

And such groups have remarkable success. Amateurs all—rarely does one find a "professional" politician among them—and sometimes unwilling even to admit that they are immersed in politics, they frequently show themselves able to marshal sufficient strength at the polls to achieve victory. Or suffering defeat the first time, they simply reorganize and come back into the fray when the issue is again presented.

With victory—or after successive defeats—the rationale for the group's existence has vanished. Its goals have been achieved, or conclusively denied it. In either case it has lost raison d'être, and there is nothing left for it to do but gracefully fade away. It then becomes mere history, to be resurrected from old newspaper files or interviews with the participants.

One last question, however, should be raised about such a group. Who are the participants, and where do they come from? The ad hoc group membership is a reflection of every race, creed, occupation, and class in the city. Although it is true that the better-educated and the more well-to-do in the city tend to participate more actively in community politics than the less well-favored citizens, the ad hoc group knows all kinds.[24] Whether the issue is a new high school, an expanded recreational or water program, local prohibition, urban renewal, or a change in form of government, the ad hoc group members—amateurs though they may be—seem to know intuitively that to be successful they must make their group as representative of the various elements of the community as their talents and energies can make it. To attempt citywide block and precinct organization, in itself, is to try to achieve representativeness.

This is not to say that the attempt to achieve a representative membership will always succeed. There will be, in fact, inevitable failures; inevitably there will be many blocks, even whole precincts, which for one reason or another cannot be effectively organized. But the attempt will be made, and it will be sufficiently successful, in most cases, to discredit the canard so often voiced that the ad hoc reform group takes to its bosom only the middle class and covertly excludes the less-favored elements of the community. But this question of representativeness can be raised again, and perhaps even more aptly, when we discuss the permanently organized political action group.

The Political Action Group. The political action group, with its political party organization and orientation, has become such a feature of city politics that it might be described as a movement. Indeed, one might, at the risk, admittedly, of indulging in flamboyance or hyperbole, call it "the unknown third-party movement in America."

These citizen organizations oftentimes function as "nonpartisan" leagues (which, of course, simply means that they have no affiliation with either the Democratic or Republican local organizations) and very frequently refuse to admit that their activities are political. Yet like the ad hoc array they are at least quasi-parties; unlike the ad hoc group they are permanent. They have an officialdom, a secretariat, a platform or succession of platforms, ward and precinct organization, a "party" war chest; and they offer slates of candidates.

The degree to which they formalize their activities, however, varies greatly. Where the caucus "parties" of Chicago's suburbia have little or no formal structure, the citizen associations of Kansas City and Cincinnati are as tightly and coherently organized as either of the two major parties. Then, too, like all politically directed societies, the action groups tend to go into hibernation between elections: it is just that for some groups the period of hibernation is longer and the state of it is deeper than for others.

[24] See, for example, Robert A. Dahl, "Who Participates in Local Politics and Why," *Science*, October 27, 1961, pp. 1340–1348.

The political action groups are to be found in large cities and small, and the success of each one, like that of the regular, old-line parties, varies greatly. The Citizens' Association in Kansas City first came into power in 1940 to fill a void left by the breakup of the Pendergast machine. Made up of independent Democrats and Republicans, it kept reasonably secure hold on city hall until 1959, when the regular Democrats won control of the council. Undaunted by this defeat, the Citizens' Association maintained its organizational integrity and succeeded to power again in 1963. The Cincinnati City Charter Committee has had a similar history, except that it is older (organized in 1924) and has had to fight off the regular Republicans rather than the regular Democrats.

In smaller cities, too, the political action groups live active lives. From 1952 to 1959 the Citizens Plan E Association of Worcester, Massachusetts, sponsored forty-three neighborhood town meetings, at which attendance ranged from a handful to several hundred. By means of these gatherings the neighborhood citizenry was able to bring to the attention of municipal officials (councilmen, school committeemen, heads of the various administrative departments) matters of vital concern to any urban neighborhood —traffic control, police protection, public works improvements, recreational facilities.[25] In Cambridge, Massachusetts, the Civic Association had the largest annual meeting in its history when in 1961 over 500 citizens attended. (Such attendance would surely evoke wonder and envy from any dedicated worker in either the Republican or Democratic vineyard.) And the University City Charter Association, a political action group supporting the council-manager form of government in that Missouri city, has been known to sponsor folk dances to stimulate interest in its political program.

We see, then, that the political action group appears frequently in local politics; that it is well organized and ably led; that it cannot only win elections but enlist citizen interest and support between elections; and that it can do battle with the regular political parties with good chance of success.

But one troubling question remains: Is the political action group truly representative of the people of the city, or is it simply a middle-class phenomenon? A quick, easy answer to this question would be that since these groups win elections (either regular elections or issue elections), they must of course be representative. But this is such an easy answer that it is probably insufficient. We need to enlarge upon the answer by posing some general (although tentative) conclusions.

First, there does certainly appear to be more appeal of the citizens' groups to the middle class than to the working class or to certain ethnic minorities. In a Kansas City study, Richard A. Watson found that only 11 percent of those in his sample who earned less than $2,000 a year were affiliated with the Citizens' Association, whereas 38 percent of those with incomes over $10,000 were association members. Using a subjective criterion (people were asked whether they were working class or middle class), he got the same results. "Persons designating themselves as members of the 'working class' definitely prefer the Democratic Coalition, while the 'middle-class' respondents prefer the Citizens' Association." [26] This conclusion is reinforced by the prevalence of citizens' political action groups in such middle-class suburbs as University City, Glencoe, and Cambridge.

A second consideration is that alienation is probably more prevalent in working-class than in middle-class districts, and the alienated person will doubtless be even more chary of the optimistic, well-educated, reform-oriented types that flock into the citizens' associations than he will be of regular Democrats or regular Republicans. He will certainly care as little about an improvement in the sewer system as he will a new wing on the art museum.

A third observation, if not conclusion, that we can make is that the leadership of the citizens' association is usually middle class. This seems to be an inevitable result of the way politics must be conducted. Although a very able block worker or precinct captain may be recruited here and there in the depressed wards, the probabilities are that he will not have the political skills to enable him to rise any further up the organizational echelon. (Exceptions to this generalization can, of course, easily be found in the Negro precincts where able business and professional leaders remain locked up in their ghettos.) Only the middle class seems to possess the necessary political skills in abundance.

The fourth point is far more of a hypothesis than a conclusion. It is that if there is a political action group, its lack of strength in working-class neighborhoods must be considered as much a political as a class phenomenon. As we have already seen, there is some evidence that working-class precincts have been voting a conservative position locally (or even a reactionary one) at the same time that they support "liberal" candidates for state and national offices. Although the Democratic platform in 1960 strongly supported urban renewal, for example, the most heavily Democratic precincts in Denver swamped the city's urban renewal bond proposal of 1964 in a tidal wave of "No" votes. This was the result in spite of the fact that the city's Democratic mayor had urban renewal as a cardinal element of his administration's program and in spite, also, of the efforts of a well-organized ad hoc group, headed by another prominent Democrat, to get rank-and-file support. Was this a political or a class reaction?

[26] Richard A. Watson, *The Politics of Urban Change* (Kansas City, Mo.: Community Studies, 1963), pp. 18–19.

In summary, we can say that the political action group, arising out of issue politics, has come close to establishing itself as a political party. No better evidence of the importance of issue politics to the urban community can be offered.

The Pressure Group. If pressure group activity is one of the most remarkable—and remarked upon—aspects of American politics at large, it is no less an important feature of urban politics. All of the many and separate jurisdictions of the urban community (city, schools, special districts, even county) and all of the many councils, boards, and rule-making and advisory bodies are subjected constantly to the petitions, memorials, and other representations of the multitude of private societies that shape (and occasionally shake) the communal structure. Every single society, in fact, no matter how small or how private, is potentially a pressure group.

A full list of the pressure groups in a city would include, therefore, every existing private society, organization, or association. We shall not try to introduce such a list here, because no community ever knows exactly how many of such groups actually exist within it and because only a few of the associations are consistently important in the formation of public policy.

If we cannot name all of the groups, we can at least make up a representative list of the important ones. Even such a partial enumeration is a formidable task: the chamber of commerce, the taxpayers' association; the neighborhood group, research bureau, or labor committee (the old CIO-PAC and the present-day COPE, Committee on Political Education); the church councils, professional societies (of lawyers, doctors, architects, accountants, teachers, and others), health societies, private businesses (contractors and engineering firms, for example), fraternal organizations (including the veterans' groups); and such associations as the League of Women Voters, the political action groups and the ad hoc organizations, which we have already surveyed. And because of the persistence of ethnic politics, that important kind of group must be added to the list.[27]

Although very few data in orderly form are available to give us real insight into the impact of these groups on local public policy, we can be reasonably sure that the impact is there, even though the extent of it has not been measured. Let us take, for example, the local chamber of commerce. Made up largely of businessmen, but including a scattering of professional people, members of the chamber have status, money, political skills, and a system of values—all of which make the organization's influence on local public policy not only inevitable but also of very great importance. And we

[27] For comment on the existence of ethnic politics, see Robert A. Dahl, *Who Governs?* (above, n. 1), p. 59; Raymond E. Wolfinger, "The Development and Persistence of Ethnic Voting," *American Political Science Review,* LIX (December, 1965), 896–908; and Michael Parenti, "Ethnic Politics and the Persistence of Ethnic Identification," *American Political Science Review,* LXI (September, 1967), 717–726.

can add still another factor bearing directly on the chamber's importance: motivation. Concerned as it is with the local economic base, the chamber is often not only more interested in this crucial element of the city's life but also more informed about it than city hall, the school board, or any of the other local governments. Notice the many chambers with full-time executive secretaries and the many others with full-time research people on their staffs. Beatrice Dinerman found that the 105 chambers of commerce in Los Angeles County devoted, on the average, 84 percent of their time to matters of strictly local concern and the remaining 16 percent to matters of county-wide, state, and national concern. Interest and information, therefore, add up to motivation—and motivation of a pronounced local character. Is it any wonder that an organization with status, money, political skills, and locally oriented values and motivation is influential in public policy formation?

Often in competition with the chamber of commerce, and rarely as influential as it is in local politics and policy formation, is the labor organization. Labor may from time to time control city hall in "labor" cities such as Flint, Michigan, but this is probably an exception that proves the rule. There is some evidence to support the hypothesis that labor has more influence in the state capitols and in Washington than in the urban communities. A case in point is the council-manager plan of city government. If not consistently unfriendly to the plan, labor has shown some disenchantment with the support given it by such associations of community "influentials" as the chamber of commerce and the League of Women Voters. Many a bitter struggle over the plan has developed between labor and liberal middle-class intellectuals, even though the two groups work hand-in-glove in state and national politics.

Why is labor not more influential in local politics than it apparently is? Although we cannot answer this question, we can offer some guesses. In the first place, labor simply cannot compete, in the urban community, with the middle class in terms of manpower possessing political skills. Nor does labor have the status or the money. In the second place, labor goals tend to be a bit provincial. They want a police force which is friendly or at least neutral toward labor display of power before the company gates or the main entrance to the downtown department store that is being organized. They are only vaguely interested in the abstract concept of a "good" police force. They want the city council and the school board to recognize and bargain collectively with public employees that are organized or can be organized. They are not particularly concerned with an orderly personnel program that applies to all public employees. (Scientific personnel management has a bourgeois "company" odor to it!) Do the day laborers receive a 20 percent wage increase and the skilled tradesmen only slightly less? Does this adversely affect employee morale in the remainder of the city's service? The labor man is apt to say, "We tend to the needs of our people; let them take care of theirs."

We can probably (but only probably) say, then, that labor as a pressure group has strong and positive influence on matters of direct concern to the workingman, but that because of limited goals, as well as other factors, labor has relatively slight influence—or at least negative influence—on major community policy.

Before we leave labor as a pressure group, incidentally, it might be well to offer another hypothesis. Because labor is frustrated locally, this frustration is reflected in the vote in labor precincts on major local policy issues. As we have already observed, there is some evidence that the working-class precincts vote "liberal" in state and national elections, but "conservative" in local elections (or, more specifically, in local-issue elections). Is labor frustration locally a partial reason for this negativism in the working-class precincts? On the face of it, this seems to be a good hypothesis, but whether it can be proved is quite another matter. At the moment it can only be speculated about.

Another type of pressure group of considerable importance, especially in the larger cities, is the research organization. Although the chambers of commerce, the League of Women Voters, the political action groups, and many others do sporadic research into questions bearing upon public policy, only the research organization devotes itself exclusively to the premise that the "facts" alone can point the way to good public policy.

How many research organizations there are is a matter for speculation, but there must be considerably over a hundred of them in as many cities throughout the republic. They are purely an American phenomenon (or, more precisely, American and Canadian), and they are rich enough and numerous enough to be organized into a national association, the Governmental Research Association, which publishes a yearly *Directory* that is a valuable annual source on the number and location of governmental research groups throughout the country. Largely business-supported, and directed principally by business and professional people, the associations show a middle- or upper-class complexion. The Greater Toledo Municipal League, for example, was dominated on its 1963–1964 board of directors by businessmen and lawyers. The members of the board of directors, identified by their organizational connections, were as follows:

Businessmen	13
Lawyers	6
Bankers	2
Chamber of Commerce	1
League of Women Voters	2

Dentists	1
American Association of University Women	2
Junior League	1
University of Toledo	2
Others and unidentified	6

Regardless of the middle-class nature of the Toledo league's membership, it is certainly the intent of the league directorate and staff to accumulate sound data on the operations of the thirty-seven local governments in the Toledo area. "The Municipal League's function is to make available the reliable, impartial facts which are essential to active, intelligent interest and sound judgment in civic affairs." (See Figure 13-1.)

Who will gainsay such a statement? So long as the facts are not partial and unreliable, they will be of use to all segments of the urban society. And it must be said that the facts gathered by the research associations are usually of acceptable quality. If they do not always point the way to the one best decision on public policy (an erroneous assumption commonly made by the members of the associations), they usually represent a net gain for discussions on policy.

Pressure-group activity in the urban community, then, is many-faceted. Its very variety is one measure of the community's complexity; the more complex it is, the greater the variety of pressure activity.

The Impact of Local Government Structure. We have already said a great deal about the organization of government locally. We need further to emphasize the importance of that organization to the distribution of community power.

The splitting up of the urban community (geographic and functional fractionalization) has been stimulated in major part by the lust (and it should be called nothing else but lust) of the various power groups for corporate identity. Acting under the guise of a spurious pluralism, and viewed tolerantly, even beneficently by the state legislature, these interest groups have sought—and successfully—to build walls around themselves by means of a legal stratagem—incorporation.

What does this corporate pluralism mean to the urban community? If a dozen local governments operate in the community, this means, probably, that a dozen or more elites participate in the control of the community. This is, if not democracy, at the very least a pluralism of elites, corresponding roughly with Dahl's pluralism, rather than a monolithic power structure as "found" by such sociologists as Hunter and the Lynds.

That this pluralism of structure has been written into our code of political values is indicated by the organization of school government in the United States. West of the Mississippi, school governments are almost

Figure 13-1.
The Urban Research Organization

FACTS ... ABOUT THE

MUNICIPAL LEAGUE　

WHAT　The Greater Toledo Municipal League
is a non-profit corporation organized to conduct
non-partisan local government research and to
distribute information supporting efficient local
government in the Toledo Metropolitan Area.

WHY　The Municipal League's function is to
make available the reliable, impartial facts which
are essential to active, intelligent interest and
sound judgment in civic affairs.

Even an interested citizen finds it impossible to
keep informed on the affairs of the 37 overlapping
local governments in this area which annually
spend more than $125,000,000 to provide a variety
of public services.

Yet, the strength of local government depends
upon the well-informed and active interest of its
citizens. The League is the only community organization devoted solely to informing citizens on
local government affairs.

WHO　The Municipal League has some 600
members, both individuals and companies, whose
tax-deductible contributions support League activities.

The League is independent, presents facts, and
is not obligated to any group or interest. Responsible, representative citizens make up the Board of
Directors. Its staff is professionally trained.

STAFF	
ARTHUR S. JOHNSON	Executive Secretary
(TO BE APPOINTED)	Research Assistant
MAY W. PHILLIPS	Office Secretary

GREATER
TOLEDO
MUNICIPAL
LEAGUE

a research association
for better government

28 YEARS OF

SERVICE TO THE

COMMUNITY

The Greater Toledo Municipal League is representative, in its membership and goals,
of literally dozens of such organizations scattered across the face of the republic.
Source: The Greater Toledo Municipal League, Toledo, Ohio (undated brochure distributed in 1964).

without fail independent municipal corporations, with their own corporate structure, boundaries, and—most important—political organization. Traditionally, the independent schools in the United States have kept
themselves rigorously free of contact with the "political" governments of

the community. Their efforts to keep out of politics have not, however, created a political vacuum. On the contrary, the school boards, the school bureaucracy, and their allies have created independent political systems of their own. One should hasten to add that there is nothing nefarious about all this; it is simply politics, built around the separate corporate existence of the schools.

What is true of the schools is equally true of the other local jurisdictions. A fire district seems about as innocuous politically as any of the community's institutions. But with its volunteer fire department, ready to do battle not only against conflagrations but also with any kind of political poachers, the district is enabled to fight effectively for its independence. The same is true with the separate park district or the suburban municipality, or any of the other municipal or quasi-municipal corporations that exist in the urban community. By means of the law they have built a separate identity, and they are perfectly capable of maintaining that identity by political action.

Toward a New Partisanship

Faced with the formidable inconsistencies in both partisan and nonpartisan elections, students of the city are hard-pressed to defend either one. This does not mean that the old forms of partisanship and nonpartisanship will disappear from the urban scene. As Arthur Bromage has observed, nonpartisanship has served many a city well and will continue to serve it well in the future. A legion of academic typewriters could not write that service out of the municipal record, either past or future.

But significant changes are taking place. If they do not alter political practices in middle-class suburban communities, they will at least redirect politics in central cities, both large and small. We can see these changes in the reorientation locally of the old-line parties and in the growth of genuinely local parties.

Old Parties Redirected. No longer can the Democratic and Republican organizations use the city simply as a building block for state and national party welfare. Having learned at the ballot box that good city government is good politics (so far has the middle-class ideal penetrated into the political consciousness of all classes!), the Democratic and Republican leaders have sought to build coherent local programs, often at the risk of lessening their potency in state and national elections.

In a decade the Cook County Democratic organization has suffered a sea change—perhaps not into something rich and strange, as the line goes in *The Tempest,* but at least into something new and different. Before 1955, except for occasional lapses into reform, both Democratic and Republican organizations in Chicago were dedicated to party victory—and to party victory at whatever cost to the city.

When Richard Daley was elected mayor in 1955, succeeding the ineffectual reform Democrat Martin Kennelly, the political soothsayers were all convinced that the Chicago democracy had taken its self-administered dose of reform and was now ready to get back to "real" politics, Chicago-style. Had not Daley grown up in the machine? Had he not learned—and used —all the tricks of the trade? Could a leopard change his spots? Could a machine politician turn into a statesman? Each of these questions answered itself, according to the soothsayers, and they one and all advised Chicago to ready itself for at least a decade of real, old-fashioned politics.

Chicago did indeed see real politics during the next decade, but hardly of the old-fashioned kind. Mayor Daley proved himself a good politician (no one had had any doubts about that), and being a good politician he knew that he could not bring back the past, even in Chicago. And he probably did not want to. Neither did he show any ambitions to occupy "higher" political office. He could make and unmake a governor or a senator; he did not want to be either one.

And so, for the first time in its history, the Chicago democracy began developing a local program of its own. To the chagrin of some organization people and to the utter disenchantment of others, the mayor exhibited incomprehensible tendencies. He seemed to have both the zest of the reformer and the real political savvy of the machine politician. Devoted to the party, he was, perhaps, even more devoted to the city. It was incomprehensible.

While all of this was going on in Chicago, to a lesser degree similar changes were taking place in New York under Robert Wagner and John Lindsay, in New Orleans under deLesseps Morrison, and in St. Louis under Raymond Tucker. Across the river in East St. Louis, Mayor Alvin G. Fields (whom the newspapers called "Boss of the East Side"), good friend and compatriot of Mayor Daley, was showing himself amenable to change.

Whether this new tack some local organizations have been sailing on during the 1950's and 1960's represents a fundamental redirection of Democratic and Republican politics locally only the years ahead will tell. The determining factor will undoubtedly be political success or failure. If, for example, Mayor Daley's organization continues to enjoy success at the polls, the new tack will become a genuine change. But whatever happens, the influence of Daley's example—and Wagner's, Tucker's, and Morrison's—on other local political leaders around the country will not go unnoticed.[28]

The Local Party. After participating actively in nonpartisan politics in

[28] Sympathetic to the urban machine, Lowi insists that it can be revived in the great cities. See Theodore J. Lowi, *At the Pleasure of the Mayor* (New York: The Free Press of Glencoe, 1964).

Wichita, Marvin A. Harder voiced a disenchantment with nonpartisanship that has become almost a typical reaction among politically active citizens:

> We are convinced that political parties are essential in the democratic process, and so we tend to view the nonpartisan election system as anarchic and chaotic.
>
> By no means, however, do we advocate national political parties at the city level . . . we believe that city issues have little in common with state or national issues . . . city parties are the most feasible approach to municipal problems. . . .[29]

In discussing the need for elective leadership in council-manager government, Dorothee Strauss Pealy came to the same conclusion as Harder. Arguing that councils should be better staffed, that the mayor should be strengthened, that the manager should become less of a public figure, Dr. Pealy concluded *"that partisan elections (preferably local parties) operate in municipalities* to encourage formulation of a coherent municipal policy where now only the manager's program exists." [30]

The local party—is this development a real possibility? Or is it a romantic illusion fostered by those people who simply cannot bring themselves to admit that nonpartisanship is a failure and must be abandoned outright? With respect to Cincinnati and Kansas City, we can answer both questions categorically: yes, the local party is a real possibility, and, no, it is not a romantic illusion. As we have seen, local parties have operated successfully in those two major cities for several decades. They have won and lost political battles, but they have continued to exist and, in doing so, have put their stamp indelibly upon local policy. In both Kansas City and Cincinnati, in spite of the anachronism of the nonpartisan ballot, municipal contests are party contests. The City Charter Committee and the Citizens' Association are by all criteria, except nomenclature, real and effective political parties. And, as we have seen in reviewing the life of the political action group, other cities also come perilously close to maintaining local political parties.

To sum up the argument, we have considerable evidence that some local organizations of the two major parties are developing coherent local programs which substantially change the classic stance of the Republican and Democratic parties locally. At the other end of the spectrum we see local political parties, usually operating within the framework of nonpartisanship, but changing the character of nonpartisanship. These two trends,

[29] Marvin A. Harder, "Nonpartisan Election: A Political Illusion?" *Case Studies in Practical Politics* (New York: Henry Holt & Co., 1958), p. 15.

[30] Dorothee Strauss Pealy, "The Need for Elected Leadership," *Public Administration Review,* XVIII (Summer, 1958), 214–216. Italics Dr. Pealy's.

taken together, make for a new kind of partisanship in urban politics. If this new partisanship continues to grow and extend itself increasingly from city to city, at least some of the contradictions in urban political practices of the past will be resolved.

Annotated Bibliography

If the locus and deployment of political and social power in the community have not been conclusively identified, the stream of literature on the subject is certainly at the flood. The two most important works, the two most widely read, and the two which best represent the polarization of the research findings into elitist and pluralist are the studies by Floyd Hunter and Robert A. Dahl. See Floyd Hunter, *Community Power Structure* (Chapel Hill, N.C.: University of North Carolina Press, 1953; New York: Doubleday & Co., Anchor Book, 1963); and Robert A. Dahl, *Who Governs?* (New Haven, Conn.: Yale University Press, 1961; also published as a Yale Paperbound, 1961). Not only do the findings of these scholars conflict, but their methodology varies greatly; and each illustrates one of the two most generally used techniques in the identification of power: reputational analysis (Hunter) and decisional analysis (Dahl).

Using methodology as a criterion, we would describe Presthus as a combination of Dahl and Hunter's techniques, since he uses both the decisional and reputational analysis in his study of two small cities in New York State. See Robert Presthus, *Men at the Top: A Study in Community Power* (New York: Oxford University Press, 1964). Jennings used Hunter's reputational technique and supplemented it with a positional analysis in a partial refutation of Hunter. See M. Kent Jennings, *Community Influentials: The Elites of Atlanta* (New York: The Free Press, 1964). Jennings' title alone indicates that he found Atlanta ruled by more than one elite. An extensive commentary on the uses and dangers of the techniques used in the analysis of community power may be found in Nelson Polsby's work. See Nelson W. Polsby, *Community Power and Political Theory* (New Haven, Conn.: Yale University Press, 1963).

A truly monumental work—the study by Agger, Goldrich, and Swanson—shows an apparent sophistication which seems capable of withstanding the erosion of time and subsequent research. See Robert E. Agger, Daniel Goldrich, and Bert Swanson, *The Rulers and the Ruled: Political Power and Impotence in American Communities* (New York: John Wiley & Sons, 1964). Other works on community power include Carol Estes Thometz, *The Decision-makers: The Power Structure of Dallas* (Dallas, Tex.: Southern Methodist University Press, 1963): and William V. D'Antonio and William H. Form, *Influentials in Two Border Cities: A Study in Community Decision-making* (Notre Dame, Ind.: University of Notre Dame Press, 1965). The last is an analysis of research done by the authors in the international city of El Paso—Ciudad Juárez. In addition, one should read Aaron Wildavsky, *Leadership in a Small Town* (Totowa, N.J.: Bedminster Press, 1964).

A wide variety of communities, including one in Norway, is to be found in Morris Janowitz (ed.), *Community Political Systems* (Glencoe, Ill.: The Free Press, 1959). A good view of British local politics may be gotten from A. H. Birch, *Small-town Politics* (New York: Oxford University Press, 1959); and from the excellent study of London, Frank Smallwood, *Greater London: The Politics of Metropolitan Reform* (Indianapolis: The Bobbs-Merrill Co., 1965).

Henry M. Alexander has written a perceptive description of an issue election in which the stakes were very high indeed in *The Little Rock Recall Election, Eagleton Case No. 17 in Practical Politics* (New York: McGraw-Hill Book Co., 1960). The Eagleton series contains other case studies of local politics. Eugene C. Lee has given us the most elaborate examination to date of nonpartisanship in *The Politics of Nonpartisanship* (Berkeley, Calif.: University of California Press, 1960). Charles Press's digest of the literature on local politics of the 1950's, *Main Street Politics* (East Lansing, Mich.: Institute for Community Development, Michigan State University, 1962), will remain a valuable bibliographical reference for at least another decade. And, finally, Richard A. Watson empirically defines the reaction of peoples in various social strata to the Citizens' Association in Kansas City in *The Politics of Urban Change* (Kansas City, Mo.: Community Studies, 1963); Edward C. Banfield examines the politics of nine major American cities in *Big City Politics* (New York: Random House, 1965); and Alvin Boskoff and Harmon Zeigler furnish us with a precise analysis of voting behavior in a metropolitan county, a suburb of Atlanta, in *Voting Patterns in a Local Election* (Philadelphia: J. B. Lippincott Co., 1964).

CHAPTER 14

The City's Income

Rags Among Riches

On a warm afternoon in early September, 1959, Mayor Anthony J. Celebrezze of Cleveland called in reporters from the metropolitan newspapers and radio and television stations. Surrounded by his financial and budgetary aids, the mayor announced that the city was not going to raise taxes for the ensuing year. "The news in this," said the mayor, "is that practically every other city is looking for new tax money, but we're not. That's like man bites dog."

Mayor Celebrezze's pride in the singularly fine state of his city's budget was understandable, because the one immediate and outstanding fact about the average city's budget in the middle of the twentieth century is that it is far from adequate to the city's needs. Faced with demands for services, which at times seem insatiable, cities are constantly engaged in an unseemly scramble for funds, which not only goes on from year to year but which seems ever to intensify. The insatiable appetite of governments—all governments—for the taxpayer's dollar is familiar even to the kindergartner, but few people probably realize that fifty years ago total governmental expenditures (state, local, and federal) amounted to almost one dollar out of every fifteen spent in the United States. Now it is one dollar out of every four dollars spent. (For a picture of the rise in per capita revenue of American governments, see Figure 14-1.)

All governments have hungered for funds, but municipal hunger has never had more than the edge taken off it. City governments are poor; more often than not, city treasuries are bare. Paradoxically, this hand-to-mouth existence goes on in the midst of the most remarkable accumulation of urban wealth that the world has yet known. It is the wealth of the city which supports the nation; the financial power of all our governments—federal, state, and local—rests upon our urban riches. Why is it, then, that cities are rich while city governments are poor?

In the struggle for governmental funds, the federal and state governments need to rely only upon their own constitutional and statutory powers. The taxing capacity of these governments is virtually unlimited, except where each government acts to limit itself. But the city's struggle for revenue is not dependent upon its own charter and internal political decisions. The city, in order to meet its financial needs, must go to the state for per-

*Figure 14-1. Per Capita Revenue
of American Governments, 1902–1964*

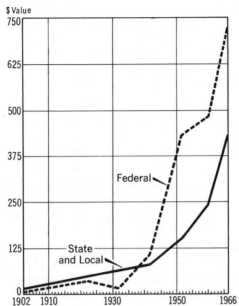

Source: U.S. Bureau of the Census, *Historical Summary of Governmental Finances in the United States, 1959*, pp. 11–13; and *Statistical Abstract of the United States: 1967*, p. 417.

mission to tax and to the state and federal governments for handouts. Such is the paradox: the city, principal source of our wealth, supports the state and federal governments, yet it has not achieved the necessary power to finance its own public services adequately.

Municipal Tax Income

Workhorse of the Tax System. The value of urban real estate in the United States is considerably in excess of $500 billion. With this tidy amount of wealth around, all of it in plain sight, it is not surprising that cities look to it as their principal tax source. In 1957, American cities received about $4.2 billion from property taxes. In 1965–1966, they received $6.9 billion.[1]

The general property tax (GPT) is a levy upon real property—land, and buildings upon the land—and upon personal property, both tangible and intangible. This tax, therefore, reaches a wide variety of property: vacant city lots, factory buildings, jewelry, and bank accounts. Although the

[1] U.S. Bureau of the Census, *City Government Finances in 1965–66* (1967), p. 5.

levy must be uniform, often cities are permitted to classify property and to provide for a different levy uniform within each class.

The general property tax is based upon the benefit principle of taxation, rather than upon the principle of ability to pay. Logically, the benefit must be considered of two types. The first is that which is received directly from local government services: protection from fire, theft, and nuisances; planning and zoning; neighborhood redevelopment; and enforcement of building codes.

The second type of benefit is of a more general kind and is too often overlooked in the evaluation of the tax. An unimpeachable theory is that property, and particularly real property, is enhanced in value by the growth and development of the community. Both the land and the buildings upon the land advance in value because of added population pressure, increased bidding for real estate, speculation in real estate, the increased economic utility of land and buildings—in short, because of all of those things which stem directly from community growth and economic vitality.

The same kind of benefit results from the building of public improvements. For example, in an area where none existed before, a sewerage system will increase the value of adjacent real estate. Since benefit is derived from public services, therefore, the property tax converts some of that benefit into municipal revenues.

In administration, two major steps are involved in the general property tax. These are (1) putting a fair value on the property for tax purposes and (2) setting the tax rate.

The first step is the assessment process. Usually the law requires that property be assessed at "fair" or "market" value, and this most difficult job is carried through by an assessing official. Although the job of the assessor calls for an inordinate amount of tact and a high degree of professional skill, too often the assessor himself is plainly unqualified to perform the duties of his office properly. The principal reason for this is that he often is elected. It is truly astonishing that, over a century after the end of the era of Jackson and over half a century after the disappearance of the frontier, we should still be filling such technical offices as that of assessor by means of the ballot. The National Association of Assessing Officers recommends that the assessor be appointed and serve under a merit system. Where such a system has been set up, it has undoubtedly raised the professional qualifications of the assessor and lessened the pressures put upon him by special interests.[2] The pressures remain, of course; they are simply channeled into other directions.

[2] Elective tax assessors in four California cities (San Francisco, Oakland, San Diego, and Los Angeles) were indicted or convicted in 1965–1966 for such felonies as taking bribes. The chief assessor of San Diego committed suicide. New York *Times*, December 4, 1966, p. 41.

Assessment jurisdictions usually are the city, county, or township. If the jurisdiction rests with the county or the township, the city government itself is powerless to reform assessment administration. The *people* of the city, true enough, may be able to effect a change by the political action of various citizen groups or even by means of the major political party organizations. Still, one must conclude that it is at least an administrative inconvenience for assessment of property for tax purposes to be placed in a jurisdiction independent of the city. Deductively, it would appear more rational for the jurisdictions that use most of the income from the general property tax (the city and the schools) to assess property than for lesser jurisdictions, such as the county and the township, to do the job.

After the assessment has been made, it may be altered in two general ways. The first is by appeal to an office of tax appeals. Here the individual's assessment is reviewed, normally by a board, and perhaps adjusted in some fashion to meet the objections of the taxpayer. If, after all possible administrative appeals have been taken, the taxpayer is still not satisfied, he may take his case into the trial courts. Another way in which the assessment may be altered is by equalization. As we have already seen, the law normally requires assessment at fair market value. If the assessment throughout a particular jurisdiction is below that value, the equalization agency raises it to the legally acceptable level.

No small task confronting the assessing official is that of insuring that all taxable property is on the rolls. In the case of intangible personal property (stocks and bonds, jewelry, and other "hidden" wealth) the assessor has an almost impossible job of finding the property; and of course if he cannot find it, he cannot very well put a value upon it. In the case of personal tangibles (automobiles, home furnishings, cattle, business inventories) the assessor does little better than with intangibles. Thus, much personal property escapes the general property tax.

With real estate (land and buildings), the mere discovery of the existence of the property is a job which will keep the assessor on his toes, but one which should not overwhelm him. With a good card index of all property within his jurisdiction, with aerial photos to check upon changes in land use, with a continuing check of property transfers and building permits, and with the recording of new plots, the assessor can keep an accurate inventory of real property. One complicating factor here is the spread of property which, under the law, is tax-exempt. This includes publicly owned property, churches, charitable institutions, cultural institutions, property owned by some business and professional groups, and property of veterans' organizations. Often it is difficult to separate tax-exempt from taxable property, and this adds to the assessor's problems. The story is told of one jurisdiction in which a valuable block of real estate was considered exempt for years simply because it was owned by a man with the name of

M. E. Church! An alert assessor might have caught this immediately, but even the best assessor cannot always find his way through the tangled maze of the property tax, particularly if he has a small staff.

Thus a discomforting fact, to the assessor as well as to those who form tax policy, is tax exemption. Exemption represents a serious erosion of the tax base, both for municipalities and for other local governments. Only by reducing tax exemption to the very minimum can the integrity of the general property tax be preserved.[3]

The second major step in tax administration is determination of the rate. After property has been discovered and evaluated, a rate must be applied against the valuation in order to arrive at the amount of tax to be paid. This rate is a percentage figure which is determined, of course, by the city council. The council, however, is subject to a good many restrictions in setting the rate. Since the total rate levied by the city is, in most cases, actually a composite of various rates, on each of which is a statutory or constitutional restriction, the council is checked at every hand. Thus one mill— and not more than one mill—may be levied specifically as a sewerage tax; ten mills might be the maximum for the general-fund levy and half a mill for policemen's and firemen's pensions. At every turn these arbitrary restrictions appear in the law. And arbitrary they are: since the fiscal capacities of cities vary widely, for some the legal rate limits are too high for safety; for others, too low. No generalized limitation can ever be valid.

What are the major criticisms of the general property tax? Though no competent student of public finance in the United States has ever suggested abandoning the general property tax, even the most ardent advocate of the tax recognizes its shortcomings. One of the serious faults of the tax has already been sketched: the egregious errors and inadequacies found in administration.

What of the other criticism? Over a century ago John Jacob Astor advised, as a sure avenue to wealth, the buying of land near a growing city. "Buy in the fringe areas of the city," he said, "and wait." Henry George, some years later, appalled at the disastrous consequences of land hoarding by the real estate speculator—disastrous, that is, to the city—wrote his extraordinary book *Progress and Poverty,* in advocacy of a land tax that would force the speculator to seek other fields in which to capture his ill-gotten gains.

Both Astor and George, in their different ways, recognized that great wealth was tied up in real estate. One would use it to enable the individual to "get ahead," the other to support governmental services and achieve social and economic reform. Yet today the general property tax is attacked

[3] For a discussion of this problem, see William O. Winter, "Tax Exemption of Institutional Property," *Municipal Finance,* XXXII (February, 1960), 143–148.

from many sides as being regressive—in other words, as bearing most heavily upon those least able to pay. Which side is right—the one which emphasizes the wealth in property, real and personal, or the one which emphasizes unequal capacity of the owners of property to pay taxes?

Both are right, of course, and the variance in the point of view depends entirely upon the orientation of the viewer. Labor and certain "liberal" interests tend to emphasize the regressive features of the tax. They point to the small property holder, to the pensioner who is living in his small cottage on an inadequate fixed income, to the young couple with a growing family, and they ask: "How can you justly expect such people to pay high property taxes?"

This regressive feature of the general property tax is well known and widely admitted, and some effort has been made to reduce the burden it imposes on lower-income groups. Some states provide for homestead exemptions, by which the first $500 to $5,000 in value is exempted from any general property levy. Where this exemption applies only to owner-occupied property, it is most certainly an aid to the homeowner and thus reduces the regressivity of the tax.

In spite of the elements of regressiveness in the general property tax, however, it still remains a highly useful source of support for municipal and other local governments. The element of benefit is so strongly present in the relationship of property—especially tangible property—to government that it can and must be used as a rationale for the property tax system.

We can summarize the critics' major suggestions for reform of the general property tax as follows:

1. *Create an administrative organization staffed by professionals*—Eliminate the elective assessor and put in his place a trained career man. The assessor's staff should also be appointed on a merit basis.

2. *Eliminate small assessing jurisdictions*—Townships, villages, and other small assessment jurisdictions are not only too small in area and population but too poor to finance an adequate assessment program. Cities and school districts are the most reasonable assessment jurisdictions.

3. *Remove arbitrary tax limits*—Blanket ceilings on taxes do not take into consideration the different fiscal capacities of local governments. Thus a 2 percent ceiling on tax rates would be meaningless to a poor city, which could not safely levy more than a 1 percent rate. To a wealthy community, however, a 3 percent or 4 percent might be both politically possible and economically reasonable.

Surely the most desirable solution to this problem, say the critics, is to eliminate the state tax-rate limit on cities altogether. Most local councils are responsible bodies, and politically sensitive, and the fears that these councils would go berserk if the limits were removed and would levy confiscatory taxes are groundless. In Great Britain, for example, the central government does not limit local property tax rates.

4. *Eliminate earmarked levies*—Special levies for everything from firemen's pensions to support of art museums are written into state permissive legislation. These earmarked taxes are not only unnecessary; they also greatly complicate the city's fiscal administration. The city should have only one levy, the returns of which should go into the general fund, to be spent as the council sees fit. Again, this point of view emphasizes political rather than legal controls.

5. *Expand the city's revenue base*—Cities must look to other taxes to supplement the general property tax. The remarkable Act 481 passed by the Pennsylvania legislature in 1947, giving cities and other local governments practically carte blanche in the use of any type of tax not already used by the state, is a classic example of the shift of tax policy-making from the state legislature to the local councils. (The same kind of shift has occurred in other states as a result of municipal home rule.) Such expansion of the city's tax base partially meets the criticism, so often voiced, that the burden of local taxation falls most heavily upon those least able to pay.[4]

In California, Pennsylvania, Illinois, New York, and Ohio, cities have received substantial grants of authority to expand the tax base. Although cities in other states have not done so well, property taxes accounted for 40 percent of total municipal revenue in 1965–1966, as contrasted with 64 percent in 1942.

The trend toward an expanded tax base for cities should continue. As a result of this expanded base, the city, though needing the general property tax, relies on it to a lesser degree than in former years. The experience of Boulder, Colorado, as given in Table 14-1, illustrates this trend and is probably typical of it.

The Municipal Income Tax: Something New in Municipal Finance. The income tax, so heavily relied upon by the federal government and by some of the states, has never been extensively used by American cities. Probably originating in Charleston, South Carolina, in the antebellum period of the nineteenth century, the income tax was extensively used by Canadian cities in the early part of this century. After the passage of Act 481 in Pennsylvania, the income tax was widely adopted by cities of that state. About the same time, Toledo, St. Louis, and Louisville enacted income tax ordinances. By 1955, 434 local income tax systems were in use in four states (Pennsylvania, Ohio, Kentucky, and Missouri) and they were authorized in two others (New York and Minnesota).[5] In fiscal year 1965–1966, ten of the 43 largest cities in the Republic were levying income taxes (see Table

---

[4] See AFL-CIO, *State and Local Taxes, Publication No. 80* (Washington, D.C.: AFL-CIO, December, 1958).

[5] Robert A. Sigafoos, *The Municipal Income Tax: Its History and Problems* (Chicago: Public Administration Service, 1955), pp. 2–5, 9.

Table 14-1. Property Tax Trends—
Boulder, Colorado, 1963–1965

Government	Mill. Levy		
	1963	1964	1965
City	14.91	14.71	9.70
County	10.15	11.15	11.50
Schools	47.28	54.15	58.26
Other (state, etc.)	2.40	2.31	2.38
TOTAL	74.74	82.32	81.76

Source: Records of the City of Boulder, Colorado, 1963–1965. The projected city levy for 1969 is 7.7 mills.

14-2), and three major cities soon thereafter joined the list (Baltimore and New York in 1966, and Cleveland in 1967).

The municipal income tax is a levy upon the income of both businesses and individuals. Usually, since the rate is very low, most taxpayers find the levy not too difficult to meet. Thus a man earning $6,000 a year will be apt to pay 1 percent of that salary to the city, or $60 a year. Notice that the tax is upon his gross salary: usually no exemptions or deductions are allowed. Another feature of the tax is that it is not graduated; the same rate is applied to all taxpayers, regardless of their varying levels of income.[6] Finally,

Table 14-2. Local Income Tax Receipts
of Major American Cities, 1965–1966

City	Income (millions of $)
Cincinnati, Ohio	17.3
Columbus, Ohio	15.7
Detroit, Michigan	45.2
Kansas City, Missouri	10.2
Louisville, Kentucky	13.9
Philadelphia, Pennsylvania	90.9
Pittsburgh, Pennsylvania	10.3
St. Louis, Missouri	27.3
Toledo, Ohio	10.7
Washington, D.C.	51.4
Total	292.9

Source: U.S. Bureau of the Census, *City Government Finances in 1965–1966*, GF-No. 12 (1967), Table 6, pp. 56–67.

[6] Both Detroit and New York, however, allow personal exemptions of $600 for each taxpayer and each dependent. The New York and Baltimore rates are graduated. Robert H. Connery (ed.), *Municipal Income Taxes*, Proceedings of the Academy of Political Science, XXVIII, No. 4 (1968), 20–21.

the tax applies not only to the income of the residents of the city but to that of people who reside elsewhere and work in the city. Businesses are liable at least to the amount of business done in the city.

The simplicity of this tax, its productivity, and its ease of administration cause officials of the city which has it to rejoice in it, and those who do not have it to look longingly for an acceptable method for introducing it into their city. But granting its several virtues, students of the tax find many weaknesses in its structure. First, it does not usually reach unearned income. This is perhaps its greatest disadvantage, and one which has given rise to vehement criticism of it. Because income from interest, dividends, rents, and capital gains is not reached, labor spokesmen have called the levy a "viciously regressive, reactionary tax." [7] Although such extravagant attacks are highly emotional, they do hit at one of the levy's most vulnerable spots. Surely the well-to-do, who receive most of the income not taxed by the municipal income levy, have an equal responsibility with all others to take their proportionate share of the city's tax burden.

That the income tax is somewhat regressive is also of concern to those who wish to bring a greater order into municipal finance. Not only does the failure to include unearned income make the tax regressive, but the flat rate and the lack of exemptions also make the tax bear most heavily upon those least able to pay for public services. The state and federal income tax systems invariably provide for a proportion of one's income which is exempt. They also provide that as one's income goes up, the rate does also. Both Canadian and Scandinavian cities have provided for exemptions and for graduated rates.[8] If these progressive features were introduced into the municipal income tax, as indeed they could be, they would greatly complicate the system. It could be argued that so long as the rate is kept very low, the tax is not unduly burdensome upon anyone.

With both residents and nonresidents subject to the city's income levy, many possibilities arise for double taxation and other inequities. In Pennsylvania the tendency has been that as soon as a central city enacts an income tax, outlying communities have immediately followed suit. After Pittsburgh levied a tax in 1954 the number of local jurisdictions in Allegheny County using the tax jumped immediately from six to seventy-three. Under Pennsylvania law, the taxpayer's place of residence takes precedence over the place of work (except for Philadelphia, where the city has exclusive power to tax the income of nonresidents, so long as that income was earned in Philadelphia itself). This means that all of the major cities, except Philadelphia, are prevented from using the income tax to force people working in the city but residing elsewhere to help pay for city services

---

[7] AFL-CIO, *Labor's Economic Review*, February, 1959, p. 14.
[8] Sigafoos, *op. cit.*, p. 26.

which they use during the working day. But this system does serve to prevent double taxation.

Because of the federal system, the conflict of jurisdictions may extend over state lines. This is precisely what happened in the St. Louis area when the central city began imposing a tax upon the incomes of those people who worked in the city but who lived across the Mississippi River in Illinois. Although vehement protests were voiced by Illinois citizens taxed by St. Louis, the levy still stands. Similarly, the protests of Canadian citizens against the Detroit income tax of 1963 were to no avail.

The experience of over 400 local governments, though mostly in four states, clearly indicates that the local income tax is a good income-producer and is apt to be continued for that reason alone. Its extension into other states will depend upon constitutional provisions and upon legislative willingness to listen to the tales of financial woe of city officials. Since about half the states now levy income taxes, it is safe to assume that in those states all that is needed is legislative authorization to permit the cities to levy the tax. Newly elected Mayor John Lindsay of New York City had not been in office many weeks before he was demanding a city income tax on both business and personal incomes. Although the city council reportedly was in favor of the tax, a major obstacle to its approval appeared in the unfriendly attitude of the governor and the state legislature. But the opposition lessened, and the state approved, in the summer of 1966, a city tax upon incomes of both residents and nonresidents.

In those states without a state income tax, it might very well be that the various constitutions stand in the way of either the state statute or the city ordinance which would attempt to levy a tax on income. The uniformity provision of the Illinois constitution (Article IX, Section 1), for example, prevents the general assembly from giving cities authority to levy a graduated tax. On the other hand, the authority clearly exists for a flat-rate tax.

As the tax is now used, its simplicity, ease of administration, and productiveness outweigh all other factors. Because of the very low rate, the regressivity of the tax is often greatly exaggerated. Yet if the tax is to become important to the American city generally, and particularly if the tax is to be used to balance off the regressivity of the sales and property taxes, a more sophisticated tax structure will have to be evolved. This sophistication in the tax system will add real worries to the municipal administrator. In the long run, possibly some kind of tie-in with state or federal tax systems promises the best solution to the problem. The city may either impose a levy which is a certain percentage of the state or federal levy, or it simply might turn over the administration of the tax to the state income tax authority. In such a case, the city and state tax bases would, for the sake of administrative convenience, need to be the same. Then the state would collect the tax and turn over the money to the city treasury, with perhaps a small charge for administration expenses. This solution would have many advantages. The taxpayer would need to file only one return; total administrative costs could be reduced; a more refined tax than the crude one currently in use could be developed; and cities, both large and small, could adopt the income levy in its refined form.

Perhaps the greatest advantage of a combination of state and city income tax systems would be that the currently regressive features of the local income tax would be eliminated. State income tax systems are generally highly progressive, even more so than the federal system; and assuming that the city adopted the state base, it would become similarly progressive. This progressiveness, as we have already seen, is an element that might eventually be built into income tax systems in order to balance the somewhat regressive nature of the general property tax and the sales and excise taxes.

Sales and Excise Taxes. When the Great Depression of the 1930's first swept over the country, state after American state, plagued on the one hand with falling revenues and on the other with a skyrocketing relief burden, turned to the general sales tax for revenue. And they found to their astonishment and delight that the levy of a penny or two on every dollar's purchase started a great and increasing flow of funds into the state treasury, even in the blackest days of the depression. State officials immediately discovered that the tax was a relatively painless way of extracting necessary state funds from the public at large: it was easy for the consumer to pay; it was quite simple to collect; and its yield was most gratifying. It is not surprising, therefore, that the most extensive use of the sales tax in the world is to be found in the American states.[9]

The sales tax differs from the excise only in a matter of degree. Whereas the sales levy applies usually to all retail sales, the excise applies only to a particular commodity or commodities. Thus, the excise is particular, and the sales tax is general. Of the two types of levies, the excise is much the older, at least as far as extensive use is concerned.

The municipal sales tax, like its counterpart at the state level, is largely a product of the economic conditions of the 1930's. Cities were at the very center of the economic whirlwind which struck most of the world in the early 1930's; indeed, grass growing in the city streets has become the symbol of severe economic troubles. With most industrial plants idle and with workers roaming the streets in a fruitless search for jobs, it was the city that first knew the desperate nature of the depression. Hard-pressed for funds as always, the city was often unable even to meet the payroll for its own employees, much less aid the rest of the populace.

If cities had been fully in control of their fiscal resources, they could have

[9] John F. Due, *Sales Taxation* (Urbana, Ill.: University of Illinois Press, 1957), p. 290.

used both their taxing and borrowing capacities to the limit to meet the crisis. But needing authorization from the state for most of their acts, they had to wait for the rurally controlled legislatures to grant them wider taxing and borrowing powers. Although some of the rural legislators actually refused to believe that great numbers of people were on the verge of starvation in the cities, the states did gradually give emergency financial powers to their cities. One such power which soon became widespread was the authority to levy a sales tax.

In 1934, New York City became the first American city to levy a sales tax. The 2 percent rate was imposed for the express purpose of enabling the city to give relief to the unemployed. It was thought of, in short, as an emergency levy which the city could happily abandon as soon as the economy recovered itself. Nothing is so permanent as the temporary, however, and though the rate in New York City was lowered to 1 percent in 1941, greatly increased pressures on the city's postwar budgets forced its increase back to 2 percent in 1946 and on to 3 percent in 1951.[10] The tax yields the city huge returns, greater than for most states, and constitutes an essential element of the city's budget.

Full control of sales tax administration by the city is a mixed blessing. A case in point was the experience of New York City before 1965. That the city was accustomed to drive hard bargains was illustrated by the sale of a hippopotamus by the New York park department to the city of Denver. The purchase price was $2,450 (apparently the going rate for hippopotami!); since the sale was made for delivery inside the city limits, the 3 percent city sales tax became applicable; and the city received from Denver a sales tax of $73.50 for its administrative foresight. From the standpoint of the taxpayer, such hard bargains were, of course, not enthusiastically received.

One of the criticisms of New York City's administration has been that its audit of taxpayer accounts is not carried out on the basis of a scientific sample. Whether justified or not, this has given rise to the suspicion that the firms and individual storekeepers selected for audit were being discriminated against on political or other grounds. A 1952 study of the auditing function revealed, according to one observer, that "while only a small fraction of accounts—from 4 to 11 percent annually—was found to be audited, virtually every audit brought additional assessments, sometimes on rather dubious grounds." [11]

That every tax administration should be stern cannot be questioned. The fairest tax can be rendered unfair if sloppily administered. But a tax must apply to all alike, else it will quickly become discriminatory. Here lies

[10] *Ibid.*, p. 315. Subsequently the tax went to 4 percent and then (after the state's levy of a 2 percent tax) back to 3 percent in August, 1965.

[11] *Ibid.*, p. 316.

one of the great difficulties of the locally administered sales tax, not only in New York City, but wherever it is still used.

Unless the city is quite large, local tax administration is apt to be, almost by nature, beset with problems. A small city may not be able to maintain an adequate enforcement program. The city sales tax, moreover, is apt to drive some shoppers to suburban shopping centers, and it is apt to increase resistance to annexation. If there is a state sales tax also, the merchants are burdened with the necessity of collecting and reporting two sales taxes, each with its own individual rate structure and tax base.

Except for large cities such as New York and New Orleans, the experience of American municipalities to date indicates that probably the best system administratively is one in which the sales tax is levied locally but collected by the state. The states of Illinois, Mississippi, and California, and the province of Quebec have had the most experience with the locally levied, state-collected sales tax. In California, however, experience shows that that which may be administratively "good" is not necessarily so politically. Because of local mistrust of the state bureaucracy, a number of municipalities, San Francisco among them, insist on maintaining their own local collection departments.

In Illinois, a 1955 agreement between Mayor Daley of Chicago and Governor William Stratton resulted in the state's giving all cities permission to levy a sales tax up to 0.5 percent. The state department of revenue was given the responsibility of collecting the tax, and to cover administrative costs the state charged the cities 6 percent of the revenue from the cities' tax. Because the cities protested this charge as exorbitant, the governor lowered it to 4 percent in 1959.

Virtually all of the 1,100-odd Illinois cities levy the tax, which was instrumental in eliminating the severe financial crisis in which Illinois cities found themselves in the 1950's. Because of the tax, some slight advantage was given to the merchant in unincorporated areas over the one in cities or villages. But even this slight inequity was eliminated in 1959 when the Illinois general assembly empowered counties to levy a 0.5 percent tax in unincorporated sections of the county and many counties took advantage of the legislation.

Most of the cities and many of the school districts use the locally levied, province-collected tax in Quebec. Introduced into the province by Montreal in 1935, with a 2 percent levy, the tax was adopted by the province itself in 1940, and since then the province has been the administrative agent. The tax is just as lucrative for local governments in Quebec as it is for those in the United States.[12]

Use of the sales tax by municipalities is supplemented by selective sales

[12] *Ibid.*, pp. 328–330.

levies, or excises, upon the exchange of goods or services. Taxes upon liquor, tobacco, gasoline, and consumption of gas, electricity, and other utility services are relatively common. Entertainment taxes, too, are often important revenue producers. Many of those consumption taxes are rationalized on sumptuary grounds: they are luxuries, it is argued, rather than necessities. People can avoid the tax simply by refusing to consume those articles or services, which they do not actually need. However much weight you wish to give this argument, the fact does remain that excises are often much less regressive than general sales taxes, simply because they are selective and do not always bear upon the absolute necessities of life.

Both sales and excise taxes are excellent revenue producers and are widely relied upon by municipalities both here and abroad. It is probable that cities will continue to depend heavily upon them for revenue, and indeed, the reliance will more probably be extended than diminished. Although usually regressive, the low rates make them palatable to the general public. The ease of collection and the relative ease with which the taxpayer can meet his obligations are also important factors in the acceptance of these taxes. Everyone benefits from city services, whether he be rich or poor, and it is perhaps not too much to expect everyone to make some contribution to the cost of operating the city government.

Service Charges and Fees. When Cleveland, in the mid-1950's, wished to enlarge its zoo greatly, the city was faced with several ways of financing the expensive expansion. At one extreme lay the choice of issuing general-obligation bonds and thus paying for capital expansion, as well as current operation, out of tax revenues. In this case the zoo would be financed by the city at large, with admission free to all comers. The alternative at the other end of the spectrum was to issue revenue bonds to pay for capital improvements and then to set up a fee schedule to be charged the customers for the retirement of the bonds and support of current operations.

The arguments that ranged around these alternatives illustrate well some of the basic differences that motivate people in public finance. The proponents of a free zoo argued that the city was obligated to furnish recreational and educational facilities to the people free of charge. If a fee were charged to view the esoteric animal and birdlife of the world, many deserving people, unable to pay the price of admission, would be denied the use of the zoo. If the zoo were expanded and operated out of general tax funds, the city could be sure that no one would be discriminated against because of inability to pay the admission fee.

People with a different set of values, or at least a different outlook on public finance, espoused the self-supporting zoo. The taxpayer, they argued, was already overburdened: he should not be asked to pay for a service which could be established on a self-supporting basis; the customers of the zoo, in benefiting from the institution, should pay for it. The city, it was also argued, should conserve its general bonding power to raise funds to build facilities that could not be self-supporting. And finally—a very convincing argument—the taxpayers of Cleveland should not be expected to pay for a service which people in the whole metropolitan area, and indeed all over northern Ohio, would enjoy. The admission charge, in other words, would require that people out of reach of the city's taxing power pay for a city service which they used and enjoyed.

Ranged against each other here were those who supported the ability-to-pay principle in public finance and those who espoused the benefit theory. Believing strongly that public services should be available to everyone, regardless of wealth or position, the former group (whether in Cleveland or elsewhere) tends to view the service charge with considerable suspicion. It must be proved to them, beyond doubt, that the charge is an absolute essential; otherwise, the city fails in its moral obligation to furnish services to all and all alike.

Those who support the benefit theory argue just as strongly that people who use public services are "consumers" just as surely as are the people who buy groceries at a private market. If the citizen consumes a service, he should pay for it. Sometimes these people, too, take up an ideological position and insist upon the moral superiority of the service charge over the ability-to-pay tax: the one is voluntary and rests upon the free choice of the individual; the other is forced upon him. Free choice, runs the argument, clearly stands above compulsion in any ethical system.

Sometimes of foremost importance in preliminary discussions of public finance, ideology tends to give way to practical considerations when a policy decision is forced upon city officials. Incapacities of the tax system, severe charter or statutory limits on the bonding power, the attitudes of the general public and of special interest groups—such considerations move to the forefront. In metropolitan areas like Cleveland the very practical objective of reaching, with a service charge, those people outside the central city who use city facilities is often given the greatest weight by city fathers. It is not surprising, therefore, that Cleveland decided upon a self-supporting zoo rather than a tax-supported one.

The service charge and the fee are virtually indistinguishable; the difference between them is largely one of nomenclature. An automobile license fee could be called a service charge for use of the city streets. A service charge for use of the city's water could be described as a fee.

Fees and service charges cover a wide variety of municipal activities and constitute an important source of city revenue. There are license fees to cover the costs of a great number of inspectional activities, particularly in the promotion of the citizens' health and safety. Fire prevention, inspection of restaurants and dairies, checking the safety of elevators, insuring that new buildings conform to the city's building, plumbing, and electrical codes—all of these essentials to a well-run city are financed, at least to a degree, from license fees. At times the license fee may be an outright revenue producer, garnering far more revenue than the city spends on the licensees. The licensing of taverns and liquor stores is one of the best examples of this phenomenon.

Service charges vary from admissions to the zoo to charges for municipal utilities. The latter type of charge is particularly remunerative. Charges for garbage collection, for water and sewerage services, and for electricity and gas supply are all lucrative sources of revenue. (See Table 14-3.) Sometimes, indeed, the municipal utility is milked of revenues to finance services that would normally be paid for out of tax revenues, and thus the service charge becomes in fact a tax.

Table 14-3. City Revenue
from Service Charges and Fees, 1957 and 1963–64

Item	1957	1963–64
Utilities	$2,378,000,000	$3,561,000,000
Current Charges	954,000,000	1,790,000,000
Interest Earnings	112,000,000	220,000,000
Other	294,000,000	419,000,000

Source: U.S. Bureau of the Census, *City Government Finances in 1963–64* (May, 1965), p. 6.

Rentals and concessions also may yield substantial amounts of income. Restaurant concessions at the park or the airport are money-makers. With air travel becoming ever more important and ever more popular, the municipal airport becomes increasingly important as a nontax source of revenue. The example of Chicago is certainly not typical of the management of municipal airports, but it indicates how nearly an airport can become self-supporting. Faced with the certainty that its Midway air terminal would soon be inadequate, particularly as jet travel became a reality, the city of Chicago reached out its extraterritorial arm and bought up land for a new terminal. This became O'Hare International Airport. In the initial stages of development, the city had to use tax money, both its own and the federal government's. But since these funds were not nearly enough, the city entered into negotiations with the major airlines. The two parties finally agreed to spend, between them, a minimum of $128 million in new airport facilities. Since this agreement required the city to raise money by borrowing, Chicago issued $120 million worth of revenue bonds and agreed to retire them from rentals and other service charges obtained from the operation of the airport itself. As a result of this canny bargaining by the city with airport users, O'Hare International became as nearly self-supporting as any airport in the nation. Similarly, Cleveland, under Mayor Celebrezze, greatly enlarged its airport in the 1950's.

In St. Louis, the governing authorities leased a corner of Lambert Field, the municipal airport, to a small aircraft company just before the beginning of World War II. The McDonnell company has since grown into one of the largest concerns of its type in the world, with a great manufacturing plant and space research center that spread over a considerable amount of city property. This arrangement has benefited the city, the company, and the national defense—all in all, a happy arrangement.

Not to be overlooked in any discussion of income from special charges are parking revenues. Unheard of a generation or so ago, the parking meter has become as common to city streets as the ubiquitous pigeon. The meter, of course, is a charge for the use of public streets or of public parking lots. Not only does this revenue aid in the repair of streets and in the planning of traffic; it is also used widely in the building of off-street parking, thus opening up the streets for moving traffic. A variation upon the parking meter is a device instituted by Milwaukee: a monthly parking charge for automobiles parked in residential streets.

Subventions from State and Federal Governments

That state contributions to local treasuries are of substantial importance is illustrated by the State of Michigan's budget. In 1956 the state paid almost one-half billion dollars, or 42.9% of its general expenditures to local units of government.[13] From 1945 to 1959, state aid to New York City increased from $93 million to $318 million.

In the practice of giving substantial financial support to its local units Michigan and New York are not alone; other states do likewise. This includes aid for such a wide variety of activities as public health and welfare, highways and streets, education, housing, and community development.

In general, state aid to cities comes in two forms: (1) shared taxes, and (2) grants-in-aid. Shared taxes are taxes levied and collected by the state and then shared with the city on a percentage basis. In Michigan the state constitution specifies that the state must return to local governments about 80 percent of the state sales tax. In Illinois the cities share in the state tax on gasoline and other motor fuels according to a formula set up by statute.

State-collected, locally shared taxes are now a standard feature of state-local finance. City officials have long insisted that municipalities should, as a matter of right, share in certain types of state taxes. Since over 40 percent of all automobile mileage is in urban areas, for example, the cities feel that they are rightfully entitled to a substantial portion of gasoline-tax revenue.

[13] Citizens Research Council of Michigan, "State-Local Financial Relations in Michigan," Memorandum 192, No. 22, August 21, 1958.

Although the validity of this argument is generally admitted by state officers, the state asks for a system of sharing which will recognize the state's primary responsibility for its local units of government and yet at the same time protect the state's own financial security.

In 1959 the state of Michigan was caught in a series of budgetary crises which were brought on, at least in part, by financial rigidity imposed by constitutional restrictions. Because the division of the sales tax between state and local units was embedded in the state constitution, even though Michigan itself was out of funds and unable to meet its general commitments, it was constitutionally obligated to send millions of dollars in sales tax revenue to the local governments. In writing Michigan's new constitution of 1963, the drafters were largely unsuccessful in eliminating this difficulty.

Grants-in-aid, like the shared tax, are payments by the state to the city and other local units. The most substantial type of grant-in-aid is for education, and in this the cities share only if, as in New York City, the schools are controlled by the city government. But even without the educational grant, state payments to cities in the form of grants-in-aid are crucial elements of the municipal budget. Grants for public welfare and highways are particularly important.

Grants-in-aid from the federal government are also of consequence to the cities; as with the state grants, federal payments have grown larger with each passing year. Without federal housing and urban renewal grants, the cities would be unable to carry out these essential functions; without federal aid, municipal welfare, health and hospital, highway, and planning programs would be hampered.

Intergovernmental revenue of American cities rose from approximately $1.8 billion in 1957 to $4.1 billion in 1965–1966. About 80 percent of this income represented state money, and about 20 percent represented money from other local units and the federal government. Although grants-in-aid and shared taxes are of greatest importance to the municipal budget, cities do not regard them as unmixed blessings. Foremost among cities' objections is their dislike of restrictions on local autonomy represented by the strings attached to the payments. Regarding state and federal aid as theirs by right, city officials consider interference with the way in which they spend money as an affront to their stewardship.

On the other hand, state and federal officials generally feel that some supervision of city spending is essential if the intent of the statutes setting up the grants, or the shared taxes, is to be carried out. If the city is not supervised in spending gasoline tax money, it might use the money to support an art museum rather than spend the funds on city streets. City support of an art museum might well be desirable, argue state officials, but not with gasoline-tax funds which the state shares with the city.

The men in city hall are apt to have the last word by pointing to the adoption of block grants by New York State and Great Britain. These payments are unconditional grants to local governments. Under the Moore plan in New York the cities are given per capita grants from the state, the spending of which is solely at the discretion of the cities. This system places great confidence in the judgment of city officials, preserves local autonomy, and at the same time recognizes the obligation of the state to its cities. The philosophy of the Moore plan is that if a city prefers an art museum to improvement of the city streets, should not that decision be made democratically in the local political arena?

The Special Assessment: Reaching the Unearned Increment

If the city paves a street in a certain neighborhood, the likelihood is that the property in the area will be enhanced in value; that is, the property will be worth more after the improvement than before. "This value stems in large part from public action and the use of public resources. The individual property holder does not create the value. At no stage of the proceedings is his participation necessary . . . to the project. At every stage, the role of government is vital, and without it the project would fail." [14]

Since the enhancement of property values which results from a public improvement is not produced by the property holder himself, but by the city, the value represents an unearned increment which rightfully belongs to the community. Thus a tax can be levied upon the property and the returns from the tax used to pay the costs of the public improvement. This levy is the special assessment.

First used in New York City during colonial days, the special assessment came into its own during the great days of American city building, 1870–1929. In the newer cities of the South and West the special assessment was a primary instrument of city building. By 1893 forty of the forty-four states then making up the union had authorized use of the special assessment by their cities. In 1913, cities of over 100,000 population received 12 percent of all their revenue from the special assessment.[15] Countless square miles of raw land were converted into municipal uses by the single device of the special assessment.

Special-assessment financing of local improvements reached its apogee in the 1920's. Caught up by the enthusiasm of the economic boom, city fathers were easy prey to the blandishments of real estate speculators; and they levied special assessments against millions of city lots, issued bonds against the levies, and then proceeded to install sidewalks, sewers, storm drains,

[14] William O. Winter, *The Special Assessment Today* (Ann Arbor, Mich.: University of Michigan Press, 1952), p. 30.
[15] *Ibid.*, pp. 12–13.

streets, water mains, streetlights—all of the necessary facilities for urban living—adjacent to vacant lots. When the 1929 market crash came, these lots had not been absorbed into the market. They were, in other words, vacant. Not being in use, they were unproductive, and the special assessments were not paid. Millions of special-assessment bonds went into default, and municipal credit was seriously damaged.

Municipal councils in the 1920's sowed the wind and in the 1930's reaped the whirlwind. With an untold number of lots unused and with special-assessment bonds by the millions going into default, even the most optimistic thought that the special assessment would never again be available to the city. The gloomy history of the 1930's, it was thought, would forever doom the special assessment.

During World War II, cities were in a state of arrested development. Because of the war they had neither men nor matériel to expand, and because of this lack of expansion, many a city came out of the war years with surpluses on hand. With the first years of peace, however, the municipal surpluses evaporated like fog under a hot sun, and city executives and councils began searching frantically for some means of augmenting municipal revenues. Quite suddenly the special assessment was rediscovered. Gingerly at first, but then with increasing confidence, municipal councils began using the special assessment to improve old areas of the city and to build new ones.

In 1949, 88 Michigan cities out of 111 surveyed reported use of the special assessment.[16] By 1953 American cities were receiving $145 million from special assessments; by 1958 this figure had increased to $234 million.[17] In 1963–1964 special-assessment income rose to $321 million. This type of income has clearly reestablished itself as an important element of municipal finance.

There are several major advantages to the special assessment. It represents a quick and easy way to reach the unearned increment, that increase in property value which is produced by public action and which, if not taken by some sort of tax levy, would result in the enrichment of individuals at the expense of society at large. It is, further, not limited by arbitrary tax and debt ceilings imposed by constitution, statute, or charter. Because of the generally straitened conditions of city budgets, it is the only means that the city can use to finance the building of certain improvements. Thus it is, surprisingly, welcomed by property holders, and even petitioned for. Of 111 Michigan cities surveyed in 1949, 58 indicated that their special-assessment projects were usually initiated by petition. In other words, in over half of the Michigan cities using the special assessment it was normal

[16] *Ibid.*, p. 90.
[17] U.S. Bureau of the Census, *Compendium of City Government Finances in 1958* (1959), p. 6.

for property holders to ask the city to levy special assessments against their properties so that they could get essential improvements installed.

On occasion, the special assessment can be a legitimate means of giving the small businessman a helping hand. Sometimes the subdivider of new lands simply does not have the capital available to install streets, storm and sanitary sewers, sidewalks, water mains, street trees, and other essentials of urban living. In such a case the city might levy assessments against his lots and install the improvements. Although this practice carries some risks —this was, after all, the ruination of the special assessment in the 1920's —it might be supported as an aid to the small contractor who is operating on a small margin.

One potential of the special assessment which has yet to be developed is in the elimination of nonconforming land uses, a common irritation of urban living, especially in residential areas. A garage, a ramshackle grocery store, or a used-car lot may exist like an open sore in an otherwise good neighborhood. The incompatible use may have existed from a period before zoning, or it may have crept in by means of spot zoning. In either case, the neighborhood may be seriously harmed; yet however much the citizens may inveigh against the nonconforming use, it can be eliminated only by purchase or condemnation, either of which requires that the property holder be reimbursed for loss of his property. If the city itself had plenty of money, it might be prevailed upon to buy the property and convert it into a park or use it in some way that would conform to the zoning ordinance and the wishes of a majority of the neighborhood. But since the city rarely has such funds available, the only avenue left open is to take the property and pay for it by the special assessment. The city moves in to eliminate the use and then levies an assessment against each piece of benefited property to pay for the elimination.

A major innovation in the city's control of its growth has lessened the extent to which the special assessment is used. This is the control of land subdivision. Though not actually new, the subdivision-control ordinance has replaced the special assessment as the principal means of assuring that streets, drains, sewers, and water mains are installed in the new subdivision before it is approved by the city. In effect, the subdivider installs all the necessary utilities and then recovers his investment by sale of the affected lots. This means that the buyer still pays, but in the form of a higher price for his homesite rather than through a special assessment levied against the property and payable separately from the purchase price.

Even if the special assessment never again reaches the importance it had in the early part of the century, it should continue as an aspect of municipal finance that cannot be ignored. As a means of rebuilding or adding urban facilities to old neighborhoods, as a means of capturing the unearned increment, and even, occasionally, as a way to subsidize small, local businesses, the special assessment has a secure place in the future.

Annotated Bibliography

The most analytical examination of the municipal income tax was written in the mid-1950's: Robert A. Sigafoos, *The Municipal Income Tax: Its History and Problems* (Chicago: Public Administration Service, 1955). Supplementing Sigafoos and bringing him up to date is: Advisory Commission on Intergovernmental Relations, *Federal-State Coordination of Personal Income Taxes, Report A-27* (Washington, D.C.: U.S. Government Printing Office, October, 1965), especially Ch. 4, which gives 1965 data on the cities' experiences with this tax. Of considerable value also is Robert H. Connery (ed.), *Municipal Income Taxes,* Proceedings of the Academy of Political Science, XXVIII, No. 4 (1968).

Other significant publications of the Advisory Commission on Intergovernmental Relations, all published in Washington, D.C., by the U.S. Government Printing Office, include: *The Role of the States in Strengthening the Property Tax,* 2 vols., *Report A-17* (June, 1963); *Tax Overlapping in the United States, Report M-23* (July, 1964); *Measures of State and Local Fiscal Capacity and Tax Effort, Report M-16* (October, 1962); and *The Intergovernmental Aspects of Documentary Taxes, Report A-23* (September, 1964).

The definitive work on sales taxes in general may be found in John F. Due, *Sales Taxation* (Urbana, Ill.: University of Illinois Press, 1957). On the special assessment, the latest complete examination is in William O. Winter, *The Special Assessment Today with Emphasis on the Michigan Experience* (Ann Arbor, Mich.: University of Michigan Press, 1952).

For the most complete general record of the financial life of the city, one has available the two valuable censuses of governments: U.S. Bureau of the Census, *1967 Census of Governments* (1968 and subsequent dates); *1962 Census of Governments* (1963 and subsequent dates); and *1957 Census of Governments* (1958 and subsequent dates).

CHAPTER 15

*B*orrowing and Spending

The Spending Power

Like all of the city's other powers, its capacity to spend the money it possesses is severely restricted. Municipal funds may be disbursed only when the object of expenditure is expressly or by implication provided in constitutional provisions or legislative acts.[1] Although both the states and the federal government have achieved objectives never envisioned by the Constitution framers, simply by appropriating money for those purposes, the city has never been able to acquire substantive power by such means. The spending power of cities, in short, is always an auxiliary or subordinate power which must be used solely to accomplish some legally defined purpose.

Since expenditures must be for authorized purposes, unless an express power exists, the spending of city funds is constantly in jeopardy. One court held, for example, that since cities were required to pay for shade trees by the special assessment, it was without power to finance the planting of trees out of the general revenues.[2] Even when the object of expenditure is so clearly within the municipal power as to convince any court of its existence, the city still may be assailed with a taxpayer's suit. Training policemen, for example, would seem to be basic to a city's functioning; yet when a North Carolina city sought to send an officer to the National Police Academy, the action was challenged. The court had no difficulty in upholding the city's power to spend, since it could be implied from the statutory authority to maintain law and order. But even though the city won its case, it was only after a worrisome and costly suit.[3] This sort of legal affliction never hampers the states or the federal government.

The devices of popular democracy might not be considered curbs upon the city's spending power, as such, but certainly they serve to limit the executive and legislative authority to make fiscal policy. In some cities an appropriation ordinance may be challenged by a petition which forces it to a popular vote. Or the initiative may be used to introduce an ordinance which tampers with the spending power, and the council is powerless to

[1] Eugene McQuillin, *The Law of Municipal Corporations* (Chicago: Callaghan & Co., 3rd ed., 1949), Sec. 39.17.
[2] *Ibid.*, Sec. 39.19.
[3] *Ibid.*, Sec. 39.17.

stop it. In extreme cases, municipal officials may be intimidated into re-scinding spending action by the threat of a recall election.

Attacked from every side, it is little wonder that city officers are unduly timid in the expenditure of municipal funds. Only in one area are they given the benefit of the doubt: when the council decides that the expenditure is for a public purpose, the courts tend to give great weight to that decision. A California court held that deciding upon public purpose rests with the city council and that the court would never substitute its judgment for that of the council unless the abuse was evident. Yet even here the municipality had better not try anything new and different. A Washington city was forbidden to spend its money on a legislative lobby in the state capital, the object of which was to get legislation favorable to the city. And a Philadelphia appropriation to aid an opera company was held not to be a public purpose.

Controlling the Purse Strings

"To make ends meet!" was the way that A. E. Buck once summarized the purpose of the budget. Because of the weak and inadequate revenue system of most cities, making ends meet becomes of overwhelming concern to the civic leader and the citizen alike. Herein lies the crucial importance of a good budget. And this is not all: even if the budget cannot be made to balance, it will serve a valuable function in showing the direction from which the unbalancing forces are coming.

Another purpose of the budget, and one that stands above all others, is to serve as the crucible within which numerous competing forces are fused. "To spend or not to spend?" is the question that constantly faces the budget-makers: to increase here, to hold the line there, to cut, to eliminate altogether. The lifeless figures on the budget sheets turn into the ambitions of department heads, the pressures of interest groups, the protestations of spokesmen for city employees. Money is to the administrative apparatus as food and drink are to animal life: it is impossible to consider budget items without at the same time considering what the city must do and what it should do. Every time a final figure is put down in the budget document, municipal policy is, willy-nilly, being formed.

The drama of the budget must be acted out, not upon one but upon two great stages. The first stage is the executive, where revenue and expenditures are carefully weighed and a budget document is formed; the second is the legislative, where the executive proposals found in the budget document are analyzed, approved, altered, or rejected. In brief, then, these stages are (1) budget-making, and (2) budget confirmation.

Budget-making is, above all, an executive function: it is the ultimate responsibility of the mayor or manager. Many a mayor or city manager in a small city must double in brass as the budget officer. In places of medium size the finance officer takes care of budget-making. In the larger cities a special office is usually assigned the task of budget-making, and this agency is usually headed by a full-time budget officer. But whatever the type of city, the budget officer (whatever his title) is the alter ego of the executive. In one of the major city charters of recent years, the Honolulu Charter Commission provided a budget officer for the city and county of Honolulu to operate directly under the mayor and to be subject to mayoral appointment and removal. The commission provided that the budget officer prepare the "annual operating budget and ordinance under the direction of the mayor." [4]

The budget officer was also to plan capital improvements, to set up an allotment system, and to analyze departmental work and evaluate departmental efficiency. He was to be, in addition to his budgeting duties, a kind of efficiency expert for the city's administrative apparatus.

Although the executive and his budget officer are at the very center of the budget-making process, they do not make up the budget document all by themselves. Rather, they call upon the entire administrative apparatus for aid, and budget-making, therefore, can be explained in terms of very definite procedures:

Step 1. Work programs and expenditure estimates. Officials of each department must plan the work of the department for the coming year and estimate the cost of that work.

Step 2. Cataloging fixed and uncontrollable expenditures. This task is the responsibility of the chief finance officer.

Step 3. Estimates of revenues for the coming year. Both departmental and finance officers make estimates of the next year's revenues.

Step 4. Preparation of budget document. The chief executive and his budget officer must analyze both revenue and expenditure estimates. If anticipated revenue does not equal anticipated expenditures—and it usually does not—the decision must be made to raise taxes, engage in deficit spending, or reduce spending; and any one of these decisions can be painful and politically dangerous. After income and outgo are brought into balance, the budget document is prepared for submission to the city council. [5]

The budget message of the executive (mayor or city manager) is one of the most important political acts of the year. Since the budget document is actually as much a political document as a financial one, the mayor or city manager must address himself, in the budget message, to the major policy

[4] Honolulu Charter Commission, *Proposed Charter of the City and County of Honolulu, Hawaii* (April 3, 1958), Sec. 5–303a. This charter became effective July 1, 1959.

[5] Municipal Finance Officers Association, *Municipal Budget Procedure and Budgetary Accounting* (Chicago: MFOA. 1942), pp. 1–2.

questions which lie hidden in the document itself. Thus the executive will describe the major programs which his administration hopes to carry out during the budget year. When he speaks of housing, mass transit, public health, public safety, police, civil rights, and poverty programs, he is talking not just to the members of the legislative body but also to the many publics in the city at large. And when he speaks of the city's revenue structure, especially if he is a big-city mayor, he is apt to be talking as much to the governor and the state legislators as he is to officials and citizens locally.[6]

Budget confirmation is a legislative task with just as exact a format as budget-making. After review of the executive budget by councilmen or by agents of the legislative body, the city council holds public hearings on the budget, in order that testimony of persons outside the city government may be taken. Upon conclusion of the hearings, the budget is approved by the council; the appropriation acts are passed; and, if necessary, so are additional revenue ordinances. With the budget enacted into law, the departments then revise work programs and spending estimates to fit the approved schedules found in the final budget document.

Execution of the Budget

Accounting Systems. When the new budget is put into effect on the first day of the new fiscal year, it must be given careful and constant attention. From this date onward the accounting system becomes of utmost importance to budget administration.

Municipal accounts may be on a cash basis, on an accrual basis, or a combination of the two. If on a cash basis, revenue is credited to an account when it is actually received by the city, and expenditures are entered against an account when the disbursement is actually made. This is a rather primitive form of keeping track of a city's finances and is not regarded favorably by professional municipal accountants.

Accrual accounts give a truly accurate picture of municipal finances. When monies are due the city, they are recorded in the proper accounts or funds, even though the city treasurer may not actually receive payment for weeks or months. By the same token, when the city obligates itself to pay for a service or for equipment and supplies, the obligation is entered against the proper fund, even though, again, actual disbursement is not made for some time.

When the combined system is used, revenues are put on a cash basis, and expenditures on an accrual basis. This is sometimes known as a modified

---

[6] For example, see Henry W. Maier, *Challenge to the Cities—An Approach to a Theory of Urban Leadership* (New York: Random House, 1966), pp. 114–129.

accrual system. Although strict accrual accounting is generally preferred by finance officers, the combined system is a very conservative one and seems to have great appeal to the people who draft state laws regulating municipal fiscal policy.

Allotment Systems. The municipality's rate of spending will vary from month to month. Such factors as climatic conditions, the movement from one season to another, and economic conditions are just a few of the influences upon the budget during the fiscal year. If the department of public works has $600,000 to spend on street repair, for example, it will not spend the money at the even rate of $50,000 per month. The rate of spending, except for cities in the deep South and in southern California, for example, will probably be high during the summer months and low during the winter, all because of the weather.

The Honolulu charter provides that the budget officer shall "review departmental work program schedules and make budgetary allotments for their accomplishment with the approval of the mayor." This procedure involves two major steps:

1. Allotting or "splitting" annual appropriations on a quarterly or monthly basis. Allotments are usually made up by department heads and submitted to the budget officer for review and approval.

2. Using these allotments or "splits" as a control device. The budget officer, in cooperation with the department heads, must use the allotments to see that agencies are not overspending.[7]

When the allotment system is not used, how are administrative officials expected to make ends meet throughout the fiscal year? This responsibility rests upon a variety of officials: mayors, managers, commissioners, department heads, and even aldermanic committees. And the old and experienced hands among these officials, knowing the spending pattern of past years, will be apt to have private and informal allotment systems of their own. No street superintendent worth his salt, for example, would willingly spend most of his appropriations during the winter and spring months knowing that he would then be forced seriously to cut back his activities during the summer. Thus even when a formal allotment system, operated from the top of the administration, is not in use, an informal one will be found in the lower echelons.

There is, moreover, a practice often used by the heads of spending agencies which can throw the budget out of kilter. Convinced that he needs more money than was appropriated for his agency, the head deliberately tries to overspend. If he runs out of money at the end of the tenth month of the fiscal year, he can not only get added funds for that year but argue more forcefully for a larger budget the following year. This is but one example of

---

[7] Municipal Finance Officers Association, *op. cit.*, p. 60.

the kind of political maneuvering that goes on behind the formal budget process. The allotment process is designed to suppress such tactics.

Transfer of Appropriations. One of the unsolved problems of budget execution is how to permit executive flexibility in administration while, at the same time, preserving legislative intent. No better illustration of this problem can be given than that involved in the transfer of appropriations.

Legislative intent is given in the appropriation ordinances. By exercising its legislative powers and prerogatives, the council has indicated the various objects for which municipal funds are to be spent during the fiscal year; and any substantial deviation from the ordinances, without councilmanic consent, would represent a frustration of legislative power.

Yet, in budget administration, the executive is forced to consider present contingencies which the council may never have considered in the past. A few short months may have changed some municipal needs so drastically that the appropriations are out of date.

The executive usually, therefore, is given some authority to transfer funds from one appropriation item to another. Just how extensive this authority should be is a question of how the city wishes to balance executive and legislative authority. The executive and his agency heads will inevitably chafe under detailed restraints imposed by ordinance. But the council will insist that if it fails to specify closely the details of spending, it will be giving up an essential right to control policy. It must not be forgotten, of course, that the executive, whether he be strong mayor, manager, or village president, has exercised legislative power in the formation of the budget. The budget is partly his, and he will be given certain rights to a flexible administration of it. Just how much power he will be given is essentially a political question that must be settled by him and the council.

Municipal authorities need the power to effect other types of transfers. Whether protected by state constitution or statute, city charter or ordinance, the earmarked fund can be a real obstacle to flexible administration. Recognizing that some earmarking is inevitable, state officials and charter drafters, therefore, often permit the council and the executive to make limited transfers of money from most accounts, just so long as those transfers do not impair any of the contractual obligations of the city.

Reduction of Expenditures. A somewhat similar problem to that of transfer of appropriations is involved in executive reduction of expenditures. Here the executive is also tampering with legislative intent, if he is given authority to reduce spending for a particular object below the level authorized by the council. As with transfers, there is no sure way of meeting the problem for all time. Yet proper budget administration required that the executive be given some authority to reduce expenditures below the level intended by the council, especially if such action is necessary to prevent a budget deficit.

Performance Budgeting. New York City was blessed with its first budget of $1 billion in 1947. Twelve years later, when Mayor Robert F. Wagner presented his 1959–1960 budget to the Board of Estimate, the citizens of New York were faced with a budget of over $2 billion, and the New York Chamber of Commerce predicted that taxpayers could look forward to budget increases of $150 to $200 million annually. That the chamber's estimate was too modest was indicated by Mayor John Lindsay's proposed budget of $4.5 billion in 1966–1967.

Nor was New York alone. The Chicago city government was spending one-half billion dollars annually in the mid-1950's, and the school district, park district, and other local units were spending hundreds of millions in addition. San Francisco spent $177 million in 1958, and Memphis approximately the same amount. By the mid-1960's most of these budgets had at least doubled.

With such vast outlays city officials are struggling to produce budget documents which are, on the one hand, adequate tools to work with and, on the other, intelligible records to the average citizen. To do this is not an insignificant task. The traditional governmental budget, whether of city, state, or nation, was of the line-item type; that is, the budget listed each department, and then allotted certain sums for personnel, for equipment, for contractual services, for travel, and for all the other elements of departmental expenses. From this kind of budget the citizen, and even the administrators of city services, could only vaguely guess at what sums were being spent for any particular kind of function or subfunction.

Municipal finance officers, mayors, city managers, and citizen groups combined to seek better budgeting methods. The result of this search was the development of performance (or program) budgeting. (For the purposes of this general analysis, performance budgeting and program budgeting will be treated as identical concepts.)

"Performance budgeting," as a phrase, first appeared in one of the reports of the Commission on the Organization of the Executive Branch of the Government, popularly known as the "First Hoover Commission." This commission, looking into federal administration, gave to the Institute of Public Administration the task of making a critical survey of federal budgeting practice. A. E. Buck, who prepared the report, long had been a student of state and local governmental budgeting practices, and he had observed that some cities and states had broken down their budgets into work programs. The budget was, in short, put together in terms of objectives rather than departments.

Popularized by the Hoover commission report, the performance budget soon became the objective toward which numerous city administrations were striving. Such widely different cities as Chicago, Richmond, and Los

Angeles have been able to develop budgets on a program, or performance, basis.

Los Angeles, by charter amendment, created the new position of city administrative officer in 1951. This officer became the technical assistant to the mayor in budget preparation. Immediately, the city moved toward instituting a performance budget.[8] Chicago soon followed suit, and its budget has been characterized by the Citizens' Budget Commission of New York as "one of the best in the nation from the point of view of presenting research material useful in performance budgeting."

It is the work unit which lies at the core of performance budgeting. Although the cost accountant has sought to use unit costs to determine the cost of performing a certain function, as well as the efficiency with which it is performed, Los Angeles budget officers reached the conclusion that "the use of unit costs in the preparation of work programs should be discarded in favor of man-hours per work unit." [9]

Although use of the work unit cannot, at least potentially, have the accuracy or the refinement of the unit cost used by the cost accountant, it has the advantage of being relatively easily arrived at, of being widely applicable to almost every type of municipal activity, and—no mean achievement—of being readily understood by even the lowliest municipal employee. Moreover, unit-cost analysis requires some arbitrary assignments of cost, which, even though done by the best accountants in the world, are apt to introduce considerable inaccuracies in the final unit. Since this problem does not occur with work units, they may be the most accurate basic measurement obtainable for municipal administrators.

Work units, as noted above, are relatively easily arrived at. In Los Angeles the budget officers set the figure of 2,088 as the number of hours worked annually by each municipal employee. To obtain the total number of man-hours for each subactivity, the number of personnel assigned to each subactivity was multiplied by 2,088. Then, the following formula was used to obtain man-hours per work unit:

$$\frac{\text{Total man-hours}}{\text{Number of work units}} = \text{Man-hours per unit}$$

Table 15-1 shows the results of such calculations for a specific subactivity of the city of Los Angeles. Since 60.4 people were credited with working at the subactivity of "Inspections," this figure was multiplied by 2,088 to ob-

[8] George A. Terhune, *An Administrative Case Study of Performance Budgeting in the City of Los Angeles, California* (Chicago: MFOA, 1954), p. 2.
[9] *Ibid.*, p. 4.

Table 15-1

Subactivity	Work Unit	Work Units	Person-nel	Total Man-hours	Man-hours per Unit
Inspections	Inspections	370,691	60.4	126,020	.34

Source: George A. Terhune, *An Administrative Case Study of Performance Budgeting in the City of Los Angeles, California* (Chicago: MFOA, 1954), p. 6.

tain total man-hours. (In fact, a slight adjustment in this figure was necessitated by overtime work.) Then the formula described above was used:

$$\frac{126,020}{370,691} = .34$$

In sum, the budget officer knew from this analysis that 370,691 building inspections were carried out, and that .34 man-hours were expended upon each inspection. Although the man-hours-per-unit figure was the basic one that the budget officer was striving for, he could also, at any time, have used it to obtain a cost figure.

As performance budgeting develops in American cities, increasingly refined techniques will unquestionably be invented. Such refinements will enable administrative officers to gauge performance and increase operating efficiency. They will also give the citizen a far better understanding of the nature and quality of municipal services than he has ever had before.

Financial Planning for the Future

In order to be secure in the present, the city must be constantly aware of the past and just as constantly at work trying to anticipate the future. Every well-run city requires a certain amount of expenditures for capital investment. This is money invested in public works, heavy equipment, and the other items of major cost and relatively long life. Since each activity of the city has recurring capital needs, which can be largely anticipated, a plan is often drawn up in which such needs are projected several years into the future. This plan is usually described as a capital budget or capital improvement plan.

The city of Madison, Wisconsin, describes its capital budget improvement plan as a programming of "public works expenditures for the coming seven years. It relates future construction to the city's fiscal capacities, land use and master planning, and services programs." [10]

[10] City of Madison, *Operations Manual for Use in Preparing Capital Project Requests for 1959 Capital Budget and 1960–65 Capital Improvement Plan* (Madison, Wis.: The City, 1958).

What does the capital budget include? In the Madison capital budget and improvement plan, the following items are included:

1. Projects for which borrowing is necessary.

2. Land purchases in excess of $3,000; construction and land improvement in excess of $5,000.

3. Equipment for new buildings and other purposes.

4. Major alterations to buildings.

5. Motor vehicles with a value over $5,000 and a life expectancy over 5 years.

6. Other capital outlays designated by the mayor.

The capital budget applies not only to all the regular administrative agencies and departments of the city of Madison, but also to the board of education, the vocational and adult school, the public library, and the water, sewer, and parking utilities.

The Madison plan, as with all other well-administered budgets for capital improvements, is made up of two distinct parts. The first part is called the "capital budget" and is for the fiscal year which lies ahead. Because of its immediate application, it is eventually written into an appropriation and borrowing ordinance. The second part, called the "capital improvement plan," is projected ahead six years beyond the end of the period covered by the capital budget. Since the second part is only a plan, it is not formally enacted into law.

Although the capital improvements program covers a period of several years, capital budgeting goes on continuously, so that at any time the city has a plan reaching several years into the future. (See Figure 15-1.) Every year, departmental heads are requested to submit new capital plans for the future. In carrying out the task, the administrator revises the old plan for his department and adds his estimates for a new year six years in the future.

This kind of projection annually goes on in all cities with workable capital plans. The Pawtucket, Rhode Island, charter provides, for example, that "it shall be the duty of the [plan] commission to prepare and *revise annually* a program of capital improvements for the ensuing five years, and it shall submit the same *annually* to the mayor and the director of finance.

Figure 15-1. Annual Revision
of the Capital Improvement Program

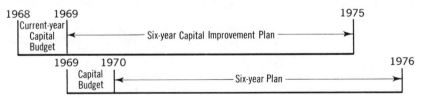

. . ." [11] Too often the capital plan is thought of as something struck off in one year and then followed carefully throughout the life of the plan. But, in fact, the well-managed plan is a projection of capital needs into the future, and it is revised annually. It is thus a living document, constantly revised and constantly brought up to date.[12]

Unfortunately for the spread of capital budgeting, state enabling legislation often does not encourage it. The situation in many states is similar to that in New Hampshire, where the municipal budget law "emphasizes expenditure limitation and restriction and gives no particular encouragement to long-range fiscal planning." [13] Nonetheless, the number of cities of over 10,000 population using capital budgets increased 17 percent from 1957 to 1964.[14]

Even where there is an adequate capital improvement program, however, it is apt to be plagued with the difficulty that it does not include all local governments. If the city alone sets up a capital program, the plan gives only a partial picture of the community's capital needs. Thus to be really accurate and to give a true picture to the citizen, the program must include all local governments, particularly the two biggest spenders, the city and the schools. If the schools are a part of the city government, this problem is taken care of automatically. If they are not, then it is the responsibility of the city council and school board to plan together for the capital needs of the future.

Living within One's Means: The Nature and Proper Function of Municipal Debt

Just as the average American family must borrow money to supply its various needs, so the city must also go into debt if it is to supply those services the citizen expects of it. It is true that some cities can meet all needs on a pay-as-you-go basis, but such cities are rare. Municipal indebtedness is as common as the summer storm. And like the thunderstorm, with its beneficial rain but destructive winds, city debt can be both an aid to municipal growth and a danger to the city's financial security.

Since World War II, city debt in the United States has risen constantly. In 1958, cities borrowed over $2.5 billion and paid off $1.25 billion of old debt, leaving a net gain of indebtedness of $1.25 billion. At the end of 1958 cities owed $13 billion in long-term, full-faith-and-credit obligations;

[11] *Charter of Pawtucket, Rhode Island,* Ch. 16, Sec. 4–1603; italics mine.
[12] See Municipal Finance Officers Association, *Capital Program and Capital Budget Manual* (Chicago: MFOA, 1964).
[13] Ernest G. Miller, *The Municipal Budget Law of New Hampshire,* Governmental Series, No. 9 (Durham, N.H.: University of New Hampshire, January, 1959), p. 14.
[14] *The Municipal Year Book 1965* (Chicago: ICMA), p. 316.

something over $6 billion in long-term, nonguaranteed debt; and $1 billion in short-term debt.[15] By 1966–67 the debt had increased to $19.6 billion (general obligation); $12.5 billion (nonguaranteed); and $3.2 billion (short-term).[16]

General-obligation Bonds. Most municipal debt is represented by bonds, which are sold to the purchaser to raise funds for various improvements and which stand for legal, contractual obligations of the city to reimburse the bondholders for specified amounts at specified periods. The reason for going into debt is to raise money for capital outlay, to provide for emergencies, or to tide the city over a short period in which disbursements are high and income is low. Municipal bonds may be classified in various ways, but the fundamental way is to separate them into two types: general-obligation and revenue bonds.

General-obligation bonds constitute a commitment of the "full faith and credit" of the city. In other words, the city guarantees the bondholder that it will use all of its taxing power and other fiscal resources, if necessary, to see that the bonds are paid off at maturity.

Because the general-obligation bond commits the total resources of the city to the repayment of the debt, rather severe limits are usually put on the city's general-obligation borrowing power, either by state constitution, state statute, or local charter. Sometimes, indeed, one will find limits on the city from all three sources. The city of Flint, for example, provides in Section 115 of its charter that the city may borrow against its full faith and credit, but that the indebtedness represented by that borrowing shall not exceed 7 percent of the assessed valuation of the city. In addition to this limit, both the constitution and statutes of the state of Michigan limit Flint's municipal indebtedness.

The state limits on general obligation borrowing vary. In New Hampshire, municipalities are held to a general-obligation debt of no more than 1.75 percent of the assessed valuation of property within the given city. From this very low figure, the debt limits rise to 15 percent in California and South Carolina, and to 18 and 20 percent in Virginia and Minnesota, respectively.[17] These state limits on municipal indebtedness resulted from the abandon with which cities of the nineteenth century borrowed and spent municipal treasure. Some cities, in that period, issued bonds in excess of 100 percent of assessed valuation.

Although the irresponsible fiscal policies of nineteenth-century cities

[15] U.S. Bureau of the Census, *Compendium of City Government Finances in 1958* (1959), p. 3.

[16] U.S. Bureau of the Census, *City Government Finances in 1966–67* (May, 1968), p. 7.

[17] Advisory Commission on Intergovernmental Relations, *State Constitutional and Statutory Restrictions on Local Government Debt, Report A-10* (Washington, D.C., September, 1961), p. 89.

have been forgotten by the cities and their citizens, the long memory of the law reaches back a full hundred years and keeps their memory green. In truth, the law here is a doddering old rake who takes malicious pleasure in reviving sins that should have been long since forgotten. Not only is there no logic to the arbitrary limits upon municipal indebtedness; the limits are, even more, positively mischievous. A statutory or constitutional limit on debt, like that on the taxing power, does not take into consideration the real fiscal capacity of the city; assessed valuation of property is not necessarily a good measure of the city's revenue capabilities, particularly since much of that revenue comes from nonproperty-tax sources. State limits of whatever kind, moreover, are an interference with the city's power to govern itself; in short, they are a violation of the principle of home rule.

A third reason for quarreling with debt limits is that they interfere with a proper management of the debt. And finally, since a city may, only rarely, go into general-obligation debt without a popular vote ratifying the ordinance proposing the debt, the notorious unwillingness of the people to approve any borrowing lightly stands effectively in the way of irresponsible borrowing.

One of the most grievous errors of tax and debt limits, taken together, is that they tend to stimulate the proliferation of governmental authorities at the local level—the kind of functional disintegration spoken of previously. With six or eight overlapping governments, all taxing and borrowing up to legal capacity, state limitations become a mockery. It would be far more effective to have one or two local governmental units controlled by an alert citizenry, than a multitude of jurisdictions which together can tax and borrow and ultimately impose severe burdens upon the taxpayer.

Revenue Bonds. The revenue bond, already described as the second major type of municipal obligation, is usually not subject to statutory, constitutional, or charter limitations on total amounts issued. This bond is a type which is retired from nontax revenues, such as the income from municipal utility enterprises. Since the service charges for a utility can be set high enough to make the debt self-amortizing, bonds can be issued against either the property or revenues of the utility and then retired from utility income. Issuance of this kind of bond is, of course, regulated by market conditions; cautious investors will not purchase revenue bonds unless the city can plainly show that it has not overextended itself. Legal debt limits, therefore, are not usually imposed upon revenue bonds, and voter approval is not necessary, usually, unless the people demand a vote via the referendum petition.

Although it is not surprising that cities resort to revenue-bond financing, considering the difficulties attendant upon issuance of the general-obligation bond, the use of the revenue bond increases the burden of city debt. The reason is that the obligation backed by the full faith and credit of the city is a more desirable investment than the revenue bond; it thus commands a lower interest rate than, generally, does the revenue bond. If the city were not hampered by state limitations on full-faith-and-credit borrowing, it could guarantee all of its bonds with all of its resources and thereby appreciably lower the carrying charges on the debt. This need not mean, of course, that all the bonds would be paid for out of tax income. In case of a bond issue to enlarge the water utility, for example, the city would simply specify by ordinance that the bonds would be retired from water revenues. After the bonds, backed by the city's full faith and credit, were sold, the necessary funds could be taken from the water utility to retire them. If this kind of arrangement would tempt municipal officials to act rashly, an alert citizenry could keep them in check.

The Special-assessment Bond. Since the special assessment may be used with or without bonding, no mention was made of special-assessment debt in the preceding chapter. Yet the building of special-assessment improvements with borrowed funds is so common that the type of financing used must be explained.

After the special-assessment district is set up, the levies made, and the assessment roll approved, the actual construction work is started. This necessitates that substantial payments be made to the contractor as the work progresses. If the city is fortunate enough to have a surplus in some fund, or if the contractor will take vouchers in lieu of cash, the city waits until the project is completed and accepted by city engineers. Thereupon the city bills the property owners for all of the cost or for one installment. If the property owners choose to pay their assessments by installment, the city usually has no recourse but to issue bonds.

Two types of special-assessment bonds may be issued: the special-general bond and the special-special. The first type is a commitment against the special-assessment installment; it may even be a lien against the property in the special-assessment district. In addition, the special-general bond constitutes a contingent liability against the full faith and credit of the city. If payments from the special-assessment district are insufficient to take care of the bonds, the city retires those remaining out of the general municipal revenues. The special-special bond is the same as the special-general except that it does not constitute a pledge of the full faith and credit of the city.

Of the two types of special-assessment bonds, the special-general is the one that is now most generally used. Because it is a safer investment than the special-special, the city receives an advantageous interest rate. According to Carl J. Faist, director of finance of Saginaw, Michigan, "bids were received for $1,200,000 such bonds in 1955 and $1,030,000 in 1956, the interest rates to the city being 1.65% and 2.076% respectively. The reason for such rates is, of course, that special-generals carry the pledge of full faith, credit and resources of the municipality." [18]

The special-general not only sells better and receives a better interest rate than the special-special; it also has fewer of the arbitrary limits imposed upon it than that other type of security backed by the full faith and credit of the city, the general-obligation bond. Ordinarily, no referendum is necessary to approve its issue, and usually it is not restricted by the general-obligation debt limit. In Michigan, the special-general has a limit of its own, 12 percent of the assessed valuation of the city. In Pennsylvania, the special-general is covered by the general debt limit of 7 percent, but the Pennsylvania law provides that the first 2 percent of full-faith-and-credit debt may be issued without a referendum.

The special-special has the advantage of being unrestricted, either by debt limits or by popular referenda, but it does not have a wide market and the interest rate it bears is invariably high, so that its disadvantages are very considerable indeed. It is no wonder that it has fallen into disfavor.

Short-term Certificates. A city may be forced to borrow for short periods of time for three principal reasons: in anticipation of taxes, for unusual emergencies, and for capital expenditures made before the issuance of long-term bonds. Sale of tax-anticipation warrants, payment of vendors or employees in vouchers (which the payee then cashes at the bank, usually at a discount), notes or other direct bank loans, issuance of vouchers to contractors—these are some of the ways cities have of quickly raising money needed for a short time.

While short-term borrowing is sometimes necessary, municipal officials avoid it as a recurrent thing, especially during a period when short-term money is scarce. But every city can be faced with an emergency situation that calls for expenditures far beyond its current budget. It is essential, therefore, that cities have and retain the power to borrow for short periods of time.

State Control of Bond Issues. In addition to laying the dead hand of legal limitations upon the city's borrowing power, some states also require administrative approval of bond issues before they may be sold. Set up in 1943, Michigan's Municipal Finance Commission has the power and duty to pass on all contemplated municipal bond issues. The Department of Internal Affairs has similar powers in Pennsylvania.

Wishing to make sure that standards would be applied to all municipal bonds, Michigan lawmakers set up various requirements for the bonds. No bond may be issued for a period longer than the expected life of the improvement; special-assessment bonds must fall due not later than two years after date of the final installment; and no bond issues may be run for longer

[18] William O. Winter and Robert W. Richey, *The Special Assessment in Illinois* (Carbondale, Ill.: Southern Illinois University, 1959), p. 36.

than thirty years, unless a special exception is made in the statutes.[19] These are provisions which the city would ordinarily wish to adhere to, without state restriction; and just as they should constitute no burden upon Michigan cities, so should they represent no arbitrary intrusion into the policy-making prerogatives of any city.

The Pay-as-you-go Principle. Some cities are well enough situated financially to be able to take care of both current operations and capital investments out of annual revenues. Several factors may contribute to this avoidance of borrowing. The city may be extremely wealthy, or it may have a long history of budgeting for capital improvements—always an aid to the orderly financing of public works—or it may have developed a revolving fund which has been built up to the point that all but the greatest expenditures may be paid for from the monies that have been accumulated.

For the most part, the cities able to operate on a pay-as-you-go basis have been able to set aside surplus income over a period of time, which enables them to build up a revolving fund. This creates certain problems. In the first place, this practice may be on the border line of legality in certain states, and various legal shenanigans are necessary for the city to set up and maintain the fund. Then, too, there is always the problem of investing the money so that it will not lie idle.[20] Still further, citizens and taxpayers' groups may be unsympathetic to the idea of the city's developing a surplus, and particularly to the level of taxation necessary to build up the surplus. If so, there may be unfortunate political consequences. And, finally, it might be queried whether citizens should be denied the right to "consume" their tax money while it lies in reserve.

After the revolving fund has been built up, all such questions—assuming the question of legality has been resolved—become academic. The situation is something like that of a hydroelectric project on a river. When the dam is finished, a certain "dead" period must ensue to permit the reservoir behind the dam to fill. Once the lake is created, however, the normal flow of the river goes through the turbines to generate electricity and maintain the level of the river below the dam. So it is with the revolving fund: when it is full, there can be a constant flow into and out of the fiscal reservoir, though this does not mean, of course, that the amount of money in the fund, like water behind the dam, will always be constant.

If a city cannot follow a strict pay-as-you-go policy, it can often use a partial one. This partial system requires that the income level be high enough so that every year some money can be put into capital investment. Even a small city should not be embarrassed by the purchase of a $20,000 fire en-

---

[19] *Michigan Statutes Annotated*, 5.3188 (25).

[20] See Advisory Commission on Intergovernmental Relations, *Investment of Idle Cash Balances by State and Local Governments*, *Report A-3* (Washington, D.C., January, 1961); also *Supplement to Report A-3* (January, 1965).

gine or by the acquisition of land for a small park. But if a million dollars is needed for street construction or expansion of the sewage treatment plant, the city can no longer use pay-as-you-go. It must instead resort to borrowing. The system is: limited capital investments on a planned basis every year from annual revenues; major capital expenditures, when needed, with borrowed funds.

During severe economic crises the city may be forced to borrow in order to meet emergency conditions. Because of high unemployment, it may be necessary to issue bonds for relief purposes. Or, unable to meet current needs, the city may be forced to borrow to meet a payroll or to defray other current expenses. Although this kind of borrowing is to be avoided if at all possible, sometimes it may prove inevitable. On the other hand, if the city has a countercyclical plan already developed, the stimulation of the city's economy from sizable public works may be sufficient to render unnecessary the measures of desperation sketched above.

Countercyclical Policy. Developed from the theories of the British economist John Maynard Keynes, the countercyclical theory is that governments should increase taxes and reduce debts in times of economic prosperity; during periods of depression, they should reduce taxes and even embark on deficit spending.[21] While this theory applies more to the federal government than to any other American government, it still has applicability to the city. By following a pay-as-you-go plan and by building surpluses during prosperity, cities can be prepared to do much in alleviating the worst periods of subsequent deflation by large spending programs. Using both reserve funds and borrowing, cities can substantially help their local economies by the development of public works projects of an essential and economically productive nature. In addition, because deflation brings lower prices, the city stands to get a bargain—public works projects built at lower cost than they would have been during prosperity.

In following a countercyclical policy, the city needs to use its spending power to create socially and economically useful projects. It needs especially to stay clear of "make-work" projects. And the way to do that is to embark only on carefully planned enterprises which have been well thought out in advance and on which a political consensus has been reached. Here the capital improvement plan stands the city in very good stead, because this plan is projected several years into the future. With such a plan, in which major projects are already thought through, the city should be capable of meeting an economic crisis with vigorous countercyclical policies. It would even be possible to telescope three or four years into one year of countercyclical activity if the political situation called for such drastic action.

[21] See James A. Maxwell, "Countercyclical Role of State and Local Governments," *National Tax Journal*, XI (December, 1958), 371–376.

Organization of the Finance Department

If the unification theme of the classical public administration theorists and the reformers has any validity anywhere, it is in the finance department. The principal financial functions seem logically to belong together: assessment of taxes, collection of tax and nontax revenues, custody of funds, auditing, purchasing, disbursement of funds, and budgeting. But deductive logic does not always translate into political logic in the American city.

Because of the lingering strength of the Jacksonian tradition, elective finance officers are not uncommon, even as we move deep into the second half of the twentieth century. And so we still have treasurers and collectors elected on the same ballot as the chief executive, and thus responsible not to him but to the people directly. And these same elective officials sometimes serve the city independent of the city manager or the mayor.

Because of the fragmentation of local government, moreover, the administration of the general property tax is often entrusted to officials who not only are elective but also serve in an entirely separate government from the city. In probably a great majority of urban centers in the United States, assessment and collection of the general property tax are responsibilities fixed upon the county and are therefore rigidly separated from the city government. The strength of this tradition may be seen even in the unified metropolitan government of Nashville, where the metropolitan tax assessor replaced the old county tax assessor, but retained his independent, elective status. (See Figure 15-2.)

Figure 15-2. Organization
of Finance Operations—Nashville, Tennessee

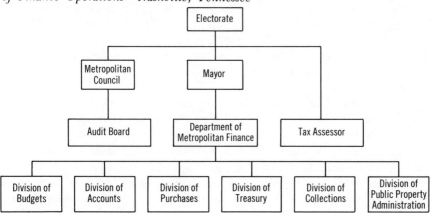

Source: *The Charter of the Metropolitan Government of Nashville and Davidson County, Tennessee* (1962). The Audit Board does not actually do the postaudit, but rather chooses an independent auditing firm for the job.

Another part of finance administration that often proves troublesome is the auditing function. There seems to be almost universal agreement that this function breaks down into two parts: (1) the executive, or preaudit, and (2) the legislative, or postaudit. The preaudit is a continuous operation, carried out daily by the executive to see that proposed expenditures have been authorized and that an unencumbered balance exists in the account to be charged. The postaudit is an annual legislative responsibility to make sure that the executive department has indeed disbursed all funds in an authorized manner. Auditing, according to this pattern, is changed from one unified function into two entirely separate and distinct functions. Even the nomenclature of finance administration will often indicate this separateness. The comptroller (or controller) is an executive official in the finance department who carries out the preaudit. The auditor is a legislative (or independently elective) official who carries out the postaudit.

If the two functions are combined, as they have been in such major cities as Denver and Philadelphia, the auditor's office may be an excellent position to be used by the minority party to badger the mayor and the party in power. From this strong point, Democrats and Republicans have alternately sallied forth to harass the administration in Denver, and the same tactics have been used by both parties in Philadelphia. Some of the results may be gathered from the following colloquy between a member of the Chicago Home Rule Commission and Mayor Joseph S. Clark, Jr., of Philadelphia in 1954:

> MR. FARR (Commission member): Who does the controller work under?
>
> MAYOR CLARK: The controller is elected; and it's been my unhappy lot to have a Republican controller ever since I've been in. The initial Republican controller was a swell guy, and we got along fine. He was tough. You couldn't get away with anything.
>
> The present city controller has been in office two months. He was elected on a platform of "throw the rascals out," and I was the principal rascal.
>
> MR. FARR: Does he have pre-audit authority?
>
> MAYOR CLARK: Well, he has; in my judgment, that is a mistake, too; I don't think he should. I was controller before I was mayor, so I know a little about it, even though I'm a lawyer. I think he should be confined to post-audit, but he isn't. He's a double-check.
>
> The principal draftsman of the charter was a very able and an extremely capable lawyer, who had been a Republican attorney-general of Pennsylvania and has a strong belief in the theory that everybody in government is a crook; and he felt that we needed not only the finance director to pass on all requisitions, whether for personnel, purchases,

or anything else; and that he should have an elaborate system of books, where you could go in and check him—but also, the controller had to approve it before it went through. And this controller has started putting monkey wrenches in that particular wheel.

The council, however, to answer your question—we have a lump-sum budget, and that's a godsend to the executive branch. We go in and justify before the council all of our appropriations in four or five categories; I can't remember them all.

One of them is personal services; another is contractual services; a third is material and supplies; and there are one or two minor ones that I can't remember. They tell us what they want the money for. They ask questions. They give us a lump-sum appropriation, and we don't have to spend it the way we say we're going to.

We are bound by rudimentary elements of good faith, and we wouldn't think of spending it in a way we haven't justified before council without talking it over with them.

This may be a little interesting example. We have a rather temperamental and imaginative director of recreation, and after the budget was passed he concluded that it [would] be a wonderful thing to have an ice-skating rink out on Rayburn Place, which is right next to the City Hall.

He got a promoter from whom he got a contract, saying he would furnish ice for 30 days; and they had a little Muzak piped in; and build it up, for $6,000, for 30 days, to make the ice. Well, there wasn't a darned thing in the budget. He didn't think about it until after the budget had been passed. We went around to the boys in the city council and said, "I think it's a good pitch." He let the contract. The city controller has said that is an illegal expenditure, and he quoted a couple of provisions of the city charter which led him to believe that. He said it's an immoral and improper thing to do, because you didn't tell the council about it.

We, in effect, said, "Nuts to him."

He's held up the requisition; but curiously enough, his lawyer is the city solicitor, and the city solicitor is my appointee, so the city solicitor is rendering an opinion telling him the holding-up of that requisition is illegal, and he has to pass it. I don't say that's necessarily good government.

ALDERMAN BECKER (Commission member): You can tell him the opinion you wanted, as a Philadelphia lawyer.[22]

The place of the budget office in the city's formal organizational structure often varies from city to city. Since budgeting is policy-making par ex-

[22] New York Municipal Reference Library, *Notes*, XXXIV (March, 1960), 270–271.

cellence, a vast amount of local politics goes into the budget and also comes out of it. The emphasis in the literature for decades has been upon the necessity of an executive budget, and this has meant to chief executives (both mayors and city managers), and to charter and statute drafters, that the executive makes up the budget and presents it as a kind of fait accompli to the council, to be nibbled at, here and there, by councilmanic critics, but not materially changed by them.

More than one councilman has chafed at this kind of executive dominance, and not, obviously, because he is fascinated by the idea of putting together hundreds of pages of drier-than-dust figures. The reason is that crucial policy decisions are being made all the time the budget is being put together, and the councilman wishes to be involved in that decision-making.

In formal terms, the council does not become involved in the budget process until it receives the proposed budget document, with the accompanying executive budget message from the mayor or the city manager. And then it has little time or staff really to give the document a comprehensive review. The charter of Nashville provides that the mayor must submit his operating budget not later than May 25, and that the council must adopt the operating budget by June 30.[23] It seems obvious that the charter drafters in Nashville did not really expect the council would have more than a peripheral role in budget-making.

The charter drafters in New York City apparently took a similar view. Not only may the New York city council not increase any item in the mayor's budget; it must also share its power with the powerful Board of Estimate (which is made up of the mayor, the comptroller, the president of the council, and the five borough presidents). So powerful is the Board of Estimate, in fact, that Sayre and Kaufman observe that the board may "accurately regard the Council's share in the expense budget process as merely formal and symbolic, subtracting nothing of importance from the Board's monopolistic position." [24]

These formal arrangements may not, and indeed probably do not, tell the whole story of the budget-making process. If the New York Board of Estimate has significant formal powers, so also has it acquired no mean informal powers—and at the expense of both the council and the mayor of New York. Similarly, councilmen, councilmanic committees, and politically potent leaders and groups will often get deeply involved in budget-making whether the law contemplates it or not. The chief executive and his subordinates will not be alone in making the decisions that go into the

---

[23] The Charter of the Metropolitan Government of Nashville and Davidson County, Tennessee, Art. 6, Secs. 6.04, 6.06.

[24] Wallace S. Sayre and Herbert Kaufman, Governing New York City (New York: W. W. Norton & Co., 1965), p. 627.

budget document. The politics of budget-making will not be confined by the formal, legal requirements of charter or statute.

Annotated Bibliography

For authoritative analyses of the mechanics of municipal finance, one can rely on the publications of the Municipal Finance Officers Association of the United States and Canada, including the quarterly journal of the association, *Municipal Finance*. Probably the best single source on the purely administrative aspects of the city's revenues and expenditures is published by the city managers' professional group—International City Managers' Association, *Municipal Finance Administration* (Chicago: The Association, 6th ed., 1962).

Several reports of the Advisory Commission on Intergovernmental Relations —published in Washington, D.C., by the U.S. Government Printing Office— give not only valuable information on city finance and administration but also considerable insight into the thinking of city, state, and federal officials about the city's financial position. On various aspects of local government debt, see *State Constitutional and Statutory Restrictions on Local Government Debt, Report A-10* (September, 1961); and *State Technical Assistance to Local Debt Management, Report M-26* (January, 1965).

A good view of the budgeting process from the standpoint of the working finance officer may be obtained from Lennox L. Moak and Kathryn Killian Gordon, *Budgeting for Smaller Governmental Units* (Chicago: Municipal Finance Officers Association, 1965). For an extended discussion of program budgeting, although with special reference to the United States military establishment, see Frederick C. Mosher, *Program Budgeting: Theory and Practice* (Chicago: Public Administration Service, 1954). One may obtain much insight into the making of the city's financial decisions by reading the book of an intellectual who is also mayor of the city of Milwaukee: Henry W. Maier, *Challenge to the Cities—An Approach to a Theory of Urban Leadership* (New York: Random House, 1966).

Although not much ever appears in the literature on the politics of city finance, one needs only to attend the gatherings of mayors and councilmen, city managers, and finance officers to realize that this is a subject constantly on the minds of the people who sit in city hall.

CHAPTER 16

The City's First Line of Defense

An army 700,000 strong mans the fire and police stations and operates the public safety equipment necessary to protect the urban population of the United States. Because urban living greatly increases the hazards to life and property over rural living, the number of public safety officers and the expense of maintaining them and their equipment have grown in geometric proportion to the population. Not merely population growth, in other words, but also its increasingly urban character and complexity have caused the public safety function to mushroom in recent decades.

The policeman and the fireman, often inadequately trained, almost invariably underpaid, and not too highly regarded by the people whom they serve, are hardly less important to society than food and drink are to the individual. Yet one need only to look at the city in disaster to see how thinly manned are society's ramparts and how a cataclysm can easily breach the defenses and overwhelm a city. Or it may be more instructive to observe how a city can be safe and secure at one moment and a fearful wilderness at the next.

Let us look at what happened during the famed Boston police strike of September, 1919. At three o'clock on a Tuesday afternoon the city was orderly. By four o'clock mobs were roaming the streets, and looting had begun. By Wednesday morning the mobs were uglier, larger, and more destructive; and Mayor Andrew J. Peters had mobilized the citizenry (including Harvard students) in defense of the city. The governor of Massachusetts, Calvin Coolidge, finally realizing the seriousness of the situation, called out the state militia on Thursday, and the city gradually fought back to normalcy. The famed Boston police strike had been broken, and a lesson had been learned about the crucial nature of the police function.

The Job of Public Safety

It is not enough to say grandiloquently that the city's uniformed, paramilitary services stand between it and anarchy and similar disasters. Only by analyzing the jobs of the fireman and the policeman can the full impact of that statement be felt.

The primary objective of the uniformed services is to prevent antisocial acts and natural events which would destroy or damage the individual's property and impair or destroy his right and expectation to a peaceful, rewarding existence. If prevention fails—whether because of human or natural agency—the uniformed services must move with discipline and determination to quell the disturbance, fight the fire, rescue the endangered, apprehend the criminal, and in other ways eliminate the hazards to life and property. Surely the city has no more worthy objectives in its long list of services.

More specifically, the city's uniformed services are faced with two compelling facts of urban existence: (1) crime and assorted kinds of social dislocation, and (2) fire and allied hazards. We should look momentarily at the crime and fire problems before discussing the organizational nature of the departments as such.

The Crime Problem. Superficially, crime may be regarded as a violation of basic personal or property rights. The criminal respects neither the person of the citizen nor the citizen's right to enjoy his own property undisturbed by aggressive acts. The criminal does not make fine distinctions between personal and property rights, nor does the citizen who is offended. Armed robbery may result in the victim's suffering a blow on the head or an agony of fear for his physical safety, but these results of the criminal's attack may well seem to him of less consequence than the loss of his wallet with its precious papers and its money.

Some types of crime may excite great public indignation: note the concern over juvenile delinquency in recent years or over crimes committed by narcotics addicts. Other types, however, may long have had a kind of public acceptance. If a man kills his wife's lover, a jury of his peers is apt to set him free. In some communities, moreover, acts which the law regards as felonies may be shrugged off as no more than misdemeanors.

Crime may result from an act of passion or from some circumstance that causes a "normal" person to act antisocially. Or it may stem from the action of an organized mob of professional criminals: the "Syndicate" or the Mafia. If it is too much to say that every sane, normal citizen is a potential criminal, it can be easily documented that a large number of persons who have never before offended against the law yearly find themselves in the criminal courts. Crime may stem from environmental factors, or it may come from emotional or psychological malfunctions which may be easily disguised or most difficult to discover. Crime, in short, is a complex phenomenon. Since it results from an extremely complicated interreaction between the individual and society, it will vary not only from person to person but also from society to society.

In order to know about the nature of crime, we need to have data on the crimes that are committed. Every competent police department will carefully record all types of crimes committed within the city and the frequency, places, and time of commission of the crimes. By analysis of these data, not only may the police chief from day to day marshal his forces at the times and places where outbreaks of crime are most apt to occur, but the department itself, in league with other city agencies, may have data available to enable them to engage in crime-prevention work. Good crime reporting may reveal, also, the beginnings of a "crime wave," a shift in activity of the organized criminal, or an increase in certain types of crime. Because there is a brotherhood among criminals, moreover, it is useful to have nationwide data on crime assembled. Using data submitted to it by city and other law enforcement agencies over the country, the Federal Bureau of Investigation compiles and publishes uniform crime reports which serve as an invaluable central reference on the nature of criminal acts in the nation.[1]

The Fire Problem. Insight into the nature of the fire problem may also be gained by the compilation and analysis of data pertaining to fire occurrences. As with crime, fires may be mapped. The locus, time of day, type of fire, weather conditions, and economic loss involved all may be valuable in preventing or combating fire hazards. Unlike crime statistics, data on fires and fire losses for the entire nation are not collected and published by an official agency; the service is performed by a private organization, the National Fire Protection Association. From these data, one may learn, for example, that in 1966 fire losses cost the United States nearly $2 billion, and that deaths from fires numbered 12,100.[2]

The fire data show that fires are largely man-made—through thoughtlessness, stupidity, taking unnecessary risks, and the ignorance of fire danger in handling combustible materials. Equipment failures, as in aircraft crashes and resulting fires—some of which may well be beyond human agency to prevent—and so-called acts of God, such as lightning, are secondary causes, though an inordinate loss of life and property often results from them.

Fires may also involve crimes. Arson is, of course, a felony in all cities. Extreme carelessness in handling combustibles could result in fire and attendant loss of life, which, in turn, could result in a charge of manslaughter. So also might negligence in the crash and burning of an automobile —criminal thoughtlessness which causes the destruction of life and property.

A study of fire-loss data and a review of the history of major fires can only impress one with the recurrent presence of human error in most conflagrations. If the story of Mrs. O'Leary's cow, which kicked over the lantern that burned down the city of Chicago, is only a fable, it is nevertheless an instructive one. A seemingly inconsequential act of carelessness or criminal negligence, that ordinarily could be easily contained, can result in a fire of

[1] U.S. Department of Justice, Federal Bureau of Investigation, *Crime in the United States: Uniform Crime Reports* (issued annually).

[2] *The Municipal Year Book 1966* (Chicago: ICMA), p. 374.

disastrous proportions. Because human error in originating the fire may be compounded by errors made long before the fire started and by others committed during the initial stages of the fire, the outbreak may easily get out of hand.

The Nouvelles Galeries fire in Marseilles, in 1938, is a classic example of how no blaze in a city is innocent until it is contained and extinguished. This fire started in a department store, apparently from a spark from a welder's torch. Twelve minutes elapsed before the first fire engine arrived; fifteen minutes later a second came. Not only was equipment useless—their hoses were rotten and burst under the water pressure—but the fire companies seemed at a loss for a way to fight the blaze. Poorly trained in the first place, they were incredibly hampered by having no central command.

Edouard Herriot, man of letters, Mayor of Lyons, sometime French premier, and leader of the Radical-Socialist party, was at a party conference in a nearby hotel when the fire broke out. Soon realizing that the entire central section of the city was in danger, he ordered the Lyons fire department to the scene, even though Lyons was 200 miles away. Still the Marseilles fire companies fumbled with the blaze, without noticeable effect. The whole center of town was ablaze; panic and looting gripped the city. Naval fire fighters from Toulon finally arrived and brought the fire under control, but not until seventy-three people had lost their lives.[3]

A welder's carelessness, causing a fire to break out in a display window, started this disastrous fire. This was a human error, but a small one compared with the ones to follow. No extinguishers were at hand, and no one seemed to have the remotest idea of how to contain the blaze. But this might not have been of great consequence had the first fire company arrived at the blaze promptly. That it did not may have been because no alarm was sent in, because of a failure in the alarm system, or because of poor training of the company and assorted other factors. That the fire equipment broke down immediately can be laid either to the foolishness of the city council in not spending the necessary funds on fire-fighting facilities or to incredible obtuseness on the part of the central government in Paris. That there was no central command of men and equipment at the scene of the fire, and no adequate handling of the crowds, was a failure of administration that could have stemmed from political tampering with personnel, lack of professional training and outlook among the senior officers (both police and fire), and other factors. It often takes monumental human error to make a monumental fire.

In order to establish a basic distinction between the police and fire function, apologists have long argued that whereas the policeman's concern is with people, the fireman's is with equipment, buildings, and other inani-

---

[3] Hugh Clevely, *Famous Fires* (New York: The John Day Co., 1958), pp. 39–41.

mate objects. Such apologists do indeed protest too much. If fires are mainly the result of human error, and the evidence certainly points in that direction, the fireman's job is to reduce that error. Thus his job is to educate people in fire safety or to force them to conform to fire safety standards. Just as the policeman's basic job is to patrol the city and otherwise seek to prevent crime, so the fireman's job is to seek out fire hazards. Both of the services have a primary obligation to eliminate hazards to life and property; in short, their task is, above all, prevention: reducing the human error which destroys life and property and endangers the public safety.

The Administration of the Public Safety Function

As we may see in the history of the American city, professionally staffed police and fire departments slowly developed during the nineteenth century. But because the paid, full-time police department appeared while the fire defense forces were manned by volunteers, the two forces took on an apartness which, sanctioned by time, came to appear as natural and which has in large measure persisted.

The full-time professional police and fire officer was the most important development in public safety in the first century of the republic. Following closely after were a number of technical changes which greatly increased the effectiveness of the uniformed forces: adequate, pressurized water supply; scientific identification; and the merit system, which reduced spoils politics in the forces and made possible a genuine career system. Later on, the internal combustion engine had a major impact on police patrol and pursuit and an equally significant impact on the fire services.

The stress on equipment continues. Indeed, because of the development of career policemen and firemen, it was and is inevitable that the professionals should search constantly for better techniques and equipment to fight fire and crime. Communications have been revolutionized by radio; the helicopter has become an effective police aid. The fog nozzle, emitting a fine mist under high pressure, introduced an important cooling and smothering device in fire fighting, and an added protection to personnel. Foam, so effective during World War II in fighting certain types of ship and aircraft fires, has found its way into virtually every fire department in the country. Robot machines, for entering places too dangerous for personnel or unavailable to the fire fighter, have progressed beyond the experimental stage. Still experimental and controversial, but indicating promise, is the use of dogs in police work; much more controversial, of course, is the use of tear gas and chemical mace in riot control.

Accompanying the rise of a professional, well-equipped career service has been the striking increase in police and fire budgets. Few indeed have been the city councils which have permitted a public safety program or department to rot on the vine, as did the Marseilles fire department in the 1930's. If there was any one universal error of policy-makers it was in their becoming bedazzled by equipment and techniques to the extent that they permitted training, remuneration, and other personnel matters to take second place. The bright new ladder truck, the too-expensive and too-elaborate police and fire communications system, and other capital items have sometimes been overemphasized in police and fire budgets.

Police Administration. In the nineteenth century the city firmly established its right to control its own police, and this principle was extended to the county and the town, or township. Even though in the last quarter-century there has been a spectacular growth in the size and importance of the state police and of federal police agencies, and even though certain major cities—St. Louis, Kansas City, and Baltimore among them [4]—have lost control of their police to the state, the principle remains substantially intact. That control of police should remain in local hands has become a basic premise of American politics.

Ultimate legal control of the local police, of course, remains with the state governments. And the states have used this power, sometimes wisely, sometimes not so well. After the great Chicago police scandal of 1960, the state of Illinois threatened to take over the police, much as Missouri had assumed control of the Kansas City force in 1939 to help give the coup de grâce to the Pendergast machine and drive the hoodlum element out of the department. Only Mayor Richard Daley's political strength in the legislature and his willingness to take drastic steps toward reform enabled Chicago to keep control of her police. For much less substantial reasons the state legislatures are prone to interfere in local administration, not only of the police but of the fire department as well. Note the propensity of legislatures to require shorter hours and higher wages for police and firemen and thus to throw upon the local councils the onus of raising the necessary additional funds.

But ultimate state legal authority involves the sweet as well as the bitter. Much of the reason for efficient, professional police administration rests on the foundation of enlightened statutory authority. If petty state rules, such as residence requirements, impair the effectiveness of the police service, they should not obscure the civil service statutes, the council-manager enabling acts, the authorizations for state administrative aids to the local police, and many other substantial contributions by the state to police effectiveness. Criticism of the state should not obscure the fact that it is at least as much a help to the city's police function as a hindrance.

---

[4] As a result of a 1962 Massachusetts statute, Mayor John F. Collins was able to appoint Boston's first locally designated police commissioner in fifty-six years. The statute also returned fiscal control of the department to the city. New York *Times*, April 8, 1962, p. 48.

By means of constitutional provision and statutory authorization the state has normally delegated to the city control over its police. Given this fact, we must look to the city council and the city's executive for all police authority save that ultimate sanction found in state law. This authority is found in both policy formation and administrative direction. In order to understand the exercise of this authority we must look at the organization and structure of the police function.

The administrative head of the police department is invariably a board or commission, on the one hand, or a single director, on the other. Except in those rare instances where the state controls the police, administrative headship stems from appointment by the executive and city council, and thus lines of authority run from the policeman on the beat, through the channels of command, to the department head (single or plural), and then to the mayor or city manager. The council's role in administration is to pass ordinances and propose amendments to the city charter, to enact the executive budget, to undertake legislative investigation of police failures, to appoint or confirm the appointment of the department head, and perhaps to have a hand in the discipline and removal of the chief or members of the police board.

The axiom that a board should be used for advice and for quasi-legislative and quasi-judicial functions, and that a single head should be used for administration, is as often applied to the police as to any other municipal service. Administrative police boards were in vogue early in the century in an effort to reduce political pressures on the force, and for a variety of other reasons. That they proved successful at times cannot be gainsaid, but they so often proved to be administrative liabilities that they have largely disappeared from council-manager and strong-mayor systems of government. We shall leave them, therefore, with only this passing reference and move on to the single-headed department.

Under the usual organization arrangement, the department is headed by a professional police officer—a career man—who is directly responsible to the mayor or city manager, and who is appointed and may be removed by the chief executive. While the trend has for several decades been in the direction of this simple, effective form of command, many variations on this arrangement still exist in the American city.

In commission-type cities a variation prevails by which an elective, civilian commissioner heads the department and may, in fact, head a department of public safety, which includes both the fire and police functions. A professional chief of police will normally serve under the civilian commissioner. Still another variation is an appointive commissioner of police who is expected to be a professional of one sort or another. Thus two recent Chicago police commissioners, each serving in effect as chief of police, have been successively a career police officer and the former dean of the University of California's school of criminology. The latter, Dean Orlando Wilson, though not a career police officer, was a man wise in the ways of the criminal and a world-recognized authority on police administration.

Once an administrative structure has evolved in a particular city, the personality and qualifications of the chief himself are of greatest moment. The chief, say most detached observers, must be a professional career man. But this is difficult to achieve in all except the largest of our cities. Both political tradition and law are prejudiced in favor of the chief's being a local man. If custom can be ignored, the law is apt to stand in the way. When Orlando Wilson was brought from California to head the Chicago police department, his tenure was not secure until the Illinois legislature had amended a statute requiring one year's residency in the city previous to appointment as police commissioner. City managers have found that their efforts to bring in outsiders to head the police have been assailed by citizen and politician alike as a desecration of hallowed community practice.

Is it any wonder, then, that a city manager writes that "intercity promotional opportunities for police chiefs are the basis for development of a professional police service"?[5] If the city manager is to be permitted professional department heads, in other words, he will look not only within his own police department but outside it for a police chief in whom he can have confidence.

If the customary and legal barriers against the appointment of an outsider as police chief are effectively breached, one of the collateral benefits will be to raise the standards of local police forces generally. Most of our city police forces now are small ones, and career opportunities within the organization itself are limited. But if a young police careerist can be confident that job opportunities will open up for him elsewhere, state or nationwide, he will be encouraged to enter a small force, in the first place, and be stimulated to keep preparing himself for the fruits of achievement which lie afield.

Police organization reflects the variety of activities carried on by the department. Although a department's functions will vary greatly from the small city to the very large one, a similarity exists among police functions everywhere. The patrol, traffic, detective, vice, juvenile, and other police activities are, in the larger cities, formalized in divisions. In the smaller departments, since the policeman is apt to be a Jack-of-all-trades, he may be a patrolman in the morning, a traffic policeman in the afternoon, and detective on special assignment in the evening.

In terms of man-hours of effort and in terms of importance to the orderly life of the community, the patrol and traffic functions loom large in every police department. Patrol is widely recognized by police authorities as the

---

[5] Bernard L. Garmire, "Appointment of Outside Police Chiefs," *Public Management,* XLIII (August, 1960), 170–175.

principal crime-prevention device available to them. It is thus the concern of every department to increase patrol effectiveness.

The motorized patrol has largely replaced foot patrol in American cities, though there are still many policemen assigned to foot patrol and some police administrators who insist on the superior effectiveness of this patrol technique. For reasons of cost alone, however, the motorized patrol is here to stay.

Considerable experimentation, intensified over the past decade, has been carried on with the one-man patrol car, and its results have been the subject of considerable debate among police administrators. The efficacy of the one-man car has been so evident that only 5 percent of the 1,334 cities reporting to the *Municipal Year Book* in 1964 used the two-man car exclusively.[6] Following San Antonio's example (one-man cars since 1939), Kansas City converted exclusively to one-man patrols in 1954. As a result, the number of squad cars on patrol almost doubled. Wrote Orlando Wilson of the change: "To cover the same number of beats with two-man cars would have required 152 additional officers at an annual salary cost of $592,800. The increased preventive value of this more intensive patrol has been credited by the Kansas City department with a 19.7 per cent decrease in major crime and a 9.5 per cent increase in their clearance by arrest. Burglaries decreased 21 per cent and robbery clearances increased 20 per cent." [7] If properly used, the one-man patrol seems to increase and intensify police coverage of the city, reduces costs of squad-car operation, and does not, seemingly, jeopardize the safety of the officers if special procedures are used.

The police dog has been adopted by many departments in order to increase overall effectiveness. The interest of the police administrator in police dogs is indicated not only by their adoption in such cities as Chicago, St. Louis, Baltimore, and Washington, D.C., but also by the rather extensive bibliography that has been built up in police literature on the use of dogs in police work.

Dogs have been used in warfare since ancient times. Probably the first noteworthy instance of dogs' being used in police work was in the late nineteenth century when the Paris police department introduced them to help eliminate the notorious "Apaches," gangs of thugs that were roaming the streets. German cities soon followed the example of Paris. Although some comment on the European development resulted in the United States, American police departments were reluctant to use dogs.[8] In the 1930's

[6] *The Municipal Year Book 1965* (Chicago: ICMA), p. 426.

[7] Orlando W. Wilson, "Police Administration: Developments in 1954," *The Municipal Year Book 1955* (Chicago: ICMA), p. 404. Also see The President's Commission on Law Enforcement and Administration of Justice, *The Challenge of Crime in a Free Society* (Washington, D. C.: U. S. Government Printing Office, 1967), p. 117.

[8] See L. F. Fuld, "The Use of Police Dogs: A Summary," *Journal of Criminal Law and Criminology*, III (1912–13), 123–127.

British cities introduced police dogs as aids to patrol, and the British police have since become enthusiastic dog users. And so have most continental police departments.[9]

In the mid-1950's Baltimore became the first major American city to use dogs in police work. St. Louis then set up a canine corps by sending a group of policemen to London for training, and Chicago did likewise by using the St. Louis police department for initial training. Washington, D.C., hired a consultant from Scotland Yard to train its first canine corps. By 1966 about 200 police departments in the United States had used dogs.

The canine corps includes both dogs and men. Using German shepherds or Doberman pinschers, the police department assigns a dog to a patrolman, and both man and dog go through an intensive period of as many as twelve weeks of training. The dog is taught to recognize his master as the only authority in his life; he must obey his master implicitly, attack on command, search out evidence, and learn how to disarm bandits and how to hold a crowd at bay. On command of his master, the dog learns to enter a burning building, jump into a car and hold the occupants, go through plate-glass windows, scale fences and walls, and search out prowlers.[10] Virtually inseparable from his master, the dog is assigned to the patrolman on a permanent basis and lives at home with the patrolman and his family.

The very presence of a dog seems to be a deterrent to crime; the criminal has even been known to run to the policeman for protection from the dog! Most of the time on leash, the dog may be used either on foot or motor patrol. The Baltimore department claims that two policemen and their dogs can take the place of eight to ten patrolmen without dogs. Thus the effectiveness of the canine corps in police work has been rather thoroughly established. Still, dogs must be used with the greatest caution. As the President's Commission on Law Enforcement and Administration of Justice reported, "the use of dogs for routine patrol, especially in minority-group neighborhoods, tends to antagonize the community and may do more harm than good." [11]

Traffic direction and control, along with patrol, are major responsibilities of the city's police department. If E. B. White's remark that American cities are experiencing "death by motor car" seems an exaggeration, the traffic policeman at a busy intersection during rush hours is apt to agree that the automobile is more of an evil than a blessing. Automatic traffic control devices, good traffic engineering, and imaginative city planning can do much to reduce the hazards and the perplexities—and the expense

[9] C. F. Sloane, "Dogs in War, Police Work, and on Patrol," *Journal of Criminal Law, Criminology, and Police Science*, XLVI (September–October, 1955), 385–395.

[10] A dog in the St. Louis police department's canine corps pawed away ten pounds of frankfurters in order to reach eight packages of narcotics hidden behind the meat in a restaurant refrigerator. New York *Times*, August 5, 1962, p. 7.

[11] *Op. cit.*, p. 117.

—of traffic congestion, but it is a rare city indeed that has all three of these assets at once.

Much of the traffic problem is outside the authority of the police department. If an expressway is built into the center of the city and adds to the existing traffic glut, the police department can do little more than assign more men to the traffic division. An ambitious off-street parking program may become totally inadequate with the erection of a major new office building. A revolutionary program for downtown, such as the Gruen plan for Fort Worth, may elicit great excitement from lay and professional groups, but may be a long time coming. In other words, the police traffic division is faced with a situation which is controlled by factors largely outside its competence and which will grow worse instead of better. Whether in the downtown section or in any congested place in the city, the motorcar has yet to be controlled. Until it is, the police department must continue to spend a great deal of money and expend much manpower on a situation which it simply cannot command.

Fire Administration. The command situation in American fire departments is less complex than for the police. Because fire departments are less subject to political pressure, because corruption and dishonesty are less frequent (the fireman has no greater moral fiber than the policeman, but the temptations are far fewer!), because the administrative board has never been widely used in fire administration, the line of command runs easily from the chief executive through the fire chief to the lower echelons of command. Two or three exceptions to this general practice should, however, be noted. In commission-type cities a popularly elected commissioner may head the fire department or, as we have seen above, a public safety department. Many special-purpose fire districts exist on the fringes of our cities, and the line of command there runs from a governing board to the chief and on downward. Finally, the very considerable number of volunteer departments in small towns and rural areas are often both fire-fighting and social organizations. In them the command structure is inevitably rudimentary.

Under direct command of the fire chief there are various officers, depending upon the size of the city and the department. Whereas the chief himself, in the small city, is apt to be in charge of training, in the large city this essential duty will be assigned to an assistant chief. At this level of command, also, officers will be assigned to fire prevention communications (including fire alarm systems) and direction of the fire-fighting companies. The next lower rung of the ladder will be made up of nonheadquarters staff, principally the captains of the fire-fighting companies.

How these companies are organized, in terms of command, depends directly upon the number of companies in existence and, again, upon the size of the city. In the smaller cities each station houses only one company, and there needs to be no intermediary command between the company captains and the assistant chief for operations. In very large cities, however, a command position—that of the district chief—may be interposed between the station command and the assistant chief.

Proper distribution of the fire-fighting forces, both geographically and temporally, is essential to the safety of the city. Most cities of over 10,000 population distribute their fire-fighting equipment and personnel around the city in order to heighten its fire defenses. In the district stations is housed the city's basic fire-fighting instrument, the engine company. Equipped with trucks carrying fire hoses, pumps (portable and fixed), a variety of tools, small fire extinguishers and other fixtures, the company is the unit around which the city's fire-fighting organization is built. In addition, there is the ladder truck company, used for rescue work and for directing high-pressure water into the upper heights of buildings afire. Finally, the station house may contain auxiliary equipment: an ambulance with an inhalator for rescue work, a tanker truck to carry extra water for rural fires, and assorted standby apparatus.

There must also be a temporal deployment of fire forces, since the city's public safety positions must always be manned. The variety of methods used by cities in manning their fire defenses is beyond the scope of this text; suffice it to say that the proper distribution of personnel around the clock is one of the perennial problems of the fire service.

Just as patrol is the police department's most important crime-control technique, so inspection and other fire preventive activities are basic to the fire department's function. In business and industrial buildings, inspection not only helps to reduce hazards but acquaints fire personnel with the buildings, so that when and if fire breaks out, the building will not be entirely terra incognita to the firemen. Fire inspection serves, also, to educate the citizen in fire prevention measures and to make him conscious of the fire hazards to his property.

Personnel Problems of the Public Safety Forces

Given an adequate career service, without which good recruitment is virtually impossible, the personnel officer must work strenuously to seek out the young man who will undertake police and fire duty as his life's work. Contrary to popular concept, there is rarely a dearth of applicants for police or fire positions. But applicants must be very carefully screened: both services seem to have an attraction for erratic, unbalanced personalities of various types. Two examples will illustrate this point. In Connecticut, a small city finally traced a number of fires of mysterious origin to an arsonist who happened to be a volunteer member of the fire department. In an Illinois city, officials discovered that they had thirty-nine applicants for one opening in the police department. By exhaustive written and oral tests they reduced the field to two candidates. As a final safeguard, they required both contenders to submit to a polygraphic examination and found, to their consternation, that the likeliest candidate admitted having committed several robberies.

If police departments have been periodically afflicted with scandals, surely one reason is the inadequacy of recruitment. The undesirables simply have not been weeded out of the list of candidates before the hiring has begun. One of the most serious restrictions upon good recruiting is the residence requirement. Often by law, just as frequently by custom, only residents of the city may apply for positions in the fire or police departments. This is, of course, a luxury, and a luxury which the city can ill afford.

When a city can throw off the residence shackles, it can reach out widely for good candidates. Oakland, California, did this in 1959, when the civil service commission received 1,460 applications for police positions after a nationwide recruitment campaign. The New York police department has considered going into Puerto Rico to recruit Spanish-speaking policemen. These are costly measures, surely, but worth doing, if the political situation permits it.

One ambitious method of police recruitment which is fairly new to the American scene is the police cadet program. By this means the city recruits young men of eighteen to twenty-one years of age and appoints them cadets in the police department. Without the authority of a police officer and usually without a uniform (in short, not a member of the service but simply an acolyte to the "priesthood"!), the cadet is encouraged to enter the service as soon as he is out of high school. This is a matter of some importance. Many young men who are fine police material become involved in other occupations before they are twenty-one, the standard age for admission to the police service. The cadet program serves to bring them into the service, to train them, to indoctrinate them, to prepare them for a police career. In New York City the police cadets are encouraged to take college work in order better to fit themselves for a police career. This kind of program can easily be adapted to the fire service.

Good training is as important to the public safety departments as it is to an army in the field or to a naval fleet at sea. Yet it is still neglected, sadly so in many smaller cities, and for a variety of reasons. If a nineteenth-century attitude prevails in the city, there is little incentive to train police and fire personnel. If the city is penny-wise and pound-foolish, the new man is given a fog nozzle or a gun and fitted out with a uniform, and little else is considered necessary to make him a police officer or a fireman.

Training is most easily divided into two parts: the training of recruits and in-service training. In the larger cities, police and fire academies are maintained to give recruits rather exhaustive classroom and laboratory work before they are put on active duty. For the small department, such academies are too expensive to maintain, and the city must rely upon the large-city academies, the facilities of the state police and fire schools, or institutes maintained by colleges and universities. If none of these avenues is open, the department must rely upon its own resources, and these are usually inadequate.

In-service training includes refresher courses for the old hands, training in new techniques, training for promotion, and training for organization fitness. Because the old hands have often had little or no formal training, especially in the smaller cities, recruit training and the refresher courses may be combined.

This kind of training may be made available to police and fire personnel in a variety of ways. In the larger cities the police and fire academies will conduct in-service training, in addition to recruit training. And smaller cities, near at hand, may be able to take advantage of such academies. Correspondence courses are available to public safety officers, and so are short courses offered by universities, the state police, and professional organizations of firemen and policemen. The National Police Academy, operated by the Federal Bureau of Investigation, gives valuable aid to local police departments by training policemen for instructional duties in their own departments.

Discipline and morale are twin concerns in police and fire personnel matters. Without discipline, the uniformed services cannot properly combat the hazards to community life and property; and if they cannot, this inadequacy reflects immediately in lower morale. Essential to discipline is a clear-cut chain of command, which is usually achieved only if the departments are directed by professional men who report directly to the mayor or city manager. The chain of command, moreover, must not be destroyed by intrusion of extraneous authorities into it. This is particularly true of interference by civil service commissions or the courts into the command function. Both commissions and courts have shown a propensity to bedevil the higher commands of police departments, especially with frivolous restrictions upon the disciplinary prerogatives of the chief.

Closely allied to discipline and morale is the honesty of the members of the force. As we have already observed, the policeman is far more apt to be involved in scandals than the fireman, not because he has less moral fiber, but because he is faced with greater temptations. Most of America's greatest cities have had police scandals within the past quarter-century. The New York department has had frequent scandals; the departments in Detroit and Kansas City were infiltrated with criminal elements shortly after World War II; and Cleveland and Philadelphia were forced to take drastic steps to reform their departments in the early 1950's. But perhaps the greatest police scandal of the century came out of Chicago in early 1960.

There a petty thief disclosed that he had been working with a group of policemen in carrying out a series of robberies in which the police guarded the premises when they were being robbed, police cars were used to carry away stolen goods, and policemen received the stolen goods. As a result the entire police force was held up to ridicule, honest policemen along with the dishonest ones. After lengthy investigations, the city hired Orlando Wilson to head the department.

Why does corruption so plague the city's police service? An expert in police administration lays the blame on bad recruitment, civil service procedures guaranteed to produce mediocrity, judicial interference into departmental management, and bad state laws setting up residence requirements for new officers.[12] To this list might be added low salary scales, the widespread belief in some communities that the police are corrupt, and the inability of the police department to clean its own house.

Who will police the police? The police? The community? The civil service commission? Civic groups? The city council? All of these, surely, will do the job, but others will too, not the least of which is the special unit within the department to investigate the kind of job the police are doing. If the so-called Scotland Yard unit in the Chicago police department had not been abolished as a result of intradepartmental politics, the department might not have had to face its Armageddon in 1960. That it was reestablished upon Superintendent Wilson's becoming head of the department was an indication of the seriousness of the city's intent to reestablish the integrity of the Chicago police.[13]

Another personnel problem of considerable consequence in public safety is that of unionization. Now widely organized in various international unions or local associations, the police and firemen have gained recognition of sorts in most of the larger cities, though this recognition will not necessarily mean that the local organization bargains collectively or that there is a formal contract signed with the city. Depending upon how strong organized labor is in the city, the executive and council will enter into annual discussions with the police and firemen, much in the same manner that private management does with a trade union of industrial workers. Or they will very gingerly negotiate with the unions and at the same time seek to give the appearance of not negotiating. Or they will stand firmly upon the traditional position of the law and refuse to have anything whatever to do with any union or association of police and firemen. Yet, as Arthur Bromage remarks, "unions of employees are now an accepted fact in Amer-

[12] Virgil W. Peterson, "The Chicago Police Scandals," *Atlantic Monthly*, October, 1960, pp. 57–64.

[13] Although the civilian review board has been highly controversial (the New York City board was abolished by popular vote in 1966), some kind of unit to preven dishonest and offensive acts by the police seems necessary. See the President's Commission on Law Enforcement and Administration of Justice, *op. cit.*, p. 116.

ican cities. Cities cannot afford to take a position of attempting to discourage and prevent unionization or to seek a company-union type of organization under official supervision." [14]

Unions of police and firemen may operate at any one or all of three different levels:

1. As labor organizations using the standard weapons of economic warfare—strikes and threat of strikes, slowdowns, union or closed shop, and similar devices. The international unions eschew the right to strike; the union locals are not averse to use of a strike threat to strengthen their demands.

2. As political organizations using standard political techniques for gaining their objectives—lobbying, support of political organizations, overt support of local political activity. The policemen and firemen are adept at this kind of operation.

3. As a negotiating instrument for presenting employee viewpoints to management. Most unions and associations operate at this level, and it is in this activity that they have greatest acceptance.

There is general rejection of the first level of activity, in spite of the locals who seem to want to use the mailed fist. Since the disastrous Boston police strike of 1919, police unions or associations of police have been especially careful to give no appearance of wanting to strike. There have been, on the other hand, sporadic examples of the slowdown, as when the police, for example, refuse to make more than a token number of arrests for traffic and other offenses. In one instance, in a Midwestern city of 80,000, a relatively minor fire turned into a major one when the city firemen refused to fight the blaze alongside volunteer companies from outlying villages. The union agent, in fact, described these volunteer firemen as "scabs"! But firemen and policemen know that such tactics are bad publicity, and since everyone has become public-relations conscious these days, that is a telling argument against use of the traditional weapons of economic warfare.

Political activity is quite another matter. Over the past several decades, all unions have become more politically conscious, or at least more closely involved in political activity, than in the neutralist days of Samuel Gompers. Lobbying by policemen and firemen, or, if this is forbidden by law, by union representatives, is widespread. Police and firemen often find that the quickest way for them to gain an increase in wages and a decrease in hours of work is to lobby in the state legislature for a bill that forces municipalities to act. Unions may also contribute support, perhaps indirectly, to Democratic or Republican organizations or candidates in order to assure themselves of friends in high places.

The widespread use of popular democracy enables municipal employees

[14] Arthur W. Bromage, *Introduction to Municipal Government and Administration* (New York: Appleton-Century-Crofts, 2nd ed., 1957), p. 357.

to bypass executive and councilmanic authority to achieve objectives under charter, ordinance, or statute which they have been denied otherwise. And police and firemen's organizations are typical municipal employee groups, in this respect. The union locals which initiate and bring to a vote proposed ordinances or charter amendments that call for pay increases or a change in working conditions are operating at this level. When resistance by police and firemen to unification of the two services in Evanston, Illinois, forced the city to vote on whether to abandon council-manager government (a maneuver which the people rejected), police and firemen were taking the kind of direct political action they so often use.

Given enlightened city officials and intelligent union leadership, the third level of operation—acting as a negotiating instrument—can be productive for public and employee alike. The give and take between organized public safety employees and the city can result, among other things, in the identification and negotiation of disputes, a constant exchange of information and points of view which will keep disputes from arising, and a stimulus to employee morale. On the other hand, a suspicious relationship between the city and its organized employees can destroy the very spirit of confidence and mutual trust which the public employee union will have as one of its main objectives and which city officials will seek to stimulate.

Unification of the Police and Fire Functions

As we have already seen, in passing, the police and fire functions developed separately, not so much because of a basic incompatibility in administrative techniques as because of historical accident. As both services developed professionally, similarities showed up as frequently as differences. Both services have the primary objectives of *preventing* growth of hazards to the public safety; and prevention, whether of crime or fire, is dependent mostly upon persuasion, education, and compulsion of the mass of urban citizenry. The old hackneyed distinction between the two services—the fireman works with machines and physical structures, the policeman with people—never too valid, is becoming ever less so. Moreover, both policemen and firemen are uniformed members of a quasi-military organization and live in similar environments of command and discipline.

Both services have weighty responsibilities for equipment maintenance, communications, personnel, and record-keeping. Both must maintain a constant vigilance: the watch over the city must never cease. Both are concerned with enforcing city ordinances and state law and with ferreting out violations of them. When there is a fire, police control of crowds and traffic is an integral part of the fire-fighting process; when there is a riot, firemen hosing down the crowds may be the prime instrument of control.

As the services have developed similar administrative patterns of behavior, one in relation to the other, great internal dissimilarities within each department have shown themselves. Note the differences between the communications personnel and the laddermen, even though both are firemen. Note also the real void lying between the traffic policeman and the detective in the vice squad. In short, great internal differences lie alongside many external similarities.

If the similarities in the police and fire functions are stressed, the logic of that emphasis is to join the forces, either partially or completely. This a number of cities have done. By 1961 some seventy-three cities and villages in the United States and Canada, mostly with populations of under 50,000, had effected either partial or complete unification of their public safety operations.[15]

No major city had attempted unification (often described as "integration") until George Bean, the energetic, iconoclastic city manager of San Diego, announced that that city was embarking on such a program. Although San Diego was not successful in carrying out unification, it was the first large city to attempt it.

Whatever the merits of unification, the final answer to whether a city adopts it will be a political one. Indeed, the main reason for us to examine unification is to observe that however logical an administrative change may appear, politics is more important in its success or failure than logic. Since firemen, who seem to be more opposed to unification than policemen, can marshal political forces in both city hall and state capitol, they can attack unification city by city or statewide. If the citizen is uninterested in the controversy—and he usually seems to be—the minority force represented by the firemen and their allies is apt to carry the day.

The Third Degree: The Police and Civil Rights

It is surely axiomatic that the very men who enforce the law should themselves remain within the law. As with most axioms, however, expressing the generalization is easier than carrying it out. Just as the line between ethical and unethical conduct is to most people often fuzzy and blurred, so one finds it difficult, many times, to distinguish between legal and illegal police action.

Further complicating the situation is the fact that there are individual standards to consider. Justice is stern; compassion, sympathetic. Shall we give the suspected criminal *every* benefit of the doubt? This question will always perplex a society which wishes to temper justice with compassion.

[15] Howard I. Bruce, *PFI, A Survey: Police-Fire Integration in the United States and Canada* (Cleveland, Ohio: Cleveland Bureau of Governmental Research, October, 1961), pp. 6–8.

Too often the discussion of the police vis-à-vis civil rights descends to an emotional defense of two untenable positions: (1) that the policeman is a thug in uniform, and (2) that the policeman is a paragon of virtue who can rarely err. Leaving such positions to those who have only visceral reactions to the perplexities of civil rights, let us move to calmer, intermediate ground and attempt to describe the role of the professional policeman.[16]

This man—the professional—is a career public servant. He is trained in his profession, trained to have respect for the law and to view seriously his role as protector of society from those who would prey upon it. If, in the passion of the moment, he acts outside the law, he does not expect the public, perhaps, to condone the act, but he does expect it, at least, to understand some of his problems. He is moved to anger, sometimes to cynicism, by those people who seem to have great charity for the accused but none for the police.

Indeed, nowadays many a professional policeman is worried over what he considers a serious deterioration in the public's determination to defend society against social marauders. It sometimes seems to him that a highly vocal minority among laymen and judges are not only interfering with tried and true police methods but are, as well, confounding the very aims of justice. When crime is apparently on the increase, he will ask, is it safe or desirable to weaken the police?

What is the rebuttal to this position? Let us look at the basic rights of those who are accused of crime. The federal Constitution and most of the state constitutions assure the accused of the right to counsel, to a speedy and public trial, to habeas corpus and protection against self-incrimination, to be free of cruel and unusual punishments and unreasonable searches and seizures. In some jurisdictions, trial by a jury of one's peers and indictment by grand jury are considered basic safeguards for those accused of serious crime.

These rules are not new; older than the republic itself, they were known in colonial times and were introduced into some of the first state constitutions. The police have always lived with them, and for the most part within them. Why are the police suddenly worried that their position is being weakened? A part of the reason centers around procedure and a part around the public regard for the police.

From the moment a crime is conceived until the criminal is arrested and convicted, the police are committed by law and by professional standards to act. But in a democratic society the policeman apprehends the accused; he does not also serve as judge and jury. In looking for evidence and in mak-

[16] A comprehensive but succinct exposition of the police role may be found in Nelson A. Watson, "The Police and Human Relations," *The Municipal Year Book 1965* (Chicago: ICMA), pp. 415–422.

ing arrests, he is limited by a considerable body of law built around the prohibition against unreasonable searches and seizures. To safeguard the innocent and to insure against the policeman's setting himself up as a punishing agent, the law forbids the use of methods which will extract involuntary confessions. Thus any physical violence—the so-called third degree —or such other methods as threats, illegal promises, prolonged confinement, or interrogation are not to be used.

An important case having a bearing on these general rules is the Mallory decision of the U.S. Supreme Court, which has caused more than a flurry of dissent in police circles. The police of Washington, D.C., arrested Mallory on suspicion of having committed a heinous crime and held him for twenty-four hours without bringing him before a magistrate for arraignment. Upon conviction in a lower court, Mallory appealed to the U.S. Supreme Court, which ruled that because the police did not take Mallory promptly before a magistrate for arraignment, his conviction should be set aside.[17] The Court cited a federal rule requiring the arresting officer to take a suspect before a judge for arraignment "without unnecessary delay." Obviously, to the majority of the Court, holding Mallory for twenty-four hours was an unnecessary delay.

Why should the police find this decision objectionable? Should not the individual, when taken into custody, have the right to consult counsel and the right to an immediate preliminary hearing? Should he not be given the opportunity to regain his freedom on bail? Will not undue restraint, in and of itself, serve as a means of forcing a confession from him?

The police position in these questions is rather simple and straightforward: when a person is suspected of a serious crime, the police should be able to hold him for a reasonable time. And this means time enough to interrogate the suspect thoroughly in private. They would insist that the Mallory decision errs in several aspects: (1) it would, if followed, hamper police investigation of serious crimes; (2) it would demand of the police that they interrupt their investigation to bring the suspect into court before they had had time even to establish a preliminary case; (3) it indicates a lack of confidence in the good faith and professional standards of the police; and (4) at the very time when crime is increasing, it indicates a lack of appreciation by the courts of the practical necessities of police administration in general and crime detection in particular. Just as we would not attempt to instruct judges on the technicalities of the law, say the police, so judges should not set aside our professional judgment on how to solve serious crimes.

The Supreme Court, furthermore, has showed itself disposed to follow

[17] *Mallory* v. *U.S.*, 354 U.S. 449 (1957); also see *McNabb et al.* v. *U.S.*, 318 U.S. 332 (1943).

the trend set in *Mallory* (and earlier in *McNabb*) by its decisions in *Escobedo* v. *Illinois* and *Miranda* v. *Arizona*.[18] Widely recognized as announcing a change in constitutional doctrine, *Escobedo* and *Miranda* have been both loudly condemned as a further assault by the Court on legitimate police practices and warmly praised as a safeguard to human dignity. Once again, procedure is at the heart of the controversy. Just as *Mallory* made clear that the Court would view with askance any "unnecessary delay" before arraignment, so *Escobedo* and *Miranda* showed the Court willing to insist that an accused be given the right to consult counsel before arraignment and indeed during the interrogation process itself. Since the police have long used the confession as an important tool in bringing criminals to justice, the critics of those decisions have seen them as a death blow to legitimate interrogation and another judicial obstacle to effective police performance. Whether they are either of these is uncertain. Perhaps society will have to live with the change for ten years to find out.[19]

The Police and Minority Groups

According to one observer, the police in Spanish Harlem are seen as "colonial troops of an unsympathetic government." And the National Advisory Commission on Civil Disorders cites the "deep hostility" between minority groups and the police as a primary cause of racial disorders.[20] But if the police are viewed with hostility by the ghetto residents of urban America, and if this ill-will has been a primary cause of riots, the police may still be only incidentally to blame for the disenchantment which the minority group member feels toward the city. Indeed, suggests the Kerner Commission, the policeman is merely the symbol of the society which, thinks the Negro or the Spanish-American, has treated him badly. The policeman, whether he is a good cop or bad, is tangible representation to the ghetto citizen of the system which frustrates him, keeps him to menial jobs (if indeed it permits him a job at all), treats him to assembly-line justice, and denies him that upward social mobility of which American society has so long been proud.

As part and symbol of that social system from which the ghetto citizen is increasingly alienated, the policeman's role is "one of the most difficult in our society." [21] Although he cannot solve the social ills that make Negroes

[18] 378 U.S. 478 (1964), and 384 U.S. 436 (1966).

[19] A monographic treatment of *Escobedo* and the whole problem of use of confessions in law enforcement may be found in "Developments in the Law—Confessions," *Harvard Law Review*, LXXIX (March, 1966), 935–1119.

[20] Dan Wakefield, *Island in the City* (Boston: Houghton Mifflin Co., 1959), p. 118; and The National Advisory Commission on Civil Disorders, *Report* (New York: Bantam Books, Inc., 1968), p. 299. Since Governor Otto Kerner of Illinois was chairman of this commission, it is commonly known as the Kerner Commission.

[21] *Ibid.*, p. 300.

and other minority groups so bitter, he can do much to ease the burdens which the ghetto citizens carry, and in doing that also lessen his own burdens. The Kerner Commission has suggested changes in police practices that could move the city toward achievement of such goals.

First, according to the commission, there is basic need for changes in police conduct and patrol practices. Officers with bad reputations in the ghetto should be transferred out, and officers sympathetic to minority-group problems should be brought in. Officers in the ghetto should be trained to understand the culture of the people with whom they associate. Above all, they should get to know the ghetto: bring the patrolman out of the car and into the neighborhood, advised the commission. If necessary, the city might give extra promotion credits and bonuses to the policeman on the beat in the ghetto. Like the ghetto teacher in the school system, the ghetto policeman too often represents the dregs of the department.

A second change of basic importance is to give the ghetto neighborhoods more adequate police protection than has existed in the past. Although it may seem paradoxical to call for more police protection for people who often seem to regard the squad car as an ill wind that blows no good, the Kerner Commission found that it was precisely because minority-group members felt neglected by the police that they increased their hostility toward the protective services. No more effective way of lessening minority-group resentment of police could be introduced than by increasing police protection.

Improving grievance machinery is still another change that could help both the citizen in the ghetto and the police. Not even the best-run internal review agency can build community confidence in the department or protect the police against groundless complaints. The commission insisted, therefore, that some kind of external review board should have jurisdiction over citizen grievances against the police.

A fourth basic change in police practices recommended by the commission is the development of clear guidelines to assist the officer in carrying out his duties. These guidelines should cover those types of activities that are most apt to cause resentment among ghetto residents: investigative methods, such as "stop-and-frisk" techniques; when to make arrests and when to use alternatives to the arrest; and how to handle minor disputes, such as those that arise between husband and wife, or landlord and tenant.

Finally, the commission found that much needed to be done to increase community support for law enforcement. If most policemen in a black ghetto are white, this circumstance alone is apt to be a "dangerous irritant," and so most departments need to increase their efforts to recruit Negro and other minority-group members. The departments need also to review promotion policies to see if they can increase the number of minority-group officers in command positions. Just as important is the need for the police to become involved in community service functions, ranging from the reporting of dirty streets to the disclosure of building code violations. Because such services are nonpolice in nature and because departments suffer from chronic manpower shortages, the police have resisted taking them on. But the commission found performance of such services essential to the building up of community support for the police in the ghetto.

Such is the gist of the recommendations of the Kerner Commission. After reviewing a mass of evidence, the members of the commission thought that these reforms would do much to improve relations between minority-group members and the police, and would make the burdens of life in the ghetto considerably easier to bear. Although basic social maladjustments such as joblessness might still remain, the reforms could well make the ghetto resident less inclined than formerly to vent his frustration upon the policeman; and that change in attitude would undoubtedly be to the benefit of the neighborhood, the police department, and the entire urban polity.

Many cities will, of course, be unable to achieve the consensus necessary to make such reforms as those recommended by the Kerner Commission. Others, arriving at the necessary consensus, will find that they simply cannot finance the implementation of the consensus without substantial state and federal aid. Congressional recognition of this obstacle came in 1968 with the passage of the omnibus crime control bill. Under the terms of that legislation, federal grants of $100 million were to be given state and local police forces in fiscal 1969, and $300 million in fiscal 1970. Although such aid was doubtless insufficient, it gave an earnest of Congressional intent to come to the aid of the urban public safety function and offered city leadership increased opportunity for implementing the reforms recommended by the Kerner Commission.

Annotated Bibliography

Undoubtedly the most important single publisher in the United States of books on police science is Charles C Thomas, Publisher, 301–327 E. Lawrence Avenue, Springfield, Illinois. The most readily current bibliographies relating to both police and fire matters are to be found in *The Municipal Year Book* (Chicago: International City Managers' Association).

There are three widely accepted textbooks on police administration: Orlando W. Wilson, *Police Administration* (New York: McGraw-Hill Book Co., 1950); International City Managers' Association, *Municipal Police Administration* (Chicago: The Association, 1961); and Bruce Smith, *Police Systems in the United States* (New York: Harper & Bros., 1960).

A good perspective on a rapidly spreading technique of policing is given in Samuel G. Chapman, *Dogs in Police Work: A Summary of Experience in Great Britain and the United States* (Chicago: Public Administration Service, 1960). Another kind of perspective, this time on police matters in general, may be obtained from an annual publication of the International Association of Chiefs of Police, *The Police Yearbook*.

The never-never land in public safety is occupied by the departments which combine the police and fire protective functions. The two definitive monographs on this type of department, both by Charles S. James and both published in Chicago by the Public Administration Service, are *A Frontier of Municipal Safety* (1956) and *Police and Fire Integration in the Small City* (1955). Also of value are Howard I. Bruce, *PFI, A Survey: Police-Fire Integration in the United States and Canada* (Cleveland, Ohio: Cleveland Bureau of Governmental Research, 1961); and *The Case for Better Utilization of Fire Manpower* (San Diego, Calif.: Office of the City Manager, 1961).

The standard textbook on the operation of the fire service is the International City Managers' Association, *Municipal Fire Administration* (Chicago: The Association, 1956). Excellent bibliographies on the police and fire services may be found in *The Municipal Year Book* issued annually by the International City Managers' Association.

A comprehensive review of the problems which arise when public employees organize and strike may be found in Sterling D. Spero, *Government as Employer* (New York: Remsen Press, 1948). Chapters 11 and 12 of this book are devoted to firemen and policemen. Unionization and collective bargaining in the public service are two important items treated at length in Kenneth O. Warner (ed.), *Management Relations with Organized Public Employees* (Chicago: Public Personnel Association, 1963).

Since the police have been of foremost topical interest during the 1960's, a wealth of material has appeared on police and community relations. Two books by professional police officers are J. E. Curry and Glen D. King, *Race Tensions and the Police* (Springfield, Ill.: Chas. C Thomas, 1962); and Juby E. Towler, *The Police Role in Racial Conflicts* (Springfield, Ill.: Chas. C Thomas, 1964). Professor Jerome H. Skolnick has produced an excellent sociological study of police problems. See Jerome H. Skolnick, *Justice Without Trial: Law Enforcement in Democratic Society* (New York: John Wiley & Sons, 1966). For a British view of police illegality, see Stuart Bowes, *The Police and Civil Liberties* (London: Lawrence and Wishart, 1966). A number of perceptive comments on the police role in society may be found in "A Symposium on the Supreme Court and the Police: 1966," *The Journal of Criminal Law, Criminology and Police Science*, LVII (September, 1966), 237–311. Finally, two notable discussions of the police function have come from presidential commissions: The President's Commission on Law Enforcement and Administration of Justice, *The Challenge of Crime in a Free Society* (Washington, D.C.: U.S. Government Printing Office, 1967), and The National Advisory Commission on Civil Disorders, *Report* (New York: Bantam Books, Inc., 1968).

CHAPTER 17

The City's Health

St. Paul once had a few words to say to St. Timothy on an important matter of health. "Do not drink water," he advised, "but partake of wine for thy stomach's sake." Although he did not understand the reasons for it, he was astute enough to see the connection between his consuming a pitcher of water and subsequent illness of one kind or another. Thus, as a practical matter, one did not drink water. Even before the days of St. Paul, however, the urban dweller had an abiding concern with the supply of pure water in goodly quantity. It was this concern, indeed, that led the Romans into achieving one of their great engineering triumphs: the aqueducts which still may be seen in many parts of the old Roman world. The Roman city was probably better supplied with quantities of good water than a majority of the cities of the Western world during the nineteenth century.

What Is Public Health?

If water has been the concern of cities for millennia, it was probably not regarded as a central health problem until the late nineteenth century. Water was regarded rather as a practical household necessity; as an essential element in fighting fires, long the scourge of cities; even as necessary for civic art—note the fountain in the public square. Water presented engrossing engineering problems: finding dependable sources and piping great quantities over considerable distances into the cities. Water had military considerations, too, for how could you defend a city if the enemy were permitted to cut off the water supply? But until 1875 water could as easily be a menace to the city's health as an advantage.

Water could not become an unmixed blessing to the city until its purity could be assured, and such assurance hinged upon the development of medical science. Furthermore, medicine had to assume a social role and a social interest or application, and it was probably not until after 1875 that it did so. As soon as scientific capabilities had reached the point of identifying the various microorganisms in water, and medicine had connected certain of these waterborne organisms with various diseases, the city's water supply became immediately of vital concern to the city's health. Maintaining the purity of the water supply in the city became fully as important as getting the water there in the first place.

Urban wastes were also an early concern. Although the Romans were as anxious to rid the city of garbage as of human offal, their concern was probably largely esthetic and olfactory. The Romans were not, however, wholly oblivious to the connection between public cleanliness and health. Sextus Julius Frontinus (circa A.D. 40–104), who was in A.D. 97 appointed water commissioner of Rome by the Emperor Nerva, showed great satisfaction in his book *The Aqueducts of Rome* in having left Rome cleaner than he had found her and less subject to widespread disease than she had previously been.

In the ancient city, public health grew out of a union between engineering and public administration. In today's city, particularly in the Western world, public health represents a mating of engineering, medicine, public administration, and many other professional interests. In the American city the citizen commonly assumes that the city's health is protected by the department of health, and that is all there is to it. Yet there is hardly an agency within the city that is not concerned, at one time or another, with health matters. Municipal codes that are essential to the city's health include housing, building, plumbing, electrical, fire protection, health and safety, and many others. And involved in the enforcement of these codes will be the departments of health, public safety, public relations, engineering, sanitation, utilities, law, finance, and the office of the chief executive. If a good game of tennis is to be thought of as a contributor to better physical and mental health, why should not even the department of parks and recreation be included in this list of "health" agencies? Nor can the important role of the schools be ignored, for everything from the child's vaccination for smallpox to his indoctrination in basic health practices will redound to the advantage of the city's health, both present and future.

Up to this point we have observed the wide scope of public health without precisely defining it. Although the boundaries of public health may be variously drawn by various people, there is a general consensus among authorities as to its approximate extent. The elements involved in this consensus are:

1. *Environmental health*—assuring the city of an adequate supply of pure water, pure food and air, adequate housing, and an acceptable standard of public cleanliness (including waste disposal and insect and rodent control).

2. *Control of communicable diseases, and the prevention of disease, accidents, and disabilities*—control and elimination of epidemics; industrial, home, highway, and other accidents; various mental and personality disorders; addiction to the use of drugs and alcohol.

3. *Public education.*

4. *Health policy formation and administration*—enactment or modernization of codes and statutes bearing upon the public health, and their

adequate enforcement; health and financial planning; political action by health groups and citizen action associations; and the further development of intergovernmental and intragovernmental relations.

5. *Research*—investigation into the social and political as well as biological hazards to the community's health.

The Politics of Health

That "socialized medicine" has been widely debated during recent years is evident to everyone who has given more than a casual glance at the popular press. Thus has a health issue intruded into political discussion. And yet this debate represents only a small part of the politics of health, for the urban community is constantly faced with the necessity of forming public policy in regard to health.

Public health measures are invariably opposed or supported by numerous interest groups in the city, whether in American cities or in those abroad. When the British Parliament in 1854 refused to extend the life of the Public Health Act of 1848, Shaftesbury bitterly identified the various pressure groups that had sought its demise. These were the civil engineers, the College of Physicians, the boards of guardians, influential men in the treasury, the agents of the water companies, and many other groups—all offended because their economic interests had been hurt, their professional pride flouted, their political power weakened. Even the *Times* opined that people would rather take their chances with cholera than be bullied into health.[1]

Health, like education, constantly poses explosive political issues in every city in the land. Let us look at the ways in which those issues are posed and met.

The Phenomenon of Public Ambivalence. During the latter part of the nineteenth century and even into the early years of the twentieth, scientific techniques in public health still lagged behind the political ones. But as the twentieth century has proceeded, science has gone ahead by leaps and bounds while politics, political processes, and even our knowledge of politics of the urban community have moved ahead slowly if at all. As science has leapfrogged into the future, the politics of the 1960's remain just about where they were in 1900. Although the public seems virtually to worship science in the abstract, it has a peculiar ambivalence toward the application of science in the city. There are at least two reasons for this ambivalence.

In the first place, the private concern with individual health matters, almost a fetish at times, seems to be foreshortened and vaguely represented in

---

[1] George Rosen, *A History of Public Health* (New York: MD Publications, 1958), p. 223.

the public arena. Physicians have a higher status in our society probably than any other professional group; vast sums of money are spent for medical services; the family without some kind of health insurance is not only exceptional but in some circles regarded as socially and intellectually marginal; and the citizen groups devoted to the pursuit of some health objective are almost legion. For all that, the public views politics and health as separate phenomena which can never be joined except in a discussion of socialized medicine or Medicare. Bring a health problem into the public arena, and the monolithic view of the great mass of citizens toward matters of private and individual health becomes a series of conflicting viewpoints. Or, to put it another way, a monistic value system rapidly is transmuted into a pluralistic one.

A second reason for public ambivalence may be found in the administrative system. Whether the administrative system causes the ambivalence or the ambivalence comes to fruition in the administrative system would be impossible to establish. But we do not need to worry over the problem of cause and effect. In the politics and administration of community health we can easily find concrete evidence of public ambivalence. Do political leaders (mayor, city manager, councilmen, and health officers—who are in politics whether they want it or not) propose a new health code? It is not unlikely that a group of landlords are immediately up in arms over the code's violation of their sacred property rights. Does the majority voice in city hall speak for an ambitious sewer program to eliminate septic tanks? Neighborhood groups shortly organize to oppose an increase in taxes, and the vigor of their opposition is directly proportional to the size of the special assessment. Does the proposed annual budget contain provision for an increase in the staff of the health department? Protests arise over putting additional snoopers on the public payroll. The individual citizen, like the *Times* a hundred years ago, will not be bullied into good health! Such is the citizen's ambivalence, however, that he will be meek as a lamb when receiving a stern warning concerning his own health from his private physician.

Patterns in the Politics of Health. Late in the 1950's a neighborhood group in a Midwestern city petitioned the city council for sanitary sewers in order to get rid of septic tanks in the area. On the recommendation of the chief health officer and the city manager, the council instructed the city attorney to draw up a resolution providing for a special-assessment district. Although no overt opposition to the group's petition had appeared, as soon as the council took the first official step toward the levy of a special assessment, an opposition appeared in force. Some people asked to have their names withdrawn from the petition; others remained favorable to the project but expressed grave fears about the cost. (The people in the neighborhood, incidentally, were essentially middle income; the houses and grounds were generally above the modest level, and a few were even spacious; and there was scarcely an automobile in the area that was more than two years old.)

The more vigorous members of the opposition brought out a counterpetition and presented it to the next session of the city council. The council received a draft of the special-assessment resolution from the city attorney; a member introduced it; and it passed on first reading. But every councilman assured the public that the resolution would not be further acted on until a thorough investigation had been made of the case.

The political argument now shifted back to the neighborhood, and both proponents and opponents began sponsoring coffees, cocktail parties, and public meetings in the nearby grade school. (Because of this new preoccupation of the neighborhood, attendance at PTA meetings fell off drastically!) The opponents hired a lawyer, and the proponents brought in a college professor who had written a book on the special assessment. Republicans and Democrats, who had been able to remain on the best of terms throughout presidential elections, now found themselves unable to bear the sight of each other. Even the children took up the cudgels, and there was a fight or two in the schoolyard between childish proponents and opponents of the health project.

After many months of controversy the issue was finally resolved, and the sewers were installed. But it took many months more for the wounds to heal, and there were some friendships that were never reestablished. Many people from other parts of the city regarded the whole controversy with amusement, but not so the active participants in it. The farther one is from a political fight, the more one can be disengaged. But in the neighborhood itself there are no neutrals.

Citizen activity of this kind is typical of the American city. It is, indeed, a part (though only a part) of the pattern that health politics assumes.

The politics of health may take the character of a neighborhood engagement, or it may be citywide; or it may involve the urban community out to its farthest reaches, as when an extensive special sewer district is proposed. An ad hoc group (or groups) may constitute the hub of the activity, as with the example described immediately above, or the hub may be a permanently organized citizens' society (or a professional one, like the county medical society). Health politics stands at the heart of issue politics, described in a Chapter 13. In addition, it takes on the character of issue politics in almost every community in which it appears.

The nature of local government organization, as well as citizen activity, helps establish the pattern of health politics in the community. Here, as in the many other instances we have seen previously, the manner in which the urban community is organized puts its stamp upon political behavior. The health district is the most numerous of all special districts which furnish urban services; thus these health districts contribute materially to the functional and geographic disintegration of the urban community. There is the health district itself, which furnishes most of the standard services offered by the city health department, but which is a separate and independent governmental entity. And then there are the water, sewer, drainage, and mosquito abatement districts, and many more. As a governmental entity each district is also a political entity. Within each district there grows up a power clique, jealous of its individuality and autonomy and ready to defend its integrity with any kind of political stratagem. The district board itself, whether appointive or elective, mans the bastions to turn aside all attacks upon the district's independence, attacks from either within or without.

Pressure group activity is a third form of behavior which puts its stamp upon health politics. Contractors and engineering firms, banks and bond houses—all have powerful influence upon the health politics of the community. If they cannot help make policy in the larger cities, they certainly can and do in some of the smaller ones. A bond house or an engineering firm—or the two in concert—may agree with the council to do about everything but cast the votes in a bond election in order to get the city's business: preliminary engineering, public relations, managing the campaign for approval of the bond issue, advertising and selling the bonds, and then installation of the improvement itself. Although this practice may not be necessarily nefarious, it can result in dishonesty; and it will inevitably result in an outside pressure group's having an inordinate amount of power over policy formation.

With the special district the opportunity for undesirable pressure group activity increases manyfold. Although the facts are difficult to come by, there is no question but that legal firms, bond houses, banks, and engineering firms actively sponsor the formation of special districts in order to increase business. So lax are many of the state laws dealing with special-district organization that it takes but a handful of citizens, tutored by a friendly lawyer and engineer, to set up a district and issue a million or so dollars in bonds.

The adjacent city, without adequate extraterritorial power and with totally inadequate power to annex territory, must often sit by in frustration while enormities are perpetuated in its urban fringe. (The county usually cannot or will not help.) Such was the case in Boulder, Colorado, when a special water district was organized and a water system installed which was little more than a piece of shoddy. After the subdivider, the engineering firm, and the bond house had taken their profits and departed, the district wanted to connect into the city's system. Imagine the consternation of the citizens when city officials told them that they would need to dig up their whole system and install new pipe. The mains and laterals were plastic and would not nearly sustain the standard pressure in the city mains!

Business and professional firms are not alone in exerting undue influence upon the urban community in respect to health matters. State and federal agencies often intrude, and not necessarily to the advantage of the urban place. State and federal programs tend to be disjointed; the governments seem to take literally the Biblical injunction not to let the right hand know what the left hand is doing. If state and federal agents cannot coerce, they can at least persuade, cajole, promote, and offer rewards in order to influence local public policy. In Illinois the state health department has for years actively sponsored the setting up of water and sewer districts, and in doing so it has added greatly to the already complicated governing structure of many an urban community.

Sometimes state and federal pressures result in particularly ludicrous situations. Take the matter of stream pollution. The state health agency has for years been trying, without noticeable results, to persuade City X to put in a sewage treatment plant. So in exasperation the agency issues a cease-and-desist order against the city. Acting under the order the city council offers a bond issue to the people, and it fails. What happens now?

A federal agency steps in and gets a federal court order directing the city to stop polluting the stream, since the pollution adversely affects interstate commerce. Once again, as required by law, the city council submits the bond issue, and once again the majority votes against it.

Or take the case of federal grants-in-aid for the construction or extension of sewage treatment plants. The mayor and council resolve unanimously to seek a grant for City X even though several of the members are accustomed to inveigh against excessive federal spending. Is this an inconsistency? Perhaps it is, but we must remember that city hall politicians tend to be eminently pragmatic and like to save their ideological dialogues for state and national politics.

The City Health Department

As we have already observed in some detail, the city's health depends upon many if not most of the city's administrative agencies. Even so, the health department itself is of central importance, and its organization is of significance to this discussion.

Looking around us, we can find that the health agency is situated in one of five places in the local governing structure. It may be an operating department within the city government, as it is in most of the major and secondary cities in the United States. For smaller urban places a county health department meets the public health needs of both city and farm areas. Still another way in which the health department is organized is to have one foot in the city and one in the county. In Michigan and Colorado, for example, the city-county health department, tied to both local governments, is of paramount importance. Sometimes, in this arrangement, the school district may also be intimately involved.

The fourth method of situating the health department governmentally is to give it operating status within the single government which controls the neighborhood or the metropolis. Thus, in Arlington and Fairfax counties, Virginia (which are really cities except in name), and in the Nashville metropolitan area, the health departments are units of the single governments which exist in those communities. And, finally, there is the health department which is a single-purpose authority, which has its own governing board and taxing power, and which is independent of the other local governments in the urban community.

These are the five principal styles of organization. Seemingly different setups in individual communities are apt to be nothing more than variations upon these five main styles. Having reviewed how the health department is situated in the local governmental structure, we are now prepared to address ourselves to the question: What functions do health departments usually perform?

One may see at a glance from Figure 17-1 the usual duties assigned the health department in the American community. The divisional duties

Figure 17-1. Organization of the Local Health Department

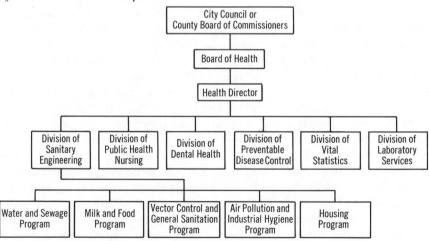

Source: Adapted from U.S. Department of Health, Education, and Welfare, U.S. Public Health Service, *Environmental Health Planning Guide, PHS Publication No. 823* (no date), p. 7.

might be described as the "basic six" of the health program. But these functions must not be thought of as exhausting all the possible activities of the department. Some cities—Denver is one example—operate departments of health and hospitals. And other functions that have been coming to the fore are mental health, safety and accident prevention, and occupational health.[2] Even noise control has become important to health.

The Central Health Functions

As we have already seen, many of the central health functions are administered outside the health department itself. We shall therefore conclude our discussion of the city's health with a discussion which is functionally rather than administratively oriented.

Water Supply. The Technical and Engineering Tasks. To meet its needs for water the city must develop a plentiful source of good, potable water; find means of conveying the water to the city; and then treat it and distribute it to the consumer. For most cities the sources of water fall into one of two categories: ready-made or developed. Fortunate indeed is the city which has plentiful fresh water close by. The city which lies near a large freshwater lake or river needs only to plan an adequate system of pumps to get the water to the filtration plants.

Without the nearby freshwater lake or major stream, the city must develop its supply. Even in regions where rainfall is plentiful, the city must dam up small streams and create reservoirs, or dig a system of wells to tap the ground waters.

For coastal cities or cities in desert or arid regions, developing and maintaining adequate sources of water is a never-ending perplexity. The first American cities to launch ambitious water-development schemes were those on the East Coast: Boston, New York, Baltimore, and Philadelphia. Because there were fewer deaths from the cholera epidemic of 1832 in Philadelphia than in other coastal cities (New York and Quebec, for example), the Philadelphia water system received considerable attention from other cities. Although no one really understood the connection between pure water and a low death rate from cholera, there was a vague feeling that some cause-and-effect relationship must exist. As a result, New Yorkers were spurred on in their efforts to install what was to become one of the most famed of the nineteenth-century water supply systems, the Croton reservoir and aqueduct. The efforts of coastal cities mounted in intensity during the last half of the nineteenth century and the first half of the twentieth, and for the most part the money expended was on developing sources in the

---

[2] International City Managers' Association, *Administration of Community Health Services* (Chicago: ICMA, 1st ed., 1961), p. 31.

hinterlands, wherever fresh water could be found. But recently the efforts have taken a new tack—the desalinization of seawater. Although fresh water has been derived from the sea since time immemorial, the problem for the coastal city is to find a method by which the conversion can be done economically.

For the desert city or the city in a semiarid region, the principal task for the political leaders may be to see to it that water is diverted from agricultural to urban purposes. Tucson uses about 50,000 acre-feet of water annually, all of it drawn from wells. About 14,000 acres of nearby irrigated lands, largely devoted to growing cotton and employing fewer than 1,500 people, uses the same amount of water. This irrigation water would supply all the needs (domestic, industrial, and mining) of an additional 200,000 urban dwellers.[3]

If Tucson cannot draw water away from agricultural uses, it will attempt other means of expanding its water sources. In 1963 construction of a pilot plant was begun at the city's sewage treatment works to explore the feasibility of reclaiming waste water for domestic and other uses. Assuming that the experiment succeeds, we can safely say that the only other problem that will remain for Tucson and other cities will be to convince their citizens that the purified waste water is perfectly good when it comes out of the kitchen faucet! [4]

Conveyance of water from source to city may require dramatic and costly engineering feats, as noted in Chapter 5. Both the drama and expense may still be seen, for instance, in the two millennia old Roman aqueducts. The treatment and distribution of water within the city are major tasks which begin as soon as the water reaches the treatment plant. If the origin of the water is deep wells, very little purification or other treatment will be necessary. But if the source is a lake or more particularly a river, the water must first be treated chemically so that foreign matter in suspension may settle out in sedimentation tanks. After sedimentation the water must be run through sand filters. Water containing a high content of iron and manganese must usually be aerated in order to oxidize the undesirable minerals. In some instances, where the water is particularly hard, cities introduce water softening into the treatment process.

To assure the purity of the water when it comes from the consumer's tap, chlorine is usually added to the liquid before it leaves the treatment plant. And recently, as an additional health measure to reduce tooth decay, the

[3] Andrew W. Wilson, "Urbanization of the Arid Lands," *Arizona Review of Business and Public Administration*, March, 1961, pp. 7–9.
[4] In water-hungry Israel, sewage water is being reused. S. Z. Hershkovitz and A. Feinmesser, "Sewage Reclaimed for Irrigation in Israel Farm Oxidation Ponds," *Wastes Engineering*, XXXIII (August, 1962), 405, 416, 421. Bakersfield, California, grows corn, sugar beets, and other crops with 8,480 acre-feet of effluent. T. M. Scott, "Effluent Grows Crops on 'Sewer Farm,' " *Wastes Engineering*, XXX (September, 1959), 486–489.

city has often added fluorides to the water (and, just as often, thereby stirred up a political hornet's nest).

Politics and Planning of Water. We have already seen some of the political controversies that arise throughout the whole field of public health. In this section, therefore, we will particularize about water politics and planning.

Planning the city's water supply requires a long-range viewpoint, a good deal of technical skill (both engineering and financial), much political savoir faire, and a great deal of good luck. The 1910 water plan for Vienna envisaged a population of 4,000,000 in 1940 and a daily consumption of 100 liters per person. The plan did not contemplate two major wars in both of which the Viennese would be on the losing side. But, more importantly, it did not anticipate the spectacular rise in water consumption by each urban dweller. (Many an American water plan went aground on the same statistic.) By 1963 the city's population of 1,630,000 was consuming more water than the 4,000,000 people anticipated by the plan for 1940. The only factor that saved the plan was a radically lower population figure than was anticipated.[5]

American cities find adequate planning for the future an exceedingly perilous enterprise. Population estimates, for one thing, are dubious pegs to hang a plan on. And who is to say, even if the population remains stable, how much water each urban dweller will need (and waste) twenty years hence? Urban councils have an unstable membership. And urban executives—mayors and city managers—also come and go.

The citizenry at large may also find it hard to look very far into the future. Will the people approve a $10 million bond issue to develop new sources of water that will not be needed, if even at all, for a decade or two? When water at present is in plentiful supply, will the people put up the hard, cold cash to provide for a margin for error or a margin for future safety?

Or how can the city anticipate the actions of the state and federal governments? Traditionally, the concern of the Colorado Water Conservation Board was with the supply of irrigation water for agricultural uses. By the beginning of the 1960's the board's interest had changed from irrigation to urban water supply. Even so, just how much help from the state the cities of Colorado can expect is anybody's guess, and the guess of the planner is probably no better than that of the average citizen.

It is equally difficult to plan on future action by the federal government. The federal Water Supply Act of 1958 authorized the Corps of Engineers and the Bureau of Reclamation to include urban water supply as a desirable element in federally supported water projects. But if this assures the

[5] *Local Government Abroad*, No. 6 (July, 1963), 6–7.

cities of aid in their water supply endeavors, it does not assure them of the amount of aid they may expect or of when that aid will come. Moreover, the partisans of navigation, flood control, and irrigation—and who would deny their effectiveness in Congress—could possibly neutralize federal aid to the cities.

In spite of the multitude of intangibles involved in water planning, it can be viewed objectively, and even scientifically.[6] The future efforts of the planner must of necessity be directed at enlarging the empirical base of planning.

The politics of water involves the clash of major interests both within and without the community. The clashes within the community—such as those involved in fluoridation and bond issues—have already been described. We need to consider some of the controversies over water that arise between and among communities.

Denver is a thousand miles from Los Angeles, and a long distance from the urban centers of Arizona. It is even farther away from Mexico, both because of physical distance and an international boundary. Yet when Denver goes west of the continental divide and takes water from the Colorado River watershed, it immediately affects vital interests of all those far-distant places. When the city of Denver, therefore, decided to build Dillon Dam in the 1950's and bring the water eastward under the continental divide to get it to the city's water mains, vigorous protests were raised against the decision by farmers and ranchers in the Colorado River basin; by the state of Colorado, which worried about its commitments under the interstate Colorado River compact; and by the federal government with its own bureaucratic interests and its interstate and foreign obligations vis-à-vis Colorado River waters.[7]

The conflict centering around the Dillon plan was highly complex. Both a variety of governments—city, state, federal, and foreign—and a variety of interests—agricultural and urban—sought to promote or oppose the scheme. Apparently all sides to the controversy worked out a satisfactory compromise in 1956, and Denver proceeded with the construction of the dam and tunnel. After an expenditure of money that exceeded $100 million, the city was ready, in 1963, to start filling the reservoir behind the dam. Opposition flared up again, and the opponents were able to obtain a federal court order against the city's closing the gates of the dam. After several months of hassling, the conflicting parties once more reached a com-

[6] See S. V. Ciriacy-Wantrup, "Philosophy and Objectives of Watershed Development," *Land Economics*, XXXV (August, 1959), 211–221; J. W. Milliman, "Policy Horizons for Future Urban Water Supply," *Land Economics*, XXXIX (May, 1963), 109–132; and Jack Hirshleifer, Jerome W. Milliman, and James C. DeHaven, *Water Supply: Economics, Technology and Policy* (Chicago: University of Chicago Press, 1960).

[7] James L. Cox, *Metropolitan Water Supply: The Denver Experience* (Boulder, Colo.: Bureau of Governmental Research and Service, University of Colorado, 1967), Ch 3.

promise. Denver had won a battle. But the agreement was hardly a treaty of peace; it was more an uneasy truce that ended the fighting in a war that would go on indefinitely.

In the western United States the battle over water between farm and city will widen in scope and increase in intensity. Throughout the republic, including the West, the battle between city and city will also doubtlessly intensify. The $2 billion California water project was approved by the voters of the state, but many a political leader in and around San Francisco still regards this great engineering project as a nefarious scheme of Los Angeles to steal water from San Francisco.

The city of Chicago supplies water to dozens of suburban cities, villages, and water districts, and there is consistent disagreement between city and suburbs over the rate at which Chicago should sell water to the other municipalities. Complicating rather than ameliorating this long-standing dispute is the intervention of the state of Illinois, which sets the rates that Chicago must charge by the worst possible method—legislative fiat.

The struggle between central city and suburb over water goes on, not only in the large metropolis, but also in relatively small urban communities. Many neighborhoods in suburbia, for example, consent to annex to the central city only because the city can supply it with a quantity of good water at reasonable cost. Still another source of conflict stems from one city's polluting a stream which is another city's main supply, as when St. Louis dumps untreated sewage into the very river (the Mississippi) from which Memphis draws its water.

Whether water is in plentiful supply or is as hard to find as an oasis in the desert, politics will inevitably affect who is to use it, how much they will use, and how much they will pay for it. The politics of water vitally affects the good health and prosperity of individual communities, and it draws the interest of the legally superior governments within the republic and of foreign governments outside it. If need for water is pervasive, no less so are the politics and political activity associated with it.

The City's Wastes—and What to Do with Them. Sewage Disposal. That a city is no better than its sewers is indicated by the experience of Des Moines with two epidemics of infectious hepatitis in the decade 1952–1961. Contributing factors to the epidemics were bad sewage disposal, low socioeconomic status of people in certain parts of the city, and housing congestion. In the neighborhoods where sewage disposal facilities had been improved and outdoor privies removed there was a reduction in the incidence of the disease in the 1960–1961 epidemic over the 1952–1953 outbreak.[8]

[8] Wiley H. Mosley, James F. Speers, and Tom D. Y. Chin, "Epidemiologic Studies of a Large Urban Outbreak of Infectious Hepatitis," *American Journal of Public Health,* LXXX (October, 1963), 1603–1617.

For over three centuries, from the founding of Jamestown in 1607 to well into the twentieth century, the concern of the city was that human wastes were somehow disposed of within the city or carried out of the immediate vicinity and dumped into river, lake, or sea. By the latter part of the nineteenth century the very latest in sewage disposal was the combined sewer, which drained away from the city both sewage and storm waters. "Why go the expense of two sewer systems," was the general thinking, "when one would suffice?"

The combined sewer served reasonably well and was certainly superior to the individual privy, as long as the body of water into which the raw sewage was dumped was sufficiently large that the wastes would be quickly oxidized. Storm water flowing through the sanitary drains, moreover, was no problem except in the instances when there was major flooding or the sewer line became obstructed.

This happy—and economical!—situation was rather short-lived. As village turned into city and city into metropolis, first public health scientists, then municipal leaders, then the citizen himself realized that raw sewage could not indefinitely be cast into any body of water that happened to be near the population center. It became obvious that some kind of treatment of the raw sewage had become a necessity. But here arose another perplexity. If a treatment plant were installed at the end of a combined sewer system, it might work well enough during dry weather, but a two-inch rain could send so much water storming through the drains that the plant would be hopelessly flooded. The older cities such as New York, Philadelphia, Boston, and St. Louis—not to mention hundreds of smaller places —were faced with the total obsolescence of their sewer systems.

Some cities reached a temporary solution to the problem by constructing bypass sewers around the treatment plants. The effect of this stratagem was to treat the sewage part of the time (when there was relatively little rainfall in the drains) and dump it raw during the periods of considerable rainfall.

Ultimately, of course, the only lasting solution was to construct two sewer systems, one for sanitary wastes and one for storm water. Older cities began requiring separate systems in the new subdivisions and reconstructing the combined drains in the older sections. New cities, like new subdivisions, sometimes of their own volition, sometimes as a result of state law, began installing separate systems from the day of their founding.

In the separate system, the storm drains carry only rain water, though sometimes uncontaminated waste water (as from air-conditioning cooling units) might be permitted in the storm drains. All other liquid wastes are deposited in the sanitary drains. It goes without saying that the two systems must be kept rigidly separate, because if storm water in the sanitary sewers greatly complicates adequate treatment of the wastes, how much more of a health hazard is the introduction of sanitary wastes into the storm system.

Yet health officers and public works officials will almost universally testify to the difficulty of maintaining the integrity of the two systems.

The modern sewage treatment plant handles sewage in three stages: primary treatment, oxidation, and sterilization. In the first stage, the solids are separated from liquids and broken down into safe, inoffensive materials by means of biological decomposition. In the second stage, the liquids are subjected to an oxidation process, usually by the activated-sludge or trickling-filter method, and the liquid is very considerably purified by bacterial action. Finally, the effluent is drained away from the plant with a chemical additive, usually chlorine, to kill whatever undesirable organisms remain after the first two stages of the treatment.

Although the modern treatment plant has reached a high standard of satisfaction and thus is an important health tool, political and economic factors intervene to lessen the impact of this scientific-engineering triumph on the urban community. For many reasons the poorer sections of almost every American city are unsewered, and the outdoor privy stands as a constant threat to the public health.

Septic-tank subdivisions are still very much with us too. Although the septic tank can work quite well for rural dwellings, mountain cabins, and similar isolated installations, in relatively crowded subdivisions it constitutes an ever-present health hazard. It is estimated that 24,000,000 persons are served by septic tanks and that one out of every three new houses being built is not attached to a sewer main. For the most part the septic tanks are installed as temporary devices, but the temporary is often transmuted into the permanent, by some strange alchemy, and then when the inevitable crisis occurs, neither the householder nor the neighborhood is prepared for it.

The financing of the collection and treatment systems is quite varied, though certain methods dominate. The special assessment has long been a common method for financing sanitary laterals and mains, and in Minnesota it is not unusual for cities to finance treatment plants by citywide special assessments. Used in connection with the special assessment, or as a means to replace it, are general-fund revenues, service-charge receipts, and subventions.

By means of the service charge the sanitary sewer system can be set up on a utility basis; both the operating and capital costs of the system can be supported by such charges. If the service charge is equated with water consumption, an approximate measurement of the consumer's use of the system becomes possible. A still more accurate measurement is possible, of course, if the wastes are metered, as in the case of a factory or creamery, and the service charge determined by the metered discharge. In addition, the city might use a flat-rate charge or a fee system based upon the characteristics of the sewage being discharged. Finally, the city may be aided by subventions. At least one state, Pennsylvania, and the federal government will make grants-in-aid for treatment plant construction and expansion.

The satisfactory treatment of human wastes in the urban community, which has reached a high level of scientific and engineering sophistication, falls short of realization because of political and social obstacles. The disorganized nature of the urban fringe, which culminates in the septic-tank subdivision; the social reluctance of the community (which is inevitably reflected in political action) to give health the very highest priority among public projects; the reluctance of the individual citizen to consent to an increased portion of his wealth being used for public purposes (and a concomitantly decreased portion for private purposes)—these are but some of the obstacles that stand in the way of achieving a truly healthful environment for the city. As a practical example, one source estimated in 1961 that at least 10,000 additional waste treatment plants were needed for all American cities.[9] We will have reached the moon long before that health goal is achieved.

Garbage and Refuse Disposal. A city piled high with garbage and refuse is a menace to all the citizens who live there. Indeed the city which cannot rid itself expeditiously of such wastes cannot function well, in either materialistic or humanistic terms.

Cities have always disposed of these wastes, and the methods used have often been picturesque. The pig or the flock of chickens in the backyard is usually thought of as a village method of garbage disposal, but it may occur in the large city. It is still not uncommon for the householder in Lima, Peru, to keep chickens, and even such animals as goats, on the flat roof of his house. This practice not only enables him to dispose of table scraps and other edible wastes; it also supplies the family with meat, milk, and eggs. And, further, it adds a bucolic atmosphere to a very old and very urbane city. The cocks crowing in the morning and the answering calls from rooftop to rooftop soften the raucous noises of automobile horns and clattering streetcars!

The pig, an eminently utilitarian animal, has served as a disposer of garbage since the beginning of the city. Not only has he existed as a family disposal unit in the backyard; he has also been brought together with his fellows in large municipal pig farms, both to eat the garbage and to help pay the expense of waste removal. When it was discovered that garbage-fed pigs often developed trichinosis and transmitted the disease to man, cities and states began requiring that garbage be cooked before it was fed to hogs. (No one has yet told us whether the pig prefers the cooked garbage to the raw.) These laws and ordinances have caused some interesting situations. When the Illinois garbage-cooking law was passed in the 1950's, literally

[9] International City Managers' Association, *Administration of Community Health Services* (Chicago: ICMA, 1961), p. 176.

hundreds of small entrepreneurs that had been accustomed to collecting garbage and feeding it to hogs went underground. And the state agriculture department, which had been entrusted with enforcing the statute, had a very difficult time suppressing the garbage bootlegging racket.

Man has long known what to do with garbage and refuse: he buries them; burns them; casts them into stream, lake, or sea; and (in the case of garbage) feeds it to animals or uses it as fertilizer. Nowadays in the United States, the preferred method is to bury the wastes. The citizen deposits all of his refuse into one container: garbage, ashes, cans, bottles, paper, tree limbs, broken toys—all of the multitude of different kinds of waste materials that accumulate around home or shop. The city then transports the wastes to bog, ravine, or isolated field and buries it. This is the sanitary landfill method, and it has significant advantages. It permits the citizen to deposit all wastes together; it is a healthful method of disposal (no rats, fires, insects, odors, or flying debris); and it may enable the city to convert a swamp into a park or an athletic field.

But there simply may not be space enough around a city for sanitary landfills large enough and numerous enough to accommodate all the wastes. Incineration then becomes the logical alternative. Unfortunately, this still leaves the city with the problem of how to get rid of noncombustibles.

Dumping of garbage and refuse is no longer to be tolerated, but it still goes on, and the open city dump is very much with us. Even major rivers can no longer accommodate the mass of refuse coming out of the city, nor can the sea—though oceangoing vessels, after having cleared port for a number of hours, continue to follow the age-old practice of dumping their wastes into the sea. (After the introduction of the submarine into the world's navies, incidentally, surface vessels soon found that the underseas craft could follow their garbage trail. This could have been, though it was not, the reason the submarines came to be known as "pig" boats.)

For garbage the disposal alternatives extend beyond the sanitary landfill and incineration. Much of this residue from the city's daily existence may be ground up and flushed down the sanitary sewer. Or the garbage may be reduced to a usable form by composting. The basic elements of this latter method should be familiar to the suburbanite, for where is the earnest gardener without his compost heap? If cities can develop an economical method of composting, they will not only solve a part of the disposal problem, but they will also be able to produce a highly desirable fertilizer and soil conditioner for their own nursery operations or for sale on the open market.[10] (Some cities are already in the soil-conditioner business by

[10] Hille I. Shuval, "The Economics of Composting Municipal Refuse," *APWA Reporter*, Part I, February, 1962, p. 24; Part II, March, 1962, pp. 16–17.

selling to gardeners the digested sludge from their sewage treatment plants.)

Air Pollution. In 1948 the city of Donora, Pennsylvania, awoke one day to find that a heavy fog had settled over the town. As the citizenry soon realized, this was no usual fog. Held snugly against the ground by a temperature inversion (warm air over relatively cold), the fog would not dissipate, and it was soon mixed with smoke, fumes from automobile exhausts, and other pollutants. People coughed, wheezed, and complained. People became ill, some violently, and twenty deaths were attributed to the poisoned atmosphere before the fog finally lifted six days later.

Some people like to call it garbage in the air. Others, more simply, call it smog. Whatever its designation, air pollution is a health menace to virtually every city—not only in the United States but throughout the Western world. It is the industrialized mechanized society, in other words, which dirties up the air of its cities.

What is air pollution? Some of it is simply dust; some of it ashes. A great deal of it comes from fires of one sort or another: from the backyard trash burner or from the smokestack of a steel mill. And a great deal of it comes from the internal combustion engine: the hydrocarbons emitted from the exhausts of automobiles, trucks, and airplanes. A 1962 study in Los Angeles found that about 69 percent of all the hydrocarbons deposited in the air each day came from automobiles, trucks, and buses.[11]

What can be done about the problem? We could, of course, follow the advice of certain intransigents at the turn of the century and go back to the horse. Since that is not a very likely prospect, we can find ways to reduce or eliminate pollution from the internal combustion engine. One way to do this is by requiring the installation of exhaust purifiers on automobiles and other vehicles.

Automotive engineers have developed fairly simple and inexpensive "blowby" controls which recirculate crankcase fumes through the motor, where they are burned. Such devices not only reduce the amount of noxious fumes emitting from the engine but may also increase engine efficiency. Since most authorities agree that the automobile contributes more to the pollution of the city's air than any other single source, a day is coming when fume-control will be as essential to the exhaust system of automobile, truck, or bus as the noise-deadening muffler. By 1961 the California State Motor Vehicle Board had worked out a program to attach antipollution controls to every internal combustion engine in the state, and such controls were enacted into law. In 1968, federal controls patterned after those in California were applied nationwide.

[11] Department of Health, Education, and Welfare, U.S. Public Health Service, *Report of the Committee on Environmental Health Problems to the Surgeon General* (1962), p. 120.

The federal government of West Germany embarked on an experiment in 1964 to determine whether exhaust fumes could be blown away. In the German city of Constance, on the German-Swiss border, the authorities installed giant blowers which sucked in fume-ladened air at ground level and propelled it straight upward at great velocity. Such artificially induced currents of air may be one answer to air pollution.

Still another answer may be found in nature itself. Dr. Chauncey Leake of the American Association for the Advancement of Science has advocated more trees as a partial means of clearing up the air. Since trees absorb carbon dioxide and give off oxygen, they act exactly in reverse to the internal combustion engine. Dr. Leake has estimated that about a dozen trees could nullify the effects of one automobile and about a hundred trees, the effects of one truck.

In all probability the air-pollution problem in cities will be met, if at all, by a variety of solutions, and as a result of both public and private action. Although action by the city will be the keystone in the arch, the city's decisions must be reinforced by many other governments. The metropolis may need an air-pollution control district, such as the one which includes San Francisco and five surrounding counties. Still further, there must be decisive action by the state governments, the minimal character of which must be good enabling legislation. To complete society's defense against impure air, there must be federal action. Indeed, in the case of a metropolis which spans an international boundary, as in the Detroit-Windsor complex, active work by all governments on both sides of the border may be a necessity.

Parks and Recreation. City parks vary from the tot-lot of minuscule size to vast expanses of invaluable real estate, such as Central Park in New York, where sale of the land alone would put the city in the black for a decade or more. City recreation programs are equally varied and range from the nonexistent to the elaborate bureaucratic establishment seeking to cater to every recreational whim of a diverse citizenship. A few cities still remain that possess no trace of a park, nor any sign of a recreational program. Some cities confine their park and recreational activities to within the city limits; others range far and wide with their programs. If the water department goes off thirty miles to the mountains to develop a lake and a watershed, the recreation department will very shortly follow it; and one can see the merging of two activities important to the city's health.

The parks and recreation department can easily take upon itself a multitude of tasks: games, gymnastics, parties, dances, music, theater, crafts, foreign language study, and many others. The department may even sponsor such activities as symphony concerts and so become involved in the city's sponsorship of the arts, which we discuss in Chapter 21 of this book.

The department receives aid from the city's sister governments locally: the school district (if independent), the independent park district, and even, on occasion, the county. It also receives aid from the park services of the state and federal governments, though the latter rarely has recreational programs, as such, immediately available to the urban citizen.

Other Health Functions. Just as the city of Amsterdam, Holland, maintains a municipal psychiatric service, so American cities are organizing mental health programs within their health departments. Noise-abatement is now recognized as a health measure, and steps in the direction of a quiet city include everything from an antinoise ordinance to provisions in the building code requiring soundproofing in both the interior and exterior walls of buildings.

If narcotics control is primarily a function of the police department, the treatment of addicts is a health activity. The city of New York operates a hospital for the treatment of offenders under the age of twenty-one; it is indeed the only hospital in the world used exclusively for the treatment of juvenile addicts (a distinction that New York would doubtless be happy to pass on to another city). General hospital services and even medical education are other health functions offered by the city.

The health department keeps track of communicable diseases, from mumps to venereal diseases, and often must go to the aid of the private physician in combating them. The chief health officer, in many cities, is the registrar of vital statistics, who must record all deaths and births within his jurisdiction and relay the information to the state health department.

Public health nursing takes up much of the time of the department and much of its funds. Public health nurses visit the homes of citizens to aid individuals and families in combating communicable diseases, mental illnesses, alcoholism, and numerous other maladies. In the well-baby clinics the nurses administer immunizations and vaccinations to infants and pre-school children, and in some jurisdictions the public health nurses serve also as school nurses, in both public and parochial schools. The nursing division of the health department also operates other types of clinics, such as orthopedic, hearing, and tuberculosis.

Every housing ordinance is also a health ordinance. In requiring that home or shop be well lighted and ventilated; in requiring cleanliness and the elimination of hazards; in making it unlawful, in other words, for a dwelling to be kept in less than habitable condition, the city is attempting to create a healthful urban environment.

Summary

The city's concern with the health and safety of its citizens may be seen not only in the activities of its health department but in the services of many other municipal agencies. Pure water, clean air, adequate and expeditious disposal of wastes, control of rodents and insects, insurance of good housing—these are environmental health factors that engross the time not only of the chief sanitarian in the health department but also of the officers and employees in water and sewers, sanitation, finance, public works, and law.

That the city is one of the primary tools available to society for protecting the public health is no better illustrated than in the political battles that arise in the community over health issues. Whether the question is one posed to the electorate at large or is limited to one neighborhood, the intensity with which people approach the issues indicates full well how much store people put in health politics. If the public decision involves a matter of health, the possibilities of its being made without vigorous debate are very slight. As soon as the question is posed, the community fragments, and out of this fragmentation comes politics.

Annotated Bibliography

Probably the two best summary statements of the community health problem may be found in John J. Hanlon, *Principles of Public Health Administration* (St. Louis: The C. V. Mosby Co., 3rd ed., 1960); and International City Managers' Association, *Administration of Community Health Services* (Chicago: The Association, 1st ed., 1961). The Hanlon work is the standard textbook in the field of public health and was written by a man who is physician, public administrator (Director of Public Health Services for the city of Philadelphia), and college professor. The ICMA publication was prepared under the editorship of Eugene A. Confrey, public health adviser to the U.S. Public Health Service, and with the advice of the Committee on Public Health Administration of the American Public Health Association.

For an excellent, brief treatment of the growth of medical knowledge and public health administration from the Greco-Roman city to the city of today, one may rely confidently on the book by George Rosen, *A History of Public Health* (New York: MD Publications, 1958). As both political and engineering history, as well as good and authoritative reading, see Nelson M. Blake, *Water for the Cities* (Syracuse, N.Y.: Syracuse University Press, 1956). This study is descriptively subtitled *A History of the Urban Water Supply Problem in the United States*.

More or less technical works on the city's health abound, some of them intelligible to the layman, others strictly for the professional. Those that fit wholly or partially into the former category are fairly easy to come by. See William L. Faith, *Air Pollution Control* (New York: John Wiley & Sons, 1959); American Public Works Association, *Municipal Refuse Disposal* (Chicago: Public Administration Service, 1961)—a fascinating book for all its unimposing title; State of California, Department of Water Resources, *Saline Water Demineralization and Nuclear Energy in the California Water Plan, Bulletin No. 94*, December, 1960; International City Managers' Association, *Municipal Public Works Administration* (Chicago: The Association, 5th ed., 1957).

In the recreation field no better book has been written than that which appears in the Municipal Management Series. See International City Managers' Association, *Municipal Recreation Administration* (Chicago: The Association, 4th ed., 1960). After three years of work the Outdoor Recreation Resources Review Commission reported to the President and Congress in 1963. The main report and the twenty-seven study reports cover national, state, local, and private recreational resources, needs, and objectives, and may be obtained from the U.S. Government Printing Office. These volumes together undoubtedly constitute the definitive study of recreation in the United States.

CHAPTER 18

City Beautiful—City Practical

Planning—A Constant Presence

Planning is no stranger to the city. Whether it was the tiny urban settlement, antedating history and sitting precariously on the edges of civilization, or the first industrial center, poking its sooty fingers out into the green English landscape, the city was planned. Urban planning has flourished as the city has flourished, and would disappear only if the city disappeared. More often than not a chaotic intermingling of a multitude of decisions, planning nevertheless has always been based upon a definite consensus (1) that the city is a physical reality, and (2) that it is—or should soon become —a political entity.

Historically, the physical and the political aspects of the city inevitably were joined together. Indeed they unquestionably developed simultaneously. If men built houses, markets, temples, shops, they could not long nurture these seeds of urbanism without the aid of community power. The aqueduct, the wall, the police force, the public ways, the art museum, the sewerage system—all of these prime attributes of urban living resulted from the agreement, or consensus, that the city was both a physical and political being.

The Development of Modern Planning

The recognition of the city as a physical reality and the use of government to control that reality were the two original elements of city planning. And they still are as basic today as they were in fifth-century Athens or eighteenth-century Savannah, Georgia. Without politics, even as without engineering and architecture, city planning could not exist.

But during the twentieth century, the concept has been greatly enlarged. No longer does planning mean simply the union of politician, planner, engineer, and architect to force a limited physical reorientation upon the city. Growing out of twentieth-century necessity, the city plan has enlarged in concept. Just as importantly, a corps of professionals has developed to plan and implement an urban ideal which, though not new, has made some startling variations upon the old, old theme of the good life in an urban setting. The professional himself is new; the city planner of this century is poles apart from his predecessor of previous epochs. Different also is the relation of planning to the community's governmental institutions.

In order to understand the effects of both the enlarged concept of the city plan and the development of a corps of professional planners, we need to glance briefly at the development of planning in recent decades. After some bold and largely successful attempts at city planning during the colonial period,[1] the brave efforts of the earlier years were forgotten with the coming of the nineteenth century and particularly with the growth of the industrial city and the ideology of laissez-faire. The controlled development of Savannah, Georgia, beginning in 1733 and based upon "little neighborhood units, scaled to human size," lasted until the War Between the States.[2]

After that the land speculator ravaged the urban landscape, not only around Savannah but around every other American city. No city escaped, not even those that had a century or more of controlled growth to guide them. The rape of the city stands as one of the most extraordinary developments of the late nineteenth and early twentieth centuries. Though this was a period of remarkable city building, it also represented the city's *abbau*, or "unbuilding," as Lewis Mumford has phrased it.

Nothing illustrates this destructive tendency quite so well as the style in which the city was platted. This was the fashion of laying out the city in the gridiron pattern. Though the grid had been known in the colonial city and in medieval and ancient towns and cities, never had it so dominated the urban scene. As Mumford observes, the medieval town planners were not reluctant to use the geometrical and the rectangular in their planning.[3] But they never made the gridiron pattern into a cult, as did the developers of the American city in the decades following the Civil War. For a cult the gridiron was to become—and to remain. Rapid industrialization and a spectacular rise in land prices supported the idea of the grid as an "efficient" way to utilize land for urban use. The physical absurdity of such cultism can be seen in virtually every American city, but nowhere better than in San Francisco. There the grid defies topography, and the streets go straight up one hill and straight down another.

The dominance of the grid indicates the state at which planning had arrived by 1875 and at which level it continued for generations. The engineer's transit was the magic wand to be waved over the landscape, to transform it. And transform it, it did. True enough, in the utopian communities, even those that were postbellum, there was planning after a grand design; here was integration of city and country, of intellectual and manual work. Here, too, was planning of the physical, intellectual, social, moral, and esthetic aspects of life. Such utopianism, however, was just an aberra-

[1] See Christopher Turnard and Henry Hope Reed, *American Skyline* (Boston: Houghton Mifflin Co., 1955), Part I.

[2] John W. Reps, "Town Planning in Colonial Georgia," *The Town Planning Review*, XXXI (January, 1960), p. 283.

[3] Lewis Mumford, *The Culture of Cities* (New York: Harcourt, Brace & Co., 1938), pp. 51–53.

tion; it was the engineer, the industrialist, the banker, the land speculator, and the Jacksonian democrat who took over the city and who kept control of it. Although the power of these elements in the community was overwhelming, they still could not control the city absolutely. Even as their dominance seemed assured, the beginnings of a new planning movement emerged.

Some people, even today, are surprised at the place of birth of the new movement. From a city settled upon the swampy flatlands of Lake Michigan, from a city forever labeled "Hog butcher to the world" by one of its adopted sons, came an exciting—yes, even glittering—prospect of an urban setting that could be as clean as it was efficient, as dramatic as it was exciting. If it was not humane, built to human scale, who could but remember that neither was the Gothic cathedral?

The city was, of course, Chicago. The glittering prospect was given to the entire continent by the Chicago World's Fair of 1893. And why should it not be Chicago? Here, the skyscaper had been invented—a tall building "floating" upon a slab of concrete. Here, Louis Sullivan was already building with integrity and originality. Here, Sullivan's peers David H. Burnham and John W. Root had designed the Reliance Building. Here, too, sons and daughters of the robber barons were founding art institutes, symphony orchestras, libraries, universities, and theaters.

Chicago had developed according to a countless number of private plans which had risen from the exigencies of the moment. Such plans reflected the needs of the free market as assessed by land speculators and other entrepreneurs. If there had been any planning by the city in the comprehensive sense, it had been in the slow development of a park system and the laying out of the streets and public ways. But in the Chicago World's Fair, David H. Burnham and his associates created on the city's lakefront a development that was at once a monument to civic pride and a stimulus to the urban imagination all over America. Filling in the swamps and tearing down the rotting piers and the decaying shanties that had lined the lakeshore, Burnham gave rebirth to the idea that a city could be planned, and on a grand scale.

Burnham's creation above all emphasized esthetics: architecture, fountains, statuary, plazas, and malls. As his idea spread across the nation, it became known as the "City Beautiful" movement. Supported largely by architects, it was concerned with esthetic rather than social or economic objectives. Supported just as strongly by businessmen, it was a grandiose advertising campaign. A relatively small area at the core of the city, built in the grand manner, daily revived the confidence of the businessman in himself and his compeers. More than that, it gave a heady message to the entrepreneurs from abroad: "Here, business is good!"

The idea spread quickly. In 1902 the L'Enfant plan was revived in

Washington; Burnham produced a plan for San Francisco in 1905 and again for Chicago in 1909. It looked as though the "City Beautiful" movement would sweep the country. Over two decades had to pass before it was generally perceived that the movement was too limited in conception, too restricted to a small geographic area, and to a small clientele to last. By some criteria the movement died; by others it simply expanded to include a wide variety of elements never seriously considered by Burnham *et alia.*

The Elements of Planning

The "City Beautiful" movement was succeeded by one which might be labeled the "City Practical." After World War I the planner began to consider more than just the downtown in his plans. He began to look at the entire city, to study the land uses throughout the city, and to recognize the vital interrelationships of those uses. He began, in short, to produce the comprehensive city plan.

Just as the planner changed his scope, so he changed his orientation and even his professional skills. It was not that the architect lost his interest in the planned city. Notice Frank Lloyd Wright and his Broadacre City, with an acre of land allotted to each dwelling unit, with broad open spaces and expansive use of land. Notice Le Corbusier, his people housed in tall towers like the Hopi Indians of Arizona—a perhaps logical extension of the idea of commonalty or community: a large number of people intimately juxtaposed. But the planner became less and less an architect and more and more a social scientist (though it should be observed that the architect was always far more the social and political philosopher than he realized; Wright's Broadacre City is a sociopolitical utopia created on the architect's drawing board).[4]

This leads us to a consideration of the comprehensive plan. The land area of every city is divided among a variety of land uses: residential, retail, wholesale, industrial, transportation, governmental, institutional, and vacant land. These uses are invariably related one to the other. To borrow a term from human ecology, there is a symbiotic relationship between and among all the various land uses within the city. The comprehensive plan is no more than a means of channeling, guiding, and anticipating this interdependence of land use. It is no more than an attempt to bring the owners of both privately and publicly held lands into a consensus.

What, specifically, does a comprehensive (or master) plan attempt to do? What are its major elements of concern? Every plan is an anticipation of the future. But in order to look ahead, one must know what exists in the present. Thus the most important initial step of the planner in construct-

---

[4] See Frank Lloyd Wright, *The Living City* (New York: Horizon Press, 1958).

ing the master plan is to determine how all the land of the city is currently used. Applying a variety of techniques the planner must conduct a land-use survey to obtain these working data. By means of this survey the planner must classify the current uses of land (a difficult process in itself) and then construct land-use maps which will accurately inform legislative and administrative officials—as well as the general public—not only about land use for a particular area but about the relation of land uses one to the other in that area. Thus the land-use inventory and the accompanying maps—which must be religiously kept up-to-date—are indispensable aids to the planner and other city officials.

Just as important to the planner is a knowledge of demography. Because all life has its place on the face of the earth, and because man is no exception to this rule, the planner is deeply interested in population characteristics and distribution. How densely people live together; their cultural, racial, and political nature; income distribution; educational background; and employment status—all of these are factors of importance. Facts on mobility of population, too, are crucial elements in the planner's repertory of information. Whether a neighborhood is growing or declining, for example, is central to an analysis of it.

Perhaps the greatest question that worries the planner is how to predict population growth. Although he attacks the problem with a number of techniques, the right answer is always elusive. He will use general census data and relate births and deaths to them. He will use house counts (either from a field or aerial survey). The schools will furnish him with enrollment and school-census figures. Both vehicle registrations and a count of utility customers he will find useful. And then he will assemble all of the data and seek to project estimates of population growth (or decline) years, even decades, ahead.[5]

Intimately related to population is housing. Knowledge of the age, quality, type, and other characteristics of housing must inevitably be incorporated into the planning process. Some of these characteristics will be found in the master plan, some in the zoning maps. If a neighborhood is predominately made up of single-family housing units, the planner must know this fact and have it recorded. Whether a neighborhood is showing signs of decay or is suffering from pronounced obsolescence will make the difference between the planner's recommending conservation or complete renewal. Public housing, too, must be entered into planning considerations.

And, of course, people are peripatetic. Every city has its circulation systems: highways, mass-transit facilities, and other transportation elements.

[5] For a description of the methods of population projection, see United Nations, *Manuals on Methods of Estimating Population: Manual I and Manual II* (New York: United Nations. 1952 and 1955); also see F. Stuart Chapin, Jr., *Urban Land Use Planning* (Urbana, Ill.: University of Illinois Press, 2nd ed., 1965), pp. 196–213.

These essential parts of urban life must be mapped and planned. Since the automobile has come to dominate the city, it must be catered to, in both its moving and stationary conditions. In most of our major cities the automobile and the mass-transit systems are engaged in a titanic struggle: the automobile has won most of the battles and may eventually win the war. Yet the planner knows that for the large city he simply cannot plan without a mass-transit facility.[6] Only by analyzing, mapping, and planning for the entire transportation network will the city be able to meet the problems that inevitably lie ahead. Only by implementing its transportation planning can the city realize its potential as a socioeconomic organism.

Parks and other recreation facilities are an essential element of planning and must be included in the city plan. Although there are many cities without parks and still others without any organized recreation programs, the public garden, the picnic area, the tot-lot, the ball diamond, the tennis court, and the swimming pool have become—to large segments of the urban population—as truly necessary to the good life as color television and new motorcars. Admittedly, there is citizen ambivalence on this point— note the frequent reluctance of the citizen to vote for a recreation bond issue—but the enthusiasm with which he uses recreational facilities when they are available indicates the value he sets on them. Recreation planning which seeks to appeal to a wide variety of popular interests may, it is true, run into political opposition from those who support one type of recreation but deplore another.

Regardless of social and political tensions, the city recreation plan must be eclectic, seeking to anticipate the needs or appetites of the citizen for recreation. As he plans to meet these desires, one of the real dangers the planner faces is that he will be misled by temporary public enthusiasm into long-range planning for a passing fancy. Planning ahead for today's recreational fads may seem downright silly ten years hence.

Up to this point we have seen that the planner faces many responsibilities. But he has still other tasks before him. Since the future of the city is bound up with its ability to produce goods and services, the planner must examine the economic base and include his examination and forecasts in the city plan. This fact means that the analysis of the city's economic base must be sophisticated in the extreme. What effect will the large-scale importation of toys from Yokohama and automobiles from Wolfsburg have upon the city's economy? Will a textile mill enhance the city's economic position or will the social costs resulting from a large influx of lowly paid workers outweigh the advantages of new industry? In planning, should city hall concern itself only with purely local matters, or with regional, continental,

---

[6] See E. F. Downs, "An Answer to the Highway Fiasco," *Public Utilities Fortnightly,* LXXI (September 15, 1960), 367–378. Downs defines the superhighway as a "curving line connecting two points of maximum congestion"!

and even worldwide problems? These are but samples of the economic questions that the city plan must pose and the planners attempt to answer.

If the city takes the regional (or wider) approach, it will use input-output analysis of its economic base. If it is oriented more closely to home, it will use the economic-base approach, with its very difficult attempt to classify basic and nonbasic economic activities.[7] The planner may set up economic flow studies, or he may simply analyze the city's economy on a matter-of-fact basis and make his predictions with the aid of these data. However he goes about it, he must make predictions; and just as in population projection, the elements of economic planning are so indeterminant and elusive (at least in a free-market society) that he must expect to be wrong frequently.

With all of this work behind him the planner is still not finished. Just as a man is no better than his arteries, so a city cannot rise above its public utilities (whether city or privately owned)—water supply, the electricity system, sewerage, and other drainage facilities. The locus, type, control, financing, and extension of these systems must be entered into the plan.

Now the planner is near the end of the plan's construction. Depending upon the city, however, he may need to occupy himself at some length with school growth, civic art, urban redevelopment, a capital improvements program, a civic center, and plans for the central business district. And when he has constructed the plan and the city has published it, he must immediately begin revisions of it—because in just the time required to formulate the plan, the city has changed and thus outdated some of the elements of the plan.

The Environments of the City Plan

Among the many environments in which the city plan exists no two are more important than the ideological and the politico-legal, for they condition it from its initial conception to its final execution.

The Ideological Environment. In ideological concept, as we have seen, the modern plan varies greatly from the city plan at the turn of the century: we have gone from the "City Beautiful" concept to that of the "City Practical." Whether this is wholly desirable, some current observers doubt. Has planning, in abandoning esthetics, lost its soul? Or, to bring the question to a mundane level: Is the city plan's very practicality the most serious flaw in modern planning?

This question is not an easy one to answer. Does the professional planner himself believe that the almost exclusive devotion of the plan to the matter-of-fact is a weakness? There is some indication that he does. Is there any

[7] See Chapin, *op. cit.*, Ch. 3.

indication in local political behavior that the citizen believes the city must be more than simply utilitarian? The evidence is overwhelming that such groups of such citizens do indeed exist and that they have considerable influence in public councils. See, for example, Chapter 21 of this volume. To put the question in the editorial words of one metropolitan newspaper: "How can the community make sure that . . . beauty continues to be a dominant element in its planning?" The editorial writer answered the question by advising the city to employ, as head of the city's plan department, one who is "not only a professional planner, but one who is devoted to improving the esthetic as well as other aspects of the city." [8]

Here is a kind of ideological ambivalence, an attempt to reconcile the antithetical ideals of city beautiful, on the one hand, and city practical, on the other. Such ambivalence might well furnish the very kind of ideological environment which the modern plan needs.

The Politico-legal Environment. Because planning eventually finds itself embodied in law, it is essential that the law be kept in mind during the designing of the plan. True, the law may be largely invisible, like the foundations of a building, but it must nevertheless be there to give the necessary support to the planning structure.

Voluntary compliance to the plan by the various elements of the community cannot be relied upon for the plan's effectuation. Compliance, rather, will come at three levels; from personal or group identification with the plan and with planning objectives; from individual respect for law qua law (force, here, is implicit only); and from enforced obedience (where force is explicit).

The development of planning has seen not the growth of new law but rather the adaptation of existing law to planning needs. The police power, eminent domain, control of business enterprise, extraterritoriality, annexation and consolidation, taxation, borrowing, and spending—all these are powers which are almost as old as the city itself. From a constitutional standpoint these are state powers which have been delegated to the city and which the city may use for many purposes—including planning. Without enabling legislation from the state the local government may dream, but it can never really plan.

If state law is essential to the city's plan, federal law can just as surely be an obstacle, or an aid. In its interpretation of the Fourteenth Amendment to the U.S. Constitution, the Supreme Court has set up certain standards that must be observed by the city in carrying out its planning function. In exercising its power to zone, for example, the city must not deprive an individual of property without due process of law. Nor may the individual's right to equal protection of the law be abridged by any kind of legislation

[8] St. Louis *Post-Dispatch*, May 21, 1961, p. 2B.

or administrative act. Thus zoning with racial bias will be repugnant to the Fourteenth Amendment.[9] And if a city deannexes territory to deprive Negroes of citizenship rights in the city, the action must fail.[10]

Fully as important to the city is the federal spending power. Under the Housing and Home Finance Act of 1954, as amended, the federal government offers planning grants-in-aid to cities. Federal grants for streets, sewage disposal, and other programs are also of importance to the plan. And, as we shall see later, the action of the federal government in public housing and urban renewal is, more often than not, the determining factor in whether the program will be initiated at all. Nor is the impact of federal activity on private housing to be overlooked. Either in insuring the mortgages on private dwellings or in making direct loans to aid veterans' housing, the Federal Housing Authority and the Veterans' Administration have shaped (some would insist that the word is "misshaped") the city profoundly.

Yet, in the final analysis, it is local law and local determination to enforce that law which determine whether the city will be planned. Though it is true enough that the local government is dependent upon the state for enabling legislation to permit it to plan, it must be remembered, nevertheless, that this legislation is, for the most part, only permissive. Thus it is quite possible—though admittedly unlikely—that a given state may have established by statute the essentials of a perfect plan and yet no city or county in the state may have utilized such a plan. We need only to go behind the legal smokescreen to see that, even with legal authorization, the city may exercise its powers only after an act of will: not only must the battle to gain political consent be won; the necessary administrative leadership and structure must also be developed to achieve the successful plan.

Two or three decades ago the city might rightly have claimed that its failure to plan was basically the failure of state and, to a lesser extent, federal law. This is not so today. Success or failure of the plan lies largely with the city, and the city must accept the burden of failure just as surely as it accepts the laurel wreath of success.

But what is local planning law? It is, as we have seen, not new law, but application of old law. The police power is far older than the republic, yet it took several decades of vigorous attack, in the legislative halls and in the courts, to expand it sufficiently to include zoning. Eminent domain is a legal antique; yet even now we have not entirely satisfied the courts that in an urban redevelopment project we can condemn private land, clear it, and then resell it to an industrial concern or to a church. Old questions of law and policy come back to plague us: What *is* public purpose? What *is* separation of church and state?

[9] *Buchanan* v. *Warley*, 245 U.S. 60 (1917).
[10] *Gomillion* v. *Lightfoot*, 364 U.S. 339 (1960).

The situation is similar with excess condemnation. If the city wishes to acquire more land than is necessary for immediate needs and then wishes later to sell off a part of the excess (perhaps at a profit) to help finance the city plan, is this legitimate? Once again, the idea of excess condemnation is not new, but the pressures upon the idea and upon the law are strikingly different, in volume and in emphasis.

The situation is similar too with fiscal powers: the extent of their use for planning and closely allied purposes has greatly expanded. Taxation as a regulatory device has long been used. But has it been used as a regulation of the use of land? Such new use of an old device theoretically has great promise.

Legal practices governing land occupancy—fee-simple title, leaseholds, restrictive covenants—these are old concepts applied to new planning situations. The regulation of street and public ways, the power to approve or reject a legal map (that is, a plat) for a newly opened urban area—these are old. Yet these lead logically to something new, the comprehensive control of entire subdivisions. Abatement of nuisances has been a power of the city for millennia: combined with the police power, it produced zoning.

These are the major legal concepts of planning. A body of old law, newly applied, becomes planning law, and this in turn becomes the politico-legal environment.

The Administration of the Plan

Since zoning is of such vital importance to the effective administration of the plan, taking a close look at the zoning process is the best introduction to the subject of plan administration.

The Central Position of Zoning. Zoning is a means of publicly controlling the use of urban land and the various structures upon that land. It may be either comprehensive or limited. It usually applies only to privately held urban property: state and federal holdings are usually exempt, and as a general rule, so are the holdings of other local governmental units unless the statutes specifically provide otherwise. Thus not only pressures from private sources but the actions of public officials from jurisdictions other than the city can very effectively render a zoning ordinance virtually useless. Indeed, there is no legal instrument—at whatever level of government—more difficult to administer than a zoning ordinance. The pitfalls along its road to success are many and formidable.

Yet, for all that, zoning has had almost complete legal acceptance. Though many bitter battles were fought in the courts and the issue was in doubt for years, the war has been completely won. The zoning authority —city or county—may determine how land is to be used, whether for business, industrial, or residential purposes; what type of building will be permitted on the land; how the building will be situated on the land; how high the building shall be and what its bulk shall be; how much minimal space may be allocated to each occupant of a dwelling; and a wide variety of other elements involved in land use and occupancy.

One of the few zoning problems that still almost defies any kind of precise definition is the one involving esthetics. Esthetics, broadly defined, could bear upon almost any aspect of planning in general and zoning in particular. City councils and state legislators have led the way in attempting to describe esthetic criteria by ordinance and statute; the courts have had great difficulty in handling that legislative initiative.

If a modern zoning ordinance is vigorously administered, there are few governmental activities that can equal its exhaustive and intimate control of human activity. Whether this represents a triumph of law and policy depends upon one's sense of values. But that it is a major device for controlling the urban environment no one can doubt. The struggle for acceptance of zoning was long and hard-fought. It therefore provides an excellent study in how public policy is formed.

The zoning movement began in Germany in the late nineteenth century, and the ideas of zoning were incorporated in the British Town Planning Act of 1909. Some of the characteristics of zoning had been previously accepted by states and cities in the United States. Philadelphia restricted the use of wooden buildings in congested areas as early as 1795. San Francisco sought to restrict laundries to nonwooden buildings, but because the ordinance was as much an effort to discriminate against the Chinese as it was a safety measure, it was ruled unconstitutional.[11] Other cities eliminated or restricted such nuisances—or potential nuisances—as abattoirs, livery stables, swamps, and junkshops, or forced into isolation land uses potentially dangerous to life and property—gasoline storage areas, for example. But this kind of sporadic restriction upon a man's use of his own land was merely a series of minor skirmishes only tenuously connected with the long and costly struggle that covered the first quarter of the twentieth century —the struggle, first, to win the political battle to get permissive zoning legislation and, then, to defend it in the courts.

It was, of course, over permissive legislation that the issue of zoning came to a head. Trace the issue's birth and growth: the springing up of pressure groups in the city—reformers, worried businessmen, civic leaders, and politicians interested in the public control of land use; then the persuasion of a group of urban legislators of both parties to introduce permissive legislation in the state legislature; immediately thereafter the cloakroom sessions, the private dinners, the appeals to friendship, family ties, church and lodge connections, the cajolery, the threats; and then the bill reported

[11] *Yick Wo* v. *Hopkins*, 118 U.S. 356 (1886).

out of committee, and the hope of success blasted by defeat on the third reading (or, what was worse, the bill emasculated at the amendment stage so that, as a law, it was a mere pious gesture toward effective land-use practice); now a wait of a year, or two or three; then a new bill in the legislative hopper; the opponents massing for a last-ditch stand, only to be overwhelmed in first one house and then the other; at long last the bill carried to the governor's desk for his signature.

Unhappily, much of the record of these exciting events has been lost or is yet unassembled. The historian, typically, has been so engrossed in national affairs that he has largely ignored one of the truly great public dramas of the early twentieth century. In California, Illinois, Louisiana, New York, and many other states, the legislatures produced laws which, if not the most desirable that civic leaders, planners, and lawyers could wish for, were of acceptable standards.

It is no easier getting zoning ordinances through the city councils than permissive laws through the state legislatures, yet a good proportion of the major cities led the way. But if the enemies of zoning had been defeated politically, they still had ample strength legally, and the assault in the courts began. This battle, even though camouflaged by resounding legal clichés, was, of course, simply political action in a different guise.

A Los Angeles zoning ordinance, which was founded upon the old legal concept of nuisance control, sought to exclude obnoxious businesses from residential districts throughout the city. Attacked in both the state and federal courts, it was upheld by both.[12] Still, this was only a very limited triumph, because no comprehensive zoning ordinance could long rest upon such slight foundations.

Because state laws and local ordinances which sought to use the broad base of the police power were being given short shrift by the state courts and because the nuisance concept was so limited, Minnesota tried a new tack. In 1920, the state supreme court upheld zoning as an exercise of the power of eminent domain: the city in this case could condemn property to interdict apartment use.[13] But this, too, was a blind alley. If, every time the city sought to zone property for residential use, it had to condemn the difference in value between residential and commercial (or industrial) use, the cost would have been enormous.

With the nuisance concept too limited and eminent domain too expensive, the city could move in only one direction—toward the police power. By 1920 a considerable number of ordinances and state enabling acts were

[12] *Ex Parte Quond Wo,* 161 Cal. 220 (1911); *Hadacheck* v. *Los Angeles,* 239 U.S. 394 (1915); see the commentary on these cases in Robert A. Walker, *The Planning Function in Urban Government* (Chicago: University of Chicago Press, 2nd ed., 1950), pp. 60–65.
[13] *State ex rel. Twin City Building and Investment Company* v. *Houghton,* 144 Minn. 1 (1920).

in existence and were using the legal rationale that zoning was necessary to the health, safety, and general welfare of the community. Two attacks upon this rationale of zoning—one upon the Massachusetts law and the other upon the New York City ordinance—resulted in important decisions by the courts in favor of zoning. In upholding the New York ordinance—probably the first great comprehensive zoning ordinance in the country—the court emphasized nuisance control, but the Massachusetts court refused to look back to the nuisance theory, and upheld the Massachusetts act on the grounds that zoning was necessary to the future development and general welfare of the community.[14]

A spate of decisions by the courts followed in the early 1920's, some of which were favorable, and some unfavorable. But the trend was in favor of zoning as an exercise of the police power. Triumph in the state courts was clearly to be seen on the road ahead. The city could take no comfort from this fact, however, because comprehensive zoning had never been approved by the U.S. Supreme Court; and no one doubted that it would eventually be challenged as a violation of the Fourteenth Amendment.

The inevitable happened, and the test came in 1926 when the comprehensive zoning ordinance of Euclid, Ohio, was assailed as a violation of the U.S. Constitution. Recognizing that the test of the Euclid ordinance could have the greatest consequences, for good or for bad, the National Conference on City Planning retained Alfred Bettman of Cincinnati to submit a brief to the Supreme Court on behalf of the conference. But because Mr. Bettman neglected to inform the court of his intention to file a brief, he was not notified of the time of the hearing and thus failed to appear. The reports were that, after the first hearing, the court was divided five to four against the ordinance.

Appealing to Chief Justice William H. Taft (a Cincinnati man!), Bettman was able to gain the consent of the court for a highly unusual second hearing. Apparently in that hearing Bettman was persuasive in his arguments, because the court ruled in favor of the ordinance by a decision of five to four.[15]

If a series of oddities had preceded the decision, the decision itself was no less unusual. The justice who delivered the opinion of the court, Mr. Justice Sutherland, was to be soundly condemned during the 1930's as a reactionary; yet he wrote a decision in which he approved a startling intrusion into the rights of property. Mr. Justice Sutherland's decision relied heavily upon the body of legal reasoning built up in the state courts. Noting that

---

[14] *In re Opinion of the Justices,* 234 Mass. 597 (1920), and *Lincoln Trust Company* v. *Williams Building Corporation,* 229 N.Y. 313 (1920).

[15] Walker, *op. cit.,* pp. 77–78. See also Charles M. Haar, *Land-use Planning* (Boston: Little, Brown & Co., 1959), p. 165, note 2; and *Village of Euclid* v. *Ambler Realty Company,* 272 U.S. 365 (1926).

the state court decisions were conflicting, Sutherland averred that the bulk of them favored the extension of comprehensive zoning controls under the police power and that this broad view was surely to prevail. The justice in particular relied upon *State ex rel. Civello* v. *The City of New Orleans,* and *City of Aurora* v. *Burns,* in which the courts of Louisiana and Illinois had reasoned well—even brilliantly—in favor of comprehensive zoning under the police power.[16]

And thus was the legal basis for zoning firmly established. This did not mean—and does not mean—that there are not numerous zoning cases that go yearly into the courts. There are. Any constitutional ordinance or statute may be arbitrarily or unconstitutionally administered. So also may a new ordinance adventurously stray from accepted zoning practices. If the courts have been tempted to intrude themselves too often into zoning administration, it has not been because of doubts about the general constitutionality of the law. The reason has been rather that the courts seem to have a penchant for intruding into administrative matters, whether those matters concern zoning or any number of other management responsibilities. And this propensity is often abetted by badly conceived or outdated statutes.[17]

The Planning Bureaucracy. Just as every creed must have its church, so every plan must have its bureaucracy. Few indeed are the public projects that are self-enforcing, and planning is not one of these. The reluctance of the people at large to accept effective planning—and its strong right arm, zoning—makes a strong bureaucracy doubly necessary.

If the desirable characteristics of such a bureaucracy are clearly defined organizational structure and a highly professional staff, most cities fail to meet the necessary standards. Haphazardly thrown together, poorly staffed (sometimes not staffed at all), the city's administrative machinery for planning is often so badly equipped for any kind of action that the plan is honored mostly in the breach, rarely in the observance.[18] It is no wonder that so many expensive plans have simply gathered dust in the municipal vaults.

Often the city has no plan at all; yet it operates under the delusion that it is carrying on a program of city planning. Literally hundreds of communities have blithely gone through the years with both civic leadership and the people assuming that zoning—and not very adequate zoning at that—constitutes city planning.

That this misapprehension of the nature of planning is gradually being

[16] 154 La. 283 (1923); and 319 Ill. 84 (1925).

[17] Charles M. Haar and Barbara Hering, "The Lower Gwyneed Township Case: Too Flexible Zoning or an Inflexible Judiciary?" *Harvard Law Review,* LXXIV (June, 1961), 1552–1579.

[18] See, for example, Richard F. Babcock, "The Unhappy State of Zoning Administration in Illinois," *University of Chicago Law Review,* Summer, 1959, pp. 509–541.

dispelled is immediately evident to anyone who follows the voluminous literature currently being published on the city. Virtually all of the great cities of the republic have well-developed planning organizations—and have had them for years. The sensational growth of council-manager government since World War II, especially in medium-sized cities, has raised municipal performance to professional levels. The city manager usually realizes that without planning he will fail, just as surely as if he had amateurish finance administration and unscientific engineering.

Finally, the role of the federal government in stimulating planning cannot be depreciated. The Department of Housing and Urban Development makes grants-in-aid for planning, and requires a basic plan as one of the seven elements of the Workable Program for urban renewal. The effect of this federal influence has been particularly noticeable in small cities which had not previously followed in the footsteps of their larger sister cities.

Up to this point we have dealt in generalities. Now is the time to go into the specific character of planning administration. In order to do so, we shall look at the planning organizations of several major cities to observe how those organizations vary.

The first example is that of the planning administration of the city and county of Honolulu. (See Figure 18-1.) Appointed by the mayor, with the approval of the council, the planning director of Honolulu is head of the planning department and is thus the central figure in the administration of the city plan. Though directly responsible to the mayor (he may be removed by the mayor without the council's consent), he is, by clear intent of the charter, a professional.[19] His major duties indicate his importance. He prepares the general plan of the city, formulates the subdivision control

Figure 18-1. Elements of Planning Administration,
City and County of Honolulu

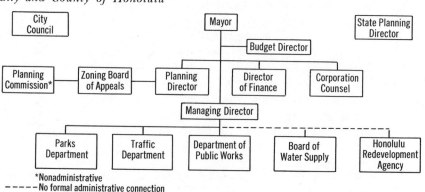

*Nonadministrative
– – – – – No formal administrative connection

Source: *Charter of the City and County of Honolulu, Hawaii.*

[19] *Charter of the City and County of Honolulu*, Sec. 5–502.

and zoning ordinances, and advises the mayor and council on the city's planning program. And he has the very considerable responsibility for administering the zoning and subdivision-control ordinances.

An advisory and rule-making body, the planning commission reinforces the planning efforts of the director and his aides. Composed of two ex officio members, the managing director and the budget director, and five other members appointed by the mayor with consent of the council, the planning commission advises the mayor, the council, and the planning director on planning programs; reviews the city plan and its modifications, as proposed by the plan director; reviews the subdivision-control and zoning ordinances; adopts regulations implementing the subdivision-control ordinance; prepares a capital improvement program; and consults with the state planning director.

In addition to the planning commission, the zoning board of appeals further aids the planning effort. Unlike the situation in many other cities, where the building department administers the zoning ordinance, the Honolulu charter fixes that duty upon the planning director. He also, as we have seen, is responsible for the subdivision-control ordinance. Inevitably, as the director seeks to carry out these ordinances, he will make decisions which citizens will appeal. These appeals must go to the zoning board of appeals.

Made up of three members appointed to overlapping three-year terms by the mayor and council, the board not only hears appeals but also hears petitions for variances to the zoning ordinances. If, for example, the ordinance provides for a fifty-foot setback for residences in a certain zone, but because of topographical considerations such a setback is impossible, the board may grant a variance.

Looking aside from Honolulu for a moment, we should note that in other cities the board of appeals may also grant exceptions—that is, permission for a type of land use not specifically countenanced for that particular zone by the ordinance. An adventurous architect may produce a design, for example, which violates the letter of the ordinance, but which still has appeal to city officials, in terms of both sound planning and neighborhood development. Such a situation arose in Baltimore, when a developer sought to build 168 garden apartments on a fifteen-acre tract of land. Approved by the board of municipal and zoning appeals and affirmed by the city court, the project was, on appeal, assailed before the Maryland Supreme Court. The latter court, though recognizing the economic advantages of the design, pointed to the express provisions of the zoning ordinance and reluctantly overruled both the board of appeals and the city court.[20] As an observer has commented elsewhere, zoning may become an

[20] *Norwood Heights Improvement Association* v. *Mayor and City Council of Baltimore*, 191 Md. 155 (1948), cited in Haar, *op. cit.*, pp. 230–233.

obstacle to innovation and deviation from the standard or the hackneyed.[21]

In general outline, the planning organization of the metropolitan government of Nashville follows the same pattern as that in Honolulu, possibly because the charters of the two cities date from the mid-twentieth century. Basically similar, too, is New York's system, with the plan commission constituting the center—though often the frustrated center—of the planning process. In Denver, as Figure 18-2 shows, most planning is under the supervision of the mayor, though one has every reason to expect that that supervision is often of a nominal sort.

It is indeed as important to know what goes on behind the organization chart as it is to understand the chart itself. There is scarcely a city agency that does not, at one time or another, become involved with the master plan, the capital budget, and the administration of zoning. The finance director, the legal counsel, and the public works director are only a few of the officials who are in a prime position to advance or frustrate the programs of the city planners. In New York, according to Sayre and Kaufman, the city planning commission's work in formulating the capital budget has incurred the wrath of the mayor, the budget director, the Board of Estimate, and other officials and agencies.[22]

Even more important are the outside forces which converge upon the planning administrator and with which he is so often unable to cope. There are other governmental jurisdictions: the federal government, the state government, school districts, adjoining cities, and other local authorities. And then there are the individuals and groups, varying from downtown businessmen to local flower clubs, with big stakes in the planning game.

Figure 18-2. Planning Organization in Denver

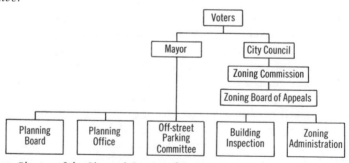

Source: *Charter of the City and County of Denver, Colorado.*

[21] For example, see Arthur C. Holden, "Zoning—An Impediment to Good Design?" *Progressive Architecture*, XXVII (November, 1946), 94–97.

[22] Wallace S. Sayre and Herbert Kaufman, *Governing New York City* (New York: W. W. Norton & Co., 1965), p. 375.

It is thus fruitless to argue about "good" planning organization, though some people like to do so endlessly. One can identify certain necessary attributes of planning organization, such as those appearing in the cities discussed above, but the ideal planning organization—ideal both politically and administratively—has so far escaped our grasp.

Some Problems of Planning Administration

Consultant or Resident Planner? The larger cities will always maintain a professional planning staff. But numerous smaller cities are faced with the decision of whether to set up a plan department and staff it or to retain a planning consultant and distribute day-to-day administration among the plan commission, the zoning board of appeals, and the building, engineering, and other line departments. The principal advantage of the latter alternative is that, by using the consulting firm, the city will have a greater variety of professional skills available to it than by using the resident planner. It is often true, also, that this method is more economical of funds, and that the outside expert, coming into town surrounded by his aides, carries with him a pomp and circumstance that is very persuasive to the local leadership.

The breaking point between these two approaches to planning administration might be given in terms of a population figure—probably somewhere between 40,000 and 50,000. Actually, however, few generalizations about when a city should change from the planning consultant to the resident planner are valid.

Intermittent advice by the consultant can probably never take the place of constant attention to the planning effort which only the professional at the head of a plan department can give the city. Let the consultant lead a major effort, such as developing the original plan or making major revisions in it; but let the city have its resident planner to bring professionalism even into the minutiae of daily administration. Let the city join forces with the county or with an adjoining municipality, if it cannot alone employ a full-time planning staff. This seems to be a digest of the experience of the present-day city.

The Problem of Intergovernmental Relations. One must always gingerly approach the subject of intergovernmental relations in planning. Few problems associated with city planning are more difficult of solution. Although we might point to Honolulu or Nashville as the model solution (if there is only one government, there cannot be intergovernmental relations, at least locally), so many vested interests have been built into the disintegrated local government structure of the typical community that emulation of the Honolulu or Nashville model, for most communities, borders on the impossible.

Yet the disintegration of local government may well reduce an originally effective planning effort to impotence. Increasingly aware of this danger, civic leaders, in league with the planners, have developed certain techniques for making the master plan an instrument of the entire community rather than simply a tool of one governmental body, the city.

What are these techniques? Extraterritoriality, an extension of municipal powers outside the boundaries of the city, is a means of bringing the urban fringe—or the unincorporated portion of it at least—within reach of the city's police powers. In North Carolina a city may zone outward for a mile and a half beyond its corporate limits; in Illinois, cities may zone and may control the layout of streets, other public ways, and public lands within the same general limits as in North Carolina. For the small urban area, even for the small metropolis, such power may have many important consequences. As soon as satellite cities and villages appear in the fringe, however, the effectiveness of extraterritoriality diminishes.

Because there is scarcely an urban community in the United States which does not contain several local governments, intergovernmental cooperation is needed both in the formation of the master plan and in its application. One means of bringing local officials together is by their appointment to the planning commission. In one instance, upon setting up its first commission, an Illinois city appointed members from the school, park, drainage, and health districts, and from the housing authority and the township—in short, from all of the overlying governmental jurisdictions save the county. The city, however, made no attempt to meet the problem of horizontal dispersion by having plan commission membership include officials from satellite cities, townships, and special districts.

Joint effort by the city and county is widely recognized as a device for coordinating efforts in the urban community. That there are not more city-county plan commissions and departments can be explained by interlocal jealousy as well as by the archaic administrative organization of the county and its rural orientation. If the city is afraid of giving up any of its prerogatives, the county is equally suspicious of any suggestions that seem to have an urban coloration. One county in a Midwestern state was so antagonistic to planning that extreme measures had to be taken to force it to act: a state university, situated in the county, obtained the introduction of a bill in the state legislature to confer upon itself the power to zone in the environs of its campus. Outraged and incredulous, but sorely shaken, the county board immediately took steps to retain a planning consultant. Only a form of polite blackmail could move the county board.

Finally, as we saw in Chapter 8, poorly conceived statutes on annexation and incorporation have contributed to the fractionalization of local government structure in the United States: these have made possible too-easy incorporation and too-difficult annexation. The city normally has much less difficulty in conceiving and executing a plan for the area within its borders than for the area without. The planning effort, therefore, could be greatly aided if severe restrictions were placed on municipal incorporations in the urban fringe and if, at the same time, the statutes were relaxed to permit easier annexation of territory than is generally permitted today.

Elimination of Nonconforming Uses. The nonconforming use—such as a business establishment in a residential zone, or a building that violates height, bulk, and lot-coverage restrictions—can damage the neighborhood, and eventually the entire community. Ideally, a plan can be developed for a neighborhood before development has begun, and some cities, by aggressive annexation, have achieved this objective. But normally the plan evolves after the neighborhood is in being and after the nonconforming uses are already in existence.

Perhaps the neighborhood has accommodated itself to the nonconformance. If so, the situation may result in no more harm than to offend the planner's sense of good order. The difficulty arises when the nonconforming property either falls into obsolescence or is about to be expanded upon. In either case the status quo is disturbed, tempers in the neighborhood are aroused, and the city must resolve the conflict. In short, the nonconforming land use, by nature unplanned, is always a potential source of conflict. The planned neighborhood shopping center, on the other hand, is as different from the ragtag corner grocery (for all the latter's claim to sentimental memories of childhood) as fire from water, even though both are commercial uses in a residential zone.

Nonconforming uses do not arise only with the introduction of comprehensive planning and zoning; they also appear when spot zoning creeps in and particularly when variances and exceptions are casually granted. These erosions of the proper use of land must be arrested, and nonconforming uses eliminated, if the stability of the neighborhood is to be maintained.

Seldom has any city attempted systematic elimination of nonconformance, yet several very practical devices are available to most cities for this purpose. The special assessment may be used: property nearby is assessed to cover the cost of purchase of the undesirable property and the elimination of its nonconformance. The amortization principle may, in some states at any rate, also be used: a nonconforming use may be permitted by ordinance to exist for a certain period beyond the date of the law's enactment. Thus a billboard might be given a three-year amortization period; a rooming house, ten years. Such periods of grace would allow the owner time to amortize at least some of his investment in the nonconforming use and time to plan for the transition to another one. They might well obviate, in addition, constitutional challenge of the law under either the due process or the equal protection clauses of the Fourteenth Amendment.

Urban Renewal. Urban renewal and redevelopment have, within the past ten years, become of such importance to the city that the master plan cannot but include them, and the plan department can but accommodate itself to the administrative and intergovernmental problems raised by this program. The situation is similar with housing and neighborhood conservation. But so important are these matters that they must be considered at length in the following chapters.

Summary

The planning of the city is inevitable. Thus, the questions to answer are: Will it plan systematically or haphazardly? Will it permit a chaos of private, limited plans to dominate the city, or will it assume public direction of the city's development in order to achieve both the private and the public good?

If the city chooses the latter course and pursues planning with determination, what will be the result? It will ideally increase the efficiency of the urban community by facilitating the movement of people and goods. It will enhance the livability of the community by raising the level of housing, recreation, sanitation, and cleanliness. It will develop the city esthetically and culturally by giving attention to things as diverse as trees and art museums.

No kind of planning will succeed, however, unless the citizenry at large is convinced of its necessity and desirability. Public acceptance will determine whether the new burst of activity in urban planning will succeed or fail. And there are signs frequently in evidence that those who people our cities either do not sympathize with planning or do not understand it. If this is true, then the planner, as a public official, must be as much a political leader as he is a professional in his trade. If this is true, then the major job of the planner is to gain popular acceptance of his ideas and his methods.

Annotated Bibliography

One cannot think of the law of planning without calling to mind the comprehensive and painstaking works of Charles M. Haar. Haar's *Land-Use Planning: A Casebook on the Use, Misuse, and Re-use of Urban Land* (Boston: Little, Brown & Co., 1959) is the best one-volume treatment in print on American planning law. For a comparative study of English and American land-use control systems see Charles M. Haar (ed.), *Law and Land: Anglo-American Planning Practice* (Cambridge, Mass.: Harvard University Press, 1964). Another useful legal study is E. C. Yokley, *Zoning Law and Practice* (Charlottesville, Va.: The Michie Co., 1953).

A devastating attack upon the ugliness of the American city (and upon the failure of planning controls) is Peter Blake's *God's Own Junkyard: The Planned Deterioration of America's Landscape* (New York: Holt, Rinehart & Winston,

1964). To see what an internationally known architect did with city planning for Sacramento and various foreign cities, one can read Willy Boesiger (ed.), *Richard J. Neutra: 1950–1960 Buildings and Projects* (New York: Frederick A. Praeger, 1959). If one wishes to find an analysis of the ills of the contemporary city and a model for the "metropolis of tomorrow," he can profitably review the work of the iconoclastic planner-architect Victor Gruen, *The Heart of Our Cities* (New York: Simon & Schuster, 1964).

For decades the literature on planning examined the political questions involved in planning under the name of "community relations" or similar euphemisms. It seems as if those who wrote on city planning were convinced that if they ignored politics it would eventually go away. But that there was a great deal of politics in the planning of housing projects was documented in Martin Meyerson and Edward C. Banfield, *Politics, Planning, and the Public Interest* (Glencoe, Ill.: The Free Press, 1955). And the many political forces that converged upon the professional planner in Minneapolis–St. Paul are described in Alan A. Altshuler, *The City Planning Process: A Political Analysis* (Ithaca, N.Y.: Cornell University Press, 1965).

For a look at the ideal city, see Thomas A. Reiner, *The Place of the Ideal Community in Urban Planning* (Philadelphia: University of Pennsylvania Press, 1963). The practical, down-to-earth approach to city planning is given in the always reliable International City Managers' Association, *Local Planning Administration* (Chicago: The Association, 3rd ed., 1959).

CHAPTER 19

A Man's Castle

The Nature of Urban Housing

One of the earliest concerns of the city was the housing of its citizenry. Even at the beginning of the urban revolution there was undoubtedly public concern for the physical conditions under which the person or the individual family lived. Archaeological evidence shows not only the existence of defense systems, which were as necessary for the protection of the physical city as of the people, but also the drains, sewers, streets, and heating and water supply systems, which must have been then, as now, basic elements of urban housing. There must also have been concern for open space and at least a tacit recognition of the intimate relation of openness to the good life in the city. Deductive reasoning alone would lead one to believe that religious and tribal controls—indistinguishable in the ancient city from civic control—were concerned with almost every facet of the individual's life, not even excepting that most important element, the way in which he was housed.

If the prehistoric city was concerned with urban housing, the modern city is no less so. Recognizing the obvious truth that the physical structure of the city is a part of the life process of urban existence—that shelter is as important as bread—the modern city gradually, almost painfully, has taken steps to protect itself from the dangers which daily beset the shelter of its citizens.

The Ancillary Services to Housing. During the Great Fire of London, little organized resistance was mounted against the flame until the latter stages of the conflagration. When Chicago burned two hundred years later, organized fire companies were on hand within minutes of the fire's beginning. Water of any kind was hard to come by in some parts of London or New York even as late as the midnineteenth century. Now the city provides itself with an abundance of pure water simply as a matter of course. The same is true with waste collection and disposal, drainage, street paving, lighting, and sometimes the production of various forms of energy (gas, electricity, steam) and their distribution.

Ordinarily, we should not need to dwell on the importance of the underground and surface utilities to housing, nor on the essential nature of police as well as fire protection. Yet so rarely do we discuss the relation of these services to housing that we must underscore their importance.

When we speak of a $20,000 house in a new subdivision, rarely do we think of more than the structure itself and the fittings to the structure. Yet consider the lot on which a house sits. Its market value is, let us say, $3,000. A few months ago it was an indistinguishable part of a cornfield, pasture, woods, or desert. But by the time this raw land was purchased and surveyed, the developer had perhaps $1,000 invested in each individual lot. In order to realize that value, he had to invest more capital. Since access to the lot was primary, he had to lay out a street; and as an integral part of the street, he had to install storm drains and sidewalks. Then, in rapid succession, he was required to lay sanitary sewers and connect the laterals into a main trunk line. Water mains came next; then came a source of energy to operate both heating and mechanical appliances. By this time he must have had a total capital commitment in the lot of at least $2,500, much of which was to become public property when the developer dedicated the storm and sanitary sewers, the water main, the street, the sidewalks, and perhaps the energy supply facilities (gas mains and electrical lines) to the city.

This is by no means the end of the natural history of a subdivision lot. As the house is built, city inspectors will periodically call to determine whether the city's building, electrical, and plumbing codes are being followed. Before the city accepts the subdivision, an engineer from the public works department must certify, after a series of inspections, that the developer has met all the requirements of the subdivision-control ordinance. This ordinance, if it is up to snuff, will require not only the usual surface and in-the-ground facilities but street trees and recreational space as well.

In other words, a discussion of housing, at least in the United States, must include a great many elements other than the building of the structure by the entrepreneur. Government plays a vital role. The first great concerted effort by government to aid housing, for example, appeared in the late nineteenth and early twentieth centuries. This was a truly mammoth effort by the newer cities in the South, Midwest, and West to supply the basic surface and subsurface amenities to housing by means of the special assessment. Without these great special-assessment programs the urban citizen could not have been adequately housed.

The Amenities of Housing. Besides the raw land and those essential capital investments in the land which make it suitable for modern urban use, the character of housing in the city has many other facets. The age of a city's housing is of no inconsiderable importance to an understanding of the housing of the urban citizen. Every decade the U.S. Bureau of the Census assembles data on the age patterns of the structures in which city people live.[1] By assembling these data and transferring them to a map, one can see

[1] U.S. Bureau of the Census, *U. S. Census of Housing, 1960* (1963), Vol. IV.

graphically the city in its youthful vigor, its middle age, and its senility. From such a map one may learn where the lower classes, the minority groups, and the elderly pensioners live and even where there exists that glittering facade of the city, the Gold Coast. Age and obsolescence seem to go together in American urban housing, and too often age means overcrowding, bad hygienic conditions, high incidence of fire hazards and crime, and assorted types of social disorganization.

Age, of course, does not necessarily need to mean obsolescence. That it does is sometimes the result of poor construction or failure of the owner to maintain structural integrity—in either case, a reflection on the city's building and housing codes or their administration. Obsolescence is also determined by cultural factors. If the novels of John P. Marquand interpret the upper middle-class culture of New England correctly—and where can one find a better interpretation?—the proper Bostonian feels that it would be déclassé for him to live elsewhere than in the ancestral home. The same is true with the remnants of the southern aristocracy in Virginia, Charleston, and elsewhere. Popular culture today, on the other hand, tends to emphasize styles or fads in housing. Note the bungalow or the Cape Cod cottage design in the 1920's, the modern colonial in the 1930's, and the ranch-type in the 1960's. These fads in housing have caused perfectly good homes to be discarded by a vast number of families simply because styles have changed. Such is one result of a popular culture which equates change with progress.

The character of housing is also strongly influenced by a collection of factors that might be grouped under the term "amenities." Site and situation are as influential as structure or underground utilities upon the nature of housing. Not everyone can have a dwelling which overlooks the sea or a clear mountain brook. But wherever the site, it should be well drained; in situation, the dwelling should be oriented to receive the maximum of light and prevailing winds. Structural density should be controlled to prevent the overcrowding of the land, to preserve open space, and at the same time to prevent the waste of land that goes into overly expansive development. Transportation facilities should be treated as an integral part of housing rather than an afterthought to be worried about after the housing is designed and built.

Except for such laws as flood-plain zoning ordinances—to interdict the building of dwelling units in river flood plains—and hesitant attempts at architectural control codes, cities as a whole have not aggressively and adventurously sought to make legal assurance that optimum amenities exist. Even the most daring subdivision-control ordinances do not attempt to force the developer to take advantage of whatever natural beauties there are to the site, or to insist upon orientation of the dwelling to the prevailing winds and to the sun.

Something new under the sun, however, something directed toward assuring the basic amenities is the housing ordinance. Given new life by urban renewal, the techniques are ones that seek to assure that housing is healthful and livable: that it provides adequate ventilation, heat, water, sewage disposal facilities, cleanliness, and structural integrity. These are basic necessities and also basic amenities which the city seeks to assure the people whom she houses.

Demography and Housing: Too Many People?

In spite of all the talk of the world's population explosion, very little consideration is given to the connection of this phenomenon with urban housing. Yet, whether in the East or West, the destiny of most men, women, and children is to flood into the cities and there to find some place to rest —if need be, in the street itself. Although this population glut has been visited upon the city many times during past centuries, the city has never learned to cope with it.

According to the Illinois Public Aid Commission (the state welfare agency), Chicago received 3,000 "relief-prone" newcomers a day during 1960. If indeed such an astonishing number as 1,000,000 people are flocking into the city every year, that fact alone does not mean that many, perhaps most, of the newcomers will not accommodate themselves sufficiently to urban life to reward themselves and their adopted city with their productiveness. In fact, most Puerto Ricans, southern hill people, and other southerners, whether white or Negro, will get work, raise families, and receive some of the rewards of urban life.[2] That the great majority of Negroes, Puerto Ricans, and hill folk do adjust to a strange new environment is not so much a tribute to race, nationality, or blood as to the human species itself.

But, unfortunately, this is not the end of the story. The impact of the population glut upon the city's physical plant, as well as upon its social and political institutions, must be recognized too.

It used to be said of Vienna that the Orient began in the city's Third District. During the flamboyant days of the late nineteenth century, semi-Oriental peoples from the far reaches of the Austro-Hungarian Empire flooded into this southeastern section of the city and multiplied in the slums of the imperial capital. Serbs, Magyars, Bulgars, Russians, Oriental Jews, Greeks, Turks, Croats—all teemed, quarreled, and starved in the working-class sections of the city. Some Viennese thought, even as New

---

[2] See Oscar Handlin, *The Newcomers* (Cambridge, Mass.: Harvard University Press, 1959). Although limited to Negroes and Puerto Ricans in New York, the study gives conclusions that can be validly applied to any city and to any group of new arrivals in the low socioeconomic stratum.

Yorkers think today, that the teeming thousands could never be assimilated; yet to walk through the streets of the Third District of Vienna now is to catch only the faintest echoes of the hundreds of thousands who crowded in upon each other during the nineteenth century. Today Vienna is one of the few major urban places in the world which is not rapidly growing. But the city on the Danube did not achieve this assimilation and this stability of population all alone. Quite the contrary, it was the breakup of empire, being on the losing side in two world wars, and the national barriers halting the free immigration of peoples which solved the problem for the Viennese.

About the same period—immediately following World War I—the raising of immigration barriers by the federal government had a similar effect upon American cities, though a less striking or long-lasting one. The subsequent rapid mechanization of agriculture and tides of migrants from Puerto Rico and, to a degree, from Mexico have forced so many people into the city that by this sixth decade of the twentieth century civic leadership is at a loss for solutions to the problem. Nor are American civic leaders alone in their perplexity. If Vienna was able virtually to solve its housing problem and thereby to eliminate slums, it is because the population glut was solved for her. But what of Paris with the teeming shantytowns filled with Algerians at her borders? And what of Lima, with the Peruvian Indians still pushing into her already overflowing slums? And what of Hong Kong and Tokyo?

It has been suggested, sometimes wryly, sometimes in deep seriousness, that major cities like Chicago, Philadelphia, and New York should set up "immigration" barriers by which they could turn away the masses of dispossessed, "relief-prone" migrants from the city. But to move, and to move about freely, is surely one of the cardinal rights of a free people. Just as the medieval serf looked to the city for his freedom, just so a millennium later his counterpart strives for the liberation of the large city.

Population movement results from, and may itself produce, both socially desirable and socially destructive situations. As people—for the most part humble people—throng into the cities of the world, they come for a variety of reasons; and their arrival has a variety of results. If they supply the city with cheap, unskilled labor, they also require of it expensive social services. If they bring racial, cultural, linguistic, national variety to the city, they also bring inevitable cultural and social conflict. No city, we should remember, has ever been able to cope with this human tide without drastic political surgery. Vienna was able to solve the problem of population glut only because the Treaty of Versailles erected national boundaries over the entire face of eastern Europe; and these became effective barriers to the free migration of peoples. Johannesburg requires that Negroes and colored not leave their reserves without passes, and that they have further passes to be in urban areas. But such drastic "solutions" commend themselves neither to the humane nor to the urbane.

It is not our purpose here to propose a solution to population glut. Perhaps, in a free society, there is no solution but only a variety of corrective approaches: urban renewal, public housing, deconcentration of industry, and the new-town movement which the British have experimented with so extensively. That such corrective measures must be pursued energetically is only too evident, for without attacking the problem of overpopulation no real strides can be taken toward the goal of a well-housed urban citizenry.

Race and Housing

We have already examined the human ecology of the city and have seen how class, race, ethnic background, and even religion react upon the spatial distribution of population. We need here, therefore, only to note the impact of that distribution upon housing. People of a similar socioeconomic class tend to live together, and their housing tends toward similarity, whether in design, economic worth, or use. As the most economically fortunate people discard their housing, the lower income groups move into it. As racial groups penetrate into a neighborhood, the movement of the "old settlers" out of it may assume the proportions of a rout. The ghetto that Louis Wirth analyzed so many years ago, though somewhat changed, still remains and still expands. Excepting for excess population, no pressure upon housing is greater than racial pressure.

The Negro, especially, finds his housing burden almost insupportable. Although all minority groups are subjected to various forms of discrimination from the dominant groups, the Negro, being readily identifiable by the pigmentation of his skin, finds perhaps his final frustration in his housing. Observe a member of the Negro middle class. Well-educated, successful in business or the professions, poles apart from the nearly illiterate agricultural worker, he seeks to separate himself physically from the masses of his own race. Class identification may thus become stronger for him than racial. (In much the same way class overcame the ethnic, religious, or national identification of such relative latecomers to the American city as the Italian, the Jew, the Irishman, and the Pole.) He attaches himself to middle-class values—money, education, achievement—but he is separated from his middle-class Caucasian peers by the barrier of race.

Why do people with the same value systems permit themselves such divisions? Though there are many reasons—or superstitions—one of the strongest has an economic basis. And it is directly related to housing. We should take a moment to glance at this factor.

As the Negro penetrates into white neighborhoods, so the argument goes, he increases the population density, overtaxes public facilities, "causes" the physical deterioration of the neighborhood, and depresses property values. "Depresses property values"!—what greater terror could strike at the hearts of the good middle-class burghers?

This widely accepted view of the Negro's effect upon property values cannot, however, stand up to close examination. Luigi Laurenti found that nonwhite entry into a neighborhood does not have the effect on property values that such "intrusion" is popularly thought to have.[3] By setting up all-white control areas and comparing the reaction of values there to values in the neighborhoods being penetrated by nonwhite peoples, Laurenti found that when Negro families moved into the white neighborhoods which he studied, the change was as apt to increase property values as to depress them. Thus those who use the economic argument against nonwhite families in Caucasian neighborhoods rest their case solely upon instances in which property values are depressed and ignore those instances in which those values are not significantly affected or are actually increased.

What role does the city play in minority housing (other than public housing)? Although it may not legally interdict the outward movement of nonwhites from their ghettos, it can without doubt create an atmosphere which will discourage such outward movement. If city hall makes it clear —informally, of course—that it will not provide police protection for a Negro family moving into an all-white neighborhood, that position alone may discourage, or effectively stymie, the move. These and other methods are used against minority groups all over the country, North or South, East or West. Incorporation, annexation, or deannexation may also be used to thwart minority desires.

An example of the limits to which a community will use its power as a municipal corporation to stop the entry of nonwhite peoples into its limits was powerfully offered by Deerfield, Illinois, a bedroom city outside Chicago. When a private corporation was at the point of building so-called middle-income housing for both white and Negro families, the local park district called for an election to authorize the issuance of general-obligation bonds to purchase the site for a city park. Just months before the park district had offered the same proposal to the people, and it was voted down. But stimulated by fears of nonwhite penetration into the community, the people approved the second offering of the proposal, and the park district moved in swiftly with its powers of eminent domain to checkmate the interracial efforts of the housing corporation. The political minority which had supported the idea of racially integrated housing for middle-class families had only a public park to sweeten the taste of their defeat.

It would be unfair to the city to paint a completely dark picture of its

[3] Luigi Laurenti, *Property Values and Race* (Berkeley, Calif.: University of California Press, 1960).

stance with relation to housing for minority groups. Under state enabling legislation, cities have attempted to forbid housing discrimination of various kinds. In 1957, New York City became the first American city—or any other governmental jurisdiction, for that matter—to forbid by law discrimination against minority groups in the rental or sale of apartment dwellings. And it has become commonplace for cities, again under permissive state legislation, to forbid discrimination in public housing.

A vigorously fought 1964 election in California resulted in the adoption (by a vote of 3.5 million to 2 million) of a constitutional amendment nullifying the state's fair-housing law which forbade racial discrimination in the sale or rental of about 70 percent of the privately owned housing in California.

This amendment had the effect, also, of setting aside any city ordinance which had been enacted to prevent racial discrimination in housing. In 1966, however, the California supreme court ruled that the amendment violated the Fourteenth Amendment to the U.S. Constitution. This meant, presumably, that local anti-discrimination ordinances were again effective.

Efforts of civil rights groups to obtain open housing legislation were not limited to the cities and the states. After long effort these groups were successful in winning Congress to their view and open housing became the most important feature of the civil rights bill enacted in 1968. Expected to apply to 80 percent of all dwellings by 1970, the new statute provided that there should be no discrimination based upon race, religion or national origin in the sale or rental of housing.[4]

Housing and Private Capital

One need only skirt the American city today—even the small one—and see the vast acreages of rural lands being converted into subdivisions (and shopping centers to serve the subdivisions) to wonder whether there is a housing problem in the United States. One is apt to conclude that there is a housing problem, yes, but only a problem such as those that usually attend a vigorous industry. How, with all this building, could there be any extensive number of people who simply cannot shelter themselves adequately?

Franklin Roosevelt used one of his typically resounding phrases to describe the situation a generation ago: "one-third of a nation ill-housed, ill-clad, and ill-nourished." After succeeding decades of prosperity, the condition of American housing is not nearly so good as we might rightfully expect, given our increase in wealth. One reason for this situation is that it is much easier to produce an abundance of automobiles and television sets

---

[4] *Congressional Quarterly*, XXVI, No. 15 (April 12, 1968), 791.

than it is to supply an abundance of good housing. Obviously, wealth is not the only determinant of housing availability: race, age, value systems, and many other factors intervene.[5]

In the mobilization of private capital for housing, the market is the most important factor. Compared with the influence of the market, government activity is of minor consideration. So long as there is any semblance of a free economy, this overall generalization will continue to hold true. Yet there are governmental aids of many types which act as a reassurance to the private capitalist and increase his willingness to invest in the building industry.

The city is intimately involved in giving that reassurance to the person with money to invest in housing. Without the constant vigilance of the public safety departments—without police and fire protection—not only would existing housing be in jeopardy, but new housing also would be discouraged. Without streets, drains, sanitary, and waste facilities; without zoning laws to interdict bad land-use practices; without the building codes and subdivision-control ordinances; without, in short, the massive protective institution which is the city, there simply could not be a free market in housing.

Nevertheless, the principal direct aid to the housing market at the present is not city at all but federal. The Federal Housing Administration, created in 1934 and made a division of the Department of Housing and Urban Development in 1965, insures the loans made by private agencies to the homeowner. Contrary to the impression held by many people, it does not itself lend money directly; it is an insurance "company" operated and financed by the federal government primarily to encourage private capital to enter the housing market. As such its impact upon the housing market has been vast, indeed, though probably not so great, for example, as the kind of aid lent housing by use of the special assessment in the half-century immediately preceding the Great Depression.

By no means an insignificant companion to FHA is the Veterans' Administration. Since the VA may only guarantee loans made to veterans of World War II and subsequent wars (and may even, unlike FHA, make direct loans), the impact of the VA program on housing may gradually diminish—if there are no other wars to create more veterans!

The ability of the FHA and VA programs to attract money into the housing market cannot be overemphasized. Particularly for lower-income groups, for young families with little ability to establish a substantial equity in a house, and even for elderly couples, the long-term, low-interest loan insured by FHA or VA has been, in effect, a subsidy in aid of those very groups which otherwise could not purchase housing. Because FHA,

[5] See, for example, Beverly Duncan and Philip Hauser, *Housing a Metropolis* (Glencoe, Ill.: The Free Press, 1960).

too, has been interested in such important adjuncts of housing as subdivision design, its policies have undoubtedly increased the desirability of the housing environment and strengthened the hand of the city in its insistence upon the developers' furnishing the necessary amenities to new housing.

Where the FHA and other federal programs have not substantially bettered the housing situation, the reasons are many and are not necessarily indictments of the programs as such. The FHA was conceived as a conservative effort to aid housing. Its very conservatism and the conservative cast of the companion housing programs perhaps made it incapable of having a truly positive impact upon the housing situation. Perhaps, too, the habit and values of the buying public diminished the effect of all governmental programs in direct aid of housing. People want housing, but they want many other things, too. In doubtlessly many thousands of family units, the decision is made every year to invest surplus earnings in automobiles rather than in improved housing. If these families are members of minority groups, they might not be able to purchase good dwellings at an acceptable price.

No discussion of the housing market would be complete without mentioning the market's distortion, as some would insist, by FHA policy. Because FHA will insure mortgages primarily on dwellings designed for single-family units, it has stimulated urban sprawl and has thus indirectly discouraged the building of multifamily units for owner occupancy or for rental.[6] This predisposition of FHA for the single-family, suburban-type home may be no more than an indication of the agency's basic conservatism. It is most certainly true that for more than a half-century, a period including extensive experience with two major types of governmental encouragement to residential expansion in the city (municipal special-assessment financing and federal mortgage insurance), the popular desire seems to be directed toward having a home of one's own. This means a dwelling physically detached from another structure and situated on roughly 7,000 square feet of ground in a part of the urban community which is not too thickly settled.

This attitude cannot be blamed upon FHA policies, any more than the popular desire for an automobile to use for all transportation needs can be laid at the feet of the auto magnate in Detroit. Still, public policy in housing, as in transportation, has been faltering and unsure, a prey to manifold ambivalences, and has been all too apt to follow the popular will without seeking to give the people real alternatives for choice.

In housing we still seem to want to live like nineteenth-century villagers —six or eight families to the acre as the maximum for land occupancy.

[6] Robert H. Connery and Richard H. Leach, *The Federal Government and Metropolitan Areas* (Cambridge, Mass.: Harvard University Press, 1960), p. 15.

And a majority of people probably agree that the best possible condition would be the one-family-per-acre conceived by Frank Lloyd Wright for his utopian Broadacre City. This romantic point of view is nowhere better illustrated than in our attitude toward public housing policy, by which we crowd families by the hundreds into great blocks of low-cost apartments and then suffer pangs of conscience that we have not given them workers' cottages with geraniums flowering in the windows. Let us now look at public housing and see what kind of strange creature we have in our midst.

Public Housing

When the Socialist workers of Vienna retreated before the superior forces of the Dollfuss government of Austria in the civil war of 1934, one of their places of refuge was the Karl Marx Hof, a great complex of low-rental apartments built by the Socialist city government several years previously. Moving up artillery, the Dollfuss forces gradually battered the housing project into rubble, and the workers were forced to surrender.

This unhappy event dramatized to the world, not only the quickening struggle between the left and right in Europe, but also the remarkable achievements of the city of Vienna in its attack upon the slums and the inadequate housing of lower-income families. Today, having almost forgotten civil war, dictatorship, and the Götterdämmerung of World War II, the Viennese can boast of the most ambitiously conceived, the longest lasting, and the widest ranging public housing program in the free world.[7] The objectives of Vienna have been nothing less than the complete elimination of slums and the housing of all lower-income families in modest, decent dwelling places. During the 1950's approximately 90 percent of all new housing in Vienna was built by the city government.

What the Viennese have done no American city, or other government, has had the heart or the will to do. Although we talk about decent housing for everyone, our public policy, at whatever level of government, has never been designed to achieve that objective. And not only has the design been inadequate, but the amount of wealth which we have been willing to devote to public housing has also been insufficient to achieve more than limited objectives.

All of this is not to say that we necessarily need to emulate the Viennese by slavishly copying their methods of attacking the urban housing problem. It is merely to point out that the Viennese, by great effort, have come far closer to achieving an elimination of slum conditions than any American city, and perhaps closer than any other city in the free world. And they

[7] For an interesting though unfriendly view of Vienna's housing program see Morton Bodfish, *Vienna's Housing—A Preface to Urban Renewal* (Bloomington, Ind.: Graduate School of Business, Indiana University, 1961).

have done so by recognizing what much of urban leadership in American cities has come to recognize—that only substantial public action can give good housing to the lower-income families in our cities.

The raison d'être for public housing in the United States is precisely this: private capital in conjunction with a free market cannot provide safe, healthful housing for all Americans. This conclusion came easily for the mayors of our larger cities, whether Republican or Democratic. But for many conservatives, such as the late Senator Robert Taft of Ohio, it came only after a great deal of soul-searching. And there is still a considerable element in all of our legislative bodies that either regards public housing with the gravest suspicion or refuses to admit that more than nominal sums should be invested in housing. For these and other reasons public housing programs in American cities have been timidly conceived, inadequately financed, and poorly administered.

Let us start, first, with administration. Although in the early part of the New Deal the federal government itself built public housing, this program was soon abandoned for the present system of local operation with oversight by the federal government. As a rule a city or county housing authority is established under state enabling legislation. Not all cities and counties need public housing, of course, and thus many have not utilized the strictly permissive laws.[8]

Once the housing authority has been set up, it becomes a quasi-municipal corporation, which is usually autonomous in its relation with the city or county. Nevertheless it must work intimately with the plan commission and with the urban renewal agency—in fact, it may sometimes be assigned urban renewal functions by the city. In North Carolina, Texas, Pennsylvania (except Philadelphia), Colorado, and California the mayor appoints all members of the city housing authority's governing board. The city, moreover, must approve proposed housing projects and agree to provide municipal services to each project when completed.

In financing low-cost public housing, the arrangements are quite complex. The housing agency is authorized by state law to issue revenue bonds which are exempt from federal taxation. Since the authority usually has no power to tax, general-obligation bonds may not be issued. Paradoxically, a general-obligation feature is attached to the bonds, but it is the full faith and credit of the federal government, rather than the city, which backs them up. Because of tax exemption and the general-obligation element, the bonds usually bring premium rates on the market. In case of adverse market conditions, however, the Public Housing Administration will purchase up to 90 percent of the local authority's bonds.

[8] At the end of 1965, something over 700,000 federally assisted housing units were being operated by 1,750 local authorities. *The Municipal Year Book 1966* (Chicago: ICMA), p. 349.

From the sale of bonds the housing authority raises the funds necessary to build the projected dwelling units. But when the units are built and rented, the authority has some rather considerable financial commitments to meet: debt service (bond retirement and interest), maintenance and other costs of operations, and payments in lieu of taxes, amounting to about 10 percent of rentals, to the local governments. Since the low rentals do not meet these costs, the federal government pays annual subsidies to the housing authority to meet its deficit.

The federal government does not, however, carry the burden alone, since several states subsidize public housing with state funds.[9] Indeed, in New York City there are three types of low-cost, subsidized housing, each aided in turn by the city, the state, and the federal government. New York City happens to be the largest landlord, not only in the nation, but in the free world.

Such is the major outline of the way that public housing in American cities is conceived, financed, and administered. The system has worked this way for almost a quarter of a century, and much low-cost housing has resulted from it. A great deal of criticism of the program has been voiced by many observers, however, and we can gain considerable insight into public housing by examining some of it.

Some Questions About Public Housing

Should Public Housing Administration Be Autonomous? Administratively, public housing has often been castigated because it has served further to Balkanize local government. Intergovernmental relations, as we have seen in previous chapters, is at best a tortuous, uncertain process, yet local governments must work together, and usually, after much backing and filling, they do. Every time an independent or semi-independent governmental power is created, this cooperation is made more difficult than before. Public housing has created literally hundreds of such autonomous units to complicate further the local governmental jigsaw puzzle. On the other hand, independence has, supposedly, certain advantages: the housing authority's autonomy does, at times, free its program from group pressure put upon city hall; the authority usually has a governing board which can gain some expertise in housing matters; and it may be able to develop a professional staff free of the spoils system. Whether these "advantages" are sufficient to warrant the formal separation of the function from the city is a value judgment. Most political scientists would say no, that the interde-

---

[9] As of December, 1961, fourteen states and Puerto Rico authorized direct state financial aid for housing to be rented or sold. *The Book of the States, 1962–1963* (Chicago: Council of State Governments, 1962), p. 460. Much, but not all, of this could be described as state aid to public housing.

pendence of housing authority and city hall is so great now, and is becoming so much greater with the burgeoning of urban renewal, that only by transforming the authority into a line department of the city (or the county, as the case may be) can the public housing program reach maximum effectiveness and, more important, achieve a measure of political responsibility.

Are There Inadequacies in Public Housing Finance? Financially, too, the program is widely charged with sins of both omission and commission. Not enough tax money is going into public housing, say the critics of the program; and city, state, and nation should raise the ante. The city of Vienna is currently spending about one-third of its income for low-cost housing, and its wealth cannot rival that of any major American city. The critics are also concerned that there are income ceilings for families in public housing. When family income exceeds a certain limit, the family must vacate public housing, only, in many instances, to return to slum housing because its income still is not sufficient to enable it to pay for decent nonsubsidized housing. The critics would have the income limits raised drastically or eliminated altogether, and would scale rentals to the higher incomes. "When family income rises above the maximum set by regulations for the development," reads one critical report, "the family should be permitted to remain, paying a larger part of the economic rental." [10] This would have the twofold effect of bringing the housing projects closer to a pay-as-you-go basis (enabling expansion of low-cost housing within the current level of public spending) and of saving families that have raised their incomes from the danger of forced return to slum housing. Once again, the Viennese experience is instructive. With no limits on the income of the dweller in public housing (anyone, whether prince or peasant, may live in, let us say, George Washington Hof), the city has still been able to rehouse the great mass of its proletariat.

Are There Errors in Fixing the Design, Situation, and Clientele of Public Housing? Many critics of public housing insist that it is poorly designed, badly situated, and discriminatory. The National Federation of Settlements and Neighborhood Centers holds that "public housing has shown too little advancement in creative design, largely because of administrative controls and inflexible standards required by the federal agency."

The site and situation of public housing come to the critics' attention for various reasons. "Public housing developments should be scattered throughout a city and should be small in most places with no more than 100 units, and a maximum of 250." Such criteria can be and are met in the smaller city. Although Vienna has had considerable success in carrying out such a policy, the large American city has had none. Even where there is

[10] The National Federation of Settlements and Neighborhood Centers, *A New Look at Public Housing* (New York: The Federation, 1958), p. 5.

general agreement that public housing is necessary, there seems to be, too often, a tendency in each neighborhood or ward to want the project in another corner of the city.

In an admirable study of the public housing struggle in Chicago, Meyerson and Banfield found that property owners near the site proposed for public housing offered objections ranging from claims that it would depreciate the values of adjoining property to insistence that it was socialism. But they also found that the protesters wanted small public projects rather than large ones.[11] And inevitably the question of race lay behind the most routine protests. Since it has been the policy of housing agencies in most northern and western cities to develop interracial public housing projects, neighborhood rank and file in such places tends, rightly or wrongly, to fear public housing. The federal government strengthened the hand of the city through the Civil Rights Act of 1964 by forbidding racial discrimination in federally assisted public housing programs. Very often, however, the housing project remains a racial ghetto.

Whether or not these criticisms of public housing are valid depends upon one's point of view. But whether valid or insubstantial they tend to show that passions of great magnitude can be generated over this segment of public policy. If housing seems so often embroiled in politics, the reasons are to be found here: with deeply felt ideas being advanced, old customs attacked, and new fears generated, politics is inevitable. But it should be remembered that politics is nothing more than a method for resolving conflict. Although politics will never achieve the ideal—in housing or in any field of human endeavor—it will nevertheless seek to accommodate as many points of view as possible. Such accommodation is the basic element in the effectuation of any policy.

Does the Local Tax System Adversely Affect Housing? As we have already seen, there is an inherent contradiction in the city's efforts to achieve good housing for all of its inhabitants and a tax system which penalizes the property owner who wishes to improve his property. In this the general property tax is the greatest offender.[12] Considering the maze of statutory and constitutional provisions which bear upon the property tax, it is a question whether the city can accomplish much in clearing up the evil without firm resolution and great effort. But the effort is worth the candle, and by enlisting the aid of the state the city can achieve it.

Rolph and Break summarize the general impact of property taxation thus. The tax is largely shifted, in the case of rental housing, from the land-

[11] Martin Meyerson and Edward C. Banfield, *Politics, Planning, and the Public Interest* (Glencoe, Ill.: The Free Press, 1955), p. 183.

[12] For a highly interesting study of the impact of the general property tax on city development, see Mary Rawson, *Property Taxation and Urban Development, Research Monograph No. 4* (Washington, D.C.: Urban Land Institute, 1961).

lord to the tenant. A tax on owner-occupied dwelling units, however, is not shifted but is borne by the owner-occupier.[13] The consensus of economists, then, is that the property tax tends to increase the cost of housing to the occupant, whether tenant or owner. In most neighborhoods this situation will not materially affect either the quality or supply of housing. It may cause a middle-income family to postpone the installation of an extra bathroom, but such "sacrifices" cannot become the concern of those who formulate tax and housing policies. For the economically marginal family, however, the impact of the property tax may be rigorous indeed.

A Policeman at Every Door: Enforcement of the City's Housing Codes

After a series of tragic fires in a slum section of the city during the winter of 1957–1958, Chicago fire and housing inspectors, aided by scores of policemen, made an intensive search of the densely populated section in which so much life had been lost and so much property destroyed. Not surprisingly, the inspectors found that the area abounded in code violations. Some of these violations had resulted from illegal conversions of their premises by slum landlords; others came from the tenants themselves. The mass of people that had come into the city from the southern hills and cotton patches moved into South Chicago as inexorably as lava from an exploding volcano. A building legally converted to house six families now housed a dozen or more. Landlords, by stealth and in flagrant violation of municipal ordinances, crowded people into every nook and cranny of the sturdy buildings that had once housed more fortunate citizens. The tenants themselves, with misplaced generosity or downright cupidity, opened their dingy flats to grandfathers, cousins, friends, and complete strangers. To say that people were crawling over one another is not to engage in commonplace exaggeration but to state a simple fact.

Population glut had infected an entire section of a great city, and while everyone knew about it—whether citizen or bureaucrat—no one was willing to attack the situation until fires had killed dozens of children and decimated entire families.

What could be done? After the army of inspectors had filed their official reports and had documented in officialese these many instances of man's inhumanity to man and of rural man's floundering ignorance in a great city, was there anyone, from mayor to President, who could act? Enforce the city's codes? A simple solution, indeed, but as one inspector grimly remarked, "To do so we'd have to station a cop at every door." But even then,

[13] Earl R. Rolph and George F. Break, *Public Finance* (New York: The Ronald Press Co., 1961), pp. 344–346.

even if the city could take such drastic steps, where were the people to go? Were they to be forced into shantytowns on the outskirts of the city—like the Algerians outside Paris or the Indians outside Lima? Should the city set up encampments for immigrants from rural America, just as West Berlin does for the refugees from Communist East Germany? Should massive public housing be instituted specifically to take care of the excess population?

To pose these questions is to suggest solutions. Yet we are not here concerned with the problem of the slum, nor even with that of overpopulation. We are, rather, concerned with the housing of the entire city, and because of that we must return to a basic question: What codes are necessary for the city to protect its housing, and how can they be enforced?

The city is concerned with the housing of its citizenry from the moment the particular structure is conceived until it is pulled down or otherwise destroyed. This concern might be broken down into three parts: (1) concern for the integrity of the structure itself; (2) concern for the use, site, and situation of the structure and its relation to other buildings; and (3) concern for the demography of the structure, that is, people vis-à-vis the buildings that house them.

That a dwelling must be built soundly and maintained in structurally sound condition throughout its lifetime is the essence of the integrity concept. To accomplish this objective there should be a coincidence of purpose by the builder, the owner, and the city. Three codes are traditionally the prime instruments used by the city to live up to its part of the bargain: a building ordinance, an electrical ordinance, and a plumbing ordinance. Although many cities work out their own legal rules governing building, plumbing, and electrical installations, others adopt the pertinent codes of the various national associations.[14] These codes govern the construction of the building, in the first place, and alterations to it thereafter. Maintenance of the building is not so apt to be the direct concern of the building, plumbing, and electrical codes as of the housing and fire prevention codes which are directly related to occupancy.

Another type of ordinance is that concerned with the architecture of the building. An architectural control ordinance may require maintenance of the historical character of a neighborhood by forbidding radical changes in building facades, or it may seek to preserve the architectural style of any section of the community. Thus if most homes are built in the French provincial style, the ordinance would try to prevent the intrusion of designs after the Frank Lloyd Wright or Walter Gropius style. The ordinance

[14] See, for example. National Fire Protection Association, *National Fire Codes* (Boston: The Association, 1965), Vols. 1–10; *Canada National Building Code* (Ottawa, Ontario: Canadian National Research Council, 1965); *Recommended Fire Prevention Code* (New York: American Insurance Association, 1965); and *Southern Standard Building Code* (Birmingham, Ala.: Southern Building Code Congress, 1965).

might even attempt to give a municipal commission authority to make esthetic judgments on prevailing styles, but this matter is fraught with legal dangers.

Codes, like the buildings they are concerned with, grow old. And if there is one flaw in municipal building codes that outranks all others, it is the antique nature of some city ordinances concerned with building matters. Although some codes now seek to require techniques and materials that meet certain minimal performance standards, quite often the ordinances specify construction materials and building techniques which have long since been equaled, if not supplanted, by new developments.[15] There is an innate conservatism in the construction industry and in the craft unions which partially, at any rate, causes this situation to develop. And the conservatism of officialdom tends to reinforce the standpattism of builder and craftsman.

One element of the concern for integrity of structure is the condemnation and elimination of buildings which not only are unfit for human occupancy but also are not capable of being rehabilitated. If the building is beyond hope of further service, it needs to be pulled down as a public hazard. But city officials and the courts are reluctant to proceed against the owners of such buildings, and the urban landscape is littered with structures which are not only dangerous but unsightly as well.

The use, site, and situation of the structure constitute the second matter of deepest concern to the city. Zoning ordinances which govern the placing of the building on the lot; the use to which the building shall be put; its height, bulk, and relation to the street; its standardization of use within a neighborhood; and, finally, its control of population density—all of these controls are essential to the entire housing complex in a city. Of like concern is the subdivision-control ordinance, directed toward maintaining open spaces, essential utilities, and many other elements. And to supplement these use and design ordinances, a specific-use law, such as that governing rooming houses, may often be essential. Since more than a million persons live permanently in house trailers, and most of these in the cities, the city must regulate private trailer parks on the grounds of esthetics, health, and safety, and must even construct public trailer parks.

The demography of housing is a third matter of deep concern to the city. Because housing is inseparable from the people who dwell in it and receive shelter and satisfaction from it, the city must assure its citizenry of both the safety and the livability of all dwelling units. To insist by means of fire safety ordinances that both owner and occupant of a dwelling unit follow established practices that would militate against fires and other acts of God is very little for even the meanest city to ask. To require by a housing ordi-

[15] See Norbert Brown, "Local Building Codes: A National Problem," *Architectural Forum*, CXVII (December, 1961), 124–125.

nance that owner and occupant meet standards of health, comfort, and cleanliness is to do no more than to insist that the city is a place for civilized man.

Annotated Bibliography

One of the few attempts to give a worldwide view of the housing problem may be found in Charles Abrams, *Man's Struggle for Shelter in an Urbanizing World* (Cambridge, Mass.: Massachusetts Institute of Technology Press, 1964). Mr. Abrams has been housing consultant to the United Nations, a visiting professor at the Massachusetts Institute of Technology, and the New York State rent administrator. An iconoclastic look at city slums may be had in Oscar Steiner, *Our Housing Jungle and Your Pocket Book* (New York: University Publishers, 1960). Since the rehabilitation of housing is an ever-present need in the city, William W. Nash offers various means of achieving it in *Residential Rehabilitation: Private Profits and Public Purposes* (New York: McGraw-Hill Book Co., 1959). There is a succinct history of public housing in Robert M. Fisher, *Twenty Years of Public Housing* (New York: Harper & Bros., 1959).

In 1945 the U.S. Supreme Court refused to hear a case in which a restrictive racial covenant was at issue. In 1948 essentially the same court ruled that under the Fourteenth Amendment state courts could no longer enforce the racial clauses in restrictive covenants. Clement E. Vose seeks answers to the court's reversal of position by looking at the interest-group activity that raged behind the restrictive covenant cases. See Clement E. Vose, *Caucasians Only* (Berkeley, Calif.: University of California Press, 1959). Other valuable books on racial discrimination in housing, appearing under the auspices of the Commission on Race and Housing and all published at Berkeley by the University of California Press, are Luigi Laurenti, *Property Values and Race* (1960); Eunice and George Grier, *Privately Developed Interracial Housing* (1960); Nathan Glazer and Davis McEntire (eds.), *Studies in Housing and Minority Groups* (1960); Chester Rapkin and William G. Grigsby, *The Demand for Housing in Racially Mixed Areas* (1960); and a general summary of the problem, Davis McEntire, *Residence and Race* (1960).

CHAPTER 20

*U*rban Renewal

Hamilton Basso, the novelist, once wrote that New York reminded him of a snake that was always shedding its skin. New York is not alone; the cityscape has always changed, since urban life first began. The patina of age in a thousand-year-old city—the Gothic cathedral in one block, the baroque town hall in another, and the modern building with a glass and aluminum curtain wall around the corner—stems from the change, as well as the stability, of the centuries.

When Vienna tore down its medieval wall in the 1850's and constructed the imposing Ringstrasse, and when Paris, about the same time, under Baron George Haussmann cut through slums and a chaotic street pattern to create the great boulevards which the American tourist feverishly treads today, those cities were engaging in what we would now call urban renewal. Urban renewal, then, in its larger and well-developed historic sense is the city's sloughing off of obsolescence, on the one hand, and its attempt to heighten the rewards of urban life by a physical reconstruction of the urban environment, on the other. It may be sheer monumentalism, an important element in the reconstruction of Vienna, as it was also in Paris— emperor, civic leader, and architect combining to make the capital a monument to imperial loyalties (in Vienna) and to French nationalism (in Paris). And the development of the remarkable Chicago lakefront was a monument to the boundless optimism of Chicago capitalist and politician.

Monumentalism, as an end in itself, surely is unacceptable. But just as surely there is a place for it in planning or urban renewal. It is fashionable today to make light of the grand gesture and the large perspective, but no one who has walked the boulevards of Paris and Vienna, or viewed the Chicago lakefront from the water at night, can doubt the value of these extravagances. If a city—in some part—is not grand, can it really be a city?

Urban renewal must, of course, be utilitarian; it must increase the city's economic efficiency and enlarge the city's tax base. It must rehouse the people, or some of them, help unsnarl the traffic, produce more open space. Urban renewal carries within itself great promise, but some remarkably difficult problems. And one of the problems is that the citizen, the city official, and most especially the federal bureaucrat forget that, in part, a city must be built (or rebuilt) on a truly grand scale.

Basic Elements

Paul Bartholomew has defined urban renewal as "a general term meaning a coordinated program of public and private efforts to remove blight and to prevent blight from affecting a neighborhood." Since the Housing Act of 1949, urban renewal has meant the mobilization of public and private capital and all of the city's political resources for the attack on obsolescence. It involves three major types of effort: conservation, rehabilitation, and redevelopment.

In some neighborhoods, still basically sound but getting a little tattered around the edges, aggressive neighborhood action, aided by the city and other governmental authorities—including the state and federal governments—can bring new vitality, pleasantness, and beauty (and increased property values!) to the area. Conservation is necessary here before blight gets a hold.

In other neighborhoods, blight is truly in evidence. New streets, perhaps a realignment of the street pattern, better drainage, a community center, a new school, a park, a public square, extensive private effort in refurbishing individual homes—these are immediate needs. Most of the housing wants attention; some of the housing should be pulled down, either to permit the building of new structures or to create open space. With the rehabilitation of the neighborhood physically there must often come also the rehabilitation of social units—individuals, families, and other groups. And, once again, many governmental authorities must be involved in the process.

In still other neighborhoods, blight has turned into a cancerous growth that has so attacked the vital organs of the area that nothing less than major surgery can save it. In renewing and redeveloping this area there must be a mobilization of all public forces: city, school, other local units, state, and federal.

There is still some confusion—or lack of consensus—over the terms "urban redevelopment" and "urban renewal." The former and older term has largely been supplanted by the latter, which was introduced to indicate the broadest possible approach to urban obsolescence—conservation, rehabilitation, and redevelopment. To a large extent, laymen and some professionals now regard all projects, built around whatever end, as urban renewal. We shall use urban renewal with this connotation hereafter.

Urban Renewal Administration

Urban renewal involves the coordinated efforts of city, state, nation, and private groups. For this reason an administrative apparatus has been built up around it which is at once elaborate and disorganized.

The prime mover for urban renewal at the local level is the city, or, more specifically, the collective sources of policy formation: the city council, the chief executive, the neighborhood group, and the thousand and one other groups that make up the local polity. From this source the web of administration spreads outward and downward to include line and staff departments of the city, quasi-independent authorities, other local governments, and various power blocs, such as the chamber of commerce (which must be considered a quasi-public entity, rather than a purely private one).

Obviously, the most complicated organization is to be found in the larger cities. As Figure 20-1 shows, the large-city renewal effort is complex indeed. For smaller cities, the administration may be greatly simplified. One may find, for example, that the plan department, a staff agency, has responsibility for the line operations of urban renewal and zoning administration. But in large city or small, there are rarely any grave obstacles which stand in the way of cooperative action on urban renewal by the operating departments of the city itself. The real difficulties arise in building up sufficient support between the officials of the city, on the one hand, and officials of autonomous agencies and other local governments, on the other.

As of July 1967, forty-nine states had statutes specifically authorizing urban renewal and development by cities, special authorities, and sometimes by counties. In addition, the District of Columbia, the Virgin Islands, and Puerto Rico have such enabling legislation. The administrative involvement of the states, however, is not great. Though a few states—New York in particular—have made substantial administrative and financial commitments for urban renewal and such allied projects as slum clearance and public housing, most of them have been content merely to give the cities statutory authority to act, and then to rest upon these legal laurels.

In 1958 the Joint Federal-State Action Committee advised the states to take a more active role in urban renewal and insisted that the governors

Figure 20-1. Prototype of Urban Renewal Administration in Large American Cities

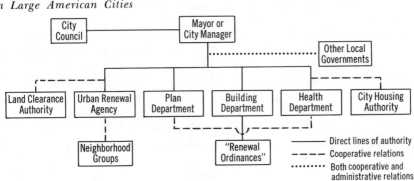

could stimulate interest initially by calling conferences on urban problems. One can say, generally, that neither the states as a whole nor the governors individually took the advice to heart.

Federal administration is concentrated in the Renewal Projects Administration of the U.S. Department of Housing and Urban Development. The administration is responsible for carrying out these programs: (1) Title I projects, authorized by Title I of the Housing Act of 1949, as amended; including general neighborhood renewal plans, community renewal plans, code enforcement projects, and demolition projects; and (2) loans for rehabilitation under section 312 of the Housing Act of 1964, as amended.

Other federal agencies intimately concerned with the renewal process are the Federal Housing Administration, which insures home mortgages; the Housing Assistance Administration, which supervises and subsidizes local public housing endeavors; and the U.S. Department of Transportation, which administers the federal-aid highway program.

The Two Faces of Urban Renewal

Urban renewal should have on its coat of arms the paintbrush and the bulldozer, one to symbolize the element of conservation and reconditioning, the other to stand for land clearance and rebuilding. Though these elements are quite dissimilar, they are administered by the same agencies and are often popularly confused. Yet the techniques are so different that they should be examined separately.

Conservation and Reconditioning. In a very real sense the city, as a whole, is a perpetual conservation area. If there is not constant maintenance, the physical plant, whether publicly or privately owned, will soon deteriorate. Constant vigilance is as much the price of a good city as it is of liberty.

A structure that is well designed, situated, constructed, and maintained will never become an urban renewal problem to the city. In order that it not become such a problem the city maintains a legal and administrative interest in every building, from its conception to its final demolition.

Because the city as yet only incidentally regulates the architectural characteristics of a building, it usually does little to impose design standards that would increase the city's attractiveness. Although New Orleans very severely restricts building or alterations in the Vieux Carré, it does so more to preserve the French Quarter's historical quality than its beauty—or at least that is the way it is rationalized in the law and in politics. Thus, in general, the city's only interest in design is related to factors of engineering, safety, health, and similar mundane elements. In a building designed without windows, for example, the city's concern would be with the adequacy of such factors as light and ventilation, not with its beauty. Perhaps we should note, however, that judges, obviously still thinking of themselves as the prime urban decision-makers, have grudgingly conceded that the city's initiative in setting esthetic standards should not be vetoed. For example, see *City of New Orleans* v. *Levy,* 223 La. 14 (1963). Nevertheless, judicial backing and filling has thrown such consternation into urban political leadership that coherent policy on esthetics is extremely difficult to arrive at.

In the location of the building the city must be concerned with its projected use and with whether that use is in keeping with the zoning ordinance and the master plan. It must be careful that the building's situation at a certain point in the city will not overburden public facilities: traffic, parking, recreation, sewer, and water. In like manner, as construction begins, the city must be concerned that the building, electrical, and plumbing codes are followed.

After the building is finished and begins to age, the city must be vigilant to see that it is properly maintained. It must see that illegal uses and illegal conversions do not corrupt its function and that the public services without which the building could not exist—from sewage disposal to fire protection—do not deteriorate. In short, the life cycle of every structure which is within the city can be traced in indelible ink through the municipal code.

The ordinances which govern the life cycle of the city's physical plant are not particularly numerous, though they may bulk large in the city code: zoning, building, electrical, plumbing, fire, housing, and health. Since these ordinances are also crucial in the enforcement of conservation measures, they might, as a group, be labeled "renewal" ordinances. But we should constantly bear in mind that the honest, vigorous enforcement of these laws would alleviate, in large part, the various urban renewal programs. They might more aptly be labeled "renewal prevention" ordinances.

Since the department of buildings often administers the zoning and building codes (building, electrical, and plumbing) and may also administer the housing code, this department is a key element in the conservation and reconditioning process. The department may, indeed, have a well-developed program for conservation, built around its traditional responsibility for building-law enforcement. Los Angeles has developed such a program, and at one time the city's general manager of the building department insisted that "if an over-all program such as the one in Los Angeles were adopted by every major city in the United States, slums would be eliminated within a 20-year period and there would be no need for tax subsidized reclamation projects as we know them today." Underscoring this opinion, the general manager decried the failure of building departments to function adequately in the past. City administrators have not permitted them to function, the departments themselves have had neither the budget nor the will for effectiveness, and the political pressures of landlords have served to hamstring good enforcement. Concluded the general manager: "Building departments must be allowed, or made, to function properly if we hope to reverse the trend that is progressively destroying our cities." [1]

Since money, as always, is a crucial factor in enforcement, one might legitimately inquire why it is so often not available for establishing even minimal administrative standards. One reason is undoubtedly the power of those interest groups which have a stake in poor enforcement. Another one is the constant financial crisis in which the city finds itself. To decrease the importance of the latter factor, the federal government, in the Housing Act of 1964, provided cities with grants-in-aid for code enforcement.

Responsible for enforcement of the building, zoning, and housing codes, the Los Angeles building department illustrates how these codes may be gathered together for enforcement. Going beyond that achievement, however, the city has set up, as an office within the building department, a conservation bureau which has as its sole purpose the conservation of the city's physical plant. (See Figure 20-2.)

As we have seen previously, the housing code is a recent phenomenon— at least in the reliance that cities place upon it—and it well illustrates the city's approach to conservation and reconditioning. We should therefore examine its nature and administration.

The housing code is essentially a series of legal standards enacted to assure decent living conditions for the city's inhabitants. In its best form, it includes such requirements as minimum space for each person inhabiting

Figure 20-2. Urban Conservation
in Los Angeles Department of Building and Safety

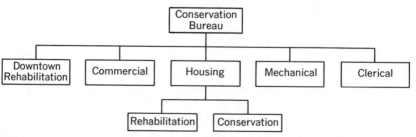

Source: Adapted from Gilbert E. Morris, *Conservation—A New Concept in Building Law Enforcement* (City of Los Angeles, Calif.: Department of Building and Safety, June, 1958), p. 40.

[1] Gilbert E. Morris, *Conservation—A New Concept in Building Law Enforcement* (City of Los Angeles, Calif.: Department of Building and Safety, June, 1958). The quotation is taken from the preface. This publication is a classic statement by a veteran public servant who seems to have extraordinary technical capacity, but little sensitivity to the manifold destructive pressures that come to bear upon the administration of "renewal" ordinances.

the dwelling unit; basic provisions for heat, light, and ventilation; indoor plumbing, structural maintenance, and upkeep of the premises; and, finally, conditions of enforcement.

Action under the housing ordinance may be initiated in a variety of ways. A complaint, from any source, of a possible violation; evidence submitted by any city inspector or other official; evidence obtained by an exhaustive house-to-house canvass by administrative personnel—any of these may be used to start the enforcement process.

Upon receipt of a complaint—or after discovery of an apparent violation—a housing inspector visits the premises and makes a formal report on the conditions there to the department. He also attempts to explain to the owner or occupier the nature of the violation and, possibly, the action the city will take if it is not corrected. In Los Angeles, housing inspectors found that the violations were usually quite evident to the owners of property in rehabilitation areas, but in conservation neighborhoods, where blight had only a tenuous foothold, the violations were a surprise to many owners.[2]

If, in the department chief's judgment, the report of the inspector requires departmental action, he notifies the owner of the property (or occupier, in some types of violations). The notification informs the property holder that the department considers a violation of the ordinance to exist and that the violations should, within a reasonable time, be eliminated.

In case of owner compliance, the case is closed. But if noncompliance continues the city may then undertake a massive inspection of the property preparatory to bringing suit against the owner. In one Midwestern city this inspection is carried out by a team led by the city manager and including the building department superintendent, the fire and police chiefs, the city attorney, the housing inspector, and the health officer! After such a visitation, if the owner is not overawed into compliance, the building department placards the building with public notice that the building is unfit for human habitation and must be vacated by a certain date.

After enforcement has run this administrative gauntlet, most violations will have been corrected by the owners. But there will always be a few landlords who stand on their "constitutional" rights to continue their peculiar form of man's inhumanity to man, and so the matter passes to the city attorney and eventually to the courts. Yet even here the case may not get beyond the filing stage. In a Chicago suburb, when the city petitioned the court for an injunction forbidding further violations of the housing ordinance by an elderly couple, outraged children and other members of the family descended upon city hall from the East Coast—and West—and even from overseas, to protect their elderly kin from the vicious designs of

[2] *Ibid.,* p. 110.

the bureaucrats. But the facts disclosed that (1) the old couple had means; (2) their permitting the violations to continue very likely stemmed from senility, not lack of resources; and (3) their children had not visited them for several years. When the family was reunited and the violations eliminated, the building inspector felt more like a social worker than an overseer of housing code violations!

In sum, the task of urban renewal is nothing less than maintenance of the urban physical structure in sound condition. Conservation starts with the design of a building and continues into supervision over site, situation, and construction. If the ordinances are then honestly enforced and structural abuse and other misuses of the building are not permitted, blight should rarely occur. But if blight does creep in, aggressive action can recondition and rehabilitate the neighborhood.

Land Clearance and Rebuilding. Observe, now, the neighborhood in which the housing is stricken with obsolescence. The frame buildings are unpainted and overcrowded; the brickwork in the chimneys needs tuck-pointing; the streets are full of holes and badly lighted; the sidewalks are broken. Every law in the municipal code is being flouted; scarcely a day passes without there being a new violation: an illegal conversion of a dwelling place, an unlawful electrical installation, a flagrant infringement of the housing ordinance. Conservation is unheard of; reconditioning, only a dream.

As living conditions worsen, more people, paradoxically, flock into the area. Slum holdings—to those who have a conscience for it—become more profitable. A city inspector finds five families in a two-family home. After the complaint against the owner has for months painfully dragged through the administrative process and the courts, a new inspection of the premises reveals seven families in the dwelling! Not even a policeman at every door could stop the flooding of population in the slum district.

What is to be done? Can the city permit the continuance of this profound disorganization, both of the urban environment and of urban society? Aside from humanitarian considerations, the city faces constantly increasing costs in policing the district, in protecting it against fire, in furnishing the various social services. And at the same time that service requirements in the district are rising, tax income from the district is going down. Although there is little question but that a tax system could be constructed which would substantially reduce the profits of the slum owner and thus enable the city to recoup some of the financial burdens imposed upon it by the slum, very little attempt has been made to achieve such a taxing plan.[3]

---

[3] See Mabel Walker, "Taxation—Cities Can't Afford Systems That Add to Ills of the Slum," *The Journal of Housing*, XVII (June, 1960), 225ff.; also see Arthur D. Sporn, "Empirical Studies in the Economics of Slum Ownership," *Land Economics*, XXXVI (November, 1960), 333–340.

Not only have city councils been generally averse to experimentation in tax design, but the state legislatures and constitutions also stand foursquare against such adventuring.

Rigid enforcement of the various municipal ordinances might ameliorate the slum situation somewhat, but such enforcement works best to prevent the slum condition rather than to eliminate it. It may be, moreover, that much of the physical structure of the neighborhood has so far deteriorated that there is nothing left but to pull the buildings down.

Although there is no ideal way to approach this situation, certainly, the prevailing method is for the local government to purchase the land and buildings in the slum district, clear the area, and then redevelop it. Although there are many perils attendant upon this process, it is the only method that seems to be fruitful.

Urban renewal, in its land clearance and redevelopment phase, has a number of reasons for being. It is used to clear away slums. It is often designed to rationalize land use: instead of a chaotic pattern of marginal land uses, the area can be rebuilt in accordance with a well-thought-out plan. It can, moreover, reduce municipal expenditures and raise municipal income. It can arrest the spread of slum conditions into surrounding neighborhoods, which can still be reclaimed by conservation and rehabilitation programs. It can substantially raise living standards in the former slum area and thus in the city as a whole.

But the effort takes money. Going into a slum area with a land clearance program, the city is faced with a real and worrisome paradox. Because of severe overcrowding in slum dwellings, low maintenance costs, and relatively low tax rates, slum property tends to be inflated in value, far above the level of similar property in other circumstances. When the city purchases the property, therefore, or acquires it by eminent domain, it must pay for value which has been established, not only by violations of the law, but also by existence of a tax system which is as faulty in administration as it is in conception. Without the necessary funds to purchase overpriced slum properties, the city must look beyond itself for help. And the help comes, in large part, from the federal government; in some small part from the states.

Before the city is eligible for federal assistance it must establish a Program for Community Improvement, commonly known as the Workable Program. Indeed, none of the programs administered by the urban renewal agency, even where grants-in-aid are not involved, may be utilized by the city unless a Workable Program is developed. Specifically, this means that the city must have an adequate system of codes and ordinances and a master plan. It must have a system of neighborhood analysis and an administrative organization adequate to carry out the tasks of urban renewal. It must have a financial plan, a plan for rehousing displaced persons, and some kind of provisions for citizen participation in urban renewal projects.

When the Workable Program is approved by the federal government, the city is eligible for grants-in-aid or other forms of federal assistance in carrying out its urban renewal programs. Now the city is ready to proceed with land clearance and redevelopment of the slum area.

Normally, the federal government will support two-thirds of the cost (actually the net loss) involved in a renewal project of this nature. The city will then pay for the remainder. After the land is acquired by purchase or condemnation, the buildings demolished and removed, the site prepared, and the necessary public improvements installed, the cost of it all is totaled. Thereupon, the land is disposed of, and the returns from its sale are deducted from the total figure. This gives the net project cost, which is shared as described above. (Note that the federal government, however, pays the entire cost of relocating residents of the cleared area.)

In an urban renewal enterprise of this nature, the community may need to use not only the city but many other local governments to meet the local one-third share of net cost. Since the local share may be borne by "noncash local grants-in-aid," a variety of public improvements newly installed in the renewal area will qualify as contributions to the local share. A study of a renewal project in the St. Louis metropolitan area revealed that the city and three other local governments could contribute to the local one-third share of the cost by building streets, police and fire stations, sewers and gutters, levees and other flood-control projects, schools, parks and playgrounds, and a number of other types of public improvements. If cash expenditures to help meet the one-third share are needed, however, the city is usually responsible for raising the necessary sums.

For all the necessity of public capital to be invested in a renewal project, private funds are still more important. Indeed, it is the genius of urban renewal that the approach is to mobilize private capital. Public powers and tax monies are utilized to prepare the way for private capital. When Atlanta began a large renewal project in 1960, the total cost was estimated at $42 million. Of this cost $17.5 million would be contributed by the federal government for land clearance; $9 million by the city in streets, schools, parks, and other improvements; and $15 million by private capital to build business, industrial, and residential facilities.[4]

Late in the 1950's Chicago embarked upon the Hyde Park–Kenwood redevelopment, one of the most ambitious projects ever undertaken in an American city. Planned to be carried out over a five-year period, the enterprise combined conservation, rehabilitation, and redevelopment. Estimated cost of the project was $130 million, of which more than half was to be private capital. Only 20 percent of the buildings in the area needed to be

[4] Atlanta *Constitution*, November 20, 1960, pp. 1, 23.

razed and replaced. The remaining 80 percent could be rehabilitated.

If these examples are not sufficiently impressive, let us take a brief but comprehensive look at urban renewal data. The expenditures on 306 projects as of December 31, 1959, were estimated as follows: local, $275 million; federal, $512 million; private, $2.9 billion. By the start of 1967 nearly 900 communities were participating in the urban renewal program.[5] Capital grants made by the federal agency had increased to upwards of $6 billion.

What are the types of projects in which land clearance and reconditioning may be used? Although any kind of classification will be somewhat arbitrary, a grouping of the uses according to major objective can be instructive and should be attempted.

Once predominant in urban renewal, but no longer, are the slum clearance and public housing projects. Although still widely used, this kind of project is in the background: both slum clearance and public housing are tools, but no longer dominant tools, for effecting urban renewal.

Central business district renewal has come to the fore. Not only does the central business district produce powerful interest groups which can influence both local and federal policy—and state, too, for that matter—but the public at large has also realized that in the downtown district are the stores and offices, the restaurants, the art and entertainment centers that are essential to urban life. As a result, some notable examples of rebuilding may be found in the central business districts of American cities. If the Golden Triangle in Pittsburgh is the best exemplification of such rebuilding (through basically a state-local-private capital affair), small-city projects must not be ignored. Thus the downtown urban renewal project in New Rochelle, New York, included in its plans a new railroad station, an office building, a civic auditorium, a department store, an apartment building, and entertainment and cultural centers.[6]

There are also renewal projects primarily devoted to cultural and arts centers: Lincoln Center, in New York City, is the best and most expensive example. And since the investment by private universities in a renewal project may be counted against the city's one-third share of net project cost, some renewal efforts may virtually be described as university-centered projects. The Hyde Park–Kenwood renewal is a case in point. Under veteran Mayor Richard C. Lee, New Haven, Connecticut, has been urban renewal prone. Not satisfied with more than $200 million worth of urban renewal projects, Mayor Lee announced, in 1966, another major project which featured a new cultural government center.

And then there are a wide number of incidental objectives in urban re-

---

[5] *The Municipal Year Book 1967* (Chicago: ICMA), p. 345.
[6] *Architectural Forum*, CXVII (January, 1961), 7.

newal. The decade-old fire that had been burning through the veins of coal under Carbondale, Pennsylvania, became the object of a federal urban renewal grant in 1959. And the growing interest in the industrial park— green and (hopefully) open industrial district—has caused many cities to include such parks in their renewal planning. Because of the expense and the legal impediments in the way of land assembly, private enterprise alone has too much difficulty, oftentimes, in undertaking an industrial park endeavor all alone. The city may, then, purchase and assemble land and receive federal aid for the loss involved. An industrial park in Providence, Rhode Island, cost the city's redevelopment agency $74,000 an acre to buy the land, $2,500 per acre to clear it, and $51,500 an acre to build the necessary improvements, or a total of $128,000 per acre. Since the land, as redeveloped, sold for about $39,000 an acre, the city and federal governments assumed the loss.[7]

In effect, urban renewal efforts include a wide variety of plans and ideas. From the standpoint of the city this is a happy turn of events. It has always been the hope and intent of thoughtful civic leadership that the entire city should be built soundly and, with proper enforcement of housing and building codes, just as soundly conserved. On the other hand, the federal government programs looked toward the rebuilding of the city especially to eliminate slum housing. (Although FHA standards for housing and subdivision designs have been aimed at a sounder city structurally, the impact has been mainly on suburban housing. Moreover, the very existence of FHA may have accelerated the rush to the suburbs in metropolitan areas.) The Housing Act of 1954 gave indication of Congressional realization of the necessity of broadening the concept of urban renewal, so that it may eventually become as broad as the best city approach has always been. Subsequent housing acts indicate that the Congress has not forgotten the need for widening its scope.

Some Questions About Urban Renewal

Does Excessive Local Pluralism Hamper Renewal? The disintegration of local government, both vertically and horizontally, has a disturbing influence upon urban renewal, just as it has on every other local governmental activity. In conception, urban renewal must reflect a combination of objectives by all overlying local governments. In financing, the same generalization holds. If the schools and the city can agree on urban renewal planning, this cooperation will considerably increase the effectiveness of

[7] Frank Fogarty, "Industrial Parks—City Style," *Architectural Forum*, CXV (December, 1959), 94–97.

the renewal efforts.[8] But as we have already seen, local interest groups, and the local governments with which they identify, are jealous of their autonomy and the prerogatives arising out of that autonomy. Cooperation with any other local government, on any local program, may seem like a step toward loss of independence. This fear may be particularly acute when the city is involved: as the most powerful local unit, whether legally or financially, the city may, with good reason, be feared by other local units. If not imperialistic today, it may become so tomorrow!

Horizontal—or geographic—distintegration presents similar problems. While urban renewal has been mainly directed toward the core city, it needs logically to be extended to the satellite city and the fringe areas in general. Obsolescence, creeping blight, and slum conditions do not stop at municipal boundaries. But it may be as difficult to achieve cooperation between two adjoining cities as between a city and an overlying school district. Local planning agencies, as well as state and federal law, have recognized the importance of planning for the entire urban community, no matter how large or how small. In the same fashion, observers of the renewal process have emphasized the necessity of thinking of renewal as extending communitywide: "urban renewal means blight prevention as well as elimination; it also means development and maintenance of sound, healthy communities. These things are as much needed in the suburbs as they are downtown." [9]

We have discovered no magic formula for curing either the horizontal or vertical fractionalization of the local community, and there is no easy solution to the problems which this condition poses for urban renewal. As much responsible as the community itself for the splinter governments, the states and the federal government can surely come to the aid of the city in resisting greater fractionalization of the urban renewal process and in stimulating cooperation among local units. An official of the Illinois state housing board said to the mayor of a large city: "By all means put your urban renewal responsibility in the local housing authority; the more administrative units you have involved in the renewal process, the greater are your chances of failure." While there were flaws in the reasoning of this state officer, the basis of the officer's judgment was probably sound: concentrate authority for the renewal process, or exaggerate the strains on the program. Somehow—perhaps in a variety of ways—the renewal process can be brought close to the fount of authority where it belongs: close to the

[8] H. Cole Williams, "How Schools Can Help Urban Renewal," *American School Board Journal*, CXXXVIII (January, 1959), 33–34. Of course, if the schools are administered by a department of the city government, it may be expected that they will follow city council policy.

[9] M. Carter McFarland, *The Challenge of Urban Renewal, Technical Bulletin No. 34* (Washington, D.C.: Urban Land Institute, December, 1958), p. 34.

city council and mayor or city manager. In New Haven, under Mayor Richard C. Lee, the renewal boss was not placed in a renewal agency at all, but was rather named executive secretary to the mayor upon the latter's election to office in 1954. Working in concert with the mayor, the renewal director, Richard J. Logue, conciliated warring community factions, unified and mobilized the resources of the city, and produced one of the most ambitious renewal programs in the nation.

Called to Boston by Mayor John F. Collins, Logue donned two hats in order to bring some coordination into the city's renewal efforts: the mayor appointed him city director of redevelopment and head of the Boston redevelopment authority, an autonomous agency. Though this coordinating effort was challenged in the courts, the mayor's action was upheld.

Not all of the disorganization in urban renewal has been at the local level, since various federal programs were, before 1965, loosely coordinated. In 1965, however, the Urban Renewal Administration, the Community Facilities Administration, the Federal Housing Administration, and the Public Housing Administration—all of the crucial agencies involved in the renewal process—were brought into a newly organized cabinet department, the Department of Housing and Urban Development. As a result, the urban renewal, public housing, and mortgage insurance programs of the federal government were brought into a more fruitful relationship than in previous years.

Have All the Major Legal Problems Been Met? One of the oldest of our constitutional precepts—and one that corresponds closest to our sense of fair play—is that although the state may take private property, it may do so only for a public purpose and after just compensation has been paid. Eminent domain, in short, may be exercised, but only under these two strict rules of the state and federal constitutions.

Just compensation is difficult enough to arrive at; public purpose is perhaps even more a problem. May the city condemn the property of householders (even though they be slum landlords) and small merchants (even though they be skid-row tavern keepers), assemble the parcels, clear the land, and then sell the land to private industry? Does this meet the requirements of public purpose? A South Carolina court said "No" when ruling that Columbia could not use eminent domain to change a "predominantly low-class residential area to a commercial and industrial" one.[10] Fortunately for urban renewal—at least in its land clearance and rebuilding phase—this court's circumscribed view of public purpose does not extend widely through the state judiciary. The prevailing view of both bar and laity has been well stated by David Rockefeller, a man whose very name raises the vision of capitalism triumphant: "the right of . . . the commu-

[10] *Edens* v. *City of Columbia et al.,* 91 S.E. 2nd 280 (1956).

nity must, on occasion (and always with due process of law), take precedence over private rights . . . in relation to land acquisition and assembly for a publicly desirable purpose through the use of the right of eminent domain." [11]

More perplexing even than whether the city may exercise eminent domain to acquire land for assembly and resale to private developers is the question whether it may resell such lands to a religious institution. What about separation of church and state? When St. Louis University, a Jesuit institution, sought land in the St. Louis Mill Creek renewal area, precisely this point was raised. Liberal Protestants supported the university's position, and so did the courts.

Without question, the legislatures and the courts have been so impressed with the urgency of the urban crisis that they have been willing to look with leniency upon new interpretations of old concepts. The result is that in virtually all of the states most of the legal obstacles to urban renewal have been cleared away.

Have the Major Financial Problems Been Solved? The American Council to Improve Our Neighborhoods (ACTION) has estimated that spending for normal urban growth, slum removal, and urban renewal needs to be doubled. Although much of this added cost would be financed by private capital, a goodly portion of it would, of necessity, come out of the public treasury.

The ACTION position strikingly underscores the need for greatly increased expenditures by local governments. But as we have already seen in our discussion on finance, there is much pessimism abroad in the land over local governments' capacity to continue to raise their expenditure levels. Whether this pessimism is entirely valid (and it should, in the vernacular, be taken with a grain of salt), it unquestionably influences the formation of public policy at the local, state, and national levels. What does it matter, really, whether a man can lift a heavy weight, if he is prevented from doing so by *thinking* he can't!

A full-scale attack upon this pessimism which gelds the city and other local governments is necessary before the city can adequately meet its urban renewal or other needs. Most of the riches of the democractic world—and most of the people—are in the cities. Given the wealth, the people, and the democratic process, cities need not feel pessimistic about their capacity to finance their needs. "The wealth is there. The crisis is of leadership, and of imagination—our leadership and our imagination." Thus Harlan Cleveland commented on the present crisis.

In addition to the necessity for the city to marshal all of its financial re-

[11] Address before the San Francisco Planning and Urban Renewal Association, San Francisco, Calif.. January 24, 1961.

sources, there is need for specific tax measures to heighten the effectiveness of urban renewal. First, there could be a substantial revision of the property tax. In urban renewal areas where conservation and rehabilitation are being emphasized, a substantial improvement in the physical condition of real property means a heavier tax burden for the neighborhood. And the better the tax administration is, in the conventional sense, the greater and more immediate will be the impact of higher taxes. And so the city finds itself working at cross-purposes: one arm seeks to arrest blight; the other penalizes those efforts by raising taxes, because there is probably no question but that an increased tax burden upon a marginal neighborhood will discourage its efforts to rehabilitate itself.

One solution to this dilemma is to declare a moratorium on increased real property *assessments* within a conservation district for a certain term of years. A more basic measure would be to separate the assessment of land, on the one hand, and capital improvements on the land, on the other. Capital improvements, for example, might be assessed at 50 percent of the market value and land at 100 percent of market value. This would have the effect of correcting some of the faults of the real property tax so eloquently popularized by Henry George in *Progress and Poverty*. If this proposal appears slightly awkward, consider the lugubrious character of the present system!

A still further reform could be made, and that is in the assessment of income-producing property. One of the reasons slum property is so highly valued is that slum landlords receive a very high rate of return on their investments. By capitalizing net income from the slum dwelling the assessor could arrive at a fair taxable value, which would normally mean that assessments on such property would rise drastically. This rise in assessment levels would tend to raise tax returns from slum dwellings and, at the same time, depress property values in slum districts. Thus slums, with their voracious appetite for police, fire, and welfare services, would pay substantially more than they presently do into the public treasury. And when the city clears the slums, it would need to pay less than presently for property acquisition. In sum, the result would be to raise revenues from slum areas and, simultaneously, reduce the cost of clearing the slums.

But neither increased tax returns nor reforms in the general property tax are sufficient. If private capital is not encouraged to invest in the renewal of the city, new blight will be created; and old slums will expand faster than remedial action can eliminate obsolescence.

Urban renewal is itself a means of attracting private capital into an area, and indeed the expectation of both city and federal officials is that most of the money flowing into the normal urban renewal project will come from private investment. When Congress, moreover, provided for liberalized mortgage insurance to enable the Federal Housing Administration to insure mortgages in blighted areas of the city more easily than previously, once more public policy provided a stimulus for the use of private capital in the building of new housing and the rehabilitation of old.

An essential local inducement to investment of private capital is energetic enforcement of the local codes, and such enforcement requires increased funds for more inspectors and other operational expenses. This should be emphasized, because city officials may jump to the hasty conclusion that renewal requires greater capital expenditures and little increase in operational costs. Yet nothing gives an investor a greater feeling of security than the realization that the city is enforcing the housing and environmental ordinances necessary for the maintenance of good living conditions. So code enforcement is, in itself, another means of mobilizing private investment of capital. This possibility may have helped bring about the introduction of federal grants-in-aid for code enforcement.

In an aging neighborhood, not only the private social plant—homes, churches, stores, apartments—is here and there touched with blight, but the public plant is also. After forty or fifty years streets and sewers, waterlines and sidewalks, street trees and storm drains are in need of substantial reconditioning. And antique streetlights do nothing to banish the fears lurking in every shadow. To meet this situation, most cities have available a device which enables the property holder to invest capital in new public works at the same time that he is investing in the reconditioning of his own property. This device is, of course, the special assessment.

The intimate connection between the physical state of private property, on the one hand, and public property, on the other, is recognized by no one more clearly than the mortgage banker. "The first sign of deteriorating municipal services—garbage and trash collection, street paving, lighting, and so forth—is a sign of danger. The first spot zoning change that permits the intrusions of an inharmonious use is a threat to all properties nearby. Neglect or overcrowding of any property in the neighborhood will have a depressing effect on the rest." [12]

Unlike general taxation, the money raised by special assessment is highly localized in its effect. If a property holder pays $500 for a new pavement in front of his home, he can see the results of his investment as surely as he can see a similar expenditure for painting his house. He can, just as well, see a revival of the entire neighborhood in the rejuvenated public plant. And so, incidentally, can the banker and other investors with capital. New public facilities alone can lift the spirit of an entire neighborhood and can be the very catalytic agency needed for arresting descent into severe blight or slum conditions.

Much like the special assessment, the service charge can also be used to great advantage. But it must be utilized adventurously. To increase utility-

[12] Wallace Moir, "Slums: Are We Creating Them Faster than We Are Eliminating Them?" *The Mortgage Banker,* July, 1954, p. 18.

type services the city may need to levy various charges that have not been levied before, especially for sewer service, garbage and trash collection, and perhaps even street cleaning. Some states have permitted cities to set up districts in which sewer service charges may be levied for installation of sanitary sewers. This principle could be extended to all renewal areas. The concept could also be enlarged. To obtain a higher level of service than is possible from general service charges (or tax levies), the conservation district could be given authority to add a surcharge for such improved service levels.

In finance, there is much that the federal government, also, might do. Compared with direct federal appropriations for agriculture, those for urban renewal and other urban programs are very small indeed. This inequity could well be adjusted in the national interest, though considering the way in which representation in Congress is warped to favor the farmer over the urban citizen, little possibility exists for such a correction, at least within a decade or so. But federal appropriations for urban renewal must surely increase if real progress is to be made in the redevelopment of our cities.

Very difficult to accomplish politically, but logically advisable, is the allocation of federal funds for renewal on an equalization basis. There are great differences, economically, among the cities and the states. Since such differences exist, federal funds might go more to the poorer cities and states, less to the richer ones. This principle has been widely used by the states in aiding school governments; it would doubtless have merit if applied to federal renewal grants. But this is abstract, not political, logic.

Finally, the stop-and-go nature of federal grants could be changed. Because of the difficulty—sometimes impossibility—of planning a capital improvements program on a year-to-year basis, federal appropriations, especially for slum clearance, need to be committed on a long-term basis. The logic here is the same as that for foreign-aid commitments.

Some As Yet Unanswered Questions

As with any complicated machine, to tamper with any of the complexity which is the modern city is to set up new and unknown forces which may have both salutary and unfortunate effects on the urban structure. Is there a delicate economic and demographic balance in the city which will be upset by urban renewal? Will renewal simply create dislocations faster than it eliminates them? Can the governmental structure at all levels be made to fit renewal? And can renewal be made to fit mankind? These are but a few of the questions of basic import which the student of urban renewal must face.

Jane Jacobs has raised some of them in her impressive book *The Death and Life of Great American Cities.* Attacking urban renewal as much more than the pulling down of great sections of the city, she shows that it is also the breaking up of viable social units, and the destruction of productive social groups—life (although a little shabby) replaced by lifelessness (the aluminum and glass curtain wall). Others have described urban renewal as a form of attack upon the Negro minority, which does not have the political skills to protect itself.

In *Urban Renewal and American Cities,* Scott Greer has a critical, sometimes almost laissez-faire attitude toward the city. Urban renewal is difficult to evaluate, he insists, because we know so little about its effects. There is its impact upon the housing market, which is difficult to evaluate. There is its impact upon the complex social processes involved in such a radical effort at social control as the Workable Program. Without knowledge, accumulated ignorance is built into the system.

On the part of mayors, city managers, and other policy leaders, there is less soul-searching than by detached observers. If these leaders are worried, it is about unduly complicated administrative procedures, lack of funds, changes in the local political climate, and other practical matters. Perhaps it is one of the serious weaknesses of the urban renewal program that there is no real discourse between the political leader and the philosopher.

Annotated Bibliography

One of the most cogent if somewhat romantic attacks upon urban renewal is Jane Jacobs' *The Death and Life of Great American Cities* (New York: Random House, 1961). Mrs. Jacobs leaves one feeling as though most answers to urban problems are to be found in her neighborhood in Greenwich Village; nevertheless her book is essential reading. Also of interest is Scott Greer's *Urban Renewal and American Cities* (Indianapolis, Ind.: The Bobbs-Merrill Co., 1965). Although Professor Greer more than occasionally indulges in hyperbole, his perspective on urban renewal clearly shows up some of its basic problems.

The Hyde Park–Kenwood renewal project on Chicago's South Side is not only one of the biggest of all renewal endeavors; it is also one of the most extensively examined, possibly because it intimately involves the lives and activities of people who write books—the faculty of the University of Chicago. For a highly personal account, see Julia Abrahamson, *A Neighborhood Finds Itself* (New York: Harper & Bros., 1959). For a study of some of the organizational roles in the Hyde Park–Kenwood renewal—city hall, the federal bureaucracy, churches, and the university—see Peter H. Rossi and Robert A. Dentler, *Remaking the City* (Glencoe, Ill.: The Free Press, 1959). A sequel to this study is Rossi and Dentler's *The Politics of Urban Renewal: The Chicago Findings* (New York: The Free Press, 1961).

There are other works of importance. See U.S. Congress, House Committee on Government Operations, *Impact of Federal Urban Development Programs on Local Government Organization and Planning,* 88th Congress, 2nd session (1964). The disturbing effect of urban renewal and the federal-aid highway program is described in Advisory Commission on Intergovernmental Relations, *Re-*

location: Unequal Treatment of People and Businesses Displaced by Governments, Report A-26 (Washington, D.C.: U.S. Government Printing Office, January, 1965). Finally, see Martin Anderson, *The Federal Bulldozer: A Critical Analysis of Urban Renewal 1949–1962* (Cambridge, Mass.: Massachusetts Institute of Technology Press, 1964).

Two books that emphasize the utility of rehabilitation of urban renewal areas rather than their demolition and entire rebuilding are Herbert J. Gans, *The Urban Villagers* (New York: The Free Press, 1962); and Bernard J. Frieden, *The Future of Old Neighborhoods* (Cambridge, Mass.: The Massachusetts Institute of Technology Press, 1964). And a contemporary Greek urban theorist states his position in C. A. Doxiadis, *Urban Renewal and the Future of the American City* (Chicago: Public Administration Service, 1966). Finally, a comprehensive book of readings on urban renewal is James Q. Wilson (ed.), *Urban Renewal: The Record and the Controversy* (Cambridge, Mass.: The Massachusetts Institute of Technology Press, 1966).

CHAPTER 21

*P*olitics and the Arts—*The Contemporary Experience of the American City*

The Case of the Egyptian Cat

A city art museum purchased a cat—not a live one, it is true; not one that would require the expensive care and nurture of a lion in the zoo, but an expensive one, nonetheless. The cat was 3,000 years old and of bronze, and it had been recovered from an archaeological "dig" somewhere in the heart of Egypt. Both the museum board and the director himself thought that the city would shout "Hosanna!" because the museum now possessed, for a mere $10,000 of the taxpayers' money, such a precious treasure of antique art. And they should have been right in their estimate, because this was St. Louis, which had as active an art life and as devoted an art following as any city in North America. If there happened to be protest as a result of the purchase, art lovers in considerable numbers would group around the museum and blunt the attack. Art, in other words, could muster an effective pressure group in its own defense.

Although the city was St. Louis, the year was 1938—and the year made a very great deal of difference. This city, like most cities of the Western world, was hungry; it was, much of it, ill-clothed, ill-housed, and ill-fed. The question might have been asked: "If the city is hungry, can the city afford to spend public money on art?"

And indeed this is precisely the question that was raised. There was a newspaper in St. Louis—a paper with a social consciousness, a paper that felt deeply in all its collective human pores the distress of the displaced and the unemployed. And so it began wondering editorially whether it was a wise act for the city to spend public money on an art object before the physical needs of all its inhabitants had been met. The controversy gained strength, and the newspaper clippings in the office of the director of the museum grew more and more extensive.

The *Star-Times* had raised more than a journalistic issue. Here were basic public questions. Could art and poverty exist by side? Could not art wait until the advent of the affluent society? If art is a luxury—and surely it must be, according to the *Star-Times* argument—can we afford to spend public money on it before the city has taken care of its necessities?

Art and politics and morality, the newspaper seemed to say, are inevitably connected.

St. Louis responded to the questions posed by the newspaper by keeping the Egyptian cat (which the museum now values at more than $50,000). But this action, taken as an answer, must be an inconclusive one, because the same questions are still being posed. Is support of the arts as important as support of social welfare programs, or public works, or police and fire protection? If a particular city gave a "Yes" to that question in 1938, it was only a qualified one. For one thing, the money with which St. Louis purchased the cat came from an earmarked levy against property, and the legal problems that would have been associated with diverting the funds from art to social welfare would have been horrendous. For another thing, the bureaucracy had made its decision, and it is no easier for the administrator to change his mind and admit that he has erred than it is for the ordinary citizen to do so.

Although St. Louis did not really decide that art was as important as other city programs, one sure conclusion can be drawn from the episode, and that is that art and politics do indeed mingle. Whenever public monies are spent for the promotion and cultivation of the arts, the question will be raised about the importance of art to the public life.

In Search of Art

This chapter is essentially about government support of the arts in the United States. "Government support in the United States!!" The incredulous will exclaim over this statement, and perhaps even ridicule it: "There is government support in Europe (city or national)," they will say, "but never in the United States."

Casual knowledge, like popular wisdom, is often neither knowledge nor wisdom. And that is certainly true in this case, because the American city energetically supports the arts; the city is government; and therefore government supports the arts in the United States.

The city itself may be an art form, even though civic leaders are all too apt to shrug off that possibility. As August Heckscher, one-time consultant on the arts to President John F. Kennedy, has remarked, "in a dramatic way the city can be itself a work of art, perhaps the most striking and durable of all man's great works." It is an easily verifiable fact of art, moreover, that the creative artist cannot exist without the city. The artist, like the prophet, may dream in the wilderness, but his dreams will be conditioned by the city, and he will eventually return to the city to implement his dreams. And he will most certainly, if one may be quite matter-of-fact, depend upon the city as an audience for his dreams.

The art that the city promotes and nurtures extends to all forms of cultural activities: music, opera, the dance, the theater; museums, galleries, and libraries; educational television and radio; civic art and architecture. No form of artistic expression can possibly escape the city's attention; or if it is possible for art to escape that attention, the demonstrable fact is that it rarely does so.

The city's nurture of the arts takes various forms. A great deal of public money goes from the city's treasury directly into some kind of support. And indirectly the city gives just as much aid, or more. When Boston decided to build a new city hall in the early 1960's, the city did not hire the architectural firm which could produce the cheapest, the most utilitarian (and most hackneyed) design, but instead held a national competition. When Boston, or one of a hundred other cities, builds a municipal auditorium, it may be viewed in the popular mind as the place for folk singers to perform or for school plays, but it may also give a home at long last to the symphony orchestra and to whatever legitimate theater that might come to the city.

As citizen interest in the arts increased after World War II, so did direct public expenditures for art. The increase in interest is generally recognized, and August Heckscher sums it up well: "Attendance at museums and concerts has increased dramatically. Symphony orchestras, community theaters, opera groups, and other cultural institutions exist in numbers which would have been thought impossible a generation ago. The artist, the writer, and the performer hold new positions of respect in our society." [1]

Not so well known is the increased public support of the arts in the past decades, mainly by the cities, although the cities are occasionally supported in their efforts by county, school, recreational, and state governments. In 1954, fifty-three cities of over 10,000 population reported to the International City Managers' Association that they spent $500,000 on symphony orchestras.[2] But in the fiscal year 1962–1963 San Francisco alone spent almost $200,000 in payments to the symphony association. Indeed, San Francisco is probably more generous than any other city in the United States in its support of the arts. In 1962–1963 the budget of the San Francisco Art Commission provided $257,480 for sculpture on the Civic Center Plaza (admittedly an unusual expenditure) and $444,289 for other activities. For 1961–1962 the city appropriated $746,000 for two art museums, and $15,000 for another. Not content with the amount of money that was going into the arts, the city enacted a 3 percent hotel tax, yielding over $1,000,000 a year, and 25 percent of the tax was allocated for cultural activi-

---

[1] U.S. Senate, "The Arts and the National Government," *Report to the President Submitted by August Heckscher, Document No. 28,* 88th Congress, 1st session (1963), p. 1.
[2] *The Municipal Year Book 1955* (Chicago: ICMA), p. 268.

ties.[3] All of these expenditures represented major increases over the money being spent by San Francisco only a decade before.

If the American city has gone to the aid of the arts, relatively little support has come from other American governments. Out of Governor Nelson Rockefeller's legislative program came the New York State Arts Council, with an annual budget of $500,000. And it was Governor Rockefeller, more than any other state political leader, who insisted upon the substantial aid given by New York State to the Lincoln Center for the Performing Arts. Most state aid, however, comes indirectly from the tax exemption given to real property and to symphony societies and other art groups, and directly through the budgets of state-supported colleges and universities.

The federal government spends a considerable amount of money overseas on "cultural diplomacy," but relatively little domestically. For the most part, the American citizen must travel overseas or to such places as the National Gallery of Art in Washington to receive any direct benefit from federal expenditures on the arts. Local art societies, of course, receive some indirect aid from the federal income tax exemption on contributions.

A new day in federal aid to the arts may have been heralded by the devotion of President and Mrs. John F. Kennedy to various art forms. Indeed, Kennedy was the first President in history to have a consultant on the arts. In accepting August Heckscher's resignation as the first Special Consultant for the Arts, President Kennedy indicated the importance he attached to federal support: "Government can never take over the role of patronage and support filled by private individuals and groups in our society. But government surely has a significant part to play in helping establish the conditions under which art can flourish—in encouraging the arts as it encourages science and learning." [4] It was undoubtedly partly the result of President Kennedy's enthusiasm for the arts that only a few months after his death, Congress approved a bill establishing the National Council on the Arts.

In Aid of the Arts

Although the city art museum is undoubtedly the most important institution aided by the city, the city library is growing in importance as it is fast becoming both an art as well as an intellectual and amusement center. From the library's record collection the citizen may borrow recordings of the best in the world's music. At noon, during some busy week, he sets aside

[3] Mel Scott, *Partnership in the Arts* (Berkeley, Calif.: Institute of Government Studies, University of California, 1963), pp. 8–9.

[4] U.S. Senate, "The Arts and the National Government," *Report to the President Submitted by August Heckscher, Document No. 28*, 88th Congress, 1st session (1963), p. viii.

his worldly chores for a chamber-music concert (live or on records) in the library's auditorium. From the music division of the library he borrows the score of a Mozart quintet. And on Sunday afternoons he sees the best in foreign and domestic films—many of which would never be shown in his city's commercial theaters.

Although the city may spend considerable sums for art subsidies, it may get surprising returns from very small sums. New York City organized the City Center on a shoestring shortly after the end of World War II, and the center has since operated on a shoestring. Even so, it has produced some remarkable results. Take the New York City Ballet, created by the City Center in 1948. Not long in establishing itself, the ballet soon became the major American dance group of its time (used incidentally by the U.S. State Department for its program of cultural diplomacy). And if much of the ballet's success must be ascribed to the genius of its director, George Balanchine, much of it also was due to the support of the city, even if sparse. As Allen Hughes has put it, "the New York City Ballet was born in the genteel and healthy poverty that has vitalized and ennobled almost every activity the City Center has spawned." [5]

The case of the New York City Center is instructive. Even if the city has not too much money for direct expenditures, it can still furnish one of the most valuable of all aids—housing for the arts. Although the art museum is the example that comes most readily to mind at this point, one must never forget the lowly and all-too-often architecturally insipid municipal auditorium. With a grant from the Ford Foundation in 1964 of $1.25 million the Mummers' Theater of Oklahoma City reached the level of affluence that could at last enable it to become a permanent resident theater. Before that financial coup, however, the city's municipal auditorium featured so prominently in the group's history that one can say that without the auditorium the Mummers would never have been able to compete for the grant. During the late 1940's the Mummers performed in a tent. When the tent wore out, the theater had only $800 in its treasury, and the players had no place to go except into the Hall of Mirrors of the municipal auditorium. Four years in the Hall of Mirrors enabled them to enlarge their audience and, just as importantly, to save $6,000.[6] As a bridge between a tent and permanent quarters, the auditorium well served the legitimate stage in Oklahoma City.

Financial support for the arts comes from the city in various ways. One of the oldest and possibly the commonest of the taxes used in support of the arts is the earmarked levy against property to be used in support of the art museum or the city library. Another common method of support is to take funds from the property tax levy without prior earmarking. Thus, in Den-

[5] New York *Times,* January 26, 1964, p. 18X.
[6] *Ibid.,* March 29, 1964, p. 3X.

ver, the total educational levy on property in 1964 was 38.1 mills, and a
fraction of the yield from this levy (one-fourth of a mill) was allocated to
the educational television station, KRMA-TV.[7]

Since the general property tax is considerably overworked, cities have
sought other sources of revenue for all kinds of municipal programs, including support of the arts. San Francisco's 3 percent hotel tax is perhaps
the best example of such a source. Enacted in the early 1960's, the tax goes
into the city's publicity and advertising fund, and about 25 percent of it is
allocated to cultural activities. The notable difference the tax made in city
contributions to nonprofit cultural groups may be seen from the budget
data presented in Table 21-1.

*Table 21-1. Impact of the Hotel Tax
on San Francisco's Support of the Arts*

	Before Tax	After Tax
	1961–1962	*1962–1963*
San Francisco Symphony Orchestra	$10,000	$ 75,000
San Francisco Opera Association	15,000	75,000
San Francisco Museum of Art	15,000	40,000
San Francisco Ballet	5,000	30,000
The Actors Workshop	no allocation	10,000
International Film Festival	5,000	10,000
Ballet Celeste	no allocation	6,000
Spring Opera Association	no allocation	5,000
Sigmund Stern Music Festival	2,000	3,000
Lamplighters Theater	no allocation	3,000
San Francisco Chamber Music Society	no allocation	2,000
San Francisco Boys' Chorus	no allocation	2,000
Total	$52,000	$261,000

Source: Mel Scott, *Partnership in the Arts* (Berkeley, Calif.: Institute of Governmental
Studies, University of California, 1963), p. 8.

Sometimes the expenditure of city funds stimulates grants or gifts from
other sources. Thus, in the case of KRMA-TV, local funds in the operating
budget for 1964 amounted to $226,163. These local funds were supple-
mented by $115,000 from public subscription and a $55,000 federal grant.
In other words, without a substantial expenditure of local tax funds, the
$170,000 from private and federal sources would not have been available to
the people of Denver.[8]

As a general rule, it seems easier for the urban community to make capi-

[7] *The Denver Post Empire Magazine,* November 22, 1964, p. 7.
[8] *Ibid.,* pp. 4, 6–7.

tal contributions to the arts than to make contributions for current operations. How much more frequent there is capital outlay for building a theater than outlay for current operations of a theater group, for example, is impossible to say from the data available. But we can be reasonably sure that capital outlays are the more frequent of the two types of expenditures. When the city of St. Petersburg in 1964 contributed land valued at $1 million as the site for the Museum of Fine Arts of St. Petersburg, it was not only assuming about half the capital costs of the museum; it was also following standard practice of cities throughout the republic. And since the museum contains several art galleries, an art reference library, and a little theater, the city was subsidizing several art forms with a single capital grant.

Not only the city itself, as a corporate entity, but also other local governments make contributions to the arts. The park district of Chicago supports about 10 percent of the budget of the Art Institute—one of the great art museums of the world—and indeed the Art Institute is physically situated on park district land. Educational television stations are often operated by the independent school governments of the city. Although the county, being rurally oriented for the most part, rarely is interested in the arts, once in a while an urban county (Los Angeles County is a notable example) will attempt some art support.

We can see, in other words, that the urban community in the United States does indeed make notable contributions from public funds in support of the arts. Even when the city's direct and indirect contributions are small, they will often mean (1) the difference between existence and collapse of a cultural activity, and (2) added prestige to the activity—a prestige that will encourage private donations to the arts.

And yet municipal support is still not enough to encourage the flourishing of the various art forms in the American urban community. It is not enough to eliminate cultural deficits, to enable enlargement of cultural programs, or to rival the contributions of European cities. For one thing, cities in the United States live constantly on the margin financially; for another, state law is rarely favorable to the arts; for still another, the local political temper is often not friendly to support of cultural activity. It is to this last phenomenon—politics and the arts—we now need to turn.

Politics and the Arts

Why does the city support the arts? Since this support is public, political decisions are involved, and such decisions are never made in a vacuum.

Since there must be an agreement on cultural goals by the political leadership, the bureaucracy, and various interest groups, a considerable number of people must become involved in both the statement and the continuing implementation of the goals. These people will push for municipal subsidy for a variety of reasons. Some of them simply like art, or at least one of the art forms; they enjoy art or, in pedestrian terms, are consumers of art. Others think of art in terms of civic pride or because of a kind of snob appeal; the opera is a place, for example, to parade one's finery between acts.

And there are other reasons for the support of the arts by civic leaders, bureaucrats, and citizens. In some instances the consent of both leadership and electorate is virtually purchased. A wealthy businessman wills a valuable collection of objects d'art to the city, and the city finds itself in the museum business, compelled willy-nilly to appropriate funds for the museum's operations. Or a rich dowager gives the city a million dollars to build a legitimate theater to be named after her father, and once again the city is forced into an active cultural role.

Moreover, because art is merchandisable, it becomes good business. For purely materialistic reasons some individuals and groups will support cultural activities. And for the additional materialistic reason of heightened social status, others will consent to public support of the arts.

There is now a brand new reason for the city's support of the arts—a reason that is at the same time a brand new political argument which the art groups may use to parlay more funds from the city treasury. This is, of course, federal aid. Following its brave step in 1964—establishment of the National Council of the Arts—Congress in 1965 set up the National Foundation on the Arts and the Humanities, and for the very first time showed serious interest in promoting the arts by making roughly $20 million annually available to the program for a three-year period. Now one can expect to hear the same argument before city councils for both the arts and—let us say—urban renewal; in order to take advantage of federal funds, the city must increase its own expenditures. This might be called the seed-money syndrome in the American federal relation.

Art Among the Pressure Groups

The principal reason that cities are investing in the arts is that there is sufficient interest in the urban body politic to force some kind of action. Political demand engenders governmental response from the mayor, the city manager, and the city council.

One of the main types of cultural pressure groups in the city is made up of the social and economic elite. If one goes down the membership lists of the symphony societies, the art museum, and the opera associations, he finds them filled with prestigious names. Cheek by jowl with the scions of old and distinguished families are the self-made (and wealthy) bankers, lawyers, and entrepreneurs of the community. From these lists, indeed, one can find the names of many if not most of those who make up the economic and social power structure of the community.

A second type of pressure group is drawn from organized labor. Because musicians must work, the musicians' union will seek city support for musical organizations of various types. The same is true with actors and stagehands. One of the probable reasons for the repeal of the New York City admissions tax was the pressure exerted on the mayor and city council by the trade unions, and the repeal represented, even though negatively, a city subsidy.

Another type of pressure group which probably exists—though it is hard to identify—is made up of the status-seeker. Art nowadays is de rigueur; because the various cultural activities of the city have always attracted high-status individuals, those in search of status will gravitate toward the groups in which they can meet the "right" people. In support of the arts, they will think, we can acquire a greater respectability than we now have.

And then, finally, there are the businessmen and the politicians who simply see art in terms of more visitors to the city, more conventions, and more tax revenues than are coming in at the present time. Whether one likes art personally is beside the point. Many people do. Art is a means of bringing those people into the city, of raising profits, and of replenishing the municipal coffers. The San Francisco hotel tax, mentioned previously, was apparently accepted by the hotel entrepreneurs of the city at least partially on these grounds.

These are some of the pressure groups. Acting in concert, as they do at times, they can be formidable. Indeed, it is surprising that they have not made more of an impact on the city's cultural policy than is evident today. Since we know very little about politics and the arts in the city, we cannot find any secure reasons for this low impact, but can at least offer some hypotheses:

1. The socioeconomic elite finds itself divorced from control of political power in the city. Dahl found this phenomenon in New Haven, and we can expect it to occur in other cities. With low-grade political potency, the very people who contribute generously to the arts from their own resources may be frustrated in their dealings with city hall.

2. This same socioeconomic elite is quite possessive of the arts. Although the board of directors of the symphony association, for example, may seek popular support through ticket sales and appeals for small donations, its power will never be threatened by this kind of popular consent. On the other hand, if the city contributes too generously to the association's support, some control at least may have to be passed to another power group. The associations would rather face the annual trauma of a deficit than a "power grab" by city hall.

3. None of the pressure groups has enough political power to impress the state legislature (or the governors) with the necessity either of state aid to the city for the arts or of state legislation that would enable the city to expand its support.

4. The trade unions directly connected with the arts (musicians, stage-hands, actors) are not sufficiently a part of the trade union fraternity to enlist the support of the other unions in the expansion of art subsidies from the public treasury.

5. Although many businessmen give generous donations to various art groups, the powerful business community as a whole is not sufficiently convinced of the economic advantage to be gained from a flourishing of art forms in the city to press for increased public support.

6. Esthetes, music-lovers, architects, and others who make up the real "art colony" of every city are not notably effective at political action. Such people, indeed, are often the politically alienated, which puts them further outside the political arena.

7. The popular mind does not automatically think in terms of public support of the arts. In spite, therefore, of the great welling up of popular interest in the arts in recent years, those who are interested in the arts are not compelled by custom and tradition to turn to the public treasury as in European cities.

We can observe a certain amount of pressure-group activity in relation to the arts. Numerically, the art-oriented citizen is becoming increasingly stronger, and yet his political effectiveness is still weak. The hypotheses given above, if at all valid, could explain some of this weakness but not all of it. We would still have to look to political leadership and the bureaucracy for other weaknesses and other strengths.

Protective Coloration: Art Among Political Leaders

In the state and national governments rarely have political leaders—Presidents, governors, legislators, or bureaucrats—shown themselves interested in the arts in any form. And yet, when the politician acts, one can see immediately the importance of political leadership to all of the art forms. As August Heckscher has observed, "in this work, as in all important work, the individual leader is at the start of things. President Kennedy in Washington, or Nelson Rockefeller in Albany, put flesh on the bare bones of policy. They make support of the arts seem not peripheral but central; they make quality and excellence seem objectives to which we can all aspire." [9] These two leaders, more than any others, made possible, respec-

[9] August Heckscher, "The City and the Arts," Wherrett Lecture on Local Government before the Institure of Local Government, University of Pittsburgh, Pittsburgh, Pa., 1964, p. 8.

tively, the National Council on the Arts, and the New York State Arts Council.

In the city, matters are somewhat different. No mayor has ever been elected because he was devoted to the musical literature of the classical period. Nor was ever a city manager appointed because of his interest in the French impressionists. Although occasionally one can find an art follower on the city council, school board, or other governmental body, those interests are peripheral to his appointment or election. And yet, since there is a tradition, even in the American city, of public support of the arts, the leaders must usually accept that support. If they were to cut it off, they would risk political damage.

Moreover, art is interwoven with civic pride. Even though the symphony orchestra or the art museum is meaningless to the leadership in personal terms, those leaders will nevertheless defend it vigorously and point to it with pride. Art has great prestige. If, like education, few people can agree on what it is or what it means, it still engenders respectful response. To put the matter another way, art is enjoyed directly by some people and vicariously by many others. And this vicarious enjoyment is important to the political leader and the citizen alike. Neither one may ever enter the portals of a concert hall; nevertheless, the art that flourishes there is a part of his world—on the margins of it, true enough, but still a part of it.

Civic pride is, indeed, a typical form of protective coloration carefully utilized by the political leader vis-à-vis the arts. Even though he may enjoy serious music and good theater, he is very likely not to argue publicly that art is one of of the highest forms of pure joy, but rather that it is good for the city for very practical reasons. One can brag about it far and wide; one can mention it in chamber of commerce promotional literature. One can even stimulate business by means of it. Civic pride can level much opposition, if it is clearly and emphatically identified with art forms.

Another form of protective coloration is to call art anything else but art. Call it many things, but call it, if at all possible, not art, but education or recreation or some other more popularly accepted activity. In spite of art's prestige, it has a far narrower public following than either education or recreation. Why has there been so little protest over the rather considerable expenditure of local tax money on educational television? The label is the possible answer. Call it "cultural" or "art" television, and the sources of public funds would rapidly dry up.

One can see evidence of this phenomenon, too, in the budgets of city recreation departments, where itemized appropriations for the arts (and particularly for the performing arts) exist uneasily alongside appropriations for volleyball and senior citizen activities! As a case in point, it is perhaps understandable that the directors of the flourishing Richmond, California, Art Center are unhappy with their niche (although a substantial one) in the city's recreation department. But in the realistic political view of the city manager, "the Art Center as a separate department would be a conspicuous target for criticism at budget hearings, and its members should be thankful that it *is* under the park and recreation department." [10] If it is anomalous for the recreational budget to provide for art (as opposed to crafts), it is an anomaly arising out of the political necessity for protective coloration.

Civic Art—A Universal Urban Function

The search for beauty in the city takes a variety of forms. For some citizens the search ends with the symphony concert or the paintings in the art museum; for many more, it ends with an imposing public structure, a fountain, or a flower bed. It ends, in short, with civic art.

What is civic art? At one level it might be defined as the kind of public display which may be photographed and printed on a picture postcard. At a different and considerably higher level, it must be thought of as an attempt to focus the urban mind upon a structure or object of more than utilitarian value. Even more, it must be a reminder of beauty, first and foremost, and only secondarily a teacher of local or national history or of political ideology. The public statue which is purely political (the kind that makes Washington, D.C., look like a public cemetery) cannot satisfy this definition of civic art. But the Buckingham fountain on the lakeshore in Chicago can satisfy it. Somewhere in between is the art that is not really art at all, but only commemorative of an artist or an art form, as with the statue of Goethe on the Ringstrasse in Vienna.

Another characteristic of civic art is that it is always political. Even when the artist, the public authority, or the private group seeks to eschew politics entirely and push it to the background, the political overtones remain. When in Springfield, Massachusetts, some fifty years ago, the Greek Revival city hall and municipal auditorium were built, in between the two buildings the city fathers raised a magnificent tower, in the style of the Italian Renaissance campanile. Contemptuous citizens immediately dubbed the three structures the Greek twins with a nursing bottle. On the other hand, if the mayor and council had decided upon a pedestrian, purely utilitarian style of architecture for the city hall and municipal auditorium and had forgotten about the campanile, they would have incurred the wrath of other citizens offended by such examples of civic nonart.

Similarly, the manner in which a private group pursues its own interests may show the inevitable connection between civic art and politics. In New

[10] Scott, *op. cit.*, p. 25. In 1961–1962, the Art Center received more than $80,000 of the $192,000 recreation budget.

York, as soon as the owners of the Pennsylvania Station announced their plans to level the grand old structure, the architects of the city rose up almost in a body to protest the egregious error. And in Chicago, when an old Louis Sullivan building was threatened with the wrecking crew, the protests rained upon city hall like shrapnel upon the battlefield. In neither case were the protests successful, but they made the political pot boil and showed even to the most skeptical the connection between politics and the arts.

The Public Building

The guiding rule for every medieval and Renaissance city was that the public building should have architectural (and thus artistic) integrity. Continued, though somewhat weakened, during the baroque period, this guiding principle was cavalierly ignored by the industrial city of succeeding centuries. And yet it would not die. Even in the United States, where there was no ruling monarchy to build monuments to itself, the principle would emerge in the most unexpected places. Something there was about the concept of the public building as art that captured the imagination, not only of the esthete, but also of the robber-baron capitalist. Why else would a world's fair laid out in the swamps along the shores of Lake Michigan start a "City Beautiful" movement that would sweep the entire continent?

Every kind of public structure above ground can, with very little additional capital expenditure, reflect the intent of civic leaders, citizens at large, and architects to create a structure of beauty, as well as one of utility. (The intent, obviously, may result in failure, particularly if the architect comes a cropper or if there is a failure of nerve in city hall.) Even the structure below ground can have beauty added to its utility, as the Opernpassage in front of the State Opera in Vienna shows so well.

The difficulty is that any attempt to spend public funds above the minimum, utilitarian level is apt to run into trouble, not only in the governing councils but among the citizenry at large and among certain pressure groups. The city is generally so strapped for funds that any attempt at good design (that is, good in the sense of artistic) is apt to be labeled superfluous and wasteful of public funds. Even when this obstacle is broken through —and we must remember that it often is—every civic leader, and a goodly number of private citizens, will be willing to pose as accomplished connoisseurs of the arts who know exactly what form the public structure should take.

If art is to be a part of the public building, the city needs some kind of policy statement concerning it. If there is an art commission, such a policy may be embodied in one or another of its pronouncements. Rarely will it be found elsewhere, whether in executive directive, ordinance, or resolution.

Perhaps the action of President Kennedy in 1962 might lead cities toward more formal policy statements than they have been used to in the past. In the directive entitled "Guiding Principles for Federal Architecture," dated May 23, 1962, the President recommended: "(1) the selection of distinguished designs that embody the finest contemporary American architectural thought, (2) the avoidance of an official style and the encouragement of professional creativity through competitions and other means, and (3) the special importance of landscaping and site development in relation to the surrounding area." [11]

History and Civic Art

Can a building acquire esthetic qualities simply by aging? Although no city will ever answer this question conclusively, many cities operate on the assumption that an old building may be more than a mere historical monument; it may be art as well. If the building was designed by a Louis Sullivan or a Frank Lloyd Wright, the presumption is that it has qualities that approach the level of art (even though one must recognize that good architects may design bad buildings). The poet John Betjeman has observed that "architecture is the most lasting monument of a civilization. After language, painting and music are forgotten, architecture remains." Surprisingly enough, a large number of civic leaders and many, many groups scattered throughout American cities would agree with him.

New Orleans has long subjected the Vieux Carre to more or less rigorous controls by the city. More recently, many other cities have moved officially to preserve buildings of historical and architectural worth. When a city acts in this respect, however, one often cannot tell whether it is respect for history or art, or both, that motivates the policy decision.

Arlington County, Virginia, early in the 1960's established a cultural heritage commission of six members to preserve structures and sites of historical and cultural worth, and under a 1961 state statute, Wethersfield, Connecticut, set up a district to preserve similar structures. Olivette, Missouri, has established a community design review board with jurisdiction over the construction, repair, or alteration of buildings varying from flour mills to apartment houses. This type of action can be particularly useful, because one can never know when a building will suddenly become "historical," or what sudden change of taste may make a building "artistic."

[11] U.S. Senate, *op. cit.*, p. 8.

Institutionalizing Civic Art

It must be known by now to all civic leaders that art has its following and that art can muster its pressure groups. One means of institutionalizing such pressures is by use of the art commission. New York can serve as a useful example.

The New York Art Commission is made up of the mayor, the president of the Metropolitan Museum of Art, the president of the New York Public Library, the president of the Brooklyn Institute of Arts and Sciences, one painter, one sculptor, one architect, one landscape architect, and three other residents of the city. The four professional artists and the three citizen members are appointed by the mayor from a list of at least twenty-one persons submitted to him by the Fine Arts Federation. The commission has jurisdiction over all works of art—from sculpture and paintings to benches, lamps, and traffic signals—which are "erected or to be erected upon or over land belonging to the city." And it also exercises jurisdiction over city buildings, bridges, and assorted other structures.

The art commission, in other words, has rather substantial power to control the design and character of major forms of civic art and of numerous minor forms as well. It has the legal power under the charter, that is; whether it has the power in fact is another question. Sayre and Kaufman suggest that the commission is a means of institutionalizing the power of a small but articulate elite group, but that the potency of the commission (and thus of the group that it represents) is significantly restricted by budgetary allotments. In the early 1960's the commission had only two full-time staff members, only a fraction of the personnel needed to carry out its charter obligations.[12]

This is an old political game, of course: you throw a sop to an interest group by giving it institutional expression in a board, commission, or other agency. Then you give it only advisory powers; or if the pressures are sufficiently great and you are forced to give it real power, you checkmate that power by budgetary strictures or by other means.

This fate of the New York Art Commission is descriptive of most of the art commissions in other American cities. Nevertheless, such commissions do undoubtedly enhance the effectiveness of the art-oriented citizen, especially with respect to civic art. All that such citizens need to do to increase their influence and, at the same time, the effectiveness of "their" commissions, is to magnify their numbers! With the growing sensitivity of the ur-

[12] Wallace S. Sayre and Herbert Kaufman, *Governing New York City* (New York. W. W. Norton & Co., 1965), p. 391.

ban citizen to the various forms of art, there is a very good chance that the art groups will indeed be able to strengthen themselves politically.

Annotated Bibliography

A bibliography on the city and the arts is at once easy and difficult to write— easy because the literature on the subject is so scant, and difficult because one is perplexed that such an engaging subject should have been so long ignored by scholars, publicists, and laymen.

There is, of course, ample, if not extensive, treatment of the subject which we might call urban esthetics, yet rarely is there any attempt in a rigorously analytical manner to relate art and esthetics to public decision-making. Mel Scott's *Partnership in the Arts: Public and Private Support of Cultural Activities in the San Francisco Bay Area* (Berkeley, Calif.: Institute of Governmental Studies, University of California, 1963), even though a modest attempt over all, appears as a substantial contribution to a casually examined field of study. August Heckscher's perceptive little essay, "The Quality of American Culture," is partly concerned with politics and the arts and may be found in *Goals for Americans* (Englewood Cliffs, N.J.: Prentice-Hall, 1960).

If one wishes a rather extensive catalog of persons and organizations that have supported federal aid to the arts, he can find it in U.S. Congress, House Committee on Education and Labor, *Aid to Fine Arts*, Hearing on H.R. 4172 and H.R. 4174, 87th Congress, 1st Session (1961). This report also contains considerable data on city support of the arts.

Two·surveys of the state of the performing arts which offer citizen and public official a formidable array of data and opinion for policy-making are Rockefeller Panel Report, *The Performing Arts: Problems and Prospects* (New York: McGraw-Hill Book Co., 1965); and William J. Baumol and William G. Bowen, *The Performing Arts: The Economic Dilemma* (New York: The Twentieth Century Fund, 1966).

Epilogue—The View from Athens

Since the first discovery of rudimentary forms of urban life in prehistory, man has been engaged with the urban revolution. And now the culmination of that revolution seems to be at hand; the city seems ready to absorb all of us of whatever race, clime, or political disposition. Gone are the hunter, the fisherman, the herdsman, and the plowman. Gradually the hardhanded yeoman, the ancestor of virtually all of us, fades into the folklore of the human race, to be romanticized, sentimentalized, and then dwelt lovingly upon by the antiquarian housed in the fortieth floor of a building in a city in which the average density of human beings is 100,000 per square mile.

The political and social changes that will come over mankind will doubtless be remarkable. Before the middle of the twentieth century very few of the men and women who had peopled the world could be called truly urban. Although in a few short years an individual from whatever stock can become urban, for entire populations it takes generations. Not until all grandfathers and all grandmothers can be remembered by their grandchildren in the shop or the factory, in the high-rise apartment or in the morning or evening traffic jam will humankind accommodate its folkways, its habits, its values, its visceral reactions to the urban pattern.

We have until now had only brief glimpses of the City of Man. In fifth-century Athens, in fifteenth-century Florence, and perhaps in eighteenth-century Boston and Charleston we can see urban life. We can catch a glimpse of it, too, in Changan during the Tang dynasty of the seventh and eighth centuries, when every city in Europe was enveloped in an intellectual and cultural darkness.

And so we know something of urban man, but little of urban mankind. We know a great deal about the city, but since the city has always been populated by essentially nonurban humanity, too recently removed from field and forest to acquire more than a veneer of urbanity, we know very little about the city peopled with urbanites. Our data are time-locked and time-distorted.

How can we, then, predict the City of Man? What will be its life, its art, its politics? We can only say with confidence that it will be different; that in the mere century that lies ahead the city, if spared the Götterdämmerung, will suffer a sea change into something rich and strange.

INDEX OF NAMES

INDEX